THREE ESSAYS

by Albrecht Ritschl

A. Ritschl

Philadelphia

Fortress Press

Albrecht Ritschl

THREE
ESSAYS

Theology and Metaphysics
"Prolegomena" to *The History of Pietism*
Instruction in the Christian Religion

Translated and with an Introduction by
PHILIP HEFNER

Library of Congress Catalog Card Number 72–75654

ISBN 0–8006–0224–2

3243B72   Printed in the United States of America   1–224

Contents

Preface

This volume of essays has been almost a decade in its becoming, and therefore it is not surprising that the debts incurred in its appearance are many. It would not be possible to mention the names of every person who has assisted me in this work, but these persons should know not only that I appreciated their helpfulness, but also that this volume was dependent upon their efforts.

Certain persons and institutions dare not go unmentioned: Professor Jaroslav Pelikan, who first broached the idea, together with the Editorial Board of the Library of Protestant Thought and the Sealantic Foundation who supported this project when it seemed that the book would appear in that series. The Rev. Robert Hanson, who worked long hours to help make Ritschl speak idiomatic English; this translation owes a great deal to him and his diligence. The men who, as student assistants, helped with exasperating details: J. William Novak, Dennis Hartsook, and John Ruppenthal. Professors Robert Fischer, Paul Jersild, Darrell Jodock, Walter Kukkonen, and David Lotz, who made critical suggestions on the translations and introduction. The scholars who furnished me with copies of doctoral dissertations—their own and others I did not know about—which made the introductory survey possible. Librarians, especially in Chicago and Hamburg, who carry on a tradition of helpfulness and expertise that is simply indispensable. Finally, to two descendants of Albrecht Ritschl, who although they have not seen this work in manuscript were always ready to help, and who made possible the photograph that appears here, Professor Hans Ritschl and his son, Professor Dietrich Ritschl.

With so many helpers, it is sobering to recognize that I take full responsibility for the errors and misstatements that may appear herein. I would appreciate having them called to my attention.

Lutheran School of Theology at Chicago   P.H.
March 25, 1972
The 150th Anniversary of Albrecht Ritschl's Birth

Abbreviations

APOLOGY Apology of the Augsburg Confession (1531)

     AS The Smalcald Articles (1537)

     CA The Augsburg Confession (1530)

     CR *Corpus Reformatorum*

Fabricius Cajus Fabricius, ed., *Die christliche Vollkommenheit und Unterricht in der christlichen Religion.* Critical edition in one volume. Leipzig: J. C. Hinrichsche Buchhandlung, 1924.

     LW American Edition of *Luther's Works.* Helmut T. Lehmann and Jaroslav Pelikan, General Editors. Philadelphia: Fortress Press, and Saint Louis: Concordia Publishing House.

R.u.V. *Die christliche Lehre von der Rechtfertigung und Versöhnung.* 3 vols.; Bonn: Adolph Marcus, 1870–1874 and several later editions.

Tappert Theodore Tappert, trans. and ed., *The Book of Concord.* Philadelphia: Fortress Press, 1959.

     ET English Translation.

Materials and notes appearing within brackets [ ] are the editor's additions.

ALBRECHT RITSCHL:

AN INTRODUCTION

Albrecht Ritschl:

An Introduction

by Philip Hefner

I. THE MAN AND HIS SETTING

The theological achievement of Albrecht Ritschl is, like that of every man, closely bound to the world in which he lived. If not a product of the environment, at least it is understandable only as a part of that environment. This may pose problems, particularly for the American reader, because Ritschl's world of nineteenth century Germany is largely unknown and even unknowable for us. Furthermore, since the definitive comprehensive study of Ritschl and his place in history is yet to be written, we are still at the stage of putting bits and pieces together from the existing studies of the man, in an attempt to understand him.[1] In what follows, we will try to show how the religious, social class, political, intellectual, cultural, and even geographical factors of his life help us to unlock the truth of what he holds for us.

HOME AND FAMILY

Ritschl was an heir of what has been called the German protestant counterpart to the Roman Catholic hierarchical clerical succession: he was at least the third generation academically interested religious professional in his family. For several generations, the family home had been in Erfurt, a Saxon town where Martin Luther had attended the university. Albrecht Ritschl's grandfather, George Wilhelm Ritschl, was pastor at the St. John's Church in Erfurt and professor

at the secondary school (Gymnasium) there. George's son and
Albrecht's father, George Carl Benjamin (born 1783, died 1858)
moved to Berlin where he was pastor of the prestigious St. Mary's
Church, earned a doctorate in theology, and in 1827 became a bishop
of the protestant church and general superintendent of the churches
in Pomerania, which today is part of Poland, with his episcopal seat
in Stettin (now Szezczin, on the border between Poland and East
Germany). The bishop was apparently an extremely diligent member
of the Prussian leading class, noted for his formality, hard work, and
unwillingness to get involved in petty bickering between cliques. He
enjoyed the respect of the emperors under whom he served,
Friedrich Wilhelm IV and Wilhelm I. Without casting aspersions
on the indisputable piety and theological earnestness of the bishop,
we must remind ourselves that his office made him a member of the
Prussian elite, what we would call today the Prussian "establishment." To be a bishop in this situation involved support for the
decades-long policy of the Prussian government to unite the Lutheran
and Calvinist churches into the Prussian Union Church. George Carl
Ritschl was a bishop of this union church and noted for his vigorous
and sincere support of the union. This made his work difficult inasmuch as Pomerania was a stronghold of "confessional" Lutherans
who emphasized their particularity over against the Calvinists and
the union church. Ultimately, the growing strength of these confessional Lutherans combined with the bishop's advanced age motivated his retirement in 1854, inasmuch as the opponents to the union
had gained enough positions in the ruling council of the Pomeranian
church to enable them to isolate their bishop.

Albrecht was the only surviving son of his father's second marriage
(although five children survived from the first marriage) to Auguste
Sebald, the daughter of the Commissioner of Justice in Berlin. His
mother apparently set a lively, light-hearted tone in the home, balancing the father's gravity of disposition. She and her husband gave
Ritschl a love for music which never waned. She was a member of
the Berlin Singing Academy (her husband was at one time on its
board of directors) in which the great theologian Friedrich Schleiermacher was also active. The anecdote survives that Schleiermacher
once exclaimed after the choir practice that Auguste was a "gorgeous girl."

Albrecht Benjamin Ritschl was born into this family on March 25, 1822. What we can safely say about his early years is that he possessed a winning and flexible personality which enabled him to live easily in love and trust with all the members of a household whose personal relationships were complicated by the fact that the two brothers and three sisters from his father's first marriage were cared for more by an aunt than by the stepmother. Albrecht entered fully into the musical life of the family and also distinguished himself by his earnest studies, graduating with a superior record from the secondary school when he was seventeen years of age. In 1839 he began his studies at Bonn, which was also at that time a Prussian city and university, where the theological faculty, under the influence of Schleiermacher, was dominated by the dogmatician Karl Immanuel Nitzsch. The theological atmosphere was marked by a supernaturalistic piety of the traditional sort (thus matching the piety of his home), combined with a commitment to the serious pursuit of academic theology, including attention to new scientific developments. Among the father's admonitions to the young Ritschl were the words that he was as concerned with his son's spiritual development as with his intellectual growth, to which he added, "faith precedes understanding, understanding grows out of faith."

The significance of this home background cannot be overlooked if we are to understand Ritschl: (1) He grew up among the intellectual, cultural, political, and ecclesiastical elite of Berlin and Prussian Germany; he was accustomed to social and professional contacts with the elite, and his family appreciated and participated in the social, cultural, and professional activities of the elite. (2) From the earliest years, he had set before him the ideal of excellence and earnestness in vocational responsibilities, as the way to contribute to the maintenance of society. (3) Deep-seated piety and belief in what we would call traditional, supernatural Lutheran Christianity permeated his life. (4) Serious concern for the practical life of the church and its political administration was inseparable from his family's piety. (5) As proponents of and officeholders in the Prussian Union Church, his family communicated to Ritschl the sense that Lutheranism was best expressed in a Lutheran–Calvinist unity, and this sense included both an intellectual-theological and a personal opposition to the conservative Lutheran particularists who comprised the "confessional" or "orthodox" party; nevertheless, as bishop, his father set the example of trying to rise above the inevitable party bickerings between unionists, confessionalists, and pietists. Each of these five elements in his early background was prominent in Albrecht Ritschl's life, up to the time of his death in 1889.

STUDENT YEARS

Otto Ritschl, in his biography of his father, comments that Ritschl's theology, even at its most abstract, is the scientific elaboration and defense of his fundamental religious and ethical convictions.[2] This comment can serve as a principle for understanding Ritschl's development in his university studies. From his first semester at Bonn, through the time of his doctorate at Halle and his habilitation dissertation at Tübingen and Bonn, Ritschl was working out his destiny on two fronts: his religious-theological beliefs and his academic-scientific methodology. From the beginning of his university days, he lived in the atmosphere in which a supernatural approach to Christian belief was fighting for its life, partly over against an also supernatural Hegelian philosophy and partly against a scientific, materialistic world view that rejected both. As he progressed in his studies, he also witnessed the dissolution of Hegelianism into its so-called right and left wings, the former returning to a traditional supernaturalism, the latter becoming a radicalizing factor, both politically and theologically, tending in the direction of the avowedly atheistic Ludwig Feuerbach.[3] At Bonn, his professors presented a traditional Christian faith that was trying to take the scientific and philosophical demands of the modern world seriously, and among his personal friendships he counted members of the confessional Lutheran party with whom he carried on intense debates until he finally worked out in his mind a respectable theological opposition to that party, substantiating academically his personal predisposition for the Prussian union. At Halle, his professors continued to pose the supernaturalistic option, with a tinge of pietism. Ritschl was impressed, but could not give his burgeoning capabilities and desire for truth to their theological schemes. Here he began his love affair with the so-called Hegelians, notably Ferdinand Christian Baur, who taught at Tübingen, but whose books, specifically his work

on reconciliation, caught Ritschl's attention. The philosopher Erd-
mann impressed Ritschl sufficiently to influence him to do his doctorate in that area, with a dissertation on Augustine. Ritschl was
determined on an academic career, and he wanted to prove himself
with Baur. His father resisted the son's turn to the philosophical and
critical position of Baur and pressed him first to spend some months
in Heidelberg, but finally consented to the study at Tübingen, where
Ritschl began work in the summer of 1845.

Besides the importance of Baur for the young Ritschl and his
development, this relationship and its rupture in 1856 goes down as
one of the important friendships and breakups in modern theological
history.[4] Baur was the first man who was able to develop a comprehensive historical theology, that is, he committed himself to the effort
to understand Christianity through a critical historical investigation
of its origins and development, with the intention to present it in
its entirety and explain its essence and its significance. Ritschl
turned to Baur because he found in him an impressive resource for
pursuing rigorous scientific studies in concert with an unabashed
Christian faith and piety. Baur was greatly influenced by Hegel,
although it is erroneous to label him a "Hegelian." He insisted that
historical study is not meaningful or "objective" unless it is carried
on under a leading idea. For Baur this resided in an understanding
of the *Geist* or Spirit revealing itself through the concrete manifestations of the historical process, mainly in the manifestations which
embody the conflict and reconciliation of opposing tendencies, in a
dialectic of thesis-antithesis-synthesis which is close to Hegel's.
Ritschl sloughed off the theoretical, speculative scheme of Baur's,
but he learned his historical-theological craft from him, and in
dialogue and conflict with Baur he worked out ideas that would
be of later importance for him. Ritschl harbored differences and
misunderstandings of Baur from the beginning of their relationship
which finally led to stormy clash, in which Ritschl's insensitivity to
Baur was an important factor, making the episode one of the more
regrettable in Ritschl's life.[5] Nevertheless, Ritschl considered himself
a member of Baur's "Tübingen school" until as late as 1856.

Under Baur's influence, Ritschl pursued a meticulous study of the
New Testament and the immediate postapostolic centuries. His
habilitation dissertation (the German prerequisite to a teaching

career) dealt with Marcion and the Gospel of Luke, concluding that the former was the original basis for the latter. This thesis won Baur's full approval, so that when Ritschl himself later abandoned it, the master was to become its ardent defender. This dissertation was accepted at Bonn, where Ritschl received the licentiate in 1846, qualifying as an unpaid lecturer in the same year, at age twenty-four.

CAREER AT BONN

Ritschl's teaching career spanned a period of just under forty-four years, at two universities—the first eighteen years, until 1864, were at Bonn, the last twenty-five in Göttingen. As a student, Ritschl had moved from a study of dogmatics, through the history of theology, to New Testament studies. At Bonn, he reversed that sequence, beginning as lecturer in New Testament until the end of the 1840s, then turning to history, with special concern for the reformation and the confessional positions of the various churches, until his appointment as extraordinary professor without tenure in 1853, when he began lecturing in dogmatics, which he was to continue until his death. From 1853 until the end, however, he continued to do research and to lecture in all three areas. Although his primary influence had been dogmatics, his last years were devoted to the history of the church and its theology, a field that he called his "youthful love," and his "escape" from the tempests of dogmatic controversy.[6]

A number of important episodes are to be noted in Ritschl's Bonn period, which ended when he was forty-two years old. (1) Ritschl entered into his first active political involvement, which turned out to be his last, also. In the wake of the February 1848 Paris uprising and because of his disillusionment with the Prussian Emperor Friedrich Wilhelm IV, Ritschl openly espoused constitutional democracy for Germany, joined the "Constitutional Union," and was elected to several offices in the Union, including that of being a delegate to a congress in Cologne in 1848. He was an observer at the famous Frankfurt Parliament, held in the Paulskirche in the same year. His was a moderate position, bitterly critical both of the radicals (the "Democratic Union") and the Prussian emperor. His disillusionment with the defeat of his party in 1849, together with the outbreak of violence in Bonn and the time-consuming demands which distracted him from his academic work, led to an early retirement from politics, although he remained active in efforts for university reform. This activity, in combination with union church sentiments and Baurian theological leanings, typed Ritschl as an activist, a critical spirit, and something of a liberal at Bonn. At this time he made a vow, which he never broke, to remain aloof from secular politics.

(2) Almost immediately after his arrival at Bonn, Ritschl began work on his book, *The Emergence of the Old Catholic Church,* which appeared in its first edition in 1850 and in its second in 1857.[7] This work, in its two editions, is significant for several reasons: (a) Whereas the first edition represents an attempt to apply Baur's method to the study of the development of New Testament Christianity into Catholicism, the second declares Ritschl's personal and academic independence from Baur and the Tübingen school, thus providing an alternative to that school for historical-theological studies which combined the same highly disciplined critical skills and concern for the overall historical significance of Christianity with a more conservative concern for the tradition and less reliance upon speculative schemes. (b) In the process of working out his differences with Baur, Ritschl solidified his fundamental interpretation of Jesus and the New Testament faith, which was to serve as a cornerstone for all of his later work. (c) The study of early Christianity laid down the basis for interpreting the emergence of the Christian church and the rise of Catholicism which was to be the kernel of the most important historical interpretation of Christianity up to our own day, that of the towering church historian, Adolf von Harnack, a later disciple of Ritschl.

Ritschl's differences from Baur did not take radical form until the second edition of the work, but they were latent from the outset. They can be summarized by saying that Ritschl on the one hand disagreed with Baur on a number of individual points of scholarly judgment, while on the other he rejected what he thought was Baur's tendency to sacrifice objectivity and the primacy of revelation to a theoretical philosophical bias, the conflict model of the dialectic of history. Although it appears that Ritschl misunderstood Baur's philosophical categories and underestimated how deeply they were rooted in Baur's historical studies, it is clear that Ritschl gave a priority to scripture which was in contrast to Baur and which constituted one of the elements of Ritschl's relative conservatism.[8] His individual scholarly disagreements with his teacher also appeared often to be conservative, since he tended to accept the authenticity of biblical documents where Baur often discredited their apostolic origins. Ritschl forsook the thesis of his habilitation dissertation, for example, only to have Baur take up the cudgels for it. In regard to the interpretation of early Christianity, on which Baur published a large work in 1853 and to which Ritschl's second edition responded, it may be said that whereas Baur had explained the movement of Christianity from the time after Jesus' crucifixion until the beginning of the third century as the struggle between Jewish-oriented Christians symbolized by Peter and Hellenistic–Gentile Christians under the aegis of Paul, culminating in the Johannine synthesis of the two represented in the Roman papacy, Ritschl to the contrary insisted that the Jewish and Gentile tendencies were more complex than Baur's conflict model allowed. Ritschl concluded that far from being a Jewish–Gentile synthesis, Catholicism was a wholly Gentile phenomenon, representing a deviation and estrangement from the Hebraic–Jewish heritage of earliest Christianity. This is the thesis that lives on in Harnack's history of dogma, where it is expanded and deepened.[9]

(3) Beginning in the 1850s, Ritschl gave increasing attention to church history and the history of theology, offering courses and writing a succession of articles on the nature of protestantism, the confessional documents, and opposing the confessionalist party. He did much basic research, which did not reach its fruition until some years later, when he had moved to Göttingen. These early efforts did help him, however, to solidify his understanding that the mainline reformation faith needed to be understood as an alternative to Roman Catholicism and that this reformation faith was best expressed by the unity of Lutherans and Calvinists, in opposition to the anti-union confessionalists. He also became even more convinced that the work of the reformation theologians was incomplete—a conviction that gave shape to his own professional vocation as a theologian.

As Ritschl probed more deeply into the reformation, he began to develop a discipline of reformation studies that were of considerable significance, even to the present time. Only recently has the work of

David Lotz[10] brought fully to light what earlier hints had suggested, namely, that Ritschl's concern for the reformation and specifically for the theology of Martin Luther was a crucial element of his own later dogmatic position and that both his concern and his specific scholarly interpretations of this period were greatly influential in the two generations after Ritschl. As a result of the studies that he undertook in the 1860s, Ritschl became one of the leading forces behind a "Luther Renaissance" which has been a major factor in twentieth century protestant and Roman Catholic theology. Even though Ritschl worked in a time before the great critical editions of Luther's works and other reformation documents were available, he established in a forceful way the thesis that Luther and the heart of the reformation faith differ from the authoritative portrayals of Luther's orthodox followers, including those of the confessionalists that opposed both Ritschl and his father in Pomerania. Ritschl established the now well-known (and in part discredited) disjunction between the theology of the "young Luther" and the mature Luther, as well as that between Luther and Melanchthon and the second generation of Lutheran dogmaticians. Ritschl's reformation studies must be placed in the context of his continuing animosities toward the confessionalists and the pietists, because these studies were used as polemical weapons against these parties. An example of how he turned this research to polemical purposes is evident in the "Prolegomena" to the *History of Pietism*, included in this volume.

(4) A vacancy in the department of systematic theology enabled Ritschl to begin lecturing in dogmatics in the winter semester, 1853–54. In the ten years that followed, until his departure for Göttingen, he developed a number of themes which became enduring characteristics for his thinking. Five of these themes deserve mention here: (a) He enunciated his position as a theologian *within* the Christian community of redeemed persons, insisting furthermore that the Christian faith must be considered a *corporate* expression of this community's faith prior to its individual expressions. (b) From this position, dogmatics deals solely with the *revelation* which is available in scripture and the tradition of scriptural interpretation. A preoccupation with revelation means that Jesus Christ is central to Christian theology and this in turn gives dogmatics its basic theme— that God's revealed will is the establishment of the kingdom of God.

(c) Preoccupation with revelation and Jesus Christ further suggests that the reconciled relationship of man with God is the arena within which theological thinking takes place. Through the sacrifice of the covenant, whose prototype is in the Old Testament, Jesus works forgiveness and justification for members of the covenant community; this justification is expressed in the community's reconciled life, which manifests itself through ethical work that builds up the kingdom of God. (d) Justification and reconciliation (the theme of the three-volume work which is Ritschl's magnum opus) appears very early, then, as a major concern for Ritschl's dogmatics. (e) From the first, Ritschl is intent upon being *systematic;* the various themes of the Christian faith must be unified in their presentation. Although his systematic penchant is the source for many of the distortions that mar his work, it was also to be his major strength as a dogmatician.

(5) Finally, we call attention to the opposition of the confessionalist Lutheran party which dogged Ritschl, even as it had his father. With the growing ascendancy of this party, which opposed both Ritschl's unionism and his Baurian background, in Prussian church affairs, the government officer in charge of university appointments and promotions consistently refused to consider Ritschl for advancement despite his growing reputation as a scholar and the recommendations of his faculty colleagues. Ritschl waited seven years to receive an appointment that would bring him a regular faculty position with salary and six more years until he was appointed to a tenured position in August 1859.

The Years in Göttingen

In the spring of 1864 Ritschl arrived in Göttingen to take over the senior chair in dogmatics, succeeding the right-wing Hegelian, I. A. Dorner. He had taken a wife five years earlier, his third child being born shortly before he left Bonn. Although his standing among his colleagues in Bonn was high, he chafed under the coolness of the government officials, and he interpreted their refusal to grant him adequate salary increases as an indication of their failure to appreciate him. Göttingen was in the province of Hannover, and Ritschl looked forward to exchanging the Prussian setting for a new one, with a new set of government and church officials.

Hannover was a "pure Lutheran" province, in the sense that it possessed no union church. The explicit program of the ecclesiastical officials was to pursue a policy of genuine confessional Lutheranism, purified of the rationalistic tendencies of an earlier generation and opposed to modernistic tendencies, yet alert to the modern world and incorporating healthy elements of pietism. Rationalist, pietist, and confessional Lutherans had all been a part of Hannover's recent past, as well as mediating theologians who attempted to synthesize orthodoxy and modern critical scholarly methods. The consequence of all these factors, however, was a situation which required Ritschl always to be wary of a resurgence of conservative confessionalism which formed a coalition with pietists, the difference here being that the ecclesiastical officials were not captive to the confessionalists. This situation was changed by the policies of Bismarck, who carried out campaigns of war with Austria, in 1866, continuing with the Franco-Prussian War of 1870. As the campaigns began, Ritschl retreated from the liberalism of the Bonn era, since he was of the opinion that Bismarck's policy was a realistic one. His status as a Prussian and as a supporter of Bismarck won him no affection in Göttingen, however, and when in August 1866, Hannover was annexed by Prussia, he felt himself severely ostracized by his colleagues. The confessionalist opposition took on added meaning, since orthodoxism now became a rallying point for Hannoverian opposition to Prussian hegemony politically as well as to Prussian unionism ecclesiastically.

Ironically, Ritschl seemed more attractive to the Prussian officials after the annexation, because he became a point of contact and a source of information for the Prussian ministers of culture and religion. In October 1869, he was appointed a delegate to the Hannoverian provincial synod, in connection with whose meetings he drew up a comprehensive report on the church-political situation in Hannover and northern Germany. This report was for the same minister who had snubbed him repeatedly in his later years at Bonn. His thesis was highly polemical: that the orthodox Lutherans in most of northern Germany were so implicated in the political situation that confessionalism was to be evaluated in political as well as in theological terms, as an expression of anti-Prussianism and "political particularism." He observed that ecclesiastical unionism and Prussian political expansionism seemed inseparable in the eyes of those who, within Prussia and without, could not share the dreams of the Prussian leaders. This report made a great impression on the minister, who called Ritschl to Berlin for further consultations, apparently even sharing the report with the Prussian king.

The unionism which Ritschl had shared by family tradition and which he undergirded with his academic studies in the nature of protestantism remained constant, even though the response it elicited from ecclesiastical and government circles varied from favorable to hostile. When this state of affairs is kept in mind, along with the ever-present pietist trends in the German church, against whom Ritschl expended as much polemical energy as he did against the orthodoxists, we can understand the existential and political circumstances in which Ritschl formed his identity as a theologian of the church. Not only his historical work, with its important emphasis upon Luther and the reformation, but also his philosophical and dogmatic work must be seen as a response, in part, to these circumstances.

At this same time, Ritschl was attempting to remain uninvolved in the specific party conflicts of the province and to avoid concrete participation in church affairs. He deliberately declined many speaking engagements and published relatively little between 1864 and 1869, on the grounds that anything he wrote or said would be used or abused by one or another of the parties. For the same reason, he discouraged his students from forming "Ritschlian" study groups among the parish pastors. He was beginning what he called his "life-work," the fruit of his vocation as an academic theologian, the three-volume *Justification and Reconciliation.* In these years, even though the temptation was great, he declined several calls to other universities, just as in the early seventies he was to decline the election as pro-rector of the university and four repeated offers of a joint position at the University of Berlin and a high post in the Prussian church administration. The concept of vocation, understood as a high ethical work related to the realization of the kingdom of God, which was so integral to his theological system, drove him to define himself more and more as an academic theologian, to the exclusion of other distractions. As a consequence, his interests and his personality became steadily narrower, to the discomfort of those who differed from him, but his life's purpose became more sharply focused and his theological contribution was progressively deepened and solidified.

In January 1869, after less than ten years of marriage, Ritschl's wife died, followed less than two years later by the death of his sister who had become his housekeeper and foster mother to his children. These deaths made a deep impression on Ritschl, whose grieving reached intense depths. We note a spirit of solemnity and even resignation entering at this time, never to leave him. For all his sternness and rigorous sense of vocation, Ritschl lived a life marked by many friendships, overcoming much of the anti-Prussian bias in Göttingen, and not by any means limited to theologians and clergy. He participated regularly in singing groups and was a party-giver of some note among his intimate circle of friends. This way of life did not disappear completely after his wife's death, but it did decline steadily. Although at the end of his life he lectured to large classes of over one hundred students, he seems to have been relatively ineffective as a classroom teacher, making much more impact with his writings than with his lectures. In the 1870s and '80s the influence of his theological thinking greatly increased—notably with the appearance of the magnum opus and his short summary of his theological system, *Instruction in the Christian Religion*. By 1879 he could write that his dogmatic position was expounded by disciples (many of whom had not studied with him, but were influenced by his writings) on every theological faculty in western Germany except for Heidelberg. But at the same time, Ritschl lamented all his life that his theology did not win the sort of positive reception that he thought it deserved. Many of his letters, at the height of his influence, speak with resignation of the "poor" hearing and negative response he was receiving. He was extraordinarily sensitive to those who became his disciples, rejoicing in their association, and at the same time equally sensitive to those who criticized him. In his later life, when controversy swirled around him, he responded only seldom to his critics and relied on his close friends to summarize the critiques, while he read only the most serious himself.

Ritschl's opposition was very hostile and vociferous, but its appearance in the late seventies and eighties was a tribute in itself to the immense impact Ritschl was making. Since, for all practical purposes, it may be said that his dogmatic achievement was complete by the mid-seventies, it is not surprising that it is only after this time that the opposition became intense, at first through the conventional channels of periodicals and newspapers, but in the early 1880s through the church-political means of seeking Ritschl's censure at provincial synods. For the most part, it may be said that his disciples, his colleagues, and the ecclesiastical officials defended Ritschl quite well—some because they were enthusiastic adherents of the man, others because they recognized that the seriousness of his achievement did not merit the kind of censure that some opponents were demanding.

The climaxing decade of Ritschl's career, 1864–1874, was devoted to the work on justification and reconciliation, in which Ritschl's creative and systematic dogmatic gifts were brought to a sharply focused expression. Roughly speaking, the next (and last) decade of his life, 1876–1886, went into the three-volume *History of Pietism.* During this time, Ritschl literally read every primary source for Dutch, German, and Swiss pietism that the libraries of his time could provide. His very last years were spent on the posthumously published work on *Fides Implicita,* which dealt with questions of faith and reason, from medieval times to the present. He had interrupted these studies to respond to critics in his essay on *Theology and Metaphysics* and also to revise the work on justification and his other books. He served two terms, in 1876 and 1886, as pro-rector of the university; during the second term he presided over and delivered the keynote address at the one hundred fiftieth anniversary of the university. Toward the end, Ritschl suffered from a number of ailments, aggravated by his feeling of loneliness at the deaths of loved ones and friends and by the generally depressing effect of controversy. In his last days, he was cared for by his son-in-law, the New Testament scholar, Johannes Weiss, and his son, the church historian, Otto. He died on March 20, 1889, five days before his sixty-seventh birthday.

II. RITSCHL'S THEOLOGICAL CONTRIBUTION

We can best understand the popularity and the opposition evoked by Ritschl's work if we turn our attention to the theological system that stands at the center of that work. The appeal of Ritschl's theology can be summarized by saying that *he presented a forceful*

contemporary statement of the Christian faith which resonated to
the scene in which he lived, and he linked this statement positively
to the tradition upon which his hearers wanted to rely, while also
expressing himself in terms of a method that was scientifically sig-
nificant. Let us look more closely at the elements of this summary:
forceful contemporary statement of faith, positive link to tradition,
and scientific method.

CONTEMPORARY STATEMENT OF FAITH

Ritschl's central statement of faith is a relatively simple, but
original, linking of a few basic ideas. The Christian faith embodies
Jesus' revelation, which is the message that God's will is to establish
his kingdom. Correlative to God's objective will toward his kingdom
is the relationship of man to God and that kingdom, a relationship
that is spoken of in terms of the classical Christian doctrines of
justification and reconciliation. Whether we speak of the kingdom
of God or of man's relationship to God in justification and reconciliation, we meet a duality (Ritschl himself called it "an ellipse with
two foci") comprised of that which man receives, as *gift,* which
brings him near to God and the kingdom, and that which man must
do, as *task,* to express his relationship to God and realize the kingdom. Forgiveness of sins, justification, adoption as sons of God—
these are terms Ritschl uses to describe the gift, or the "religious"
side of the duality, whereas reconciliation (as the evidence of justification), ethical vocation, love, are terms that spell out the task,
or "ethical" side. The kingdom of God is the highest good—God's
highest good in that in it he draws near to man and fulfills his own
will, man's highest good in that the kingdom involves reconciliation
and the ethical activity which fulfills man's own nature. The sacrifice
of Christ for the covenant community, the church, forgives sins and
thus brings man near to God, justifies him, and makes possible the
life of love in the ethical vocation which fulfills man and the will of
God in the kingdom.

This view of the Christian faith is first of all corporate, since it is
only in the community of the believers that one receives the revelation of God in Jesus Christ, and the realization of the kingdom of
God is a corporate reality embodied in the interrelation of justified
and ethically responsible persons. But the individual is also chal-

lenged, since it is his fulfillment and his ethical vocation which the
Christian faith speaks to most directly, just as it offers him a vision
of his own reconciliation with God. The kingdom becomes God's
highest good, in that his will is fulfilled in it. But the impact of the
kingdom is knowable only as man's highest good, and as such it
resolves the basic dilemma that confronts every man, namely, that he
is a part of nature and seemingly subsumed within the gigantic system of the natural world, thus deprived of his distinctive spiritual
value which tells him in his own mind that he is more than nature
and therefore not to be subsumed under it. Ritschl's statement of
the Christian faith, therefore, is focused on the fact of human life
(later, we shall call this "a way of living," or *Lebensführung*), indeed
a theology of *life,* which speaks not only of reconciliation with God
but also with self and the world, not only of the religious dimension
of life but also of the ethical. His theology is a theology of the inner,
or spiritual, life, and the key to understanding this statement of
faith is that it encourages man on the one hand by telling him that he
is free to participate in the world through his vocation in society,
which actually serves to build God's kingdom, while on the other
hand it consoles him with the assertion that even if external conditions are unaffected by his vocational activity, God's providential
working incorporates man within the system of God's kingdom, a
system that does not subsume him under nature but rather relates
him to nature in a way that preserves his spiritual distinctiveness
and value.[11]

POSITIVE LINK TO TRADITION

Ritschl's statement of the Christian faith appealed to his hearers'
religious and ethical needs; it showed them how to live with God
and with the world and their fellowmen. But it did so in a way that
gave special confidence to pastors and students of theology, because
it based its premises on the tradition of religious faith which those
pastors and students had been taught to respect and upon which they
wanted to rely. First of all, Ritschl turned his hearers toward scripture and Jesus Christ. The message of justification and reconciliation
in the kingdom of God is central to the preaching of Jesus, and the
New Testament is a reliable resource for learning of that preaching,

just as the Old Testament is a necessary presupposition for it. Furthermore, this message of the kingdom is central to the tradition of scriptural interpretation in which we have shared in the ongoing church of Christ. Although his thesis concerning the rise of catholicism held that the post-apostolic developments perverted the biblical faith in a Gentile environment, Ritschl nevertheless was able to document a continuous tradition of interpreting the message of Jesus which led through the Middle Ages, up to Luther's reformation and on to his own work as a successor to the reformers. He could document the deviations from this tradition, but he did so in a way that explained why the deviations took place, most often showing sympathy for the men who were compelled by circumstance to take a deviating position in spite of their own best intentions, while also very forcefully demonstrating why those deviations must be rejected in favor of a return to the authentic message. He led his readers through a continuous tradition which emphasized Jesus, the apostolic community, certain medieval figures including St. Bernard, Luther, and Calvin, to a certain extent Melanchthon, Kant, Schleiermacher, German Idealism, up to Albrecht Ritschl. It is no accident that he entitled his short systematic summary of Christian doctrine *Unterricht in der christlichen Religion,* which is the same phrase in German which entitles John Calvin's reformation summary of doctrine, *Institutes of the Christian Religion.*[12]

LIFE-STYLE AND HISTORICAL THINKING

In 1853, Ritschl himself laid down a principle of method that fairly represents his own work: "The principle of theological knowledge must be a synthesis of personal religious knowledge with the full understanding of the history of the reciprocal relations of piety with scripture and the understanding of the world."[13] His biographer restates the same principle thus: "The basic element in his teaching concerning Christianity is his biblical theology, which has been worked into dogmatics in terms of a certain shape of protestant piety, with theological concepts whose validity he had demonstrated in thorough investigations of the history of theology."[14] Two elements are described in these statements: (a) piety or life-style and (b) thinking through this life-style in historical perspective.

Life-Style

At the center of Ritschl's method was the conviction that religion is first of all a "way of living" (*eine Weise des Lebens*), a "way of conducting one's life" (*Lebensführung*). A way of living was what Ritschl's historical studies examined, it was the focus around which he organized his theological system, and it is that which he aimed to influence in the church and society of his day. This is not to imply that Ritschl reduced religion to ethics, because he put "way of living" in a full context of religious and dogmatic considerations; but he focused his study of religion on the existential moral, philosophical, and psychic problems which attend the conduct of life. As we have seen, this way of living was described in terms of the objective will of God in his kingdom and the process of justification and reconciliation which takes place within man. Each of these two sets of concepts deals with the balance or equilibrium between that which man *receives,* which sustains him and brings him near to God, and that which man must *perform,* the imperative which commands his will and flows from God's will. Although he did not develop this category of "way of living" until relatively late with fullness and precision, it was a concern which antedated his earliest work and in a less refined way directed even the first edition of *The Emergence of the Old Catholic Church.* The category is clearly determinative for the work on pietism (included in this volume). Ritschl's presentation of the "way of living" category made plain certain implications which he presupposed, as well as certain consequences that followed from it. For one thing, it incorporated within itself Jesus' theme of the kingdom of God, a theme which Ritschl applied in a new and original way for his time by using it as the primary interpretive key for understanding Jesus. At the same time, the category of "way of living" belonged within the framework of the familiar justification concept that was central for Luther. Finally, it also built upon the ethically oriented kingdom of God concepts of two imposing figures in what was then recent German intellectual history, Immanuel Kant and Friedrich Schleiermacher, as well as the contemporary Richard Rothe.[15] Thus, when Ritschl's readers dealt with his category of "way of living," they sensed that they were dealing with familiar strands of thought that had been dealt with prominently in their intellectual and religious tradition, even though they also sensed that they were witnessing an original reshaping of those familiar elements.

Justification and Reconciliation

When Ritschl spoke to his readers about justification, the central doctrine for Luther and Lutheranism, he confronted them with the sharply stated opinion that the Lutheran reformation, Luther included, had left unfinished theological business for their generation, in that justification had not been related adequately to regeneration and good works, and further that the older Luther and his followers had distorted the purity and power of the young Luther's insights into the nature of justification and reconciliation by increasing objectivism and metaphysicizing.[16] Justification is solely the act of God aimed at man; it involves no placating of God by Jesus Christ, since it is man alone who is estranged and needs reconciling, not God. Justification is a judgment by God that the sinner's transgressions no longer stand as a barrier to the nearness of God and the intimacy of man's relationships to God. Justification provides the answer to the sinner's question, "How can I stand before God in my imperfections?" The answer comes back, "Your sins are deprived of their alienating consequences by the God who has drawn near to you in Christ's sacrifice." Justification calms the conscience of the sinner who needs consolation in his guilt,[17] and reconciliation is the empirical evidence of that justification. To Ritschl's audience, this radical emphasis upon Luther and his central doctrine was something not shared by other dogmaticians of the day,[18] and it turned students and preachers directly to Luther rather than to orthodox dogmas, philosophical schemes, or pietistic spiritual processes. It also emphasized, in a new (and perhaps erroneous) way the consoling aspects of Luther's doctrine rather than the wrath toward sin and the consequent human inner torments, which were generally emphasized in treatments of Luther's thought.[19] This consolation of God's judgment freed man, in Ritschl's interpretation, for participation in the kingdom of God, and in this way the latter concept was the reverse side of the "way of living" category which incorporated justification.

The Kingdom of God

The kingdom of God is also a pure gift of God to men, consoling them in their situation, because it offers them adoption as God's sons and the possibility of participation in a system of meaning which preserves their spiritual status as human beings. In the process of offering this consolation, however, it is also a mandate for the ethical action which realizes this kingdom. The marks of Kant, Schleiermacher, and Rothe are clear. Kant's great contribution was his single-minded emphasis on the significance of will and ethical action as the chief character of man, opening up man's relationship to God and the total human community; in his own way, Kant linked this to the Christian concept of the kingdom of God. Schleiermacher added to this a more direct concern for the kingdom of God and spoke of the "highest good," which motivates man's action and which serves God's own highest good as expressed in the idea of the kingdom. Rothe underscored the developmental character of the kingdom as it stood as overarching key to the movement of history, progressively realized by man's ethical action.[20] As Norman Metzler points out, this prior thinking presented Ritschl with the clear concept of the kingdom of God as a duality—representing God's highest will for the world and man, thus an eschatological concept, and also offering to man his ethical mandate, which brings with it self-fulfillment.[21] But Ritschl, while taking over the thought of these predecessors, forcefully redirected it by arguing that this complex of thought was the key to interpreting the preaching of Jesus and that it is attested by the New Testament.[22] To Ritschl goes credit for having ensconced the idea of the kingdom so emphatically and irreversibly at the center of Christian dogmatics that it became determinative for his entire dogmatic system and unavoidable for his successors.[23] He also developed it more fully, calling attention to the dual character of the kingdom as gift and task, religious and ethical. Thus, Ritschl synthesized Kant and Schleiermacher—two of the towering intellectual influences in nineteenth century German culture, tempering Kant's ethical emphasis with Schleiermacher's concern for feeling and religion[24] and grounding them both in reformation and New Testament faith.

Life-Style and Method

The category of life-style or "way of living" belongs in a discussion of Ritschl's method, because he insisted on the one hand that the unity of his generation with Luther, with the prior Christian tradition, and with Jesus and the New Testament consists in the unity or agreement with this form of life-style.[25] On the other hand, as a matter of scientific principle Ritschl laid down the axiom that theology's task was not to describe God and his actions "from above," that is, as if the theologian stood in God's own mind, but rather in terms of the corresponding moral and religious actions which are stimulated or called forth by God. In other words, the only medium in which we can discern and describe God's action is in the style of life which the justified Christian lives; that style of life is both the substance of God's revelation in Jesus and the common link that Christians have with preceding generations of the church.[26] This represents a concentration upon man's life and particularly upon the psychic and spiritual dynamics that pertain to his religious and ethical choices, dynamics which have been of decisive significance for Christian theology.

Ritschl spelled out in detail the characteristics of this style of living. They consist of confidence in God's providence (this confidence is the expression of one's justification), which liberates man to enter into relationships of love, primarily through the faithful exercise of his vocation. Freedom to live in the world under God's providence is the hallmark of Ritschl's conception of Christianity. Humility and patience go along with this liberated life, as well as prayer and participation in corporate worship. Prayer and worship remind the Christian of Christ's revelation and example, and thus they are to consist chiefly of praise and thanksgiving for the gifts of forgiveness and freedom which God has given.

Historical Thinking

We have clarified the way in which Ritschl's method focused upon the Christian style of life, elaborated in philosophical and theological concepts which gave force and clarity to that style. But both Ritschl and his son Otto spoke also of the biblical and historical connections of this concept. We have already suggested how Ritschl drew upon historical and biblical sources for the materials of his concept of the Christian life, relating it specifically to Luther, the reformation, the New Testament witness to Jesus, as well as to Kant, Schleiermacher, and Rothe. But in terms of Ritschl's method, which was so compelling to a generation of theological students and pastors who adhered to his thought, there is more at stake than the fact *that* Ritschl appealed to history (including the Bible)—there is the question of *how* he approached history.

Baur

Ferdinand Christian Baur taught Ritschl two lessons that he never forgot. The first lesson was that the nature of Christianity is to be ascertained by subjecting it to critical historical inquiry in its total historical development from the beginning to the present; any single phenomenon in Christian history can be adequately assessed only by understanding the previous generations upon which it built, its own historical circumstances and the contribution it made to that situation and bequeathed to the next generation; and the whole of Christianity can be understood only by tracing these successive contributions under the interpretive guidance of a leading category which is appropriate to the study. Ritschl's leading idea was his category of Christian life-style. The second lesson was that the study of Christianity in terms of its history must be carried out by immersion in the concrete dynamics of the historical process by means of attention to the original sources; one must deal with as many of these sources as possible, and his interpretations must take intelligent account of all of them.

In part, Ritschl's break with Baur was due to his opinion that the teacher had not followed his own principle in this regard faithfully enough. With this twofold lesson firmly a part of him, Ritschl's corpus of works, especially (but not only) the magnum opus on justification and reconciliation, forms a whole.[27] He operated with his leading interpretive idea of "way of living," working through all of Christian history from the Old Testament backgrounds through the rise of catholicism, Middle Ages, reformation, and protestant developments up to his own time. He showed the twists and turns which the development of his leading idea had taken, always balancing the two factors, gift and task, within his discussion. He dealt both with the internal dynamics of the development (which Baur had emphasized) and the external factors affecting it (which Baur did not deal with so fully). Thus, he could explain not only *that* a Gentile deviation in understanding the Christian style of life had occurred, but also *why* and *how* it happened (due to pressures in the Roman Empire which alienated Gentile Christians from their origins), and he could sympathetically clarify how second and third century Christians were forced to their deviation, even though he emphatically rejected their deviation. In the same way, he could show how and why Melanchthon and the second generation of Lutherans were compelled to distort the reformation impulse through the objectivizing and legalizing pressures in their environment, and he could even understand how pietism, his *bête noire*, represented a sound reaction to his other bitter foe, objectivizing orthodoxy. He developed a theory of "vestigial leaves" (*Keim-blättchen*) which antedated Harnack's "kernel and husk" theory, even though it achieved little prominence. According to this image, Ritschl judged that the second generation of a powerful movement was obliged to erect certain rigidities of thought and practice in order to preserve the truth of the movement, as a seedling develops hard vestigial leaves. From the plant, however, we learn that these early rigidities are to be sloughed off as soon as possible, when the plant is strong. The catholicizing trend in early Christianity and the dogmatizing trend of the reformation sustained the rigidities past their usefulness and turned them into deviation.[28] These reflections from his historical studies gave him a sense of being a new reformer which, although at times overbearing and exasperating, lent clarity and forcefulness to the alternative which he clearly posed to the deviations he had uncovered, past and present.

Interpreting the "Present Age"

Michael Ryan has probed deeply into Ritschl's use of historical method, relating it provocatively to Schleiermacher and to nineteenth century German historiography, particularly the theories of the secular historian, Leopold von Ranke.[29] Ryan believes that after his break with Baur, Ritschl became indebted to Schleiermacher more than to any other person. From Schleiermacher's method, Ritschl accepted the suggestion that dogmatics deals with the historical knowledge of the present moment "considered with a view to the future development of Christian doctrine," or, in other words, dogmatics builds on historical theology so as to develop an interpretation of the present, for the present.[30] Ritschl thus worked under the imperative of interpreting the "present age," which was determined for him by the movement from Kant through Schleiermacher in which was developed a category of the "religious-moral community" and in which Kant's emphasis upon the moral law and will was modified by Schleiermacher's concern for religion and feeling. To be sure, Ritschl also used Kant to criticize Schleiermacher. Ryan's analysis receives a corroborative counterpart in Norman Metzler's thesis describing a Kant-Schleiermacher-Rothe development in the concept of the kingdom of God and the highest good.[31]

The significance of Ritchl's attempt to interpret his present age must not be underestimated. The tendency is to underestimate the attempt, since Ritschl himself spoke misleadingly about his own theology as having no apologetic interests whatsoever and since he is also frequently characterized as self-assured and confident of the world in which he lived, the implication being that he was unaware that he was living in the last days of the modern era that began with the enlightenment and ended with World War I. Horst Stephan's remark that Ritschl's emphasis upon the church as the theologian's starting point led to theology's isolation from cultural matters has been influential.[32] It is not clear how conscious he was of the significance of his epoch and its imminent demise, but it is certain that the options he took for his work do represent a response to his times, and we dare not overlook the potential fruitfulness of those options. Several strands of thought must be brought into one focus in order to make this clear.

Ritschl was obviously aware, in the first place, that the scientific world view which was burgeoning in his time was crucial for the lives of all men. He understood the impact of this world view to reside in its tendency to include all of the world and man within a vast nexus of cause and effect which deprived man of his free will and which eliminated any qualitative differences between man and the rest of reality. He expressed this as the contradiction which man feels when he knows himself to be a part of this world and subject to its cause and effect system even as at the same time he knows himself to be created in God's image and different from, in a sense superior to, the world. Man's basic religious striving is toward wholeness, which means that he seeks to become a part of a whole which does not compromise his essential being. The scientific world view tells man that he is part of a whole which *does* compromise him by making him no more than any other constituent of nature. It is quite possible to interpret Ritschl's entire theology as an attempt to deal with this challenge of the scientific world view. Such interpretations have prompted some critics to charge that Ritschl's total presentation of the Christian faith is simply an effort to bend God to the task of meeting man's need for rescue from the cause and effect system of modern science.[33]

Ritschl also seemed to be well aware that the synthesis which Schleiermacher and Hegel had effected between speculative metaphysics and scientific modes of thought, or between Christian faith (metaphysically conceived) and the contemporary world views, was breaking down.[34] This breakdown was evident in his student days, and especially at Halle in the early 1840s when he was actively engaged in thinking through the Hegelian option and its development and dissolution in its right and left "wings." What Ritschl did was to reject metaphysics and speculation as constitutive for theology and faith (see the essay, "Theology and Metaphysics" in this volume). Paul Wrzecionko has described what Ritschl put in the place of metaphysics.[35] He took the epistemology of his Göttingen colleague, Hermann Lotze,[36] who explicitly attempted to construct a metaphysics that could harmonize with the scientific world view, and thus to open up a vast interpretation of human existence and God's relation to that existence, while "bracketing out" all metaphysical categories, including Lotze's own. Lotze's epistemology brought ontology and psychology together in its assertions that the separation between the knowing subject and the object it seeks to know is overcome when we recognize that in the temporal manifestations which occupy human processes of knowing the object is fully present through its effects— even that "object" which is the Ultimate. These effects, in form and operation *are* the object we seek to know, and thus it is mistaken to suppose that we must "get behind" or "above" or "below" these effects to another world where objects are "real." To this Ritschl linked Kant's and Schleiermacher's high regard for the ethical life of man and for the processes of his self-consciousness, and by means of Lotze's epistemology he could assert that a full and exclusive concentration upon this human spiritual life of ethical decision and religious self-consciousness would bring man knowledge of and participation in the "real." Of course, he centered on the religious self-consciousness and ethical decision that are expressed in the life of the Christian community of believers, in constant dialogue with the revelation of Jesus Christ in the New Testament and in later tradition. Encounter with this revelation, localized in the self-consciousness of the church, brought man into relationship with the ultimate reality of God, whose kingdom was the whole which preserved man's essential nature as spirit and related him to the rest of the world.

Little wonder that Ritschl could channel great energy into historical examination of the Christian sources of revelation! That was the place where the data of God were to be found, and he could challenge men to wrestle with this revelation in their own lives, since the impact of revelation upon their conscious lives was the impact of God. Ritschl's attention to Christian history was an alternative to metaphysics, whereas for Baur it had been the completion of metaphysics. Lotze further helped Ritschl to formulate his insight that the ethical response discernible in men's conscious lives is response to the activity of the real, God. This alternative to speculative metaphysics, which turned toward the examination of the mutual relationships between a concrete historical tradition and the human self-consciousness, liberated theology from being a metaphysical, supernatural enterprise which was rapidly being discredited by the natural scientific perspective.

The obverse side of this retreat from metaphysics and the threat of science was Ritschl's statement to his age that the "natural" processes in which they participated were more than they themselves would often admit, since they were actually the correlates of the divine reality. Furthermore, he challenged his times to acknowledge that the leveling of human self-consciousness and man's psychic life to a place of subjection within a natural nexus of cause and effect would in the end be a destruction of the very human spirit which they exalted. Wrzecionko sees this as a pointed apologetic which demonstrates how seriously (and in Wrzecionko's view, wrongly) Ritschl took the spirit of his times, a spirit which proudly and even arrogantly sang the praises and glories of the human spirit and its achievements.

Before we interpret Ritschl's antimetaphysical bias and his strategy of concentrating solely on Christian community and revelation as a retreat from the ferment and challenges of his age, we must be clear in what ways he was accurately interpreting the thrust of his era. This was an era marked by the demise of the older metaphysical God and the metaphysical method of talking about God. Ritschl was concerned to carry on both an attempt to overcome his age and to offer an apologetic to it. It goes without saying that his was a *relatively* conservative approach among many liberal alternatives. His rejection of metaphysics went along with an unquestioning acceptance of God and the traditional picture of God as heavenly father (he fully expected to be reunited with his wife after death, in heaven), and he was convinced that his innovations were a return to Jesus and the authentic reformation. But he was only relatively conservative; he made no attempt to rescue metaphysics or supernaturalism or to gloss over their passing.

Ritschl's Norm

We can conclude our survey of Ritschl's method by describing in more detail the factors that were normative for his historical method, most of which have already been discussed implicitly in our survey. Many interpreters of Ritschl, including myself, have argued for a single norm in his work—Jesus Christ as set forth in the New Testament, Luther, the historical tradition as such, and his constructive category of the dual relationship between God and man which received expression in his concept of the kingdom of God.[37] Effective arguments have recently been made for each of these. As a result of these several arguments and their mutual criticisms, we are probably wisest to conclude that there are several normative elements in Ritschl's thought, each of which can appear paramount when his system is viewed from a certain perspective. Three of these suggested norms belong together as historically received factors—Jesus, Luther, the tradition—while the concept of a duality of religion and ethics is a constructive category built of dogmatic and philosophical elements. Ritschl was convinced that his dual concept of the God-man relationship, expressed powerfully as the kingdom of God, was at the heart of Christian faith and that it was a word his generation needed to hear. He was also convinced that this was a faithful representation of what Jesus preached as the revelation of God and of what the authentic Christian tradition, including Luther, witnessed to. Ritschl could not have effectively interpreted his tradition from Christ to his own nineteenth century, nor participated in that tradition, if he had not possessed such a category of meaning and interpretation. At the same time, he could not, in good conscience, have affirmed this concept of Christian life if he had not been convinced that the authoritative persons and moments in the tradition witnessed to its substance and its importance. His attention to history gave breadth and persuasiveness to his dogmatic concepts, but we cannot avoid the judgment that those concepts (and their philosophical undergirding) rendered his reading of the historical sources partial and, in some respects, seriously defective. History and dogmatic creativity were so closely wedded in his method and in his person that it seems impossible to argue that one or the other was normative over the other, even though his own intention was to let historical revelation rule his dogmatics.

III. RITSCHL'S SIGNIFICANCE FOR HIS OWN TIME

We have argued, partly in reliance upon new studies of Ritschl, that he worked under the consciousness that he had a message for his own day and that this consciousness helped to shape his total theological work. We have examined that message and its methodological principles in some detail; now we must ask about its significance. *Positively*, we may say that Ritschl's significance lies in his effectiveness in bringing together more creatively than any of his contemporaries the theological concerns of his age and its recent past, and in his ability to synthesize those concerns with his own categories in the formulation of a message persuasive to a great variety of his contemporaries. *Negatively*, we must say that Ritschl also made a great number of his contemporaries feel that the wind had been taken out of their sails by his system. The one judgment explains his popularity and influence, the other the bitter criticism he drew from his opponents. Because he drew together so many elements in his work, very few of his colleagues in the church or in the theological and philosophical faculty were left untouched by him. We can test this thesis by briefly observing Ritschl's impact on a number of his contemporaries.

To the Hegelians and the Tübingen school of F. C. Baur, Ritschl seemed to be a conservative traditionalist. He stung them by insisting that a concentration upon the revelation in the New Testament demanded a revision of their overarching theoretical schemes for interpreting Christianity, viz., their concept of the Spirit manifesting itself in history and fulfilling itself through the movement of conflict from thesis to antithesis and synthesis. Since they considered this scheme to be essential for objective scientific thought, Ritschl's demurrer appeared to be a lack of nerve, a retreat from the critical implications of historical truth. To many pastors and theological students, however, Ritschl's insistence that speculation must be subordinate to biblical revelation was more consonant with what they conceived to be the imperatives of their faith. Alongside this explicit polemic and appeal, however, lies the implicit strategy of Ritschl's antimetaphysical stance which wagered its future on a surmise that the metaphysics of Hegel and Baur was passing away, in which event theology was better advised to concentrate on the obvious historical sources available and their significance for life. Ritschl's advocacy of revelation over speculation was also a decision that in the future Kant's critique of metaphysics would prove correct. But while he was rejecting the superstructure of Hegel and Baur, he took over their critical apparatus and brought it to even greater refinement and inspired his disciples to surpass himself in this regard. In the process, he retained the Hegelian-Baurian concern for the whole of history and for the interpretation of Christianity in terms of its total development.

In his decision against Hegelian metaphysical speculation, Ritschl relied upon the Kantian critique of metaphysics and the Kantian emphasis on will and the moral law, in concert with Schleiermacher's ethics and religious emphasis. Ritschl was sharply critical of Schleiermacher's romanticism and individualism, which he thought were pietistic in their consequences. But in his decision for Kant and his subsequent concentration on the ethical and religious self-consciousness of man, he found Schleiermacher's detailed and methodical discussion of that self-consciousness invaluable. In the long run, Ritschl linked his work to Schleiermacher's in both historical studies and in probing the dynamics of the religious consciousness, albeit modifying the latter with a Kantian concern for the will.

Ritschl's relations to orthodox, confessional Lutherans and pietists were especially significant, since they formed a hostile environment for him and his father before him. He very nearly defeated the confessionalists on their own ground, since he championed Luther and the confessions every bit as strongly as they, devoting years and many treatises to demonstrating that he was in fact the true Lutheran. And, as Lotz has shown, even though Ritschl was greatly mistaken in some of his Luther-interpretation, his work—especially as it was an impulse for the work of Karl Holl—may have been more significant in the long run than that of the more orthodox Lutherans, even that of Theodosius Harnack.[38] Far from leaving his adherents without a strong sense of Lutheran identity, he intensified it in men like Wilhelm Herrmann and Adolf von Harnack. It might be said as much as anything else, that Ritschl's work was a vigorous description of what it meant to be a reformation Christian in his day—at least he thought it was.

As for the pietists, they consumed as much of Ritschl's time and effort as the confessionalists. He said that his ten years of work on the history of pietism was necessary in order to hold up to his pietist contemporaries their own history and demonstrate openly how wrong they were.[39] This seems an almost compulsive dedication of a decade's work, but it also indicates what Ritschl thought was at stake. In one sense, focusing as he did on the Christian style of life or *Lebensführung*, he was in direct competition with the pietists and therefore had to beat them at their own game. He had claimed that unless the reformation of Luther, Calvin, and Zwingli could foster a strong piety or life-style, it could not claim to be a true interpretation of Christianity.[40] He did not, in other words, believe that a preoccupation with piety and a living religion were in error; rather, he disagreed with the specific option which pietists set forth. He considered the pietists to be the manifestation, within churchly protestantism, of the same perversions that were rooted in medieval catholicism and its left-wing protestant (i.e., for Ritschl, nonchurchly protestantism) offshoot, the anabaptists. Several observers have rooted Ritschl's success in the healthy version of piety which he fostered. He rested it in the New Testament and in Luther, thus stealing the thunder of the pietists with one hand and attempting to eradicate them with the other.

A number of Ritschl's theological peers had committed themselves to mediating between the modern world view and critical scholarship on the one side and traditional faith on the other. This group, practically speaking, simply had to accede to Ritschl, since he fulfilled their program with more skill and force than they could themselves.[41] The case of Martin Kähler is an instructive example, since we now know from recent studies that far from being an alternative to Ritschl, he stood with Ritschl on many of his most important emphases and even borrowed from him for some of his most characteristic ideas.[42]

One of the reasons that Ritschl's opponents failed in their attempts to have Ritschl censured is that his popularity was simply too great. Another, perhaps less important reason but nevertheless worthy of mention, is the high regard he enjoyed in governmental, university, and some ecclesiastical circles. It is ironic that the "new thing" that Ritschl did theologically and philosophically did not possess within it a thrust for new things culturally, politically, and socially. His was not the image of a typical conservative or "establishment" figure although his social and political impact led to such a characterization. When in 1886 protests were at a high pitch in confessional circles— leading to an attack at the 1887 provincial synod—Ritschl was receiving forty-seven out of a possible fifty-eight votes in his election as pro-rector of the university. Colleagues and provincial officials took over much of his defense at the synods. He had earlier declined four calls to the Berlin faculty where the confessionalist leader Hengstenberg was strong. Yet as revolutionary as many of his ideas were, his social impact was conservative, probably due to his call for vocational obedience, his thorough authoritarianism, which marred his emphasis on divine providence, and his success at linking his theological opponents, the confessionalists, to an anti-Prussian political position. Ritschl had been in the Prussian elite since birth and he knew how to conduct himself discreetly. Although he was controversial, he never permitted his person or his name to be attached to a specific party or to partisan newspapers or periodicals. As thickly involved in controversy as he was, his political shrewdness deserves some admiration.

Finally, Ritschl's thought attempted to help the protestant church of his day bolster itself against the onslaughts of both a rising secularistic culture which despised the church (and for protestants, these critics were joined by catholic opponents) and a modern scientific world view which threatened the faith of the church. David Lotz has argued suggestively how Ritschl's interpretation of protestantism can be viewed as an almost point-for-point refutation of the anti-protestant polemic of two prominent contemporaries—Jakob Burckhardt of Basel, with whom Ritschl may not have been familiar, and Paul de Lagarde, who was a colleague and sharp foe at Göttingen.[43]

Lotz focuses particularly on the formal address which the university
faculty senate (with Lagarde dissenting!) delegated Ritschl to deliver
in 1883 on the occasion of the four hundredth anniversary of Luther's
birth. But in a sense all of Ritschl's work comes into play here, especially the work on justification and reconciliation. The substance of
the several critiques of protestantism was that protestantism undercut human freedom and the need for a moral reordering of society
by its insistence that God alone ordained man's salvation through a
justification to which man could contribute nothing and by its
tendency to retreat from involvement in the practical affairs of
society into a world of objective, partially obscure dogmatic propositions. Lagarde's school of historical studies insisted that since the
doctrine of justification was polemical in Paul's writing, it is of only
occasional importance and therefore cannot be considered to be the
essential theme of Christian faith. The anti-protestant critics also
charged that the reformation was responsible for the cultural disin-
tegration of the great ancient and medieval traditions of western
society and that its true colors were evident in the libertinism and
anarchism ascribed to the anabaptists. Ritschl's work bears within
it a clear, if implicit, answer to these charges. He insists that the
essence of the Lutheran understanding of justification was that God
liberated man to live freely *in* the world, through his vocation, without reliance upon artificial props whether in the form of an ecclesiastically controlled state or a repressive sacralized social order. The
freedom of the Christian man which the reformers proclaimed was
the very antithesis of the anabaptist theology, since it committed the
Christian to working for the righteousness and justice of society at
every level and valued every worldly occupation and institution in its
own right, without demanding that it be "Christian." True reformation faith was thus eminently practical and only secondarily dogmatic
in its expression. It may be that Ritschl's sensitivity to this kind of
attack on protestantism contributed to his insistence that Christian
faith supports vocational obedience to the established order.

We have already clarified Ritschl's assessment of the modern
scientific world view and its threat to faith by reducing man's significance in a vast chain of cause and effect which subordinated him to
nature. Ritschl challenged this view by insisting that the failure
properly to distinguish between physical and psychic (and spiritual)

realities meant a failure to understand man. With this challenge he offered the kingdom of God as a holistic system that incorporated both man and nature with God in a way that preserved the authentic being of both.[44]

If it is true that in Ritschl's age traditional supernatural and metaphysical religion, as well as traditional views of man and traditional protestantism were on the defensive, it seems that the aggressive forces were those that threatened the death of metaphysics, which would later be the death of "God," and substituted an age of "one-dimensionality," which would be the death of man. Ritschl felt the strength of these forces and plotted a strategy to meet them. The death of metaphysics he did not mourn, and he devised a strategy for living without it. The death of man through one-dimensionality was more fearful for him, so he challenged it with a theology that insisted that every action and reaction within man's dimension was correlative to another dimension which was God.

Although Ritschl's foes and competitors were at many points correct in their criticisms of his thought and even though their own work was at points more satisfactory than his, and, furthermore, even though it cannot be said that he won every battle (the ecclesiastical scene in Germany, for example, was hardly relinquished by the confessionalists and pietists), it must be said that no other single theological work of his generation gathered in itself so many strands of intellectual, religious, and cultural meaning and synthesized them in a creative manner—both intellectually stimulating and practically edifying (even "preachable")—as Ritschl's did. This is his significance for his own day: that he spoke his particular message to an epoch that was shaped religiously by confessionalists, pietists, and Prussian unionists; philosophically and theologically by Kantians, Hegelians, and Schleiermacher; culturally by free-thinking liberal and anti-protestant secularists; as well as by classical German protestantism and Vatican I catholicism, by great social unrest, and in politics by the Prussian state and its radical opponents. The passion that marked both his friends and his foes is explained by the fact that he entered the fray on so many fronts and deeply touched so many raw nerves. As a consequence, his work dominated many university theological faculties. The succeeding generation of Ritschlians includes outstanding men in every field of theology. His influence was felt in Sweden, England, and in America (where the social gospel and many liberal religious thinkers were impressed by his thought). In Europe, the generation that was to overthrow Ritschlianism was largely trained by Ritschlians.

IV. RITSCHL'S SIGNIFICANCE TODAY

We have portrayed Ritschl in terms of his times and his own thought, suggesting the significance of the word that he spoke to his contemporaries. Now we ask: What is the assessment of our own day? What is his significance for us?

After the bitter controversies that centered on Ritschl himself had died down, the number of articles and book-length studies subsided to a trickle after 1910. Even though the Ritschlian school taught and trained most of the next generation of dialectical theologians, these pupils in the main chose to gloss over their own ties to the Ritschlians and focused instead on what may be termed a vigorous and even malicious attempt to discredit Ritschl himself and, to a lesser extent, his school. The silence concerning origins and the ensuing denunciation had their effect. Emil Brunner tarred Schleiermacher and Ritschl with the same brush of criticism, whereas Karl Barth restored Schleiermacher, only to blister Ritschl with disdain in what must go down as one of the most influential ten-page essays in the history of theological interpretation.[45] Barth's point was that Ritschl was not all that important anyway, when compared to Schleiermacher, and that he represented the effort to repristinate enlightenment theology, to give religious and theological support to bourgeois nineteenth century German society.

Since 1960, however, there has been a resurgence of interest in Ritschl which can be explained by the fact that the passing of the anti-Ritschlian dialectical theology has liberated us to look more honestly at the nineteenth century. The present attitude toward Ritschl is that his theology represents a significant input to the present theological situation and that it is therefore necessary to carry on dialogue with him, whether his work is evaluated positively or negatively. We can understand how Ritschl is a man to be reckoned with. On the one hand he so energetically brought together in his work the elements of his generation that all theology now stands on his shoulders, even that which goes beyond him and/or rejects him.

On the other hand, since the generation of theologians which dominated the first half of the twentieth century suppressed an adequate
critical evaluation, it is only now that theologians are free to engage
in an open self-conscious dialogue with Ritschl's work.

One of the tests by which the validity of any work of the mind
and spirit is determined is its usefulness in stimulating further
thought—sometimes even a work that is marred by serious errors
is rendered valid by history in the sense that it is provocative of significant subsequent developments. With this in mind, we ask: What
seems to have become of Ritschl's powerful statement to his own
generation and what seem to be its prospects now?

In his recent study, Rolf Schäfer demonstrates how Ritschl appears
to us as a curious blend of conservative and liberal, even though he is
invariably (and rightly so) viewed as a figure in the history of German liberal theology. Our survey has shown some of the grounds for
this ambivalence. He saw the need, philosophically and theologically,
for a "new thing," and to a large extent he carried out his vision.
But his vision did not include a rejection of much tradition, and it
did not call for a change socially and politically. We have described
how Ritschl was a child of the Prussian system in which he grew up
and in which he and his father served with distinction, and how his
call for obedience within society's vocations had a conservative
thrust. Obedience and work in those vocations was the force for
realizing God's kingdom. Ritschl is not conservative because he did
not envision creative and reforming actions within those vocations
(for example, educational reforms, which he supported as a member
of the provincial examining committee), but rather because he gives
no hint that those vocations might be shattered by changes in society
and thus rendered more fluid or radically reshaped both in their own
form and in their relation to other vocations.[46] Ritschl was not un-
critical of his society, and there is no evidence that he divinized it,
but he simply had no inkling that there was any other societal form
in which God's kingdom might be served. Thus, in an ironic way,
his impressive concern for the world, his intimate wedding of religion and ethics, and his vision that the kingdom of God pertains to
this world—all of these were undercut by his commitment to the
vocational structure of his own society. Formally, there is no reason
why his thought cannot be a force for change and liberation; but

materially his own investments of meaning gave an unfortunate conservative thrust to his work. For example, in his day there was great
ferment for the democratization of society and greater social justice.
Despite Bismarck's fairly advanced welfare policies, conditions among
the working class population in Germany were miserable. In this
setting, Ritschl's emphasis on the high possibilities of vocational
obedience must have seemed ironic to persons outside the middle and
upper classes—unless he meant that the worker and the political
revolutionary had a vocation to change society, which he did not!
Ritschl must not be pictured as a man who was content with his
times and their achievements, nor as one who did not challenge the
establishment of church and state, university and culture. We must
conclude, however, that he was almost totally captive to his own
elitist social class, and that his feeling for the transience of the metaphysics of his day was not matched by a sense of the impermanency
of its societal forms. And this aspect of the man and his work has
proven to be singularly unproductive, up to this day, because to a
post-World War I generation this aspect made Ritschl seem culture-
and time-bound to the "other side" of the dividing line between
modern and postmodern epochs.

Theologically, Ritschl's ambiguous conservative/liberal stance has
contributed to his being a bridge figure spanning the modern and
postmodern periods. His work has been rejected or simply left
unregarded at those points where his cultural conditionedness tied
him indissolubly to the modern age, that is to the enduring validity
and adequacy of the nineteenth century system of society, religion,
and values. It was this that the dialectical theologians of the first
half of the twentieth century rejected, and it is this conditionedness
that perhaps angered Karl Barth the most—a man who took social
and political differences almost more seriously than theological disagreements! They were the theologians who witnessed the collapse
of the pre-World War I European dream, and they naturally spoke in
terms of man's precariousness, the evil and weakness of institutions,
and the fragility of human existence in a way that qualitatively
marks them off from Ritschl and his achievement—even though,
as we shall discuss later, they had close affinities with Ritschl theologically. A good deal of Ritschl's ethicism, drawn from Kant and

Schleiermacher has appeared to be a dead end, since it breathed an air of authoritarianism and exhorted obedience to the cultural and religious system—an obedience which our century's experience must conclude is more than a system has a right to demand. Furthermore, the philosophical and historical supports for the ethicism in Ritschl's system are also now being called into question. The mysticism, anabaptism, and pietism that he rejected in a single-mindedly neo-Kantian manner we now see were elements of creative ferment within the modern system.

It is clear, however, that as a bridge figure Ritschl was able to make a massive contribution to later generations. We can summarize under four categories the elements of his achievement that have proven productive of fruitful development, even up to the present time.

IMPETUS FOR HISTORICAL-CRITICAL STUDIES

We have already called attention to this aspect of Ritschl's work. His own historical work is impressive, including comprehensive treatments of early church history, reformation developments, the history of pietism, and the history of the doctrine of justification and reconciliation. The output of the so-called Ritschlian School is staggering: Adolf von Harnack's studies of the history of dogma, Ernst Troeltsch's historical work in ethics, not to mention hosts of others in every field of church history, including the often overlooked Ritschlian influence on Karl Holl and other early workers in the "Luther Renaissance." It is not that these men were wholly under Ritschl's influence (which they were not) nor that without him they would not have been excellent historians (they surely would have been). Rather, the point is that Ritschl personally encouraged them and inspired them and his influence upon them is unmistakable. Even more important for our assessment of Ritschl's meaning and significance is that his decision, based on what he learned from Baur, to commit his own resources to a critical-historical investigation of Christianity and to insist that such an investigation be a foundation for the constructive dogmatic expression of the Christian faith has not only been vindicated, but has become so productive of fruitful advance that it is reckoned a basic assumption for theological work.[47]

RESOURCES FOR DIALECTICAL THEOLOGY

That the dialectical theology of Karl Barth, Emil Brunner, Rudolf Bultmann, and Friedrich Gogarten lived in a different world from Ritschl and branded him its arch-heretic cannot obscure the fact, as Paul Jersild has brought out, that the main contours of Ritschl's theology furnished a framework which dialectical theologians could incorporate for their own ideas.[48]

Here we must distinguish between the Barthian and the existentialist wings of dialectical theology. Three of Ritschl's most important and most strenuously argued assertions provide formal resources for his twentieth century Barthian antagonists: his insistence that theology must base itself on the revelation of God in Jesus Christ as portrayed in the New Testament (what developed into Barth's so-called Christo-monism); his adamant rejection of any "natural" theology or philosophical statement of the Christian faith; and correlative argument that the theologian must irrevocably take his stand within the community of believers, the church, and do his theologizing from that standpoint. Other assertions that Barthian theologians share, at least formally, with Ritschl are a concern to reappropriate Luther and the other mainline reformers for dogmatics, a rejection of Schleiermacher's emphasis upon feeling as the main resource for theology, a rejection of historical positivism, and a rejection of romanticism, mysticism, and aestheticism in theology. In these areas of commonality, it is not a question of isolated points of agreement; rather, we are dealing with issues which Ritschl and the Barthians alike made central to their programmatic efforts to renew dogmatics in their respective generations. For some of these members of the dialectical theology, these elements were mediated through Wilhelm Herrmann, a close friend and disciple of Ritschl, who was a respected teacher of both Barth and Bultmann. Paul Jersild has shown that despite Barth's rhetoric of rejecting Ritschl, there remains a surprising bond of continuity between the two theologies, specifically in their doctrine of God. Perhaps the fundamental bond, however, is their common effort to build a theology exclusively upon the distinctive Christian revelation in the New Testament message of Jesus and their common effort to maintain this position polemically against other options in their times.

Some of these very Ritschlian elements which the dialectical theologians found useful are now proving less fruitful, both in their Ritschlian and in their dialectical forms. The restriction to the New Testament revelation, with its corollaries of restriction to the community of believers and rejection of philosophical resources for stating the Christian message, as these found expression especially in Barth, have proven confining to many in the present generation, since they seem to offer little resource for taking seriously the secularization and unbelief which press upon us today in a form that neither Ritschl nor Barth felt. Nevertheless, we must not forget that these so-called restrictions may also be interpreted as a *response* to secularization in both Barth and Ritschl and not simply as *retreat* (see pp. 26–29, above).

For the existentialist wing of dialectical theology, represented in the work of Bultmann and Gogarten, Ritschl's preoccupation with the self-consciousness of man was of great significance. This dimension of his thought was particularly mediated to them through Herrmann, and it provided an antecedent thrust toward their existentialist orientation. Their reliance upon the philosophies of Heidegger and Buber, for example, can be construed, as Wrzecionko has done, as a direct elaboration of Ritschl's methodological decision to avoid metaphysics by turning to the self-consciousness of man (see the essay "Theology and Metaphysics") as the arena within which theology was to probe the encounter with historical revelation.

HISTORICAL AND HERMENEUTICAL METHOD

Ritschl is a remarkably contemporary partner in dialogue for theologians and historians who are today concerned over the question of historical method and its function in the art of interpreting the past, and his suggestions for his own time have proven to be of continuing usefulness. We refer here not simply to Ritschl's insistence upon critical-historical tools and techniques for historical and theological study, but also to the way in which he stated theology's relationship to historical methodology. We note three aspects of this relationship: (a) the insistence that Christianity must be understood in terms of its *whole* development; (b) the acknowledgment that every theologian and every generation stands in a relative position within the historical process, from which is carried on a dialogue with the past and the present; (c) the necessity, for the adequate carrying out of this method, of perceiving the dynamics of the historical consciousness of man, that is, the need for a phenomenological description of man's historical consciousness.

(a) The concern for interpreting Christianity and its individual manifestations in light of the whole development of the Christian religion through its successive periods is now so deeply rooted in the consciousness of German and most western theology, that it hardly needs mention. It is one of the most important methodologies for biblical studies, where it functions as "tradition criticism" and "redaction criticism," but it is also prominent in studies of the history of later periods and in theology itself. Ritschl insisted in employing this totalistic approach in interpreting the doctrines of justification and reconciliation, and in his studies of Luther, orthodox confessional Lutheranism, and pietism. He placed his own theological proposal as the contemporary climax of the interpretation of Christianity's development.[49] In systematic theology, the work of Wolfhart Pannenberg, in dialogue with the philosophy of Hegel and Hans-Georg Gadamer, as well as the work of Gerhard Ebeling, building on both Barth and Heidegger, are two of the most important examples of how Ritschl correctly assessed the significance and ongoing fruitfulness of this methodology, which he did not originate, but which he did plant irrevocably in the discipline of dogmatics.[50] Ritschl himself, although his perspectives were impressively broad and inclusive, is superseded in the even more inclusive work of these men, who reckon not only in terms of the Christian tradition, but also place that tradition more effectively in its cultural setting than did Ritschl.

(b) When we take the historical approach, interpreting Christianity in terms of its total development, critically investigated, we are ultimately forced to recognize the relativity of each phenomenon and epoch—including our own—within the whole process. Consequently, we are engaged in a dialogue with past and present, on the basis of which we speak our own word in our own epoch, with a view toward the future possibilities of that word. Gerhard Ebeling has put this in classical contemporary form for theology in his book, *The Problem of Historicity*; Ebeling's argument shows how close Ritschl was to the contemporary discussions in his explicit awareness of the dialogical character of the historical approach. This is borne out especially in Ryan's analysis of Ritschl's kinship with Schleiermacher, Dilthey, and Ranke in respect to historical methodology. Ritschl devoted considerable effort to interpreting his own "present age" so that he could carry on dialogue with it and through it with past and future. In other words, Ritschl's method made its investments in a line that has proven fruitful, even among those who feel uncomfortable with the specific results that he obtained in his own time. Studies by Schäfer, Wrzecionko, Lotz, and myself all point to a basic defect which mars Ritschl's intentions to carry out this dialogical principle.[51] Although each of these writers expresses the defect in slightly different terms, they stand agreed that the presuppositions which Ritschl brought with him to the dialogue with past and present served not only as a key to unlock the meaning of Christianity's historical development, but also as serious blinders that vitiated the impressive skills and breadth of intention with which he approached the dialogue.

(c) The past two centuries of western experience with the historical mode of thinking have taught us that man does not merely *use* the historical method, but rather he *is* a historical being. This insight has gone hand in hand with a close phenomenological analysis of man's psychic and intellectual processes as he is caught up in the historical process of assessment and dialogue. To mention only a few who have made great contributions to this analysis: Schleiermacher, Dilthey, Heidegger, and the contemporary phenomenological school, including Gadamer, Ebeling, and Paul Ricoeur. This phenomenological analysis has attained a high level of sophisticated description. Ritschl stands in this tradition. In fact, his entire polemic against the use of metaphysics in theology was predicated on the argument that metaphysics could not distinguish between physical and spiritual entities, and therefore it could not do justice to the distinctiveness of man and to that dimension of human existence where the encounter with God and the theological enterprise take place. In connection with this argument, he produced a rudimentary phenomenology of man's psychic processes, mainly in his effort to show that classical metaphysics distorts our understanding of these processes. His argument requires a more profound depth of analysis, however, and here, we must conclude, is the place where Ritschl contributed least to the future of the historical method. He stands well below the others in this tradition in his grasp of how man functions within the dialogical process of history. This must be said, even though his concentration on the psychic life of man, as the arena within which the encounter with revelation was to be charted, gave a formal impetus for full-scale phenomenological work and encouraged his followers to do what he did not do.

Ritschl himself seems to have been content to understand the dynamics of human life in generalizations drawn from his own style of life. He found it almost impossible to understand from within and thus with fairness those religious and cultural movements (uncongenial to him) which were deeply concerned with the inner dynamics of man's psyche and mind—pietism, mysticism, romanticism, and the concentration upon human consciousness which was part of Schleiermacher's theological legacy. Since these movements were all active at the same level as he was—committed to discerning the encounter with revelation within man's own self-consciousness—he seems to have looked upon them more as foes to be vanquished than as comrades in the same battle. Schäfer's critique is here much to the point, that although Ritschl formulated a clear and healthy image of Christian life-style, he slighted—with regrettable consequences—the interior life of individual persons, submerging this dimension in his concern for the corporate practice of religion and in his formal ethicism.[52] Lotz joins Schäfer and Jersild in calling attention to the way in which this seriously flawed Ritschl's understanding of Luther and his doctrine of justification, since he could not deal adequately with human despair over one's sinfulness and the inner torments which accompany the religious and ethical life.[53] Thus, in his *Instruction in the Christian Religion,* Ritschl could devote more attention to the ambiguities concerning the pursuit of recreation than any other specific ethical problem!

To summarize: The tradition of historical interpretation in which Ritschl stands has given great attention, at least since Schleiermacher, to two factors: man's stance in a process of relative moments in history with which he carries on dialogue, culminating with a word spoken to his own generation; and the description of the inner dynamics of man's life as a historical being. Ritschl attended carefully to the first of these and contributed to our understanding of it. And although he acknowledged the importance of the second factor and framed his argumentation so as to be dependent upon it, he contributed much less to it. The result of this was that his dialogue with past and present was in some respects extraordinarily stunted, primarily in the direction of an ethicism which achieved a dominance which Ritschl himself did not intend and also in the direction of an insensitivity to the dark side of despair, ambiguity, and inner torment in human existence.

THEOLOGY CENTERED ON THE KINGDOM OF GOD

Ritschl stood in a tradition, from Kant through Schleiermacher and Rothe, that understood the importance of the kingdom of God for Christian faith and which interpreted the kingdom in both eschatological terms as a religious reality given by God and as an ethical mandate governing man's life. He made a decisive contribution to this tradition by demonstrating that the kingdom of God was central to the New Testament picture of Jesus and his preaching, and that the Jesus of the Gospels simply cannot be understood apart from this message. Whereas an earlier study by Christian Walther negatively assessed Ritschl at this point, newer works by Schäfer and Metzler have reacted more positively to his achievement.[54] Ritschl was the first to make the kingdom of God "the crucial, all-embracing term of systematic theology," so forcefully implanting the concept in the doctrinal system that eschatology could never again simply be left for the end of the catechism.[55]

In 1892 Ritschl's own son-in-law, Johannes Weiss, followed by Albert Schweitzer (who built on Weiss's studies, even though he received more notoriety for the view), leveled a fundamental criticism at the Ritschlian view, only three years after the latter's death. He charged that even though Ritschl is correct in emphasizing the centrality of the message of the kingdom of God for the New Testament picture of Jesus, his conception of the kingdom actually owes more to the enlightenment ethical interpretation that dates from Kant and Schleiermacher than it does to New Testament sources. Weiss himself claimed (and Schweitzer supported him) that it was impossible to hold a concept of the kingdom that was both eschatological and ethical, both God's gift and his ethical demand for men, and further that the New Testament clearly pictures Jesus as emphasizing the eschatological rather than the ethical. Weiss concluded that the New Testament concept was unusable for dogmatics and that Ritschl's ethicized view was to be preferred to the biblical concept. Ritschl's disciples, notably Herrmann, Troeltsch, and Walter Rauschenbusch in America, followed suit. In the years that followed, this critique gained ground and was seen as the decisive negation of Ritschl's views, albeit generally accompanied by the opinion, contrary to Weiss, that Ritschl was *not* to be preferred to the New Testament, although the interiorizing of eschatology by the existentialist theologians is not far from Ritschl's ethicizing of it. Walther continues this recent trend of pitting Weiss against Ritschl, to the discrediting of the latter. Schäfer reopened the question by challenging Weiss's interpretation of the New Testament and suggesting that Ritschl's views are more viable as biblical exegesis than the critics have allowed. Thus, he continued to pit Ritschl and Weiss against each other. Norman Metzler, with support from Wolfhart Pannenberg, speaks in contrast of the "Ritschl-Weiss historical-theological nexus,"[56] whose value is enduring and whose real implications are just now being fully unfolded by the current "eschatological" school of theology, which includes Pannenberg, Carl Braaten, and Jürgen Moltmann. The suggestion is that Ritschl and his tradition were correct, that the kingdom of God in the New Testament and in Christian dogmatics *is* both eschatological and ethical, but not in the precise way Ritschl set forth. That is, the kingdom is not to be conceived, as Ritschl did, as a reality which is to be realized in and through man's concrete ethical actions, actions which thus fulfill both God's highest good and man's, offering self-fulfillment for both God and man. Rather, the kingdom is a future reality realized only by God, but which proleptically gives shape to man's ethical action. That is, it gives shape to present action, even though it is a future reality to be consummated. This is so because man lives under the impact of that coming kingdom which was also present in Jesus through his resurrection. I have previously suggested that Ritschl's success in concretely relating the kingdom to the dynamics of human action is notable and still stands as a challenge to the eschatological school.[57] However one evaluates the discussion, it appears that Ritschl's insights on the kingdom as a central, if not all-embracing, issue for Christian faith is another example of the fruitfulness which his theology has had for succeeding generations. Metzler goes so far as to say that "the Ritschlian concept of the kingdom must be considered the norm and touchstone of any modern discussion of the kingdom of God."[58]

V. CONCLUSION

We have interpreted Albrecht Ritschl by applying his own historical method to the phenomena of his own life and work. He spoke a word to his own age that was so appropriate and so in resonance with his contemporaries in Germany that despite its weaknesses it became the dominant theology of his generation. It has proven fruitful up to this day in several major areas of theological concern, even though parts of it have been rejected or permitted to lie dormant. Such an analysis of Ritschl—in light of his significance for his own day and his fruitfulness for subsequent generations—is only possible because of the numerous new studies of the particular facets of his thought. A full picture of Ritschl and his significance is not yet possible, since there is still much in his work that lies unexamined, but we can now assess him appreciatively and critically in a way more responsible than at any previous time since the 1870s. We are in a position to discern that even though many of his specific interpretations now appear faulty and even though he himself did not always match his intentions with performance, he nevertheless still stands as a significant guide for the *manner* in which Christian theology is to be done, that is, for theological methodology.

NOTES

1. The primary source for Ritschl's life is the biography in two volumes written by his son, Otto, shortly after his father's death. Unless otherwise noted, it is the source for all of the biographical details in this essay. See Otto Ritschl, *Albrecht Ritschls Leben*, 2 vols. (Freiburg, i. B.: J.C.B. Mohr, 1892 and 1896).

2. Ibid., I:3.

3. Ibid., I:45–50. Also Peter C. Hodgson, *The Formation of Historical Theology: A Study of Ferdinand Christian Baur*, in Makers of Modern Theology, ed. Jaroslav Pelikan (New York: Harper and Row, 1966), chapter 2. Also Karl Löwith, *From Hegel to Nietzsche* (Garden City: Doubleday Anchor Books, 1967), Section V.

4. See Darrell Jodock, "F. C. Baur and Albrecht Ritschl on Historical Theology" (Ph.D. diss., Yale University, 1969).

5. Ibid., pp. 175–85.

6. Otto Ritschl, II:315, 317.

7. *Die Entstehung der altkatholischen Kirche.* Eine kirchen- und dogmenge-schichtliche Monographie (Bonn: Adolph Marcus, 1850: Zweite, durchgängig neu ausgearbeitete Auflage, 1857). Jodock's work is a thorough study of the significance of the differences between these two editions. The following discussion is based on his study.

8. Jodock, "F. C. Baur and Albrecht Ritschl on Historical Theology," chapter 4. See also Rolf Schäfer, *Ritschl.* Grundlinien eines fast verschollenen dogmatischen Systems (Tübingen: J. C. B. Mohr, 1968), pp. 161, 176.

9. Adolf von Harnack, *History of Dogma,* trans. Neil Buchanan from 3rd German edition (1893), 7 vols. (New York: Dover Publications, 1961).

10. David Lotz, "Albrecht Ritschl's Interpretation of Luther's Theology: An Exposition, Analysis, and Critique" (Th.D. diss., Union Theological Seminary, New York, 1971).

11. See Philip Hefner, "Albrecht Ritschl and His Current Critics," *The Lutheran Quarterly* 13 (May, 1961): 103–12.

12. Unfortunately, this fact (which Ritschl explicitly noted) was not taken into account by the first English translator of the work, and so it has gone down in English as *Instruction in the Christian Religion.*

13. Otto Ritschl, I:101.

14. Ibid., II:391.

15. The following works are useful for this discussion:

   Norman Metzler, "The Ethics of the Kingdom" (Doctoral diss., Evangelical-Theological Faculty of the University of Munich, 1971).

   Michael Ryan, "The Role of the Discipline of History in the Theological Interpretation of Albrecht Ritschl" (Ph.D. diss., Drew University, 1967).

   Rolf Schäfer, *Ritschl* (see note 8, above).

   Christoph Senft, *Wahrhaftigkeit und Wahrheit.* Die Theologie des 19. Jahrhunderts zwischen Orthodoxie und Aufklärung (Tübingen: J. C. B. Mohr, 1956).

   Christian Walther, *Typen des Reich-Gottes Verständnisses.* Studien zu Eschatologie und Ethik im 19. Jahrhundert (Munich: Chr. Kaiser, 1961).

   Paul Wrzecionko, *Die philosophischen Wurzeln der Theologie Albrecht Ritschls* (Berlin: Töpelmann, 1964).

16. Lotz, "Albrecht Ritschl's Interpretation of Luther's Theology," pp. 91–98. Philip Hefner, *Faith and the Vitalities of History: A Theological Study Based on the Work of Albrecht Ritschl,* in Makers of Modern Theology, ed. Jaroslav Pelikan (New York: Harper and Row, 1966), chapter 2.

17. Lotz, "Albrecht Ritschl's Interpretation of Luther's Theology," pp. 117–28.

18. Ibid., p. 19.

19. Ibid., pp. 117–28.

20. Walther, *Typen des Reich-Gottes Verständnisses,* chap. 6. Also Metzler, "The Ethics of the Kingdom," pp. 105–10.

21. Metzler, "The Ethics of the Kingdom," pp. 2–3, passim. See also, Philip

Hefner, "The Concreteness of God's Kingdom: A Problem for the Christian Life," *The Journal of Religion* 51 (July, 1971): 189–93.

22. Metzler, "The Ethics of the Kingdom," pp. 201–4. See also, Rolf Schäfer, "Das Reich Gottes bei Albrecht Ritschl und Johannes Weiss," *Zeitschrift für Theologie und Kirche* 61 (1964): 66–88.

23. Metzler, "The Ethics of the Kingdom," p. 204.

24. Ryan, "The Role of the Discipline of History," pp. 336–58.

25. Hefner, *Faith and the Vitalities of History,* chapter 3, especially pp. 99–100.

26. Ibid., p. 100. Wrzecionko, *Die philosophischen Wurzeln,* pp. 141–42, 218–19.

27. Hefner, *Faith and the Vitalities of History,* pp. 70–90.

28. "Prolegomena," *History of Pietism,* see pp. 51–147 below.

29. Ryan, "The Role of the Discipline of History," especially chapters 4 and 7.

30. Ibid., pp. 329 f.

31. Ibid., pp. 335–59. Metzler, "The Ethics of the Kingdom," pp. 207 ff. Schäfer, *Ritschl,* pp. 121–213.

32. Horst Stephan, "Albrecht Ritschl und die Gegenwart," *Zeitschrift für Theologie und Kirche,* N.F. 6 (1935): 21. See David Mueller, *An Introduction to the Theology of Albrecht Ritschl* (Philadelphia: Westminster, 1969), pp. 149–50.

33. This is the opinion of Ernst Haenchen, "Albrecht Ritschl als Systematiker," in his *Gott und Mensch* (Tübingen: J. C. B. Mohr, 1965), pp. 409–75. Also Senft, see note 15, above, and Karl Barth, see note 45 below.

34. Hodgson, *The Formation of Historical Theology,* pp. 70–73.

35. Wrzecionko, *Die philosophischen Wurzeln,* pp. 22–33.

36. Ibid., pp. 52–140.

37. Jodock, Ryan, Schäfer argue for Jesus in his New Testament witness. Lotz emphasizes Luther, although not as an exclusive norm. Hefner has argued for the tradition as such. Wrzecionko argues for the philosophical norm, as does Gösta Hök, *Die elliptische Theologie Albrecht Ritschls*: Nach Ursprung und innerem Zusammenhang (Uppsala Universitets Årsskrift, 1942), p. 3.

38. Lotz, "Albrecht Ritschl's Interpretation of Luther's Theology," p. 202 f.

39. Otto Ritschl, II:320 ff.

40. "Prolegomena," *History of Pietism,* see pp. 51–147 below.

41. James Hastings Nichols, *History of Christianity, 1650–1950* (New York: Ronald Press, 1956), p. 285.

42. Schäfer, *Ritschl,* pp. 113–14. Ryan, "The Role of the Discipline of History," pp. 22–23.

43. Lotz, "Albrecht Ritschl's Interpretation of Luther's Theology," pp. 209–18.

44. Hefner, works mentioned in notes 11 and 21 above.

45. Karl Barth, "Ritschl," in *Protestant Thought from Rousseau to Ritschl* (New York: Harper and Row, 1959).

46. Schäfer, *Ritschl,* pp. 123–28. In 1887, on the occasion of the 150th anniversary of the university, Ritschl as pro-rector gave the keynote address. He used the opportunity to analyze the three main political forces at play in the life of the university—clericalists, free-thinkers, and social-democrats. He leveled sharp criticism at the first two, which drew their fire in return in newspaper editorials aimed at Ritschl. The speech argued that university professors should be freed from political pressures and distractions. For an extended discussion of Ritschl and his relationship to his cultural milieu, see Fritz Fischer, "Der deutsche Protestantismus und die Politik im 19. Jahrhundert," *Historische Zeitschrift* 171 (1951): 473–518, esp. pp. 499–501.

47. Ryan, "The Role of the Discipline of History," and Schäfer, *Ritschl,* both give full accounts of Ritschl's wedding of history and dogmatics. Hefner, *Faith and the Vitalities of History,* summarizes his historical studies and their conclusions.

48. Paul Jersild, "The Holiness, Righteousness and Wrath of God in the Theologies of Albrecht Ritschl and Karl Barth" (Doctoral diss., Evangelical-Theological Faculty, University of Münster, 1962). Excerpts in *The Lutheran Quarterly* 14 (1962): 239–57, and 328–46.

49. See Ryan, "The Role of the Discipline of History," passim, and Hefner, *Faith and the Vitalities of History,* passim.

50. Wolfhart Pannenberg, ed., *Revelation as History* (New York: Macmillan, 1968). See also his "Redemptive Event and History," "Hermeneutic and Universal History," and "On Historical and Theological Hermeneutic," in *Basic Questions in Theology: Collected Essays,* Volume 1 (Philadelphia: Fortress Press, 1970). Gerhard Ebeling, *Word and Faith* (Philadelphia: Fortress Press, 1963), especially "The Significance of the Critical Historical Method for Church and Theology in Protestantism," pp. 17–61. Also his *The Problem of Historicity* (Philadelphia: Fortress Press, 1967) and "Sola Scriptura und das Problem der Tradition," in *Schrift und Tradition,* ed. K. E. Skydsgaard and Lukas Vischer (Zurich: EVZ Verlag, 1963).

51. Schäfer terms this restriction "biblicism"; Wrzecionko describes it as a philosophical bias; Lotz calls it a tendency toward ethicism; Hefner argues for a restricted view of life-style. Both Ryan and Jodock seek to rescue Ritschl from this charge.

52. Schäfer, *Ritschl,* pp. 178–81.

53. Lotz, "Albrecht Ritschl's Interpretation of Luther's Theology," pp. 129 f., 151–61.

54. Metzler, "The Ethics of the Kingdom," pp. 438 ff.

55. Ibid., p. 204.

56. Ibid., p. 438.

57. See note 21, above.

58. Metzler, "The Ethics of the Kingdom," p. 1.

"PROLEGOMENA"

TO *THE HISTORY OF PIETISM*

"PROLEGOMENA" TO *THE HISTORY OF PIETISM*

The History of Pietism was the product of Ritschl's last active period, consuming the decade 1876–1886, after his major works in dogmatics were complete. He undertook a thorough study of the original sources, a task that made great demands on the libraries he used, since he had to call for books that had long been out of use. He dealt with every available treatise, devotional booklet, or other literary vestige of Dutch, German, and Swiss pietism. The reading had a great effect on him and his moods, at times exciting him and at others depressing him, since he was always aware that he was dealing with a phenomenon that was alien to himself. The great and intriguing question is why a man would devote ten years of his life to the study of a movement to which he was opposed. The answer may lie in the fact that pietism was so concerned with the Christian life, which was also Ritschl's major concern in his academic thought. At any rate, the work grew to three volumes of what is Ritschl's clearest, most easily comprehended writing. The "Prolegomena" lays out more lucidly than anything else he wrote how he employed the categories of "way of living" as a key for interpreting the Christian religion and its various groupings.

This "Prolegomena" first appeared, in a slightly different form, in the *Zeitschrift für Kirchengeschichte* in 1877. Apparently Ritschl wanted to float the idea before putting it in more permanent form. The first volume of the work appeared from Adolph Marcus in Bonn in 1880, followed by the other two volumes in 1884 and 1886. This is the first English translation of this work.

"Prolegomena"
to *The History of Pietism*

I. THE SCOPE OF THE TASK

There have been contradictory assessments of the nature and significance of that phenomenon in the history of the protestant churches which we call pietism, just as there have been totally different judgments about its extent. This twofold disparity in comprehending pietism strikes one when he compares the two monographical studies by Max Goebel and Heinrich Schmid which have been undertaken in the last generation. Schmid[1] recognizes under the rubric of pietism only that series of manifestations within the Lutheran church of Germany which were occasioned by Philipp Spener[2] and which reached their term in the course of the controversy between Joachim Lange in Halle[3] and Valentin Ernst Loescher in Dresden.[4] He rightly denies the allegation that Spener was conforming directly and intentionally to his older contemporary, the reformed separatist Jean de Labadie,[5] when he reluctantly established the conventicle. Accordingly, however, he separates the manifestations of pietism in the Lutheran church from similar events in Calvinism with the result that he pays no attention at all to the latter and does not even raise the question of whether the two phenomena are to be derived from the same source. In addition, he is so convinced that Spener's movement is central to pietism that he makes the false estimate that pietism originated in the Lutheran church and subsequently spread from there into the reformed provinces as well (p. 468). Moreover, it is surprising that he excludes from his *Die Geschichte des Pietismus* [*The History of Pietism*] not only the founding of the *Brüdergemeinde* [Moravian brotherhood] by Zinzendorf and its historical development, but also the phenomenon of Württemberg pietism and the theology of Johann Albrecht Bengel and his followers. This branching of pietism, in itself, contradicts the estimate by which Schmid makes the transition from his historical portrayal to a judgment concerning the nature of the pietist movement: "Pietism continued to stimulate and win individual souls, but from an ecclesiastical perspective it also proceeded to work in a disintegrating and destructive manner" (Ibid.). Is it further the case, for this historian, that the series of manifestations in which pietism clearly showed itself as representative of ecclesiastical interests and revealed its efforts to subject under its own domination those souls which would not permit themselves to be won over to it, does not even exist? Or does he deny that, in terms of church law, pietism attempted to hold these persons on a leash like a child and even to silence them? It might even seem an insignificant thing to try to understand this incorrect delimitation of the material which the Erlangen church historian has set before us, but a comparison of this work with Johann Georg Walch's *Historische und theologische Einleitung in die Religionsstreitigkeiten der evangelisch-lutherischen Kirche* [*Historical and Theological Introduction to the Religious Controversies of the Evangelical Lutheran Church*][6] pushes us irresistibly to attempt such an understanding. Schmid's book is neither more nor less than an elegant extract from the fifth chapter of Walch's work, which deals with the pietist controversies and extends from the middle of the first volume through the middle of the third. Using this method, Schmid thus elicits the impression that the history of pietism consists solely in controversies, whereas the documents of pietism are actually for the most part ascetical books and hymns. A particular verification of my suspicion about this book is offered by the fact that Schmid enlarges upon Gottfried Arnold[7] and Christian Thomasius[8] in a postscript (p. 472), as Walch does, presenting both men at the conclusion of his portrayal of the controversies, separated only by a series of mystical enthusiasts to whom Schmid correctly gives attention. If my conjecture is correct, that the material of Schmid's *History of Pietism* is only an extract from the work of Johann Georg Walch, then it is fully understandable that we look in vain for Zinzendorf and Bengel in his book, because Walch dealt with them only in the sequel to the above-named work, which first appeared in 1739. One is tempted, as a proof of that piety with which dogmatics, alone among the sciences, is favored, to recommend the Erlangen church historian's enterprise for everyone to read and marvel at—that is, that in 1863 he has restricted his presentation of pietism to the perspective of 1730! The only mitigating circumstance would be the fact that even in Schmid's own book (p. 454) there is a reference to Loescher's comment that piety also possesses desires, drives, and demands which have been ordered and established in a perverse manner. By the very fact that Schmid has appropriated Loescher's expression as an evaluation of pietism's worth, he will be all the more vulnerable to the criticism of his historical perspective which follows from this very reasonable observation. He finds that the error of this sort of piety is rooted in a doctrinal error of Spener. In his judgment, Spener was in agreement with Lutheran doctrine as a whole, but differed on the question of what was the correct estimate of the organization of the Lutheran church. The establishment of the conventicle supposedly called into question only the "third order" of the church, namely, the congregation, whereas it justified its churchly activity solely on the assumption that this "third order" worked in cooperation with the other two orders (pp. 436, 445).[9] In addition, Schmid also takes exception to pietism on the grounds that Spener's manner of emphasizing the necessity for *active* faith (i.e., good works as the test of justification) created a confusion of this faith with sanctification (p. 448).

The phenomenon of pietism is not at all exhausted by this interpretation and derivation. One receives this impression immediately when he surveys Goebel's description of these same manifestations in the reformed and the Lutheran churches.[10] His research of the entire material has led this author to suggest the interpretation that pietism, in all its types, is the diminished or attenuated form of the same movement which appeared as anabaptism in the sixteenth century. Goebel's interpretation opens a wide horizon for church-historical research, and the value of his observation is totally independent of the use which he himself makes of it. Since he comes to his work with a personal commitment to pietism, which he considers to be a powerful force for renewal in the face of the stagnation and corruption of the protestant church, he also makes a very favorable judgment on anabaptism. Alongside the violence of the anabaptist movement, he recognizes their efforts to reform the ethical and political order as a *more thorough, more decisive,* and *more perfect* continuation of the reformation of Luther and Zwingli (I, 137–39). This evaluation of pietism and anabaptism requires all the more justification since Goebel himself could not withhold certain qualifications of his positive interpretation, for he termed the reform of the anabaptists at the same time a degeneration of Luther's reformation and he considered the renewal which pietism opened up for the protestant church to be one-sided. This uncertainty in Goebel's judgment also indicates that his observations on the phenomena he studies are neither complete nor exhaustive. Both the pietistic phenomena and anabaptism demand more precise investigation if their relationship to each other is to be confirmed and their common form perceived with certainty. For every conscientious study of pietism will have to concern itself with the scope of the vista which Goebel has opened up for us. In this sense I have imitated his work. It is also my personal desire, however, to testify how provocative Goebel's diligent and many-sided research has been in guiding my own work. Even where I have had to contradict his judgment and where his presentation has not satisfied my own demands, I have nevertheless been reminded of his eager diligence and his characteristic accuracy. Just as he has won for himself a lasting place in the writing of church history through the aforementioned work, so also I, and indeed all who have known him and had associations with him, will never be able to forget his friendliness, helpfulness, impartiality and unpretentiousness.

II. THE REFORMATION IN THE
WESTERN CHURCH OF THE MIDDLE AGES

Wherever it exists, pietism claims to have reformation significance for the protestant churches. No less have the anabaptists felt that they themselves brought the work of restoring the church—which was begun by Luther and Zwingli—to its proper end. Therefore, both phenomena stand in strong analogy to each other and, accordingly, it is not improbable that pietism might stand in the close relationship to anabaptism which Goebel suggested. But even if a protestant theologian did recognize in pietism the diminished form of that tendency by which anabaptism wished to reform the church, we would still require more than the simple assertion that anabaptism is the logical fulfillment of Luther's reformation, especially since Luther and Zwingli and their own contemporary followers were of a totally different opinion. They saw a renewal of monasticism in anabaptism, which was something quite different from their own ends and means, and a protestant theologian cannot rightly disregard this judgment of the reformers nor deviate from it. Rather, one must ask himself very precisely whether anabaptism merely displays a *quantitative* difference from the reformation of Luther and Zwingli (as the consistent extension and carrying out of a task common with theirs) or whether there is a *qualitative* difference, a difference in kind, between the two attempts to restore the church. We have not yet fully realized the task which arises from this dilemma, and this defect is closely related to the fact that protestant church historians have had an excessively narrow interpretation of the concept of "the reformation," a concept they have subsequently used to throw light on a whole range of phenomena.

It is well known that certain tendencies in the second half of the Middle Ages have been designated by protestant church historians as "reforming," as the prehistory of the reformation of the sixteenth century, as the forerunners of "our" reformation which is seen as the only distinctive one. As criteria for their judgments, these historians have divided their sources, making use partly of the rejection of the veneration of saints and the like and partly of the actual or apparent acknowledgment of the doctrine of justification by faith and the acknowledgment of the exclusive authority of holy scripture for Christian doctrine. In addition, however, they have also counted opposition to the constitutional representatives of catholic ecclesiasticism as a chief mark of the reformation character. They have even gone so far that, for a long time, they considered the dualistic thought and ascetic life of the Albigensians to be a "forerunner of the reformation," simply because they set themselves in opposition to the Roman hierarchy. With similar justification, one could with certainty also convince himself that there is the closest relationship between the anabaptists and our reformers, merely because the

former stand in an even sharper opposition to the Roman church than
the latter. If this criterion is essential and decisive for the concept
of the reformation of the church, then in the name of Luther and
Zwingli we would have to abdicate in favor of the anabaptist or
Manichean reformation. It is a pity that both are choked in blood!
This interpretation of history, which culminates in Karl Ullmann's
Reformatoren vor der Reformation [*Reformers before the Reformation*],[11] merely serves to confuse everything. This interpretation originally grew out of the esteem which these historians held exclusively
for Luther's reformation, but by means of the categories to which
they have restricted themselves in comparing historical phenomena,
they have only succeeded in effacing the distinctiveness of the reformation. In particular, this method of historical comparison is guilty
of the greatest injustice against the Middle Ages of the western
church. The Middle Ages is always regarded only as the footstool
for the Lutheran reformation and is almost never examined on the
basis of the tendencies which were intrinsic to it and which are thus
justified relatively in the light of the existing circumstances. The
basis for this inadequacy lies in the too-narrow and illiberal concept
of reformation which is employed. By "reformation," these historians always mean first of all opposition to the legitimate or traditional form of the church, and they seldom are receptive to the
question of whether or not it might be possible to have reformations
in the church which were accomplished directly by ecclesiastical
authority or in cooperation with it. Consequently, they do not understand even Luther's reformation in a full and correct manner.

Gotthard Viktor Lechler,[12] to be sure, recently betrayed some
misgivings about this failure of church historians to secure a broader
concept of the reformation for themselves. As he undertook to
portray the *Vorgeschichte der Reformation* [*Prehistory of the Reformation*] (i.e., the reformation of the sixteenth century) in order to
put his hero John Wycliffe[13] in proper perspective, who should he
discover in his path but Pope Gregory VII[14] as the leader of a reform
party which strove after the *moral purification* and the *liberating of
the church* from its dependence upon the world, i.e., upon the power
of the state (p. 37). Similarly, he recognized the impulse for an
inner renewal and reform of Christendom in the two great mendicant
orders of the thirteenth century (p. 80). Now these are truly the

two epoch-making realities which give shape to the history of the western church and which transmit to us, at the same time, the material by which we are able to amplify any concept of the reformation of the church. And it will become clear that this amplification does not hamper our understanding of Luther's reformation nor lessen our esteem for it. But Lechler has not made use of these observations; he quickly blurs their significance for the history of the church in the Middle Ages by comments which grow out of his bias in favor of the particular forms of the Lutheran reformation, on the one hand, and which make success or failure the criterion for judging historical intentions, on the other. Lechler decides that he should not dwell on the reforming significance of Gregory but, instead, quickly turns to the varied manifestations of opposition to the church whose reforming intentions he validates in familiar fashion as forerunners of Luther's work. Why? Because one can hardly sense "the warm pulse of the pious Christian heart" in the great pope, because the priestly celibacy which he established for the moral purification of the church accomplished precisely the opposite of what he intended, and because the elimination of lay investiture[15] did not accomplish the desecularizing of the church. But is this a justifiable assessment of Gregory? How would we judge Luther's reformation if we used this criterion? Does the "pulse of the pious Christian heart" beat in the controversy over the doctrine of the Lord's Supper, or is it not much more the concern to guarantee objective ecclesiasticism? Furthermore, is there really a correspondence between the result of Luther's reformation, namely a separate church which stands under the constraint of scholastic doctrine, and his reforming intention to guide all Christians in the direction of their religious freedom over the world and their moral obligations toward human society? He who weighs Luther's reformation against concerns of the "pious Christian heart" and the intention of the reformer himself against his success could well miss the significance of the reformation of the sixteenth century—and many have done this. But if we do not permit ourselves to be confused in our assessment of Luther by the experiences of the mystics and converts to catholicism in the epoch subsequent to syncretism and romanticism, then we ought not let Lechler's comments falsify Gregory's reform either! Lechler also deals very superficially with the reform of St. Francis.[16] He does not even describe its goals and means; but merely says that the well-known divisions in the Franciscan order dampened the very hopes which the order itself aroused. If this is supposed to mean that there was no success at all in efforts at reforming the church in this manner, then, as we shall see, Lechler is quite wrong.

Now then, if we are to survey adequately the scope of phenomena within the history of the medieval church that are pertinent to the concept of the reformation, we must take the following into account. The two reformations which Lechler allows—that of Gregory VII and Francis of Assisi—have their common point of origin in the monastic reforms which permeate the history of the medieval western church in all possible forms and degrees. In particular, the liberation of the church from the power of the state, which the great pope undertook, has its roots in the reform of the Benedictine order which culminated in the congregation at Cluny. And Francis based the reform of the church which he sought on the establishing of the Franciscan order which, like all newly established orders, carried within itself the intention to reform monasticism. Now in the catholic interpretation of Christianity, that monasticism which turns away from the world stands as the true, perfect Christian life. In comparison with it, the worldly Christianity of the laity is wholly subordinate, even as they are admonished to a merely passive discipline through the sacraments. By "reformation," the Middle Ages understood quite explicitly only the renunciation of the world, which continually had to be intensified from time to time. Romans 12:2, in the Vulgate,[17] is determinative for this point of view: *Nolite conformari huic seculo, sed reformamini in novitate sensus vestri* ["Do not model yourselves on the behavior of the world around you, but let your behavior change, modelled by your new mind"]. Reformation of monasticism, or the defense against the always-spreading secularization of monasticism, therefore, qualified in the Middle Ages as reformation of Christianity generally. When judged in this light, the history of the western church in the Middle Ages is an almost unbroken chain of attempts at ecclesiastical reformation. Against this general background, the Cluniac reform of the Benedictine order and the establishment of the Franciscan order stand out as the epoch-making events. This assessment is borne out concretely by the fact that the Benedictine rule at Cluny was intensified by the vow of silence and that through Francis the renunciation of personal property, even by the monastic community, was introduced into the general monastic obligations. Both had identical aims— to preserve the freedom from the world to which men felt themselves called and for which they strove, within the forms of monasticism, against backsliding into worldliness. If it is true that all reforms of the monastic orders and all the foundations of new orders proceed on the basis of this common goal, then it is also true that the reform of the relationship between church and civil power which Gregory VII conceived was only the application to the legal ordering of the whole Christian church of that principle which governed the authentic Christian life. If it were so that the Christian life, in the form of monasticism, should be freed from the worldly factors which had stunted its growth, then it did not seem fitting that the power of the secular state should interfere in the legal ordering of the church of Christ. Now it is not accidental that a Cluniac monk should set for himself this task of liberating the church, since the reformed congregation at Cluny was brought into touch with the concerns of the whole church by virtue of the fact that it was directly under the supervision of the pope. Also, since Cluny was well aware of the significance of this position during the time of its flowering, it followed that the Cluniac monks attempted to lay down the rule that secular spirituality [the spirituality of Christians outside the monastic orders] should accept the canonical pattern of life, i.e., a pattern in the closest possible analogy to monasticism. Within this same line of development, we also find the view that marriage of priests should be eliminated. It was through this prohibition that Gregory VII thought that he could most effectively undergird his liberation of the church from the state. The Cluniac reform of monasticism, therefore, brought along with it the monastic reform of the clergy; and a church which was represented by such a clergy could not tolerate dependence upon the secular state: this is the context in which Gregory's epoch-making significance as reformer is to be understood.

We can form an adequate assessment of the significance of the Cluniac and Gregorian reform, however, simply by tracing the course which this movement took within the Middle Ages itself. In the first place, the goal of reforming monasticism does an injustice to the great masses of church members. Furthermore, the ever-recurring necessity for reforming monasticism is a clear proof of the purposelessness of undertaking to shape Christian perfection in the statutory forms of simplistic renunciation of the world. Finally, the fact that a church, richly endowed with property and legally struc-tured, is independent from the state is no assurance that that church is liberated from what we would call "the world" in a moral sense, for in this latter sense property and law are thoroughly secular conditions and structures. The church which wishes to be structured substantially by the marks of material property and legal functioning is plainly a part of the world. We must also add that the same church had to exalt itself to dominion over the world since it could not exist in the same place (or should we say persons) in indif-ference to the state once it had freed itself from imperial investiture. And since the church presented itself as the original possessor of the secular sword it therefore betrayed the fact that it was first led down the road of secularization by Gregory. But this result had received its *de facto* rectification already in the Middle Ages. Not, to be sure, in the reform councils of the fifteenth century, but in the system of national churches. It is a direct abrogation of the Gregorian reform that in England, Spain, and France—indeed, through a formal concession by the pope in the two last-named lands—the *appoint-ment* of the bishops came to be in the hands of the kings. Even in Germany a system of state churches was created to the extent that the Holy Roman Empire transformed itself into a confederation of secular and spiritual princes, and the possession of the bishoprics in Germany was made useful to the social and political demands of the upper and middle aristocracy.

Nevertheless, the reformation of St. Francis of Assisi designates a new epoch in the western church during the same period in which the Gregorian system unfolded its farthest-reaching consequences. To be sure, as the founder of a new order, Francis thought that he was simply attaching himself to the line of his predecessors; and he thought that his efforts to insure that the Franciscan brothers remained far removed from the world through the severe means of total poverty differed only in degree from previous founders of monastic orders. In spite of this he had the unmistakable intention to renew authentic Christianity, that is to say, the religion of Jesus, through his order, and his contemporaries understood the success of his life in precisely this sense. The older, more detailed Rule of St. Francis, comprising twenty-three chapters, lays down the rule in the introduction: *Vivere in obedientia et in castitate et sine proprio, et domini nostri Jesu Christi doctrinam et vestigia sequi, qui dicit . . .* ["To live in obedience and in chastity and without property, and to follow the teaching and example of our Lord Jesus Christ, who said . . ."]—and it cites Matt. 19:21, 16:24, Luke 14:26, and Matt. 19:29.[18] The approved rule of Honorius III, which came later and which encompassed twelve chapters, determined that the *vita fratrum minorum* [life of the Franciscans] would "observe the gospel of our Lord Jesus Christ by living in obedience, without property, and in chastity."[19] It is a matter, therefore, of the monastic vows of continence being intensified, but with the intention that they should correspond to the general commands of Jesus upon his disciples and to Jesus' own example. Accordingly, the precepts of the individual orders also made constant reference to the principles of universal service and forgiveness which the gospel sets forth, and in particular the monastics of St. Francis were literally charged with the precepts which Jesus gave to his disciples that they should travel through the world without purse, money, or staff, and that they should always greet those whom they met with peace and seek hospitality. Added to this was the obligation to preach to the masses with the intention that, so far as possible, the Christian principles of universal self-abnegation might also be recognized as valid and actually practiced among the laity which the church had neglected up to that time. Peter Waldus had previously attempted to do the same thing, but the ecclesiastical authority had not permitted him.[20] In spite of this, Francis and Dominic simultaneously with each other took up the same task again a generation later and they received ecclesiastical approval both of their motives and of the means by which they set out to accomplish their goal. Such preaching for repentance or commendation of the ascetical life to the laity meant that an attempt was being made within the catholic church itself to resolve the alienation that existed between the Christian perfection of the monastics and the utterly passive Christianity of the laity. It was explicitly recognized by both contemporary and later witnesses that these undertakings, particularly that of St. Francis, amounted to a reformation of the church, i.e., the restoration of primitive Christianity.[21] Neither the warm pulse of the pious heart nor the earnest concern for the judgment of the gospel is missing from the reformer of Assisi; rather, the entire life-style of this extraordinary man indicates a level and inner profundity of Christian sensibility, as well as a breadth of human love, which none of those other men have attained to, whom we otherwise distinguish with the title "reformer of the church." The reforming intention of St. Francis has been anything but a failure—but we need not insist that the consequences of his work must be identical with those of Luther and Zwingli in order for them even to qualify as manifestations of a reformed Christianity. For Francis's goal, which was to transport the ascetical life out from behind the walls of the cloister into the society as a whole, is totally unlike the intentions of the reformers of the sixteenth century, just as the specific means which Francis employed would be quite foreign to those men.

It is said that St. Francis's preaching for repentance was a powerful impetus for the masses to enter the cloistered life. That is quite understandable since the principles which Francis proclaimed as the substance of catholic Christianity had only been exercised up to that time in the particular form known as monasticism. Therefore, it was up to the reformer to introduce the ascetical form of life into the civil society as well. To this end, in addition to the men's order of the *fratres minores* and the women's Order of Poor Clares, he established the *ordo tertius de poenitentia* [third order of penitence] which was composed of lay congregations of men, and women as well, for whom he provided a comprehensive rule of twenty articles.[22] Thus we see the direct consequence of his restoration of primitive Christianity in this half-monastic association of laity who remained in their secular situations. Entrance into these tertiary communities—which was possible only after a certain period of testing—was meant to obligate the entrant so fully that he could leave only if he were transferring to a full-fledged monastic order. Married women required the permission of their husbands before they were accepted. Members were required to draw up their wills soon after their entrance into the order, so that they could relinquish all concern for their property. They were prohibited from participation in revelling and dancing, specifically from dramatic presentations, and even from indirect support of such entertainments. The vow was granted to the tertiaries only in specifically designated cases since taking an oath was forbidden in the circumstances of daily life. Bearing arms was permitted only for the defense of the Roman church and the fatherland, for in general they were held to complete pacifism. A cheap cloak was prescribed for clothing, neither black nor white— hence, grey. In addition, the tertiaries were held to diligent attendance at worship services, observance of the canonical hours, frequent confession, regular communion, four weekly fast days, visiting the sick within the order, participation in the burial of members of the order, and, finally, subjection to the regular visits of their superior (*ministri*). Similar associations grew out of the groups that followed the Dominican order and the later orders of the Augustinians, the Minims, the Servites, and the Trappists. The Jesuits also formed such congregations of laity. Thus, in this respect, the impulse of St. Francis has been efficacious in the Catholic church throughout the epoch that followed his own life. As far as the Middle Ages is concerned, however, the Franciscan and Dominican preaching proved its reforming intentions in the spreading of an asceticism which accommodated itself to the conditions of living among those who were married and active in civil pursuits and thus it narrowed, at least, the gulf between monastic and laity. In general, this undertaking corresponded more fully to the Christian imperatives of equality and corporate unity than the reform in the first half of the Middle Ages which restricted itself to monasticism alone. When we look at the means which were employed for its purposes, however, it is particularly clear that the significance of the Franciscan reformation is only relative—namely, that it amounted simply to the foundation of a new type of monastic order.

In just this manner, the Franciscan reformation stood intentionally in service to the medieval system of the western church, in that it concentrated on the catholic perspective on the Christian life. The principle of absolute poverty and renunciation of property which St. Francis set forth for his order was, in itself, an occasion for conflict between the ascetical reform of the church and the papal dominion of the world. The representatives of the papacy were well aware that the spiritual sword could neither gain nor maintain dominion over the secular sword unless the preponderance of worldly property was in alliance with spiritual authority. Arnold of Brescia[23] had had to do penance with his life for entertaining the opposing view, namely, that the clergy and monks who possessed property could not be blessed. Therefore it is understandable that the popes would not tolerate the principle of complete renunciation of property, even in the limited domain of the Franciscan order, for they must have recognized in that order a quiet rebuke of their system, and they must also have feared that a general rebellion against the property rights of the church which laid claim to worldly goods would come out of it. The "spirituals" in the Franciscan order actually did raise this opposition to the highest imaginable degree. Thus we see here the phenomenon of a reformation, as fully catholic in its conception as the Franciscan, turning about, at least partially, to oppose the ecclesiastical system. And, as a logical conclusion from the reforming principle of their master, the "spirituals" judged that the papacy and the church actually followed the Antichrist, since they did not revert to the example of apostolic Christianity but, rather, sought to repress the Christianity of the "spirituals," which corresponded to the gospel of Christ himself. They concentrated their efforts, however, on actions which would leave to the future the reformation which would be equal to the level of degradation which the church had reached—a future in which the eternal gospel of the Spirit would be efficacious. Such an outlook is perhaps a silent admission that even the intensifying of the Franciscan ascetical means for reform was not sufficient to lead the church directly toward perfection. I will grant that the hope for the future reformation through the eternal gospel was directly determined by the conviction that there would also be a final judgment of damnation upon the antichristian degradation of the church along the lines depicted in John's Apocalypse. The medieval church thus became the master of this movement. After the storms and conflicts which the "spirituals" aroused in the thirteenth and fourteenth centuries, for which many of them had to do penance on the funeral pyre, they permitted themselves to be pacified by virtue of their recognition as the *fratres regularis observantiae* [Brothers of the Strict Observance] by the Council of Constance. From then on, for the remainder of the Middle Ages, none of their repugnance for the Roman church appeared on the surface. Nevertheless, it is difficult to believe that this voice could be fully confined to the circle of the order. The silent obedience of the monks disguised many impulses from the distant observer which could become the common property of many within the smaller circle simply through partial hints. Even if the fifteenth century did not offer us a single document indicating that the Franciscan-Observants had propagated their fundamental objection to the secularization of the Roman papacy among themselves and their tertiaries, it would not follow, from this absence of documents, that their objection had died out completely in that period.

The phenomena of the Middle Ages that I have set forth in this short survey fall under a concept of "reformation" which has a much broader scope than the one which dominates the protestant view of history. "Reformation" in this sense is the restoration of the proper relationship between Christianity and the world which is based on the assumption that that relationship has passed over into a confusion of Christianity with the world. This general concept refers both to the individual Christian life and to the position of the church in the world. The two reformation epochs which I have described are particularly conditioned by the fact that they are governed by the catholic interpretation of the Christian life as being monastic in nature, as well as on the catholic view of the church as a legal entity. For this reason, these examples of reformation had as their goal, on the one hand, carrying out the ever-recurring and ever-intensified task of detaching monastic perfection from life in the world and, on the other hand, the spreading as widely as possible monastic perfection to the laity who were to remain in their families and in their civil occupations. Thus, the reformation of the church which Gregory VII undertook was concerned with detaching the divine legal structure from the influences of the secular state which was spoken of as the organism of sin. But the reformation strategy, which the "spirituals" had in mind, meant the liberation of the church from secularization in general—certainly, the degree and extent to which this was attempted remain in the dark since the enterprise was left to a supernatural intervention of God in the future and was not taken directly in hand by any man.

It is especially noteworthy that the Franciscan reformation of the catholic church was based on the principle of the primitive church, which was still free of confusion with the world (see p. 63). This

view was certainly not restricted to the circle of the Franciscan enterprise, nor is it to be considered an exclusive characteristic of theirs.
On the contrary, the example of the societal situation of the earliest
church in Jerusalem was the standard for nearly all of the reformation movements in the second half of the Middle Ages. It first
appeared in the writings of Joachim of Fiore (died 1212).[24] Simultaneously (about 1170) Peter Waldus, the forerunner of St. Francis,
was engaged in restoring the apostolic life through the actual
observance of the commands of Christ, in voluntary poverty, and,
above all, through evangelical (i.e., ascetical) perfection. Against
the popular tradition which asserts the close relationship between
this phenomenon and the reformation of the sixteenth century, it is
always necessary to refer to the testimony of Herzog that this
"reform stands on catholic soil and was rooted in it."[25] Even though
Peter Waldus did not represent this demand to restore the primitive
church from the very beginning, the Waldensians have been accustomed to legitimizing themselves through that claim.[26] Furthermore,
the Bohemian Matthias von Janow (died 1394)[27] entertained the
idea of a similar reformation. After 1457 the community of the
Bohemian Brethren undertook a form of life in his example, similar
to that of the Waldensians, in the territory which was set in tumult
by the Hussite wars. Through their founder, Brother Gregory the
Barefoot, they seem to have been derived from the Franciscans.[28]
This imitation of the church in Jerusalem maintained its specific
catholic character even as late as the sixteenth century. This same
ideal also governed that double form of the "modern devotion"
which occurred in the Netherlands—the Windesheim Congregation
of regular Augustinians and the Brothers and Sisters of the Common
Life—associations whose specific catholic character cannot be denied.[29] Just how fully this norm corresponds to the catholic way of
reforming can be seen, finally, in the fact that the Jesuits have
extolled the Indian congregations which they founded and supervised in Paraguay as being replicas of the earliest Christian congregations.[30]

I will demonstrate later how the reformation of the sixteenth
century relates to the concept of reformation which has emerged as
the decisive one for the western medieval phenomena that I have
just assessed. But the historical outline of the western church which

I have suggested here does entail a measurable reduction of the category of "forerunners of Luther's reformation" which has been current since the time of Flacius. The manifestations that I have discussed above in reference to the Franciscan reformation would have to be stricken from Flacius's category. It would be still another task to define the catholic counterreformation of the sixteenth century according to that category. Meanwhile, as we come to the conclusion of this discussion, it should be recalled that the eastern church exhibits nothing similar to the reforming efforts which have kept the western church perpetually in turmoil. That church has been at peace since the sixth century as far as its liturgy and ecclesiastical customs have been concerned. In its territories church and state have been closely intertwined, because the ecclesiastical customs are also folk customs and because the church can either identify with the patriarchal despotism of the state or remain so neutral in respect to that despotism that there is no conflict. Since it is concerned only with the stability of the liturgical structure and custom, the church can maintain this stance. In the territory of the eastern church it is much more possible for the Russian Czars to rule the church in their realms indirectly, as the Byzantine rulers did at an earlier time, and—conversely—for the Patriarch of Constantinople to be provided with judicial powers and rights of taxation within the Turkish empire, as the political head of his comrades in the church or of his nation. The problem of the relationship between church and state does not even exist for the eastern church while in the west it has exercised the church and occupied the attention of the state continually for centuries.[31] The eastern church has had equally as little occasion to reform monasticism or to found new orders, nor has the stance of monasticism in relation to the laity come into question, nor the relationship of the secular clergy to the monks. Neither do we find any particularly ascetical congregations among the laity, nor has the marriage of priests been challenged. On the other hand, the married priests have never set themselves against the privilege of the cloisters, from which the bishops are chosen. No reformations in the western sense have appeared there, either because all of these things have always remained in their stable order in the eastern church or because men have not felt deeply the disorder which might exist.

Apparently the western church stood in the same relation to the empire of Charlemagne which the eastern church enjoyed with respect to the Byzantine emperors. The church appeared to be incorporated within the Frankish state; the organs of the church stood at the disposal of the chief of state, to be employed for moral discipline and schooling; even the church councils were under the guidance and confirmation of the emperor, who was designated the regent of the holy church. Only the fall of the Carolingian monarchy made it possible for the papacy to achieve independence and ecclesiastical dominion over the state. But the rise of the papacy was not accidental, nor did it come about simply because of the fall of the Carolingian empire; it would be incorrect, moreover, to assume that the western church would have continued in a relationship of dependence upon the state, like the Byzantine church, if that empire could have maintained itself. For the western church possessed a spiritual legacy in Augustine's teaching concerning the superordination of the city of God over the earthly city, and this legacy pressed to disrupt the Byzantine combination of church and state. Byzantine Christianity lacked this sort of fundamental ethical-political vision. Therefore, that church was indifferent towards those changes in the equilibrium between Christianity and the world which have caused the western church to open itself to repeated reformations, the effects and countereffects of which have both filled out and distinguished its history.

III. THE DISTINCTIVENESS AND ORIGIN
OF THE ANABAPTISTS

According to Goebel, anabaptism is the more basic, more decisive, and more perfect reformation, which is to be recognized as "the child of the reformation" which Luther and Zwingli undertook, even though they abandoned it in 1522 and 1524 respectively. If we follow through with this assertion, we can trace the lineage of anabaptism back to Luther and Zwingli in two senses: first, the earliest manifestations of the movement appeared several years after the reforming work of Luther and Zwingli had begun; secondly, many of its leaders were first adherents of the two reformers, prior to their own obvious deviations from those reformers. But these circumstances do not adequately prove that the one phenomenon is the descendant from the other. That which comes later is not, by virtue of the fact that it is something different, necessarily caused by its predecessor, and the adherence of later anabaptists to Luther and Zwingli could be coincidental; it all depends on whether these two reformations *specifically* held to the same purpose and course. But such is simply not the case. Luther defined the Christian life thus: that through the religious virtues of humility, confidence in God, and patience, the Christian is free lord over all things, subject to no man, and that through the moral exercise of his civil occupation, he is obligated to every man. The same holds true for Zwingli, even if it is not so precisely formulated. Both men interpret the moral law as free and independent recognition of the demands which duty imposes; they place the Christian life in the realm of civil society, and they recognize the legal structure of the state as the chief guardian of the exercise of the Christian life, of the ordering of public worship, and of the work of religious instruction. In comparison, one can ascribe a superiority of perfection to the anabaptist pattern of life, only if he believes that detailed statutory rules for the external conditions of life are a necessary and valuable supplement to the freedom that goes along with the moral law. Moreover, one might judge that the anabaptists were more thorough in their reform of life if he holds that it is more useful and more successful to practice Christianity by renouncing as far as possible the ordinary conditions of human life, rather than transfiguring and purifying the given structures of human society through the motives of universal love for neighbor. Finally, one might extol the anabaptists for their greater decisiveness, in that they blazed the trail for a statutory sanctity or, to put it more bluntly, for a statutory sinlessness. But just how little these means succeeded in attaining autonomy and purity in formation of the character is demonstrated by the ease with which these marvelous holy people fell into antinomian aberrations. Thus anabaptism pursued the task of reforming the Christian life in a direction that is diametrically opposed to the intentions of Luther and Zwingli. As reforms, both phenomena are comparable and, in a few situations, similar; but when they are compared in terms of the distinctive characteristics of their respective movements, they appear as complete opposites, rather than as related to each other.

For protestant theologians it is clear that the reformation of Luther and Zwingli, at least in principle, moved beyond the stage of Christianity which unfolded from the second century on and which is described in particular as the catholic stage of Christianity. In contrast to this, it is evident that the motives and goals, the means and the specific regulations on which the anabaptists stand are, as a whole, of medieval lineage, and that that age provides the closest analogies to their movement. For proof of this assertion I reach back to the accounts of Heinrich Bullinger.[32] In that the anabaptists defined themselves as the one, righteous, God-pleasing church of Christ, they put the weight on the active life and on the "visible improvement" of that life in their circles—something which was sought after as little in the protestant as in the papal church. On this basis they censured the protestant doctrine of the satisfaction worked by Christ and justification by faith, since this doctrine seemed to assert that men became righteous before God through faith and not through works. They further censured the teaching that the law cannot be fulfilled, since scripture prescribes keeping the law. In these two principles of life the anabaptists stood on the side of catholicism. From the Christian imperative of love, they deduced furthermore that the Christian should not be permitted to hold property or goods, since love would much rather prefer to hold all things in common with the brethren. This principle is only the generalization of a rule which, up to that time, was held as a condition of Christian perfection by monasticism.[33] Moreover, the anabaptists held themselves partly indifferent and partly averse to the state and its arrangements. They denied that religion belongs to the competence of the state and that the Christian has any need to live by civil laws. According to their view, Christians do not resist force, and they have prepared themselves for suffering—therefore they do not seek legal protection from the state. This means that they cannot occupy any office of authority, nor are they permitted to bear arms or use them, nor may they take an oath. These principles grow out of a differentiation between the Christian religious community and the secular state, a differentiation which has its closest analogy in the principles of Gregory VII, and it ultimately refers back to Augustine's polarity between the city of God and the city of man. The logical conclusion of all of these principles is that the community of the righteous and guiltless should separate itself from members of the protestant and papal churches. Since they could never tolerate a passive adherence to the community of the sanctified, as these latter churches acknowledge in their practice of infant baptism, but rather only the active, ascetical qualities of their group, the anabaptists were led to practice adult baptism as the only correct form of reception into the true community of Christ—or else the rebaptism of those who were baptized as infants. Among all the principles of this group this one innovation is to be understood as a necessary consequence of their way of structuring life, and its individual features can be shown to be more or less developed in medieval catholicism.

Bullinger designated these marks of the anabaptists as those which were in part common to all their sects (except for individual modifications) and in part (excluding deviations) served as characteristics of the masses for which he recommended the term "general or common baptists." Generally, they fall into two groups: the one depends on individual inspiration, and the other on the letter of the Bible. The first group originally appeared in the Zwickau prophets, the other in the Zurich prophets. It is customary to say that in each respective group we find a heightening of the reformation principles of Luther and Zwingli. The intensification of the authority of holy scripture is said to be evident in Conrad Grebel's[34] deviation from Zwingli, and the revelations of the Holy Spirit among the baptists are said to be simply the natural development from the immediate certainty of salvation to which the individual is led by the doctrine of justification by faith. But this series of phenomena presents yet another side. When we compare the biblicism of Grebel and Zwingli, we see that it is but a means of defending totally different claims concerning the Christian religion. Biblicism was the easiest and, for that time, the most self-evident means available for such a defense. For his part, Zwingli stood with Bible in hand to represent the gospel of divine grace and the moral law, whereas Grebel represented a social and ethical organization of the Christian church as binding, even though it was derived from a historical epoch that lay far in the past. The educated people of the time tended to restrict themselves to the general principles which Grebel set forth, but we must enlarge our picture of these phenomena by comparing the response of

these educated men with the actual application which was made of
that principle among the uneducated adherents of the movement.
The "apostolic baptists" looked only at the letter of scripture, according to Bullinger. Since they relied on the example of the apostles,
they traveled around as preachers without staff, shoes, purse, or
money; because the Lord had said that the apostles should preach
from the rooftops what was whispered in their ears, they climbed
up on rooftops and preached from there; since it is written in scripture that one should become a child among children, they behaved
as children; because discipleship to Christ supposedly entailed that
one should abandon wife and child, house and trade, they became
tramps and let themselves be supported by the brethren. A related
group, the "separated spiritual baptists," wanted to have nothing
more to do with the world, and therefore they regulated both the
material and style of dress, eating, drinking, sleeping, standing, and
walking; whenever they saw someone laughing, they called down
woes upon him in the name of the gospel; for the same reason, they
shunned all weddings, festive meals, singing, and stringed music;
in addition, they rejected the fraternal and guild associations in
which they might have to mingle with different types of people, and
also the bearing of arms. Would one really wish to interpret these
oddities—whose only analogy in church history is the monomania
of the Russian Old Believers[35]—as being the logical continuation of
the movement which Zwingli began? One might be forced to this
assumption by the legend that the "formal principle"[36] predominated
in Zwingli's reformation. But on the basis of the anabaptist consequences that followed from this so-called principle, one could also
be convinced that actual life never follows such wretched schemes.
Zwingli's view of Christianity differs from that of his anabaptist
opponents in its profoundest depths, namely, his view is far from
the catholic form of life, whereas theirs links itself closely to the
ceremonial-legal tendency of catholicism. The fact that both base
their directly contradictory claims on the binding character of the
word of God and the holy scripture indicates that this norm is not a
distinctive characteristic of the reformation of Luther and Zwingli,
but that, on the contrary, it has played a role in other movements as
well. The ceremonial-legal substance of this norm gives us cause to
suspect that its roots lie in the Middle Ages.

The appearance of ecstasy and inspiration which the other groups of anabaptists gave has likewise nothing in common with the personal assurance of salvation which comes from faith based on justification through Christ. It is rather the case that those pathological manifestations which portray the most arbitrary, most worthless, or most wanton impulses as if they were divine commands stand completely removed from the humility and patience, as well as from the faithfulness to the pursuit of one's vocation, in which the evangelical assurance of salvation sets itself forth. The nearness of the return of Christ and his judgment, which the anabaptists proclaimed in their ecstatic excitations as the means by which his kingdom will be established, are indeed similar to the presupposition of the coming end of the world which went along with the work of Luther and his comrades. But while it is true that these presuppositions of the two parties are identical in content, the Lutherans never made them a particularly important part of their gospel, whereas the anabaptists made them the chief substance and leading motif of their preaching for repentance. Ecstasy and inspiration are the kinds of phenomena which are much more at home in monasticism, since they are possible effects of the ascetical life, and thus they received a certain esteem in the Middle Ages. Therefore, this mark of anabaptism is also oriented in the same direction as the ones we assessed before. The ecstatic proclamation of the nearness of Christ's return likewise finds its analogies in the Middle Ages; but its particular location will be designated in the later course of this investigation.

Everywhere, anabaptism sprang from the bosom of the urban artisan population. This reforming movement was basically untheological, in spite of the fact that it won for itself many clerics and monks whose level of education enabled them to lead the movement and defend its principles through speaking and writing. For example, the mystical theology represented by Andreas Carlstadt[37] and Hans Denck[38] and the general thrust toward restoring the so-called apostolic stage of Christian society were, in themselves, totally indifferent to one another. Now I will grant that mysticism is reputed to stand in a particularly close relationship to the Lutheran reformation. But it is really only a much more pronounced phase of catholic piety, as I will show in the following section. And even though Luther shared this theological tendency for a time, it nevertheless did not lead him to those ideas through which he became a reformer; rather, the traces of mysticism in his writings disappear as his reformation viewpoint clarified itself. The vision of the Christian life that is distinctive to Luther, as it is presented in *de libertate christiana* ["Concerning the Liberty of the Christian Man"],[39] is directly opposed to mysticism. Mysticism teaches escape from the world and renunciation of the world, and it places the significance of the ethically good action and the formation of virtues far beneath ecstatic union with God. Luther taught that the Christian religion leads to spiritual dominion over the world, and he placed the same value on the service of ethical action toward other men as on those activities which comprise man's reconciliation with God. Mysticism in the Christian church is actually a growth of neoplatonism, for the leading idea, which is common both to this philosophy and to mysticism as well, is that God is not the world but that he is the denial of the world. This idea is the expression of a paganism that has despaired of its own foundations and is in itself subchristian for that very reason. Furthermore, the piety which corresponds to this idea of God, which seeks ecstatic reunion with God so that the world in general and creatureliness in the form of one's own person can be denied—this piety is possible only if the ascetical renunciation of the corporeal and social conditions of human existence has preceded it. For this reason, and since it declared the monastic asceticism invalid in general, Luther's reformation cannot be related to mysticism. Indeed, the two exclude each other: the teaching of Luther is that human existence is to be understood in terms of the opposition between sin, for which we are responsible, and the divine grace in Christ; whereas mysticism sets man's self-assessment within the opposition between creatureliness on the one hand and its dissolution on the other hand into universal, divine being. Furthermore, mysticism does not set forth a higher religious view than that which Luther opened up for us; nor does Luther's theology find its natural fulfillment in the mysticism of Carlstadt and Denck. Rather, Luther's structure for understanding salvation is of incomparably greater significance than the mystical method, which is high-flying but unfruitful. Therefore, since mystical theology is at home in the circle of the anabaptists, this demonstrates that the anabaptist reformation received its *Leitmotiv* from the catholic-ascetical Christianity of the

Middle Ages, to which mysticism, at the very least, is quite congenial.

But now what is the particular area within medieval Christianity from which anabaptism sprang? In order to answer this question,[40] we must first of all keep in mind that this reformation, which is alleged to be more thorough, was without a doubt first set in motion essentially through the example of Luther and Zwingli. With very few exceptions, the adherents of this reformation were first attracted through the reformation of Luther and Zwingli prior to the time they hit upon those differences which distinguished their tendencies from those of these men. The Lutherans could make good use of the saying (1 John 2:19), "they went out from us, but they were not of us." But how is it to be explained that men who were oriented toward legalistic and ceremonial sanctity and toward the restoration of a perfectionist social system for the church could even temporarily put their trust in Luther and Zwingli? We can imagine that the later anabaptists were won over by the fact that these reformers exalted the authority of the preaching of the divine word, because this had always stood as well in their own circles as the highest standard for the reform of the Christian life. If we may accept this presupposition, then it is understandable how the preaching of Luther and Zwingli won the urban masses for them so quickly, and also how they lost these same masses, as it became evident that their preaching of the gospel did not lend itself to the purposes of a particular ascetical sanctity in whose terms these masses were accustomed to judge the significance of Christianity. Now the "preaching of the gospel" is also the proper rubric for understanding the reformation of St. Francis, although the tendencies of this reformation were totally different from Luther's efforts. Accordingly, the question of the origins of the anabaptists and of the basis for the changing attitudes which they assumed both as adherents and foes of Luther and Zwingli, leads one to the assumption that a resuscitation of St. Francis's reformation made its appearance in them and that it was aroused by their efforts to emulate Luther and Zwingli. When I first set forth this research in the *Zeitschrift für Kirchengeschichte* (vol. II, no. 1),[41] I sharpened this hunch into the hypothesis that the anabaptists emerged directly from the circle of the Franciscan tertiaries, in particular, from the Observants.[42] Since I could not support this hypothesis through any documentary evidence at that

time, I wanted to give an interim sketch of how the study of the
documents which I was suggesting should be carried on. Should it
turn out that nothing concrete could be ascertained on this point,
I would not persist in this particular hypothesis since that which is
pertinent to anabaptism can be clarified even without it.

Therefore the anabaptists, whose piety itself bore the mark of the
monastic and the ceremonial-legal, gave notice that they originally
understood something different by the term "reform of Christianity"
than what they had learned from the reformers; and this was expressed through the opposition to Luther and Zwingli, which followed after their original adherence to those reformers. With few
exceptions, the anabaptists were men of literary education who
belonged to the lower artisan class. However, for three hundred
years this class had been the sphere of activity for the mendicant
orders that had settled in the cities, of which the Franciscan orders
were the more popular. To be sure, the mendicant orders showed
various signs of secularization in the fifteenth century, and in many
places in Germany they gave the civil authorities occasion to inter-
pose themselves with reforming action. But this did not diminish
their impact upon the masses. They applied themselves to preaching,
and therefore also to the task of interpreting holy scripture, and thus
they gained the upper hand over the parish clergy, who were uneducated and lived gluttonous lives. While they were adept in bringing
these clergy into contempt on the one hand, on the other they
impressed the masses, according to Erasmus's testimony, with their
appearance of sanctity.[43] If we try to picture to ourselves the kind
of Christianity that had spread among the lower classes in the cities
at the end of the Middle Ages, we can only think of the pattern of
the Franciscans, even if we omit for the moment the existence of
the congregations of tertiaries. And if one spoke of the reformation
of the church in these circles, it would only be understood in a
Franciscan sense, namely, as the direct reform of mores. George
Witzel[44] came to Luther with this expectation, *omnia fore purius
christiana* ["that all of Christendom would become more pure"],
only to find later that he did not know what to make of Luther, since
the latter undertook no direct measures to this end. All the proph-
ecies of a general reformation of the church which were mentioned at
the end of the fifteenth century and which were later referred to

Luther were, without a doubt, meant in the sense of this expectation. The customs and intentions of the anabaptists coincide so precisely, in part with the rule of the Franciscan tertiaries and in part with the first rule of St. Francis, that one cannot deny that herein there is a genetic relationship. It is thus all the more striking, precisely at this point, that this similarity has not been noted by any church historian up to this time. The "apostolic baptists" to which Bullinger refers, who set out to preach under the conditions which Jesus laid down for his disciples (Mark 6:7–9), correspond literally to the heading in the first rule of St. Francis, article 14, *quomodo fratres debeant ire per mundum* ["In what manner the brothers ought to go forth through the world"].[45] Bullinger does admit, but in an offhand manner, that among the apostolic baptists who had relinquished private property there were "several new Barefoot Ones, that is, men who were like the Franciscan monks," who held that it was a sin to travel at all with money, whereas others were not opposed to the money as their share of the common property. The anabaptists based their rejection of the idea that the state had any competence within the church on the premise that Christians were called to suffering and therefore did not need civil protection against injustices. This fully corresponds with St. Francis's admonition, in the same source, that his brothers in the world should govern themselves directly according to Matt. 5:39–42. Accordingly, one can also understand that the anabaptists exceeded the restrictions concerning taking oaths and bearing arms which were placed upon the tertiaries by making them into absolute commands. They were well enough acquainted with the Sermon on the Mount that they could subject themselves to this gospel of Christ under all circumstances. Modest clothing, gray in color and cut specifically in the style of the monk's cowl, was prescribed for the tertiaries, and participation in worldly pleasures was forbidden. Concerning the "separated spiritual baptists," Bullinger reports that in order not to appear like the world they issued regulations for clothing and they censured all manifestations of joy and cheerfulness "exactly like a new monastic order." In all these points of reference, the identity of the anabaptist reformation with that of St. Francis springs to mind. But there is yet another very instructive point in this connection. When the movement put its very existence within the civil order at stake through its abrupt renunciation of taking oaths and bearing arms, Melchior Hofmann,[46] who was so influential everywhere, acknowledged once again his obligations to the state in respect to the oath and bearing arms. In this instance, he actually returned to the stipulations which corresponded to the rule of the Franciscan tertiaries.

From all these marks of agreement, we are quite well justified in concluding that the anabaptists were the kind of people who were filled with the Franciscan ideal of Christianity, even when they thought that they could discern the instruments of a corresponding reform of the church in Luther and Zwingli. They felt themselves obligated to take up the reformation of St. Francis after they found their expectations disappointed, since Luther and Zwingli had apparently turned away from the work of raising the level of asceticism among Christian people. The fact that the anabaptists almost universally preached the return of Christ and the establishment of his earthly thousand-year kingdom is another point of agreement with my hypothesis. The despair that is expressed in this regard, over improvement within Christianity by means of the ordinary forms of ethical training, exhibits a distinctive strand within that thinking which renounces the world. The dominant motif within that strand of thought is the view that the task of Christianity is not to formulate the moral rules of life in the world and order them supernaturally; rather, the ordinary regulation of moral life in the world and the rule of Christianity are mutually exclusive. This is also the fundamental view of all monastic asceticism, be it inside or outside the walls of the cloister. This urgent expectation of a forcible rupture of all human ordinances through the return of Christ clarifies once again the monastic substratum of the anabaptist movement. But the fact that the heavenly kingdom of Christ is to appear on earth, that is, under the continuation of the conditions of the world, seems to stand in contradiction with the point of view to which I have just referred. This aspect of anabaptist thought springs from the other motif within medieval Christianity, the Augustinian-Gregorian assumption that the kingdom of God must accommodate itself on earth through ethical-political ordinances. There may be a contradiction between the monastic principle of escape from the world and the hierarchical principle of the political dominion of

world and state, but since it embraced both elements of this contradiction, the system of western catholicism was not rendered
impracticable. The anabaptists, however, merely effected a modification of this catholic synthesis, in their monastic tendencies despairing at the secularization of the hierarchical system of the vicar of
Christ on the one hand, while considering the earthly kingdom of
Christ itself as a practicable form of the Christian life, on the other.
If it is thereby established that medieval images are at work precisely
in this expectation, then this particular expression of that expectation points us again to the soil which has been seeded with the well-
known set of dualisms which the spiritual Franciscans posited. I will
grant that things are more ambiguous after the Observants were
legalized through the Council of Constance. As a matter of fact, we
see a thoroughgoing, harmonious reciprocity between the papacy and
the Franciscan orders in the fifteenth century. Indeed, Erasmus
observed that the mendicant orders took pains with their relations to
the pope when it might bring them an advantage, but otherwise the
holy father was no more a reality for them than a dream.[47] One has
to assume that this inner independence from the papacy was stronger
and more widespread among the Franciscans than among the
Dominicans, for the latter were charged with the Inquisition and
therefore were more closely bound to the papacy. This is also verified by the fact that Luther's opposition to the pope received wide
approval among the Franciscans. That this approval was due to the
gospel of God's free grace and justification by faith more than to a
basic censure of the secularization of the church and the papacy is
doubtful. In any case, the artisans who had been affected by the
diverse activities of the Franciscans recalled again, when they heard
Luther, how the church had been secularized under the papacy;
nevertheless, they also experienced the inability to break through
this secularizing of the church in Luther's reformation. With this in
mind, it is quite understandable that in their ascetical impulse for
reform, their recollection of the eternal gospel also became more
vivid—a gospel whose fulfillment seemed to stand all the nearer to
them as the hopeless, antichristian character of the church became
clearer. But now, in the sixteenth century, the slogan of the movement was "the visible return of Christ himself," rather than "the
eternal gospel, based on the Holy Spirit." This expression was also

set forth in the Joachite Books,[48] and without a doubt this vision from the apocalypse was more popular than the vision of the eternal gospel based on the Holy Spirit. With this modification, therefore, the anabaptists' expectation is nothing but the renewal of the storm caused by the spiritual Franciscans.

Finally, the fact that the anabaptists shared the perspective of mystical theology can be fully explained by recalling that the preaching of the members of the mendicant orders transported mystical piety from its usage within the cloisters out into the parishes. When the anabaptists followed leaders such as these, who extolled resignation to God as the highest calling, and when they not only experienced ecstasies and visions but even believed that in them they received impulses from God, they indicated thereby that they had stood for some time under the influence of the mystical traditions which had come down from the mendicant orders to their particular congregations. Therefore, there is nothing that is included in the dominant views of the anabaptists that is not explicable in terms of the impact that the mendicant orders, specifically the Franciscans, made upon the urban lower class masses. For this reason, when viewed from the outside, the reformation which the anabaptists undertook appears more decisive and complete than that of Luther and Zwingli. Luther did not even intend a reform of Christian life, but, rather, a reform of doctrine and worship as well as of the teaching office, and he had only an indirect effect on the practical amendment of life, to the extent that he established the proper foundation for moral training. Zwingli, to be sure, aimed directly at improving mores, in that he brought the restricting legal power of the state into relationship with the power to arouse which preaching on matters of faith and obedience possessed. But who can continue to give a favorable assessment of anabaptism, in light of the fact that it bases amendment of the Christian life on renunciation of the world and contempt for the civil order, in view of the fact that it prescribes communal ownership and the cut of the clothes, forbids cheerfulness and joyfulness, and in view of the fact that it points the way for a fundamental freedom of the flesh through its imagined sinlessness? Such principles as these aim at goals which are diametrically opposed to the intentions of Luther and Zwingli, and the antinomian side of this movement is not an accidental appendage.

If the norm of the Christian life is to be arrived at, in any sense, through ascetical rules in statutory form, then one might let himself be impressed by the facade of the anabaptist impetus for reform. But if the Christian life has to do with the totality of character formation on the basis of the law of freedom, then the error of the monastic and statutory position of the anabaptists is clear beyond any doubt. This is what demonstrates that this reform is not the more thorough and complete, but rather that it is simply another kind of reformation, diametrically opposed to that of Luther and Zwingli. This conclusion is fully clarified by the probability that anabaptism took its origin from the sphere of the Franciscan reform, since the opposition between this reform and Luther's is established. It is true that a number of Luther's and Zwingli's adherents afterwards appeared as anabaptists, but even this phenomenon does not destroy the hypothesis I have set forth. The attachment of those ascetically inclined artisans to Luther and Zwingli was possible because the authority of the divine word and the holy scriptures was just as decisive for the adherents of the Franciscan reformation as it was for Luther and Zwingli. It is true that that authority was understood in totally different ways in the two types of reformation and that opposing styles of life are derived from it. Although the masses of ascetically inclined urban artisans first permitted themselves to be drawn to the side of Luther and Zwingli through the slogan of "reform based on God's word," they turned away from those two reformers just as quickly and struck out on the path of anabaptism when they failed to find their ascetical ideal confirmed in those reformers. Under these circumstances, it is also understandable why the authority of the holy scriptures could not settle the differences between these two movements, since it was a purely formal authority which was utilized differently by each side. As a consequence, the decision against the anabaptists was actually occasioned by the force of the civil authorities, rather than by the force of a theological norm.

IV. CATHOLICISM AND PROTESTANTISM

The fact that the authority of holy scripture is invoked both by our reformers and by the anabaptists at the same time, but with opposing meanings, indicates that we can neither explain nor adequately describe the distinctiveness of our reformation through the commonly used formula of the "two principles of the reformation."[49] Actually, the so-called formal principle, which asserts the exclusive authority of holy scripture for faith, life, and theological knowledge, was already acknowledged by the Franciscan monastic theologian, Duns Scotus.[50] The fact that the theology of the Franciscans nevertheless incorporated a great deal of the ecclesiastical tradition did not diminish the significance of the scripture principle for them; neither did the fact that protestant theology transmitted a mass of ecclesiastical traditions from the very beginning compromise the significance of holy scripture for protestants nor their fundamental esteem for it. Such a position makes Duns a representative of the reformation tendencies of the founder of his order rather than an isolated "forerunner" of Luther. Neither did this same scripture principle take on specific meaning for Luther and his comrades until they found themselves in opposition to the Dominicans and Thomists and to that action at Trent[51] which made the equation of tradition with scripture the fundamental principle of the catholic church. It would be much sounder to claim that the original meaning of the reformation of the sixteenth century is based on the so-called material principle, the doctrine of justification through faith. Even though this concept was already expressed before Luther—for example, by St. Bernard[52]—it was only in an accidental manner, with no real tie to the opposition against the catholic system which gave Luther's doctrine its significance. But a *principle of doctrine* cannot be established on the basis of Luther's assertion of justification by faith. On the contrary, it is only a characteristic conclusion to be drawn from the principle of divine grace, which, *when it is related to* other knowledge, serves for ordering and evaluating the Christian life in a relevant way. The formula of the two principles of the reformation, and the manner in which it is customarily employed to interpret the reformation, expresses an inadequate assessment of this epoch-making phenomenon. Such an assessment would only lead one to believe that the reformation of Luther and the others called a new form of theological school into being, and not that it had set in motion a new phase of the Christian style of life [*Lebensführung*]. In addition to this shortcoming, the formula of the two principles was put together in a very fortuitous manner, with no comprehensive reflection upon the facts.[53] Schleiermacher has explained how the formula may be rightly interpreted and what its usefulness is, namely, that within the diversity of protestant theologians, the acknowledgment of these two principles is the least that must be attributed to a theologian if he is to qualify as a protestant [*evangelischer*] theologian.[54]

In light of the common characteristics of western Christianity which were presupposed at the time, the distinctiveness of ecclesiastical protestantism—that is, that which is common to the reforms which Luther, Zwingli, and Calvin carried out—over against Latin catholicism, can be set forth under as few as three headings. These are: the substance of the image which serves as the norm for the Christian life [*Lebensideal*], the estimate of what is most important in the Christian community, and, finally, the judgment of the relation of the state to the Christian religious and moral community.

If the reformation of the sixteenth century had exhibited no ideal for the Christian life [*Ideal des christlichen Lebens*], we would be hard put indeed to demonstrate with certainty that it possesses epoch-making significance and lasting validity alongside the catholic form and phase of Christianity. And, in the light of the three-hundred-year history of the progressive splintering of its community, our faith that God will sustain protestantism until the end would be shattered. Catholic Christianity finds this governing image for its style of life [*Lebensideal*] in monasticism, in the bond created by the obligations of poverty, chastity, and obedience (to the superior in the order). These are understood as touching upon the universal law of God. In these particular virtues, it is said that one attains the supernatural destiny which Christianity holds out for man, a destiny which was not provided for in man's original creation. Since man enters into the life of the angels in this way, the monastic condition, thus conceived, is really Christian perfection. That protestants are filled with a sense of the quantitative imperfection of all their accomplishments is by no means a conclusive antithesis to this catholic position. This qualification does not deny the catholic position in any fundamental way; rather, it only clouds the issue. The works-righteousness or self-righteousness which popular opinion teaches us to ascribe to the catholics is no more frequent among them than it is among orthodox and pious Lutherans. If protestantism is to prevail against the practical weight which catholicism carries in its cultivation of monasticism and in the spreading of monastic piety, even among the laity, then it must be able to produce a standard of qualitative perfection. And it has been able to do just this.[55] Just as a chief characteristic of the condition of sinfulness is the lack of fear and trust in God, so also—according to the Augsburg Confession[56]—perfection consists of fear and trust in God through all the conditions of life; this is more fully expressed as fear, trust in God's merciful providence, prayer, and the conscientious carrying out of one's vocation.[57] Such a description of perfection is expressly intended as the antithesis to the catholic view of monasticism. It is true that this idea is not prevalent in Luther's private writings,[58] and Melanchthon gives it no place in his doctrinal writings. Thus, it is all the more significant that the Apology of the Augsburg Confession[59] not only frequently echoes this idea, but even gives it classical expression at one place.[60] There the meaning of the assertion of justification by faith is demonstrated—namely, that such justification clarifies how the sinner comes to possess trust in God's providence in all the situations of life in which he finds himself and whence he actually derives that trust.[61] This is the distinctive test of reconciliation with God, that one is also reconciled with the course of the world which God directs, no matter how hard it may strike him. In contrast, the doctrine of justification by faith has no *direct* intention of explaining the good works of the believer or engendering them. If that were the intention, we would have to prefer the catholic doctrine of justification. And it is in this context that the practical significance of the Lutheran doctrine comes to light, the practical significance which gives it its place as the *primus et principalis articulus* [first and principle article]. That is to say, the importance of this doctrine becomes clear only as Christians have to strive after their perfection precisely in the midst of their regular intercourse with the world and in their vocations within the domain of the secular society. How can their worldly anxieties and temptations to cowardice give the monastics cause for such faith in God's help, defense, and redemption from tribulations—these monastics who are free from these weaknesses, according to the testimony of St. Bernard?[62] Therefore, in our reformation's governing image of life-style, faith in God's providence stands next to prayer and regard for secular vocation as the place where love for man is practiced in mutual reciprocity. This interpretation of the secular vocation is similarly a specific principle of protestantism; it is the practical expression of the fact that protestantism is conceived as filling and penetrating the world, rather than renouncing it. This significance and effect are inherent in the principle, even though they are not systematically grounded and derived from it by the reformers.[63]

But, I can hear someone say, the concept of perfection is a subordinate matter for the reformers, since it only occurs in their polemic against the catholic concept of perfection.[64] If I were to understand this remark as an assertion that the concept of Christian perfection is a matter of indifference for the total reformation view of life as such, then I would have to concede that it is supported by the fact that the concept is seldom enough discussed. Apart from this, however, it seems to me that even if this concept of perfection does flow from the pens of the reformers only when they polemicize against the catholic regard for monasticism, that in itself is an indication that it holds a primary significance for them. Or am I mistaken in asserting that the distinctiveness of the reformation of the sixteenth century is to be understood at one single point, over and above its specific agreement or disagreement with catholicism? And is it not true that monasticism stands as the authentic form of Christianity in catholicism? A person who has spent his life in the nineteenth century, untouched by catholic patterns of life, might form the opinion that a concept which is antithetical to monasticism would be in itself of subordinate significance for the reformers. But this would not be true for the sixteenth century, despite appearances to the contrary. And even though the Augsburg Confession seldom speaks of the term "perfection," nevertheless the substance and significance of the concept is attested by the interpretation of Adam's perfection before the fall, which Luther and Calvin both set forth, in agreement with each other,[65] inasmuch as the redemption spoken of in Christianity is supposed to reinstate the perfection which Adam possessed in relation to God. But the description of Adam lacked one thing which was necessary for the reformers' own situation, namely, the imperative which confronts the Christian to prove his Christianness within his secular vocation through good or publicly useful action; however, they emphasized this one mark of perfection so consistently that it tended to make up for all the other marks.

This principle fundamentally transformed the entire society and gave the catholic opponents, for example, Georg Witzel,[66] occasion to assert that the reformation led to epicureanism and paganism. If the reformers never doubted the importance of worldliness, but rather always lifted it up, regardless of the fact that there was also a pejorative form of worldliness (which was also relevant to the practice of their principle), should we then assume that they wanted to be known as the patrons of a distinctive imperfection in the moral life? Should we not, rather, understand them in this respect as representatives and guardians of a distinctive perfection of Christian life? Let me posit the converse: The reformers took no constructive interest in the matter and spoke only from a polemical perspective when they reflected upon the ideals of Christian perfection that were current in their own time; therefore, they did not possess any internal impulse to set forth an image which in its wholeness would govern the Christian style of life [Lebensideal]; all they could do, or wished to do, therefore, was to give fragmentary rules for Christian living. Here I would admit that protestantism stood at an immense disadvantage vis-à-vis catholicism, and I recognize that I must take pains to justify my concurrence with the former. Perhaps I should assume that the weakness I have described is counterbalanced by the amplification which pietism sought to make effective within a Lutheranism that was in itself imperfect; then, however, the question would arise whether the last state were not worse than the first. To put the matter briefly, if the independent significance of the reformation concept of Christian perfection is denied, then I cannot help but regard that the soul-saving significance of pietism really begs the question. Indeed, the image of life-style [Lebensideal] or evangelical perfection which the reformers asserted describes the distinctiveness of their undertaking, particularly in that the discriminations between perfect and imperfect Christians, monastics and laity, or pietists and nonpietists, are made with a norm which is the same for all. To a certain extent, St. Francis pursued the same intention; but through just the opposite means, so as to extend monastic piety as far as possible throughout the laity. The basis for this effort in the Middle Ages was found in a reformation patterned after the example of the church in Jerusalem. This authority was also brought up against the reformers in Wittenberg by Georg Witzel, in criticism of their undertaking as it pertained to the ethical imperative.[67] But Melanchthon, with his sure sensitivity, recognized the monastic style of this example. If it should be confirmed that pietism is similarly sustained by the authority of the example of the primitive church, then Melanchthon's critical judgment against Witzel is especially noteworthy, since it presupposes the familiar idea of Christian perfection.

The second major point of comparison between catholicism and protestantism is the determination of the relation between the religious and legal communities that are included under the rubric of the church. The catholic principle at this point reads as follows: that these two functions coincide throughout, that there is no religious function of a Christian type which does not fall within the framework of the legal structure of the western church, and that this legal structure serves as the direct warrant for the correct exercise, maintenance, and propagation of all religious functions within the community. Accordingly, either of these functions could be legitimated as the end and the other would stand as the means, in reciprocal fashion. In protestantism, on the contrary, the common legal structure of the church stands unconditionally only as the means for the corporate religious activity, or, in other words, the latter is always held to transcend the framework of the legal structure, and it would never be said that it coincides with the former.

Third, catholicism understands the state either as a form of the sinful world or as God's means for ordering the world, with the stipulation that it is of less value than the ecclesiastical legal structure and must unconditionally accommodate itself to the claims of that structure. In the protestant interpretation, the state is a good thing, as the legal structuring of human activity which is as such legitimated by God; to be sure, of less value than the religious community within Christianity, but in itself nevertheless a support of that community, since the care of the law is the corresponding means for the freedom of religious and ethical activity.

If one asks, on the basis of the aforementioned marks of protestantism, how this relates itself to the concept of reformation spoken of in the twelfth chapter of Romans, it certainly appears as if protestantism is far removed from this standard. "Do not model yourselves on the behavior of the world around you!" [Rom. 12:2].

Is esteem for one's vocation in society together with rejection of monasticism not in direct contradiction to this admonition? Is esteem for the state as a special support of the combined religious and ethical activity within Christianity not a significant concession to the world, especially when one recalls that from this relationship the transfer of the church's legal structure to the state first came about? To the contrary, I would observe that with respect to one's vocation in society the important thing is that the vocation be carried out in a spiritual rather than in a worldly fashion; and with respect to the state's legal supervision of the legal functions of the church, the important thing is that the religious activities of the community —which in fact make it the church—be bothered as little as possible by legal, that is, worldly, concerns. The thrust in both cases is therefore governed throughout by the other clause, "but let your behavior change, modelled by your new mind" [Rom. 12:2]. But at the same time, it is precisely the fundamental differentiation between the legal and religious functions within the church and the fundamental regard for the disparity in their respective worth that stands in direct harmony with the first admonition. The catholic view of the church, however, runs directly counter to it. Law is primarily the concrete, secular ordering of man's common life; all ecclesiastical law is therefore also secular. The catholic view concerning the law of the catholic church, that this law is directly and unconditionally divine and supramundane, involves a specific conforming of Christianity to the world. Accordingly, protestantism has not renounced the principle of reformation, but is sustained, contrariwise, by the intention to conform to it to a greater extent than is the case in catholic Christianity. Which of these two forms of Christianity nevertheless gives the greater impetus for secularization is a question that ought not be discussed here.

Thus far in my comparison between the two forms of western Christianity, the catholic concept of Christian perfection has been determined by the traditional formulas of monasticism. Officially, catholic perfection is exhaustively described by the three monastic virtues; nevertheless, the full scope of this perfection is actually arrived at only through the contemplative form of piety to which the monks are held. We cannot afford to overlook this phenomenon at this point, because it is only through it that the opposition between the protestant and catholic concepts of perfection is fully understandable. For faithfulness to one's secular vocation is opposed to the three monastic virtues. Furthermore, what is the importance of the fact that faith in God's providence and the prayer which that faith supports are counted as part of protestant perfection? These functions find their corresponding opposite in the contemplation which is imposed upon the monastics and which, on the surface, seems to aspire to much higher things. It must be noted, however, that in the second half of the Middle Ages, this devotion was, in part, expressly counted as a mark of the monastic and, in part, had also extended itself among the masses, as was the case with the tertiary orders and related forms, like the Friends of God,[68] and the Brothers and Sisters of the Common Life.[69] However, the prototypical statement of this devotion, and the one that was normative throughout the entire Middle Ages, was set forth by St. Bernard in his eighty-six sermons on the Song of Songs.[70] Without a knowledge of this typical outline of devotion, one can have no full understanding of catholicism. Bernard made such a highly influential application of the allegorical exegesis and ecclesiastical use of the Song of Songs that he explained the bride of Christ no longer as the church, but rather as the individual believing soul. To be sure, the familiar interpretations of the church fathers also occur in his work, and once (56, 1) he also gives expression to Athanasius's exposition that the visit of the bridegroom to the bride refers to the incarnation of the divine word. In advance then, one can imagine that, when compared to these expositions, Bernard's interpretation was especially important for determining the direction piety took. I will note here that in his lectures Luther expressly rejected Bernard's explanation, since he interpreted Song of Songs as applying to Solomon's political rule.

The background for the range of Bernard's ideas, which we want to consider at this point, was a most comprehensive acknowledgment of divine grace. It is well known that this stands generally in his sermons as the highest and dominant theme; consequently, his concern for human freedom, which is shown in his theoretical theology, drops totally out of sight. From this perspective, Bernard serves to establish for us the fact that a thrust identical to that of our reformers had its roots in medieval Christianity. Nevertheless, it is pertinent to try to find the boundaries of this consensus in the practical consequences of St. Bernard's reform movement. To do this, it is appropriate to undertake a precise analysis of the piety which is inherent in the sermons on the Song of Songs. Thus, for St. Bernard, it was firmly established that believers had to lead their lives in trust in the fullness of God's mercy, and not trust in their own merit or in the feeling of their own powers (14, 4; 21, 11); and on occasion he was able to give as precise an expression of justification by faith as a protestant could desire (22, 7, 8, 11). In another connection, to be sure, the compassion of God through the forgiveness of sins is acknowledged as the effective ground of merits (61, 5; 68, 2). One ought not view this as though catholic piety were disposed predominantly or overwhelmingly toward works-righteousness. This tradition of interpreting catholicism among protestants is shaped by judgments that grew out of Luther's special and very one-sided experiences, and it is in need of considerable correction. Still, the fact that Bernard does not give up on merit completely, in spite of his energetic stress on God's grace, but rather maintains it intact, causes one to doubt from the outset that the basic presupposition in his work which is common to us both will lead to wide-ranging consequences which we can both accept. In this connection we must above all pay attention to the fact that Bernard's sermons are directed only to monastics. Their situation, however, is such that they enjoy in the cloister "peace from the cares of the world and the vicissitudes and afflictions of life, in that they are directed to lead a life that is exceptional in its holiness and virtue" (46, 2). Consideration of the first verse of the Song of Songs, "O that he would kiss me with the kisses of his mouth," leads to the conclusion that we "extend ourselves in trust (*fiducia*) to the same degree that we grow in grace" (3, 4). But in this context this verse finds an application totally different from what it would have to find to retain a protestant sense. For the sphere to which the protestant Christian is directed for testing his trust in God is simply nonexistent for the listeners of St. Bernard who are protected from the manifold cares of life in the world (see pp. 86–87 above). Rather, the trust in God which he means points to the sphere of individual contemplation and to the benefits which are sought therein; and at the same time this trust to which he refers is motivated by something other than the simple acknowledgment of reconciliation with God through

Christ. In the third sermon, Bernard proclaims that one does not get
to kiss the bridegroom's mouth before he has succeeded in kissing
his hands and feet. The first kiss is the act of penance for sin; it
directs itself toward the feet of the stern Lord, which symbolize his
compassion and his righteousness; in the reciprocal relationship of
these factors, however, the Christian does not long continue in either
despair or in false security (6, 6–8; 11, 2). Since the penance would
nevertheless be pointless if its results were not firmly established
through abstaining from sin and through works of piety, the second
kiss signifies the whole spectrum of active sanctification, in which one
is supported by the hand of the Lord. Thus growth in grace is
signified, and it consists in extending oneself in trust in God. Only
he who has experienced divine grace in the first two kisses, that is,
in the consummated penance and in the active sanctification which
consummates itself, is permitted to claim with more ardent love and
increased trust the wonderfully sweet and gracious kiss from the
mouth of the bridegroom, the kiss in which he becomes *one spirit
with the Lord Jesus*. Therefore, one experiences this kiss only on a
level of perfection which seldom exists (4, 1). "My beloved is mine
and I am his" (Song 2:16)—no one dare strive for this height of
reciprocal love, to which the soul is entitled through wondrous grace,
who has not merited the experience through special purity of disposition and holiness of body (67, 8). Or whoever longs for peace in
contemplation has to take the lead through exercise of the virtues
of that sacred peace, since the enjoyment of contemplation is due
only to him who is obedient to the commandments (46, 5). One
has only to read how Bernard at one point counts up his good works
and afterwards proceeds to say that all of these come from habit, not
from inner sweetness; therefore, he who has only produced what he
owes is termed a useless servant in the gospel. "Perhaps I do fulfill
the commandments in one way or another; but in so doing my soul
is like land without water; therefore, let him kiss me with the kisses
of his mouth, so that thereby my sacrifices might be rich" (9, 2).

The protestant Christian, who also considers himself a useless
servant since he is only doing his duty, at the same time entrusts his
salvation to the reconciliation with God which he has experienced in
Christ. St. Bernard's stance is somewhat different however, even
though he, too, experiences no salvation in his fulfilling of the

commandments. For him, this experience is a trial both of God's grace and his own merit—it is a trial through which he gives himself to be aroused to that trust in God or thirsting for God which will bring him satisfaction in his bridal love for the Lord Jesus. In the interpretation of this image, the marks of the *humiliated* and suffering Son of God emerge at times very significantly, whereas the marks of his divinity and dominion are, according to the circumstances, intentionally repressed through the description of the love which is directed toward him. On the other hand, the satisfaction which is sought in the bridegroom is affected by the fact that he is also the word of God and that he stands in place of God. Accordingly, in the portrayal of the contemplative processes, God can be interpolated for Christ without any difficulty. It is all the more striking then, that the description of love which Bernard intends here expressly pushes aside the barrier between God (Christ) and the person of the believer which is set by God's sublime nature.

> The soul loves ardently, it is so intoxicated with its own love that it does not heed the majesty. Oh what power of love, what trust in the spirit of freedom! Perfect love casts out fear (also awe?) (7, 2). I am driven by ardent desire, not by reason; raise no complaint against the presumption toward which passion drives. Caution warns us, certainly, but love outweighs it. I know very well that the king's honor desires judgment, but love, rushing precipitately, disregards judgment; love will neither be moderated by counsel nor bridled by modesty, nor governed by reason (9, 2). The beloved is present, the master is away, the king disappears, propriety has left, and awe is laid aside. Between God's word and the soul a very private dialogue is carried on, as between two neighbors. Mutual love and tenderness flow into each from the one source of love. Accordingly, words sweeter than honey soar from both sides, and there hover about the glances that are filled completely with ecstasy. Finally, he calls her 'beloved' and names her 'the beautiful one'; he repeats himself, and he receives the same endearments in turn from her. Truly, this is sublime vision, in which the soul is lifted to the level of trust and then again to the level of acceptance where it comes to know Jesus, the Lord of all things, no longer as Lord, but rather only as beloved (45, 1, 6). The soul that loves is driven by desires, drawn on by yearning, it conceals its merits; the soul closes its eyes to majesty, opens wide its longing in the sense that it directs it toward salvation and bestirs itself with full confidence toward that salvation. Finally, without trembling and without reserve (*inverecunda*) it calls

God's word back to itself and confidently begins the game (*deliciae*) again, in which, with her accustomed freedom, she calls him not Lord, but Beloved (74, 4; see also the even stronger expressions in 79, 1).

Bernard even concedes that this love for the God-man is in a certain sense sensuous.

> Notice that the heart's love is to a certain extent fleshly (*carnalis*), because it is directed more to the flesh of Christ and because what Christ does and commands in the flesh grasps the human heart. And when that heart is filled with this love, it is easily incited to that sort of talk.

But the love which is supposedly passionate in this connection is said, at the same time, to be prudent and powerful—prudent in that the sensuous movement of that love itself renders the attractions of the flesh ineffective; powerful in that it hews to the line of the church's rule of faith (20, 4–9). Besides this, however, we notice that the sensuously formed excitements which the text of the Song of Songs sets before us are transformed allegorically into spiritual functions. The soul, which is called happy in Song 2:6 because it lies on Christ's breast and in his arms, is reminded that it has to prove itself through fear and hope (51, 5). Generally, however, the goal of contemplative ecstasy is that one should attain the purity of the angels, that in the knowledge of God one would not remain entangled in sensuous images, but rather would transcend the illusions of corporeal likenesses. One cannot hope for the peace that he strives for until this prior goal has been achieved (52, 4, 5).

We must ascertain precisely the characteristics of this love for Christ which I have described, this love which is attributed to the perfect believers; for from the very beginning it is alien to protestant piety. Above all, however, we must observe that this sketch of passionate love for Christ contradicts the common protestant assumption that the catholic approach is to posit the God-man only as a strict judge set at the greatest possible distance from the believer. Just as, in accord with Luther's experience, we frequently judge that catholic Christianity consists in striving after works-righteousness in the timid fear that accompanies servile work, so too, the assumption has taken root among us that, for all practical purposes, Christ stands for catholics only as a strict, inaccessible judge, whose grace is surreptitiously obtained through the intercession of the saints. We have every reason for wanting to set this opinion straight. It is true that in catholic piety Christ holds this position I have just described in penance (see above, p. 93), that is, at the beginning of the religious life, but not in an exclusive sense. St. Bernard's thinking is not just different in form from the stereotyped picture of Christ as stern judge—it contradicts that picture. As I have suggested, the reason why most comparative studies of Lutheranism and Roman Catholicism do not introduce this dimension into their discussions goes back to the accidental fact that Luther had no experience of it in his monastic life. But in reality, Bernard's method, which leads the believer through the context of divine grace to passionate love for Christ, serves us as a direct introduction to the flowering of monastic piety. Luther, on the contrary, became acquainted as a monk only with the withered shell of monastic devotion which was already emptied of its fruit. According to the introduction which St. Bernard provides for the monk who is firm in his sanctification, love for Christ should disregard the divine sublimity; the soul on whom God has bestowed grace should experience and enjoy the benefits through which the God-man satisfies his yearning as if he and Christ were on a level of equality. The soul may be just as quick to rejoice in the fact that it has been lifted above its original position as it is to take God's humbling of himself as the occasion for its sensuous passion to be aroused toward him. Since the opposition of these two points of view has never been clearly delineated, the latter has prevailed to the extent that this passion for Christ has served to neutralize the drive for this world's goods and the pleasures that go with them. Only under this supposition does the other view come into force, namely, the view that the sensuous intuition of the God who humbles himself turns into the formless spiritual immersion in God which characterizes the ecstatic goal of blessedness in which the benefits of eternal life are even now experienced in advance. The balancing of these opposing methods of the spiritual life proceeds according to the laws of feeling itself [*Gefühl*]—the one method pulling Christ down in the interests of drawing close to him in a passionate and sensuous manner, at the cost of his sublime nature; whereas the other method seeks a union with him in one spirit through an elimination of sensuous elements and by participating in his sublimity. Since the sensuously colored passion for the God-man also includes in itself a spiritual intention, the apparently purely spiritual elevation of feeling to the state of ecstasy can be understood as resting on the expectation that the tension of the overexcited sensuous drives will be lessened. This is why I say that the balancing of these contrasting methods proceeds according to the laws of feeling.

Although such a devotional method rests upon clear images of Christ, since, indeed, it points us to excitations of feeling which have to be linked to Christ, those images are nevertheless by no means uniform. For Bernard, the image of God who humbles himself is twofold in nature; in the first place, it is framed with no reference to his sublimeness, only afterwards to become entirely commensurate with that sublime nature which guarantees that the soul is elevated over its own creaturely limitations. In contrast, the protestant Christian is under the imperative to find personal religious meaning in the fact that the God-man who humiliates himself is identical with the sublime divinity, and also in the converse. For this reason, we must be careful not to overestimate Bernard's apparent agreement with the protestant point of view in the following explanations. Bernard recognizes the love of the bridegroom in his works of redemption and says that every redeemed man must to some degree hold them vividly in mind. In connection with this theme he raises two points, namely, the form and the consequence. The form is the humiliation of God, the consequence, our being filled with God (11, 3). To be sure, it is particularly important for Bernard that these conditions be effective as the basis of the distinctive devotion which his sermons aim at eliciting. The work of redemption, therefore, should not be understood here as if it could explain for every believer how he has been restored in the image of God and to dominion over the world (21, 6, 7), rather, it is to be understood as that which "allures in a coaxing manner, justifiably compels, closely binds, and sharply arouses" love, the passionate excitement for Christ. In addition, however, it is emphasized that one must make real for himself individually the whole spectrum of efforts through which the God who humbles himself has authenticated his love. For the same God who without effort created the world through his simple command endured in his earthly preaching those who would oppose him; in his actions, the hostile onlookers; in his torments, the scoffers; and in his death, those who would malign him. See how he loved! Learn, therefore, from Christ how you should love him (20, 2, 4).

The basis for the protestant faith which subordinates itself to Christ is simply the regard which the believer has for the love of God which is efficacious unto redemption in the obedience of Christ, whereas the passionate love of equal for equal which Bernard represents, demands that the total achievement of Christ's love be divided up into its individual strands. Consequently, Bernard explains in connection with Song 1:13 ("My beloved is to be a bag of myrrh, that lies between my breasts"):

Since the beginning of my conversion (i.e., my entry into monasticism) I have undertaken to bind this bag to myself and to lay it on my breast—a bag which is made up of all the anguish and bitterness of my Lord, especially that which has to do with the distress of the child-like life, that is, the toil of preaching, the weariness in travel, vigils in prayer, the temptations in fasting, weeping in sympathy, and finally dangers from false brothers, the invectives, blows, mockery, abuse, nailing, and the like. Among the many types of this scented myrrh, I have not omitted that which he drank on the cross and with which he was anointed at his burial. I wish to express my remembrance of the fullness of the sweetness of these things as long as I live; in eternity I wish to remember these mercies in which I have found life (43, 3).[71]

He applies this interest differently in the exposition of Song 2:14 ("O my dove, in the clefts of the rock, in the shelter of the cliff"). Here Bernard presents an explanation which he borrows from another, but which he represents with his own conviction, namely that

the clefts of the rock refer to Christ's wounds, for the rock is Christ. The sparrow makes its house in these clefts and the turtledove its nest; in them the dove finds safety from the hawk. And truly, where may the weak find safety and peace except in the wounds of the savior? Men pierced his hands and feet and stabbed his side with the lance, and through these openings, it is permitted to me to drink honey out of the rock and oil out of the hard stone; that means that I may taste and see that the Lord is sweet. The secret of the heart is revealed through the rents in the body, the secret of piety and the depths of God's compassion. Are these depths not laid open through the wounds? Where would it be clearer than in your wounds, Lord, that you are sweet and mild and richly compassionate? (61, 3, 4).

We can see that the most important elements are preserved also in these words, and in accordance with the principle that it is only by contemplating the humiliated God that one attains the vision of his majesty. "For the direct exploration of his majesty is full of terror, whereas the exploration of his merciful will is as comforting as it is devout" (62, 5). In spite of this, St. Bernard starts down a very steep path when he emphasizes the reciprocal relationship between the suffering form of Christ, which he has to explicate in its individual aspects, on the one hand, and the passionate love, on the other hand, which goes beyond Christ's majesty and embraces him as an equal, as a neighbor, and as a friend.

It is clear that Bernard wishes to lay hold of the mercy of God in the suffering form of Christ or, in other words, he wishes to contemplate the suffering God in individual manifestations of Christ's passion, a passion that testifies to his concern for men. From such a perspective, he is concerned throughout with the divine significance of Christ. He expresses this when he says that in his feeling for individual acts of suffering he finds the "fullness of sweetness" and that in the wounds of Jesus he receives the impression that the Lord "is sweet and mild and full of compassion." This estimate of Christ's suffering is to be made in the context of the believer's relations of equality with the bridegroom. Since, in Jesus' undeserved and voluntary suffering, one gets to know the fullness of his love for the individual who practices contemplation, one should permit himself to be moved to a correspondingly high level of reciprocal love and sacrifice for Jesus. This particular thrust of the total view which Bernard sets forth comes from the statement that the bitter experiences of Jesus should be appropriated in a sweet taste of his love, and they should bear the shape of the same. It is clear from this that Bernard does not wish to conclude that one should lose himself in the inexhaustible pity and dejection which arise from comparing his own guilt with the guiltlessness of Jesus. He really intends a religious impression of an entirely different sort. But the question arises, nevertheless, whether the method which he prescribes really does necessarily lead the believer through the bitterness of suffering with Christ to obtain a taste of sweetness from his suffering, and further, whether in striving for this impression one really does justice to the full significance of redemption. As a theologian, Bernard knows very well that the power of faith to overcome the world arises from one's inner realization of the majesty, divinity, and dominion of Christ over the world (21, 6, 7). Moreover, at one point, Bernard is able to articulate in exemplary fashion the significance of Christ's person as the God who humbles himself.[72] Still the taste of sweetness to which he was able to penetrate in contemplation upon Jesus' love in the bitterness of his sufferings—this taste of sweetness does not necessarily follow from nor is it the clear test of the divinity of Christ's love. When we observe the phenomena of medieval piety, which nourished itself directly on the contemplation of Christ's suffering, we see that endless numbers of people never went beyond the point of aimless pity and dejection. In the devotion of the monks and the nuns, we get a much deeper impression that this devotional method led to gloomy abasement than we do that it served to elevate and liberate.

Furthermore, the fact that Bernard could transform the impression of bitterness into sweetness through contemplating that the meaning of Christ's suffering was really that of love, or that he could harmonize the desirable and the repugnant or joy and pain—this is by no means a trustworthy proof that he impressed both the divine sublimeness of Christ and the experience of his human humiliation upon his memory at the same time. To be sure, there is a certain analogy between Bernard's remembered impressions, which constitute a problem of cognition, and the experiences of Christ, which are questions of a complex sense-impression. In the divinity of the man Jesus, seemingly contradictory opposites do have to be thought together. And when the manifestations of Christ's suffering are tasted at the same time as bitter and sweet, we are presented with a paradox. In itself, this paradox contains no contradiction; for the bitterness follows from the impression of suffering, whereas the sweet taste adheres to the thrust of the love which permits Christ to suffer voluntarily. Outside of this, however, this love which is perceived as sweet points to no fundamental mark of divinity which would necessarily exceed the measure of human being. On the contrary, it is simply the ideal man, who lives for me, who lets me have his perfection [*Schönheit*], whose suffering causes the experience of bitterness to find an echo in the pleasure of sweetness; and Bernard is able to experience the feeling of sweetness only because he relates to the Lord Jesus on the basis of equality in this situation. The amalgam of bitterness and sweetness that we have to interpret before we can understand and assess Bernard's position possesses a character customarily associated with spiritual epicureanism, and therein it reveals rather a close relation to certain sensuous excitations of feeling than an analogy to the problem of how one comes to know the phenomenon of God-manhood. Even if it were true that this cognition impresses itself upon a person through the intuition of the suffering of Christ and from that gives the impression of redemption, still it is not advisable to venture into the specificities which Bernard recounts and to arouse the pain and ecstasy of sympathy from them; rather, one must assure himself of the total significance of redemption in the fact of the power of Christ's obedience to overcome the world. For the perception of Christ's divinity lies in the fact that his love wins victory over the world in his suffering; and we test this perception in feeling when we experience the elevating impulse for our own dominion over suffering and the world on the basis of reconciliation with God through Christ. This is the protestant understanding of the matter, which does do justice to the divinity of Christ. On the contrary, Bernard's contemplation can elicit a passionate love for neighbor and a willingness to serve which also transforms the most bitter into sweetness; but that is merely the cult of the ideal man which modern sentimentality has learned to apply to others besides the Lord Jesus. Thus at this point, we come to a perfectly clear opposition between protestant and catholic piety which we dare not overlook.

Since Bernard attended to the reciprocal relations between the soul and its bridegroom as if they were real, the question arises as to how this reality is to be put to the test. How can we disregard the objection that what we are dealing with here is the activity of the imagination? To this we hear the answer:

When I feel that the sensitivity for understanding holy scripture is being opened up for me, or a wise saying wells up, as it were, from my inmost depths, or mysteries are unveiled by a higher light, or, as it were, the inner depths of heaven are spread out before me and from above a rich fullness of contemplation in the spirit is poured out, then I do not doubt that the bridegroom is present (69, 6). . . . The soul should not consider itself to be perfectly united with God until it has the strong *feeling* that God abides in it and it abides in God. I am one spirit with God when I am once convinced that I cling to God as those who are in love (71, 6). . . . Sometimes when the word has come to me, I have not been able to feel just when it happened. I have *felt* its presence and afterwards remembered it; sometimes I could sense its coming in advance, but I could not directly sense its coming again or its leaving. By what means would I have recognized its coming? It is lively and powerful; as soon as it enters into me, it awakens my sleeping soul, sets it in motion, it soothes and wounds my hard heart. I have recognized the presence of the bridegroom only by the movement of my heart, and I have experienced his power when my sins ran away and the desires of the flesh were restricted (74, 5, 6).

Although sense experience generally does not distinguish between the feeling subject and the object which arouses that experience, the reason which always coexists with sense experience does posit this distinction. As a consequence, it is possible to become one spirit with God through the intentional elevation of religious desire (which is also supported by sufficient corporeal means) and still make this normal rational distinction between oneself and God. For this reason, Bernard holds the expectation that the goal of the mutual relationship of love is the vision of God, though not without some limitations. For he reserves the vision of God as he really is to life in the beyond, and he grants only that God appears in the present to those whom he will, as he will (31, 2). Occasionally he even circumscribes this vision of God according to the experience of Moses, so he says that man cannot see God's face, but rather only his back (61, 6). Nevertheless, the most important assertion in this regard is that

this experience of the soul and its commingling with God's word which lies beyond any bodily feeling and beyond the power of the imagination, is produced only through God's condescension, when the ardor of holy desire and the incessant groanings of prayer draw the bridegroom close (31, 4–6).

One could be tempted to assess this assertion as magic, except that the mystical union is ascribed throughout to the will of God or of the bridegroom and is seen as conforming to an expanding experience. For

> when a person seeks the bridegroom through vigils and *entreaties*, through many exertions and a rain of tears, and when the bridegroom does make himself present, then he slips away suddenly just when one thinks that he holds him fast, and when he again confronts the weeping soul that pursues him, he does, to be sure, permit himself to be grasped, but not to be held fast, since suddenly, as it were, he vanishes away once again (32, 2). . . . When the soul feels grace, it recognizes the presence of the word, when not, it protests his absence and strives after his presence. Thus, the word is called back through the yearning of the soul which has once had his sweet presence bestowed upon it. But the word comes and goes according to his own will, as when he pays a visit at twilight and shows himself unexpectedly (74, 2, 3).

Therefore, it is always only in a momentary way that it is possible to substantiate the presence of the bridegroom through the passionate excitations of feeling. The price of these pleasures, however, is the barrenness and slackness into which the soul falls, ever deeper and for even longer periods of time, in proportion to the unnatural character of these exertions which precede the pleasure (9, 3; 14, 6; 32, 4; 74, 7). And it is hardly appropriate to give the admonition that the enjoyment of grace is not to be counted as a securely held possession, inviolate through inheritance, as if this advice would keep one from losing courage and becoming unnecessarily disconsolate when the bridegroom withdraws himself (21, 5). For a constant certainty of grace is not achieved in the isolation which Bernard describes thus: "The soul that beholds God beholds him as if it were itself beheld only by God. In such confidence, the soul enters into this mutual relationship between God and itself as if nothing existed at all outside itself and God" (69, 8). At this point, I would only add the observation that this postulate of mysticism does not find a counterpart in that piety which is properly protestant. Churchly protestantism gives no sanction for such egoism. Yet Bernard is in a position to rebuke the monastics for claiming this privilege of mystical vision only for themselves, because on another occasion he reminds them that in truth the

church is the bride and that the prerogatives of the one catholic
community which comprises the purpose toward which the world
tends cannot be claimed by any individual soul who belongs to the
church, no matter how great its sanctity might be (68, 7).

> For which of us is able to possess any of the gifts of grace perfectly, in
> such a way that he is not at some time unfaithful in his speech and half-
> hearted in his works? But it is the church which in her totality never
> has a defect from which it is intoxicated or odorous. For what is lack-
> ing to the church in one person, it possesses in another. The church is
> odorous in those who make friends for themselves among unrighteous
> mammon, and it is intoxicated with those servants of the word who
> sprinkle the earth with the wine of spiritual joys, make the earth itself
> intoxicated, and harvest its fruits in joy. This church can call itself the
> bride with boldness and certainty. Therefore, although none of us
> takes it upon himself to call his soul the bride of the Lord, nevertheless,
> since we belong to the church, we justifiably claim our share of this
> honor. Without contradiction, we can say that each one of us shares in
> that which we all possess together (12, 11).

This is actually a confession which cuts across all of the previously
portrayed claims of the soul to be the bride, by referring back to the
older exegesis of the Song of Songs. All of those statements about
the special distinction of the individual soul, whereby it seems to
be made autonomous from all the other members of the church, in
immediate relationship to God and Christ—all of these are rendered
invalid in the light of Bernard's assertion concerning the church!
But I will not draw this conclusion, since it appears that each alternative is valid for the speaker in the place where it appears—or each
is imagined.

But this much is clear indeed, that the mystical vision which comprises the particular immediate relation of the individual soul to God
under such equivocal conditions did not at all intend that this relation should develop beyond its catholic forms into protestantism, and
there turn into the kind of evangelical Christian who is filled with
awe and trust in God in the midst of life's distresses and who is
exceedingly diligent in the service of God within his secular vocation. The two forms of piety are different or, to be more specific,
they are opposed in their fundamental characteristics. And no little
weight should be placed upon the fact that the sentimental piety with

its mystical thrust is expected only of monks who have no opportunity to test their faith in the temptations which arise from the cares of human life. This consideration serves perfectly to determine the character of the opposition between catholic and protestant Christianity. Grace is the dominant factor for protestant piety, but not, on that account, exclusively the possession of protestants, since it is also central to catholic piety as well. But the consequences and the applications of this highest principle are different for the monastics who live a life free from cares and for the protestant Christians who remain within the midst of their secular conditions of life and who must stand the test of their faith within the inescapable cares of those conditions. The latter must so conduct themselves through trust in God and the prayer which proceeds from that trust that, on the basis of their reconciliation with God or their redemption from guilt and evil they overcome the forces which hold man's life in check. In contrast, the monastics and their devotees in the catholic church may prove their redemption through Christ in the exercise of equality with him in sentimental pathos and sentimental desire which reaches to the height of the unity of their spirit with Christ and God—at least as long as this enjoyment lasts and does not deteriorate into the barrenness of experience. From this we may conclude that the certainty of reconciliation as it is expressed in trust in God is the necessary presupposition of sanctification for the protestant Christian, whereas for the catholics the enjoyment of redemption in tender intercourse with the redeemer is a possible appendage to their sanctification.

V. LUTHERANISM AND CALVINISM

If we may suppose now that pietism, in principle, restored the thrust of the anabaptists within the sphere of the Lutheran and Reformed churches, we still have the further question of which of the two protestant churches was more receptive to pietism's seed. And from this general investigation, our first task is to isolate the prior question of how far one may carry the analogy between Zwingli's reforming intention and that of the anabaptists. Although it is well known that the theocratic form in which Zwingli developed his plan for reformation did not become or remain normative for the formation of the Reformed church in Switzerland, nevertheless

that tendency of his is pertinent to at least a portion of the anabaptists. Zwingli clearly did not impute to the state merely the direct
task of protecting Christianity and reforming the church; he also
considered it advisable that the state should extend this reformation
through political force. In a similar manner, the anabaptist group
which was led by Hans Hut,[73] considering itself to be the true Israel,
proposed to exterminate all godless Canaanites by the sword, and
the anabaptists in Münster acted on this same impulse. This violent
attitude, to be sure, is an exception to the basic peaceableness and
subservience with which the anabaptists generally responded to the
force applied against them. Nevertheless, this deviation is quite
understandable as anticipatory of the coming power of Christ to
judge and rule, which the anabaptists expected. Thus the theocratic
perspective engendered on both sides a sanctioning of force for the
purpose of carrying through the Christian reform. Of course, there is
a great disparity between the two—Zwingli applied the means of
the existing state to the ends of a truly moral ordering of life; the
anabaptists, on the contrary, sought with their morally questionable
and reprehensible ends to overthrow the civil order. Accordingly, the
Münster theocracy of the anabaptists can hardly be viewed as the
consequence of Zwingli's Zurich theocracy. Indeed, there is neither
a logical nor moral connection between the moral and antimoral
ends, respectively, of these two tendencies, between Zwingli's legal
attachment to the existing civil order and the radical overturning
of the civil order in Münster. The constitution of state and church
in Zurich, directly under Zwingli's leadership, is therefore least of
all disposed to grant the anabaptists' claims concerning the validity
of their perfect Christianity. On the contrary, in fact, the opposition
to them in Zurich was so forceful precisely because the people there
were confident of the Christian justification for the existing civil and
moral order.

Even in his own lifetime, none of the Swiss social classes accepted
Zwingli's theocratic perspective, and in Zurich itself this highly
significant proposal was abandoned when the catastrophe occurred
in which Zwingli met his death. From then on, within the entire
sphere of the sixteenth century reformation movement, the principle
came to be accepted that the service which the state could render
to the Christian religion could be justified only by individual terri-

tories and that it could only be a protective service. In other words, Christian unity was sought only in unity of confession, not in unity of legally constituted organization, and hardly even in unity of liturgical forms. We need not discuss here how the commonality of confession split apart in the Lutheran and Reformed groups. By contrast, one other function of the church does come to mind, besides the ones already described, which brings with it a different manner of classifying the territorial churches. I am referring to the church's function of discipline. The polemical theologians of the sixteenth century were not clear in their own minds that there are divergences of considerable significance between the Lutheran and Reformed churches in their regard for church discipline. Even in our own century adequate attention has not been given to this matter.[74] It is very easy to demonstrate, in this respect, however, that Calvinism stands opposed not only to the whole of Lutheranism, but also to the ecclesiastical order of German Switzerland, or to the actual sphere of Zwingli's activity. Calvinism was able to occupy this area with its doctrine and its official confession (with the exception only of Basel), but not with its discipline; and even in the matter of doctrine, a Zwinglian undercurrent has always remained active. In addition, Calvinism has not been able to make its form of discipline stand in the German territories which acknowledge its authority in doctrine, as in the Palatinate, Bremen, Hesse, Anhalt, etc. In this regard, it has been able to establish its validity only in the areas outside Germany, and in Germany it was able to take hold in eastern Friesland, as well as in Julich, Cleves, and Berg only by reaching out from the Netherlands. Therefore, if church discipline is considered a worthy basis for classifying the reformation churches, Calvinism outside Germany must be set in opposition to the German sphere, which embraces Lutheranism and Zwinglianism. Indeed, Calvin could not carry out his work of establishing the church in Geneva except on the basis upon which the shaping of the reformation churches took place in the spheres of Luther and Zwingli, namely, through the authority of the state. Under such circumstances, church discipline came to be in the hands of the civil authorities throughout the German and Swiss territories. But there were various principles at work in bringing this to pass. In part, the medieval practice of church discipline assumed the form of secular penalties which the state simply took over in the wake of the reformation. In part, the one distinctive penalty of the church, exclusion from the Lord's Supper, could not be left to the individual pastors but had to be taken over by the provincial consistories. Or where a particular authority was established to exercise the ban, as with Bucer (1531) in Ulm (four men from the town council, two pastors, and two members of the congregation), it was prescribed that this authority could excommunicate only at the command of the town council.[75] Nevertheless, this course of things within the German sphere (particularly the Lutheran) of the church's development did not take place simply because of external, accidental considerations; rather, from the very beginning this development was governed by a certain theory concerning the respective competencies of church and state.

The two branches of the reformation between which we are differentiating here agree on this point: that church discipline is not necessitated simply by general considerations for social order, but, rather, by consideration for the honor of Christ or for the particular character of the Christian community.[76] As we know, Calvin concluded from this that the church must be in possession of specific legal organs for excluding public sinners. These organs could not be developed without support and even cooperation from the state, but yet they were to be independent of the state in their activity. In any case, the power of the state was to stand as a ready servant of the disciplinary decrees of the consistory and not as a higher authority over them. For the power to discipline is in God's behalf and, according to the prescriptions of holy scripture, it is an inviolable attribute of the church. But the Lutherans deviated completely from this norm. Franz Aepinus, in the Church Order for Stralsund (1525), and Johann Brenz, in the Church Order for Schwäbisch-Hall (1526),[77] agree that the church bears only the organs of grace, and that, accordingly, the maintenance of the Christian life through means of law or discipline is ultimately an attribute of the secular authority or of the state.[78] Accordingly, Brenz asserted that discipline was exercised in the ancient church in conformity with Paul's precept only because no Christian governmental authority was then in existence. Since general legal authority has come into the hands of Christians in the meantime, the necessity for church discipline has largely disappeared. In those specific cases where Brenz does prescribe church discipline, however, it is only in the sense of a substitute action because and for so long as the state does not hold sex offenses to be punishable, even though they transgress both divine and *imperial* laws.

The idea is clearly expressed in this discussion that in principle the church can have no punitive authority over its members since it is the community of divine grace and the bearer of the proclamation of grace. And therefore, when it does occur that this authority is attributed to the church, this can be explained only as an accidental defect in the relation between church and state in a certain epoch. However, when the state is conscious of the moral character of its penal authority, within a Christian frame of reference, the church must dispense with its disciplinary authority, in order to mold in a more definitive manner its own character as a religious community. This conclusion that the necessity of discipline is only conditional for the church stems from a contemporary of Luther, who actually only attained a second-rate significance. Although none of the later church orders include similar ideas, this man's discussion must be regarded as normative for the direction this issue took in the sphere of the Lutheran reformation, because his thinking conformed the most precisely to the dominant concept of the church at the time. When a person judges that it is a mark of the weakness of the German reformation that, in part, it left the church's power of discipline directly to the state and, in part, subordinated it to the judgment of the state-church administrative authorities, he unconsciously has the Calvinist ideal in mind. What is considered a "weakness" is justified in principle by the Lutheran thought which Aepinus and Brenz represent, that as the organ of divine grace, the church cannot be a fundamental organ of punitive authority at the same time. And this standpoint is confirmed indirectly by still other witnesses.

In the second generation of the development of Lutheran churches, the man to whom I am referring, Erasmus Sarcerius, superintendent of the worthy earldom of Mansfeld, wrote a volume entitled, *Von einer Disciplin, dadurch Zucht, Tugend und Ehrbarkeit mogen gepflanzt und erhalten werden* [*Concerning a Discipline whereby Culture, Virtue and Honorableness Might Be Planted and Maintained*] (1556), wherein he discussed the urgent need for this discipline and the means for restoring it.[79] It strikes us in reading this work that he has the German people rather than the ecclesiastical community in mind as the subject of his discipline. The conscience of the people is to be developed on account of the decline of morals, and, as proof of this need, he compares the present with the description of the Germans given by Tacitus. Accordingly, he makes the claim for the secular authority that it is the vicar of God for the purpose of restoring discipline; and when he adds that the clergy are also called to the same task, his exact words are that they are obligated by their office *to assist* in establishing a discipline. One has further reason for doubting that this book is concerned with an imperative of church life when, on the basis of examples taken from both Christian and pagan periods, the legislative and judicial functions of the state are recommended as means for establishing such a discipline, specifically the imperial parliament, the provincial parliaments, municipal ordinances, and all types of courts. This undertaking will further alienate many contemporary theologians since the author brings these proposals to bear upon complaints about the immorality of the royal courts and of the jurists—matters which have no bearing on the church's interest. Such a structure of demands and proposals in which the secular legal basis for discipline is combined with the ecclesiastical basis, would be entirely unintelligible if one thought that the term "a discipline" referred to the catholic and Calvinist practice of separating public sinners from the cultic community. But this meaning of the word seldom comes into force in Sarcerius's usage. By "discipline" he normally means the much more comprehensive imperative of *good morals,* which are the fruit of true penance and whose restoration is effected chiefly by the preaching of the gospel, that is, next to the law of the civil order. The customary meaning of discipline, as the punishment of the church upon those who publicly transgress God's will, "for their own improvement and as a horrible example for other persons"— this meaning is only appended by Sarcerius to the means and ways by which the divine law is brought to realization among the people.

> We would make a more beautiful and more worthy beginning toward a discipline if every citizen would reform one man; then in time, everyone would be reformed. Thus, the head of every house would first lay the foundation for a common discipline in his own house, for himself and his kin, in that every man would bring his wife, children, and

servants up to their best. Then it would be that much easier for the
authorities and the clergy to set up a common, public discipline
(namely, through punitive force).

Since Sarcerius also prescribes for the clergy by what means they
have to restore a discipline, ten chapters of the work in question
deal with their personal attitude, the proper management of their
houses, their faithfulness in preaching on penance, grace, duties, and
virtues, and with the holding of synods and visitations; and only
after this are they advised to exercise ecclesiastical penalties and to
impose public penance. The final two chapters are very characteristic
of the whole book, in that the establishment of good *schools* and,
again, common fraternal admonition are suggested as particularly
effective means for setting up and maintaining a discipline.

When we recall in what sense the reformers of the sixteenth century took over the imperative of ecclesiastical discipline from the
catholic tradition, and in what sense it formed the imperative for
Calvin's life at the same time, then we recognize that Sarcerius has
shifted the meaning of this imperative considerably. The dicipline
which he wishes to carry out is the *moral training of the entire
nation.* To this end he could bring civil legislation and government
together with the principles on which the Christian religion structures the common life, and even in such an order of priority that the
latter takes precedence as means for the secular authority. However,
since he bore in mind the original meaning of ecclesiastical punitive
discipline he could rightly maintain that it is feasible and effective as
a means for restoring public morality only when it can rely on the
substructure of the moral training of the nation. Nevertheless, the
conviction does emerge rather clearly that the ecclesiastical process
of punishment will seem superfluous to the extent that the task of
training the nation is successfully carried out.

> For where there is discipline, there everything goes well and right in an
> orderly manner; there every citizen does in his vocation what it is his
> obligation and duty to do; there is obedience and everything good;
> there is peace and unity; there men render to God what is God's and
> to the civil authority what belongs to it.

If one wishes to know the Lutheran position with respect to
church discipline, he dare not restrict himself to the perception that

this discipline has somehow been curtailed because it was transferred to civil organs. Currently, this point of view usually also includes the judgment that thereby an essential function was lost to the Lutheran church, and that Calvinism surpasses Lutheranism because it retained this function. When one is in such a mood he generally disregards the fact that discipline has been no less impracticable in Calvinism than in the Lutheran church. However, in order to understand the position of Lutheranism authentically and fully, one should recognize what a much more comprehensive and sound enterprise Sarcerius has set forth as a replacement for traditional church discipline. And this enterprise, in spite of all the difficulties, has not remained unheeded in protestant Germany. When one reads in Sarcerius's book the profoundly bleak descriptions of the moral conditions of his time, as well as the complaints lodged against the conduct of the upper classes in his society—persons whom he nevertheless expected to accept his admonitions—then one must marvel at the power of his practical idealism and the patience which accompanied his belief that the task could be carried out. From this line of thinking, it is also plain that the Lutheran acceptance of church discipline is only a conditional one. It is expressed in the following formulation: "If church discipline is to take place, then it is only possible under the assumption that there has been a prior civil and religious training of the nation in morality." Meanwhile, it will be objected that Sarcerius is not a sufficiently legitimated representative of Lutheranism. As though it were to be reckoned to Luther's adherents—Sarcerius among them—that they had disposal over their own ideas! The essence of his point of view can be authenticated directly in Luther himself.

In the exposition of the prophet Joel which Veit Dietrich published from Luther's lectures of 1547,[80] Luther concerns himself with the widely held view that the ban, as exclusion from the Lord's Supper, had fallen into disuse partly through the carelessness of the clergy and partly through the disfavor of the civil authorities. Against this, he asserted that the guilt for this lay with the entire Christian society. Everyone failed in this task, namely, to warn and admonish his neighbor against injustice and lack of discipline, so as to reform him. Thereby, out of the fear of men and due to their own anxiety, people assured themselves that they would be treated in similar fashion by others. The actual cause of the decline of the ban, then, was the circumstance that true Christians were so small in number. This view of Luther led to the conclusion that if the ban were to come into usage, it would be necessary, above all else, to train the nation in true Christian morality. But at the same time Luther calls attention from another point of view to the fact that the ban has only a relative worth for the church, for it directs itself only against public scandals. Nevertheless, as Luther explains, the private sinners who share in the sacraments of the Christian church are also banned, *de facto,* by God. Thus they fall under God's judgment even though they deceive men by their appearances. From this it follows that the exercise of ecclesiastical punishment against public sinners does not achieve its purpose of purifying the church of sinners; rather, the fear is aroused through this activity that the hypocrites are the ones who will present themselves in the church as worthy. Even if Luther did not use these precise words, he nevertheless suggests these considerations, since they serve to verify his argument for the purely relative significance of the ban for the church. As much as he argues *in thesi* for the usefulness of the ban and the clergy's duty to exercise it—even in this context—he still is hardly of the opinion that the church has had one of its essential functions curtailed simply because the ban has fallen into disuse.

Calvin's opposing point of view finds its clearest manifestation in the manner in which he brings the authority of the New Testament to bear in this case. As a man of the second generation of the reformation, he stood less free vis-à-vis the authority of holy scripture than did Luther; as a matter of fact, he distinguishes himself at this point from Lutherans in general. This disparity occurred because Calvin regarded not only the religious train of thought of the New Testament, but also certain social structures of the first Christian communities as permanently binding, whereas Luther and the true Lutherans abandoned the latter. In Calvin's opinion, the installing of pastors and doctors of theology as leaders of the church after the apostles, without permitting a distinction in rank among them, was a holy, inviolable, and eternal law—a structure which God had established, and not a human invention (*Institutes,* IV, 4, 6, 7). Similarly, discipline as punitive power was seen as an attribute of the church which the Lord had foreseen as necessary (IV, 12, 4).

The threat of punishment which Paul raised in the name of the church against the members of the Corinthian congregation stands for Calvin as the divine sanction for the entire range of discipline which is granted to the church. Brenz, on the contrary, could discern only a momentary need of the church in this passage, since there was not yet any Christian civil order at that time. In this divergence, the difference between the Lutheran and Calvinist views is clearly not merely one of discipline but rather one of the use of the Bible in the church as well. With regard to what pertains to the social ordinances of the first Christian communities, the Lutherans could look upon the New Testament as the document of bygone conditions, which are no longer binding under altered historical circumstances. But Calvin perceived inviolable norms to which the church had to be led back, both in the precepts of the apostles concerning discipline as well as in the first century congregational organization to which the New Testament witnesses.

The manner in which Calvin understood the necessity of the ban and the application of the authority of the New Testament meant that he moved over to the side of the anabaptists to the same degree that he distanced himself from Lutheranism. The point here is not simply the question of discipline, however, although the anabaptists also reproached the Lutheran preachers for neglecting it, according to Bullinger's testimony. In this connection one could assert, rather, that when the two say the same thing, it is not the same thing. For the Calvinist interpretation of the Christian religion and Christian morality differs too much from the anabaptists' legalistic and monastic striving after sanctity to make an actual affinity between the two conceivable. And the similarity that exists between the two in their regard for the ban is simply not strong enough an argument, that it can serve as basis for such an affinity. Even if we suspend this consideration, there is still clear agreement between the two that the authority of the New Testament is to be applied not merely in respect to the religious world view and the image of God, but also in respect to the binding character of certain practical ordinances which occur in the first generation of the church. This agreement is not destroyed by the differences between the two in the scope of their application of that principle. The anabaptists concluded from the authority of the New Testament that Christians as such could

not participate in the secular state and that instead they could only
be admonished to be patient in the face of injustice from all sides—
because such was the situation of the first Christians. Although Calvin was far enough removed from that position, he still asserted the
necessity of punitive force in the church and the elimination of all
distinctions in rank between the teachers and pastors of the church,
only because it had been so in the first generation of Christianity—
and the structures of that generation were unconditionally binding
upon him since they were documented in holy scripture. As far as
we can presently judge, therefore, the normative image for the
Christian life-style [*Lebensideal*] which Calvin held is totally different from that of the anabaptists; for that reason, discipline carries
a different weight for each of them. For the anabaptists, it is the
means for restoring the actual sanctity of the true church. For
Calvin, it is, under all circumstances, a means of external order
to which one is obligated for the sake of the honor of Christ and the
moral well-being of the individual members of the church (*Institutes,*
IV, 12, 5). In spite of this, the manner in which this is derived
from the New Testament, as though it were an inspired law book,
echoes the principle of St. Francis's reformation, namely, that the
social order of Christendom is to be referred back to the conditions
which obtained during the first generation. On the basis of this
formal agreement, it is certainly not likely that Calvinism possesses
within itself a particular inclination to accept or reproduce Franciscan
or anabaptist forms of life. Calvin's understanding of the Christian
structuring of life is identical with the Lutheran position in this
respect, that it is linked to the exercise of one's vocation and to one's
placement within the civil order. On these grounds, nevertheless,
Calvin imparted a moral structure to his church for the maintenance
of discipline—a structure which modified considerably the governing
image of life-style [*Lebensideal*] which was common to protestantism. In order to make this understandable, we must also take
Calvin's personal moral endowments and nationality into consideration at the same time.

It is certainly worth noting that the French who entered actively
into the reformation of the sixteenth century were very decidedly
intent upon church discipline. Prior to Calvin, in this regard, we
may refer to William Farel and Franz Lambert.[81] Especially instruc-

tive, however, is this former Franciscan's [i.e., Lambert's] attempt
to provide the church of Hesse with a disciplinary structure. Luther
had expressed the devout wish for a community of those who earnestly desire to be Christian in his *Deutsche Messe und Ordnung des
Gottesdienstes* [*The German Mass and the Ordering of the Service
of Worship*], which he published in 1526. He meant that these
people would have to designate themselves with the name "Christian" and gather in a particular house for prayer, Bible reading, and
the use of the sacraments. In this community and according to these
conditions, one could discern, punish, reform, exclude, or put under
the ban those who did not comport themselves as Christians. But
Luther added that he could not establish such a community, because
he did not yet have the people for it, and he did not observe many
who would be suited for it. He also feared that there would have
been an uproar if he had carried out the plan for this community on
his own. "For we Germans are a wild, rough, raving people, with
whom it is not easy to begin something new unless there is the most
urgent necessity."[82] This correct, if unflattering, testimony by Luther
about his people, with its prior fear that the implementation of his
plan for forming more restricted communities would bring with it
an uprising, is undoubtedly to be understood as a reasonable assessment of the fact that the Germans as a whole would not have gone
along with his system. Herein an insight is expressed which is
doubtless correct, that the Germans lack the feeling for the equality
and for the involuntary adherence to law which is required for a
system of church discipline. Consequently, the project of forming
such a restricted community, which would condescend voluntarily
to the exercise of discipline, was a fantasy of a devout wish which
did not occupy Luther's thought further in any demonstrable manner. But the Frenchman Lambert had nothing which was more
urgent to him than to incorporate the project of Luther into the
church order which he wanted to use at Homberg as a means of
instituting the reformation of the Hessian church. In the fifteenth
chapter of this church order,[83] he prescribes that after the Sunday
worship service, those men and women should come together who
earnestly practice Christianity and who are to be counted in the
number of the sanctified. They should pledge to place themselves
under excommunication, if it should be necessary, and this pledge

should be written down. This community should pursue all of its concerns under the direction of the bishop; it should not only choose its officers, but should also take in hand the process of excluding persons from the community and receiving them back into it. Everything which is necessary for admonishment should also be communicated to this restricted group. Anyone in the congregation who does not earnestly amend his ways within fourteen days after the protestant preaching begins is to be excluded not only from the Lord's Supper but also from the preaching service and all fraternal relations. Thus, the protestant congregation would be placed on the same basis as a congregation of tertiaries! This man from southern France, a former Franciscan, thought that he could offer such fare to the Hessians without taking warning from Luther's estimate of the German people! It is true that his church order remained, on paper at least, even after the advice which Luther gave, on request, to Landgrave Philip. In his letter[84] to this prince he emphasizes chiefly that laws are useful only when some degree of morality exists to support them; having said this, however, he also confirms the judgment as to why the Germans would not permit the establishment of church discipline. In line with the roughness and intractability that Luther censured among the Germans, there is also the feeling for individual liberty, and, in addition, the feeling for freedom in matters of morals, which are the real reasons why they resist a universal law of church discipline. Since the Frenchman, to the contrary, considers it to be self-evident that the disciplinary prescriptions which seem to be set forth in the New Testament should be put into immediate practice, he counts on that drive for equality and that inclination to permit oneself to be disciplined in all things, which are precisely the factors which differentiate his people from the Germans.

The factors which these men linked with the reformation of the sixteenth century—legal strictness and the task of disciplining the masses—are the characteristics through which the general attitude of the French has distinguished itself in the history of the church. I recall that the monasticism which developed in ancient Egypt was first received with enthusiasm in Gaul, and, further, that in the first half of the Middle Ages the monastic reforms and restorations manifested themselves at Cluny, Chartreux, Citeaux, and Prémontré;

and it is more important to see this fact as a clear testimony to the character of French Christianity than it is to note that the founders of two of these orders were Germans. At the same time, France is the home of the crusades. In the second half of the Middle Ages, the University of Paris was also the center of significant ecclesiastical movements, and that community of learning was always a splendid demonstration of how large numbers of men could be disciplined. Since the epoch of the sixteenth century, the ascetical tendency of the French has burst forth partly in the work of the founding of the order at La Trappe,[85] partly in Jansenism,[86] and not a little in the quietistic mysticism which found its most significant representation among the French, even though it did not originate among them. In addition to these, the work of Vincent de Paul should be recalled.[87] Finally, since the Revolution and the Restoration, French Catholicism has been disciplined ever more intensely as an instrument of the papal efforts at world domination. Moreover, this disposition of the French seems to become all the more distinct as the religious state of affairs becomes more insufficient and weak— a development which presently seems to be linked with the social and political undertakings of the papacy. As representatives of strict church discipline who definitely count on this discipline being carried out, the French reformers of the sixteenth century belong to the tradition of French Christianity, despite their deviations from its doctrine; and they fill in a gap in this tradition since the Roman Catholic spirit did not produce any noteworthy effects in the sixteenth century.

Calvin did impose certain tendencies upon the branch of protestant Christianity which he founded, in the interests of church discipline, which express an unmistakable approximation of the monastic renunciation of the world. In principle, he was indeed in agreement with Luther that the Christian life is to be conducted and tested within the framework of civil vocation, in the state. But, since Calvin needed no personal recreation for his own life, he considered the normal forms of social intercourse and the manifestations of luxury that went along with them to be merely the most pressing temptation for sin. Now it is true that church discipline can assert itself to be churchly only if it is relatively infrequently applied. For this reason, Calvin drew the conclusion that the temptations for

immorality which derived from social intercourse, and which therefore would be occasions for ecclesiastical punishment, had to be
eliminated. This is the reason that Calvin fought against all that
pertains to the cheerful and free enjoyment of life and art; and since
he appointed like-minded French immigrants to the governing council in Geneva, he succeeded in imposing upon the patterns of common life which he supervised an attitude of alienation from the
world which was similar to that of the Franciscan tertiaries. For
among the latter there was a prohibition against participation in
social enjoyments, particularly the theater, just as surely as there was
among the Calvinists.

Accordingly, we can now determine fully the opposition between
Lutheranism and Calvinism in their regard for discipline. The
Lutheran formulation goes like this: "If there is a need for church
discipline to be carried out, then there is a need for general moral
training of the whole society." The Calvinist formulation is expressed
thus: "Since church discipline is necessary, the life of the whole
society must also be restricted even more, particularly with respect
to social intercourse and the public theater." To the extent that
Calvinism's governing image of the Christian style of life [*Lebensideal*] is anticatholic, it has sprung from Luther's inspiration. To the
extent that it diverges from Luther's point of view, it has turned
back to the tradition of the Franciscan image of the style of life
[*Lebensideal*]. It seemed to be clear already from our previous
analysis that Calvin's application of the authority of the New Testament to the establishing of church discipline was reminiscent of
the Franciscan and anabaptist principle: The earliest and most elementary forms of the Christian church should be normative for all
time. This formal agreement is now amplified through the aversion
to social intercourse and public theater which was common to both
groups. Therefore, if pietism has sprung from the same view of the
Christian life of the masses that was active in the Franciscan and
anabaptism reformation, then it is to be expected that Calvinism is
more disposed to accept and reproduce this pietistic tendency than
German protestantism, be it of the Lutheran or Zwinglian variety.

It is well known that Calvin could carry out his organization of
the church in Geneva only through the authority of the state. Consequently, he also took a number of governmental officials into the

agency of church discipline, the consistory. But he also wanted to be certain that the decisions of this ecclesiastical authority would be altogether exempt from the legitimation of the state. In the light of this concern, he struggled for the fundamental autonomy of the church from the state. Differing circumstances proved to be useful for carrying out this principle in different areas of Calvinism. In France, the Reformed church owed its autonomy from the state to the fact that the state opposed the reformation altogether. In Scotland, on the contrary, the essence of that autonomous relation, which was continually striven for and partially achieved, was expressed in a medieval view of the state which the founders of the Reformed church embraced. In particular, John Knox and George Buchanan shared with their teacher, John Major of St. Andrews, the conviction that the state, including, therefore, the monarchy, has its direct basis in the will of the people without any detriment to the divine ordinance, and that the people are justified in deposing an unjust prince.[88] This assertion, which rests on the authority of Thomas Aquinas,[89] depends on the additional argument that the church, representing divine authority directly through its organs and leaders, is of greater worth than the state and for this reason is autonomous, even from a legal point of view. In keeping with this, John Knox implanted the analogous view in the Scottish church, that Christ, as the head of the church, guarantees directly the divine authority of its organization, its liturgical ordinances, and its discipline.[90] Knox borrowed this formulation from John Laski, who, as chairman of the immigrant congregation in London, was pressed by circumstances to establish the church which later came to be called "independentism." The fugitives from the Netherlands and France, whom he served as pastor in London until they fled from Bloody Mary, had to give up, as aliens, all claims to support for their church life by the government; their independent legal constitution placed Laski under the protection of the kingdom of Christ and made his office a direct product of the legislative power of that kingdom. The basis for this view was the harmony of that church's constitution with the ordinances which existed in the primitive church. This image of the church, put into force by these immigrant congregations primarily in response to an emergency, and impressed upon the theory, at least, of the Scottish church, won the upper hand, over the episcopal and presbyterian forms of the church in England, for a time at least, in the seventeenth century. Because, as a consequence of the independentism of Laski, the power of the state was disallowed in respect to the legal ordering of the church, the unity of the state church was also abandoned in favor of the autonomy of every individual congregation. In this manner, a conformity to the church of the primitive period was achieved which extended even beyond Calvin's intention. However, what we have here is evidence of the fact that, to the degree that Calvinism's anticatholic image of the church is consistently followed, that image develops into an independentism which once again approximates the anabaptist congregations. And it is not accidental, either, that the independents' image of the Christian life [*Lebensideal*] also goes back to that of the anabaptists. The congregations of the English independents rested their claims basically on the ascetical sanctity that was revealed in their members, namely, in their strict repudiation of all secular recreation and all games. Since they were for the most part baptists as well, they also came to reject infant baptism. At the same time, theocratic-revolutionary phenomena manifested themselves in their groups in the seventeenth century which were similar to those which appeared among the German anabaptists one hundred years earlier. To be sure, these conditions appeared only in a particular sphere of Calvinism and then under particular circumstances. But they were possible nevertheless only insofar as they were consequences of principles which differentiate Calvinism generally from Lutheranism and state-church forms of Zwinglianism, and which conform, as a whole, to the image of the life-style [*Lebensideal*] which was prevalent in the Franciscan and anabaptist reformation. Since this agreement led to the extensive reversion of independent English Calvinism to the tradition of the anabaptists, we may say that the general inclination of Calvinism has thereby been demonstrated to accept and reproduce anew forms of practical life which correspond to the Franciscan reformation.

This inclination is present in Calvinism in spite of the fact that the founder of this form of protestant Christianity earnestly took precautions that the thrust of his churches toward moral perfection should not result in separatist consequences.[91] In anticipation of this consequence, he insisted that the substance of the church is tied only to the correct teaching of the gospel and the administration of the sacraments; and since he described the imperative of the moral purity of the church as a temptation, he required as virtues which followed from this purity the qualities of forebearance and patience —qualities which are customarily lacking from the virtues of the separatists. It is significant however that he did ascribe the predicate "good" to these strict and impatient persons. Accordingly, these strict and impatient representatives of moral perfection in the church consequently consider themselves to be good people, indeed, the best people in the Reformed church, and, therefore, they treated with contempt all the arguments with which Calvin had opposed them in advance. These arguments are nevertheless worthy of our attention. Calvin appealed first to the fact that Paul viewed the Corinthian church as the church of Christ, even though it was full of moral faults, and also the Galatian Christians who had even abandoned the gospel. He recalled for them, further, that the church was founded on the forgiveness of sins and continued to maintain itself on this foundation. Finally, he characterized as a self-deception the opinion that a person would simply be giving up fellowship with the godless, if he separated himself from the existing church. Such a step was more likely to bring with it the general destruction of the church. Calvin linked these reflections and admonitions against separatism only to the phenomenon of anabaptism in his time. He did not confront similar deviations within the churches he had himself established. However, it is almost as though he anticipated that his intention to develop the legal and disciplinary sanctity of the church would lead the faithful adherents, whom he himself termed good, into the error of separatism. This very thing happened, while these arguments of Calvin, which have just been cited, were fully lost on those people who were precisely the ones who intended to proceed consistently toward the goal which Calvin had set.

VI. THE NECESSITY FOR REFORM IN CHURCHLY PROTESTANTISM

The need for renewed or more extensive reform within protestantism seems to depend first of all on the intensity of the internal and external difficulties which the individual reformers experienced in carrying out their own original ecclesiastical mandates. These difficulties were most significant in the case of Luther and Melanchthon. It was not simply because of their own internal difficulties that they took such great effort and needed more time to break away from their attachment to the given forms of liturgy and church organization; in addition, they experienced particular restraints because of the conditions which the Holy Roman Empire placed upon them. In both of these respects, Zwingli occupied a much more favorable position than the reformers in Saxony. In the first place, he was not hindered by the power of the Holy Roman Empire, not the least because he lacked the devotion to it which animated Luther and Melanchthon. Furthermore, he attained a decided clarity at an early period concerning his religious convictions and their consequences for liturgy and organization. Calvin stood in an even more favorable position in this respect, for as an epigone he had the advantage of being able to take possession of a tradition which had already freed itself from the apron strings of the medieval church. Not only did he take possession of that tradition with his characteristic clarity of reason and strength of will, in that he gave it the most consummate theological expression, but in addition, he yoked that tradition to tasks which had been alien to it up to that time. Furthermore, he found a field for his work of establishing churches which was even further removed from the influence of the empire than Zwingli's area of activity. Through these differences among the reformers, one is able to gauge why the formation of the protestant church in the sphere of the German empire gives the impression of a persisting incompleteness and, at the same time, appears to stand closer to the practice of the catholic church than the churches established by Zwingli and Calvin. Many elements of medieval origin have actually been propagated, or reproduced with modification in the Lutheran church which have disappeared in the other churches. Accordingly, it appears that a need for reform would have manifested itself sooner in the Lutheran church than in the Calvinist-Reformed church. But, of course, this is not the case. The established church of England embodied even more striking compromises with the catholic past, in the ordering of the liturgy as well as in organization. For this reason, the reforming movement of the Puritans began in that church immediately after the external security of the English

church was established by Queen Elizabeth. In addition, the imperative for completing the reformation was seized upon in the Reformed
church of the Netherlands before the German Lutheran Church
could realize the proper conditions for real reformation efforts. In
order that one might be prepared to understand pietism's reformation thrust within the Lutheran church, a historical explanation is
required of the scholastic restriction of Lutheranism, since, as the
well-established assumption has it, it is this restriction which points
to the need for reform within that form of church life. I need only
add beforehand that Calvinism shares this need equally with Lutheranism. That this fact is customarily overlooked can be explained by
the fact that such a characteristic of Calvinism is compensated for
and veiled by legalistic tendencies in morals and discipline—characteristics more prominent in Calvinism than in Lutheranism.

But the error we are describing did not make its appearance simply
as a later manifestation within the Lutheran or the Reformed church;
it is grounded, rather, in the circumstances under which the reformation arrived at its particular church forms. It is well known that
the political circumstances in the Holy Roman Empire favored
Luther's reformation just as much as they restricted it. The loose
character of this political alliance permitted a number of princes not
only to protect the reformers, but it also allowed alterations in the
liturgy and the actual severing of the new teaching office in their
churches from the power of the bishops. But on the other hand the
stability of the empire and its association with the Roman church
inhibited the autonomy of protestant church life, in contrast, for
example, with Switzerland, where the church was established simply
by the decision of the municipal authorities to accept the reformation. Since the protestant princes were no less interested in the
stability of the empire than those princes who were inclined to the
papal church, they felt compelled to retain the substance of the
one catholic church to which the political validity of the empire
had been linked at one time. Theirs was the task of establishing their
evangelical interpretation of the destiny and conditions of the one
catholic church in all sections of the empire. As long as they did not
succeed in this, and as long as they strove for it through religious
negotiations, the protestant princes acknowledged themselves and
their church structure, in effect, as a party within the church.

Similarly, they considered the papists to be the other party. This perspective not only dominated the Augsburg Confession of 1530, it also conditioned the religious Peace of Augsburg in 1555, which did not rule out the possibility of a compromise. This political manifestation of parties within the church can be regarded, theologically, only as a difference between schools. The set of doctrines and liturgical principles which were recapitulated as such in the Augsburg Confession (some as noncontroversial and some as controversial) is the direct expression of a scholastic point of view in the church, in which the opponent is also assumed to be a school. No other situation would have been possible, given the conditions which obtained then in the Latin church and in the Holy Roman Empire, since, in the second half of the Middle Ages, an opposition between schools was accepted within the church and in the universities which were legitimated by the church. As long as the assumption was maintained that these parties could come to an understanding through religious negotiations, that is, in a scholastic manner, there could be no official recognition that the controversy of the sixteenth century was concerned with interests much more practical than those which had separated the Thomists and the Nominalists from one another.

In reality, every study of this sort reminds us that the opposition between those parties in the church which were held together by the political forces of the empire cannot be viewed as if it were the opposition between two schools. Moreover, the theologians of the reformation never did restrict themselves to this point of view, but rather interpreted the Roman church to be the false church and the protestant church to be the true one. The Smalcald allies had already adopted this position by 1537, when they refused the invitation to the council.[92] This kind of argumentation was unavoidable, especially since both catholicism and protestantism upheld as Christian world views and images of life style [*Lebensideal*] which were quite different. If their differences were simply of the kind that exists between schools, both parties would subordinate themselves under the same definition of the purpose of Christianity. Therefore, after 1537, the protestants no longer held back their assertion that the church designated by the Augsburg Confession was the catholic church, whereas the papal church was actually a perversion. In one

sense, however, the claim that the new church forms should be considered as types of a school was upheld and never excluded. To be
sure, it was always asserted that this new church served the purpose
of salvation through the gospel it represented, a purpose which was
missing from the catholic side because of all sorts of errors. This indicates that the protestant church includes within its self-definition *a
total understanding* of the correct world view and proper ordering
of the Christian life. But this implication is put aside and over-
shadowed by the insistence that we possess the correct *doctrine* of
the gospel in the Augsburg Confession and that we prove ourselves
to be the catholic church by upholding the ancient confessions of
that church. It is precisely at this point that the "school" element is
asserted as though it were the principal characteristic of the church's
existence; and this judgment is confirmed by the fact that Melanchthon, the spokesman in these matters, conceived of the church as
a kind of school, in order to uphold his conviction that it was not
to be conceived of as a state.[93] Nevertheless, we do not have to hold
Melanchthon solely responsible for this fateful assertion. Rather, it
is the consequence of the type of struggle through which the reformation had to pass if it were to free itself from medieval ways of
church life, and thus it was inevitable that this original form of
argumentation would continue to be effective in the self-consciousness of the protestant church.

Whenever it happens that a new form of Christian truth appears,
we know that those who find the old wine better tasting than the
new exercise their wisdom in the following manner: they pluck
out those particulars of the new point of view which offend them,
and they vigorously oppose them as though they were individual
points of doctrine without first placing themselves in the total context of the new manifestation. In most cases, these premature
opponents of the particulars are as incapable as they are unwilling to
put themselves in this total context which the new sets forth. Moreover, if the representative of a new point of view permits himself
to respond to all such fragmentary attacks, he exposes himself to the
danger of fragmenting his accomplishment—whose value consists
in the wholeness of its form—into many particularities which, as
such, do not retain their recognizable relation to the whole. This is
true of Luther who generally gave battle for his convictions which

deviated from the traditional opinion before he had established the totality of his view of Christianity in his own mind and put it into organic form. He permitted himself to be forced by his opponents into controversy over individual points, and he never compensated for this by producing a systematic presentation of his interpretation of the gospel. In addition, Melanchthon, after all, was only able to use the loose scheme of the *Loci theologici*,[94] which actually produces the opposite of a theological system. And finally, as much as the character of the Augsburg Confession differs in this respect—to its credit—from the private writings of the reformers, we still confront in this document a disconnectedness in the presentation of the controversial doctrines and ordinances. As a compendium of the controversial doctrines, this legal foundation of the new church serves this end precisely: it assures that the "school" element in the church took on a preponderance over the other necessary functions from the very beginning. There is yet another consideration that intensified this situation. In order to legitimate the protestant church as catholic in the eyes of the emperor and the empire, Melanchthon (as well as Luther) attached major importance to the ancient confessions, and he even granted precedence to them over the new protestant interpretation of the *beneficia Christi* [benefits of Christ].[95] Now the Nicene form of the doctrine of the person of Christ was originally of direct practical consequence for the Greek church and was a vehicle for the soteriology that was distinctive to that church. However, that formulation was no longer normative for the Christian understanding of salvation, even for the Latin church, in the Middle Ages. It had become, much more, a possession of the schools in that epoch and, as such, no longer corresponded to the vital interests of medieval piety. The same is true of the reformation. Thus, Luther could interest himself personally in that dogma only because he reinterpreted it and interpolated his understanding of the love and the grace of God in Christ into the formula concerning the two natures. It was Melanchthon, however, who gave the keynote for his successors, and for him the doctrines of the person of Christ and of the Trinity were only difficult scholastic problems which he did not understand as being directly pertinent for the protestant understanding of salvation.[96] Therefore, if the protestant church were to link its existence and its validity to these doctrines which had become unintelligible, then, in that very act, the school element would be acknowledged as the fundamental condition of protestant church life.

The foregoing will explain the scholastic delimitation of the understanding of salvation in the Lutheran church—it came about through the restrictions which the German reformation experienced from its theological opponents and from the political demands of the Holy Roman Empire. This delimitation made itself manifest through the fact that the Lutheran church expounded its self-consciousness only through a series of doctrinal propositions, rather than by setting forth its perspective in a practical and usefully structured whole. In addition to this, the defective academic disposition which we observe in the sixteenth century theologians who followed Melanchthon's example also made a very distinct impact. This defective disposition consists of the inability or unwillingness, first of all, to consider the Christian religion in terms of its total aim, and then to identify the world, together with God and man, as the only three points through which the course of religion can be viewed as a whole and opened up to human understanding. Frankly, it is shocking that there is no mention of the practical aim of justification by faith[97] in the fourth article [on "justification"] of the Augsburg Confession. And if we explicate this aim in any terms other than those of blessedness, within present experience, and if we do not take the believer's attitude toward the world into consideration, how is it to be understood as distinctively protestant? But these considerations are never asserted as being theologically normative. With such a norm, it is easy to establish the aim of justification by faith on the basis of the Augsburg Confession, namely, that it gives certainty to the human self-consciousness over against the world through God's providence. But the necessity for viewing things in this way was hidden from the theologians of the sixteenth century. Because they were not in the position to place the practical world view of protestantism as such clearly under the above-mentioned categories, the individual doctrines which they formulated remained in a scholastic fragmentation. Thus, if they did not actually hinder the ordering of the Christian life, they certainly did nothing to facilitate it. In addition to this, John Gerhard brought about the direct perversion of protestant teaching through "school theology," in that he adopted—in accord-

ance with an ill-chosen norm of Thomas Aquinas—the so-called
natural religion or theology, and he explained faith in God's providence as a conviction that springs from a natural source when, in
fact, it is a specific mark of our reconciliation with God through
Christ. I have referred elsewhere to the fact that the Lutheran
ascetics maintained the truth which John Gerhard's successors, in
their acknowledged orthodoxy, placed under a bushel.[98] To be sure,
the impact of saving faith upon the believer's attitude toward the
world did not wholly sink into oblivion, even among the theologians
of this period; but neither was it viewed as being of the first order
of importance. Franz Balduin, Gerhard's older contemporary and
professor at Wittenberg from 1605 to 1627, puts the question in his
work on casuistry thus: "When we ask what, among those things by
which the human spirit is cultivated, produces the most excellent
faith, what things in man's spiritual activity ought to be considered?"
He mentions as marks "of those things that we can point to, by
which the human spirit is cultivated to true faith," first of all the love
that accompanies spiritual activity; but in addition, secondly, trust
in times of calamity; fifthly, prayer, which counts as its fulfillment
that which is in accordance with the divine will; sixthly, firmness of
hope in times when help vanishes.[99] In between these, however,
there appear, thirdly, humility before God and the neighbor; and,
fourthly, the confession of faith. Thus we can see that also this
theologian did not recognize the full significance of faith for the attitude of the believer toward the world. And although he derives from
the examples of David and Job the insight that trust in God overcomes all the billows of misfortune, he nevertheless does not always
count on this support for his faith, since he adds apologetically that
faith is often weak in similar situations, but that even in its weakness it is a proper faith. But on the contrary and more to the point, it
is necessary in such a situation to encourage faith to strong confidence
in God rather than to furnish it with a basis for formal correctness
in its weakness! That is precisely the scholastic point of view, not the
practical one. The former merely provides a support for slackness.
And if the faith which experiences justification through Christ must
necessarily consist in trust (*fiducia*) in God in order to achieve the
result of comfort and a quiet conscience—that is, the restoration of
self-confidence from a previous insecurity[100]—then we cannot even

clearly perceive what the conditions of faith are unless this trust in God is contrasted with that situation in the world which causes one's self-reliance to be disturbed.

From the very beginning, this clarity and distinctness of principle was never achieved for the Lutheran reformation. By contrast, Calvin's portrayal of the concept of faith achieves the greatest possible fullness since here, as elsewhere, he shows himself to be the most circumspect of Luther's interpreters in regard to the structuring of the order of salvation. If we were to form a synthesis out of the different attempts at defining justification by faith which he sets forth in consecutive manner, we would find that faith consists in the moving, and therefore personal, conviction which is mediated through the feeling [*Gefühl*] of the significance of the grace of God that is apprehended in Christ.[101] Of particular importance is the fact that one must not interpret this statement as though *fiducia* were meant only as an inference from faith. Without a doubt, Calvin intends the derivation of trust from faith mediated through an apostle as an analytical judgment, for he defines the man who really believes as the one who also sets this trust in God against the evils in the world and who extends it to include all of the gifts of life which a person anticipates from God.[102] Should one not expect that this insight would have been ineradicably impressed upon the theologians of Calvin's school? On the contrary, the greatest of these, Gisbert Voet, professor at Utrecht from 1634 to 1676, as well as the entire Calvinist school, did not include *fiducia* in the concept of *fides* but distinguished it, rather, as an inference from faith. Thus he understood Calvin's statement in the fifteenth section of the *Institutes* as synthetic. Accordingly, he understands the principle that man's stance toward the world is discovered through faith as though it were only a different application of faith itself. In his disputation *de praxi fidei* [*Concerning the Practice of Faith*], the matter comes up under the category of "the acts which follow from faith, which are efficacious not in themselves, but in other theological virtues—and such are the acts of elicited hope, love, the new obedience, patience, and renewed repentance."[103] But it is only in the form of patience, cited here, that he asserts that faith maintains its power in favorable as well as in unfavorable conditions of life, in temptation and in death— and not in the form of trust in God. Thus Voet recognizes the thing that matters, but he acknowledges it merely as a postscript to faith in Christ; and he always defines even this by concentrating solely upon the theoretical act of knowing Christ.

All this adds up to the fact that the scholastic aridity of all religious knowledge is even stronger in the Calvinist-Reformed church than in the Lutheran. Calvin gave this impetus, despite his insight into the nature of faith, as cited above, through his rejection of the catholic tolerance of *fides implicita* [implicit faith].[104] Calvin rejected the idea that one might be prepared to believe all that the church prescribes, even without understanding the dogmas, on the grounds that faith does not consist in ignorance but in knowledge, and that of reconciliation through Christ.[105] As he strove to actualize this knowledge among his contemporaries in the church, he asserted that it was to be unfolded clearly and in detail, that it was to emerge from regular reading of the holy scriptures, and that it was to master a body of knowledge that was not insubstantial in scope. In other words, it was to be scholastically precise. Calvin freely admits that the faith of Christians will remain confused in many cases, that much of God's dispensation would remain hidden, and that many passages of scripture would not be understood; in these circumstances, one must simply acknowledge Christ as the best teacher. But in reality, this admission means very little when one considers the high level of religious knowledge which Calvin presupposed and strove after, above all, in his work of establishing churches. For example, when he went to Geneva he required that the citizens subscribe to a confession consisting of twenty-one articles. That was simply not practicable. In spite of this, he attempted all the more zealously to instill in the church members that which he had found missing from the very beginning—a scholastically ordered knowledge of Christian doctrine; and he attempted this through his catechism and public catechizing, imposing upon everyone the obligation to participate. For this reason, even in his church, the intellectual meaning of faith took on such preponderance that actual conviction in the content of faith assumed the position of a postscript, necessary and valuable as that might be. Now, if faith became arid and scholastic in this area also, the basic reason for it lies once again in the need to differentiate the reformation churches from catholicism. Thus, in order to differentiate oneself personally from catholic faith, the body of knowledge of the reformed system had to be appropriated by every member of the church. It was assumed that conviction, with all of its practical effects, would follow. Unfortunately, practical conviction was not necessarily linked even to such a rich deposit of traditional knowledge. For this reason, after a few generations, there were open complaints in the Calvinist areas against the barrenness and the lack of spirituality present in the literalistic faith, just as there were in the Lutheran church.

Nevertheless, it is interesting to see how a theologian from the Netherlands, Hermann Witsius, in Franeker in Frisia, expressed himself on the question of implicit faith 120 years after Calvin.[106] This man shared the complaint about the depravity and lack of spirituality in literalistic Christianity, on the one hand, but, on the other, he is very far from depreciating the scholastic imprint of the same. However, since he was a practical man, in a special sense, at the same time, he could not overlook the fact that those who were uneducated from an intellectual and Christian point of view made liberal use of implicit faith. He justified this on two grounds, one which is catholic in nature, the other, a theoretical self-deception. In other words, he first assumes that these believers grant that holy scripture is, in general, the inerrant source of all the necessary articles of belief, even when those articles are not understood; he then assumes that they hold the fundamental truths firmly in the consciousness, from which other truths are derived as necessary. This is small consolation since we cannot see how it could profit a person to know fundamental truths from which *others* may be able to derive the remaining necessary truths, even though he cannot. And yet Witsius recognizes the situation in which "someone to whom God has measured out a small portion of knowledge might nevertheless be *most firm* in the faith, *even* in *martyrdom.*" And what does he derive from that? That one ought nevertheless not consider ignorance to be the source of faith and piety! And the result? The believer must necessarily know, in general, the divine authority of scripture, and, in particular, that he himself is alienated through sin from the true life in God, that the Lord Christ is full of grace and truth, and that it is necessary to be united with Christ through the Holy Spirit and faith, not simply for justification, but also for sanctification and surrender to his dominion. This amount of theoretical knowledge is prescribed as the minimum that the believer must know! But then, how can even a slight degree of that firmness of faith be based on this knowledge which would be remotely comparable to the decision for martyrdom? Is the structure of the necessary articles of knowledge determined simply by fitting congruent components together? I should have special knowledge that I am alienated from God in sin and, only afterwards, should I know generally the grace of Christ and its possible effects! To that special knowledge of the unworthiness of my own sin must be added the special feeling of my selfhood and my significance, that I am a child of God despite sin. Without this, all the religious knowledge in the world has no meaning for strengthening faith. Therefore, if implicit faith is conceded at this point, as it must be, can we speak about it usefully in any other terms except to say that all things work for the best for those in the Christian church who love God? This knowledge is demonstrable only as personal conviction and, in this case, as the concrete perspective on the world and on life that is mediated specifically through Christ. The most telling confirmation of the fact that the Reformed church also suffered gravely from complacency toward intellectualism and was in need or reform in this respect lies in the fact that this point was not understood by them, even though they had long understood that the intellectual content of their faith was insufficient.

This error, the product of circumstance, would not have asserted itself as strongly as it did, however, if the men of the reformation epoch had not suffered from a distinctively restricted spiritual inclination. What I have in mind is their unfamiliarity with feeling [*Gefühl*]in general and with its particular conditions and relationships in the spiritual life. To be sure, the men of that era did feel, and they also permitted themselves to be moved by desire and aversion in the religious life; but it remained hidden from them that the soul exercises a third activity alongside knowing and desiring. Indeed, even a pietist writer of the seventeenth century, Jodocus van Lodensteyn by name, who took feeling very seriously into consideration, nevertheless recognized only knowing and willing in his scheme for understanding spiritual activities. However, in the sixteenth century, protestantism seems generally to have been little disposed toward religious feeling. Even the asceticism of that

period produced a stiff, doctrinaire discourse, as Stephen Praetorius's *Geistliche Schatzkammer* [*Spiritual Treasury*] indicates.[107]
It almost seems as though protestantism, since it had given up the
life of the cloister, had closed itself off from access to the exercise
of the religious feeling that was indigenous to the cloister. Or was
even the cloister barren in fifteenth century Germany? In short, in
light of the fact that men in reformation circles generally did not give
attention to the life of feeling [*Gefühlsleben*] and did not rightly
esteem it, the doctrinaire portrayal of religion in the sixteenth century
and the tendency to consider this portrayal as the only valid one are
all the more understandable.

The comprehensive view of Christianity which the reformation
assumes is thus not given adequate expression in an exclusively
reason-centered presentation of the doctrines of the gospel. Rather,
it is fragmented on the one hand and muffled and clouded over on the
other. On the contrary, it is only another kind of implicit faith that
is exercised in this doctrinaire interpretation of faith which was
intended to be set against the catholic version of implicit faith. The
reason-centered position which I have described did not enable a
person to possess the feeling of personal worth that accompanies
trust in God in a clear knowledge of the nature and significance of
this feeling itself, even though it is the mark of reconciliation through
Christ; rather, this position confused this feeling with the pride of
possessing pure doctrine or, at best it made the feeling a postscript
to the latter. The distinctiveness of protestantism is still sufficiently
discernible that almost all who count themselves as its adherents
recognize that its original manifestation was stunted or deformed.
All that is pietist and rationalist agrees in *this* judgment; and of
course even those whose ideal futilely consists in the orthodoxy of
the sixteenth and seventeenth centuries are so deeply permeated by
pietism and rationalism that they do not find fault with the scholastic
narrowing of the reformation in that period. But I mean to amplify
this observation through the opposite view—that the reason-centered
narrowing of protestantism, which was unavoidable under the circumstances, was also salutary under those conditions and useful for
maintaining the reformation. I prefer to compare the doctrinaire
narrowing of the reformation to the vestigial leaves which protect the
seed [*Keimblättchen*] as it grows into a young plant; these leaves

must remain until such time as the plant forms and grows its own leaves, which are necessary for its further life. The vestigial leaves are not of the same type as the plant's own leaves, but rather they are adequate to the conditions in which the seed is fertile. In comparison to the plant's own leaves, these protective leaves appear to be stunted or deformed, but at the same time they are indispensable and salutary for the first period of the plant's life. I wish to leave to others the judgment of whether pietism and rationalism are such vestigial organs of protestantism, which correspond to its nature as leaves correspond to the nature of their particular plants; but the efforts of the confessionalists have meant that the plant of protestantism always had to exist with only a modified type of vestigial leaf. I will agree that these comparisons are pertinent only to a limited extent. Protestantism is a common spiritual movement which, until now, has not yet gone under, in spite of the fact that it has also not yet produced an appropriate organizational form, but rather, still more stunting has followed from its original deformation.

In this respect, structures of man's common spiritual life can tolerate more than the forms of organic nature. The rule is always observed that distinctive new thrusts are not appropriated by men directly, especially in their purity and fullness; on the contrary, the habituated thrusts and traditional norms always continue in some relation to that which is new. Such compromises between the new and the old might appear subsequently to be illogical and intolerable; but for the men who are involved, the compromises are not only possible, but they are practicable precisely because they guarantee that continuity of the spiritual life which the majority of men apparently cannot do without. The individual has his continuity, even though his life achieves a meaning which is diametrically opposed to its previous course, be it through the discovery of a new direction in life or through conversion. The masses, who are not spiritually productive, but rather, at the most, are in various degrees receptive, cannot be won over to something new unless accommodations are first made to the old, or unless reversions to the old appear within the new. The masses of those who are simply receptive in nature would be corrupted if they had to experience a rupture in their spiritual life in all clarity and bluntness. But afterwards, it is necessary that these compromises not be solidified again as venerable ordinances, when they have lost their original validity and, in principle, should be disposed of.

The reversions to which I refer have appeared in the various branches of protestantism. In the Lutheran church, the institution of confession belongs under this category. It is simply a modification of the catholic sacrament of penance and, like penance, has the purpose of making the masses sensitive to the moral and religious authority of the church—an authority that they are in need of, even in protestantism. Of course pietism cast doubt on whether the purpose were being realized by this means to the extent which was desirable. At any rate, this institution does not conform to the protestant concern for the doctrine of justification. The insistence upon confession always expresses the idea that God's accepting man is actually and ordinarily dependent upon good works, and that forgiveness of sins is only a substitute because one's good works are defective. In such a context, forgiveness of sins is brought to bear only as the exception, as in catholicism; but in protestantism, the significance of forgiveness is that it is the regular basis of corporate and personal religious life. Be that as it may, this reversion to a catholic institution in the Lutheran church was popular in the sixteenth and seventeenth centuries, and it was probably no obstacle to the assimilation of protestantism's thrust by the masses. This tendency did not occur in the Reformed church. Such a circumstance, along with other factors, is usually used to support the judgment that the Calvinist-Reformed church far surpasses the Lutheran church which remained half catholic, in the purity of its protestant structure. Such is the meaning of the phrase "our church, which has been reformed according to God's word," which is opposed to the Lutheran church, which has been reformed according to God's word, but also with consideration for the Holy Roman Empire and the customs of the "coarse common man." Now this reputation of the two churches is not wholly accurate. Such a phrase seems to infer that Calvinism wishes to imitate the primitive church in organization and in world-renouncing mores to the degree that its existence within the state will allow (see p. 119 above). Calvinism does indeed comport itself so as to exclude all the institutions and cultic forms of the medieval church; but insofar as it was possible within the state, Calvin linked the thrust of the world-renouncing, holy church to Luther's principles. Now this thrust corresponds to a similar drive for reform which existed among the masses at the end of the Middle Ages, as anabaptism demonstrates. Through his personal interpretation of this element and its incorporation in his work of establishing churches, Calvin gave his congregations a power of resistance which was not native to Lutheranism; but this was still simply a reversion of the medieval ideal of reform within the scope of Luther's reformation. In Calvinism, therefore, foreign elements are bound together to a greater extent than in the so-called half catholic Lutheranism. Thus the need for reform in the two branches of protestantism is similar in respect to the doctrinaire narrowing of their understanding of faith, but it is different in respect to their retention of catholic patterns of life. The reform that pietism undertook is therefore similar in both branches of the protestant church as a reaction against an exclusively literalistic, reason-centered Christianity [*Verstandeschristenthum*]; but in spite of this, we should not expect that pietism within the Reformed church would react against the world-renouncing element in that tradition in the same way that it manifested itself in opposition to the institution of confession in the Lutheran church. Rather, in this regard, diametrically opposed phenomena manifested themselves in the two churches. The task of the history which follows [in the three subsequent volumes] is to become acquainted with the complexities of this movement.

If it should seem pertinent to begin by seeking the starting point of pietism, I would observe here that it did not begin with Valentin Weigel (pastor in Zschopau bei Chemnitz; born 1533, died 1588) and Jacob Böhme (born in Görlitz 1575, died 1624). These two men do indeed share pietism's reaction against the dominant rationalism in the Lutheran church, and they did set forth conditions for the Christian life that were of an interior and practical kind. But in all other aspects, they were unlike the pietists. Both men directly forsook the doctrine of justification by faith and therefore stood on ground that is foreign to the Lutheran church; the same is true of their philosophical interests. As followers of Theophrastus Paracelsus (professor of medicine in Basel; born 1493, died 1541), they intertwined the redemptive significance of the Christian religion with a theoretical understanding of the world which was dominated by the correspondence between nature and the spiritual life, and which, at one moment, took a turn toward pantheism and, at the next, toward dualistic materialism. It is obvious that this theosophical tendency does not stand on the same ground as the reformation. Paracelsus, a contemporary of the reformation, was and remained catholic. The fact that his world view deviated from the official pattern of Thomism does not make it either related to or analogous with the reformation. Since, as a nature-philosophy, it provides rather an impulse for referring spiritual phenomena back to powers of nature, it contradicts the tendency of the reformation, which gave practical assurance concerning the superordination of the religious and moral life to all of nature. Apart from the theosophical aspect, which took a totally pantheistic form, Weigel's practical world view stands closest to the movement of the spirituals. He relied on the fact that his view of life would come to completion in the approaching age of the Holy Spirit, when the heavenly kingdom of Christ would exist on earth through the dominion of Christ in us. He believed that the law would be perfectly fulfilled by the believers, and he prescribed the surrender of the will, so that Christ would be allowed to be efficacious within us. He counted on the complete transformation of the civil society; Christ's law rather than Justinian's would be in force; the authorities would be allowed to levy no tax, decree no capital punishment, wage no war. Common ownership of property would prevail; business would be designated as unchristian; procreation of children, and also, therefore, marriage, would be regarded as ordinances of sin. What is to be found here, then, that is not analogous to anabaptism rather than to the Lutheran reformation? The only difference between Weigel's work and the public manifestations of anabaptism is that Weigel quietly entrusted his opinions to paper in writing. And this is also true of the followers whom he found and whom Gottfried Arnold rescued from oblivion in his history of the church and heresy.[108] Weigelism had only a literary existence. Or, as the case of Ezekiel Meth[109] and Isaiah Stiefel[110] in Langensalza demonstrates, there was a circle of family and friends that was interested in Weigel's ideas at one time.

Jacob Böhme differs from Weigel in that he brought only the cosmological speculation into relationship with the Christian idea of redemption, but made no projections about the transformation of civil society. For this reason, his direct influence is also traceable only in the ties of personal friendship among those who shared his temperament. This continued to be true as individual adherents of his were filled at the same time with practical impulses from Weigel. Such was the case with John George Gichtel (1638–1710) and the "community of the brothers of the angels" that took its origin with him, and further, with the English group of the "Philadelphians," Jane Leade (1623–1704), John Pordage (1608–1688), and Thomas Bromley (1629–1691). German pietists, of course, busied themselves a great deal with reading Böhme's writings; individual groups of pietists also took over certain practical principles from Gichtel; but these practical followers of Böhme gave as little direct stimulus for the rise of pietism as did their older relatives from Weigel's party.

NOTES

1. Heinrich Schmid, *Die Geschichte des Pietismus* (Nördling: Beck, 1863).
2. [Philipp Jakob Spener (1635–1705) is considered to be the "Father of Pietism."]
3. [Joachim Lange (1670–1744) was a pietist theologian who is noted for his strong stand against dancing, card-playing, theater, and the like on the grounds of their possible immoral consequences.]
4. [Valentin Loescher (1675–1749) was one of Lange's chief opponents, who insisted that God's creation is to be enjoyed to the fullest.]
5. [Jean de Labadie (1610–1674) was a Spiritual Franciscan who became a Calvinist in 1650. He was active in France, Geneva, and the Netherlands.]
6. Johann Georg Walch, *Historische und theologische Einleitung in die Religionsstreitigkeiten der evangelisch-lutherischen Kirche*, 3 vols. (Jena: Johann Meyers, 1730).
7. [Gottfried Arnold (1666–1714) was an important early protestant historian who recognized the importance of unconventional and heretical movements in Christianity.]
8. [Christian Thomasius (1655–1728) was professor of Law at Leipzig and Halle, a pietist who was close to Spener and Francke.]
9. [In the medieval understanding of religious orders and their congregations, the first order consisted of male religious, the second order of women members, and the third order, or tertiaries, of lay people who remained in their secular occupations while living under the spiritual direction of a religious community.]
10. Max Goebel, *Geschichte des christlichen Lebens in der rheinisch-westphälischen evangelischen Kirche*, 3 vols. (Coblenz: Bädecker, 1849). The third volume was edited by Theodor Link, after the author's death on December 13,

1857. Volumes two and three are pertinent to the task that lies before us; the continuation of the work up to the nineteenth century was made impossible by Goebel's early death.

11. Cf. my *A Critical History of the Christian Doctrine of Justification and Reconciliation*, trans. John S. Black (Edinburgh: Edmonton and Douglas, 1872). [The reference is to Ullmann's *Reformers before the Reformation, principally in Germany and the Netherlands*, trans. Robert Menzies (Edinburgh: T. and T. Clark; London: J. Gladdings, 1855).]

12. [Gotthard Lechler (1811–1888) was a Leipzig professor noted especially for his work on English church history.]

13. Gotthard Lechler, *Johann von Wiclif und die Vorgeschichte der Reformation*, 2 vols. (Leipzig: Hinrichs, 1878), vol. 1. ET, *John Wycliffe and his English Precursors*, 2 vols. (London: C. K. Paul, 1878).

14. [Gregory VII was a great reforming pope of the eleventh century, who impressed celibacy and papal supremacy upon the church.]

15. [The practice whereby the secular authority invested the bishop with his authority was termed lay investiture. Gregory VII challenged this practice, thereby making the church independent of the kings.]

16. [Francis of Assisi (1182–1226) was responsible for one of the most powerful reform movements in western Christendom prior to the sixteenth century, culminating in the establishment of the Franciscan order.]

17. [This translation is from *The Jerusalem Bible*.]

18. [This reference is to *S. Francisci Opuscula sincera*, "Regulae non bullata," 1. In Heinrich Boehmer, *Analekten zur Geschichte des Franciscus von Assisi*, 3rd ed. (Tübingen: J. C. B. Mohr, 1961), p. 1.]

19. [Ibid.]

20. [Peter Waldus was a merchant from Lyons, France, who took the vow of poverty in 1176 and established the Waldensian sect, a peripatetic preaching group, committed to personal repentance.]

21. Jacobus a Vitriaco (died 1244), *Historia occidentalis*, chap. 32: "In those days the Lord added a fourth institution of religion (namely, the Franciscan order). If, however, we diligently heed the circumstances and ordering of the primitive church, we see that he did not add a new rule so much as he renewed the old; he lifted up the falling and he awakened an almost dead religion in the evening of a world traveling towards its death, at the time when the son of perdition was near, so that he might train new athletes to fight against the dangerous times of the Antichrist and so that he might preserve the church by fortifying it."

Ubertinus de Casali (Minorite at about 1312), *Arbor vitae crucifixae*, book V, chap. 3: "Jesus chose the final command for the church at the fifth period of time, awakening the men of noble truth, who by the example of their lives sharply reproved a deformed church and by the words of their preaching aroused the masses to repentance. . . . Among these men, Francis and Dominic singularly exhibited the type of an Elijah and an Enoch. . . . Because in truth, all the evil of the fifth period of time consisted in the corrupting action of a manifold vanity which takes its nourishment from the cupidity and abundance of temporal things, for this very reason that man who separated himself more radically from the temporal things that pertained to himself and his station, that man (Francis) is spoken of as the *principle reformer* of this period." See: Johann Karl Ludwig Gieseler, *Lehrbuch der Kirchengeschichte,* 6 vols. (Bonn: A. Marcus, 1835–57), II/2:325, 350. ET, *A Textbook of Church History,* 5 vols. (New York: Harper and Bros., 1871–80). [The material within the first two sets of parentheses is Ritschl's; the material within the last set is from the source he is quoting.]

22. Cf. Lucius Holstenius, *Codex regularum monasticarum et canonicarum auctus a Mariano Brockie,* 6 vols. (Budapest: Eggenberger, 1759), vol. III. Similar material occurs also in the other monastic rules which St. Francis composed.

23. [Arnold of Brescia was a powerful figure in Rome in the middle of the twelfth century. He was a compelling preacher, enthusiast, and ascetic, who influenced the masses.]

24. See Gieseler, *Kirchengeschichte,* II/2:353. "However far removed all modern religion may be from the form of the primitive church, it can nevertheless be comprehended by many people." Of the sayings of Joachim which the Franciscans applied to themselves, Gieseler's judgment is that the following is genuine (p. 354): "It is necessary that there come into being a true likeness to the apostolic life, in which the possession of an earthly legacy is not acquired, but rather is given up."

25. Johann Herzog, *Die romanischen Waldenser* (Halle: Anton, 1853), pp. 131, 141, 189.

26. Their catholic opponents deny them this claim. See Gieseler, *Kirchengeschichte,* II/2:565.

27. L. Krummel, *Geschichte der böhmischen Reformation in 15. Jahrhundert* (Gotha: F. A. Perthes, 1866), pp. 89 ff.

28. Anton Gindely, *Geschichte der böhmischen Brüder,* 2 vols. (Prague: C. Bellmann, 1857–58), I:21, 26 ff. Cf. A. Ritschl, "Georg Witzels Abkehr vom Luthertum," *Zeitschrift für Kirchengeschichte* II (1878):397.

29. Johannes Gerhardus Rijk Acquoy, *Het klooster te Windesheim en sijn invloed,* 3 vols. (Utrecht: Gebr. Van der Post, 1875–80), II:336, 671.

30. Gieseler, *Kirchengeschichte,* III/2: 675.

31. The Starowerzen [See note 26, above] were excluded from the Russian state church, and the latter manifested a fanatical aversion to them. But this was only an accidental consequence of the refusal of those Old Believers [See note 25, above] to use the reform of the liturgical manuals which had been carried out by the Russian authorities to correct their own corrupted tradition.

32. Heinrich Bullinger, *Der Wiedertäufer Ursprung, Fürgang, Secten, Wesen* (Zurich: C. Froschauer, 1560).

33. It is not accidental that the first argument for this principle in the sixteenth century stems from Thomas More (in *Utopia*), a man of thoroughly ascetical patterns of life and a martyr for the primacy of the pope.

34. [Conrad Grebel (1498–1526) was one of the earliest anabaptists, and he

is considered to be a founder of the movement. His activity was largely confined to his home city of Zurich.]

35. [See note 25, above.]

36. [See Ritschl's article, "Ueber die beiden Principien des Protestantismus," *Gesammelte Aufsätze* (1893), pp. 234–47.]

37. [Carlstadt (1480–1541) was a co-worker of Luther.]

38. [Hans Denck (1500–1527) was a teacher in Nuremberg who became a spiritualist and anabaptist.]

39. [*LW*, 31.]

40. Karl Adolf Cornelius, in his *Geschichte des Munsterischen Aufruhrs*, 2 vols. (Leipzig: T. D. Weigel, 1855–60), II:10 ff., seeks the roots of the anabaptists too superficially, namely, in the manner in which the uneducated people appropriated the access to the Bible which was opened to them by Luther. Heinrich Erbkam, in his *Geschichte der Protestantischen Secten im Zeitalter der Reformation* (Hamburg and Gotha: F. and A. Perthes, 1848), p. 485, points, on the contrary, to the substance of medieval sectarianism that existed prior to the reformation and was aroused anew by Luther's activity. Nevertheless, this is not a clear interpretation.

41. [Ritschl refers to an article which embodies the first four sections of this present treatise, "Prolegomena zu einer Geschichte des Pietismus," *Zeitschrift für Kirchengeschichte* II (1878):1–55.]

42. [The Observants were a rigoristic party within the Franciscans which separated into its own congregation during the fifteenth century.]

43. Gieseler, *Kirchengeschichte*, II/4:290–302.

44. Compare my study of him in *Zeitschrift für Kirchengeschichte* II (1878): 390. [See note 28, above.]

45. [*S. Francisci Opuscula sincera*, "Regula non bullata," 14. See p. 9 of the work by Boehmer cited in note 18, above.]

46. [Melchior Hofmann (1500–1543) was one of the early leaders of the anabaptists, who was active in Sweden and the Baltic area.]

47. Cf. Geiseler, *Kirchengeschichte*, II/4:302.

48. Cf. Hermann Reuter, *Geschichte der religiösen Aufklärung im Mittelalter*, 2 vols. (Berlin: W. Hertz, 1875–77), II: 364, note 17.

49. [See note 36, above.]

50. *In primum librum sententiorum,* in *Opera Omnia* (Paris, 1893), VIII, Prologi Qu. III. 14: "Sacred scripture contains sufficiently the doctrine necessary for life."

51. [The Council of Trent (1545–63) embodied the ideals of the counterreformation and led to church reform in the wake of the protestant reformation.]

52. [St. Bernard of Clairvaux (1090–1153) was a Cistercian monk who founded the monastery at Clairvaux and grew to hold great power and widespread influence in the church, because of his asceticism, his preaching, and his mysticism.]

53. See my study "Ueber die beiden Principien des Protestantismus" in Brieger's *Zeitschrift für Kirchengeschichte* I (1877): 397–413. [Reprinted in

Gesammelte Aufsätze (Freiburg, i.B. and Leipzig: J. C. B. Mohr, 1893), pp. 234–47.]

54. "Ueber den eigenthümlichen Werth und das bindende Ansehen symbolischer Bücher" (1819), *Friedrich Schleiermacher's sämmtliche Werke*. Erste Abteilung, zur Theologie, 12 vols. (Berlin: G. Reimer, 1836–49) V:451. See p. 404 in my article cited in the previous note.

55. Cf. my lecture, *Die christliche Vollkommenheit* [Critical edition by Caius Fabricius (Leipzig: J. C. Hinrichs, 1924)] and my *Justification and Reconciliation*.

56. [See note 12, above.]

57. *CA* II, "all men who are propagated according to nature are born in sin. That is to say, they are without fear of God, are without trust in God, and are concupiscent." XVI, "[Our churches] also condemn those who place the perfection of the Gospel not in the fear of God and in faith but in foresaking civil duties." XXVII, 49, 50: "For this is Christian perfection: honestly to fear God and at the same time to have great faith and to trust that for Christ's sake we have a gracious God; to ask of God, and assuredly to expect from him, help in all things which are to be borne in connection with our callings; meanwhile to be diligent in the performance of good works for others and to attend to our calling. True perfection and true service of God consist of these things and not of celibacy, mendicancy, or humble attire."

58. *De votis monasticis* (1522) *WA* VIII, 573–669. *LW* (ed. James Atkinson), 44, 245–400: "The state of perfection consists of disdaining—with spirited faith—death, life, glory, and the whole world, and serving all with fervent love." 344: "The obedience of sons, husbands, slaves, captives is better and more perfect than the obedience of monks. . . . Therefore, if one must make the transition from imperfect to perfect, he must make the transition from monastic obedience to the obedience to parents, masters, friends, rulers, adversaries, and all others." "Temporal Authority" (1523), *WA* II, 245–80; *LW* (ed. Walther Brandt), 45: "Perfection or imperfection does not consist in works, nor does it confer external status among Christians; rather, it resides in the heart, causing one to believe more and love more; that man is perfect, whether he is externally husband or wife, prince or peasant, monk or laity." *Hauspostille über Matthäus 22:34–46, WA* 52, 489–93: "A Christian says: 'To be perfect is to fear God and love and do all possible good to the neighbor; for God has commanded nothing else.' "

59. [The *Apology* was written to answer objections to the *Augsburg Confession*.]

60. *Apology*, XXVII, 37: "All men, whatever their calling, ought to seek perfection, that is, growth in the fear of God, in faith, in the love of their neighbor, and similar spiritual virtues." [Ritschl lists other references to the *Apology*, but, due to typographical errors in the original, it is impossible to ascertain just which passages he was referring to. He may have been referring to IV, 71, 232; XII, 25, 61. See also *CA* XXVII, 49–50.]

61. *CA* XX, 24–25: "Whoever knows that in Christ he has a gracious God, truly knows God, calls upon him, and is not, like the heathen, without God. For the devil and the ungodly do not believe this article concerning the for-

giveness of sin, and so they are at enmity with God, cannot call upon him, and have no hope of receiving good from him." *Apology* IV, 4, 46, 180–82. XII, 73, 74. [References to *Apology* are misprints, corrected by editor.]

62. In *Sermons on the Song of Songs*, XLVI, 2: "In the cloisters, we live quietly, far from the impulses of the world and the worrisome cares of life."

63. In respect to Calvin, one might compare briefly, *Institutes of the Christian Religion* [ed. John T. McNeill, Library of Christian Classics 20 (Philadelphia: Westminster, 1960)], III, 2:10, 10:6.

64. Martin Kähler's review of P. Lobstein's *Die Ethik Calvins*, in *Theologische Literaturzeitung* III (1878):295–97.

65. Luther's Commentary on Genesis 1:26; 2:17, 21. *WA* 42, 41–51. *LW* (ed. Jaroslav Pelikan), 1, 55–68. Calvin, *Institutes*, I, 2.

66. [Georg Witzel (1501–1573) was a Lutheran pastor who became a Roman Catholic.]

67. See my study, "Georg Witzels Abkehr vom Lutherthum," *Zeitschrift für Kirchengeschichte* II (1878):386–417.

68. [This group emerged in the Netherlands in the 1380s, as a society of both clergy and lay, around the person of Gerhard Groote.]

69. [The Brothers of the Common Life was a movement that emerged in the mid-fifteenth century as a result of the impulse for a nonmonastic Christian form of life engendered by the *devotio moderna*. The movement flourished in the Netherlands and western Germany, where it formed numerous communities, of which the central one was at Hildesheim. Communities of Sisters were also formed.]

70. [Saint Bernard, *On the Song of Songs: Sermones in Cantica Canticorum,* trans. and ed. by A Religious of C.S.M.V. (New York: Morehouse-Gorham Co., 1951).]

71. Among Bernard's hymns, the one which is devoted to this idea is *Rhythmica oratio ad unumquodlibet membrorum Christi patientis a cruce pendentia.*

72. In *Sermons on the Song of Songs*, VI, 3. [Here Ritschl cites a long section in which Bernard speaks of Christ's human nature.]

73. [Hans Hut (ca. 1490–1527) was a chiliast and anabaptist who worked in southeast Germany.]

74. I might adduce here that Schmid, *Die Geschichte des Pietismus*, p. 442, had the insight that there was a difference between Lutheranism and Calvinism at this point; but he did not interpret it clearly, because he assumed from Goebel the concept of the church which he imputed to the Reformed churches, as if there were no Reformed confessions which in their own circles had as great value as the Lutheran confessions to which Schmid was obligated.

75. Richter, *Evangelische Kirchenordnungen* (Weimar: Verlag des Landes-Industrie comptoire, 1846), I, 158.

76. Calvin, *Institutes*, IV, 12, 1. Brenz's church-order for Schwäbisch-Hall (1526), in Richter, *Evangelische Kirchenordnungen*, I, 45.

77. [See note 26, above.]

78. Richter, *Evangelische Kirchenordnungen*, I, 25: "Two things are neces-

sary for Christianity to exist, that one hear God's word and believe in it and that one love his neighbor. The preacher's office is to preach the word of God clearly and purely; to the secular authority belongs the task of governing in an orderly fashion, that Christian love and harmony may be maintained and what is forbidden by God's word may be hindered, yea even punished." [Ritschl adduces an entire page of quotations from Richter which elaborate on this same point.]

79. This writing is not taken into account in the study by Moritz Frhr. von Engelhardt (currently professor at Erlangen), "Erasmus Sarcerius in seinem Verhältnis zur Geschichte der Kirchenzucht und des Kirchenregiments in der lutherischen Kirche," *Zeitschrift für die historische Theologie* XX (1850): 70–142. Nevertheless, the dominant thinking of Sarcerius himself is suggested on p. 89.

80. *Opera latina*, Wittenberg, IV, 514b. Walch, VI, 1632–33.

81. [Farel (1489–1565) was a leading Reformed preacher and organizer in Switzerland. Lambert (1486–1530) worked in Germany, where he was professor of theology at Marburg in his last years.]

82. Richter, *Evangelische Kirchenordnungen*, I, 36.

83. Ibid., I, 62.

84. January 1527, *WA Br.*, 4, 157–58.

85. [The Cistercian cloister in Normandy, where the Trappists emerged in 1664, was founded by Jean le Bouthillier de Rancé.]

86. [A rigorist Catholicism that attracted the upper classes in France during the seventeenth century. The movement grew up around Cornelius Jansen, but was repressed by the Jesuits and the curia.]

87. [Vincent de Paul (1576–1660) founded the Sisters of Charity, the Lazarists, and other charitable groups, as well as the *caritas* movement.]

88. Julius Köstlin, *Die Schottische Kirche, ihr inneres Leben und ihr Verhältnis zum Staat* (Gotha:Perthes, 1852), pp. 26 ff.

89. Johann Baumann, *Die Staatslehre des Thomas von Aquino* (Leipzig: Hirzel, 1873), pp. 23 ff., 141.

90. *R.u.V.*, III, 368. *ET*, section 44.

91. Calvin, *Institutes*, IV, 1, 13–27.

92. See my study, "Die Entstehung der altkatholischen Kirche," in *Gesammelte Aufsätze* (Freiburg and Leipzig: J. C. B. Mohr, 1893), pp. 186–87.

93. Ibid., p. 201.

94. [Melanchthon's *Loci communes rerum theologicarum* was his theological magnum opus. The first Lutheran textbook in Christian doctrine, this work ran through sixty editions, of which the 1521 edition was the first. Its organization features a series of propositions, rather than a logical or theological system.]

95. "Entstehung der altkatholischen Kirche," pp. 191–92.

96. Ibid., pp. 179–80.

97. [Tappert, pp. 31 f.]

98. *R.u.V.*, III, 158. *ET*, section 24, pp. 159–60.

99. Franz Balduin, *De casibus conscientiae, Opus posthumum* (Frankfurt a. Main, 1654), p. 670.

100. *Apology*, III, 178–84.

101. *Institutes*, III, 2, 7 (McNeill, 551): "Now we shall possess a right definition of faith if we call it a firm and certain knowledge of God's benevolence toward us, founded upon the truth of the freely given promise in Christ, both revealed to our minds and sealed upon our hearts through the Holy Spirit." III, 2, 8 (McNeill, 552): "that very assent itself—as I have already partially suggested, and will reiterate more fully—is more of the heart than of the brain, and more of the disposition than of the understanding. For this reason, it is called 'obedience of faith.' " III, 2, 14 (McNeill, 559 f.): "When we call faith 'knowledge' we do not mean comprehension of the sort that is commonly concerned with those things which fall under human sense perception. . . . But while it is persuaded of what it does not grasp, by the very certainty of its persuasion it understands more than if it perceived anything human by its own capacity. . . . From this we conclude that the knowledge of faith consists in assurance rather than in comprehension." III, 2, 15 (McNeill, 561): "But there is a far different feeling of full assurance that in the Scriptures is always attributed to faith. It is this which puts beyond doubt God's goodness clearly manifested for us. But that cannot happen without our truly feeling its sweetness and experiencing it in ourselves. For this reason, the apostle derives confidence from faith. . . . By these words he obviously shows that there is no right faith except when we dare with tranquil hearts to stand in God's sight."

102. *Ibid.*, III, 2, 16 (McNeill, 562): "Briefly, he alone is truly a believer who, convinced by a firm conviction that God is a kindly and well-disposed Father toward him, promises himself all things on the basis of his generosity. . . . No man is a believer, I say, except him who, leaning upon the assurance of his salvation, confidently triumphs over the devil and death; as we are taught from that masterly summation of Paul (Rom. 8:38)." III, 2, 28 (McNeill, 573 f.): "Now, in the divine benevolence, which faith is said to look to, we understand the possession of salvation and eternal life is obtained. For if, while God is favorable, no good can be lacking. . . . By this they intimate that when God is reconciled to us no danger remains to prevent all things from prospering for us. Faith, therefore, having grasped the love of God, has promises of the present life and of that to come. . . ."

103. *Selectae disputationes*, II, 501.

104. [*Implicit faith* refers to the readiness with which a person, especially an unsophisticated or unlearned person, may assent to propositions of belief on authority even when he does not understand them.]

105. *Institutes*, chap. 2: "Is believing, therefore, to know nothing, but only to submit your mind obediently to the church? Faith does not arise in ignorance, but rather in knowledge. . . . For we do not find salvation in that which we are prepared to embrace as true whatsoever the church prescribes, but rather when we know God the father to be our propitiation by the reconciliation worked through Christ, the Christ truly given to us for justification, sanctification, and life." Chap. 3: "Faith in God and Christ rests on knowledge, not on reverence for the church."

106. *Exercitationes in symbolum apostolorum* (Franeker, 1681), Ex. III, 9, 10.

107. [Stephan Praetorius (1536–1603) was an author of devotional literature.]

108. [See note 7, above.]

109. [Ezekiel Meth was a nephew of Isaiah Stiefel (see note 110, below), whose ideas he propagandized.]

110. [Isaiah Stiefel (1560–1626) was a disciple of Thomas Müntzer. He separated himself from the Lutheran church and actively propagated what are now considered to be anabaptist beliefs, in the province of Saxony, for which he was frequently persecuted and imprisoned.]

THEOLOGY AND

METAPHYSICS

THEOLOGY AND METAPHYSICS

Ritschl finished his magnum opus, the three volumes on justification and reconciliation, in 1874, followed in the next year by *Instruction in the Christian Religion*. This meant that his theological system was complete and in the public eye, with the result that it was fair game for the critics. After 1875, Ritschl and his disciples came under increasing fire in the journals, and beginning in the 1880s, his critics among the confessionalist Lutherans and the pietists began to attack him in pastoral conferences and provincial synods. Ritschl himself felt that he had been extraordinarily patient in the face of attacks, scarcely responding in public. In 1881, however, the attacks on his own work, as well as those on *The Doctrine of Christ's Divinity*, by a friend and disciple, Hermann Schultz, moved him to action. He was convinced that his opponents were blinded by adherence to an outmoded metaphysics which they confused with their Christian faith, and when in April a journal appeared with three articles that intensified his opinions, he interrupted his work on the *History of Pietism* to write a rejoinder. He wrote this essay between April 15 and June 6 of 1881, aiming it specifically against Luthardt of Leipzig, Frank of Erlangen, and Hermann Weiss of Tübingen. The first two were confessionalists, the third a pietist. The essay shows some signs of hasty writing, and it is acknowledged that Ritschl tends to obscure the fact that he is relying on Kant as much as on Lotze in his attack on metaphysics, just as he is vague on some of his own problems of methodology. Nevertheless, the piece gives a clear insight into what Ritschl thought was at stake in his rejection of metaphysics and what he considered to be the foundations of dogmatic theology.

The first edition appeared in 1881, from Adolph Marcus in Bonn, in the same volume with the second edition of *Instruction*. A second edition in 1887 is virtually unchanged from the first. This translation is the first to appear in English.

Theology and
Metaphysics

Towards Rapprochement and Defense

I

Christoph Ernst Luthardt,[1] on page 62 of his *Compendium der Dogmatik* (5th ed., 1878), expresses the opinion that my theology, "since it eliminates all metaphysics, places Christianity exclusively within that framework in which we concern ourselves with the value which every particular thing holds for the moral determination of man's will; this moralizing evaluation of Christianity cheapens it because it constitutes a rationalistic misunderstanding of Christianity's divine nature." This judgment, which serves as the Leipzig professor's introduction of me to his students, has caused Professor Wilhelm Herrmann to doubt whether this "censor" has ever read my *Christliche Lehre von der Rechtfertigung und Versöhnung* [*Christian Doctrine of Justification and Reconciliation*] or whether he had read it thoroughly and with the care it deserves.[2] Herrmann, on my behalf, attests to Luthardt that I have devoted the utmost diligence precisely to the effort to differentiate between the specifically religious element of Christianity (justification by faith) and the other element that stands together with it, namely, that which is attainable through moral striving. Furthermore, he stresses the fact that I have sought to insure that this differentiation would not be overlooked. With regard to this [Luthardt's] judgment upon my work, there are several further points with which I find fault. According to Luthardt (p. 11), "Restricting religion to feeling engenders mysticism; restricting it to knowing, rationalism; and restricting it to human willing or doing, moralism." If his opinion holds true, that I have cheapened Christianity itself through a moralizing evaluation, then, by his own formulation, it is not possible for me to have misinterpreted Christianity rationalistically at the same time. Finally, if it were a mistake to eliminate all metaphysics (from what? from theology, that is all I have said!) I would expect some instruction in the *Compendium* as to what metaphysical knowledge is necessary for theology. But I have looked in vain for such information, everywhere it might be given, even for the word "metaphysics." This judgment lacks the care which would have been helpful for Luthardt in opposing me, his disclosed intention being to warn others about me, *Hic niger est, hunc tu Romane caveto*[3] ["A very shady customer is he. Roman, beware of him!"].

So be it. I take Luthardt's first accusation as occasion for examining what claim metaphysical knowledge has to make in theology. This very question is the source, I find, for all possible kinds of misunderstandings among my colleagues in theology. In the hope of getting this discussion off to a good start, I have the good fortune of being able to call upon Luthardt himself who, three pages after the opinion ascribed to me, surprises me most pleasantly with the following assertion. He begins the doctrine of God in section 22 as follows: "The Christian doctrine of God is the doctrine of God as the revelation of redemption." He also adds in a note: "On this point Luther expresses himself repeatedly in opposition to the scholastics, as, for example, in his commentary on John 17:3,

> Notice how Christ, in this saying, weaves and binds together his knowledge and his Father's, with the result that therefore one knows the Father only in and through Christ. I have often said, and I say it continually, that even after I am dead, one should meditate thereupon and guard himself from *all teachers (as if they were driven and led by the devil) who begin to teach and preach from the pulpit about God alone in isolation from Christ, as, up to this time, men have speculated in the schools and have played* with his works above in heaven, as to *what he might be and think and do alone by himself.*[4]

On the basis of these statements, one would be entitled to certain expectations. They are: that the author would thereupon sketch, according to the biblical-theological method, a picture of the person or work of Christ; that he would establish upon the principle of knowledge so derived all the parts of the Christian view of the world and life, giving preeminence to the necessary concept of God. We would expect him to build his dogmatics upon the principle of knowledge derived from Christ, because it is the authoritative revelation of God for the Christian church. But this expectation is not fulfilled by the said dogmatician. On the contrary, section 23 deals with the natural revelation of God:

> All knowledge of God rests on revelation. There is, first of all, the general self-revelation of God the Creator within men and through the world. The consciousness of God that is thus established finds its truth fulfilled, however, only in that which is mediated through the history of salvation [*heilsgeschichtlich*].

This paragraph stands on the same page as Luther's assertion, but it is on the reverse side and thus, analogically and in fact, it turns its back on Luther's utterance. This coincidence imposed on the long-suffering page constitutes the only rational relationship to be found between the two assertions. Rather, if one has experienced the fact that he knows God in Christ and only in Christ—and this fact arises from his existence within the Christian community that theology is to serve—then other revelations of God are, at the most, only of interest when one can measure them against the revelation that is mediated by the Son. And if this revelation is not set forth within an orderly biography of Christ, the only result is a confusion produced in dogmatics by the misrepresentation of a "natural" revelation of God. As a result, the character of all the assertions in section 23 is thoughtlessness compounded by confusion.

"All knowledge of God rests upon revelation." The apostle Paul knows a widespread knowledge of God which rests upon a perversion of revelation. "Revelation is, *first of all*, the general self-revelation of God the Creator within man and through the world." In many religions, men do not believe in God as creator of the world; but all religions do believe in God or gods as the helpers and defenders of man. What the dogmatician expresses in this second assertion is not at all *close* to the first assertion but is, on the contrary, quite removed from it. This is true even when we grant its validity within the Pauline limitations just cited. In fact, the second assertion stands *close* only to Luthardt's own resolve to copy the books of certain authorities in order to bring a *Compendium of Dogmatics* into existence. "The consciousness of God that is thus established finds its truth fulfilled, however, only in that which is mediated through the history of salvation [*heilsgeschichtlich*]." If this so-called natural consciousness of God finds its truth fulfilled only through something else, then, in itself, it has no truth. Thus, in itself, it is a false doctrine of God. Or, should this natural theology stand somehow as a half-truth until it is augmented by the revelation of redemption to full truth? Unfortunately, falsity would nevertheless cling to this proposition, because the truth is not to be found by adding together the heterogeneous halves.

Nevertheless, this natural revelation of God and a part of the "Proofs for God" (section 24) form the nest in which metaphysical knowledge of God has been nurtured in the past. But, since Luthardt has not acknowledged this fact directly, I shall attempt to prove that the cosmological and teleological proofs for the existence of God belong to metaphysics and that, on that account, they do fall short of their goal. Indeed, in this manner, I shall have also justified the fact that I refrain from this use of metaphysics in theology.

"Metaphysics" is familiar as the quite fortuitous title of Aristotle's "First Philosophy." This discipline devotes itself to the investigation of the universal foundations of all being. Now the things that our cognition concerns itself with are differentiated as nature and spiritual life [*geistiges Leben*[5]]. Therefore, any investigation of the common foundations of all being must set aside the particular characteristics by which one represents the difference between nature and spirit and the means by which one knows that these groups of things are dissimilar entities. Thus natural and spiritual manifestations or entities occupy the attention of metaphysical knowing only insofar as they are to be grasped generally as "things." For the conditions of knowing that are common to the manifestations of both nature and spirit are established in this concept of "thing." The "First Philosophy," therefore, indicates the knowledge which may temporally precede or follow the preoccupation with the particular circumstances in which things are partly nature and partly spirit, but metaphysics does not surpass the philosophy of nature and spirit in value.

For either all parts of philosophy are of equal value in a formal sense, or those parts of philosophy which explain reality more exhaustively are of more value than others. According to this latter standard, however, the philosophical cognition of nature and spirit surpasses metaphysical cognition in value since, when metaphysical cognition investigates both nature and spirit, these entities are treated only generally and, therefore, superficially under the general concept of "thing." But metaphysical cognition of nature and spiritual life as "things" is *a priori*; it establishes the forms which originate in the cognizing spirit of man. These forms alone enable the spirit to rise above the flow of impressions and perceptions in order to proceed to the fixing of conceptual objects. Thus, metaphysical concepts do indeed embrace and dominate all other concepts that are directed toward the particularity of nature and spirit, and these metaphysical concepts clarify the fact that through experience the human spirit fixes its specific perceptions on things and differentiates them accordingly as natural things and as spiritual entities. However, it does not follow from the superordination of metaphysics to knowledge based on experience that one arrives through metaphysical concepts at a more basic and more valuable cognition of spiritual entities than would be the case through psychology and ethical examination of those entities. For it is only these latter forms of cognition that succeed in reaching to the reality of spiritual life. By itself, metaphysical analysis of a spiritual entity is not capable of differentiating that entity from natural entities. Such an analysis is inadequate for grasping the form and peculiarity of the spirit, and in that sense is without value.

Within the boundaries just described as thinking about things, metaphysics is ontology. In addition, it encompasses *a priori* concepts in which the manifold of perceived and presented things is ordered again into the unity of the world (be this conceived necessarily as limitless or as a whole); that is, metaphysics is also cosmology. From the concept of the "thing" which is neutral or blind toward the distinction between nature and spirit, it follows however that metaphysical cosmology is also neutral toward this distinction. Furthermore, metaphysical thought about the world is indifferent to the distinction in value by which the metaphysician, as spirit, knows himself to be set off from all nature and feels superior to it. It is at this very point that the disparity between metaphysical cosmology and every religious world view emerges. In all of its forms, the religious world view is established on the principle that the human spirit differentiates itself to some degree in value from the phenomena within its environment and from the workings of nature that press in upon it. All religion is interpretation of that course of the world which is always perceived, in whatever circumstances, an interpretation in the sense that the sublime power which holds sway in or over that course of the world sustains or confirms for the personal spirit its own value over against the limitations imposed by nature or by the natural workings of human society.

In opposition to these conclusions, the most widely circulated assumption is that religion and metaphysics either belong close together or that they are related to each other in the most intimate way. This assumption finds its most characteristic expression in the assertion, met often enough, that religion is the metaphysics of the masses! Now this combination of religion and metaphysics rests historically on the fact that Aristotle regarded it as suitable to link the word of God with the concept of the final end of the world. The fragmentary perception which orders things through the concepts of means and end, which he broadened to become the law of the cosmos, demands augmentation through the assumption of a final end according to which all things move themselves. For the final end moves all things indirectly, in that as the unmoved and self-originating conception of itself, it claims the perfection of being pure reality. Aristotle calls this end or destiny of the cosmos "God," although the final end of things does not transcend the concept of the cosmos itself. But it is devious to entitle this metaphysical postulate "God." The idea of the final end of the world does have a certain similarity with God conceived as unique in his kind; and that which Aristotle calls "God" does bear comparison with the monotheistic thrust which accompanied Hellenic polytheism. But the difference between the Aristotelian idea of God and the view of the divine being in Hellenic religion is greater than the similarity. The compassion for men in the midst of the difficulties of life, which even the Hellenic religion acknowledged was demonstrated by the gods, is excluded in the unmoved *actus purus* which the philosopher conceives of as the destiny and ordering ground of the world in general.

No veneration of God can attach itself to this idea. Similarly, the Aristotelian God is only the representation of the fate that governs even the gods. Still, this idea does indeed have a monotheistic appearance even though it is the denial of religion altogether. Where it gained validity among the Greeks, it expresses a skepticism concerning the religion practiced among them, that is, the irrepressible misgiving that the gods, who were so involved in nature, did not possess the power to fulfill the expectations that their votaries entertained concerning them. The result was fate, to which the Hellenic gods themselves were as subject as the men who prayed to them. Fate can no more be venerated as the true God than the entity in the world, which Aristotle calls God, can attract religious veneration to itself, because fate leaves men caught in their misery.[6] This entity therefore cannot rightly carry the title God. Or, if the title God does seem justified for the Aristotelian concept of the final end of the world, this is so only for heathen circles in which the specific differentiation between the world and God has not yet arisen. This state of affairs must also be taken into account in the concept of God in later Platonism, represented by Philo and the neoplatonists, which was accepted by the Christian Apologists as valid. The illimitable Being which they call God because it exists in a realm beyond the appearance of a world that is itself divided and ordered in antitheses, the entity which embraces all and excludes from itself all determinations—this entity, although it is represented as the ground of the world, is indeed merely the idea of the world itself and nothing more. Only on the level of heathenism, however, is it possible to entertain the idea of the world as God since it knows only divine beings who are involved in nature.

Two conclusions follow from this discussion. If God is the power in or over the world, venerated by man because it sustains his spiritual self-consciousness [*Selbstgefühl*] against the limitations of nature, then the idea of God does not belong to metaphysics since metaphysical knowledge is indifferent toward the distinctions of kind and value that exist between spirit and nature. In addition, when Aristotle and the Platonists (though in a different manner) set forth an idea of God which is really the correlate to their philosophical evaluation of the world in general, they manage to come to this view only within the same horizon of ideas which Hellenic reli-

gion incorporates when it commingles the divine essence with the
natural world. That is, their idea of God either does not transcend
the world or it merely represents the idea of the world. From this it
follows that if one is able to differentiate the conditions of the religious world view from those of a metaphysical cosmology, then as
a Christian, he cannot grant a metaphysical knowledge of God on
which one believes for his salvation. Or if a Christian commits himself to metaphysical knowledge of God he thereby relinquishes his
Christian orientation and moves to a position corresponding in
general to the level of paganism. For paganism asserts as divine,
entities which in the judgment of Christians properly belong to the
world.

The cosmological and teleological proofs for God are metaphysical
because they disregard the difference between nature and spirit, since
they regard the content of the world as a chain of effects and causes.
Illustrations of these proofs indeed are normally taken from the
analysis of objects of nature and major attention is directed to these
objects, only in respect to their general character as neutral things.
Now it is remarkable indeed that the author of the *Compendium*
excuses himself from working out these proofs, and is content,
rather, to direct his students to all sorts of references and citations
which here and there demonstrate the argument of the cosmological
proof. Finally, when he does mention that in Kant's judgment the
concept of causality does not reach beyond the boundaries of the
sensible world, he adds: "And indeed this argument leads *chiefly*
only to a 'world-ground' which can also be an immanent 'ground' in
the pantheistic sense." Luthardt himself, then, as the representative
of the opinion that metaphysics is an essential and valuable element
of theology, agrees with me at this point: the cosmological argument
is no proof for the existence of a God who is the originator of the
world. For *if* one *postulates*, from a subjective standard of knowledge, that the nexus of objects is a *closed* nexus of causes and effects
or that it is *a whole*, and if he proceeds correctly, then he can arrive
at no other point but the knowledge that the world is one substance,
one thing. The usual thrust of the argument, that the *causa sui* [the
self-originating cause] which forms the end of all *res causatae*
[caused things] is God, is false. The *causa sui* is each thing in itself,
since at the same time, *in another relation*, it is conceived of as the

res causata. One reaches the end of the causal nexus only by assuming a *causa sui* which is under *the same circumstances* also *causa omnium* [cause of all things]. Therefore, this "cause" is the expression of the oneness of the world which we attain on this level of reflection both at the outset and as the end result of our thinking. But insofar as this reflection is metaphysical, it has no further relation at all to the Christian religion and therefore also no specific significance in theology—and Luthardt is rather clearly aware of this. He shows that he has decided to forget this *especially* when he says that it is only *possibly* the case that the conclusion of such metaphysical reflection can be understood in "a pantheistic sense." However, this characterization of the matter is already an evasion and this agreed-upon concept of a unified world ground does not by any means enable us to arrive at a representation of God. The world ground is the representation of the world which is posited as the ground or, rather, as the causative unity of the otherwise endless number of imaginable things. Anyone who clothes this representation in terms of a "pantheistic sense" is not thinking metaphysically, but rather in Brahmanic terms. He does not, in any case, hold to the scholarly precision that is demanded in a compendium. Luthardt continues:

> But that which obtrudes urgently upon our immediate sensibilities, namely that the observation of the world in itself engenders the idea of God, also validates itself in our thinking (cf. Matthias Claudius, in his *Chrie*).[7] The finite world cannot be its own ground; *nor can nature engender spirit, nor the spirit nature.* Therefore, this world calls for a cause outside itself and not simply for a world-substance.

This would be another possible way of elaborating the cosmological argument, but how does he carry out this elaboration? Even Luthardt should recognize that "immediate sensibilities" only correspond to individual manifestations and impressions as the elemental spiritual activity and that the sensibility which accompanies our representation of the world is very much a mediated one. However, even when the consideration of the world does engender the idea of God—as in the case of Matthias Claudius—we do not construct a metaphysical argument in order to discover the idea for the first time. Rather, it is the case that an acquired and nurtured *religious* faith in God the maker of heaven and earth is brought into primary relationship with one's consideration of the world. This is quite different from the cosmological argument, and Luthardt abandons the field of this argument when he finally postulates God as being over the world, because neither nature nor the spirit that resides in the world permits itself to be derived from the other. Indeed, the essential character of the cosmological argument lies precisely in its ability to comprehend things as causes and effects, irrespective of their differentiation as nature or spirit. As a metaphysical line of thought, this argument actually leads only to the idea that the world is the substance of all things, the one thing that subsists in all appearances. Insofar as Luthardt entertains the possibility that the cosmological argument leads to the supramundane God—in addition to what I have just mentioned—he places upon that same argument the task of differentiating between spirit and nature and the task of clarifying the distinction between things according to these qualities, and from this thrust he concludes with the postulate of the supramundane God. However, this differentiation is not the thrust of the cosmological argument, but rather it is a reflection that emerges out of the regard for the spirit that is based on the Christian religion. And if, therefore, Luthardt attains his proof, or rather, his postulate, for the existence of God on the basis of this presupposition, then he himself accomplishes at this point the very thing for which he reproaches me—the elimination of metaphysics from theology. It has taken only a little effort to clarify his opinion of the cosmological argument. I find that this work is permeated by an unmistakable carelessness and this appears precisely in regard to that object which alone makes a compendium desirable. I will let others judge how a novice in theology would find the right path through the blinding variation of assumptions that come together on this point.

The paragraph of section 24 which deals with the teleological argument also omits the necessary information about the form of this argument and a clear judgment as to its possibilities for success. "The inference from the purposefulness of the world to a highest Intelligence" is by no means a proof for the existence of the supramundane God that we believe in as Christians. Just as we consider ourselves justified in forming the concept of a world-whole on the assumption of an ultimate purpose as the result of our observation of the purposeful relations between things, so also we find that Aristotle has already clothed this concept with the idea of highest Intelligence. When we turn to this side of the matter, the ultimate purpose of the world is to be represented as the world soul. But if one proceeds with the teleological induction in a statistically precise fashion (others have already shown that one can substantiate innumerable cases where purposeless relationships and purposeful relationships between things exist side by side), then one reaches no goal at all in this metaphysical view of the world, least of all the safe inference of a supramundane God. The result, rather, like the familiar natural reason of the Buddhists, is that the world which embraces so many purposeless relationships within itself cannot be referred to a rational Source at all but, on the contrary, one can only conclude that it ought not to exist at all. But if the opposite seems true (namely, that the world is purposeful), the validity of that truth for us Christians is not based on a more correct metaphysical knowledge, since such knowledge is indemonstrable, but rather on an opposite religious world view. Moreover, the exclusive claim of this religious world view is certified by a totally different point of view, to which a Buddhist can scarcely be open, rather than by some reasonableness that is common to all men. The following quotation, "Insofar as *man* reflects upon the world and upon himself, he finds God in both and through this justifies for himself his immediate consciousness of God," expresses the totally hollow argumentation of section 24. I decline the task of judging the oraclelike comments on the so-called ontological and moral proofs for the existence of God which occur in these sections, since they are not pertinent to metaphysics. These arguments do not at all portray a possession common to all human reason. Rather, the ontological argument merely serves to dispel a doubt which the representatives of Platonic idealism have felt under certain circumstances concerning the success of their way of thinking. Kant's moral argument, however, stands under the unmistakable influence of the Christian world view.

II

I shall now proceed to another investigation of metaphysics in the Christian doctrine of God. Franz Hermann Reinhold Frank of Erlangen has written a curious essay[8] in which he aims to show

the error of a portrayal of the *Christian* concept of God which I
attempted in my doctrine of reconciliation, and, in the same essay,
he also strives to maintain intact the necessity of a metaphysical
origin of the doctrine of God in dogmatics. I affirmed that as a
dogmatician one has to assert the idea of God which takes its place
in the Christian view of life and the world; that one has to define
God fundamentally as he is revealed in Christ; and that one is permitted, accordingly, to take the brief Johannine assertion, "God is
love," as a theme of the doctrine of God. On these points I certainly
did not expect opposition from a Lutheran theologian. Even though
my enterprise might not be a common one for such a theologian, I
nevertheless thought that its correctness and obligatory nature would
have occurred to him as a Christian and would have been clear to
him as a Lutheran, especially since Luther so decisively rejected the
opposite enterprise and so clearly stigmatized it, as the passage cited
by Luthardt to which I referred above indicates. In my work on
justification I amplified the opinion that the assertion of the personal
character (*Persönlichkeit*) of God can only be firmly established
upon the substance of love and in the directing of the will [which is
implied in that love] toward the kingdom of God; in other words,
the world view of the Christian church is fully established upon the
Son whom God loves eternally. Everything else that pertains to the
concept of God must be demonstrated within this framework. I
assumed that everyone would recognize the appropriate substance
which amplifies the name of God in this concept of love, a concept
which entails within itself the relationship between Father and Son,
as well as the purpose which embraces the world. Furthermore, in
the will to love so defined, everyone could perceive the differentiation between God and the spiritual creatures who, according to their
form and limitations (i.e., as members of God's kingdom), become
subjects of that will to love. I interpreted John's words with this
understanding and I thought that I would be so understood by every
theologian who seeks to establish the Christian concept of God and
no other. But, on the contrary, Frank holds fast to the beginning
point of my discussion without paying attention to the way in which
I established the essential relations of the concept of love as the
title for God. Accordingly, he explains (p. 308):

God is neither exhausted nor even conceptualized when one simply assumes such a concept [i.e. Ritschl's concept of God] to be a positive concept of the divine being; for one finds, since [Ritschl] never brings it to expression, that he must always add 'the specifically divine' *since Ritschl's concept, per se, does not clarify the difference between God and the creaturely.* It is love, indeed, but divine love; personhood indeed, but divine personhood.

I reject this censure as thoroughly pointless. Because, as I explained at the end of the section to which the preceding comments refer:

God is love insofar as he establishes his own inner purpose [*Selbstzweck*] in drawing mankind into the kingdom of God as the supramundane purposiveness of man himself. . . . The kingdom of God which is formed of men is, therefore, the correlate to the divine inner purpose, and it is the goal of the creation and ordering of the world.[9]

Frank indicates where he wants to come out on this matter in the following sentences.

The predicate of absoluteness is always present where man, i.e., *a Christian*, perceives God. By means of this predicate, he distinguishes what God is from all of the factors that make up the world, not merely as an empty denial of the world, devoid of substance, but as a thoroughly positive concept, namely, as the only position which can support the *Christian* in the world and the world as concomitant with the Christian, the rock that begot us, the God who gave birth to us (Deut. 32:18). There is *nothing that is more positive than the expression of that which exists through itself* [*Durchsichselbstsein*], *in itself* [*Insichselbstsein*], *and which is in full possession of itself* [*Seinselbstsein*]. This expression of the *absolute* is the form in which man experiences God practically, not a means of rendering God dialectically accessible. On this basis the God who was before the mountains were formed is our refuge and on this basis when we are with him, the rock of our hearts, we do not inquire after heaven and earth, or about the ultimate fate of our flesh and hearts. This *positive concept of absoluteness* is the fundamental one in all expressions of the *Christian* consciousness of God. Through this concept, to be sure, the distinction between God and the world is maintained while, at the same time, however, the other predicates like personhood [*Persönlichkeit*] and love are elevated into the sphere of the divine. (Pp. 309, 310.)

It is a shame that so much pathos is lavished on a totally false assertion! What is asserted here is not true, in any case not demonstrable,
even though these assertions are made with direct reference to the
religious reflection of Christians and, through Old Testament catch-
words, with indirect reference to the pious ones of Israel. Much
more, rather, the Christian affirms with Paul: "If God is for us, who
is against us? He who did not spare his own Son but gave him up
for us all, will he not also give us all things with him? In all these
things, we are more than conquerors through him who loved us"
(Rom. 8:31–32, 37). And the Old Testament believer acknowledged
Jehovah as his rock, because he knew him as the covenant God of his
people. But, I hear the opponent contradicting, behind the love of
the Father of Jesus Christ and behind the covenant grace of Jehovah,
the Christian, like the Hebrew, must nevertheless think of the God
of his salvation as the absolute, as the subject of the love and of the
covenant grace!

I can see in Frank's postulate, however, nothing but an unseemly
mingling of metaphysics with revealed religion. Still, one would
remain on the ground of religious reflection if he commented thusly
on the Pauline passage just cited: That One must indeed be thought
of first of all as the all-powerful One who, as the father of Jesus
Christ, shows us his love through Jesus' sacrifice in death for our
sake, and who thereby establishes the certainty that he procures for
us all good gifts; therefore we believe in him as the all-powerful One
who possesses in himself the characteristic of love for the community
of his son. We would have to believe that behind his love God stands
as the subject of all-powerfulness. But this line of thought is not the
only possible one. In contradistinction, it is also possible to conceive
of God as loving will—and this arises from his orientation toward
that community which he elected before the creation of the world,
that it might adore him. To this community his loving will appears
to encompass the world and, for this reason, is recognized as the love
that possesses the characteristic of all-powerfulness. I think that I
may assume that this latter line of thought stands closer than the
other to the pattern of thought that dominates the New Testament
sources, but enough of that for now. Frank does not make the concept of all-powerfulness the valid one for referring to the bearer of
love; rather, he stresses the concept of the absolute (*sensu neutro*)

—even though he grants that when this concept is understood as a divine predicate, it should be interpreted by reference to the same phenomenon among created beings, to which it stands in contradistinction. The absolute! How exalted that sounds! I can still recall, if only dimly, how that word occupied me in my youth, when the Hegelian terminology threatened to draw me, too, into its vortex. But that was long ago. Now, since I do not find any far-reaching ideas designated by it, the word has become largely alien to me. Literally, it means that which has been severed, which stands in no relation to another. Frank understands it thus, since he substitutes for it the expressions "to exist through oneself" [*Durchsichselbstsein*], "to exist in oneself" [*Insichselbstsein*], and "to exist in full possession of oneself" [*Seinselbstsein*]. On this basis, my opponent asserts that this concept, "is the form in which man experiences God practically, not a means of rendering God dialectically accessible." If that is correct, then at the very least the man in whom God dwells is a different subject from the Christian in general, to whom the earlier comments pertained.

The absolute, as Frank defines it, is indeed something similar to what the Brahmins assert, and the mystics in Islam and in the Christian church experience and explore it practically in that they temporarily lose themselves and their self-consciousness in universal being, but not in order to place their trust in it as the Christian does in his Father in Christ. But if the absolute is conceived as existing only for itself, outside all relationships to others, it cannot rightly be designated as "the rock which has begotten us, the God who has given us birth." For these words designate a being who does enter into relationships with others, and if these relationships are correct predicates, they are either excluded from the concept of the absolute or they call into question the definition established above. In both cases it is clear that the absolute is not a product of religious reflection, but rather is a metaphysical concept which is entirely foreign to the Christian and is current only among the mystics in the religious groups we have mentioned. In metaphysics, however, the concept of the absolute (as Frank defines it) does not possess the highest place or the most comprehensive breadth, but rather it enjoys a severely restricted realm of operation. In the explanation that Frank includes in his work, the word "absolute" designates that which can be conceived of only in terms of the unity of its internal relationships. It is something, therefore, that is represented as being incomplete since we recognize an autonomous entity as being complete, first of all, in its qualities, that is, in its effects upon our perception and upon other things. When appearances are perceived within a restricted realm in a position or in a series that remains constant and whose changes are perceived within certain limits and order, these appearances focus our thought, so that we conceive of the unity of the thing in analogy to the perceiving soul, which feels and remembers itself to be an enduring unity in the midst of the alterations which correspond to its sensibilities.[10] Accordingly, the thing that we represent to ourselves exists in and of itself. And as the soul asserts itself as the source of its changing sensibilities under the stimulation of the appearance of an object and also perceives itself, in these perceptions, as the purpose of its own self, so also the soul represents the isolated object in its characteristics as both *causa sui* and *finis sui* [cause and goal of itself]. Accordingly, the isolated object is thought of as existing through and for itself. But when it is so conceived, the object is deprived of all specific qualities. It is a purely formal concept without content. Thus we see how trivial the concept of the absolute is— the very concept which Frank proclaims as God with such gravity! But when we designate for ourselves the position that this idea rightly holds, then another factor must be taken into consideration. Namely, the absolute is not at all conceived of as complete, except in a preliminary way, when we visualize it across the boundaries of our cognition as an isolated object outside of the relationship to us which makes it possible for us to sense its qualities and represent its unity in itself. And if we wanted to deny this obvious relationship, even in regard to the isolated object, we would be talking nonsense, because an object in and of itself would be inaccessible to our perception and representation. And, finally, if we were to affix the predicates of personhood and love to the absolute which Frank designates as the basic representation of God—in order that one could raise the concept "into the sphere of the divine"—we would discover that this cannot be easily done. Both of these predicates express relationships to another. Love is conceivable only with an object, and personhood only as a distinctive relationship of the spiritual life to the world or to other persons. If the absolute, isolated and without qualities, is conceived of with such predicates, then either these predicates contradict their subject, or it is not possible for us to infer the assumed subject from these predicates. One can say all he wants, therefore, about the object which stands outside all relationships to another possessing love for others or even indeed being that love—but such talk has no useful meaning. And with his absolute, Frank really establishes nothing else but a metaphysical idol which, moreover, cannot support the distinction between creator and creature.

For many men there must be a singular attraction in the prospect of knowing something about God *a priori*. Frank sacrifices every other consideration to this attraction; the unclear, confused idea of God that he forms is set forth as the foundation of religion. But at the same time he freely grants that this idea does not exhaust the necessary religious knowledge of God. But he does have to take account of the familiar representations such as personhood and love, which arise from positive religion and to which the metaphysical concept of the absolute cannot relate itself. Consequently, he has attached them quite externally to the metaphysical concept, with the result that the concept of God is expressly established as an aggregate, as an edifice of several stories whose foundation is incapable of sustaining the superstructure. Friedrich Adolf Philippi's *Kirchliche Dogmatik*[11] has already set forth such an aggregate, whose parts are layered one upon another and which is characterized by numbered parts, like a column of figures to be added. In this work, the attributes of God are ordered according to the "three phases in which the divine being discloses itself to us, in ascending stages": God (1) as absolute substance, (a) eternity, (b) omnipresence; (2) as absolute subject, (a) omnipotence, (b) omniscience; (3) as holy love, (a) wisdom, (b) righteousness, (c) goodness. This is a clear renunciation of the proper concept of God, namely, one that articulates his unity. This error, however, stands in direct relationship to the fact that the individual "phases" of the divine being are derived from differing epistemological bases which do not enjoy equal validity in theology.

I have still another claim to establish in this matter. Frank, since he chooses a metaphysical construct to be the vehicle of his Christian cognition of God, thereby permits himself to be led astray into a peculiar error, when he judges my thinking which is contrary to his. He deceives himself in thinking that I go astray by defining the will of God, as it is revealed in Christianity, in an *a priori* fashion with the concept of love—as if I proceeded in the same way he does in his definition of the absolute. He analyzes a formulation of mine, which he had previously left unnoticed, that God is recognized as love in that he actualizes his purpose for himself [*Selbstzweck*] and his purpose for the world in the kingdom of God. In an attempt to demonstrate once again his concept of the absolute, he makes the following comments against this statement:

> The execution of this purpose (of the kingdom of God as God's purpose for himself) cannot actualize itself save in a way that is commensurate with the nature of man, namely, that man comes into communion with God as a person with free choice. God can determine man to such communion, and he can create him and equip him accordingly; he can also guarantee to man, as a sinner, the possibility of returning to this communion, but always under the condition that man will accomplish this actualization of his will as a person in free autonomy, since he has intended man to be a person and created him thus. However, if one conceives things in such a way that God, out of love, makes the purpose of his kingdom the correlate of his own purpose for himself, without adding absoluteness to love as its basis, then one of two things will happen: *either* God will carry through this correlate of his self-purpose under any and all circumstances, *or* if he does not carry it through, then when he abandons the correlate he abandons his purpose for himself at the same time. The one alternative is as impossible as the other. God cannot compel man to take part in his community. . . . It is just as impossible, however, to conceive that God should cease to be himself, which would logically follow upon his abandoning his purpose for himself. This unacceptable consequence is the result, therefore, of the unacceptable presupposition.[12]

True! Except that the unacceptable presupposition is my opponent's and not mine! If he had read my presentation fully, instead of reading only one paragraph and stopping before he got to the following comments, then he could have seen (cf. *R.u.V.*, III (2nd ed.), 265. *ET*, section 34) that (in accordance with the testimony of Christ and the well-established experience that rests on faith in him) I presuppose the kingdom of God in the community of Christ as being in some sense real when I speak of the relation between the

love of God and the men who are united in the kingdom of God.
For I have derived the description of God as love only from the
knowledge which Christ has mediated to his community. If my
opponent deceives himself that I spoke in this connection *a priori*, in
the sense of a hypothesis, then he subsumes me under a heading
diametrically opposed to that which I truly represent. These two
absurd alternatives, which he wishes to place upon me, grow only
out of his presupposition that I choose a starting point for my theology as untenable as the one he has chosen for his.

And what does he gain from his own hypothesis of the absolute
by way of contributing a resolution of the difficulty which he has
fashioned from the two impossible consequences of his misunderstanding of my teaching? He says:

> Things take on an entirely different form when we take the creation's
> being-for-God up into God's being-for-himself as an expression of his
> absoluteness and then establish on this basis the love of God which is
> included in the divine being. For here, then, there is an implicit insist-
> ence that man's being-for-God can and must actualize itself even when
> he sets himself against *the loving will of God, which itself exists in
> man's being created for God.* For even the repression of the sinner
> under the divine ordinance against his will is the realization of his
> being-for-God; this being-for-God must come to the fore, for the sake
> of God's absoluteness, even when it cannot do so in the form of a
> voluntary being-for-God to which God's loving will relate itself.

When one grasps this line of reasoning, he may indeed be astonished.
Frank attempts to incorporate the thrust of mankind's tendency
toward the absolute within the concept of the absolute as that concept serves as the basic formulation for God. But how is this possible, since every relationship to another is excluded from the concept
of the absolute, including also every relationship of another to the
absolute itself? For in this case a reciprocal relationship is indicated
over against which the absolute excludes itself. This is no exercise in
consistency but merely a play on words. But let us go on! Is it possible for my opponent to think that the loving will of God lies in the
thrust of mankind toward the absolute? What a strange way to
express oneself! What expectations this lays on the powers of the
imagination! Is the attribute of love for God equivalent to the concept of mankind's thrust toward God? Or is it set forth as a direct

correlate of this thrust? I do not know. Toward what kind of a theologian is this assertion directed? I take the liberty simply to reject such theological instruction. What it amounts to for my opponent, however, is this. He combines the thrust of mankind toward the absolute with the absolute itself, that is, with the isolated object (that possesses no qualities) which he equates with God. He does this in order to make the attributes of love and legal righteousness into correlates of equal value with the freedom of the created spirits, so that he can hang them like alternately coordinated characteristics on both arms of the great "X" which is the appropriate image of his idea of the absolute. With this, he opens our eyes to another chapter of natural theology which really does not exist. I decline this opportunity, however, to go into the question of God's recompensing righteousness and the covenant of works.

III

It is understandable that one would make use of metaphysical concepts, assigning to them the highest priority in systematic theology, if he understands the task of systematic theology to be the harmonization of Christian revelation, that is, the Christian world view, with that comprehensive secular world view which is thought to be preeminent because it claims to be both universal and rational. But the preceding discussion has shown that such an attempt in systematic theology is, by its very nature, a rationalistic misuse of reason in theology which diminished the value of the knowledge of God that we obtain from revelation—even though both Luthardt and Frank may affirm or demand such an attempt. Moreover, this is Luther's judgment also, as may be seen in the above-cited passage from Luthardt. It is more difficult to understand the supposition of metaphysical concepts in the interpretation of certain Johannine passages where Christ speaks of his unity with God the Father (cf. John 10:30; 17:11; 21:22). I am not referring to the interpreters old and new who impose dogmatic propositions upon every passage that even faintly echoes them as they expound the biblical writings. Calvin has already protested such practices, in comments on John 10:30:

> The ancients misuse this passage when they prove that Christ was consubstantial with the Father. For Christ did not dispute about the unity

of substance, but rather, concerning the unity of mind that he had with the Father; whatever is clearly performed by Christ is confirmed by the goodness of the Father.[13]

Heeding this admonition, Friedrich Lücke, August Meyer,[14] and Luthardt understood the meaning of Jesus' saying in accordance with its context, that Jesus here clarified the equality of his power with God's, and, as Meyer rightly adds, in qualification, this equality lies in the unity of activity in carrying out the redemptive will of God. But this exposition of Meyer is accompanied by another comment which reintroduces the interpretation just discarded: "The homoousion is *presupposed* as the essential basis of this communion between the Son and the Father, because of the metaphysical relationship of the Son to the Father which is clearly attested, particularly by John." Luthardt considers this postscript to be correct, inasmuch as he attaches similar reflections to his interpretation of the text. These two also agree in their exposition of John 17:11, 21, 22, that the unity between the Father and the Son, as it is compared with the unity of the faithful among themselves, pertains not only to the will and disposition but designates beyond that something that is different and higher. As Luthardt expresses it:

> The Father and the Son should be the element in which the faithful live and move in a mystical union (*unio mystica*). . . . The faithful are not only united with the Father and the Son in their will and disposition, but rather, in their *own actual being*, without ceasing nevertheless to be creaturely and sinful.

It is very easy to write such a thing and let it be published, but it is very difficult for others to understand it and more difficult still to accept it as a true representation of the ideas Jesus had in mind. These few statements of Luthardt appear to me as so many unbearable burdens which the author himself will not even lift a finger to help us carry. I am to imagine that my will—that is, my disposition in which I form my purposes and designs and which calls forth and directs my activity in the community of the faithful, my will which moves itself in the direction of God and his purpose—I am to imagine that all of these are not actually my own being, but are really only a derived and apparent being! Indeed, in the light of this being which is unreal and not my own (according to Luthardt) I know myself, exercise my responsibility, have the feeling of my own distinctiveness and worth. And, in relationship to this being, I rebuke myself before God or experience my blessedness. But I know nothing about this thing Luthardt calls my "actual and authentic being," that is, my metaphysical being. I experience nothing of it and cannot orient myself according to it. And Luthardt himself cannot teach me anything about it, since he too knows nothing of it. Further, it is said that "the Father and the Son are the *element* in which the faithful live and move: *unio mystica.*" I would demand an explanation of the word "element," if I were not further enlightened as to his meaning by the term *unio mystica*, which Luthardt attaches as a synonym. As a "repristinating theologian,"[15] he undoubtedly intends the concept, a feature of seventeenth century Lutheran dogmatics, to be predicated of every individual believer. Thus, after justification, the Trinity takes residence in the believer with the proviso that this *unio cum patre, filio et spiritu sancto* [union with the Father, Son, and Holy Spirit] is neither *substantialis* [substantial] nor *personalis* [personal] but, rather, *mystica* [mystical], which is to say, indeterminable. This means that one should not think of this unity, as did Philipp Nicolai,[16] as one in which the believer is amalgamated with God into one cake or lump and thus partakes of divine nature, nor should one assume, as did Stephen Praetorius,[17] that the believer is divinized and therefore can rightly say that he is Christ. I assume that I am dealing, in these distinctions, pertinently with the idea Luthardt expresses in *unio mystica.*[18] According to his view, therefore, our Lord Christ had in mind this concept of *unio mystica*, as we have defined it, since he did not apply the unity of the believers to their disposition as such, analogous to his substantial unity with the Father, but rather to their actual and authentic being and only by implication from that to their disposition. If these remarks do not deal pertinently with the author's meaning, then I can only complain that he does not speak clearly.

Therefore, I shall recapitulate here Luthardt's probable meaning on the basis of the two assertions which are not fully in accord with each other but, rather, which are ranged against each other. The will, even though it is orderly and stable in its disposition, whether for good or evil, and is necessarily accompanied by a corresponding cognition and governing self-consciousness, still does not set forth the actual and authentic being of a man. Since this is true of the will, we must also say that the unity of the believer with the Son and the Father, patterned after the unity between God the Father and his Son, is not to be understood in terms of the unity of will that exists among all men in the purpose which the Son (and in him, the Father) carries out in establishing the redemption of the believers. Rather, this unity between the believer and the Son and the Father is to be understood as a more significant reciprocity between these parties, and this reciprocity, which lies behind the volitional unity, is neither an identity of essence nor of personal life but an identity which, according to its nature, is indeterminable, that is, the *unio mystica.* In this line of reasoning we observe that a metaphysical distinction is placed between the unreal, inauthentic being of spiritual persons (which is equated with will and disposition) and their real being which is posited only for the sake of the concept which Luthardt esteems so highly, the *unio mystica cum tota sancta trinitate* [mystical union with the complete Holy Trinity]. The saying of Christ is explained on the basis of the religious concept of the *unio mystica* and not directly in a metaphysical manner even though the explanation is analogous to the metaphysical distinction between the authentic and inauthentic reality of man. These ideas of the metaphysical and the religious are ranged against each other but they share one common ground, they are both totally unclear. The only thing we experience in the "real and authentic being" of man is that it does not consist in his disposition. What can we say of the *unio mystica?* I can only assume—in line with the older dogmaticians—that our proponent means that the *unio mystica* is to be conceived of neither as *substantialis* nor as *personalis.* Therefore, if the *unio mystica* is the key to understanding this saying of Christ, then metaphysics is not the direct criterion of Luthardt's interpretation of it at all. Thus one cannot perceive here a misuse of metaphysics which compares to that noted in earlier examples of his theology.

Indeed, there is such a close relationship between mysticism and *this kind* of metaphysics that it is immaterial whether one counts certain affirmations as mysticism or as false metaphysics. In order to perceive this one must define mysticism in its original sense and scope as a method of religious life and yearning, rather than in the special formulas of the later Lutheran dogmaticians. In the mystical method, the important thing is to go beyond the individuality of the spiritual life which maintains itself in discursive knowledge and in ethical action that contributes to the common good. Rather, one must transport oneself to the realm of one's real and authentic being. This is to be achieved when one loses himself, either through theoretical intuition or through the negation of one's own will, in the universal being which is considered to be God. The only conceptual scheme in which this process is intelligible is the neoplatonic with its deprecation of all particular, determinate being and life in favor of universal being. Thus, according to the criterion of universal being, the particular and determinate are predominately deceptive and unreal whereas the universal being is the real, with the added meaning of being authentic. Therefore, a manner of life which bases itself on this understanding will consequently lead one to conclude that his goal is the dissolution of his own distinctiveness into universal being. Hence, mysticism is the practice of the neoplatonic metaphysics, and this metaphysics is the theoretical norm of the so-called mystical enjoyment of God. But it is a deception to believe that the universal being into which the mystic wants to melt is God. For the only consonance between the idea of God and the concept of the universal, indeterminate being lies in this, that God is not the world and that the universal, indeterminate being is the negation of all those characteristics by means of which we know the world which fills our perceptions. At the same time, we may say that the neoplatonic God is also the idea of the world; and as such it is the universal, colorless scheme in which all particularities and interrelations of things are eliminated but which, as an idea in the Platonic sense, is nevertheless set forth as the real, authentic being.

Gottfried Arnold has rendered a most noteworthy witness to the collapsing of this sort of metaphysics into practical mysticism.[19] For example, at one point, he shows in parallel columns the three paths to the secret knowledge of God according to the instructions of the books of the most all-wise King Solomon.

The secret learning of God, belonging to the *path* which unites, illumines, and *reconciles*, is taught, respectively, in Proverbs, Ecclesiastes, and *Song of Songs*. . . . In like manner, there is a threefold love of wisdom, *Ethica, Physica*, and *Metaphysica* which deals with morals or external works, with natural things, and with *spiritual matters.* In such a manner Solomon would teach love of wisdom in his position as an ethical teacher who deals with virtues and would instruct his children as a father; as a teacher of natural things he would differentiate things according to their natures and as a physician would heal the sick; similarly, as a teacher of supernatural things *he points to the divine and as a learned man of God would lead men to God. . . .* That teaching which Solomon considered most necessary was how to live peacefully in the world, despise the vain and unworthy, *and through love to enter into communion with God. . . .* So that man might know how to live well in the world and to subject the world, after he had recognized it, to himself, *that he might ascend to the embrace of the bridegroom.*

These juxtapositions continue for ten pages. Nevertheless, I have the following comments to add to the statements just cited. Metaphysics and mysticism were identified by Arnold; and ethics was subordinated to them as the most elementary and least valuable stage of knowledge and practice. Indeed, even physics was placed above ethics. Meanwhile, one also recognizes that the combination of the second stage of wisdom with the Preacher Solomon is related to the rejection of the natural world in asceticism in accordance with his saying, "All is folly." Therefore, if the first stage is meant to be *natural* morality, then it is clear why he ranks asceticism above it, since asceticism is the rejection of the natural. Then the second stage is, at the same time, characterized by man's *knowing how to subordinate the world to himself*, since this ascetical predicate is excluded from the ethical life of the first stage. I would here refer incidentally to my description of the ethical determination of man in Christianity. In keeping with the concept of the kingdom of God, I emphasize the supernatural and supramundane character of man's ethical calling, and I have expressly shown how the believer exercises spiritual dominion over the world in accordance with his justification through faith.[20] Thus I deplore the fact that Luthardt, in his reproach of my "moralizing interpretation" of Christianity which he considers erroneous, thereby also loses the ability to distinguish between natural morality on the one hand and supernatural, world-dominating piety and ethical action on the other. In comparison, however, I do not find the so-called higher metaphysical path to mystical union a more valuable method than this ethical life-style [*Lebensführung*] which I characterize as Christian, nor do I recognize the mandate of Christianity in the goal of mystical union.

I return now to Christ's saying whose exposition gave rise to these controversies. Why have Meyer and Luthardt not simply contented themselves to explicate the unity of the apostolic community (identical with the unity of the Son with the Father) in terms of its basis in a common purpose of the will or disposition? Why have they deliberately made its meaning unclear by mixing a metaphysical distinction and an unintelligible mystical formula? Because a mixing of metaphysical concepts is at hand in the Nicene definition of the relationship between the logos of God and God. This mixture rings in their ears and dominates all the impressions which they might have gotten from the scriptural manner of viewing things, even though they are obligated to expound this point of view in the context of scripture's own terms. Thus, when less clear sayings present themselves in a piece of scripture, as in the Johannine witness to the unity of Christ with God, then these passages are to be clarified by comparing them with parallel sayings which are clear in their own way. Meyer has done this with John 10:30, where he explains the unity of Christ with God in terms of the identity of their working for man's salvation. But it is interesting to note that he fails, at the same time, to go into the passage in which this thought first appears, namely, 4:34, and he only notes the later expression in 17:4. Meyer's interpretation of 4:34 transposes the metaphorical expression "food" in the following sense: "It is my pleasure to carry out the work of God." But it is much more appropriate to the context if one says: "Carrying out the work of God *is the means by which I maintain myself.*" Luthardt has not interpreted this passage at all; he has simply designated it as full of meaning. He can hardly hold it against me, therefore, if I use it as the key for the interpretation of the less clear sayings of the Lord. For the Son's unity with the Father, or the coinherence of both [*Ineinandersein*] should indeed designate something real. Within a person's life, however, reality cleaves to his spiritual activity and to nothing else. And he who can honestly say of himself that the total activity of his vocation is the work of God can demonstrate this alleged unity with God in his life-work [*Lebenswerk*]. Therefore, the ethical perspective still obtains here. If anyone recognizes in what I have just said something that is unworthy of the divine level of Christ's self-consciousness, then he must hold to Arnold's understanding of the conditions of the will; namely, that the will can be conceived only as the bearer of natural morality. Meanwhile, it is precisely from Christ himself as he appears in all of the Gospels, that we learn that under his guidance the human will is destined to grasp the supramundane goal which corresponds to the cosmic purpose of God as he set it forth in Christ, namely, the salvation of man. The overcoming of the world which Christ designates as the accomplishment of his own life is the proof that his solidary unity with God is actual in his will, to which he holds fast even under the opposition of the God-defying tendency of the world. This conclusion corresponds to the exposition of Christ's words in John and it takes as its criterion the context itself.

What would it mean if one understood the passages in question metaphysically? Metaphysical concepts are the elementary cognitions in which one determines the objects of cognition as such, as things in general, in their isolation and moreover in their given positions vis-à-vis each other. In this way of looking at things, one avoids the task of distinguishing whether objects of cognition are nature or spirit. Therefore, the metaphysical method only allows one to perceive spiritual entities superficially, incompletely, and not in their distinctiveness. If Christ, therefore, in the sayings which lie before us, designates the unity he shares with God as that which actually exists between him, a spiritual person, and God, who is spirit and will, then (of necessity) he did not practice a metaphysical way of thinking. Nor should we think that Christ was capable of ordering his self-consciousness according to the categories of metaphysical and ethical knowledge; for he was certainly not a philosopher. And even if he were such, or were to be compared with philosophers, it would be absurd to attribute such distinctions to him. For even a philosopher, if he is a wise man, will not express the distinctive self-awareness, by which he knows himself, in metaphysical concepts as such, nor will he express himself by blending the images by which he designates himself as a spiritual person with metaphysical concepts.

From the point of view I am representing here, that classification is also valid which includes the unity among the disciples with the

unity that exists between the Son and the Father. Both of those interpreters note Johann Bengel's saying in reference to John 17:11: *Illa
unitas est ex natura, haec ex gratia; igitur illi haec similis est, non
aequalis* [That unity is one of nature, this one, of grace; therefore,
this one is similar to that unity, not equal].[21] Neither interpreter
could understand this comment to mean that the one unity is metaphysical, whereas the other is ethical; for both are metaphysical
according to Meyer and Luthardt. But I would be able to appropriate
Bengel's comment when I interpret both instances of the unity
ethically. That which pertains to Christ is *ex natura* ["of nature"]
insofar as Christ is presented to our cognition in that communion
with God which remains constant and without change; so that what
he performs in his life (*sein Lebenswerk*) is the work of God. To
the degree that a man wants to be a Christian, he has this datum
which he must acknowledge as given: the relationship to God which
is expressed by Christ and sustained by him through his death and
resurrection. One must avoid all attempts *to go behind this datum*,
that is, to determine in detail how it has come into being and
empirically how it has come to be what it is. These attempts are
superfluous because they are ineffectual; and it is dangerous to give
oneself to these attempts since they are superfluous. The corresponding unity of the community with Christ and God, however, is *ex
gratia* ["of grace"] because in the community we only see men who,
in themselves, cannot give testimony to this unity with God. Moreover, in themselves, these men give the appearance of changeableness
which is not present in the given appearance of Christ, thereby indicating that this unity can only be accounted for through God's grace.

IV

In their presentation of the dogmatic teaching about God and
in their exegesis of the Johannine Gospel, I have shown that my
opponents are guilty of an improper and unsuitable use of metaphysics. Their exegetical work also brought before us the use of a
false metaphysics. This false metaphysics was mixed in with their
exegesis only because my opponents dispersed it over the entire
range of their theological perception. I do not think that Luthardt
has paid attention to this fact, since he has counted it an error in
my work that I eliminate all metaphysics from theology. But his

aversion to my theology and his inability to judge it justly arises from the fact that I use a different epistemology and the way I grasp the object of knowledge is different from his work, which represents what has been established and handed down. Because I determine the contents of theology in a manner to which he is not accustomed, he cannot understand why I teach many things that have not occurred to him, and why I leave many things aside on which he sets great value. And my relationship with him is similar to my relationships with many others. Therefore I am all the more interested in demonstrating that the metaphysics and, specifically, the ontology (i.e., the use which one makes of the concept of that which is the object of knowledge) which I use differ from that of my opponents. And, at the same time, I will also demonstrate that my opponents, in that they represent the theological tradition, utilize a false epistemology. In addition, it will hopefully become clear that when they allege that they surpass me in their concern for Christianity, it is only a deception which mirrors their unexamined faith in a false epistemology.

There is a commonplace view of the things we know which, upon closer examination, is shown to suffer from an error, namely, that it is uncertain in its ability to make distinctions as well as premature in its tendency to unify things. In this commonplace view, the impressions [*Empfindungen*] mediated through our senses [*Sinne*] are the first and last guarantee that the things we perceive through the sensations [*Empfindung*] they excite are actually present or real. And this view is held in spite of the fact that we deceive ourselves in many of the perceptions which accompany our sensory experience [*Empfindungen*] and which subsequently even confirm these deceptions. We consider that things we perceive and sense are real even when we can only recollect our sense-impressions [*Empfindungen*] of them from our memory, because we justifiably assume that others have had perceptions just like ours in the meantime. And it is precisely at this point that the commonplace view draws the conclusion that the things which are present to us can be grasped as they are *in themselves* through subsequent precise representation and study. This fixed distinction between things as they are in themselves outside any relation to our sense-impressions [*Empfindung*] and perception and their existence *for us* is the first error of the commonplace view. Because things are separated here which, in the light of the origin of the process of knowing, belong together.

In addition to the relationships in which we perceive the existence of things generally, there also belongs (necessarily and unfailingly) the relation of those things to us as subjects of the acts of receiving sense-impressions, perceptions, and mental images. And even though a person can forget this additional relationship in many instances, it should never go unheeded in scientific reflections, i.e., precise and complete reflections. For things which we might posit and define for experimental purposes, in and of themselves but not in their relation to us, are necessarily unknowable to us. Yet a person conceals this truth from himself when he thinks that in the relationship of things to us there is only a mass of false, deceiving appearances, and when he tries to guard himself from these appearances by grasping things in and of themselves, as they exist for themselves. But indeed, by this procedure, one is really only yielding again to the appearance, namely, that in the relationship of things to us, there is always deception and only false appearance.

Now even if it were taken for granted that the above were correct, it could not be verified; there could be no criterion for judging the matter. But one quickly ascertains the reliability of appearance (admittedly, a limited reliability) when, in several different instances, the consensus of many persons' perceptions establishes that things are indeed what they have appeared to be to us. And if God belongs to the objects of cognition of scientific theology, then there is no satisfactory basis for the claim that one can teach something about God in himself, something that is allegedly knowable for us apart from his revelation which, however it is fashioned, is sensed and perceived by us. Yet this claim is made by my opponents. By Frank when he pretends to think of God as the absolute; by Luthardt (in section 29 of the work referred to above) when he teaches about the characteristics of God's nature *in itself* which, he thinks, can be known prior to those attributes of God that are efficacious for us. In these instances, therefore, they adhere to the false metaphysics of the commonplace level of human reason, a metaphysics which is not scientific truth, even though it has found its place in the textbooks of metaphysics since the time of Christian Wolff.[22]

The second error of the commonplace view of things lies in the fact that the image we form in our memory, in which we fix the repeated perceptions of a thing, does not take into account certain alterations which we have subsequently perceived from time to time in that very thing. The recollected image [*Erinnerungsbild*] is attached to the thing through intentional abstraction from the changing appearances of the thing. Under such circumstances, the recollected image asserts a solidity and clarity in the ordering of its characteristics which does not correspond precisely to any of the individual observations in which the thing was originally given to our perceptions. Yet the essential characteristics of the thing, characteristics in which it exists as actual in distinction from the accidental characteristics in which it appears as changeable, are ascribed to this recollected image. In our original sense-impressions we persuaded ourselves both of the reality of the thing itself and of the reality of its changing appearances [*Affectionen*]; the sense-impressions are aroused within us by these appearances, and we compensate for their changeableness by means of the continuity of our own self-consciousness. Now the placid image of a thing in one's memory certainly does not stimulate the kind of sense-impressions that we actually receive from the appearances themselves as they strike our senses. Yet an interest, a feeling for the value of the thing, attaches itself to the recollection. The recollected image preserves this interest so that it directs, abbreviates, and facilitates future observations of the recollected thing. This feeling for the value of a thing, in one's recollection of it, is then made equal with the sense-impression which originally authenticated the reality of the thing in its immediate perception. And so ordinary human reason carries with it two kinds of impressions of the reality of a thing; and as long as this reason continues in its conventional manner, it does not take time to scrutinize them precisely and fully. But if on this level of cognition one is led to undertake a comparison between the immediate perception of a thing and the image of that thing in one's memory, that is, between the perceptible changeableness of the thing in its appearances and the solid and clear delineations of the recollected image, then the way is open, under such circumstances, for him to observe an error in his cognition. A person entertains the recollected image in a dimension which lies behind the circumstances in which the immediate perception of the thing unfolds. Thus he separates all those aspects of the perceived object which stimulate our senses directly from the characteristics which make our recollection firm and clear. We can conceive of that which stimulates our sensibilities in no other way except as the relationship, movement, and activity of the thing itself. Therefore, we can justifiably posit a thing as real only as it stands before us in the realm of appearance. We must judge our recollected image—which we have placed in a realm "behind" the thing—to be unreal to the extent and in the sense that its placidity and indifference hold it aloof from the activity of our senses. Yet, in these circumstances, ordinary reason makes its judgments as if the thing whose recollected image carries with it both placidity and indifference were actually presented in that fashion to us in the *moment* that our sensibilities were stimulated by the movements which we perceive in the "front realm." Nevertheless, the discrepancy between the "back realm" position of the recollected image and the "front realm" position of the thing as it stands in the flux of time does not at all permit us to transfer the characteristics of the thing to its recollected image. For in the arrangement of the momentary and the lasting realms, one behind the other, the two images of the same thing are bound to be opposed to each other despite all their similarities. Thus the one realm is dynamic, changeable, and possessed of efficacy, while the other is placid, indifferent, and without relationship to anything else. Therefore a contradiction results when a thing, presupposed to be placid, indifferent, and powerless in our recollection, is at the same time represented as moved and moving, changing and alterable. Such inconsistencies do not matter to unscientific thought. But it is insidious when this false combination of recollected image and direct perception of things is also found in scientific metaphysics. For the assumption that one can know things in themselves, i.e., spatially "behind" and temporally "before" their appearance, is nothing but a deceptive distortion of the recollected image which one acquires "behind" the first observations and which he carries with him "before" subsequent observations. The recollected image is overvalued or improperly cherished when a person substitutes it for the actual reality of a thing, even though we rightly treasure it because it serves to simplify and stabilize our cognition. I will grant that the solidity and clarity which the image bears in itself seem to justify themselves since these characteristics bid fair to satisfy the drive for cognition. But there are, on the other hand, other aspects of the recollected image, namely pallor and indeterminacy, which stand over against the apparent solidity and clarity and frustrate them as warrants of its reality.

What I have been designating here is that element of cognition whose generalization forms Plato's doctrine of ideas. In his meaning of the term "idea," the recollected image is the generic concept for a multiplicity of things that are similar in most of their characteristics and are, therefore, of the same kind. Nevertheless, these generic concepts that we form are held to be the real things. In relation to these concepts, the things of sense-perception exist only insofar as they participate in the ideas. These eternal primal images of all individual existence exist purely for themselves, in the locus of the mind, accessible only to thought, and untouched by the alterations of those things that only participate in them. Individual things are only the shadow-images of the ideas. The ordering of the ideas (only hinted at and yet maintained as a postulate) expressed Plato's difference from the Eleatic philosophy which held that the being which was most real was constituted by a plurality within unity rather than by an undifferentiated unity. However, the idea of the good, which orders the plurality of ideas, does not refer to the morally good but rather to the first cause and final purpose. This world view perpetuates the same errors that are indicated in our treatment of ordinary human reason. Plato leads us precisely to the point of thinking about the thing in itself, quite apart from its individual appearance for us. He posits further that these things-in-themselves are the causes of the behavior which attaches to the individual things since the individual things exist only insofar as they participate in the ideas. Granted, this is quite unclear, but lack of clarity is not in contradiction to the tendency of this entire world view. Historically, this world view grew out of the challenge to guide cognition between the sophistical assertions of the Eleatics that all reality is only simple being and the principle of the Heracliteans that all reality is only the flux of appearances. But Plato's answer to this problem does not precisely determine the relation between cognition and being. For we must amplify the statement that ideas are only generalized images of the memory by observing that these images become more and more dim and imprecise and even, in themselves, uncertain, to the extent that they are called upon to include more and more specimens or subspecies. Is the idea of an apple a solid and clear representation? The generic characteristics of size, shape, color, taste, inner structure, etc., must always be represented in a limited but sliding scale. It is self-deception therefore to expect that one can achieve a solid and clear cognition in the concept of genus. To the extent, however, that a person purifies a generic concept of the fluctuation within it and gives to it contours that are solid and clear—to that extent one can be certain that the concept is only a shadow-image of the actual thing in our memory and that no reality belongs to it. But this understanding is just the opposite of the Platonic assertion that individual things are the shadow-images of the ideas. Accordingly, the concept of universal, undifferentiated, indeterminate, and boundless being which Plutarch, Philo, and the neoplatonists posit as God is nothing but the shadow of the world. This confusion is to be attributed to the Greeks, since they were never able to differentiate with certainty between the mundane and the divine. To a lesser extent, the confusion can be attributed to Philo the Jew. I shall not comment again here on the fact that Christian theologians persist in this same confusion as warrant for the Christian cognition of God.

The representation of a thing arises out of the different sense-impressions which attach themselves in a certain order to something which fixes perception in a limited space. We posit the apple as round, red, and sweet because the impressions of the senses of touch, sight, and taste attach themselves to the place where the corresponding relationships of form, color, and taste are perceived. It is precisely from these relationships which converge in the same place in repeated perceptions that we focus the representation of a thing. A thing "exists" in its relationships and it is only in them that we can know the thing and only by them that we can name it. The significance of the relation of these characteristics, ascertained through sense-impressions and expressed in the judgment, "This thing is round, red, and sweet," is that we get to know the subject of this sentence only in its predicates. If it were possible for us to let these predicates drop from our sight or for us to forget them, then the thing with which we were acquainted under these characteristics would also fall out of our cognition. There is no reason at this elementary level of the formation of the concept of a "thing" for us to posit the thing and its characteristics (sensed and perceived together) in two dimensions, one behind the other and separate from each other; nor is it necessary to assert that it is possible to know the thing "behind" its characteristics or "before" the naming of those characteristics. But, there is also no occasion for attempting to amplify the concept of "thing," by saying that we learn to understand the characteristics of a thing as the apparent functions of a cause [*Ursache*] and as instruments of a purpose [*Zweck*], or that even though a thing's characteristics are perceived as variable up to a certain point the whole is seen as functioning in the orderly variation of its qualities, or that, finally, a law can be conjectured from the perceived history of a thing. Rather, the thing is the cause of its functions and the purpose governing the orderly succession of its apparent variations.

The impression that the perceived thing is one despite the variation of its characteristics arises from the continuity of the self-consciousness within the succession of sense-impressions which the thing arouses in us (cf. above, p. 166). Furthermore, the comprehension of a thing as cause and purpose of itself emerges from the certainty that I am cause and purpose of the functions that I myself originate. We would do no violence to the evidence that is obtained from perceiving a thing in its characteristics and recognizing its reality in its effects upon us (in accordance with which we judge the thing in itself) and upon other things with which its effects stand in reciprocal relations—to repeat, we would do no violence to this evidence unless we indulge in an improper use (described above) of the individual recollected image of a thing and its universalization in the concept of genus. But a person teaches something that is contrary to the evidence and incomprehensible when he uses the analogy which the common understanding is wont to use. When he does use that analogy, he follows the direction of Plato's thought by positing the thing as pure being or as a reality without properties, to which one only accidentally and subsequently attaches its relations and its specific properties, in order to establish the thing clearly and solidly and to guard it against the disturbances of the variations which are perceived in it by our senses. Furthermore, such thinking introduces a kind of conception which is akin to myth. Myth represents things

of nature as bearers of spiritual life. False metaphysics holds that pale
and wavering recollected images of generic concepts are real. And
even though these images and concepts have been relegated to a state
of motionlessness through the scaling off of all the conditioning elements associated with concrete functioning, a kind of intentionality is
attributed to them under indeterminable circumstances in order to
ascribe a functioning to these images and concepts that was previously
expressly denied to them. And this functioning is to be understood
as constituting no variation in the things, since it is posited as accidentally related to the things that are motionless in themselves, since
they always remain in themselves the same. This whole line of reasoning is neither consistent nor clear. It is completely foreign to our concrete behavior in regard to things of nature and spiritual persons. This
behavior is never guided by such abstractions but always by the
evidence that the individual apple we eat is real and that the man
we get to know through the direction of his will and the states of his
self-consciousness is himself. There is no being "behind" these
appearances of the man that is somehow more authentic to him or
more real, which has to be taken into consideration in order for us
to understand him and assume a meaningful relation to him. Nevertheless, the false metaphysics to which this distinction of Luthardt
(between a thing and its appearances) belongs, carries within itself
a force of prejudgment, a fact to be considered in view of the presentation of ontology in the *Metaphysics* of Lotze, which proceeds in
a constant refutation of that assumption. I will use the following
quotation from this work as a conclusion to my effort to clarify the
issue:

> Metaphysics does not have the task of making reality, but, rather, of
> acknowledging it; it is the task of probing the inner ordering of what
> is given, not of deriving the given from what is not given. In order to
> meet this task, metaphysics must guard itself against the misunder-
> standing which regards the abstractions, through which metaphysics
> fixes the specific determinations of what is real for its own purposes, as
> positive and independent elements which can be used again, as they are,
> to construct the structure of reality. We have seen metaphysics fre-
> quently caught up in this misunderstanding: it formed a concept of
> pure being and gave a meaning to this concept that is cut off from all
> the relationships which alone show forth reality; it ascribed to a con-
> cept of reality, *per se*, which is without properties the reality that can

only belong to that which is fully conditioned; it spoke of laws which would stand as an imperious power between or outside the very things and events in which alone laws have real validity.[23]

V

Apart from the doctrine of God, Christian dogmatics offers no opportunity to set forth directly a metaphysical concept as if it were theological. All of the remaining theological themes are so specifically spiritual in nature that metaphysics can only come into play as the formal pattern for the cognition of religious entities or relationships. In view of this, every theologian, as a scientific worker, is under the necessity or obligation to proceed according to a certain epistemology of which he is himself aware and whose correctness he must demonstrate. Thus it would be ill-considered and unthinkable to assert that I would eliminate all metaphysics from theology. For if I am capable of working in theology in a scientific manner—and in general no one has yet contested that—then I must follow an epistemology which proceeds according to a concept of "things" in its determination of the objects of knowledge; that is, it proceeds metaphysically. Therefore, the question at issue between Luthardt and me can be formulated correctly only in the following manner: "Which metaphysics is justified in theology?"

The theory of knowledge which can claim to hold a dominant place in the theological tradition is the Platonic, in which everything is deduced from above by means of general concepts. My opponent represents this position whereas I have given it up. The above discussions against Frank have demonstrated adequately that he and Luthardt have subordinated the knowledge of the God and Father of our Lord Jesus Christ to an idea, to a general concept which is called the Absolute, Substance, that is, Thing or Object. The conventional form of dogmatics teaches that one knows God as the subject of characteristics that are in and of themselves inert; this, in turn, enables them to focus their attention next on a presentation of God in his actions toward the world. Knowledge of Christ is subordinated to a general concept of his preexistent divinity, whose incongruity with the corresponding Johannine train of thought is clear; and then the futile attempt is made to authenticate the divinity of Christ in his historical existence. Furthermore, this dogmatics sets forth the concept of Christ's full person before it even brings that person to our attention through his distinctive works. When this dogmatics deals with the doctrine of sin, its general concept of sin is put forth as the passive, inherited corruption of human nature and afterwards actual sin is judged and clarified. Finally, the entire structure of this dogmatics is not oriented upon Christ as the bearer of revelation but, rather, upon the perfection of Adam; for sin is judged in reference to Adam's nature and the redeemer from sin is judged in reference to sin itself. Once again, the first men before the fall are understood only as the idea of man which is brought into existence through God's creation.

Within this method that I have outlined, we can account for the fact that Professor Hermann Weiss[24] of Tübingen recently rebuked me because I do not allow room in my theology for the *unio mystica*, that is, that I omit a demonstration of the direct personal unity of the believer with God.[25] For, he asserts, "the spirit is indeed not simple (that must mean: simply) will, but also a certain kind of being and living, and certainly herein it possesses an objective side that is akin to nature" (p. 410). In response to this assertion, intelligible to me in spite of its confusion, I can refer to what I have said concerning the same assertion by Luthardt in regard to John 17. This most recent opponent continually misinterprets or distorts my assertions, despite his efforts to understand me, since, as a quasi platonist, he wants to understand the issues "from above" through general concepts before he gives himself to the scrutiny of individual entities as they actually exist. In an article published a few years ago, "The Christian Idea of the Good," he dealt first with the idea of the Good in general and only subsequently with the Christian idea of Good. I remember very clearly the error into which the author fell because of this approach. The "Good in general" cannot be described except, perhaps, in a pale, indeterminate fashion which stands neutrally over against all determinate forms and stages of ethical communities that have appeared in the course of history. Since Weiss needed to bring more concrete phenomena into this part of his article, he transposed a mass of Christian interpretations of the Good into the framework of the Good in general. I cannot trust the author of such a theological work to have the necessary predisposition to understand my own style of theology since it rejects the method of proceeding from the realm of the universal which exists "up above." Accordingly, the picture of my position that he draws with his peculiar reasoning is only a caricature. Weiss always seeks only the conventional categories, and it is into these that he wants to squeeze me through his critique. He asserts that my presentation is inherently contradictory since I alternate in my description of the subjective religious processes between the perspective of divine grace and that of free human action (as if there were any other way!). He intimates that something like an objective nature can be identified behind free human action; a nature to which God can be directly and immediately present. It is upon precisely this metaphysical peg in the human spirit that he hangs the concept, determinative for him, of the *unio mystica*. He further alleges that this concept of the immediate personal relation of the believer to Christ is the truth which I deny. My reply to this is that the concept of the *unio mystica* is either unintelligible and impractical, as in the older dogmatics, or else it blots out the normal protestant confidence in salvation, as in pietism. Weiss asserts that it is evident that the well-known Pauline formulations and the Johannine farewell discourses compel a theologian to affirm the *unio mystica* as a truth necessary for salvation! I contest the evidence upon which this presupposition rests. I reject this use of scripture—a literalistic notation of certain passages without any attempt to interpret them, in order to stamp a favorite truth as necessary for salvation. In the light of such a procedure by an academic theologian, I cannot see how one could criticize or even be amazed at the way the anabaptists or the Russian Old Believers use the holy scriptures.[26] Indeed, it is clearly written: "What you hear whispered, proclaim upon the housetops" (Matt. 10:27); "If anyone comes to me and does not hate his own father and mother and wife and children . . . he cannot be my disciple" (Luke 15:26). Therefore, the anabaptists preached from the housetops, abandoned their families, and wandered about. It also stands written: "What comes out of the mouth, this defiles a man" (Matt. 15:11), and that we should "attain to the measure of the stature of the fullness of Christ" (Eph. 4:13). Therefore, the Starowerzen[27] refrained from smoking tobacco as a great sin and cared for their beards as if it were a command from Christ. I find the New Testament passages that Weiss applies literalistically as proof of the *unio mystica* no more compelling than the justification of these sectarian principles on the basis of the New Testament passages just cited.

It is either a remarkable coincidence that the same issue of *Studien und Kritiken* which contains Weiss's attack on me also presents an essay by C. F. Georg Heinrici[28] entitled *Zum genossenschaftlichen Charakter der paulinischen Christengemeinden* ["Concerning the Character of the Pauline Communities as Fellowships"], or else it is a testimony that my friend, the editor, follows no particular "party." For in this essay, following a contrary interpretation, the same controversy appears which figures in Weiss's objections to me, the controversy between a judgment based on universal concepts and the derivation of a broad perspective that emerges from the observation of the individual and the particular. Carl Christian Johann Holsten[29] is the representative of universal concepts in comprehending the situation of the Corinthian church, and Heinrici refutes both his method and his conclusions. Weiss and Holsten stand together harmoniously; and the same epistemology with which Weiss thought he could win the victory over me suffers a defeat at the hands of Heinrici. Holsten holds the following concept of the church:

> The nature of God should be brought to expression in the church; the transcendent power of God's spirit shapes the plurality of the believers in the church of God into an organic unity; therefore the church of God is an organism of God's spirit.[30]

But when Holsten undertakes to interpret the evidences contained in the Pauline letters concerning the situation in the Corinthian church according to this universal concept he finds, in Heinrici's estimate, that that church has asserted a formlessness which stands diametrically opposed to the unity which was asserted in principle. From the heights of his universal concept he has not recognized in which functions of the church's life the Holy Spirit is active and, therefore, present. As Heinrici (p. 515) summarizes his opponent's opinion, Holsten seems to be saying that it is much more important to understand that transcendent and ideal powers hover over a formless and unorganized aggregate of believers since "where the Spirit dwells in the hearts of the faithful, he also remains as a transcendent power." In opposition to such a position, Heinrici introduces the argument that if the Holy Spirit is not authenticated concretely in the harmonious and corporate movements and activities of the faithful, then his transcendent presence is fruitless and worthless. Weiss's argument against me is similar to Holsten's argument about the Corinthian church. He goes so far as to assert that I have simply wrenched the Holy Spirit out of the organic whole of Christian doctrine. Indeed, as he further alleges, I have conceived of the Holy Spirit as the ground of the common consciousness of God's sonship, as the motive and divine power of the church's supramundane religious and ethical life, and therefore as the necessary concrete determinant of Christian personhood! That is not enough for Weiss, and he misses the significance of these assertions for precisely the same reasons that Holsten does not recognize the functions of God's spirit in the church at Corinth: a preoccupation with the transcendence of that Spirit. Weiss triumphantly draws his conclusion out of my interpretation of the Holy Spirit: "Therefore, the Holy Spirit is in no sense something real or actual," etc. Naturally! What is real, in his sense, must be *asserted* before and quite apart from all its particular functioning. The Holy Spirit in man is set forth as real according to the same standard as that which asserts that "the human spirit is not just will, but, rather, also a certain kind of being and living, and, in this sense, possesses an objective side which it shares with nature." In this fog, spun out of the metaphysics and the physics of human spiritual life, one is supposed to be able to recognize the reality of the Holy Spirit. Furthermore, this fog is supposedly the place where the *unio mystica* is to be found *quite apart* from the given functions of the Christian life in which the Holy Spirit is grasped as something active and real. The Tübingen professor ought to test the order of his own concepts first before he criticizes someone else; particularly before he insinuates that I have deprived Christianity of one of the essential parts of its world view.

My opponents' charge (whether direct or indirect) that my theology devaluates Christianity is based on nothing else than their conviction that their own modes of knowledge are in solid agreement with Christianity. Their claim contains the indirect suggestion that I ought to accustom myself to their platonizing and mystical-metaphysical epistemology if my reputation as a theologian and my salvation are dear to me, since one cannot be saved in a Christianity that is devalued and mutilated. I reply that I have protected myself from the implied consequences of their reproaches by my continual willingness to criticize myself. Therefore, if my opponents are right in attacking me in the interest of Christianity, then I would have to resolve to acknowledge the customary universal concepts of theology and the derivation of particular perceptions from these concepts—terrible as that might sound—since those universal concepts authenticate at the same time the reality of the relationships which they designate. If I did not acknowledge those universal concepts, then I would not be a reliable theologian and Christian. But I find such a demand to be a deadly analogy to the talk of those men who in their own time came from Judea to Antioch saying, "If you do not permit yourself to be circumcised, you cannot be saved." For just as, in that instance, the particularity of a national custom was forced upon Christianity as a condition of its validity, so now the particularity of an epistemology is held up to me as the condition of the integrity and correctness of a theological presentation of Christianity and, as a consequence, a condition also of my own personal character as a theologian and a Christian. But the sacrifice which the Judaistic Christians demanded of the Gentiles and the *sacrificium intellectus* [sacrifice of the intellect] which I am supposed to offer have equally little in common with Christianity. For Christianity is neutral over against the differences between Jewish and Hellenistic customs, just as it is religiously neutral over against the different epistemologies through which its intellectual content might be scientifically ordered. Consequently, the collision between the different epistemologies which has occurred in the objections my opponents make against me can only be correctly judged as a scientific controversy, and this is the way I myself have understood it. The only result of Weiss's critique is to show that I theologize differently from the manner to which he is accustomed and that my theology is absurd when judged by the criteria of his beloved universal concepts. His efforts in this connection remind me of the treatment which the famous Procrustes gave his guests. Therefore I cannot acknowledge the comfortable bed of universal concepts as the rightful norm of my theological knowledge; rather, I find that

Weiss's treatment of my work is a kind of torture by which he suc-
ceeds in making my assertions give *him* a meaning different from that
which I intended and expressed. His example, Procrustes, was mani-
festly and without doubt gifted, but he was brutal at the same time;
in the realm of scientific knowledge these two characteristics flow
together to form sophistry.

Weiss and Luthardt give evidence of their metaphysical inclination in their joint assertion that the reality of the human spirit is
not to be grasped in its volition which, naturally, includes knowing
and the dominant feeling of self-consciousness but, rather, that one
must conceive of man's real and authentic being "behind," "under"
or "over" these functions in an objective form that is also proper
to nature. These two gentlemen have not clarified their thoughts any
more than this. They have not demonstrated that this conception of
man, this hovering mist, is reality; and, further, that it is a reality of
more persuasive power than the concrete functions in which every
man knows his own actuality, partly as experienced by him (i.e.,
passively) and partly as his own activity (i.e., actively). I do not
level any particular reproach against them for this; the circumstances
in which my own controverted assertions emerged did not allow
me to furnish any such proof either. Moreover, both of these men
intend only to assert the firm deposit of faith contained in tradition.
But the kind of proof I demand is one that they can never produce.
Such a proof would have to be carried out in a manner somewhat
analogous to the ontological proof for the existence of God. That is,
it would have to be a proof that representations of the nature of
man that are formed quite apart from all experience do nevertheless
correspond to reality by virtue of their universal and ambiguous content. I do not wish to take the lead over my opponents in formulat-
ing such a proof; rather, I put the challenge before them here and
now. But before they try to put off this responsibility in some proper
fashion, I will add this on the basis of the conditions that I have
already set forth for metaphysical knowledge: The elementary
knowledge that spiritual life is something real is only preparatory
to the knowledge of the distinctive character of spirit in the functions of feeling, knowing, and willing—chiefly, however, in willing.
Furthermore, one cannot authenticate the impact of others upon the
human spirit except in the context of active and conscious sense-

impressions [*Empfinden*] which comprise the raw material for the articulate self-consciousness of the "I." This raw material is the key to all knowing and the occasion for recognizing the motives of the will. Only in this realm of the actuality of the spiritual life can one understand the actions of God which furnish the basis for religion. But since we can only perceive God in his actions toward us, which correspond to his public revelation, so it is that we perceive God's presence for us precisely in these actions. Of course the evidence for this is different than it would be for individual sense-perceptions [*Sinneswahrnehmung*]. But this difference does not lie in the fact that sense-perceptions are immediate whereas the religious evidence of God's presence is frequently mediated. For even the simplest sense-perception which appears to common sense as immediate is actually a complex of sense-impressions and the faculty of judgment mediated through habit. Rather, the religious evidence for God's presence depends upon a connection of religious community and education with ethical self-formation and self-criticism. I shall not describe them here since my opponents can authenticate this for themselves if *they* wish. The historical side of this connection in religious experience also has its perceptible characteristics but these are so far removed from the act that I have in mind that they come into view as of secondary importance, even when one analyzes the matter in detail.

But it is precisely at this point that I encounter the sharpest criticism of my opponents. In their opinion, it is a defect of Christian conviction that I and others with me refer only to the effects of God or Christ[31] which the believer experiences in himself as a member of the community through the mediation of the preaching of the gospel. They say, rather, that one must be in possession of an unmediated personal relation to Christ our redeemer.[32] Against this opinion I dare to adduce the following in my defense. If one correctly conceives of effects, he conceives the cause in the effects. It is only the false judgment of popular common sense which asserts that a person places the causes in an imagined space "behind" the space in which he sees the appearances which he believes to be the effects of those causes or that he places the causes at an earlier point in time than the effects themselves. In these schemes, one does not really conceive of the perceived appearances as effects of those causes because these two concepts (i.e., cause and effect) properly stand in such a relation to each other that they can be referred to one another only within a unity of space or time. Our separation of these concepts in time and space is only a provisional operation of thought in which we establish firmly for ourselves the order of the relationships we have differentiated in our observation of the thing. Indeed, when we have once grasped the unity of a thing or the connections between things, we do away with the scheme which separates these elements spatially. Therefore, what we substantiate religiously as the activity of God or Christ within us authenticates the presence rather than the distance of the author of our salvation. And it does this according to the model of the relation that exists between persons. For God punishes me in remorse; Christ consoles me and gives me courage when I sense the worth of his example or when I direct myself toward the motives which, since they are focused and made actual for me in his person, make him the originator and perfecter of my salvation. If, in spite of this, my opponents should ascribe this admission simply to my subjective fancy, because it does not fall within the formulae of reality that are familiar to them, then things must rest as follows: They themselves posit pale and wavering images from their memory as the reality of things, and from them they have abstracted their universal concepts without any sort of proof, even when these universal concepts are themselves borrowed from some tradition.

On the contrary, when the human spirit orients itself toward those effective and worthwhile motives which give distinctive substance to its life, it appropriates those motives in the form of a precise and detailed recollection. This is a better way to understand the phenomenon of recollection. The self-consciousness of our actual spiritual life is thereby the sufficient ground for knowing the reality of all that which contributes to our reality, that is, to our worthwhile and effective existence in the world. The personal interrelationships of life are mediated, in particular, through precise recollection. Thus, for example, one person continues to be efficacious in the life of others and is therefore present to them when they act on the basis of education or other stimulation which they have derived from him. In the broadest sense, this is the case with the religious bond between our lives and God—mediated through the precise recollection of

Christ. But one should not consider such relationships to be immediate ones—particularly the relationship to God—else he is really
suggesting that they are imagined. For without mediation, nothing
is real. The personal relationship of God or Christ to us, however, is
and remains mediated through our precise recollection of the word,
i.e., of the law and the promise of God. And God works upon us
only through the one or the other of these revelations. The basic
assertion of the immediacy of certain perceptions and relationships
raises the question of distinguishing between reality and hallucina-
tion. Those who maintain the pretension of having an immediate
personal relationship to Christ or God are apparently not well-read
in the literature of mysticism. They could, for example, learn from
the nun Catherine of Genoa and from her description of her life
what sort of content is possible in the immediacy of relationship to
Christ which they maintain![33] Therefore, without the means of the
word of God as law and gospel and without the precise recollection
of this personal revelation of God in Christ, there is no personal
relation between a Christian and God. I want to clarify and justify
this correct and useful insight of the reformers by my comments. I
am not obligated to any other doctrine, nor am I justified in holding
to any other. Nevertheless, it is remarkable that a theologian like
Weiss should dare to judge me at this point according to his pietistic
pretensions whereas I should maintain my position along the line
laid down in the teachings of the reformation. It is even more
instructive, in the present confusion between pietistic and orthodox
tendencies, when a person can observe in a Lutheran who is considered to be correct that he lays considerable weight on his immediate personal relationship to Christ and that when he permits
himself to be greatly persuaded by it, he consequently betrays
Lutheranism and becomes an enthusiast.[34] This is precisely what is
so distressing and offensive about the contemporary situation of
theology and the church—that the flag of churchliness and confessional loyalty flies over so much pietistic cargo which does not belong
under that flag because it is of an opposing and conflicting nature.

The subtitle of Weiss's treatise, "Critical Survey, with Particular
Relationship to Ritschl's Theology," provides me a further opportunity to confirm that he himself has only cursorily surveyed the
emergence and structure of the later Lutheran doctrine of the *unio*

mystica, a doctrine which he wishes to retain and which I hold to be impractical. He recalls the conclusion of Matthias Schneckenburger (pp. 409–10), "who has recently fallen into a shameful obscurity and not been appreciated," that the Reformed and the Lutherans understood *unio mystica* in different ways. While it is true that I am not one of those who has forgotten Schneckenburger, I have nevertheless shown (*Geschichte des Pietismus,* I:167) that the Reformed theologian Jodocus van Lodensteyn[35] represented the same position which was first introduced into Lutheran theology by Justus Feuerborn[36] and Johann Hülsemann,[37] in the same way that Philipp Nicolai[38] and also Johann Arndt[39] and Balthasar Meisner[40] had previously enunciated it. Lucas Osiander the Younger[41] testified quite to the contrary in his writing against Arndt (1624), that up to that time Lutherans had understood the *unio mystica* to apply only to the image of the body and the members of Christ; that is, to the framework of the religious community, within which they conceive of the rebirth and continuance of faith in the individual believer. This means that before Arndt the Lutherans explained this matter exactly as Calvin did in the *Institutes* III, 1, 1 and 2, 30, 35.[42] And I know a few ascetical books before and after which confirm the same opinion. Thus it is precisely at this point that Schneckenburger's observation is neither complete nor correct. Rather, both explanations of the *unio mystica* (i.e., as referring to the believer's relationship with God and to his relationship with the church) appear in both Reformed and Lutheran understandings, and the Lutheran Meisner puts them in his academic lecture: "We are Christian together"—but he did not make it clear that the different perspectives do not coincide with each other. The *inhabitatio totius trinitatis* [the presence of the entire Trinity] as it is used for example in the Formula of Concord[43] and by Johann Gerhard[44] means nothing more than regeneration as a way of understanding good works. It is not until the work of Philipp Nicolai and Balthasar Meisner that the concept of this *unio mystica* took on the meaning of being the basis for the joyous mood of the faithful and for their royal and priestly character. Thus the effects which inherently correspond to justification by faith were carried over to the concept of the *unio mystica* and these same combinations of ideas were repeated by Johann Andreas Quenstedt[45] and Abraham Calov.[46]

This is the basis for asserting that this new doctrine was only later brought into competition with the doctrine of justification. For when one attends to Philipp Nicolai and Johann Arndt, he is persuaded that the original doctrine of the reformation was set aside and rendered practically ineffectual, in order to glorify the ambiguous and apocryphal concept of this *unio mystica*, which was supposed to authenticate blessedness. One can judge accordingly whether Luther's occasional use of mystical formulae establishes—as Weiss would have it—an attitude toward those formulae which is characteristic of the reformation. Did Luther base his reformation on the doctrine of justification by faith or on the doctrine of the *unio mystica*? The original formula of the *inhabitatio trinitatis* is without a doubt to be traced back to the thought of Andreas Osiander[47] where it is made the basis of active sanctification. It also has found a place in the Formula of Concord, III, 54 and, in the same sense, Philip Melanchthon[48] already acknowledged it in his *Postille*. Naturally, one could not acknowledge that this formula is the correct expression for justification; however, the image which it calls to mind of God's dwelling in believers seemed to be important enough that a formula which corresponds to this notion of God's indwelling should be permitted as an explanation of how sanctification follows upon the decree of justification. This tendency appeared first in the seventeenth century when Nicolai and Arndt, disregarding and opposing the Formula of Concord and reviving medieval modes of thought, appended the kinds of relationships to the *unio mystica* through which it was finally made into the doublet of the doctrine of justification, with the result that justification became simply a theoretical presupposition for it. Finally, Johann Arndt and, later, Christian Hoburg[49] and others explained the actuality of this union with God as referring to the tender relationship of love between the soul and its bridegroom. Since I am defending the doctrine of justification in its original formulation and for its well-known practical relation to belief in providence, humility, patience, and prayer, I must reject the aforementioned doctrine of the *unio mystica* which arose only in the seventeenth century. I hope I have answered Professor Weiss's insinuation that it is not a Kantian moralist antipathy which leads me to this position; and I hope I have also shown that the naïveté on this matter which he boasts of (p. 408) grows out of a defect in historical knowledge which renders his advice to me unusable.

Finally, I cannot resist touching upon still one more characteristic point in my opponent's deductions. As one might expect, Weiss brings Friedrich Schleiermacher[50] into the concerns which he represents. He is said to be so liberal that he forsakes the scholastic form in which the Lutheran dogmaticians *developed the details* of the doctrine of the *unio mystica*. One might also ask whether Weiss has ever looked at Quenstedt's or Calov's treatment of this doctrine. I observed only a concise delimitation of the doctrine in their work rather than a more or less detailed development. But everything in Weiss's work is unclear and imprecise. He disclaims the scholastic form and he

> holds fast only to the kernel of the matter, as it is indubitably witnessed to in the New Testament, and, *in his own way*, reproduced also by Schleiermacher—that through faith there is formed a personal and therein real spiritual union between God and the believer, a union which provides the lasting foundation for a real spiritual union between them, that is, a meaningful common life.

Now the fact of the matter is that Schleiermacher did indeed use these expressions which were current for him out of his Herrnhut[51] background, but he reinterpreted them to refer to the *effects* which extend from the redeemer to the believers within the church. In addition, he analyzes all of the circumstances that are here suggested within the framework of the subjective life. With respect to method, therefore, he is my forerunner; I have learned my method partly from him and partly from Schneckenburger! Weiss apparently has not perceived or retained this in his recollection of Schleiermacher's theology—a recollection which is probably already somewhat obsolete. Therefore, out of regard for his faded recollection, I must add that Schleiermacher is also opposed to me. Thus it is that theologians like my opponent, who desire what is old but not in the superannuated costume of the scholastic forms; who always guard themselves in every possible way from heretical deviations; who thus narrow their scope until they finally revolve only about themselves; who always criticize and never get along with others—these unfruitful theologians, I must say, always claim Schleiermacher's patronage for themselves. But it is not Schleiermacher as he really was but rather their idea of him, their dull recollection (which they have "dressed up") of the great theologian's teaching, to which they ascribe at the same time all their own intentions and merits. Thus he is idealized according to a flaccid "mediating theology,"[52] set upon the scene, and claimed to be in harmony with the views of men who have taken their roots in places other than his and whose thought is projected from methods quite opposed to his. To the many amenities which one is accorded when he tries to make his way independently as a theologian must be added this, that he is trumped by the Schleiermacher who has been accommodated to the needs of these men. But that is a dishonest game.

VI

The controversy over original sin which Victorinus Strigel, Jacob Andreae, Tilemann Hesshus, and Johann Wigand[53] carried on against Matthias Flacius[54] furnishes an instructive example of the value of judging theological assertions metaphysically. To the utterance that original sin is *accidens* [accidental] to man, made by Strigel in the Disputation at Weimar (1560), Flacius responded with the opposing assertion that original sin is of man's *substantia* [substance]. It was only in 1567 that he published the tractate *De peccati originalis aut veteris Adami appellationibus et essentia* ["Concerning original sin, or the names and essence of the old Adam"], in the *Clavis scripturae sacrae* [Key to the Holy Scriptures], which explained and preserved that familiar concept. Flacius's assertion was not intended to be as offensive and exaggerated as it appears. For one thing, it is directly related to the framework of ideas in which Luther used to portray original sin and in which he taught that it should be abhorred. In addition, Flacius did not wish to ascribe a simple diabolicalness to Adam's progeny but, on the contrary, he wanted to ascribe some good to them, in spite of his assertion. To this end, he differentiated two meanings of the concept *substantia: substantia materialis* [material substance] and *forma substantialis* [substantial form]. In respect to the former meaning, he allows that despite corruption it remains the bearer of some good; in respect to the latter, the substantial form, he makes the judgment that without exception it has become the bearer of evil, just as through creation it had been the bearer of the divine image. Even in respect to this first distinction, Flacius's meaning remains ambiguous because it is spelled out only in metaphysical concepts. That is, what he says about the material substance is unintelligible:

> The mass of mankind established at the beginning, although it is deeply corrupted, has nevertheless remained to this day, in the same way as with wine and spices, when their airy and fiery substance evaporates, only an earthy, watery substance remains.[55]

This example from chemistry does not make the metaphysical notion any clearer. What Flacius strove for in this connection becomes clear when one understands that sin is to be conceived within the structure of volition. For it is in the conscious will that sin appears as an effect. Thus the law of the will consists in the power, either to convert the propensity of its drives toward lust into actual intentions, projects, resolutions and transactions, or through these means to moderate and divert that propensity. The will is evil, however, insofar as it sets its projected *course* on unrestrained lust or on lust that has been intentionally limited so that its pleasure might be intensified accordingly. The will is good insofar as it circumscribes its drives through the good intention which it holds, that is, converting those impulses into means for doing good. This formal law of the will corresponds to the *substantia materialis* [material substance]; that course of the will which is specified by a purpose with a certain content corresponds to the *forma substantialis* [substantial form]. When the nature of character is to be judged by the criterion of which values in life [*Lebensinhalt*] the will directs itself toward, then the judgment that the character is evil must include the same appraisal of the negative value of sin which Flacius certainly meant to imply in his assertion. But none of this is clear in the inadequate metaphysical categories in which Flacius and his opponents expressed themselves. In other words, it never became explicit that the controversy dealt with the appraisal of the value of sin—and it could not become explicit because this insight is based on feeling, which stands between the concrete course of the will and the presentiment or knowledge of man's destiny.

Hence the controversy revolved around the question of whether sin is the *substantia* of man or *accidens* upon his *substantia*. The

Aristotelian traditions preserved in Melanchthon's *Erotemata dialectices* (1547)[56] served to facilitate the decision. This work describes substance in the following manner: "Substance is a thing which has the property of being and which sustains accidents." Accident is thus defined: "An accident is that which does not subsist through itself, nor is it a part of substance, but it is changeable into something else" or "that which is present or absent over and above the corruption of the subject." However, it depends on how the characteristics under which a thing manifests itself are classified between the categories of "substance" and "accident." According to the way this is done, the concept of substance becomes either fuller or emptier. The tendency Melanchthon followed was toward emptying the concept, since he did not reckon the qualities as substance, but placed them with the accidents. He says: "Quality is the form through which a substance makes itself efficacious, or that which stimulates the senses." He assumed that *habitus, potentiae, naturales, affectus,* and *figura* were qualities.[57] These *forms of the efficacy and perceptibility of things* were therefore *excluded from the concept of the thing.* To take an example, that would mean that the characteristics under which a thing is perceived as round, triangular, or square are irrelevant to its existence as a thing! Flacius rejected this differentiation between substance and accident. He reckoned the qualities, particularly the shape, to things and to their substance. Accordingly, in his opinion, the will belongs to the substance of man. For the good will was established through creation as the essence of the first man; therefore the evil will in Adam's progeny is of their substance. Now it is interesting that of Flacius's opponents, two (namely Strigel and Andreae) join with him in rejecting Melanchthon's distinction,[58] even though they distinguish between substance and accident differently from Flacius in their interpretation of the will. They posit the will, generally, as the substance of man; its constitution as good or bad is, however, accident in their opinion. Wigand came to the same result much more simply and, finally, Hesshus did too. They reckoned that on the whole neither reason nor will was man's substance, but rather accidents *quae in substantia sunt mutabilitar* [which, in substance, are changeable]! Naturally, then, original sin is also accident. But as what, then, is the essence of man to be known? As an indeterminate thing without relations, without effects, the doublet of Frank's "absolute," differing from that "absolute" only in the indemonstrable assertion that that absolute is God, whereas the soul is created. The assertion that original sin is accidental to man's essence is every bit as intolerable as the opposite, that it is the substance of contemporary humanity. But even more fatal is the fact that the assertion of Flacius's opponents found a place in the Formula of Concord, Solid Declaration I, 57.[59] For that would mean that there is a contradiction in the interpretation of original sin as *corruptio totius naturae et virium* [corruption of all nature and of men] and, at the same time, as something *quod adest praeter subiecti corruptionem* [which is present over and above the corruption of the subject]. At the same time, it is this formula of the corruption of nature which prevented the original, intended deviation from catholic teaching, a teaching which included the substance of man's essence, the *liberum arbitrium* [free will] under original sin (Council of Trent, session VI, 1), thus holding that original sin should be thought of as *accidens praeter corruptionem subiecti* [accident over and above the corruption of the subject]. This all came forth because someone undertook to define this point of Christian teaching with metaphysical concepts, but its application had already made a correct formulation of the question impossible since such an application could not possibly correspond to the religious and ethical appraisal of sin.

The conceptual definitions and distinctions which extend throughout the Formula of Concord demonstrate how influential the tradition of the popular metaphysics which Melanchthon favored was upon the formation of the second generation of reformation theologians. But Luther's conscious intention follows just the opposite method, since his intention was embodied in his comprehension of the total task of theology as oriented toward our salvation. I would call to attention some of his sayings: that knowledge of God's essence, as such, as it is undertaken by the scholastics, is without redemptive value and ruinous; that knowledge of God's gracious will can only be understood as the correlate of knowledge of Christ; that Christ's divinity can only be understood in his activity to fulfill his vocation. Hermann Schultz has brought these sayings together recently.[60] All of these ideas follow the rule for knowledge that a thing is known through effects which manifest themselves and that, therefore, a spiritual person exists in his volition as it is visible and present to us. This idea dominates as well the total reformation usage of terms such as *evangelium* [gospel], *promissiones* [promises], *fides evangelii* [faith of the gospel], and *fides promissionum* [faith of the promises]. Pietism erroneously judged the value of these formulae. Wilhelm Brakel and Friedrich Adolf Lampe[61] overlooked the security of Christ's presence that is in these formulae, and they believed that they themselves offered promises so great that, if they were right, they surpassed the promises of the Lord himself. In this instance, however, the impulse toward out-of-the-ordinary piety can oppose the idea of the reformers only because it misunderstands the correct epistemology.[62]

Furthermore, the formula in which Melanchthon defined the task of theology generally in the first edition of the *Loci theologici* (1521) corresponds to this correct epistemology. Thus: *Hoc est Christum cognoscere, beneficia eius cognoscere non quod isti (scholastici) docent, eius naturas, modos incarnationis contueri* ["This is what it is to know Christ—to know his benefits, not what those (scholastics) teach, to survey his natures, his modes of incarnation."].[63] Therefore the substance and worth of Christ should be understood in the beneficent actions upon us Christians, in the gift of the blessedness which we sought in vain under the law—not in a previously held general concept of his divinity. For we will never be able to make this concept coincide with our necessary contemplation of the man Jesus. Moreover, the theory of kenosis,[64] which is currently in vogue, expresses the same thing as the Platonic formula concerning the individual, namely, that Jesus only partakes of divinity. What Melanchthon says about sin is no less characteristic: "Scripture does not call this original sin and that actual sin. For even original sin is plainly a certain perverse lust which is actual."[65] This perspective is also expressed in the first half of the second article of the Augsburg Confession, whereas the second half of that same article presents again the general concept of passively inherited sinfulness. Melanchthon's original intention is to conceive of the sin that is common to all as an active indifference to and mistrust of God and, also, as a self-seeking desire. His intention was not, however, to posit as real a general concept of sin behind those rebellious acts, a concept which is unintelligible. For a passively inherited circumstance cannot be thought of as sin. In respect to the doctrine of sin, as well as in the doctrine of Christ, Melanchthon did not carry things out to a proper development of the theme.

He applied this principle of knowledge more clearly in the sketch of the doctrine of God, where the corresponding explanations of Luther guided him. As is well known, he passed over these in the first edition of the *Loci*. Contrariwise, in the second edition of 1535, the doctrine of God is found, where it is linked to the doctrine of the Trinity. This amplification was certainly occasioned as much by the inner necessity of the theological task as it was by the outward position of the protestants vis-à-vis the Roman church or by Servetus's argument against the doctrine of the Trinity. This amplification was already present in the lectures of 1533, and out of this vividly presented statement I extract the following. Melanchthon begins by saying that one must proceed from the saying of Christ in John 14:9, "He who sees me sees the Father."

Let us hold to this admonition, that we may learn to seek God in Christ; for in him he wishes to be disclosed, to become known and to be apprehended. . . . For if we allow ourselves to be drawn away from Christ, as if we could know either the nature or will of God without Christ, our souls fall into fearful darkness, because nature is not able to perceive God. . . . The human mind does not comprehend the nature of God by speculations, nor in fact is it able to judge the mercy of God toward us; but when the mercy of God is apprehended in Christ, then it begins to discern the goodness and presence of God, and to understand God in some way. And that does not happen by speculative knowledge, with the result that I may speak with common words, but it happens in practical meditation, that is, when hearts terrified by the knowledge of sin, throw themselves back upon Christ and in him apprehend the promised mercy. Then they know consolation and life, and they know that their lives are returned to God, they know in truth that God is present and merciful. This is the wisdom of Christians. This method does not proceed *a priori*, that is, from the hidden nature of God to knowledge of God's will, but from knowledge of Christ and of the mercy revealed in him to the knowledge of God. To strengthen and confirm souls in this knowledge is far better than to philosophize about the hidden nature of God.[66]

This is an unambiguous position and a candid definition of the doctrine of God. However, the methodological execution of the position does not follow from the task which is here set forth. Rather, on the very next page, Melanchthon frustrates the reshaping of the doctrine of God which he himself lays down by a formula which he describes as the summation of the biblical affirmations about God, but which, in reality, represents a capitulation to the neoplatonic and scholastic position.

> Scripture testifies that God is a spiritual substance. It assigns to him eternity, infinite power, etc. Moreover, this substance is perceived not as that which sustains accidents but, rather, it signifies most properly the essence that subsists in and through itself. Wisdom, goodness, justice, mercy, are not accidents of God, but, just as we do not sunder power from its substance, so we separate neither wisdom nor goodness from their substance. For power is itself wisdom, goodness, etc.[67]

Since the beginning of his service in Wittenberg, Melanchthon had cultivated the dialectic with success, that is, the Aristotelian doctrine of categories and logic. He busied himself with these matters in three treatises, carrying different titles, in 1520, 1528, and 1547. In the last of these, *Erotemata Dialectices* [Dialectical Inquiries] which is published in *Corpus Reformatorum,* XIII, we find the same definition of God as in the *Loci*, with the explanation: "Human minds learn this description from demonstrations *outside the church and without special revelation.*"[68] Could one speak more clearly? This description is simply to be augmented in the church through the application of the name and structures of the Trinity. Although this realm of knowledge is amplified through the customary proofs from scripture and the traditional formulae, even so, the contrary point of view also assumes a certain validity here, namely, that the divinity of Christ and that of the Holy Spirit is recognized in the effects and demands which they exercise upon the believers.

> Thus scripture teaches us, concerning the divinity of the Son, not so much speculatively as practically; this it commands so that we might invoke Christ, so that we might have confidence in him—for in that way the honor and divinity is truly given to him—and thus scripture wishes us to know the divinity of the Holy Spirit in that same consolation and vivification. . . . It is useful for us to consider these offices of the Holy Spirit. . . . These offices intend for us to contemplate rather than dispute concerning the Spirit's nature. . . . In this invocation, in

these exercises of faith, it is better to know the Trinity than to engage
in otiose speculations which dispute concerning what the persons of
the Trinity do among themselves, but not what they do with us.[69]

The situation is such, in the second edition of the Loci (1535),
that the two opposing epistemologies within the doctrine of God
carry equal weight. In the third edition, the doctrine of God drawn
from theoretical knowledge (*firmae demonstrationes*) and ecclesiastical tradition carries the preponderant weight. While it is true that
the reference to John 14:9 remains, the protest based thereon,
against *a priori* knowledge of God, has fallen to the side. And it
corresponds to the move from the demonstrable and therefore generally rational concept of God to a concern for the structure of his
revelation in Christ that now the first question raised concerns the
essence of God and secondly concerns his will.[70] These indicators
are but another test of the fact that Melanchthon, to the extent that
he was or became independent over against Luther, did not keep in
force the characteristic thrusts which Luther set in motion. I will
say that I do not reproach him for this, nor do I derive a judgment
of disrespect from it. *Ultra posse nemo obligatur.* [No man is required
to do more than he is able.] But since it is the current fashion to
overestimate Melanchthon, it appears to be incumbent upon me to
curb this trend in the interest of truth. Thus he relinquished the new
epistemology which Luther had set forth, and he led theology back
again into the old channels of scholastic apriorism to whose deductions the positive data of revelation are attached in a loosely struc-
tured manner. So it has remained, and the new wine was handled
to such an extent that it could no longer burst the old wine skins.
I am not in the least surprised that the outline of the new theology
which Luther drew up eluded the patrons of the old skins completely;
nevertheless, I will let this example work to my own advantage. Now,
if one is inclined to compare the thrust of Melanchthon's doctrine of
God in the texts of 1533 and 1535, he will soon see that the controversy between Frank and me is, actually, the open controversy
of Melanchthon versus Melanchthon. This is possible since the one
Melanchthon is the representative of Luther's thought, whereas the
other Melanchthon is the representative of himself, the Aristotelian,
the metaphysician, and, at the same time, the representative of
unexamined tradition. As I have already shown, Luthardt is still in

the same position of acknowledging the two opposing methods simultaneously on one page of his *Compendium*. Between me and Frank, these two methods are handled as opposites which exclude each other and I consider this controversy to be a gain.

Calvin's *Institutes of the Christian Religion*, in its full form of 1539–59, is so laid out that he progresses from natural religion to revealed religion, from God as creator to God as redeemer. This is precisely a sketch, similar to the scholastic, which holds to the path on which Melanchthon once again guided the theology of the reformation. But that does not hinder Calvin from giving unambiguous expression, on occasion, to the contradictory viewpoints of Luther and Melanchthon. Insofar as he specifies the structure of faith he teaches that God is known as a gracious will in Christ, and Christ is known in the picture of his beneficial deeds and gifts which accompanies the word.

> This, then, is the true knowledge of Christ, if we receive him as he is offered by the Father: namely, clothed with his gospel. For just as he has been appointed as the goal of our faith, so we cannot take the right road to him unless the gospel goes before us. And there, surely, the treasures of grace are opened to us; for if they had been closed, Christ would have benefited us little. . . . He [Paul] understands by this term ["doctrine of faith" in I Tim. 4:6] the new and extraordinary kind of teaching by which Christ, after he became our teacher, has more clearly set forth the mercy of the Father, and has more surely testified to our salvation. . . . First, we must be reminded that there is a permanent relationship between faith and the Word. He could not separate one from the other any more than we could separate the rays from the sun from which they come. (Therefore, there is no immediate relation to Christ!) . . . In understanding faith it is not merely a question of knowing that God exists, but also—and this especially—of knowing what is his will toward us. For it is not so much our concern to know who he is in himself, as what he wills to be toward us . . . for it is after we have learned that our salvation rests with God that we are attracted to seek him. . . . Accordingly, we need the promise of grace, which can testify to us that the Father is merciful. . . . Now we shall possess a right definition of faith if we call it a firm and certain knowledge of God's benevolence toward us, founded upon the truth of the freely given promise in Christ, both revealed to our minds and sealed upon our hearts through the Holy Spirit.[71]

A theology which was laid out as an analysis of this assertion would distinguish itself very favorably in comparison with the traditional form which is analogous to the scholastic.

But also, on yet another point, Calvin follows the method of authenticating a thing in the manifestation of its appearances, that is, a specific action of God in the sequence of the human acts which correspond to it. In contrast to the reproaches of Weiss, it is very interesting to me how Calvin judges the "repentance that for the Christian man ought to extend throughout his life" (Chap. 3, par. 2). Concerning this human life-style [Lebensführung] which is conceived of as expressing itself spontaneously in mortification and vivification, he says in paragraph 9:

> I interpret repentance as regeneration, whose sole end is to restore in us the image of God. . . . And indeed, this restoration does not take place in one moment or one day or one year; but through continual and sometimes even slow advances God wipes out in his elect the corruptions of the flesh . . . consecrates them to himself as temples renewing all their minds to true purity that they may practice repentance throughout their lives. . . .[72]

Weiss, therefore, does not need to adduce this chapter of Calvin as yet another testimony for *his unio mystica*.

✶   ✶   ✶   ✶   ✶

In what I have written here, I have shown that the epistemology which I use in theology corresponds to the actual intention of Luther, in particular, his aim to break with the scholastic methodology. He was not able to perform this task. Melanchthon, for his part, was not equal to it either. On the contrary, this leader of theology in the church of the reformation set out on a return trip to the scholastic methodology—slowly but with progressively greater decisiveness. Up to now, at least methodologically, our theology has remained, as a whole, in the channels of scholasticism. Even Schleiermacher shares in the fundamental error of this mode of theology, in that he portrays the pious self-consciousness as the first part of theology, which is presupposed in every excitation of Christian sensibilities and yet, at the same time, is also always contained within it. That is, as with Melanchthon, his general doctrine of God is natural theology. I know of only one theologian who has broken with this whole tradition: Gottfried Menken.[73] He opens his *Versuch einer Anleitung zum eigenen Unterricht in den Wahrheiten der heiligen Schrift* ["An Attempt at an Introduction to My Own Instruction in the Truths of Holy Scriptures"] with the following assertion:

> A people has never been found, indeed, not even a single man has been found, who had a natural religion—i.e., such a religion whose concepts, truths, commands, usages, and hopes were innate to him, or who had come upon his religion prior to all instruction, all education and intercourse with men, who had come upon his religion through reflection and speculation without any teaching, tradition, or history. No man has been found who wanted to consider his religion as the result of his own speculation rather than as holy teaching of divine origin.[74]

Logically, the rejection of natural religion means, at the same time, a rejection of all universal concepts which one might possess prior to the particular structures of revealed religion or apart from the actuality of those structures in the founder and in the community.

These are the viewpoints by which my attempt at theology is guided. In general, it does not amaze me that this attempt has encountered misunderstanding and hostile misinterpretations. Specifically, however, the range and the kind of distortions in which men have brought me to exhibition and made me a horrible example has exceeded my furthest expectations.[75] And, worst of all, in their zeal to degrade me, my opponents have left themselves in a most vulnerable position without thinking that a corresponding judgment could follow upon the heels of their criticism. Many of them really appear to me to be very much like the Corinthian speakers in tongues. I have been silent for six years in the face of the slanders of my doctrine of atonement, and even now I have decided not to change my behavior. This present writing intends neither to make retaliation nor to advance the scandal. Rather, first of all, it aims at rapprochement and it makes defense only to the extent that it seems necessary to explain the matter itself in the light of my opponents' assertions. Whether I will achieve my goal, I do not know. Up to now, I have simply reconciled myself to the fact that the worst distortions of my viewpoint will be reckoned to me as my own work, and I have no direct means of cutting off the water to the mill of accusation in which I am constantly being ground to powder. My patience even endured the attacks of Frank and Luthardt for a long time. But one day, at the beginning of April, the controversy over metaphysics in theology was carried on so close to me, at the same time, though from different sides, that I decided to discuss the topic openly. Having entered the battle, I could not resist settling accounts with my opponents in Erlangen and Leipzig, even at this late date. At the same time, Weiss's discussions came into my hands, and they showed so much agreement with the prejudices of the theologians just named that I could only regard it as providence to take this opponent into my discussion as well. Besides, I do not wish to conceal the fact that, under these circumstances, I owe him a certain debt of gratitude, because he gave me so many opportunities to defend my convictions which were offensive to him.

Now, in order to bring this to a good end, I beg my opponents' indulgence as I recall still another man who handled metaphysics in a manner such as theirs and with the same unclear results—and that 200 years ago. Philipp Jakob Spener expressed things correctly,[76] saying that metaphysics is the doctrine of universal concepts which are used in all disciplines. But, at the same time and in the same sentence, he also pronounced the true metaphysics (which was not yet in existence) to be "a solid knowledge of the *doctrinae spiritum* [doctrine of the spirits]." Is it not true that this could only refer to the doctrine of angels? And one can understand Spener only with this presupposition, that metaphysics is the specific knowledge of divine things. But how is this assumption related to the correct definition of metaphysics, of which Spener is also sure? He evidences this same confusion in still other places.[77] In the controversy over the conditions necessary for theology, whether the theologian could be unregenerate or must be regenerate, he grants to his opponent George Conrad Dilfeld[78] his first assertion that the true knowledge of God is to be understood in a logical sense. But he nevertheless denies his opponent's assertion that the true knowledge of God is to be understood in a metaphysical sense. For in that case he would mean that the criterion for true knowledge of God is that *such knowledge must include everything which belongs to divine knowledge.* This would not be intelligible unless metaphysical knowledge were meant here to be equivalent to knowledge that takes its origin from religious interests, and this confusion is possible only if metaphysics is taken to be identical with the knowledge of God and of divine things. One can see that the nest of confusions which I have attempted to resolve is of fairly ancient standing. May I permit myself the hope that I have not merely shaken it up, but that I have destroyed it, so that no more barren and deformed theological eggs can be laid in it?

Written on the second day of Pentecost, June 6, 1881.

NOTES

1. [Christoph Ernst Luthardt (1823–1902) was an orthodox "neo-Lutheran," who was professor of New Testament and Systematic Theology at Leipzig. Ritschl's references to his *Compendium* are from the fifth edition (Leipzig: Döffling und Franke, 1878).]

2. Wilhelm Herrmann, *Die Religion im Verhältnis zum Welterkennen und zur Sittlichkeit* (Halle: M. Niemeyer, 1879), p. 14. [Herrmann (1846–1922) was one of Ritschl's greatest students.]

3. [Horace, *Satires*, Bk. I, 4; lines 155–56. Trans. by Henry H. Chamberlin, *Horace Talks* (Norwood, Mass.: The Plimpton Press, 1940).]

4. In J. G. Walch, *Dr. Martin Luthers Sämmtliche Schriften,* 23 vols. (Saint Louis: Concordia Publishing House, 1880–1910), VIII, 697.

5. [The German term *Geist* and its various forms are translated generally throughout this essay as "spirit." The term refers to the psychic life of man, and it is not necessarily religious in its meaning, although the connotations deriving from German Idealism which relate man's spirit to the Absolute Spirit cannot be set aside completely. The term often emphasizes man's intellectual or mental activity and in some instances it is translated with the word "mental." In the present passage, Ritschl provides an excellent description of *Geist*.]

6. Cf. Herrmann, *Die Religion im Verhältnis*, pp. 123 ff.

7. [Matthias Claudius (1740–1815) was a noted literary figure who emphasized the inner awakening of the human spirit.]

8. Franz Hermann Reinhold Frank, "Aus der neueren Dogmatik," *Zeitschrift für Protestantismus und Kirche,* n. s. LXXI (1876):301–22. [Frank (1827–1894) was prominent in the "Erlangen school" of theology, which was more confessional and conservative than Ritschl.]

9. *R.u.V.* III, 242–43. See *ET*, 282, 283.

10. Rudolf Hermann Lotze, *Metaphysik*, 2nd ed. (Leipzig: S. Hirzel, 1884), p. 185. *ET: Metaphysic*, trans. B. Bosanquet (Oxford: Clarendon Press, 1884), p. 168. [Lotze (1817–1881), a philosopher, was Ritschl's colleague at Göttingen.]

11. Friedrich Adolf Philippi, *Kirchliche Glaubenslehre*, 3rd ed. (Gütersloh: Bertelsmann, 1883), II:20 ff. [Philippi (1809–1882) was a confessional theologian associated with "neo-Lutheran" movements. Ritschl erroneously refers to this work as *Kirchliche Dogmatik*.]

12. Frank, "Aus der neueren Dogmatik," p. 319.

13. John Calvin, *Commentary on the Gospel According to John*, 2 vols. (Grand Rapids: Eerdmans, 1949), I:417.

14. [Friedrich Lücke (1791–1855) was a middle-of-the-road theologian at Bonn. Ritschl probably refers to Heinrich August Wilhelm Meyer (1800–1873), a Hannover church official who founded a celebrated commentary series on the New Testament.]

15. ["Repristinating theology" refers to a nineteenth century German Lutheran theological trend which emphasized adherence to the Lutheran confessional documents, with special opposition to rationalism and to "union" attempts which aimed at uniting the Lutheran and Reformed churches in Prussia.]

16. [Philipp Nicolai (1556–1608) was a Lutheran theologian and hymn writer.]

17. [Stephen Praetorius (1536–1603) was a pastor who wrote devotional tracts during the period of the reformation.]

18. See my *Geschichte des Pietismus*, II: 19, 23, 32.

19. Gottfried Arnold, *Historie und Beschreibung der mystischen Theologie oder geheimen Gottesgelehrtheit* (Frankfurt: Thomas Fritschen, 1703), pp. 132 ff. [Arnold (1666–1714) was an important early protestant historian, who recognized the importance of unconventional and heretical movements in Christianity.]

20. [See, for example, Ritschl's comments in *Die christliche Vollkommenheit*, critical edition by Cajus Fabricius (Leipzig: J. C. Hinrichs, 1924), pp. 8 ff. Also *R.u.V.*, III, 343–45, 472–73, 489–90, and section 49; *ET*, 362–64, 501–2, 519–21.]

21. [Johann Albert Bengel, *Gnomon of the New Testament* (Philadelphia: Perkinpine and Higgins, 1888), I:705. Bengel (1687–1752) was a noted pietist biblical scholar.]

22. [Christian Wolff (1679–1754) was an Enlightenment metaphysician who attempted to synthesize science and ontology.]

23. Lotze, *Metaphysik*, p. 163.

24. [Hermann Weiss, a contemporary of Ritschl, was professor of theology at Tübingen.]

25. Hermann Weiss, "Ueber das Wesen des persönlichen Christenstandes; Eine Kritische Orientierung mit besonderer Beziehung auf die Theologie Ritschls" in *Studien und Kritiken* LIV, 3 (1881):377–417.

26. [The anabaptists comprise a movement within the reformation, generally termed "left-wing," which emphasized a second birth for Christians. Luther and Calvin were very critical of the anabaptists, an attitude which their followers maintained in Ritschl's time. The Old Believers is a sectarian movement which originated within the Russian church in the seventeenth century, in protest against ecclesiastical and civil authority. The movement included broad sections of the common people, and it tended toward fanaticism.]

27. [Starowerzen refers to the Russian Old Believers.]

28. [C. F. Georg Heinrici (1844–1915) was professor of New Testament in Marburg and Leipzig.]

29. [Carl Christian Johann Holsten (1825–1897) was professor of New Testament in Heidelberg.]

30. [The citation is quoted from the article by Heinrici, p. 510.]

31. Perhaps it would be interesting to examine Spener on this point. *The-ologisches Bedenken* (Halle: Wäysen-Hauses, 1702), Vol. 1, chap. 1, section 34: "What is the actual *formal element* of the spiritual life in the soul of the regenerate? Grace or Christ or faith or the powers granted us? Christ himself is not the *formal element*, rather he belongs much more to the *efficient cause*; and the spiritual life is something that, as it were, flows from him. And if on the basis of Gal. 2:20 ("It is no longer I who live, but Christ who lives in me") or Col. 3:4 ("Christ who is our life") it should be said that Christ is made the *form* of our life, that is nevertheless not the intention of those passages; rather, they only show that our spiritual life comes from Christ, that he—far more than we—is efficacious in it. . . . Again the grace of God is not the *formal element,* but rather belongs to the efficacious cause; for just as we are reborn because of the grace of God, so also, therefore, our life flows out of that same grace. . . . Therefore, I do not know how to characterize the *formal element* other than as the new manner of the new man or new divine nature in him (II Peter 1:4); this new manner consists in a divine light of a lively knowledge of God and in the divine power, out of which the regenerate person is not only able to do good, but he also has a drive toward the good and is like-minded with the divine will."

32. See, for example, Hartung's review of Hartmann's *Die Krisis des Christenthums in der modernen Theologie,* in *Theologische Literaturzeitung* VI, 8 (1881):191–92.

33. [Catherine of Genoa (1447–1510), daughter of a wealthy family, became a mystic, noted for her writings.]

34. ["Enthusiasm" refers to the ecstatic phenomena associated with the anabaptists.]

35. [Jodocus van Lodensteyn (1620–1677) was a Reformed theologian and revival preacher.]

36. [Justus Feuerborn (1587–1656) was professor of theology at Giessen.]

37. [Johann Hülsemann (1602–1661) was professor of theology in Wittenberg and Leipzig, noted for his Lutheran orthodoxy.]

38. [See note 16 above.]

39. [Johann Arndt (1555–1621) was one of the principal figures in the emergence of pietism.]

40. [Balthasar Meisner (1587–1626] was an important theologian of orthodox Lutheranism in the century after Luther.]

41. [Lucas Osiander the Younger (1571–1638), together with his father, represented the strong Swabian theological tradition after the reformation.]

42. [John T. McNeill (ed.), Calvin: *Institutes of the Christian Religion,* Library of Christian Classics 20 (Philadelphia: Westminster, 1960), pp. 537, 576, 582–83.]

43. [The *Formula of Concord* of 1580 is one of the chief confessional documents of the Lutheran tradition. It was the last of these documents in time, coming after a period of bitter controversy among Luther's followers. The standard text is found in Tappert.]

44. [Johann Gerhard (1582–1637) was one of the most significant Lutheran theologians in the century after Luther.]

45. [Johann Andreas Quenstedt (1617–1688) was a major orthodox Lutheran theologian.]

46. [Abraham Calov (1612–1686) was a major orthodox Lutheran theologian.]

47. [Andreas Osiander (1498–1552) was a contemporary of Melanchthon who was a leading force for conservatism and strict orthodoxy, although in the issue discussed here by Ritschl, Osiander was considered unorthodox because of his insistence that justification must mean that Christ dwells within the believer, since it is not enough to say (as the more orthodox did say) that the believer is *declared* righteous. In this connection he used the concept of *unio mystica* to express the indwelling of Christ.]

48. [Philip Melanchthon (1497–1560) was Luther's co-worker and chief disciple. See also Ritschl's essay from 1878, "Die Entstehung der lutherischen Kirche" ("The Emergence of the Lutheran Church") in Gesammelte Aufsätze (Freiburg and Leipzig: J. C. B. Mohr, 1893).]

49. [Christian Hoburg (1607–1665) was a pietist and appreciative of mysticism.]

50. [Friedrich Schleiermacher (1786–1834) is often termed the greatest modern protestant theologian. He was strongly influenced by pietism and romanticism.]

51. [Herrnhut is the site of a famous Moravian pietist community where Schleiermacher lived for some years during his youth.]

52. ["Mediating theology" refers to a nineteenth century German protestant theological tendency which attempted to hold the rising scientific liberal spirit and traditional Christianity together—thus mediating between repristinating theologians and liberals.]

53. [Victorinus Strigel (1524–1569), Jacob Andreae (1528–1590), Tilemann Hesshus (1488–1540), and Johann Wigand (1523–1587) were all strict orthodox Lutheran theologians who were active during the reformation period.]

54. Cf. Johann Wilhelm Preger, *Matthias Flacius Illyricus und seine Zeit*, 2 vols. (Erlangen, 1859–61), II:310 ff., 395 ff. [Matthias Flacius (1520–1575) was a co-worker and contemporary of Melanchthon and Luther. See also "The Emergence of the Lutheran Church," cited above, note 48.]

55. Ibid., p. 313: "massam hominis initio conditam adhuc utcunque remansisse, tametsi valde vitiatam, sicut si in vino et aromatibus, exspirante aerea et ignea substantia, remaneret tantum terrena et aquea."

56. [Cf. *CR* XIII, 507–752. The discussion of substance and accidents is taken from pp. 522, 528–29.]

57. Ibid., pp. 534–35. [These five philosophical categories are difficult to translate. Ritschl's point is that Melanchthon did not reckon a person's empirically observable actions and appearance as a part of his essential self.

Thus, we may render the terms as actions of habit (*habitus*), possibilities of action (*potentiae*), necessary action by which we adjust to our world (*naturales*), action aroused by the effects of others upon us (*affectus*), and our physical appearance (*figura*).

58. Preger, *Matthias Flacius*, pp. 397 ff.

59. [Ritschl erroneously cites Section II, paragraph 57, in his text. See Tappert, p. 518.]

60. Hermann Schultz, "Luther's Ansicht von der Methode und den Grenzen der dogmatischen Aussagen über Gott," *Zeitschrift für Kirchengeschichte* IV, 1 (1880):77–104. Also, "Lehre von der Gottheit Christi," pp. 195 ff.

61. Ritschl, *Geschichte des Pietismus*, I:296, 299, 436.

62. Weiss proceeds quite analogously, since he is intent upon demonstrating that I set God aside in a deistic manner. Simply because I do not—on every page where the complex relationships of the Christian life are being examined in light of the inescapable form of spontaneity [*Selbstthätigkeit*]—buttress his memory with the reminder that this all has its present basis in the love and gracious will of God—because of this, he asserts that the concepts of love and grace hold no place in my work. Immediately thereupon (p. 397), he reproaches me: "The idea, however, that individuals obtain the basis and content of their religious life *totally only* from the community is, despite Ritschl's assurances to the contrary, catholicizing." I want to come to the assistance of the Herr Professor's memory with (Luther's) *Large Catechism*, part II, 40–42: "I believe that the Holy Spirit makes me holy. . . . How does he do this? By what means? Answer: Through the *Christian church*, the forgiveness of sins. . . . In the first place, he has a unique community in the world. *It is the mother that begets and bears every Christian through the Word of God*, etc." Yet I do not conceal the fact that this enterprise, in its attempt to fasten upon me, in one breath, the opposite error has momentarily shattered my equanimity. But I regain it through reflection upon the probable basis on which Weiss made his judgment of me. To begin with, he is a pietist, or at least he sees everything through the pietist glasses, and therefore he has no idea of and no concern for the practical interests of the reformation. Further, as a disciple of Max Landerer (Cf. my review of Landerer's *Neueste Dogmengeschichte* in *Theologische Literaturzeitung* VI, 4 (1881):77–81), he has learned to investigate other persons for all possible heresies. Finally, however, he betrays the source of his virtuosity and violence in this way, that also a drop of critical oil from Baur's legacy has gone to his head.

63. *CR* XXI, 85.

64. ["Kenosis" comes from the Greek "emptying," and it refers to a theory concerning Christ, that he emptied himself of his divinity, in order to become incarnate redeemer. Cf. Phil. 2:7.]

65. *CR* XXI, 97.

66. Ibid., 255.

67. Ibid., 256.

68. Ibid., 530.

69. Ibid., 366, 367.

70. Ibid., 607–10.

71. [Calvin, *Institutes,* III, 2, 6, 7 (McNeill, 548–51). Material in parentheses is Ritschl's.]

72. [Ibid., 601.]

73. [Gottfried Menken (1768–1831) was a pietist theologian.]

74. Gottfried Menken, *Versuch einer Anleitung zum eigenen Unterricht in den Wahrheiten der heiligen Schrift,* 2nd ed. (Bremen: W. Kaiser, 1825).

75. Spener already had his experience with this theological evil. He writes in 1680 in *Die Allgemeine Gottesgelehrtheit aller gläubigen Christen und rechtschaffenen Theologen* (Frankfurt, 1680), I:326: "It is a grievous rudeness of our time, that men are so ready and quick with glee to bring under suspicion a teaching simply because it may not be commonly heard, or because it is set forth with words that are not familiar, or because it is set forth by a man whom one otherwise holds in suspicion; or else men handle it in some other unpleasant manner—even if that teaching is commensurate with the holy scripture and Christian doctrine, it is brought under suspicion of error, immediately discredited publicly, even without sufficient proof; but generally a teaching in which one finds even the smallest bit of an ancient heresy or a new one, is immediately burdened with the name of the heresy, even when that doctrine has some agreement with the words which a Christian teacher has used." [Philipp Jakob Spener (1635–1705) is considered to be the "Father of Pietism." Ritschl dealt at length with Spener's work and thought in his *Geschichte des Pietismus,* II.]

76. Philipp Jakob Spener, *Theologische Bedenken,* I:420.

77. Ibid., III:535.

78. [George Conrad Dilfeld, deacon in Nordhausen, rejected Spener's insistence that theology could not be undertaken by reason alone, solely as an academic discipline.]

INSTRUCTION IN THE
CHRISTIAN RELIGION

INSTRUCTION IN THE CHRISTIAN RELIGION

This work is a summary of Christian doctrine that Ritschl originally prepared for use in the upper grades of German secondary schools. His activity on the provincial examining committee, which supervised graduation requirements, convinced him that religious instruction needed improvement. The book never succeeded as a school text except where Ritschl's students used it and supplemented it by their own explanations, thereby rendering it less difficult to understand. Some distinguished theologians began their careers teaching school, using this book, including Wilhelm Herrmann, Adolf von Harnack, and Theodore Link. Since Ritschl incorporated their suggestions into later editions, we might say that his text had exceptional field-testing! Ritschl saw, however, that the future of the book lay with theological students, and he rewrote later editions with that in mind. It did succeed in gaining him many followers among theological and philosophical students in his day, since it is the only complete survey of his doctrinal system in print.

The title of this book in German is the same as that which translates Calvin's *Institutes of the Christian Religion.* Ritschl chose the title deliberately, as he wrote in 1875, when the work first was published,[1]

> It is not food for babies, but on the contrary very strongly concentrated nourishment. . . . I hope that it will be worthy of the attention of theologians also. For this reason I choose the title, so as to indicate that I wish to pick up from Calvin and (implicitly, of course) also from Melanchthon's *Loci* and Lombard's *Sentences.* Don't I have high-flying aspirations?

Thus, it should be titled in English so as to carry the connotations Ritschl intended. However, inasmuch as the first translation by Alice Swing in 1901 has gained wide usage, her error is continued here.[2]

The first edition from Adolph Marcus in Bonn is dated 1875, with revised editions in 1881 and 1886. Unaltered printings of the third edition appeared in 1890 and 1895. Cajus Fabricius issued an excellent critical edition in 1924 which includes all the variant readings of the three editions, and a new printing of the first edition has recently appeared in German. The translation which follows, from the third edition, is a revision of Swing's with important variations from the first edition in footnotes.

1. Otto Ritschl, II:273.
2. In Albert Swing, *The Theology of Albrecht Ritschl* (New York: Longmans, Green and Co., 1901).

Instruction in the

Christian Religion

INTRODUCTION

1. Since the Christian religion has its origin in a special revelation, and exists in a special community of believers and worshipers, its peculiar conceptions of God must always be interpreted in connection (a) with the recognition of the one who bears this revelation and (b) with the right appreciation of the Christian community, if the total substance of Christianity is to be understood correctly. A system of doctrine which ignores either of these two elements will prove defective.

2. Christianity claims to be the perfect religion, in contrast to the other kinds and levels of religion; it furnishes man with that which is striven after, but only dimly and imperfectly realized in other religions. The perfect religion is the one within which the perfect knowledge of God is possible. Christianity claims to have this perfect knowledge of God because its community derives itself from Jesus Christ who, as the Son of God, ascribes to himself perfect knowledge of his Father[1] and because it derives its knowledge of God from the same Spirit in whom God knows himself.[2] These conditions of the existence of the Christian religion are referred to when we are baptized in the name of the Father and the Son and the Holy Spirit.[3]

3. Any understanding of Christianity can do justice to its claim to perfection (par. 2) only when undertaken from the point of view

of the Christian community itself. But because this point of view has often been shifted in the course of history, and because the intellectual horizon of the community has been clouded by outside influences, it stands as the fundamental principle of the protestant church that Christian doctrine is to be obtained from the Bible *alone*.[4] This principle refers explicitly to the original documents of Christianity gathered together into the New Testament, for the understanding of which the original documents of the Hebrew religion gathered together in the Old Testament serve as an indispensable aid. These books are the foundation of a competent understanding of the Christian religion from the point of view of the community, because the gospels set forth in the work of its founder the immediate cause and final end of the community's religion, whereas the epistles make known the original state of its common faith. The epistles do this, moreover, in a form not yet affected by the influences which as early as the second century stamped Christianity as catholic.

4. The instruction in the Christian religion must be so divided that the conditions referred to in paragraph 1 are adhered to. Moreover, that portion of doctrine which pertains to the life of the individual Christian will be governed by the communal conditions of the religion and its ethical development as set forth directly in the preceding paragraphs. The instruction in the Christian religion may be divided into the following doctrines:

1. Concerning the kingdom of God.
2. Concerning reconciliation through Christ.
3. Concerning the Christian life.
4. Concerning public worship.

I. THE DOCTRINE OF THE KINGDOM OF GOD

5.[5] The kingdom of God is the divinely ordained highest good[6] of the community[7] founded through God's revelation in Christ; but it is the highest good only in the sense that it forms at the same time the ethical ideal for whose attainment[8] the members of the community bind themselves to each other through a definite type of reciprocal action.[9] This meaning of the concept "kingdom of God" becomes clear through the imperative which is simultaneously expressed in it.

6. The righteous conduct through which the members of Christ's community share in effecting the kingdom of God finds its universal

law and its personal motive in love to God and to one's neighbor.[10] This love receives its impulse from the love of God revealed in Jesus Christ (pars. 13, 22). The broadening of the concept of neighbor to include men as men, i.e., as ethical persons, opposes the kingdom of God to the narrower ethical communities (par. 8) which are limited by men's natural endowment [*Ausstattung*] and by the natural restrictions on their common activities.[11] The law of love appears in contrast to the arrangement of human society based merely upon private right,[12] and it goes beyond the principle of personal regard for others set forth in the Mosaic decalogue.[13]

7. The Christian concept of God's kingly authority—to which the kingdom of God corresponds as the union of subjects bound together by righteous conduct—arose out of similarly expressed thoughts in the religion of Israel, thoughts which in turn indicate its original purpose.[14] These thoughts are, in their historical development, elevated by the prophets to the expectation that through God's supernatural judgment his dominion will be realized in the righteousness of a morally purified Jewish people and will be recognized even by the heathen.[15] This idea is to be distinguished from the heathen designation of their gods as kings, partly because of the background of the free creation of the world by God, and partly because of the humane content of the corresponding law (par. 6, n. 13); for these reasons it engenders the expectation of the religious and moral unification of the nations. The Christian meaning of this thought goes beyond its Old Testament form, in that the ethical intention of the dominion of God is freed from adulteration by the political and ceremonial conditions under which the Old Testament idea and the Jewish hope labored.[16]

8. The kingdom of God which thus (pars. 5–7) presents the spiritual and ethical task of mankind as it is gathered in the Christian community is *supernatural*, insofar as in it the ethical forms of society are surpassed (such as marriage, family, vocation, private and public justice, or the state), which are conditioned by the natural endowment of man (differences in sex, birth, class, nationality) and therefore also offer occasions for self-seeking. The kingdom of God is *supramundane*, even as it now exists in the world as the present product of action motivated by love, insofar as we understand as "mundane" the nexus of all natural, naturally conditioned and organ-

ized existence. And the kingdom of God is at the same time the highest good of those who are united in it, to the degree that it offers the solution to the question propounded or implied in all religions: How can man, recognizing himself as a part of the world and at the same time capable of a spiritual personality, attain to that dominion over the world, as opposed to limitation by it, which this capability gives him the right to claim? The supernatural and supramundane kingdom of God continues to exist as the highest good of its members even when the present mundane conditions of spiritual life are changed (par. 76).

9. Although actions prompted by love and charitable human organizations are empirically perceptible as such, the motive of love which inspires them is in no case completely open to the observation of others. Therefore, the presence of the kingdom of God within the Christian community is always invisible and a matter of religious faith.[17] Especially must it be noted that the real continuance of the kingdom of God is not identical with the continuance of the Christian community, as the latter is visible as the church in public worship.[18]

10. The equality of all men as such, regardless of differences of nation or rank (par. 6, n. 11), and the duty of universal brotherly love are recognized even in classical paganism. Greek poets recognize the equality of slave and freeman.[19] Stoic philosophers witness to the brotherhood of all men, and from this conception of human nature derive the virtues which are to lead to the establishment of the most comprehensive human fellowship[20] and all of this apart from any thought of God. Nevertheless, it is a fact that the transformation of human society in accordance with these views was a development of Christianity, not Stoicism. Two reasons account for this: *First*, a diametrically opposite conclusion from that of the Stoics may as easily be drawn from their conception of the nature of man, depending upon the empirical view which informs this conception. *Second*, a knowledge of universal ethical precepts, as such, is never sufficient to call forth and organize the activity that is appropriate to those precepts. This activity follows only when a special, indeed a religious, motive or ground of obligation is linked with knowledge of the universal precept. Accordingly, the principles common to some degree to both Stoicism and Christianity became fruitful only

upon the soil of the latter where they were taken up into the underlying principle of obligation of that particular religious community.
The highest criterion for those obligations is the thought of a supramundane, supernatural God.[21] Accordingly, the exercise of one's
humanness is all the more reliably connected with the thought of a
supernatural God rather than a fluctuating concept of human nature
when the union of men, *qua* men, at which it aims, bears in itself
the stamp of the supernatural and supramundane (par. 8).

11. The complete name of God which corresponds to the Christian revelation is "The God and Father of our Lord Jesus Christ."[22]
This name includes the fact, already recognized to some extent in the
religions of all civilized nations [*Culturreligionen*], that God is a
spiritual person. It includes also the characteristics brought out first
in the religion of the Old Testament, that God is the only being of
his kind, [23] that he is not encumbered with nature and thus did not
come into existence with the world like the many heathen divinities;
that rather, he is the creator of the universe who, as the will that
determines himself and all things for himself,[24] in particular designs
a community of men for religious communion with himself and
ethical communion with one another.[25]

12.[26] Indirectly included in the complete Christian name of God
(par. 1), "The God and Father of our Lord Jesus Christ," is also
that he is the Father of all, of whatever nationality, who are united
in the community of the Lord Jesus Christ. Therefore in the abbreviated name, "God our Father,"[27] the thought is expressed that the
one God directs his special purpose to this community, whose highest
good and common imperative is the kingdom of God (par. 5). Now,
however, the complete name of God means that he has assumed this
special relationship to this particular community only because he is
already and first of all the Father of Jesus Christ, who is recognized
as Lord by his community. In this capacity, however, Christ stands
nearer to God, nearer than any other, because he shares in God's
attributes of being the end of creation[28] and recognizes himself as set
apart from the world in his position of sonship to God the Father.[29]
The key to the relationship between God the Father and the Son of
God is found in the declaration that God is love.[30]

13. In the complete name of God the fact that God is the Father
of human beings is connected with Jesus Christ insofar as he is recog-

nized as the Lord of a particular fellowship (par. 12). Through Christ's mediation this community of human beings is also designated as the object of divine love.[31] Such a relation would be inconceivable if God's purpose were merely the maintenance of the natural existence of the human race. In this case men would not be of like nature with God (par. 12, n. 30). The concept of God as love corresponds to that idea of mankind which sees man destined for the kingdom of God and for the activity directed toward this kingdom, i.e., the mutual union of man through action springing from love (par. 6).[32] This destiny, however, is realized by men only in their union with the community of their lord Jesus Christ.

14. The correlation between the concept of God as love and the kingdom of God as the final purpose of the world is confirmed by the statement that God's decision to establish the community of the kingdom of God was decreed before the foundation of the world.[33] The eternity of God which this implies is not sufficiently contained in the affirmation that his existence reaches out beyond that of the world without beginning or end and that God therefore has a measure of time different from that of man.[34] Rather, we recognize God's eternity in the fact that amid all the changes of things, which also indicate variation in his working, he himself remains the same and maintains the same purpose and plan by which he creates and directs the world.[35]

15. The religious acknowledgment of the omnipotence and omnipresence of God, implied in the creation and preservation of the world by God's will,[36] does not undertake to explain the continuance of natural things in whole or in part,[37] but rather always seeks to emphasize that God's care and gracious presence are certain for the pious man, because the world-creating and world-preserving will of God has the well-being of man as its purpose. Therefore, the thought of the omnipotence of God finds its consistent fulfillment in the thought of his wisdom, omniscience, and disposition to meet the needs of men.[38]

16. The first perception to arise out of the thought of the omnipotence of God is the insignificance of man. However, inasmuch as the same thought is also the foundation of our impression of God's constant readiness to help (goodness, grace, pity),[39] omnipotence receives the peculiar stamp of *righteousness* in the particular revela-

tion of the old and new covenants. By "righteousness" the Old Testament signifies the consistency of God's providence [*Leitung zum Heil*], validated on the one hand in the existence of pious and upright adherents to the old covenant,[40] and undertaken on the other hand for the community whose salvation would bring God's government to completion.[41] Insofar as the righteousness of God achieves his dominion in accordance with its dominant purpose of salvation, in spite of all the difficulties which proceed from the Israelites themselves, it is *faithfulness*.[42] Thus in the New Testament also the righteousness of God is recognized as the criterion of the special actions by which the community of Christ is brought into existence and led on to perfection;[43] such righteousness cannot therefore be distinguished from the grace of God.

17. The religious view of the world is based on the fact that all natural occurrences stand at God's disposal when he wishes to help men (par. 15). Accordingly, remarkable natural occurrences with which the experience of the special help of God is connected,[44] are regarded as miracles, and thus as special tokens[45] of his gracious readiness to help believers. Therefore, the conception of miracles stands in a necessary correlation to a special belief in the providence of God and is quite impossible apart from such a relationship.[46]

18. God administers the government of the world—and adjusting of the relation between man and the world—by means of retribution. This legal conception is employed in Christianity, as in all religions, because several of its characteristics correspond to the relations which are recognized in every religious view of the world. For law as well as religion has to do with regulating *the position* of the individual *vis-à-vis the world* in accordance with his social or moral worth, and has to do further with the fact that this position is assigned or recognized by an external will (of society, or the state, or God). Thus the concept of divine reward and punishment is also employed in Christianity.[47] The analogy with law extends also to the fact that as the exercise of the right of punishment in the state is only a means of upholding the public well-being, so also the divine punishments which are visited upon godless and persistently rebellious men are always subordinate to the purpose of perfecting the salvation of the righteous and maintaining their cause in the world. But in his purpose these dispensations of God are never a matter of equivalents.

On the contrary, there is in this divine administration of justice, *first of all*, no admission of human right over against God,[48] *secondly*, no equality between reward and worthiness on the one hand, and punishment and unworthiness on the other,[49] and, *thirdly*, no immediate congruence between misfortune and guilt or prosperity and goodness in individual cases, as might have been expected from the divine power. Any such congruence is referred rather to the future, particularly to the final judgment and the future life.[50] Therefore, the familiar conclusion drawn by the pre-Christian manner of judgment, i.e., that great misfortune was evidence of great guilt, is especially invalidated,[51] and the probability is introduced that a high degree of worldly misfortune may exist precisely in connection with religious and moral worthiness.[52] Finally, a point of view is introduced that substitutes an organic relation of cause and result[53] for the mechanical relation between reward (punishment) and worthiness (unworthiness) which is recognized in human law. That such a principle as this is operative in all cases can, in truth, be discerned only at the end of time. In the course of history clear examples of this principle are surrounded and obscured by manifold instances of exactly opposite nature. But the Christian faith does not allow itself to be confused as to the consistent direction of the world by God through the apparently purposeless complications of the present and the suffering of the righteous in consequence of the guilt of the unrighteous,[54] because the regular experience of an exact and immediate connection between happiness and worthiness would endanger the freedom and dignity of the moral disposition.

19. The imperative of the moral association of all men as men could become effective as a practical principle only insofar as it grew out of the religious motive of the specifically Christian community (par. 10). Moreover, since that imperative raises itself above all naturally conditioned moral motives, its authority in the Christian community finds its necessary criterion in the idea of a supernatural God developed in paragraphs 11–18. Moreover, the peculiar fact of such a community, which sets itself to the realization of this universal task as the thrust of the kingdom of God, is not a natural "given" but is comprehensible in its distinctive nature only as the work of Christ's own establishment (par. 13). Therefore, in order for us to understand and rightly participate in the existence of this

community, it is necessary to acknowledge and understand the permanent relation which exists between the community of the kingdom of God and its founder Jesus Christ.[55]

20. The historical connection of Christianity with the religion of the Old Testament (par. 7) makes it natural that Jesus should in general represent himself as a prophet sent by God who was ordained in God's decree concerning the world and mankind.[56] However, he sets himself above all the preceding prophets of the Old Testament by making himself known as the Son of God and the promised king of David's race (Christ the anointed),[57] who need not first prepare the way for the kingdom of God but effects *the* work of God,[58] i.e., himself exercises immediate divine rulership over the new community of the sons of God, and establishes it for the future (par. 5, n. 7). The prophetic vocation of Jesus is not annulled by his claim to messianic dignity, but only modified by it, since he exercises his right as lord only through his morally effective teaching and by his readiness to engage in the action of servant—not by the compulsion of legal judgment.[59]

21. In the moral world all personal authority is conditioned by the nature of one's vocation and by the connection between one's fitness for his particular vocation and his faithful exercise of it. Accordingly, the permanent significance of Jesus Christ for his community is based, *first*, on the fact that he was the only one qualified for his special vocation—bringing in the kingdom of God;[60] that he devoted himself to the exercise of this highest conceivable vocation in the preaching of the truth and in loving action without break or deviation;[61] and that, in particular, as a proof of his steadfastness[62] he freely accepted in willing patience[63] the wrongs brought upon him by the opposition of the leaders of the nation of Israel and the fickleness of the people, all of which were so many temptations to draw back from his vocation.

22. *Second*, the imperative of Jesus Christ's vocation, or the final purpose of his life, namely, the kingdom of God, is the very purpose of God in the world, as Jesus himself recognized.[64] The solidarity between Christ and God, which Jesus accordingly claims for himself,[65] has reference to the whole range of his activity in his vocation and consists therefore in the reciprocal relation between God's love and Jesus' vocational obedience.[66] Since he is the first to actualize in

his own personal life the final purpose of the kingdom of God, Jesus is therefore unique, for should any other fulfill the same task as perfectly as he, he would be unlike him because of his dependence upon Jesus. Therefore, as the prototype of the humanity to be united into the kingdom of God, he is the original object of God's love (par. 12), so that the love of God for the members of his kingdom is also mediated only through him (par. 13). Therefore, when this person is valued at his whole worth, this person who was active in his peculiar vocation, whose constant motive is recognizable as unselfish love to man, then we see in Jesus the complete revelation of God as love, grace and faithfulness.[67]

23. In every religion, not only is some sort of communion with God (or the gods) sought after and attained, but there is also a search at the same time for such a position of the individual vis-à-vis the world as will correspond with the idea of God which guides that religion. Hence, *third*, Jesus Christ's prerogative, that the rulership of the world is delivered over to him,[68] corresponds to the solidarity of Jesus with the supramundane God in the realization of the supramundane (par. 8) kingdom of God, which as the final purpose of God is also the final purpose of the world. The significance of this attribute is not secured if we suppose that Jesus did not exercise it, but allowed it to remain inactive in his public historical life. Moreover, he did not merely exercise it indirectly, as if by his deeds and his words and his patience in suffering he prepared the way for the kingdom of God in his community, so that his dominion over the world would be established only in the world-historical progress of that community. Rather, he exercised this dominion directly, not only in the independence of his action from the standard of religion peculiar to his people,[69] but also in his very readiness to suffer everything even unto death for the sake of his vocation.[70] For through this suffering he transformed the world's opposition to his life purpose into a means of his glorification, i.e., into the certainty of overcoming the world by the very fact of this momentary subjection to its power and assuring the supramundane continuance of his life.[71] Accordingly, his resurrection through the power of God is the consistent fulfillment, corresponding to the worth of his person, of the revelation effected through him which is final in respect to both the actual will of God and the destiny of man.

24. In Christ's vocational activity, directed to the divine purpose of the kingdom of God, the same acts of love and patience are both manifestations of the grace and faithfulness which are essential to God himself and proofs of his dominion over the world.[72] These relations, which are necessary to the full appreciation of Jesus and are evident in his life, are referred to in the confession of the God-hood of Christ which the Christian community has made from the beginning. That is to say, this attribute of Godhood cannot be maintained unless the same activities in which Jesus Christ proves himself man are thought of as being simultaneously and in the same way also distinctive predicates of God and the peculiar means of his revelation through Christ. If the grace and faithfulness and dominion over the world, which are evident both in Christ's active life and in his patience in suffering, are also the essential attributes of God and decisive for the Christian religion, then the right appreciation of the completeness of the revelation of God through Christ is assured by the predicate of his Godhood, in accordance with which Christians are to trust in him and to worship him even as they do God the Father.[73]

25. The estimate of Christ set forth in paragraphs 20–24 is intentionally directed with the greatest possible exactness to the historically certified characteristics of his active life, but at the same time it is undertaken from the standpoint of the community of the kingdom of God founded by him. These two criteria, historical and religious, for the understanding of his person should coincide[74] inasmuch as Christ's purpose was directed at founding the community in which he was to be acknowledged in religious faith as the Son of God. And if this purpose is in any measure historically realized, it follows that the perfect historical estimate of Christ is possible only for his religious community and that this estimate will be religiously correct in proportion as his community remains faithful to its historically unquestionable task. Accordingly, it is essential to the continuance of the Christian community as such, that it should keep alive within itself the memory of the finished life-work of Christ[75] and that accordingly the personal impulses of its founder should be ceaselessly operative in like efforts on the part of the members of his community.[76] In the fulfillment of these conditions we see the visible side of the mystery of Christ's exaltation to the right hand of God,

which is acknowledged by his community[77] as a guarantee that the purpose of his life was not frustrated but rather fully accomplished in his death.[78]

II. THE DOCTRINE OF RECONCILIATION
THROUGH CHRIST

26. In the Christian community the concept of the perfect common good included in the notion of the kingdom of God and the concept of personal goodness included in our understanding of God and in our view of Jesus Christ lay the foundation for a corresponding concept of sin and evil. Everyone judges himself by this concept of sin and evil to the extent that he stands in reciprocal relation to the world, i.e., to that structure of human society which in all conceivable degrees and variation is in contradiction to the good as recognized in Christianity.[79]

27. The imperative of the kingdom of God is assigned to the members of the Christian community, since their capacity for good in general is to be presupposed according to the revelation of God's love in Christ and its special effect upon them (par. 13). But it must also be remembered that we conceive the kingdom of God, insofar as the Christian community is active in its realization (par. 5, n. 9), to be in the process of becoming; it therefore is mingled at all points with the opposing currents of evil springing up on every side from the merely natural impulse of human will. Thus, while everyone born of Christian parents is born into the community of Christ, he is, at the same time, put into connection with evil, against which his natural will as such does not contend.[80] Sins are evil volitions, but they are also corresponding intentions, habitual inclinations and dispositions, not only insofar as these thwart the intended union of men into the kingdom of God or offend against the moral law of Christ (par. 6, n. 10) or run counter to the glory of God (par. 11, n. 24),[81] but in addition, insofar as they manifest in varying degrees a lack of reverence and trust in God.[82]

28. The possibility and probability of sinning, and this only, can be derived from the fact that the human will, which should decide for the recognized good, is a constantly growing power whose efficacy is not accompanied from the outset by a complete knowledge of the good. A universal necessity of sinning can be derived neither from

the natural endowment of man nor, least of all, from a discernible purpose of God.[83] The fact of universal sin on the part of man, in accordance with experience, is established by the impulse to the unrestrained exercise of freedom, with which everyone comes into the world and meets the manifold attractions to self-seeking which arise out of the sin of society. Therefore, it happens that some degree of self-seeking takes form in every person, even before a clear comprehension of the state of society's self-consciousness is awakened in him.

29. Sins are, in particular, actions or other volitions which come into conflict with increasingly severe social and legal ordinances, as is the case with rudeness, immorality, careless or intentional wrong, and crime. For at the same time, they oppose the highest law of good. Even actions and dispositions, which follow a justifiable end in a narrower sphere (par. 57, n. 162), are sins when they follow it in such a way as to come into conflict with higher common ends. On the other hand, we also recognize various degrees of sin in comparisons between a single action and a propensity to or a habit of sinning, between a carelessly and a willfully sinful act, between prudent self-seeking, unbridled passion, vice, insolence, and malice. Although all these forms of sin are alike in their opposition to the good, yet they are different in the degree in which they are detrimental to it and in the possibility still existing of improvement and conversion.[84]

30. The cooperation of many individuals in these forms of sin leads to a reinforcement of the same in common customs and principles, in standing immoralities, and even in evil institutions. So there develops an almost irresistible power of temptation[85] for those who with characters yet undeveloped are so much exposed to evil example that they do not see through the network of enticements to evil. Accordingly, the kingdom of sin, or the (immoral, human) world[86] is reinforced in every new generation. Corporate sin [die gemeinsame Sünde], this opposite of the kingdom of God, rests upon all as a power[87] which at the very least limits the freedom of the individual with respect to the good.[88] The limitation of the freedom of the individual for the good, by his own sin and by entanglement with the common condition of the world, is, strictly speaking, an absence of the freedom to choose the good [Unfreiheit zum Guten].

Apart from the kingdom of God, however, this is the common condition of all men, because the form even of the partial good is assured only through the existence of the whole.

31. It is true that the full extent of the existence and guilt of sin appears only from a comparison of sin with the imperative of the kingdom of God (par. 26). Yet its character—contrary as it is to the destiny of man, to the freedom of the will, and to the commands of God—is made evident in all the preceding levels of moral development through a self-condemnation which, arising everywhere as an act of the individual, in some measure grows into a common conviction. At the heart of all individual as well as corporate condemnation of evil is the feeling of guilt as an expression of the individual accountability included in the freedom of the will. This sense of guilt is a witness to the fact that even the single sinful act does not by any means come to an end with the act, but continues to work as a disordering or perversion of moral freedom; it further testifies to the fact that the consciousness of an opposite destiny, so necessary to freedom, maintains itself in spite of the sinful action and desire. The feeling of guilt, in the form of this unavoidable judgment of condemnation, springs from the conscience,[89] whose presence in every man is to be counted upon as long as he has a measure of free will in connection with his sin. To be sure, the feeling of guilt, as such, does not have the power to undo the sin or to limit the continuance or increase of the sinful propensity. Rather, in many cases this feeling of guilt becomes the occasion for a stubborn maintenance of the sinful propensity or an increased rejection of God or, at least, an aversion to his authority. In yet worse cases, through the growth of this sinful propensity, the conscience itself is weakened and the feeling of guilt is practically lost, even in great sin. In spite of this, it is not consistent with our regard for human worth to admit, even in the cases of those apparently most hardened, the complete absence of this manifestation and thus the impossibility of repentance.

32. By evils, we mean natural events which, proceeding partly from the course of nature and partly from the operation of man, limit the exercise of our freedom for the attainment of our purposes. In part evils are, directly or indirectly, the result of sinful actions. The pre-Christian world held to a view which regarded great common misfortune as divine punishment and therefore as necessarily

the result of unusual transgression against the gods; to this was added the corresponding principle that all evils without exception are only the consequences of one's own sins and God's punishments. This pre-Christian perspective is in part out of harmony with experience and in part contrary to the view of the world set forth in Christ.[90] Thus it is that, in general, the estimate of evil by different men varies according to their strength of will or their habit and is therefore subjectively conditioned. On the other hand, Christianity teaches us to recognize that through our very devotion to our faith we necessarily draw suffering upon ourselves as the result of our coming into collision with present historical forces (par. 18, n. 52). The Christian view of the world differs therefore from the heathen and Jewish views in that tenderness of feeling which prevents us from reckoning a man's personal sufferings as divine punishments.[91] It follows, finally, that the Christian regards death, even though it may have entered the world as a universal decree in consequence of the first sin of man,[92] neither as a punishment of his personal sin nor as at all the specific hindrance to his communion with God or to his salvation, and therefore not as the greatest evil.[93]

33. Strictly speaking, only the individual person himself can determine that the misfortunes which come upon him are divine punishments for sin, when he thus reckons them to himself because of a feeling of guilt. This is true as much when through redemption one has attained to trust in God (par. 51) as it is in the case of defiance toward God. Still worse, to be sure, is the condition of a sinner who regards deserved misfortunes as injustice, or connects no thought of a divine government of the world with his experience. So far the analogy holds between the punishments inflicted by God and those decreed by human law. In both cases the curtailment of rights which follows upon the illicit extension of those rights is evident in connection with the occasion of misfortunes. But punishment in the religious relation to God, apart from external misfortunes, is the lessening or dissolution of the designed or desired communion with God. Accordingly, the continuance of unforgiven guilt, whether felt more or less strongly or even not at all, is to be regarded as divine punishment in the fullest sense, as the real condemnation, insofar as it is connected with that lack of trust in God which gives expression to separation from God (par. 27, n. 82).

34. As a member of the Christian community one is called to the kingdom of God as man's highest good and his highest common duty (par. 5), because it is the final purpose of God himself (par. 13). At the same time, however, by the very recognition of this destiny there comes an increase of the feeling of guilt and separation from God which arises from our own sin and our solidarity with the sin common to all men. Thus Christianity seems to require of us a self-contradictory judgment of ourselves, but at the same time it does away with this contradiction in that it also brings the certainty of a God-given *redemption*.

35. Redemption in Christianity has both a thoroughly internal and a universal religious significance. From the first rubric, it follows that we are not, as in the Old Testament, to include under redemption the removal of social evil, especially political dependence upon foreign nations, to say nothing of the establishment of economic prosperity.[94] The second rubric implies that redemption does not pertain directly to the setting aside of the condition of sin which dominates the individual.[95] For while this condition is common to all, it is also distinctive in each individual and, therefore, can be contended against and set aside only by means of a particular opposition in the form of the resolution of the will, after one has experienced for himself religious redemption. In Christianity, such redemption denotes the forgiveness of sins or pardon through which the guilt of sin which separates man from God is removed, provided that neither indifference to nor defiance of God is joined with the feeling of guilt.[96]

36. The forgiveness of sins or justification [*Gerechtsprechung (Rechtfertigung)*], which guarantees the existence of the Christian community, is, as a divine purpose of grace, part of a free judgment. That is to say (without taking up at present the conditions to be considered in pars. 39–44), sinners are given by God the right to enter into communion with him and into cooperation with his own final purpose, viz., the kingdom of God, without their guilt and their feeling of guilt acting as a barrier thereto.[97] The freedom and independence of this divine judgment consist in this, that on man's part, situated as he is, no moral work (merit) is conceivable which might call for this positive judgment of God or actually establish it. Rather, this judgment needs only religious faith[98] or confidence in the

free grace or righteousness of God (par. 16, n. 43) in order to become actual and effective.

37. The more specific conceptions of reconciliation with God and adoption as his children coincide with the forgiveness of sins, pardon, and justification. These specificities merely add something individual. In reconciliation, for example, the forgiveness of sins appears no longer merely as the purpose of God but also as the result of that purpose. According to the conception of reconciliation with God, the individual has in faith and trust appropriated to himself the final purpose of God and given up his opposition (enmity) to God.[99] In adoption (acceptance as children of God) the gracious purpose of the judgment of forgiveness or justification is put into effect, so that God confronts the believer as a father and gives him the right to the full confidence of a child.[100] But these effects of divine redemption find practical application only on the condition that the believer at the same time takes an active part in the recognized purpose of God's kingdom and has given up the pursuit of selfish ends and inclinations, whether intentional or habitual.[101]

38. The forgiveness of sins, or reconciliation, as the common fundamental condition of the Christian community, within which the individual appropriates this gift of God,[102] is as essential to the peculiar character of that community as is the fact that it is called to realize the kingdom of God or the fact that the impulse to this realization is contained in its calling. It is a regression to the point of view of the Old Testament religion, or a falling back into the catholic conception of the matter, to preach forgiveness of sins merely to individuals as such, in relation to their personal feeling of guilt and their need as thus measured, or to preach it as a good which is always yet to be attained.[103]

39. Forgiveness of sins cannot be inferred as necessary from any universally established conception of God.[104] Rather, as the positive fundamental condition of the Christian community, it is to be gained from the positive Christian conception of God. Therefore its validity (par. 38) is linked to the peculiar work of Christ (par. 19).

40. Redemption or forgiveness of sins is not assured to the Christian community through Christ simply because he made, in his role as prophet and thus revealer of God, a universal promise to that effect (par. 20). On the contrary, that is just what he did not do.[105]

Rather, he himself beforehand and after him the earliest Christian witnesses linked such a result to the fact of his death. And this takes place insofar as his death is capable of comparison with the Old Testament sacrifices[106] which, in accordance with the grace of God, were offered for the whole people of Israel, partly to indicate their own entrance into the covenant with God and partly to serve in yearly repetition for the forgiveness of sins, i.e., to maintain the integrity of the covenant.[107]

41. The death of Christ has the value of the covenant-offering and the universal sin-offering, not because his enemies put him to death but because he obediently yielded himself to this fate as being, in the providence of God, a sure result of his distinctive vocation.[108] This significance of Christ's death is also expressed in the relationship between the images of the priest and the sacrifice, since in bringing his life-work to completion he conformed to both of these images.[109] Therefore his death stands as a sacrifice offered for the purpose of bringing forgiveness to his community or consummating their new covenant with God only insofar as we connect him with the very offering of the sacrifice or with the priestly self-awareness which dominates all of his vocational activity.[110]

42. The obedience of Christ to his vocation can be interpreted as a gift of God or as a sacrifice and priestly offering, because his righteous life, his patience and his preachments of truth were the result not only of his divine charge but also of his free consecration of himself to God. For by this vocational obedience he maintained the special fellowship of reciprocal love between God and himself.[111] Now he rendered his vocational obedience not only for its own sake, but at the same time necessarily for the purpose of bringing mankind into the same relation toward God which he occupied, as their father.[112] For this very purpose, furthermore, he also accepted with patience and resignation to God's will increased sufferings and death as a proof of his fellowship with God. And, finally, in this way he performed everything that was necessary to prove the genuineness of his fellowship with God and the possibility of a similar fellowship for all. In these respects, therefore, he represented the community before God as its royal priest for the purpose of establishing it completely.[113]

43. Now if we compare the fact of the existing community of

Christ to which we ourselves belong with his purpose in its foundation and with the priestly significance of his life and suffering unto death, there appears clearly in his death, i.e., in the completion of his life from the point of view of sacrifice, an analogy between it and the Old Testament types. For the universal meaning of the symbolic actions performed by the ministering priest, that the sacrifice might be accepted by God, is rightly expressed by Peter when he says, in speaking of Christ, that believers are thereby led to God,[114] are brought near to him in the sacrifice.[115] In the case of the community to be founded by Christ, this bringing near of men takes place because they are originally separated from God by their sins and feeling of guilt. Therefore, the sacrificial act of Christ's priestly completion of his life-work serves to equip the new community with the divine forgiveness of sins, because as their intentional representative he transforms this separation of man from God into fellowship with him as their father.

44.[116] Christ's victory over the world through patience in the suffering made necessary by his vocation is not only a mark of his Godhood in his office of revealer (pars. 23, 24) but is also the mark of the completeness of his work as priestly representative of the community which he is bringing to God. The same scope of Christ's vocational obedience which filled his life and came to fulfillment in his death is conceived under the two contrasting viewpoints of the office of royal prophet and the royal priesthood, the representing of God to men and of men (in the community) before God. Of these two sides of his vocation (or offices), the latter is, it is true, subordinate to the former. But in this double value of his life Christ is the mediator of the highest conceivable fellowship between God and man.[117]

45.[118] The distinctiveness of the community founded by Christ is not determined by his life in its aspect as representative and revealer of God, that is, as God himself,[119] for in this relation Christ stands over against the community. But the character of the community which is itself reconciled to God, as is every individual within it who appropriates justification through faith in Christ,[120] corresponds rather to the position that Christ took as representative of the community in relation to God and the world. Since his dignity as Son of God is also his because he sacrifices his life for the sake of the community,[121] so the adoption as children belongs to the members of his community as a result of the reconciliation with God (par. 37, n. 100). Because his patience in suffering and death establishes his dominion over the world for the sake of his believers, so faith in Christ includes in itself spiritual dominion over the world,[122] i.e., eternal life or Christian freedom.[123]

III. THE DOCTRINE OF THE CHRISTIAN LIFE

46. The individual believer within the Christian community does not appropriate to himself the call to the kingdom of God and reconciliation or acceptance as a child of God without simultaneously experiencing these effects of grace as impulses for corresponding personal activity.[124] Therefore, conversely, in the religious estimate of our total life-work which corresponds to these impulses, we recognize everything good as the effect of divine grace in us.[125] This agreement between these impulses and the purpose of God, and their similarity in different individuals, is grounded in and assured by the Holy Spirit in the community.[126] This is to say that the impulse to right conduct, i.e., to fulfilling the imperative belonging to the kingdom of God, and the impulse to give practical proof of our sonship with God have as their criterion the knowledge of God as our Father which is given to us in Christianity. However, the Christian knowledge of God, springing as it does from definitive revelation, is congruent with God's knowledge of himself. Hence, seen from the divine point of view, the development of the Christian community (resulting from the exercise of love in accordance with this knowledge of God) is a part of the divine self-revelation (par. 13, n. 32). From these considerations, it appears that the common spirit through which the members of the community receive their like knowledge of God and their like impulses toward the kingdom of God and toward sonship with God, is God's Holy Spirit.[127]

47. Practical proof of sonship with God in spiritual freedom and dominion over the world and labor for the kingdom of God fill out the Christian life which is a new creation of God, when compared with the sinful state which is presupposed in man.[128] It is as certain that these two activities stand in reciprocity with one another (par. 37, n. 101) as that the ends and motives in both cases exist on the same supramundane level. The reciprocal relation of these activities,

the first religious and the second ethical, is evident in the fact that the religious imperative of dominion over the world demands the same effort of the will as the ethical imperative of the kingdom of God, even as the latter includes in itself religious elevation above the world. The unity of this twofold destiny of life is evident in the joy or blessedness which springs from them both.[129] This is the feeling of religious-ethical perfection.[130] Insofar as blessedness is expected in the Christian life, the possibility is also therein admitted of perfection, which is set before us as an imperative in those two dimensions of our striving—for God's kingdom and its righteousness and for the exercise of freedom over the world.

48. Of course it is true that the series of dutiful actions, which we would represent to ourselves as the embodiment of the ethical task of our lives, always remains imperfect, partly because in our conceptualizing such a series can be carried out into infinity and partly because in any single moment our responsibilities may seem staggeringly heavy. In reality, it is not the fact of the actual continuance of sin,[131] but this external and quantitative conception of the imperative of the Christian life which is the ground of the traditional assertion that defect in good works is unavoidable and the possibility of Christian perfection is therefore out of the question. Nevertheless, in spite of the unavoidably defective quality of human conduct, we must uphold man's destiny as one who may attain personal perfection, since this destiny is correlative with the qualitative judgment that the religious-ethical life is a whole in its own right [*ein Ganzes in seiner Art*]. Now the concept of the whole signifies that the component parts of an organic existence are in a special way united by a common end. In accordance with this conception, Christian perfection consists in the process which fosters a person's ethical life-work[132] and in the development of ethical and religious character.[133] Included in this is the fact that one directs his action toward the end of the kingdom of God in a particular ethical vocation[134] and authenticates his sonship with God and his dominion over the world in the particular conditions of life into which he is placed.[135]

49. The struggle against and suppression of selfish impulses and habits are included in sanctification or the formation of Christian character.[136] The task here is not rooting out any impulse or affection, but ennobling and purifying it by the opposing force of moral prin-

ciples (par. 72). This task cannot and should not be accomplished by special scrupulousness or special ascetic practices before the beginning of right action or the attainment of positive virtues. The similar attempt of monasticism to avoid certain temptations to sin by isolation from the fundamental institutions of human society is also a mistake. For evil inclinations and habits are rendered ineffective only by the development of contrasting good inclinations and habits; while virtues are produced only by the reaction of dutiful or righteous action upon the will itself.[137] Therefore, the Christian imperative of perfection and the consciousness of continual sinfulness are balanced in the command to strive for the common good with the idea that as a member of the Christian community one is no longer alive to sin.[138] This is also the intended purpose of all honest and effectual repentance, to which, in the process of sanctification, one is all the more inclined as he becomes more sensitive to the effect of sin upon himself.[139] Such repentance, however, is not attained when one dulls his perception or observation of his own particular sins by mirroring them in the uncertain reflection of the immeasurable general sin of a society. It is in the constant readiness for real repentance that the change of heart prescribed by Jesus stamps the whole life.[140]

50. The Christian perfection which corresponds to the personal example of Christ himself[141] is shaped by the religious functions of sonship with God and dominion over the world (i.e., faith in the fatherly providence of God, humility, patience, and prayer) and by the ethical functions of dutiful action in one's particular vocation and the development of ethical virtues.[142] In this coherence of the spiritual life the individual person possesses the significance of a whole which exceeds the significance of the entire world which is viewed as the order of a divided and naturally conditioned existence.[143] Included in this is autonomy from every particular authority.[144] This consequence of the Christian religion is the goal of that impulse which is found in all religions (par. 8), namely, to make certain through the appropriation of the divine life or the evident divine purpose the significance of our spiritual life in the midst of the limitations which grow out of its involvement in nature or the world.

51. Faith in the fatherly providence of God is the Christian world view in an abbreviated form.[145] In this faith, although we

neither know the future nor perfectly comprehend the past, yet we judge our momentary relation to the world on the basis of our knowledge of the love of God and on the basis of what we derive from this knowledge, namely, that every child of God possesses a significance greater than the world which God directs in accordance with his final purpose, i.e., our salvation.[146] From this faith there springs that confidence which in all its gradations is equally far removed from the gnawing anxiety which might arise from our relation to the superior power of nature, as it is from dull indifference or bold recklessness or from stoic imperturbability, since none of these are an expression of ongoing spiritual freedom. More specifically, faith in providence furnishes a standard by which the first impression of evils as limitations of freedom or as divine punishments is transformed into an interpretation of them as blessings, i.e., as means of education or testing.[147] In this assessment of evil occurrences he who trusts in providence gives evidence of his dominion over the world, as well as his redemption from the guilt and power of sin and his reconciliation with God. In an equally clear manner, faith in providence illumines the experiences of prosperity or happiness as gifts of God which call for our thankfulness to him and the purification or moderation of our self-reliance.[148]

52. Humility is that quality of feeling which springs from the knowledge of God's fatherly guidance and either accompanies this knowledge or, as a constant readiness to concur with all the dispensations of God, takes the place of the conscious exercise of trust in his providence. As a distinctively religious virtue, it is again that power of self-consciousness which leads us to assess both unpleasant and agreeable experiences as dispensations of God, and in such a way, therefore, that we are neither crushed nor unduly exalted by them.[149] The humility of the Christian does not spring from a constant consciousness of his sin, but neither is it indifferent to it. Rather, it involves a more lively sense of God's grace in view of sin and accordingly a hesitation to regard our religious and moral convictions, however well intended, as God's cause or to defend them as such. The religious man is unconscious of his own humility,[150] and still less is that humility an object of observation and exhaustive judgment on the part of others, since it does not manifest itself directly in any moral quality or mode of action.[151] Least of all does

it find its necessary manifestation in ceremonially proper ascetic actions, although from the first, thanks to a dualistic view of the world, a low estimation of the natural conditions of human life has been accepted as an especially clear proof of humility toward God.[152]

53. Patience under the hampering limitations of the world,[153] which arises from the judgment of faith in providence through the feeling of humble submission to God's fatherly guidance, accepts deserved evils as divine punishments and also as a means of education, undeserved evils as tests, or, perhaps at the same time, as the honor of martyrdom. Patience is fundamentally always a determination of the will; but it may take the form of a quality of feeling and thus unite itself closely with humility, when the original determination of the will proves adequate for countering the concrete limitations which the world continually sets before it. Since, however, the Christian world view holds that the difference between the significance of evil and prosperity is a relative one, patience as a religious virtue has room for exercise not only in experiences which appear at first as direct limitations, but also proves itself of value in connection with humility as a moderation of self-reliance in the context of experiences of prosperity, which can spoil men and make them dependent on the world.

54. Prayer, whether as thanksgiving or as petition, is the conscious and intentional exercise both of faith in God's providence[154] and of humility. It is also, as thanksgiving, the proof of patience and, as petition, the means of gaining or of strengthening patience. In these respects prayer is the proof of his reconciliation which the individual gives before God and to himself as well as being the means by which he establishes himself in the same. As the common offering of the community, it has still other characteristics (par. 79).

55. The answer to the prayer for specific blessings which we direct toward God in the midst of life's difficulties, although it seems to be assured without any limit,[155] is nevertheless limited by the reservation that the petition must accord with God's providence over us,[156] and that the one who prays must be engaged in the fulfillment of the divine commands.[157] Finally, the significance of the petitions addressed to God is made independent of the test of their direct and complete fulfillment by the fact that to know that God hears us is also to know that we have the blessings which we requested.[158]

56. The ethical imperative of the kingdom of God (par. 47) is performed as the most universal imperative of the Christian community, but only when the ultimate motive for all conduct is love for one's neighbor. We carry out this action in naturally conditioned moral communities which are narrower in scope (marriage, family, civic and social life, the nation), and we do so according to the specific principles that govern each. For the universal is always realized only in the particular. If the opposite were true, and one wished to fulfill the Christian imperative outside the natural orders of life, he would give a false particularity to that which should be universally valid and create something bizarre.[159]

57. Conduct in the narrower and naturally conditioned communities is subordinated to the most universal end of the kingdom of God and brought into direct relation to the same, when the regular activity incumbent upon each one in these communities is exercised in the form of an ethical vocation (par. 50, n. 142) for the common good.[160] The intention to serve the common good, with which the work of every vocation in society should be undertaken, does not exclude personal interest in its success or the acquiring of property; this latter becomes a motive to selfishness, however, unless it is balanced, in this ethical conception of vocation, by the communal ends. Accordingly, fidelity to one's vocation is at the same time following the example of Christ.[161] Moreover, this assessment, which sees ethical vocations as constitutive elements in the kingdom of God, overcomes the temptations to selfishness which adhere as such to the particular circumstances of each area of life[162] and disproves the catholic assumption that one lives a spiritual life only in separation from worldly vocations.[163]

58. The significance of marriage as the union of two persons of different sexes into one (monogamy), which is set forth in the Old Testament and recognized by Christ as God's original ordering,[164] not only implies that in marriage husband and wife are of equal honor [Wert], and that their union is indissoluble during earthly life,[165] but also proves itself in the fact that in this relation the self-sacrificing power of love for one's neighbor can and should test itself in the most intense and blessed manner.[166] Nevertheless, when love is demanded of the husband and obedience of the wife,[167] it is because of that difference in the spiritual nature of the two sexes which leads

the wife to subject herself to her husband as the representative of their mutual union.

59. Since the realization of love for one's neighbor, which is intensified in marriage, is further continued in the care and training of children by their parents, the relation of these children to Christianity is already assured by their birth from Christian parents.[168] The children, in turn, during their upbringing realize their Christian destiny in that obedience to parents which in general is fitting.[169] Moreover, as brothers and sisters, the children of a household are admonished both to develop a consciousness of mutual rights and to form especially close friendships with one another. In these two respects their relation serves them as a school for their necessary participation in the public community of rights and in common ethical interaction. And the real effectiveness of the latter depends precisely upon the broadening and solidifying of the ethical individuality of each one through the winning of friends.

60. Law [das Recht] is the ordering of mutual or concerted actions which have reference either to personal ends (civil law) or to such common ends (public law—constitutional and criminal) as are of narrower scope than the ethical end of the kingdom of God. Inasmuch as judicial law directly controls only actions, actions which are in accordance with the law are not necessarily nor always the expression of a corresponding disposition; rather, judicial law is always accompanied by a compulsion to enforce right-doing among those who are otherwise disposed. But since law, when completely understood, is conceived of as the means by which ethical freedom attains its ends and therefore as an ethical product, the right ethical disposition includes necessarily a disposition to uphold the law, and in the community of laws we customarily presuppose such a disposition on the part of every individual.[170]

61. Therefore, the legal constitution of a people or a state is in itself indifferent to Christianity, regarded either as worship or as the practice of the kingdom of God;[171] yet the state is acknowledged as God's ordering, and obedience to judicial authority is prescribed as a religious duty.[172] This is because the community of laws, being a necessary means for securing ethical freedom, is also the indispensable condition for the Christian, if he is to fulfill the imperative of the kingdom of God in all the spheres of ethical interaction.[173]

62. Accordingly, while active participation in the state, insofar as it springs from patriotism and a general sense of justice, is not an activity which belongs directly to the kingdom of God, yet (as we may conclude from par. 61) it is not only compatible with the Christian life but the two activities have a necessary reciprocal relation to one another.[174] On the one hand, the Christian will find it incumbent upon him to promote the legal authority of the state for the very purpose of gaining room for striving after the kingdom of God. On the other hand, the pedagogy by which a Christian people is brought to its humanity, a pedagogy demanded by the welfare of the state, is founded upon an effort to realize the kingdom of God and must be regulated by an insight into the morality suitable for it, an insight which a statesman in a Christian nation can ill afford to be without. To the degree that this disposition pervades the different nations, it strengthens regard for their mutual rights. But as long as statecraft has to defend the rights of a people or a state against hostility from others, although it is never justified in the use of criminal means to this end, yet it is not bound by the same rules which hold for the legal and ethical action of the individual Christian in his relation to the state and in intercourse with other men.

63. Virtue and duty are concepts which, in that form, are derived from philosophical ethics. Both concepts must be used in Christian ethics, however, because their content is included in the right apprehension of the Christian life. Ethical virtues and actions regulated by the concept of duty are the products of a will directed toward the purpose that is ultimately good. The difference between the two is that actions in accordance with duty go forth from the will, while virtues are acquired in the will itself; the former relate to intercourse or association with others and the latter belong to the individual as such. When, nevertheless, we judge actions to be virtuous, we have in mind not their relation to interaction with others, but rather their relation to the distinctive personal force of the doer himself. On the other hand, when it is declared a duty to become virtuous, this concept of duty, against its own nature, departs from the usual concept of duty, and that departure is likely to cause confusion. In other words, such an expression is in part an unnecessary circumlocution with regard to personal rights, e.g., that of self-preservation or the choice and maintenance of the ethical vocation,

and in part an expression, permissable in pedagogics, of the necessity for the immature to acquire virtues.

64. In reality, dutiful actions and the acquisition of virtues are separate from each other in neither time nor space. On the one hand, the very means by which virtues are acquired is constant dutiful action (par. 49, n. 137); on the other hand, virtues are already being employed in the formation and implementation of the right concepts of duty.[175] And as they are exercised they are confirmed or rather acquired in ever higher degrees. This is not the description of a self-contradictory and hence falsely conceived and impossible process. The ethical will is a force whose effect upon others and whose effect upon itself stand in an inseparable reciprocal relationship to one another. For the ethical development of the individual will is utterly inconceivable apart from social interaction with other persons.

65. The virtues are derived from the various relations in which the will that is directed toward the highest purpose is to be recognized as a whole. To the extent that the will subjects the impulses of the individual disposition to that purpose which is ultimately good, it gains *self-control*. To the extent that it establishes firmly for itself the condition upon which the ethical vocation depends (par. 57), whether this results in the limiting or in the strengthening of that vocation, it gains *conscientiousness*. To the extent that it orders its planned activity in consistency with its intentions, purposes and resolves, it gains *wisdom, discretion, decisiveness* and *constancy*. To the extent that it directs the good disposition through the motive of love toward the individual persons with whom one is in moral association, the will gains *kindliness, thankfulness*, and *justice*.[176]

66. The *first* group of virtues—self-control and conscientiousness[177]—makes for autonomy and honorableness of character. In the opposite vices, sensuality, intemperance, immoderate ambition, imperious dogmatism, unscrupulousness, untrustworthiness—the will is lacking in the capability of determining itself in a consistent manner. Honor is the moral autonomy of a man insofar as it is recognized by other autonomous men. Thus the man without virtue has no moral honor. Moreover, no one gains honor by winning for himself the regard of his companions through yielding to the prejudices or immoralities of a special group. Finally, honor must not be confused

with that negative regard which is to be accorded to the dignity of the human being *qua* human being, which is accorded even those who are without virtue.

67. The *second* group of virtues—wisdom, discretion, decisiveness, and constancy[178]—makes for clarity and energy of character. For the good end at which one aims is without effect upon one's character if he is wavering in his purpose, reckless in his principles, indecisive in particulars and changeable as to the whole. In the accomplishment of conduct which is systematic and also expedient for the moment, prudence alternates with discretion,[179] the latter estimating the intended measures according to one's resources, the former according to the resistance to be expected from others.

68. The *third* group of virtues—kindliness,[180] thankfulness, and justice—makes for a good disposition or amiability of character. It is at the very least a lack of virtue when, out of a thoroughly good intention, the moral ends of society are treated in a purely, or largely, impersonal manner, hence with a harshness and lack of consideration for the very persons to whom one nevertheless wishes to show love. The full scope of love proves itself rather when, in kindliness, we gain facility in adjusting our manner of action to the claim which others have upon our love; when in thankfulness we gain the readiness to depend upon the kindliness of others; when in justice we gain the disposition so to bear the lack of kindliness and of thankfulness in others as not to allow ourselves to be led by our perception of that fault into harshness toward them. Thus justice will not exercise the necessary severity toward others without tempering it with a perceptible measure of kindness.[181]

69. The moral law is expressed with such generality in Christ's precept of love to one's neighbor (par. 6) that all morally necessary and desirable actions fall within the scope of this rule. But it has direct reference to the disposition alone, and leaves undetermined all the other conditions under which the necessity for individual benevolent action is to be recognized. To these conditions belong not only the determination of the ways in which love is to be exercised (par. 72), but also the judgment whether in any particular instance we have to deal with a neighbor in the full sense, or with one who is undeveloped in character and in need of education, or with an enemy (par. 6, n. 11). And, finally, it must be determined

whether in a particular instance one ought, at all cost, to act from the disposition of love or should refuse to act. A firm decision concerning these conditions must be included, however, if one is to be able to assure himself that a particular action, or its omision, in any given instance accords with the moral law.[182] But these conditions are so innumerable that they could never be dealt with exhaustively in any systematic, statutory exposition of the moral law.[183] For a judicial law can be laid down as statutory and exhaustive in its definite commands and prohibitions only because the actions which are neither commanded nor forbidden are permitted, i.e., remain legally undetermined. The moral law on the contrary reckons upon a measure of virtuous autonomy in the individual, according to which he has to determine his moral duty in each instance (par. 64, n. 175), namely, whether he is obliged by the universal moral law now to act in accordance with it, or under the circumstances not to act at all. Under these conditions the moral law, perfectly understood, becomes the law of liberty.[184]

70. Therefore, moral duty is the judgment of the virtuous man that in a particular instance, determined by an estimate of the personal and objective circumstances, the moral law requires him to act from the disposition of love. The element of freedom, inseparable as it is from this judgment of the necessity of a loving act, entails that in the same instance one individual may be under obligation to act and another not to act. But the disparity allowed by the conception of duty does not imply lawlessness. For since it is in his own particular ethical vocation (par. 57) that each one is to work at the common task of the kingdom of God and fulfill the universal moral law, most of the moral duties are thereby determined in advance. Thus the duties of one's vocation are the ordinary duties of love.[185] And the disparity in the duty of different individuals in the same instance is explicable from the difference in their ethical vocations. In addition, those actions not provided for by one's particular ethical vocation are also recognized as necessary or obligatory when found to be analogous to those of one's own calling. In these instances a person forms the judgment that through particular circumstances he is called to the exercise of an extraordinary duty of love.

71. Yet the network of ordinary (belonging to one's vocation)

and extraordinary duties of love does not extend so far as to cover all the voluntary expressions of good character. It is a question, therefore, whether all that action which one assumes is morally allowable, and which one is thus accustomed to withdraw from the direct application of the conception of duty, is (1) to be regarded as altogether morally indeterminable, or (2) still to be subsumed under the severity of the concept of duty, or (3) perhaps to be regulated morally in some other way. The *first* case is improbable, because the coherence of the good character would not admit to the morally indifferent nature of such a large range of its activities. The pedantic rigorism of the *second* case is not to be recommended for the very reason that we must be able to assure ourselves of our moral freedom as such, when it encounters legal necessity in the concept of duty. For instance, we must be able to preserve our freedom by not following any prior duty in the choice of our particular vocation; by being under no obligation to marry any particular person or to marry at all; by not being obligated in all cases to defend our vocation against hostile attacks. In these respects one exercises, rather, only rights which may be ignored or exercised in a choice that is not amenable to any concept of duty. However, the way in which this exercise is ethically measurable will become clear when the other realm of what is morally allowable is taken into consideration. This realm is, namely, that of recreation, partly as rest from exertion of work and as sensuous and intellectual enjoyment, i.e., as luxury over and above the indispensable needs of life,[186] partly as social entertainment and amusement, and partly as a combination of both. Rest from moral activity and for enjoyment is occasioned by the dependence of our spiritual life upon bodily conditions. Social amusement in bodily and mental exercise is occasioned by the nature of our spirit, which seeks the individual artistic self-expression that exists along with the necessity for moral association. Thus it corresponds more to the dignity of man to seek his recreation from useful work by entering into all possible artistic activity than in sitting still by himself. The nature of recreation is therefore essentially such as not to be directly subordinate to the moral concept of duty. Only when health is impaired is one led to recreation from a sense of duty to oneself or to one's usefulness in his vocation. Nevertheless, recreation is limited indirectly and negatively by duty.

The kind and duration of recreation is to be so regulated that one will not be less fitted for the fulfillment of his vocation after the recreation than before. Whenever this is the case, recreation is contrary to duty and morally prohibited. Hence, since the regulation of recreation by the concept of duty does not extend further, the *third* case holds good, because all recreation, especially social recreation, must work to maintain virtue. In all recreation conscientiousness, self-control, discretion, kindliness, thankfulness and justice are to be maintained, and all amusement and all entertainment are prohibited which interfere with the exercise of these virtues. Thus it follows that in this realm the same thing is permissible for one and not for another, to the degree that these virtues are exercised therein or not. Finally, it is evident that even in the exercise of personal rights as discussed above, virtue must also make its contribution as the moral standard.

72. The duties of love, which are to be derived from the general disposition toward love, may be divided according to the varieties of the application of this kindliness; and hence specific principles follow which facilitate the decision concerning particular duties. Kindliness authenticates itself either in the positive loving *regard* for other persons, or in the *support* of their justifiable ends, or in *forbearance* with the defects in their virtue. In the first instance, the principles of *modesty* and *sincerity* result; in the second the principles of *rectitude, readiness to serve, benevolence, truthfulness*; in the third the principles of *compatibility* and *willingness to forgive*.

73. Loving regard for others includes the negative regard for the dignity of the human being as such and care for the possessions (of whatever sort) of others as such, these being antecedent conditions of love, maintained even by the order of public justice.[187] For in and of itself this negative regard can be exercised in connection with complete indifference toward others, and leads therefore to no moral fellowship. But the principles of modesty and sincerity do imply such a regard for another, since by action and speech we do enter into moral fellowship with him. Modesty is that limiting of the sense of self to which we are obliged because we acknowledge in the person that the fellowship into which we are entering is of value.[188] Sincerity is the expression of the constant spirit of solidarity with others [*Gemeinsinn*] (to which we are also obliged) which

recognizes the value of the other for the purpose of the fellowship we are entering into.[189]

74. The loving support of the justifiable purposes of others includes righteous behavior in all our relations to them which are governed by contract. For since the administration of justice is the means of assuring the exercise of moral freedom, the disposition to uphold justice is included in the disposition to love (par. 60) and orders our legal duties to others by the principle of rectitude.[190] Rectitude has reference, it is true, to those relations with others which depend upon mutual advantage while, on the contrary, the trait of unselfishness (that is, the surrender of our own advantage in the assistance of others) is necessarily involved in readiness to serve, benevolence and truthfulness. Yet the distance between the principle of rectitude and these other principles is lessened by the fact that the principle of rectitude includes equity in dealing with those who are under legal obligation to us and can lay claim only to our rectitude. Of course, equity is no measure of our duties of love, but it expresses the recognition that our relations to others, while ordered momentarily only by contract, are not exhausted by legal justice. Rather, he who is presently under legal obligation to us possesses at the same time human dignity and moral freedom, and he can at any moment give us occasion to exercise the duties of love. The real duties of love first arise, however, when no question of mutual right is involved and thus when unselfishness is possible. This is the case when the justifiable ends of others are supported in helpfulness by giving personal assistance—in benevolence by the sharing of property, in truthfulness by the sharing of knowledge.[191]

75. Benevolent forbearance in the face of a lack of virtue in others expresses itself basically in compatibility during existing intercourse, and in the willingness to forgive when this intercouse has been interrupted by strife. Both are distinct from a weak indulgence toward wrong, in that they are connected with sincerity.[192] Moreover, right action in accordance with these and the preceding principles (with the exception of rectitude) is limited by the consideration whether the kind and degree of formation of moral character in others allow moral fellowship with them at all, or to what extent.[193] The exercise of rectitude is imperative, however, under all circumstances.

76. Perfection, which, on the foundation of the grace of God and in conformity to the redemption through Christ, consists in the exercise of religious and moral virtues and in the performance of the duties of love regulated by our ethical vocation (par. 50), is necessarily accompanied by a feeling of blessedness (par. 47).[194] But insofar as individuals have succeeded in attaining this height of Christian character-formation and in maintaining it in the conflict with their own sin and in patience under external limitations, they will, as a result of their intensified sensitivity of feeling, be the very ones to judge themselves full of defects and imperfection. Therefore, these will be the very ones to refuse to organize a group of the perfect, so as somehow to form a narrower circle of the same within the community of worship.[195] But the Christian faith, which is certain of eternal life through the reconciliation in Christ (par. 45) and maintains this blessing in the exercise of righteousness as well as in sanctification, orients itself upon the hope that the consummation of the kingdom of God as the highest good will be realized upon conditions which extend beyond this world of experience (par. 8).

77.[196] Christ and the apostles looked forward to the coming of this end and these conditions in the near future. Following the Old Testament prophets, they counted on the divine judgment of the world as a perceptible event upon this earth, through which the way was to be prepared for the dominion of Christ over the kingdom of God on earth.[197] This epoch was to be introduced (and at the same time differentiated from the previous epoch) by the resuscitation of the believers who had died and by the visible reappearance of Christ himself.[198] This form of future expectation has not maintained itself in the church, though it is still held in sectarian circles. The hope cherished in the church gives up the expectation that this earth will be the scene of Christ's dominion, while it holds fast the practical truths of the divine judgment and the separation of the blessed and the lost, as well as the final attainment of the highest good in the case of the former.[199] Since a consistent eschatological theory cannot be gained from the data of the New Testament, the hints of the New Testament as to the condition of the blessed and the lost lie beyond the possibility of a clear presentation.[200] The important thing, however, is not the satisfying of curiosity but the assurance that no one is blessed except in union with all the blessed in the kingdom of God.

IV. THE DOCTRINE OF PUBLIC WORSHIP

78. Prayer is not simply an act or a need of the individual believer (par. 54), but it is intended as well for a public exercise.[201] Prayer is the most spiritual form of divine worship. Therefore, in the perfect religion of Christianity, it has replaced all the material offerings and sacrifices used in the worship of God in other religions.[202]

79. In the generic concept of prayer, petition and thanksgiving are not equally important parts. Otherwise, the error would be encouraged that self-seeking petition may serve as justifiable worship of God, and that one has to return thanks to God only when his petitions are granted. Prayer is represented, rather, as a whole and under all circumstances as thanksgiving, acclamation, praise, recognition and worship of God.[203] The "confession of his name" is thus the recognition of God as our Father, inasmuch as he has revealed himself as such to us through his Son,[204] and proven himself such in the direction of our destiny (par. 54, n. 154). Petition is a variation of the prayer of thanksgiving. For the humble and unselfish recognition of God, or thanksgiving, governs in all cases the petitions which issue from the needs of the one who prays.[205] This also indicates the limits within which we may be confident that our petitions will be granted (par. 55). In particular, petition cannot be public except in the certainty that what is desired will serve not only our need but also God's glory. There is thus the assurance that such petitions will be granted as are offered in the name of Jesus Christ,[206] i.e., aimed at the bestowal of the blessings which are directly related to the purpose of the revelation through Christ. The right and the duty of mutual intercessory prayer is thus preeminently established.

80. The prayer which Christ taught his disciples at their request[207] offers a characteristic confirmation of Paul's direction that every prayer be accompanied with thanksgiving, and it offers the key to the sense in which the confession of God's name is to be understood as a sacrifice of praise. For, in the first place, all the individual petitions of this prayer are clearly subordinate to the invoking of God as our Father, and are embraced in this confession of his name. Further, every petition includes in itself the recognition that God assures to the praying community the blessings to which the petitions relate in varying degrees. The desire that God's name be hallowed presupposes that God has made his being and his power

known to man[208] and therefore that the hallowing of his name, or the recognition of him,[209] is in the same measure possible. On the lips of his disciples, the petition that God's dominion may come presupposes that in the full sense this dominion has already been set in motion by Christ precisely in their own circle (par. 5, n. 7). The prayer for daily bread presupposes the assurance that God cares for the maintenance of the one who prays;[210] and for him, however, who has won the bread he needs by his own toil the petition bears the character of a thanksgiving for divine blessings he has enjoyed. The petition for the forgiveness of sins in no sense gives expression to a just claim on God's favor because it is conditioned upon our forgiveness of others. This condition signifies rather that we are engaged in the exercise of ethical duty characteristic of that community (par. 6, n. 11) which is bound together through the forgiveness of sins, or reconciliation with God (par. 38). The petition for the continued or ever-to-be-renewed application of this gift of forgiveness presupposes therefore the recognition that it is a universal datum in the life of this community. Finally, the petition that we may be spared the temptation that grows out of the particular relationships to the world into which we have been placed or preserved from the evil likely to arise out of those relationships is inconceivable apart from a recognition of God's direction of the world and his loving purpose to direct it for the good of his children.

81. Since Christians call themselves *ekklesia*, church, their uniform and common prayer is considered the essential mark of their unity. For even though this community is at the same time called to the ethical task of carrying out the kingdom of God, yet this activity does not assume a direct, empirically measurable manifestation (par. 9, n. 18). But common prayer, as the manifestation of the religious worship of God, is not only in itself the church's purpose, but serves also to mediate the believers' sense of solidarity in the task of God's kingdom. Apart from this, therefore, the confession of God's name (as our Father) in common prayer is the mark which corresponds to the church's nature as the religious community of Christ. In its exercise all Christians are priests.[211] In addition, the confession before men of Jesus as the Christ or as our Lord is the characteristic of this community which corresponds to its placement in world history.[212]

82. As every religion relates itself in some way to divine revelation, no religious community maintains its peculiar character without resting upon a repeated series of similar revelations, or upon the original revelation as it is held in remembrance and reproduced in speech. It is particularly indispensable for the existence and authentic maintenance of the Christian religious community, that its activity of prayer be regulated by a common and publicly controlling remembrance of its founder and the revelation of God presented through him (pars. 19, 25). Therefore the word of God or the gospel is also the mark of the Christian religious community or church. By "gospel" we mean the revealed divine will of grace which has as its end the kingdom of God and therefore includes the right interpretation of Christ—that he makes actual the grace and faithfulness of God (par. 22) and, as the one who reconciles sinners with God, founds and represents the community of the kingdom of God (par. 42). The entire content of this knowledge is called the word of God, since it is set forth in the form of the will of God and his purpose that we be destined for the kingdom of God (par. 5), and for freedom over the world (par. 45). So constituted, the word of God is effective not only for gaining knowledge, but also for the corresponding stirring of the feelings and the will; it is therefore effective for personal conviction and effective as the motive and criterion of that worship of God which forms the essential active characteristic of the Christian community (par. 81). Given such content and effectiveness, the word of God, even as spoken by man, has its significance as God's word.[213]

83. The two acts of baptism and the Lord's Supper, which Christ instituted and whose observance is maintained by the piety of the Christian community, are in their uniform repetition also marks of the unity of the Christian church.[214] In their visible form, they are cultic acts of the community and are inconceivable apart from that community. Accordingly, they are of the same nature as common prayer and, like it, are acts of confession on the part of the community.[215] But inasmuch as the Lord's Supper refers to the event of Christ's sacrificial death, which includes the founding of the community (par. 42), this cultic act of the community at the same time assures the continuance of the forgiving grace of God by virtue of which Christ founded the community. This is also true of baptism

insofar as it has reference to the revelation of the Father through the Son and through the Holy Spirit bestowed upon the community (pars. 54, 55). Their validity as sacraments or means of grace rests upon these considerations.

84. The catholic concept of the church makes the significance of the common Christian faith and liturgy dependent upon acknowledgment of the specific canons of the catholic church. Now a right appreciation of the community or church of Christ belongs of necessity to the religious view of Christianity as a whole. This not only involves a right appreciation of the community in its relation to the kingdom of God as its highest good and common task (par. 5), but also in its existence as a community of faith and worship that is directed by God's word (par. 82) and, as such, itself maintains the efficacy of the revelation of God in Christ. Therefore it is necessary, even in the protestant view, to believe in the church under these marks when one is a participant in its worship of God. But in the protestant sense one believes thus in the church without reference to the authorized forms in which it exists.[216] For, although the religious elements of the church could not have become historically effective without the mediation of authorized forms, yet the perspective of the community of religious faith and prayer, in which the Christian church universal really consists (par. 86, n. 222), is thoroughly indifferent to the canons which vary from one segment of the church to another.

85. Understood according to its nature and true destiny under the marks already discussed (pars. 81–83) as the fellowship of believers in one and the same divine worship, the Christian church as such entered into the public sphere of history on Pentecost.[217] But it did not attain to permanence without developing within itself functions other than those which are primarily essential to it. For example, the ordering of fellowship in the liturgy and its propagation in succeeding generations necessarily led to the creation of an official class whose privileges over the community had to correspond to the legal as well as to the moral obedience due them.[218] But this organization of the Christian community attained a larger scope than the immediate exigency demanded, because the Christian church found itself originally placed over against a society whose moral ordinances were determined either by pagan or Jewish religion and

whose legal ordinances left no place for the Christian community as a religious body. The latter was thus forced by historical circumstances, not only to develop its customs in contrast to the surrounding society, but also to protect them by legal ordinances and to entrust the management of these structures to the officers of the liturgy. As early as the apostolic age the Christian church began, by means of free-will offerings and regular alms, to attain economic independence, to decide questions of private justice among its members, and to develop a new marriage code;[219] it continued this development by exercising the punitive law of excommunication (the ban) against unworthy members and recognizing the bishops as divinely appointed organs of those judicial forms. In these functions the Christian church—holding itself distinct from the Roman Empire—itself became a state without national foundations. After three centuries it was recognized as such a state in the Roman Empire, and the Roman Catholic church emphasizes now more strongly than ever its claim to the divine establishment of this her organization. On the other hand, according to the protestant view, all the attributes of a state are excluded from the concept of the church. Yet inasmuch as the liturgical fellowship as such is in need of lawful ordering, this ordering is limited essentially to the maintenance of the preaching office.[220]

86. The unity of the liturgical community of Christ is such an essential part of the world view which belongs to the Christian religion[221] that the splitting of the church into a multitude of divisions and sects, and the ceaseless continuance of controversy among them, forms a great hindrance to the convincing power of this religion. Still, in the *first place,* this very fact is a proof of the significance of Christianity as the religion of humanity. For the divisions and controversies of the church are occasioned by the fact that all possible religious, moral, and intellectual tendencies of pre-Christian humanity are to be brought into union with Christianity. This phenomenon, therefore, which is impossible in any folk religion, which does not appear in Buddhism and only to a very limited extent in Mohammedanism, is a proof that Christianity attracts to itself all the formative elements of the human spirit, even at the risk of its own deformation. Besides this occasion of divisions, in the *second place,* the unity of Christian liturgy as a matter of fact may be recognized

in all divisions and sects in that they without exception make official use of the Lord's Prayer[222] and thereby maintain the *intention* of a pure understanding of God's word. Nevertheless, divisions arise because variations, partly in the different cultic forms, partly in the understanding of God's word, are regarded as necessary grounds of separation. For this reason, however, the Christianity which is embodied in the different churches varies not only as to kind, but also as to the level of its development. Therefore, whenever one is conscious of sharing a higher degree of Christian development in that branch of the church to which he necessarily belongs, a degree not possible in other branches, he is under moral obligation just there within his own church to fulfill the universal imperative of Christianity—religiously, liturgically, and ethically.

87. The liturgical community becomes at the same time a school, in that it expresses its understanding of the pure word of God or the religious world view of Christianity in universal statements of truth or dogmas.[223] Variation in dogma (doctrine, system of doctrine) is not the only possible source of church division. The eastern and western catholic churches were originally one in doctrine, but separated because of differences in cultus, church ethos and church order. On the other hand, the great division of the western church, even in cultus, is based on variations in doctrine. A protestant Christian interprets this to mean that as such he occupies a more mature level of Christian development than the catholic church offers (par. 45, n. 123). The positive interest of protestant Christians in the doctrinal system of their church, a system which is the natural consequence of this interest, is regulated by two conditions. *First*, the doctrinal system of the church must be normed by scripture (par. 3) and, where it is appropriate, corrected by scripture. *Secondly,* the doctrinal system always marks the church as a school. It brings confusion, therefore, when the doctrinal system is designated exclusively as the "confession of the church," without regard to that which is set forth in paragraphs 79–81. For the ecclesiastical doctrinal systems which stem from the reformation period can only be appropriated through a *fundamental* theological training, even though theological training generally cannot be expected of the members of the church as such. Membership in the protestant church is to be determined, rather, by what constitutes Christian perfection

according to protestant teaching (par. 50, n. 142). By this means, the distinction is also made clear between churchly protestant Christianity and the sects (including sectarian tendencies within the former) who in the protestant church tend to define Christian perfection in terms other than those set forth in the Augsburg Confession.

88. The properly limited and privileged preaching office (par. 85, n. 220) aims at morally directing the church toward the attainment of the destiny that is embodied in its liturgy. The principle of the German reformation that the religious-ethical authority of the preaching office is not a legal-political authority, nor to be confused with the same,[224] is maintained without difficulty, since a protestant parish is constituted as community [Gemeinde] by its property and the administration of the same, and as church by the maintenance of the office of the word and the administration of the sacraments. The official preaching of the divine word (par. 82) may, as occasion demands, take the form of rebuking certain specific persons for their errors and immoralities, and under certain circumstances the local parish may be obliged to deny individuals the privilege of participating in its worship. But even this exercise of a natural right of the community is properly understood only as a moral influence and the application of moral entreaty. The protestant church acquires a legal character in the proper sense of the term, bearing the characteristics of external compulsion, only when the many local parishes wish to become a unity and at the same time stand forth as a corporation privileged by the state. This calls for a legal organization with a gradation of offices, as well as the supervision of those holding office in the interest of the whole; however, the legal compulsion which is necessary for such purposes cannot be exercised by the church as such, but only by the state[225] which recognizes and protects the church as a public corporation. For, as the legal representatives of a Christian people, the authorities [Organe] of the state cannot be indifferent to the church. In Germany, at least, historical circumstances brought it about that in the sixteenth century the authorities in representing the territorial churches bestowed upon them their legal organization and assured its operation by special state-church officials. This for a time produced anew a general confusion of religious and legal authority, since under the influence of medieval per-

spectives the chief object of the state was considered to be the direct furthering of the Christian religion and its morality. On the other hand, within Calvinism, several forms of church constitution were developed which were independent of or indifferent to the state. Of these forms, however, the synodical constitution of the old French church could not have existed without forming a state within the state and in contrast to it. The independence movement in England and America abandoned the legal organization of the whole church, making the local parishes sovereign and recognizing only a moral bond between them. Finally, in Scotland, a synodical church constitution arose, partly in union with the state and partly independent of it, whereby, however, a church absolutely identical in cultus and faith is divided in polity.

The provincial government of the church in Germany is now a condition for the union of the different protestant provincial churches within themselves and with each other and ought not be judged and depreciated by the example of the conditions in America or Scotland. According to protestant doctrine, there is no exclusively ideal form of church government, and the course of protestant history in Germany justifies the assertion that the maintenance of the unity of the provincial churches has protected the protestant church against being split into sects and conquered again by Romanism. Nevertheless it is true that the legal foundation of the provincial government of the church should be guided in a way very different from previous methods. That provincial government can no longer be derived either from the so-called religious purpose of the state, nor from a fictitious transfer of the catholic episcopal office through the princes, nor from the scope of state sovereignty as such. Yet the legal government of the church by the princes as an independent addition to their sovereignty is still comprehensible, since the national state, for the sake of the spiritual well-being of the people, must maintain the protestant church as a whole, and since all public administration which involves compulsion falls within the sphere of the state. And such administration is necessary, because it would be no advantage to the protestant church itself were it to form a state within the state through legal autonomy, and because its autonomous religious calling would be injured if it should be forced into this course. And the governing of the protestant church by the provincial authorities preserves the fundamental distinction between religious and legal authority in the church. For, on the one hand, the provincial officials spare the pastors from extending their office to include the government and administration of the whole church and thus impairing their moral authority; on the other hand, the provincial authorities are to be trusted to maintain the peculiar character of the protestant church, both in worship and in doctrine, and to impose nothing upon it that offends against the gospel. At present it remains undecided how far it will be possible to strengthen the existing church government by establishing synods and, at the same time, preclude the danger of dissolving the provincial church.

89. Baptism (immersion) *in* the name of the Lord Jesus, or Jesus Christ, or in the name of the Father, Son, and Holy Spirit,[226] is in its visible form an act of the community, by which it pledges the individuals joining that community to the revelation of God to which it owes its existence. This pledging includes the purification and renewal of the spiritual life which is signified symbolically in the washing of the body and to be understood factually as acceptance into the circle of forgiveness or reconciliation.[227] The rite, however, is not to be understood merely as the confession of the individual who enters as a believer into the community, but as a sacrament, because it is an act of the community, since the continuance of the community depends upon the revelation of the Father through the Son and as such assures the distinctive blessing of this revelation to the one newly received. This significance of the act is clearly expressed in the baptism of infants.[228] Although this practice rests only on very old tradition, and not on the command of Christ or precedent of the earliest church, yet it finds its justification in connection with religious and moral education within the church. On the other hand, the principle of the baptist sects that only adults and such as can be recognized as sanctified and regenerated may be baptized rests on the mistaken supposition that one can attain to the formation of Christian character outside the community.

90. The Lord's Supper in its visible form is an act of the whole community (and of the individual insofar as he presents himself as a member of the community), by which it thankfully recognizes the significance of Christ's sacrifice of his life for the establishment of the community.[229] As Christ himself, however, set forth the sig-

nificance of his approaching death to the community of his disciples as the sacrifice of the new covenant (par. 38, n. 102), so the repetition of the Lord's Supper in the same form becomes analogous to the sacrificial meal of the Old Testament. And since, further, the community founded through the sacrificial death of Christ stands in the relation to God characterized by the forgiveness of sins or reconciliation, the act is not only an act of confession on the part of the community, but also a sacrament. This significance of the act to the individual participant follows from two considerations, one more important than the other. First, the community within which he partakes of the Lord's Supper assures to him the forgiveness of sins, the forgiveness which forms the foundation for the community's existence.[230] But at a deeper level, however, Christ himself assures this to the believer, insofar as the act is repeated through which, in advance, he appropriated the reconciling efficacy of his death for the community. Accordingly, the Lord's Supper has the practical significance of intensifying the sensitivity of moral feeling, of stimulating the life emerging from reconciliation that moves toward humility, trust and patience (par. 50), and finally of arousing the lively sense of fellowship in the community.

Christian churches of different confessions are divided as to how the body and blood of Christ, represented by the bread and wine, are combined in the act of the Lord's Supper with these elements. Catholic doctrine asserts the transformation of the natural elements of bread and wine into the body and blood of Christ while retaining the appearance of bread and wine; the Lutheran doctrine asserts the nonspatial coexistence of these substances within the space of the natural elements; and both teach the oral reception of the body and blood of Christ. The Calvinist doctrine teaches that the administration of the body and blood by Christ for spiritual participation coincides in time with the oral reception of the bread and wine. The controversy between these doctrines cannot be settled by an appeal either to the words of Christ at the institution of the Supper or to the later explanation of Paul. And especially is this true, since none of the confessional doctrines take into consideration the fact that the broken bread and poured wine make present the body and blood of Christ under the characteristics of his violent death. Finally, it is unquestionable that Christ established this sacrament in order that all might unite in it, and not in the expectation that they would be divided as to its meaning and content and so separated from one another in its celebration.

NOTES

1. Matt. 11:27.

2. 1 Cor. 2:10–12.

3. Matt. 28:19.

4. *AS* II, 2: "The word of God shall establish articles of faith and no one else, not even an angel." Also *Formula of Concord,* Epitome 1.

5. [In the first edition, 1875, this paragraph reads as follows: "The kingdom of God is the universal end of the community that was founded through God's revelation in Christ, and it is the corporate product of that community, since the members of that community bind themselves to each other through a definite type of reciprocal action."]

6. Rom. 14:16–18. The kingdom of God is the divinely ordained end of the preaching of Christ, extending the invitation to a change of heart and to faith (Mark 1:15), and forming the principle subject of prayer to God (Luke 11:2; Matt. 6:10). The value of the highest good is especially set forth in the parable of the wedding feast (Matt. 22:2–14; 8:11; Luke 14:16–24; 13:29). In John the promise of eternal life has the same significance.

7. Christ in his office of revealer actualizes the kingdom of God (Matt. 12:28); in order to assure its task for men, he calls the twelve disciples so that they may be with him (Mark 3:14; Luke 12:32), may learn the mysteries of the kingdom (Mark 4:11), and enter into the same fellowship with God which he himself maintained (John 17:19–23); in accordance with this purpose he distinguishes them (the sons of God) as a special religious community, distinct from the Israelite community of the servants of God (Matt 17:24–27).

8. The parables (Mark 4) which set forth the mysteries of the kingdom in figures of the growth of grain, etc., always signify by "fruit" a human product, springing out of an individual activity called forth by the divine "seed," i.e., by the impulse of the divine word of revelation. The parable of the laborers in the vineyard has the same meaning (Matt. 20).

9. Fruit is the figure for a good deed or for righteous conduct (Matt. 7:16, 20; 13:33; James 3:18; Phil. 1:11). The kingdom of God consists in the exercise of righteousness, in the peace produced by it among all its members, and in the joy of blessedness proceeding from the Holy Spirit (Matt. 6:33; Rom. 14:17, 18). As to peace, compare Mark 9:50; Rom. 12:18; 14:19; 2 Cor. 13:11; 1 Thess. 5:13; Heb. 12:14. As to joy and blessedness, compare Gal. 5:22; James 1:25; and Luther's Small Catechism, II, 2: "That I might live under him in his kingdom and serve him in everlasting righteousness, innocence, and blessedness."

10. The law which Christ points out in the two chief commandments of the Mosaic law (Mark 12:28–33) has reference to the conduct suitable to the

kingdom of God. Love to God has no sphere of activity outside of love to one's brother (1 John 4:19–21; 5:1–3).

11. One's neighbor is no longer one's relative or compatriot alone, but possibly also the benevolent citizen of a hostile people (Luke 10:29–37); thus love of one's enemy in its generally permissible manifestations is included in the Christian love which embraces all mankind (Matt. 5:43–48; Rom. 12:14, 20, 21). This special command does not mean that we shall support an enemy in what he is doing against us, but we shall have regard for his dignity as a human being. The ordinary duty, of course, is love of the brethren (1 Pet. 1:22; 3:8; 1 Thess. 4:9; Rom. 12:10; Heb. 13:1), to whom one is also bound to extend forgiveness (Luke 11:4; 17:3, 4); but since the Christian community is the special body in which the members of different peoples are bound together into a moral fellowship whose principle is brotherly love, the circle of the kingdom of God is in this latter command also extended to include all men (Gal. 3:28; 5:6; 1 Cor. 7:19; Col. 3:10–11).

12. The surrender of private rights which follows from the law of love is the rule in intercourse with the brethren (Matt. 5:23–24, 38–42; the evil doer referred to in 5:39 must also be understood to be a brother).

13. The Mosaic decalogue, except in the command to honor one's parents, prescribes negative regard for the personal rights of everyone, in the sense of not inflicting injury (Exod. 20:12–17). This negative care for the rights of others is always the presupposition of the positive regard which finds its completion in the love of others (Rom. 12:10); this love manifests itself in the positive demand for the good of all, therefore in the exercise of public spirit (Rom. 12:16–17; 15:7; Phil. 2:2–4; 2 Cor. 13:11; 1 Thess. 5:11; Heb. 10:24; 1 Pet. 3:8). Thus the "royal law of love" includes in itself the decalogue and has a broader reach than its prohibitions (James 2:8–9; Rom. 13:8–10).

14. The one and only God who created the world and therefore is the king of all nations (Jer. 10:10–16; Ps. 47; 97; 103:19–22) will especially lead his chosen people as their king, on condition that they by obedience keep his covenant (Exod. 19:5–6; Judg. 8:23; Isa. 33:22). As their ruler God administers justice among all peoples (Ps. 9:7–8; 1 Sam. 2:2–10; Isa. 3:13), but especially among the chosen people, partly as their leader in war, maintaining their cause against other peoples (Exod. 7:4; Ps. 7:6–13; 76:4–9; 99:1–5), and partly procuring justice for righteous individuals against their insolent oppressors (Ps. 35; 37; 50).

15. Isa. 2:2–4; Mic. 4:1–4; Jer. 3:14–18; 4:1–2; Isa. 42:1–6; 51:4–6; 56:6–8.

16. Mark 10:42–45; 12:13–17; 2:27–28 (Compare with Isa. 56:2–5); Matt. 17:24–27.

17. Luke 17:20–21; Heb. 11:1.

18. The name of the community of believers (church, *ekklesia*, Heb. *Kahal*), as a result of this harmony with Old Testament use of terms, refers directly to the visible liturgy (sacrifice, prayer) (par. 81). But this religious community must at the same time unite itself to the kingdom of God by the mutual exercise of love. By virtue of the different nature of these two activities and the different conditions under which they arise, it follows that they are never exercised to an equal extent during the historical existence of the

community. The community of believers must fulfill its mission in these two relations in such a way that the two lines of their activity shall stand in reciprocal relation to one another, but it is a mistake so to identify the two as to use the same name interchangeably for them both. For the actions by which the community becomes a church are not those by which it unites itself to the kingdom of God, and vice versa. And it is particularly misleading to claim, as the Roman Catholic church does for itself, designation as the kingdom of God because of a certain juridical form [*rechtliche Verfassung*].

19. Menander: "The slave becomes base, when he learns merely to bend himself to every service; give freedom of word to the slave and he will surely become the best of the good" (*Ex incertis comoediis,* 254). "Serve in a free spirit and you are not a slave" (Ibid., 255). Philemon: "Even he who is a slave, madam, is still none the less human, since he is truly a human being" (Ibid., 29). "Though one be a slave, he is yet of the same flesh; for nature never created a slave, it is only fortune that has thrust the body into servitude" (Ibid., 84).

20. Antiochus of Askalon, in Cicero's *De finibus bonorum et malorum,* V. 23:65 [trans. H. Rackham, Loeb Classical Library (New York: Macmillan, 1914), pp. 467–69]: "But in the whole moral sphere of which we are speaking there is nothing more glorious nor of wider range than the solidarity of mankind, that species of alliance and partnership of interests and that actual affection which exists between man and man, which, coming into existence immediately upon our birth, owing to the fact that children are loved by their parents and the family as a whole, is bound together by the ties of marriage and parenthood, gradually spreads its influence beyond the home, first by blood relationships, then by connections through marriage, later by friendships, afterwards by the bonds of neighborhood, then to fellow citizens and political allies and friends, and lastly by embracing the whole of the human race. This sentiment, assigning each his own and maintaining with generosity and equity that human solidarity and alliance of which I speak, is termed justice." Compare the collection in Schmidt, *Die bürgerliche Gesellschaft in der altrömischen Welt,* 306. Seneca expresses himself similarly.

21. Concerning a standard of this relation which comes closer to us, cf. par. 19.

22. 2 Cor. 1:3; 11:31; Rom. 15:6; Col. 1:3; Eph. 1:3; 1 Pet. 1:3.

23. 1 Sam. 2:2; Isa. 45:18, 21–22; Exod. 20:2–3. The Old Testament conception of the gods of the heathen is accordingly either that they are nothing or vanity (Lev. 19:4; 2 Kings 17:15; Jer. 2:5; 8:19) or, insofar as their existence is granted, that they are subordinate organs of the government of the only God (Deut. 4:19; 10:17; Ps. 95:3; 96:4; 1 Cor. 8:5–6). As the only God, the true God is the Holy One (1 Sam. 2:2), who is unattainable by the way of natural knowledge, exalted above all sense perception, unimpeachable.

24. Gen. 1; Isa. 45:12; Matt. 11:25. That God as the absolutely free will determines himself and as the creator determines all that together makes the world is united into the statement that God is the end of the universe, or that the course of the world ministers to his glory (1 Cor. 8:6; Rom. 11:36; Eph. 4:6). The conception of the creation of the world by God lies entirely outside of all observation and ordinary experience and therefore outside of the realm

of scientific knowledge, which is limited by these. Thus, even though we are able to obtain from experience a clear idea of natural causes and effects, the creation of the world by God cannot rightly be thought of as analogous to these forms of knowledge. It can only be analogous to the original force of our will as it is directed toward a goal and comprehended in such a way that the world as a whole, and not just its individual parts, is compared to God.

25. Scientific observation of nature is directed toward the causal relationship of things. Since it regards organic beings (plants, animals) with reference to the end which they have in themselves, it denies itself the occasion to recognize them as necessarily existing for the sake of man. Such a relationship is apprehended everywhere only by the religious judgment; thus in the Old Testament everything is subservient to the world supremacy of the people of Israel.

26. [In the first edition, this paragraph reads as follows: "As with all religious interpretations of the world (cosmogonies), the biblical account of God's free creation of the world necessarily also moves to a discussion of human ends and the establishment of a religious and ethical community of men with God. This idea is given further specification in Christianity with the assertion that the world is directed toward the kingdom of God, i.e., to the ultimate end that a kingdom of created spirits should come into being whose essential nature is perfect spiritual union with God. That the world is directed toward God himself or his glory is in perfect harmony with the fact that it is directed also toward the kingdom of God so long as we understand God in terms of the concept of love." This paragraph was elucidated by the following footnote (note 12a in the original, Fabricius's edition, p. 41): "This goal of all religious cosmogonies is only a generalized statement of every particular religious view of the world. Whenever, in a religious judgment, we derive an empirical event in the world from God's dispensation, we are thinking of a purpose of God that is directed toward us, but which reaches out beyond the event itself. In the scientific understanding of certain natural entities, we conceive of a nexus of causes and their effects, also in the form of a purpose. But when we think of the purpose of an organic being (planet, animal), a purpose which it has in its own right, we conceive of that purpose being necessarily subordinated to man's purposes, although we have no scientific basis for doing so. The scientific understanding of nature, therefore, defines all phenomena as orderly effects of causes, and it defines organic beings according to their own intrinsic purposes; the religious view of the world defines all creatures according to their usefulness to man (Gen. 1:26–31)."]

27. In the majority of the inscriptions of the New Testament epistles.

28. As the end of creation (Col. 1:6; Eph. 1:10), Christ is also the central reason [*Mittelgrund*] for creation from the standpoint of the divine purpose (1 Cor. 8:6). As Lord over all he is the one "to whom every knee shall bow," that is, he receives divine worship (Phil. 2:9–11). But note that God the Father is placed over him (1 Cor. 3:23, 8:6).

29. Matt. 11:27. That God alone knows the Son signifies that he is set apart from all the world. God's knowledge of him, however, includes in itself a productive voluntary purpose (1 Pet. 1:20; Rom. 8:29). Thus Jesus, knowing his peculiar existence to be grounded in the love of his Father (John 10:17,

15:10), places this relation above the coherence and existence of the world (John 17:24).

30. 1 John 4:8, 16. Love is the *constant* purpose to further another spiritual being of *like* nature with oneself in the attainment of his authentic destiny [*Bestimmung*], and in such a way that the one who loves in so doing pursues his *own* proper end [*Selbstzweck*]. This appropriation of the life-purpose of another is not a weakening negation but a strengthening affirmation of one's own purpose. Thus if God is revealed as love in that he directs his purpose toward Jesus Christ his Son, the love of *God* will be revealed in proportion as this purpose encompasses even the world of which this Son is Lord, and causes it to be recognized as the means to the end, this end being Christ as the head of the community.

31. 2 Cor. 13:11, 13; Rom. 5:5–8; 8:39; 2 Thess. 2:16; 1 John 4:9–10; Heb. 12:6.

32. In the love shown by Christians to their brothers the love of God is perfected (1 John 2:5; 4:12), i.e., it finds its complete revelation.

33. Eph. 1:4–6. "God has chosen us (the Christian community) in Christ (as Lord of the same) before the foundation of the world, that we might be holy and without blame before him; having in love predestined us to the adoption of children through Jesus Christ to himself, according to the good pleasure of his will, to the praise of the glory of his grace."

34. Ps. 90:2, 4.

35. Ps. 102:25–27.

36. Ps. 24:1–2; 115:3; 135:6; 139:7–12.

37. This is the application given to these divine attributes in the theological doctrine that God as the first cause is present in all mediate causes. This doctrine consists, nevertheless, of a confused mixture of religious and scientific observation. The idea of God is not at the disposal of a scientific explanation of nature, and any such explanation would indeed offend against the content of the idea of God, if it should make him, under the concept of causation, similar to the natural causes which are intelligible by observation. The religious view of nature, however, does not limit itself to the explanation of natural phenomena as such, but subordinates their existence for the sake of man to the will of God (cf. n. 25, above), which is entirely different in kind from natural causes.

38. Ps. 139 (as a whole, culminating in verses 23, 24); 33:13–19; 104; Job 5:8–27; 11:7–20, 36, 37.

39. Ps. 145:8–9; Exod. 34:6; Ps. 103:8; Acts 14:15–17; James 5:11; Rom. 2:4; 2 Cor. 1:3.

40. Ps. 35:23–28; 31:2, 8; 48:10–12; 65:6; 143:11–12; 51:16.

41. Isa. 45:21; 46:13; 51:5–6; 56:1.

42. Hos. 2:18–21; Zech. 8:8; Ps. 143:1.

43. 1 John 1:9; Ps. 51:14; Rom. 3:25–26; John 17:25, 26; Heb. 6:10 (1 Cor. 1:8, 9; 1 Thess. 5:23–24).

44. Ps. 105; 107; 71:16–21; 86:8–17; 89:5–14; 98:1–3; 145:3–7; Job 5:8–11.

45. Miracles and signs, Ps. 135:8, 9; Exod. 3:12, 13:9.

46. Mark 5:34; 10:52; 6:5–6. We shift completely the religious conception of miracle when we begin by measuring it against the background of the scientific acceptance of the orderly coherence of all natural events. Since this scientific concept lies outside the horizon of the men of the Old and New Testaments, a miracle never signifies to them an occurrence contrary to nature nor a disruption of the laws of nature by divine arbitrariness. Hence the belief in miracle in the sense referred to above, as a gracious providence of God, is perfectly consistent with the probability of the coherence of the whole world in accordance with natural law. If, nevertheless, certain accounts of miracles in the Bible appear to be contrary to these laws, it is neither the duty of science to explain this appearance nor to confirm it as a fact, nor is it the duty of religion to recognize these narrated events as divine operations contrary to the laws of nature. Neither ought one base his religious faith in God and Christ upon a preceding judgment of this kind (John 4:48; Mark 5:11–12; 1 Cor. 1:22), especially since every experience of miracle presupposes faith. Beginning, however, with faith, everyone will meet the miraculous in his own experience; in view of this, it is entirely unnecessary to ponder over the miracles which others have experienced.

47. Matt. 5:12, 6:1, 2; 1 Cor. 3:8; 2 Thess. 1:8, 9; Heb. 10:29.

48. Job 41:3; Rom. 11:35. In general, the view of human life set forth in the biblical writings moves within the limits set by the covenant grace of God. When, therefore, the righteousness of God is appealed to for the reward of righteous men (Ps. 7:8–10; 17:3; 58:11; 139:23; 2 Thess. 1:5–7), the mutual legal relation thereby indicated is only apparent. For the righteousness of God signifies in these cases also only the consistent completion of the salvation of the righteous (par. 16), which, however, has the appearance of reward because it deals in these cases with a condition of innocence and righteousness that is already present in men. Properly, the recompense of the righteous is the work of the grace of God (Ps. 62:12); that of the wicked is their exclusion from (his grace =) righteousness (Ps. 69:24–28). Reward and punishment are not coordinated as expressions of the righteousness of God, but only as visible acts of his exercise of justice, i.e., of his government of the world (Ps. 94:1, 2; 58:10, 11).

49. Exod. 34:7; Mark 4:12; 10:29, 30. The divine punishment in its common Old Testament representation as the wrath of God, because of the nature of the emotion involved in the term wrath, excludes the idea of an exact weighing of the amount of the punishment.

50. The poets of the Old Testament find themselves completely disappointed in their natural expectation that the good would be prosperous and the wicked unhappy. They must content themselves with praying to God for the righting of the wrong condition of affairs in the future. Thus the establishment of the right order awaits the future judgment of God in the Old as well as in the New Testament.

51. Eliphaz draws this conclusion in the book of Job (4:7, 22:4–11); on the other hand, consider Job's assurance of his integrity (6:28–30; 23:10–12). As against this combination compare John 9:1–3; Luke 13:1–5.

52. Matt. 5:11; Mark 8:34, 45; Phil. 1:28. Cf. par. 32.

53. The scheme of retribution in the final judgment (Rom. 2:6–12; 2 Cor. 5:10; 2 Thess. 1:6, 7; Eph. 6:8) is surpassed by the analogy of the seed and the harvest (Gal. 6:7–8). The final result in the case of the good as in that of the evil is but the appropriate legitimate effect of the power of the good or the evil will. By comparison, the transitory temporal experiences of a contrary nature are not worthy of consideration.

54. Rom. 11:33–36. From par. 13 there follows the universal law of the divine government, maintained everywhere in the Old as well as in the New Testament, that all punishment or destruction of the wicked by God serves as a means to the complete salvation of the righteous. It is not, however, a means to the end of God's own glory or righteousness, as is set forth in Luther's and Calvin's doctrine of predestination.

55. In all folk religions the person of the founder, even when known (Zoroaster, Moses), is a matter of indifference, because the religious community, consisting of the whole race or people, is determined by nature. On the other hand, in universal religions (Buddhism, Christianity, Islam), allegiance to the founder, or worship of him, is prescribed, because only through the founder does the corresponding community exist as it is, and only by allegiance to him can it be preserved. In these cases the difference in the estimation of Mohammed and Christ is to be explained by the difference in the nature of the two religions.

56. Mark 6:4; 9:37; John 4:34; 5:23, 24; 6:44. It comes also under the prophetic conception (Exod. 33:11; Num. 12:8) that Jesus speaks what he hears from God (John 8:26, 40; 15:15) and has seen of him (John 6:46; 8:38).

57. Mark 12:1–9; 8:29; 14:61–62; John 4:25–26.

58. John 4:34; 17:4.

59. John 18:36; Mark 10:42–45.

60. The fitness of Jesus finds expression in his assertion of the mutual knowledge existing between himself and God as his Father (Matt. 11:27; John 10:15; compare Luke 2:49). He does not know God as his Father without being himself conscious that he is *the* one called of God to found the kingdom of God in a new religious community. This conviction vouches also for all the other sides of his spiritual endowment for this vocation. because all the characteristics of his life witness to his perfect spiritual soundness, and there is not the least trace in him of fanaticism or self-deception.

61. The sinlessness of Jesus (John 8:36; 1 Pet. 2:21; 1 John 3:5; 2 Cor. 5:21; Heb. 4:15) is only the negative expression for the constancy of his disposition and conduct of his vocation (obedience, Phil. 2:8; Heb. 5:8) or for the positive righteousness in which he differs from all other men (1 Pet. 3:18).

62. Heb. 2:18; 4:15; Mark 14:33–36; 1:13.

63. The principle of Matt. 11:28–30. The two Greek words *praüs kai tapeinos* ("gentle and lowly") point to the use of one Hebrew or Aramaic word, *anav,* which indicates the regular characteristics of the righteous in their suffering under the persecution of the godless (Pss. 9:12; 10:12–17; 25:9; 37:11;

69:32). The addition of *te kardia* ("in heart") denotes that Jesus in his righteousness is ready to endure all the undeserved sufferings which follow from the reaction against his activity in his vocation. Thereby, however, he makes a distinction in kind between himself and the righteous of the Old Testament, who always seek to be delivered from their undeserved suffering.

64. John 4:34.

65. John 10:28–30, 38; 14:10; 17:21–23.

66. John 15:9, 10; 17:24, 26; 10:17; 12:49, 50.

67. John 1:14; Exod. 34:6, 7; compare par. 16.

68. Matt. 11:27.

69. Matt. 17:24–27; 8:11, 12; Mark 12:9.

70. Matt. 11:28–30. Compare n. 63, above.

71. John 71:1, 4, 5; 16:16, 33. Accordingly, the view of Jesus' life given by Paul in Phil. 2:6–8 is not complete. The path of obedience even to death is for Jesus only apparently a degradation beneath his dignity. It is in truth the form of his self-exaltation above the world and above its usual standards (Mark 10:42–45). That is to say, one *becomes* great through degradation in service only because one *is* already great in unselfish obedience (Phil. 2:1–5).

72. In apostolic usage, the Old Testament name of God, "Lord," is applied only to the risen Christ, exalted to the right hand of God (Phil. 2:9–11). Yet this conception can only be understood on the condition that this attribute is discernible also as an actual characteristic in the historical life of Christ (par. 23). But this dominion of Christ over the world has no other sphere of activity save such as is maintained through the power of a will concentrated upon God's supramundane purpose of love. Also the apostles regard Christ as creator only in this respect, that because he comprises typically in himself the goal of the world, i.e., the kingdom of God and the glory of God, he furnishes in the divine creative will the means for the creation of the world (Col. 1:15–18; 1 Cor. 8:6; Heb. 1:1–3). This line of thought, however, leads over into the territory of theology proper and has no direct and practical significance for religious belief in Jesus Christ.

73. Melanchthon, Loci (1535, *CR XXI*, 366): "The scriptures teach us the divinity of the son not only speculatively, but practically, i.e., they command us to pray to Christ and to trust in Christ, for thus is the honor and divinity truly accorded to him."

74. There is a complete misconception of the problem, and the understanding desired is rendered impossible, if the principle is followed that historical knowledge of Christ is possible only insofar as one is divested of religious devotion to him.

75. Accordingly, his death will be regarded, not as a just punishment for blasphemy as his enemies intended it, nor as the result of fanatic daring, but as the completion of the work of his vocation, which he accepted with dutiful determination because he recognized in it God's purpose for him. This significance of the death of Christ, set forth by the apostles, marks also the right and complete understanding of Christ's obedience in life, as it was completed in his death. (Cf. n. 110, below.)

76. Gal. 2:20; 3:27; Rom. 6:5, 11; 8:2, 10; 12:4, 5; 1 Cor. 12:12.

77. Rom. 10:9; 1 Cor. 15:3–20; 1 Pet. 1:3; 3:21, 22; Heb. 13:20, 21.

78. Mark 14:62; John 10:17, 18; 17:4, 5.

79. It is impossible to arrive at the view of sin which is in accordance with Christianity before arriving at the knowledge of what Christianity regards as good. Therefore it is a peculiarly inconsiderate demand, that one should recognize his own and universal sin in their full extent, in order from this alone to derive a longing for a redemption such as is promised in Christianity.

80. Augustine's doctrine of original sin, i.e., the original inclination to evil transmitted in procreation which is for everyone both personal guilt and subject to the divine sentence of eternal punishment, is not confirmed by any New Testament author. Paul draws from his scholastic exegesis of the account of the fall only the conviction that the universal decree of death for man was the consequence of the sin of the first human beings, and the conclusion that their descendants have sinned since that fate was theirs also (Rom. 5:12–19). Neither Jesus nor any of the New Testament writers either indicate or presuppose that sin is universal merely through natural generation. The expressions in the Old Testament which approach this view (Ps. 51:5; Job 14:4; 15:14) are not didactic in character and not suited to determine the Christian conception.

81. Gen. 8:21; Matt. 5:28; Gal. 5:16–21; 1 Cor. 6:9, 10; Titus 3:3; 1 Thess. 4:3–8; Luke 15:21; 1 Cor. 6:18–20; 8:12; 1 John 3:4.

82. *CA* II, 1: "Since the fall of Adam all men who are propagated according to nature are born in sin. That is to say, they are without fear of God, are without trust in God, and are concupiscent."

83. Therefore the sinlessness of Jesus (cf. n. 61, above) does not contradict his human nature.

84. This gradation is indicated in 1 John 5:16, 17. It is also signified when Jesus represents sin or the world as an object of redemption on the one hand (Mark 2:17; Luke 13:2–5; 15:7, 10, 24, 32; 18:13) and incapable of salvation on the other (Mark 8:38; Matt. 8:22; 12:39–45; 13:49; 16:4). In the same way with reference to Num. 15:27–31, a distinction is made between sins arising from ignorance or mistake and therefore receiving forgiveness (1 Pet. 1:14; Eph. 4:17–19; Acts 17:30; 1 Tim. 1:13; James 5:19, 20) and those which are committed freely or with firm resolution and bring destruction in their train (Col. 3:5, 6; Eph. 5:5, 6; Rev. 21:8).

85. James 1:14, 15 and Mark 9:43–47 represent individual impulses and their bodily organs as causes of the temptation to sin, insofar as the impulses are directed to worldly good and the organs mediate that attraction. Along with this, the power of social custom as well as the authority and example of others furnish seductive occasion to sin (Mark 4:17; 9:42; 1 Cor. 8:13, 21; Rom. 14:13, 21; Rev. 2:14). But also the suffering of the good, when not understood, works in the same way (Mark 14:27, 29; 1 Cor. 1:23; 1 Pet. 2:8).

86. James 4:4; 1 John 2:15–17. The expression "the kingdom of sin," to be sure, is not directly biblical; yet it is indicated in the representation of the devil as the prince of this world (1 John 5:18, 19; John 12:31; 16:11). Of

course this nexus of sin is unlike the kingdom of God, in that it is controlled by no positive purpose.

87. Rom. 3:9; 5:20, 21; 6:12–23.

88. The absolute inability to good, which the reformers wish to find expressed in the sinfulness of every individual, is not asserted in the New Testament and is limited even in the reformers themselves by the recognition of *justitia civilis* as the work of sinners.

89. The manifestation of conscience in involuntary self-condemnation for a deed done is to be understood as an exercise of freedom, i.e., of self-determination to good, but this of course takes place only on the presupposition that one is brought up in a moral fellowship. An evil conscience is a positive manifestation, a so-called good conscience the absence of the same. In the New Testament the former is referred to in Heb. 10:2, 22; and the latter in Acts 23:1; 2 Cor. 1:12; Heb. 13:18; 1 Pet. 3:16; and both together in Rom. 2:15. That a good conscience has only a relative value in proving a mode of action to be right is shown in 1 Cor. 4:3, 4. As to the conception of the positive law-giving conscience, cf. n. 177, below.

90. John 9:1–3; Luke 13:1–5; compare n. 51, above.

91. Luther, for instance, failed to exercise this tenderness of feeling when he declared Zwingli's tragic end a divine punishment for his heresies (*WA, BR,* IV, 332, 352).

92. Rom. 5:12.

93. Rom. 14:7, 8; Phil. 1:21–24; Rom. 8:35–39.

94. The deliverance of the people of Israel from Egyptian bondage into an independent national life and the establishment of their own true religion (Exod. 15:13; 20:2), is the type by which all similar expectations of the prophets are governed, in each recurring subjugation of the people to foreign nations (Ps. 111:9; Isa. 35:10; 45:17; 51:11). The conversion or the spiritual renewing of the people is, to be sure, included in this conception as well (Isa. 10:21; 32:15–18; Ezek. 36:24–30; Ps. 130:8).

95. This is not even the definite meaning of such passages as Rom. 11:26, 27; 1 Pet. 1:18, 19; 2:24; they depend rather upon being made clear by the line of thought which follows.

96. Redemption is like forgiveness of sins (Col. 1:14; Eph. 1:7; Heb. 9:15; 10:16–18) and justification or acquittal (Rom. 3:24–26); this latter again is also forgiveness of sins (Rom. 4:5–8). The figure of the forgetting or covering of sins by God does not mean that God commits an intentional self-deception as to the existence of human sin, but it has the meaning expressed in the conception of pardon, that the result of transgression, namely, the interruption of intercourse between the guilty individual and the representative of moral authority, is purposely brought to an end by the latter. This meaning follows from the comparison of the divine forgiveness with the human (Luke 11:4; Matt. 11:25).

97. It is utterly purposeless to compare the catholic and the protestant conceptions of justification [*Rechtfertigung,* to be declared just], since they stand in relations which are completely indifferent to one another. That is to say, the

catholic conception of justification [*Gerechtmachung*, to be made just] through the imparting of love to the will is intended to explain how sinners are made capable of good works. This thought has therefore a different purpose from that of the protestant formula referred to above; in themselves both might be true at the same time and in force side by side without conflicting with one another. Yet the catholic formula sets forth a spiritual occurrence in a mechanical and materialistic way and is not consonant with the normative biblical conception. The conception of *dikaioun* ("righteous") adopted by Paul (Rom. 3:26, 30) follows the meaning of a Hebrew verbal form (*hizdik*), which denotes the pronouncing of one as righteous by the sentence of a judge (Rom. 4:11).

98. The justification established by God's gracious judgment (*dikaiosune theou*, "righteousness of God") depends on faith (Rom. 1:17; 3:22, 26; 9:30; Phil. 3:9).

99. 2 Cor. 5:18, 19; Rom. 5:10; Col. 1:21.

100. Matt. 17:26; 1 John 3:1; Gal. 4:4–7; Rom. 8:14–17. Luther's *Large Catechism,* III, "God will lead us to believe that he is our real father, and we are his real children, to the end that we, in all boldness and confidence, may ask of him as dear children of a dear father."

101. Since the Christian life is only complete in the fulfillment of both of these conditions—assurance of reconciliation (or adoption) and the seeking of the kingdom of God and its righteousness—these two lines serve as a mutual proof of their rightness and genuineness, or mutually condition one another. This appears in the following propositions: (1) Assurance of reconciliation is not justified when the life is either directly sinful or marred by a predominating form of self-seeking. (2) A life directed by a constant good purpose fails of its end when the assurance of reconciliation is marred by a predominating self-righteousness. (3) Insofar as the moral life must be judged incomplete in general, and also because of sin's interruptions, this lack is balanced not only by the assurance of divine forgiveness but also by the purpose to make greater effort and improvement and by the carrying out of this purpose. The commonly received idea opposed to this rests upon the error that in Christianity forgiveness of sins is a substitute for what is supposedly the original arrangement, wherein one might attain the right relation to God by mechanically fulfilling the law.

102. This is evident from the fact that Christ, in the institution of the Lord's Supper (Mark 14:24), refers back to Jeremiah's prophecy (31:31–34) of the new covenant, whose foundation is the forgiveness of sins. As the prophet holds out the prospect of this covenant only to the whole of the people Israel as the continuing community of the true God, so Christ in agreement with this thinks of the community as existing in the twelve, for whom he makes the covenant of forgiveness efficacious by the sacrifice of his life—cf. Luther's *Small Catechism,* second part, third article, "in which church God daily and abundantly forgives all my sins and the sins of all believers." See also *Large Catechism,* II, 40–42 and *CA* I, 5 and "Treatise on the Power and Primacy of the Pope," 24 (Tappert, p. 324).

103. In the catholic system the idea of forgiveness of sins is made clearly

efficacious only in the ceremony of the priestly absolution of the individual in the sacrament of confession. A similar procedure is maintained in the Lutheran confessional, without there being any reference in their liturgy to the specific principle of the reformation, namely, that in consequence of the redemption mediated through Christ we belong to the community founded upon the forgiveness of sins and accordingly we do not make confession of past sins, in the sense that we have lost the state of grace and therefore receive forgiveness as something new. This confessional practice rather furthers the fateful error (cf. n. 100, above) that churchly forgiveness of sins is a substitute for a defective striving after the good.

104. Although the love of God has been occasionally construed as the ground of a reasonable leniency on God's part toward the weakness of men, yet it does not furnish the datum for a so-called natural religion, which indeed does not exist. But even were it otherwise, leniency toward the imperfections of human conduct is an entirely different thing from Christian forgiveness of sins. Such leniency accepted as a divine substitute for human weakness would sacrifice the seriousness of moral obligation and would utterly fail to assure a fellowship of men with God, in which the task of the kingdom of God calls forth the constant effort of the will.

105. The instruction to pray for the forgiveness of sins (Luke 11:4) and the command to exercise a forgiving spirit (Mark 11:25) apply to the community as existing already in the twelve disciples and express the thought that in this community one cannot appropriate to himself the forgiveness of sins without at the same time giving proof by a forgiving spirit, or the love of one's enemies, that one is engaged in the ethical work of the kingdom of God. (Cf. n. 101, above.)

106. Mark 14:24 refers to sacrifice in the covenant (Exod. 24:3–8). Insofar as the Israelites entered by this act upon their vocation as the possession of God and as a kingdom of priests (Exod. 19:5, 6), compare Acts 20:28; Rev. 1:5, 6; Titus 2:14. Rom. 3:25, 26 and Heb. 9:11–14 refer to the type of the general annual sin-offering (Lev. 16). 1 Pet. 1:18, 19 refers to the passover, which belongs to the deliverance from Egypt. Eph. 5:2 makes no distinction between these various kinds of sacrifice.

107. The sacrifices prescribed in the Mosaic law, as well as the sacrifice concluding the covenant, signify that by these acts the covenant community approaches its God; the sacrifices depend therefore upon the certainty of his covenant grace. This is also true of the sin-offering which has reference only to such transgressions as do not involve a breach of the covenant (Num. 15: 27–31).

108. John 10:17, 18; 14:31; 15:13, 14; 17:19; Rom. 5:19; Phil. 2:8; Eph. 5:2; Heb. 5:8, 9. Compare n. 75, above.

109. The combination in the epistle to the Hebrews, especially in 2:17; 4: 14–16; 6:20; 9:11, 24–26.

110. It is remarkable that the epistles have so few reminiscences of the life of Christ. Hence it appears as if the emphasizing of his death as the act of redemption counted upon an interpretation of this act which is in complete contrast to the assessment of his life. Yet it is plain that the apostles under-

stood the divinely purposed death of Christ to be a sacrifice only as it was connected with his obedience in his life's vocation. This highest proof of the obedience of Christ serves thus as a redemptive sacrifice, because it can be understood as summing up in itself the value of his life given in the service of God and of the community to be established. Mark 10:45: "For verily the son of man came not to be ministered unto, but to minister, and to give his life a ransom for many."

111. John 15:10; 10:17, 18; compare n. 66, above.

112. John 17:20–26.

113. The view that Christ, by the vicarious endurance of the punishment deserved by sinful men, propitiated the justice or wrath of God and thus made possible the grace of God, is not founded on any clear and distinct passage in the New Testament. It rests, rather, on a presupposition of natural theology, clearly of Pharasaic and Greek origin. This presupposition is that justice is the fundamental relation between God and man to which religion is subordinate. And along with this a principle is accepted which is contrary to every judicial system, namely, that on the whole justice may be maintained as well by vicarious punishment as by the regular course of law. But these two ideas cannot be coordinated. For the object of justice is the universal well-being of a people or a company of men, and punishment is comprehensible only as a subordinate means to this end (par. 18). Now all law is binding only because the lawgiver shows himself a benefactor, a maintainer of the public weal. Thus the goodness of such a benefactor is the motive for the recognition of his law by the society he founds. Applied to God, this principle shows that the experience of God's goodness or grace is precedent to every law which gives expression to mutual rights between God and man. Therefore the "covenant of works" cannot be regarded as the fundamental relation between the two, and hence the "covenant of works" cannot rationally be transformed into the "covenant of grace" by Christ's fulfilling the conditions of the former and so doing away with it.

114. 1 Pet. 3:18; compare Eph. 2:16–18; Heb. 7:19; 10:19–22. The same thought is expressed in saying that the community is sanctified by the sacrifice of Christ (John 17:19; Heb. 10:14), for "to sanctify," "to make his possession," and "to cause to come near" all mean the same thing (Num. 16:5).

115. The symbolism of all lawful animal sacrifice in the Old Testament has the following content: The ministering priest, who is authorized, in the place of the people or of the individual Israelites, to bring their gifts (corban, that which is brought near) into God's presence, fulfills this purpose in sprinkling the blood containing the life of the animal upon the altar where God meets with the people (Exod. 20:24) and in burning the animal, or certain parts of it, in the fire, where God is present (Lev. 9:24). By these actions, which present the gift to God, the priest "shields" the people or the individuals from the God there present. This accords with the presupposition that no living being can come uncalled into God's presence without being destroyed. But the gift, brought according to the divine order, is the covering or protection under which those in covenant with God are ideally brought into his presence. In the sin-offering there is no rite prescribed which would signify any different

conception from that of the burnt-offering and the peace-offering. In the annual general sin-offering only the blood of the goat is sprinkled on the cover of the ark of testimony (ark of the covenant), because this is a higher symbol of the gracious presence of God than the altar of sacrifice. When God thus suffers the national community, who are conscious of sin, to draw near him in prescribed ways, then in these acts the relative separation from him resulting from sin is done away with. This bringing near to a gracious God, thus accomplished, is the ground of the fact that sins are forgiven, i.e., that they no longer separate men from God.

116. [In the first edition, this paragraph reads as follows: "Since the particular kind of communion with God that a religion embodies is linked with a corresponding stance of men toward the world, dominion over the world has been referred to Christ as an attribute which was incorporated into his distinctiveness as the Son of God and became efficacious in the obedience to his vocation which was directed toward establishing the kingdom of God (par. 23). Overcoming the world through patience in suffering was also incorporated into his obedience to his vocation to the extent that that obedience displays his role as priestly representative of the community which he is to lead to God. From this it follows, however, that for this community also, the calling to spiritual dominion over the world is inseparable from its complete reconciliation with God. Conversely, the hostility toward God which one abandons when he is reconciled with God, must be seen as servitude to the world. It is inconceivable that the man who is reconciled with God would be indifferent to the world. Therefore, spiritual dominion over the world belongs necessarily with reconciliation to God or sonship to God."]

117. Heb. 3:1; 9:15; 12:24.

118. [In the first edition, this paragraph reads as follows: "The same scope of Christ's vocational obedience which filled his life and came to fulfillment in his death is conceived under the two contrasting viewpoints of the office of royal prophet and the royal priesthood, the representing of God to men and of men (in the community) before God. In this double significance of his life, Christ appears as the mediator of the highest conceivable communion between God and man. For this reason, the community established by Christ fulfills this communion with God as its father and assures to every individual membership in this community as well as forgiveness of sins or justification and his position as child of God through faith in Jesus Christ. In relation to the world, this religious faith is the state of Christian freedom, not simply negative freedom from guilt and the power of sin, but rather the positive freedom and dominion over the world in which that negative freedom also comes into our experience."]

119. Thus the idea of Athanasius, that the positive result of redemption through Christ is the deification of the human race, is untenable.

120. Mark 8:29; James 2:1; 1 Pet. 1:7, 8; 1 John 5:1; Heb. 2:3; Rom. 3:21, 22; Acts 4:10–12.

121. John 10:15–18.

122. Mark 9:23; 11:23; Rom. 4:13; 8:31–39; 1 Cor. 3:21–23; James 1:9; 1 John 2:25; 4:9; Rom. 5:1, 2, 17; 1 Cor. 4:8.

123. John 8:36; Gal. 5:1; Luther, "The Freedom of a Christian," *LW* 31: "Now just as Christ by his birthright obtained these two prerogatives, so he imparts them to and shares them with everyone who believes in him according to the law of the above-mentioned marriage, . . . Hence all of us who believe in Christ are priests and kings in Christ, as 1 Pet. 2:9 says" (p. 354). "First, with respect to the kingship, every Christian is by faith so exalted above all things without exception, that nothing can do him any harm. As a matter of fact, all things are made subject to him and are compelled to serve him in obtaining salvation" (Rom. 8:28; 1 Cor. 3:21–33) (Ibid.). "The power of which we speak is spiritual. It rules in the midst of enemies and is powerful in the midst of oppression . . . Lo, this is the inestimable power and liberty of Christians. Not only are we the freest of kings, we are also priests forever . . . , we are worthy to appear before God to pray for others and to teach one another divine things" (p. 355). "From this anyone can clearly see how a Christian is free from all things and over all things so that he needs no works to make him righteous and save him since faith alone abundantly confers all these things" (p. 356). In this interpretation of the freedom founded on faith we find the specific difference between catholicism and protestantism. Catholicism prescribes in its place the *timor filialis* ["filial fear"], the continued anxiety lest one offend God by transgression of the law. This anxious fear before the lawgiver conforms to the whole catholic system and holds men in slavery beneath the structure of supposed guarantees of salvation, which reach their culmination in an infallible pope. The protestant, on the other hand, lives in reverent trust in God our Father, a trust which imparts courage to strive after the righteousness of God, and he needs no other guarantee than the grace of God revealed in the man Christ Jesus (Rom. 5:15).

124. 1 Pet. 1:15; 1 Thess. 4:7. The opposite condition is abnormal (2 Cor. 6:1).

125. Phil. 2:12, 13; Heb. 13:20, 21.

126. 1 Pet. 1:2; 1 John 3:24; 4:13; Heb. 6:4; 10:29; 1 Thess. 4:7, 8; Gal. 5:5, 6, 22–25; 1 Cor. 3:16, 17; Rom. 8:4, 13.

127. 1 Cor. 2:10–12; Gal. 4:6; Rom. 8:15, 16. Melanchthon, *Loci* of 1535, *CR*, XXI, 366, 367: "Scripture desires us to know the divinity of the Holy Spirit in consolation and renewing. It is useful to consider these the offices of the Holy Spirit. In this invoking of the Son in these exertions of faith, we get to know the Trinity better than in useless speculations which argue over what the persons of the Trinity do among themselves not what they do for us."

128. 1 Pet. 1:3, 22, 23; James 1:18; Gal. 6:15; Eph. 2:10; Rom. 6:4, 6; 12:2; Col. 3:9–11; Eph. 4:22–24. New birth, the usual expression for the ideal beginnings of the Christian life, corresponds to none of the expressions used in these passages. It is necessary to be on one's guard against wishing to make certain of this foundation of one's own Christian life by direct experience or at a definite time. Objectively, the new birth or new begetting by God or admission into the relation of sonship with God coincides with justification, as well as with the bestowal of the Holy Spirit. This again is the same as admission into the community. Thus for the one who attains to the independence of his Christian life through the innumerable means of education belonging to

the Christian community, it is quite impossible as well as unnecessary to mark
the beginning of this result. What individuals regard as the beginning is at best
to be considered only a step in their Christian development.

129. Rom. 5:1–4; 8:31–39; 14:17, 18; James 1:2–4, 9, 25; 1 Pet. 1:3–9;
Phil. 4:4.

130. James 1:4; 3:2; 1 Cor. 2:6; Phil. 3:15; Col. 1:28; 4:12; Rom. 12:2; Heb.
5:14; 6:1; 1 John 4:18; Matt. 5:48.

131. 1 John 1:8.

132. Not individual good works, but a complete consistent life-work, is the
duty set forth in the chief writings of the apostles (James 1:4; 1 Pet. 1:17;
Heb. 6:10; 1 Thess: 5:13; Gal. 6:4; 1 Cor. 3:13–15). Good works are to be
considered only as the manifestation of a consistent state of life (James 3:13;
2 Cor. 9:8; Col. 1:10).

133. In James under the name *sophia* ("wisdom") (1:5; 3:17), in Paul and
elsewhere under the name of *hagiasmos* ("holiness") (1 Thess. 4:3–7; 1 Cor.
1:30; Rom. 6:19, 22; Heb. 12:14; 1 John 3:3).

134. This is clear in the case of Paul, who grounds his expectation of the
completion of his salvation upon that which he accomplished in his calling
(1 Thess. 2:19; Phil. 2:16; 2 Tim. 4:8; 1 Cor. 3:5–9). Cf. par. 57.

135. [Ritschl uses the term *sittlicher Beruf* frequently in the paragraphs that
follow. The term is translated here as "ethical vocation." As Ritschl says
clearly in paragraph 57, he is referring to the ordinary vocation or occupation in
which a man carries out his daily work, by which he earns his livelihood, contributes to society, and fulfills his own personal destiny. To refer to this as
one's ethical vocation may be misleading, because it could imply that an *ethical*
vocation is a different vocation from the regular occupation in which one
lives his life, or that it is an additional vocation. By describing the vocation
as *ethical*, however, Ritschl is speaking about the attitude which a man holds
toward his regular occupation and the status it assumes for him. The attitude
should be a very serious one, because the occupation must be carried out in
high ethical responsibility, precisely because one's daily occupation carries a
very high status as the vehicle in which a man fulfills his destiny as a son of
God who contributes his own labor to the work of God's kingdom. An *ethical
vocation*, therefore, is an ordinary, worldly vocation which is entered into and
carried out with high ethical resolve and religious understanding.]

136. James 4:8–10; 1 Pet. 2:11, 12; Rom. 8:13; 13:12–14; Col. 3:5–10.

137. The exercise of righteousness serves for sanctification (Rom. 6:19, 22;
compare Heb. 12:14), i.e., for the attainment of a godly character.

138. Rom. 6:11. It is analogous to this that the perfect no longer look upon
that part of their career which is behind, but on that which is ahead (Phil.
3:12–15).

139. 1 John 1:8.

140. Mark 1:15; 2 Cor. 7:9, 10. Luther's first thesis of Oct. 31, 1517 (in
"Explanation of the Ninety-Five Theses," *LW*, 31, 83): "When our Lord and
Master Jesus Christ said, 'Repent,' he willed the entire life of believers to be
one of repentance."

141. The example of Christ, it is true, is only appealed to in the New Testament in particular respects, as love (Eph. 5:2), devotion to the public good (1 Cor. 10:33; 11:1; Phil. 2:2–5), patience in suffering (1 Pet. 2:21).

142. *CA* XXVII, 49–50: "For this is Christian perfection: honestly to fear God and at the same time to have great faith and to trust that for Christ's sake we have a gracious God; to ask of God, and assuredly to expect from him, help in all things which are to be borne in connection with our callings; meanwhile to be diligent in the performance of good works for others and to attend to our calling. True perfection and true service of God consist of these things and not celibacy, mendicancy, or humble attire" (contrast to the catholic conception of Christian perfection as attained only in monasticism). This contrasted conception of perfection corresponds to the conception of sin in *CA* II, 1 (see also n. 82, above).

143. Mark 8:35–37: "Whosoever shall lose his life for my sake and the gospel's the same shall save it. For what shall it profit a man if he shall gain the whole world and lose his own life? Or what shall a man give in exchange for his life?" The valuing of life as an incomparable good, superior for us therefore to the value of the whole world, is here presupposed as a universal conviction. But at the same time, a truth is also presupposed which is in direct opposition to this conviction, namely, that the loss of life, which awaits every man, proves the insignificance of life in the presence of the regular order of the world. But if one assures his life through union with Christ, even though it be by losing it according to the order of the world, then, on this special condition, the correctness of the claim felt by every human being to have a value surpassing that of the world is established, and any experience of an opposite nature is rendered invalid.

144. 1 Cor. 3:21, 22.

145. *CA* XX, 24: "Whoever knows that he has a Father reconciled to him through Christ . . . knows that God cares for him." The goal and the test of justification by faith in Christ are reverence toward God and trust in his help in all times of need. Compare *Apology*, XX. This reciprocal relation between a special trust in providence and the certainty of reconciliation with God is not rendered less valid by the fact that Seneca also says (*De providentia*, 2): "The brave man is more powerful than all external circumstances. I do not say that he does not suffer, but he conquers. . . . He ponders the actions that are appropriate for all things. . . . The god of the fatherland gives his attention to brave men." For in the first place, these sentences do not signify that trust in God's providence is a datum of the so-called natural or rational religion that all men are said to possess. Instead, it is a special mark of the Stoic philosopher and not common to paganism as a whole, since *natural religion* can attain to this idea neither in its polytheistic form, nor in tragic poetry, nor in the course of philosophy as a whole. But these sentences from Seneca are also not at all like the Christian expressions which they resemble, because they stand in connection with all the hardness of the Stoic sense of self and consciousness of power. [Here Ritschl cites further passages from chapters 2 and 4 of Seneca's work, taking issue with Seneca's admiration of heroic suicide.] According to the Christian standard, suicide is only conceivable as a result of an utter lack of faith in the providence of God.

146. Rom. 11:33–36. Cf. n. 54, above.

147. This knowledge breaks through occasionally even in the Old Testament (Jer. 30:11; Prov. 3:11, 12; Ps. 118:18). In Christianity this knowledge follows from the necessary explanation of the sufferings of Christ the righteous one (Mark 8:34, 35; James 1:2, 3; 1 Pet. 1:6, 7; Heb. 12:4–11; Rom. 5:3, 4; 8:28).

148. 1 Thess. 5:16–18. Thankfulness to God is in general the motive for joy, which is expected to be the pervading tone of the Christian life. Cf. also Rom. 14:17; 15:13; Phil. 4:4.

149. Humility is most clearly expressed in the "fear of God" (1 Pet. 1:17; 3:2; Phil. 2:12; Rom. 11:20; 2 Cor. 5:11; 7:1), which is the "beginning of wisdom" (Prov. 9:10), i.e., godly righteousness.

150. "Humility is like an eye, which sees everything else, but not itself; real humility does not know that it exists." (Scriver) Here the line is drawn against the self-conscious pride of virtue in Stoicism, and the self-conscious pride of religion in all kinds of Pharisaism. The healthy emotional life, expressive of constant harmony with one's self or with the world and with God, moves along under the escort of unclear conceptions. Thus religious experiences of conscious and hence heightened happiness are always infrequent and of dubious value, since their discontinuance is usually experienced with dissatisfaction. We must judge in accordance with this the cases of conscious religious happiness and the universal desire for religious enjoyment.

151. Humility will, it is true, usually be accompanied by modesty toward others (both meanings meet in *tapeinos* ["lowly"], Phil. 2:8; Matt. 23:12; Col. 3:12; Eph. 4:2; Phil. 2:3; 1 Pet. 5:5), but also, on occasion, by anger and zeal against the wicked (Mark 3:5).

152. Such a case is judged as "false humility" in Col. 3:20–23. Jesus judges as hypocrisy (Matt. 23—*hypokrites*, "actor") the ceremonial legal exhibition by the Pharisees of humility as a special devotion to God. The zeal which seeks to impose upon others this or similar ceremonial legal forms of humility, or to put them into effect by force, is fanaticism.

153. James 1:3; 5:10, 11; 2 Cor. 6:4; Rom. 5:3; 12:12. Calvin's *Institutes*, (McNeill, 708): "Yet such a cheerfulness is not required of us as to remove all feeling of bitterness and pain. Otherwise, in the cross there would be no forbearance of the saints unless they were tormented by pain and anguished by trouble."

154. Peter Martyr Vermilius: "This is the character of the sons of God, that they frequently take time for prayers; for that is what it means to perceive the providence of God."

155. Matt. 7:7–11.

156. Mark 14:36; 1 John 5:14.

157. 1 John 3:21, 22.

158. 1 John 5:15. That is, the certainty of God's care in general is not disturbed by the fact that many petitions for individual blessings are not directly answered, but rather it furnishes a compensation for the fact that certain petitions are not answered with exact literalness.

159. This is the error of the catholic view that monasticism implements real Christian virtue or the ideal of the supramundane angelic existence just because it is outside of the natural forms of morality. The giving up of family, private property, complete independence and personal dignity (in obedience to superiors) does not in itself assure a more positive and a richer development of the moral nature, but rather threatens it. For these blessings are absolutely essential conditions of moral health and the formation of character. Pietistic inclination approaches the error of the catholic system in this matter.

160. 1 Cor. 7:20–24. If here even the condition of slavery is viewed in the light of an ethical vocation and so made morally endurable (1 Pet. 2:18, 19) this is certainly true of all kinds of free labor. As to labor, 1 Thess. 4:11; 2 Thess. 3:10–12; as to public spirit, Phil. 2:2–4; Rom. 12:3–5; Cf. *Apology,* XV, 25–26. The demand of Christ in Mark 10:21 has reference to the condition on which the calling of the disciples was to be exercised at that time and does not prescribe monasticism for all times.

161. *Apology,* XXVII, 48–50. (As to the conversation of Christ with the rich young man, Matt. 19:21): "Perfection consists in that which Christ adds, 'Follow me.' This sets forth the example of obedience in a calling. . . . Callings are personal, but the example of obedience is universal. It would have been perfection for this young man to believe and obey this calling. So it is perfection for each of us with true faith to obey his own calling."

162. The ethical blessings of family, station, and patriotism can be perverted into a narrow-minded pride of family, pride of station, and national vanity.

163. Luther, "To the German Nobility," *LW*, 44: "Just as those whom we call clergy (*die Geistlichen*) are distinguished from other Christians only by the fact that they are to administer the word of God and the sacraments—this is their work and office, in the same way secular officials hold the sword to punish the wicked and to protect the pious. A shoemaker, a smith, a peasant, each one has the work and office of his own craft, and yet they are all at the same time consecrated priests and bishops, i.e., spiritual persons [*geistliche Personen*], and each one ought to be useful and serviceable to the other in his office or his work." From "Concerning Monastic Vows": "The obedience of sons, wives, servants, and captives is more perfect that the obedience of monks. Therefore, if we are to move from the imperfect to the perfect, we must go from the obedience of monks to that of parents, masters, tyrants, enemies, and all others."

164. Mark 10:6–8; Gen. 2:24. *Apology,* XXIII, 11–13: "The union of man and woman is by natural right. Natural right is really divine right, because it is an ordinance divinely stamped on nature." Therefore the positive institution of the legal marriage contract falls under the control of the state. Christian marriage is legal marriage between Christians, and does not, therefore, first derive its Christian character through consecration by the church.

165. Mark 10:9–12; 12:25; 1 Pet. 3:7. Exceptions to the indissolubility of marriage appear early, Matt. 19:9; 5:32; 1 Cor. 7:15.

166. Eph. 5:25–29.

167. Col. 3:18, 19; Eph. 5:33; 1 Pet. 3:1.

168. 1 Cor. 7:14.

169. Col. 3:20; Eph. 6:1–3.

170. The view of the Middle Ages, shared even by Luther, that we could get along without legal ordinances were it not for sin, because then everyone would do what is right from love, is false. This view does not take into account the necessary organization and gradation of the ethical principles for the different spheres of life, whereby we are spared a waste of energy. The use of legal enactment thus makes active life an easier matter than would be possible if at every step it were necessary to consider the highest possible standards and their application to ordinary civic duties.

171. Mark 12:17.

172. 1 Pet. 2:13–17; Rom. 13:1–7.

173. Society, when unorganized into a state, whether in a revolutionary or nomadic condition, is an absolute hindrance to the Christian task of the kingdom of God. Even the Israelites were obliged to abandon the nomadic life in order to perform the duties of their religion, whose fundamental promise was that they should acquire a permanent dwelling place (Gen. 12:1–3).

174. CA XVI, 6: "Therefore Christians are necessarily bound to obey their magistrates and laws except when commanded to sin, for then they ought to obey God rather than men (Acts 5:29)." This limitation of the duty of obedience to the state deals with a very distant possibility. The expression of Peter referred to asserts rather the duty of Christian confession in direct opposition to unjustifiable limitations proceeding from a churchly authority.

175. Paul clearly recognized this (Rom. 12:2; Phil. 1:9–11; cf. Rom. 2:18). This proving of what is different, the good and the bad, denotes the finding out of duty, i.e., of what is necessary to do in a particular case. Col. 1:9, 10 refers further to the reciprocal relation, that by wisdom we recognize what God's will is as to a particular course of action, while by the performance of the recognized duties the ability to recognize duty is increased.

176. This table of virtues is complete. All others referred to in ordinary discourse are either synonyms (as faithfulness with conscientiousness or kindliness) or subspecies of self-control (chastity, frugality, moderation) or principles of duty which correspond to the virtue of kindliness (modesty, uprightness, readiness to serve, etc.). This may be seen in the fact that kindliness is to be present always, while these special activities cannot be exercised in all cases, since they must be suspended in intercourse with certain persons.

177. The exalted importance of conscientiousness (Luke 16:10; 1 Cor. 4:2) appears in the fact that it serves as an abbreviated standard of right for the actions of one's regular vocation. It does not, it is true, serve to determine the necessary manner of conduct outside of the regular calling. It is, however, often enough applied as a rule in this realm, through a belief in the authority of conscience as a trustworthy and final standard for all ethical conduct. But the correctness of such a belief is confuted by the fact that there exists also an erring or weak conscience (1 Cor. 8:7–12; 10:28–31; Rom. 14:1–4), which is to be respected in the person of its possessor but is also to be recognized as a tribunal needing correction by higher standards. Still less can the conscientiousness of individuals determined for themselves by false judgment be accepted as a general law for others. When one, for instance, not only erro-

neously makes ascetic rules a part of his own Christian vocation but also wishes to judge others by his own conscientiousness so determined, his conscience is spotted or scarred (Titus 1:15; 1 Tim. 4:2, 3), because he must have suppressed his doubt as to the rightfulness of his proceeding.

178. Wisdom: 1 Cor. 3:10; 6:5; Luke 21:15; Matt. 23:45; 25:2. Discretion, soberness: 1 Pet. 1:13; 5:8; 1 Thess. 5:6, 8. Determination: Rom. 14:22, 23; Col. 4:15; Eph. 5:15, 16. Constancy: Luke 8:15; Heb. 10:36; 12:1; Rev. 2:2; Rom. 2:7.

179. Matt. 10:16; Luke 16:8.

180. 1 Cor. 13:4, 5; Gal. 5:22; Col. 3:12; Eph. 4:32; Phil. 4:5.

181. The moral peculiarity of individuals depends upon the different degrees in which the several groups of virtues are developed, and the various combinations thus arising. At the same time it is also conditioned by the nature of one's vocation, the grade of intelligence and the kind and grade of artistic ability which belongs to each one in general and affects his own moral self-expression.

182. This principle decides against Jesuitic morality, which, because the general moral law does not extend to definite actions, treats the conception of obligation as itself indefinite; it accordingly withdraws the individual possible actions from any definite determination and teaches that they are to be decided according to the authority or assurance of individuals in harmony with the precept that "the end justifies the means."

183. This appears clearly in Christ's Sermon on the Mount (Matt. 5–7), the particular precepts of which are sometimes applicable only by analogy, and sometimes have reference to intercourse with brethren, i.e., with men of like moral disposition. Thus they always take for granted the free judgment of circumstances which cannot be enumerated in the rule.

184. James 1:25.

185. Because the duty of one's vocation is the regular and ordinary form of the duty of love, its fulfillment is rightfully recognized as a part of Christian perfection (see n. 142, above). For the determination of the duties belonging to one's vocation, the virtue of conscientiousness which corresponds to the vocation is, in the formula of the authoritative conscience, the ordinarily sufficient subjective standard. Hence conscientiousness seems to extend also to the judgment as to whether one is called to the performance of certain extraordinary duties of love. Yet this is the very realm where the erring conscience (see n. 177, above) has full play, when one forgets that his own vocation has its limitations, and that some actions are really less analogous to it than one easily imagines.

186. Calvin, *Institutes*, III, 10, 2 [McNeill, 720–21]: "Now if we ponder to what end God created food, we shall find that he meant not only to provide for necessity but also for delight and good cheer. . . . Did he not, in short, render many things attractive to us, apart from their necessary use?"

187. This is the underlying principle of the second table of the commandments (see n. 13, above).

188. The right conception of modesty must always be distinguished from such a false ascetic conception as that which Thomas á Kempis expressed (*De Imita-*

tione Christi, I. 7): "If you possess anything good, then believe the better of other people, so that you may preserve humility. It does no harm for you to subordinate yourselves to others; but it does great harm for you to place yourself above others." This rule contradicts the natural impression of many experiences and involves a constant reflective self-scrutiny in comparing ourselves with others, and it is even more unwholesome, since the result sought after can often enough be reached only by ignoring the truth. For in modesty the important thing cannot be that one regards an immature man as more mature than himself, etc.; but the important thing is that one subordinate himself as an individual to the worth of the fellowship which is sought, in that he puts himself both in speech and action in relation to another. When we are forbidden to judge [*richten*] others (Matt. 7:1–5), the giving up of all moral judgment [*Beurteilung*] of others is not demanded of us. It appears rather from a comparison of that rule with James 4:11, 12 and Rom. 14:4, that such judging of others is wrong when it elevates itself indirectly above the lawgiver or ignores the value of another in God's sight. For thereby the significance of this one for our fellowship would be denied also; but the necessity of such fellowship is established by the law of Christ and by the common dependence of all upon God. One can thus, for instance, make clear to himself the lower moral grade of another in accordance with the truth and yet show him modesty, i.e., the loving regard for his personality which makes one care for his education or improvement.

189. The sincerity which duty demands of us is not the same as natural frankness, though it is made easier by frankness, and the material of individual self-communication is contained in them both. But frankness cannot come to its full expression in sincerity without a restriction by the common end which one is seeking in contact with others. This limitation of natural frankness in sincerity varies according to the character of those with whom one has to do—the two negatives, immodesty and insincerity, denote direct and positive violations of regard for others, the latter as falsity under the guise of sincerity. Non-sincerity or reserve is to be distinguished from these as a purely negative manifestation.

190. Therefore rectitude is possible apart from the disposition of love, as is the negative regard for the person and property of others (see n. 187, above). Both are included in the conception of civil justice which according to the doctrine of the reformers is possible even in the sinful state. It is, however, to be remarked that even in this conception of rectitude the standard is found not in the positive law but in the idea of justice. For this rectitude also excludes such forms of fraud as under certain circumstances are not subject to punishment by the letter of the law and the administration of justice connected with it, for instance, usury, i.e., using another's distress to one's own profit under the form of a legal contract.

191. These three principles have a common opposite in the fundamental unwillingness to please which refuses personal services, gifts and information (in disobliging taciturnity or reserve). Truthfulness has, however, a more distinct opposite in lying, or in a fundamental mendacity. Not every untrue statement is a lie. In the realm of art, in jest, in the deception of children or the sick or enemies, an untrue statement is occasionally permissible or even

desirable. But a lie is an untruth told with the purpose of injuring another or of gaining an unwarrantable advantage for one's self, or both. Mendacity is the habitual inclination to untruthfulness, arising either from such a purpose, or from such an indifference to truth as excludes the purpose of being of service to others through truthfulness.

192. Matt. 5:23, 24.

193. Matt. 7:6.

194. [In the first edition, this paragraph stands as follows: "Perfection, which consists in the exercise of religious and moral virtues and in the performance of the duties of love regulated by our ethical vocation, is necessarily accompanied by a feeling of blessedness. In the present worldly existence, only a few persons succeed in attaining this pinnacle of Christian character-formation and in asserting it in the struggle with their own sin and in patience in the face of external restraints, since ethical sensitivity only throws stronger light on all the defects and faults which present themselves to that sensitivity. Moreover, it is not possible to create a community of the perfect as such, so as to establish a smaller circle, so to speak, within the larger community of those who worship God. For men's striving after the kingdom of God is never evident to the observation of others in such a way as to allow us to enter into a particular alliance for the purpose of advancing that effort. Furthermore, the task of education which is implied in the imperative of the kingdom of God would be hindered rather than advanced if Christians of highest character isolated themselves from the rest of the community as a particular, more restricted group. Nevertheless, the communal concern of the Christian religion is not satisfied by the confidence that a few persons will always be able to scale the heights of Christian perfection. For this reason, this communal concern engenders the hope that those Christians who have attained their own personal form of perfection will attain the higher communal goal of life and blessedness under conditions of existence other than those that prevail in this world of experience."]

195. Such an order appeared originally in Buddhism, then in Manichaeism, then was applied in the estimate of Christian monasticism, and finally appears again in pietistic circles. In all these similar manifestations, there is prominent a religious bias toward an abstract denial of the world, which in varying degrees is common to these religions and tendencies. At the same time it is true, a separation of the *perfecti* from the *auditores* (as they are classified in Manichaeism) only appears when at bottom there is a strong tendency toward a ceremonial-legal conception of religion.

196. [In the first edition, this paragraph reads as follows: "Eternal life grows out of the common destiny which Christians possess by virtue of reconciliation through Christ and therefore is a result of God's grace; but, since this eternal life belongs to the Christian as the distinctive goal that is to be attained within the community, it is conditioned by the exercise of justification and by sanctification. Furthermore, as the supranatural and supramundane consummation of the humanity which is uniting itself in the kingdom of God, this eternal life is only conceivable under circumstances in which the natural conditions to which our spiritual life is bound in this present world will either be removed

or altered in the future. Christ and the apostles expected the appearance of this consummation and these circumstances to come more quickly than actually was the case, and they did so in terms of the dramatic images of God's judgment over the world, which had been utilized by the Old Testament prophets. Natural science also sets forth, by its methods, the end of the present world order, particularly the dissolution of the solar system, by which the earth processes are determined. In contrast, the religious estimate of our spiritual and ethical life that arises in Christianity provides the basis for hope that that spiritual and ethical life will be maintained and strengthened in communion with God and in the kingdom of perfected spirits. As decisive as the subjective certainty of this consummation may be in our own feeling regarding the significance of our lives—formed as they are by Christian influences—there remains necessarily a lack of clarity in our concrete vision of the means by which this consummation will be actualized and shaped in the hereafter, because our present experience cannot touch upon those things. For this reason, all of the forms set forth in the New Testament concerning the last things possess a symbolic significance. Similarly, those structures of thought which we have to acknowledge as the framework for religious hope cannot be filled out with a content that is directly perceivable."]

197. Mark 8:38; 9:1; 1 Pet. 4:7; James 5:8, 9; 1 John 2:28; 1 Thess. 4:15; 1 Cor. 10:11; 15:52; Heb. 10:35–37. Compare, on the other hand, 2 Pet. 3:4–9; Rev. 19:11–22; 1 Pet. 4:5; Heb. 10:30, 31; 2 Cor. 5:10; Matt. 25:31–46.

198. 1 Thess. 4:16, 17.

199. CA XVII, 1: ". . . at the consummation of the world Christ will appear for judgment and will raise up all the dead. To the godly and elect he will give eternal life and endless joy, but ungodly men and devils he will condemn to be tormented without end."

200. Here belongs the expectation of continued existence in a body corresponding fully to the spirit (1 Cor. 15:35–53; 2 Cor. 5:1; Phil. 3:20, 21); as well as the destiny of those who are not saved, of whom it seems uncertain whether they shall suffer endless punishment or be annihilated (Mark 9:43–48; Rev. 19:20; Rom. 2:9, 12; 9:22; Phil. 3:19; Rev. 17:8, 11; Matt. 7:13).

201. The same community which, in mutual moral action, forms the kingdom of God is through reconciliation with God at the same time destined to unite itself in public worship (see n. 18, above).

202. The fruit of lips which confess God's name is the sacrifice of praise (Heb. 13:15; cf. 1 Pet. 2:5), a sacrifice which occasionally, even in the Old Testament, is recognized as the opposite of, and the most complete substitute for, material sacrifice (Hos. 14:2; Ps. 50:14, 23; 51:15–17; 116:17; Isa. 57:19).

203. The word "prayer" is a real hindrance to the recognition of this fact, since the first thought it suggests is that of petition. But one only needs to look through the Psalms, which in Hebrew are called *tehillim* (songs of praise), to recognize the norm of the matter in the statement above.

204. The calling upon God as our Father through Jesus Christ (par. 12) distinguishes Christianity from all other religions, including that of the Old Testament. For although God stands in the Old Testament as the father of the chosen

people Israel, which is his son (Exod. 4:22; Hos. 11:1), the right is first given to the members of his community by Christ to regard themselves individually as sons or children of God, while he designates the Israelites as strangers, i.e., as servants of God (Matt. 17:24–27). Accordingly, it is characteristic that Paul, in the opening of his epistles, identifies himself with the community he addresses by giving thanks to God as our Father and as the Father of our Lord Jesus Christ and does so on the ground of the existence of the Christian religion in that community (1 Thess. 1:2–5; 2 Thess. 1:3, 4; Gal. 1:3–5; 1 Cor. 1:4–9; 2 Cor. 1:3–7; Rom. 1:8; Col. 1:3–6; Eph. 1:3–6; Phil. 1:3–7; cf. Acts 2:11, 47).

205. Phil. 4:6; 1 Thess. 5:16–18.

206. John 14:13, 14; 15:16; 16:23, 34.

207. For various reasons the text of this prayer and the occasion for it as given in Luke 11:1–3 are to be preferred to the text and the context in Matt. 6:9–13. In the former the prayer consists of five petitions [Here Ritschl includes the Greek text of the Lord's Prayer]. What is added in Matthew proves to be only an enlargement of the second and fifth petitions. For the coming of the kingdom of God consists in God's will being done on earth as in heaven (Ps. 103: 21), and being delivered from evil is identical with being kept from temptation.

208. This is the meaning of the "name of God" (Ps. 9:10; 69:36; Deut. 28: 58; 32:3; Isa. 30:27; 50:10).

209. Isa. 29:23; Ezek. 36:23.

210. Matt. 6:31, 32.

211. Priests are those who are permitted to draw near to God (Num. 16:5). In this sense the Israelites were originally a kingdom of priests (Exod. 19:6). The exercise of this right was then limited in being restricted to the mediation by the sacrifice of the official Levitic priests. In Christianity this condition is done away with, since in its community only the sacrifice of prayer is offered; thus all Christians are priests (1 Pet. 2:5, 9; Rev. 1:9; 5:10; Heb. 7:19; 10:22; 13:15).

212. Matt. 10:32, 33; Rom. 10:9; 1 Cor. 12:3; Phil. 2:11. This confession of the church corresponds both to its historical peculiarity and to its universal human destiny. By this confession Christians are to be distinguished from all other religious communities, but at the same time they are to extend their community until it embraces humanity.

213. Mark 4:14; John 5:24, 38; 8:31; 14:23, 24; Luke 10:16; Acts 4:29; 1 Pet. 1:23–25; Rom. 1:1; 1 Cor. 14:36; Col. 1:25; 1 Thess. 2:13.

214. Eph. 4:4–6; 1 Cor. 10:17.

215. 1 Cor. 11:26; Matt. 28:19. The marks of the unity of the church are not similar in nature to one another, and no one of them ought to be emphasized in a one-sided manner. The preaching of the divine word in the church must be evaluated with reference to its goal, namely, that the church may be united in the prayer-confession of God through their Lord Jesus Christ, and the two acts instituted by Christ fully attain their divine sacramental significance only when they are performed as acts of worship on the part of the com-

munity. Thus the definition of the church in the *CA* VII, 1: "The assembly of all believers among whom the Gospel is preached in its purity and the holy sacraments are administered according to the Gospel," is incomplete, because it lacks the characteristic of uniform prayer. But further, a right understanding of the matter would not be reached if the word of God, prayer, sacraments, were only enumerated side by side as similar characteristics of the church. For the contrast must be maintained between the word *of God* and the prayer *of the community*, in order to recognize the reciprocal relation between the two, and it must be made clear, in the case of baptism and the Lord's Supper, that the reciprocal relation between the *act of the community* and the *gracious gift of God* is expressed in one and the same act.

216. Belief here has reference to the church as the union of believers in the Holy Spirit and as the sphere designated by the forgiveness of sins (see n. 102, above). This belief recognizes these determinations of value as belonging to the church and recognizes the church in these relations as a reality whose existence is assured by God. Legal forms, however, are not definitions of value for religious faith, and thus it ignores them in establishing the religious significance of the church.

217. Acts. 2:1–11.

218. 1 Thess. 5:12, 13; 1 Cor. 16:15, 16; 1 Pet. 5:1–5; Heb. 13:17.

219. 1 Cor. 6:1–6; 7:10–17.

220. *CA* V, 1. The fact is overlooked here that the preachers of the divine word are at the same time the liturgists, i.e., those who offer prayer for the congregation. Now as prayer is an activity in whose exercise all Christians are priests (see n. 211, above), there can be no objection to designating those who offer the public liturgical prayers as official priests. In so doing the right of the catholics to limit this title to the sacrifice of the mass is denied, since in the protestant sense no other kind of sacrifice belongs to the priest than that which belongs to all, the sacrifice of the lips—prayer.

221. John 10:16.

222. Baptism and the Lord's Supper, in spite of their original intent (see n. 214, above), unfortunately can no longer be called actual characteristics of the unity of the church. The Lord's Supper is almost everywhere without hesitation made the confessional sign of churchly schism. Baptism also is no longer what Luther considered it, a common characteristic of all sects. In the Greek church, which practices a threefold immersion, the sprinkling of the western church is not so fully recognized that Latin Christians may not be baptized at the option of the individual priest. The numberless sects of Baptists do not recognize infant sprinkling as baptism at all. And lately the Roman Catholics have been departing from the former recognition of heretical baptism and occasionally rebaptize converts from protestantism.

223. The earliest document of the kind, the so-called Apostles' Creed, cannot rightly be regarded as the uniform confession of the *whole* church. For in the Greek church it is neither in official use, nor is it generally known, since there its place is occupied by the Nicene-Constantinopolitan formula of the rule of faith.

224. *CA* XXVIII, 12, 21: "Therefore, ecclesiastical and civil power are not to be confused. . . . Hence according to the Gospel (or, as they say, by divine right) no jurisdiction belongs to the bishops as bishops (that is, to those to whom has been committed the ministry of Word and sacraments) except to forgive sins, to reject doctrine which is contrary to the Gospel, and to exclude from the fellowship of the church ungodly persons whose wickedness is known, doing all this without human power, simply by the Word."

225. Luther, "To the German Nobility," *LW*, 44: "Since secular authority is ordained by God, to punish the wicked and to protect the good, they shall be suffered to exercise their office unhindered throughout the whole body of Christendom, regardless as to whom it may affect, be it pope, bishops, priests, monks, nuns, or whomsoever it may."

226. Acts 2:38; 8:16; 10:48; 19:5; Rom. 6:3; Gal. 3:27; Matt. 28:19.

227. Acts 2:38. Many passages of the New Testament which are generally understood as referring to the Christian baptism of the *individual*, do not have reference to this, but to the *general* renewing of man by the Spirit of God, which is symbolically referred to in the Prophets as cleansing and quickening through water (John 3:5; Titus 3:5; cf. Ezek. 36:25, 26; Isa. 32:15; Joel 3:1).

228. *CA*, IX, 2: ". . . children offered to God through Baptism are received into his grace." Here the baptism of children is rightly represented as a consecrating of them by the community, an action which is effective because of the relation of the community to God.

229. 1 Cor. 10:16, 17; 11:23–26; Mark 14:22–24; Matt. 26:26–28; Luke 22:19, 20.

230. Luther's *Large Catechism*, V, 32: "Now, the whole Gospel and the article of the Creed, 'I believe in the holy Christian church, the forgiveness of sins,' are embodied in this sacrament and offered to us through the Word."

INDEX

Index

BROWN-EYED GIRL

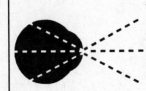

This Large Print Book carries the
Seal of Approval of N.A.V.H.

Brown-Eyed Girl

Lisa Kleypas

THORNDIKE PRESS
A part of Gale, Cengage Learning

GALE
CENGAGE Learning·

Farmington Hills, Mich • San Francisco • New York • Waterville, Maine
Meriden, Conn • Mason, Ohio • Chicago

LIBRARY OF CONGRESS CATALOGING-IN-PUBLICATION DATA

Kleypas, Lisa.
   Brown-eyed girl / Lisa Kleypas. — Large print edition.
     pages cm. — (Thorndike Press large print core)
     ISBN 978-1-4104-7733-0 (hardback) — ISBN 1-4104-7733-9 (hardcover)
   1. Large type books. I. Title.
PS3561.L456B76 2015b
813'.54—dc23   2015022287

Published in 2015 by arrangement with St. Martin's Press, LLC

Printed in the United States of America
1 2 3 4 5 6 7 19 18 17 16 15

For Eloisa James and Linda Francis Lee,
who make me happy when
skies are gray.
Love always,
L.K.

ONE

As an experienced wedding planner, I was prepared for nearly every kind of emergency that might occur on the big day.

Except for scorpions. That was a new one.

The distinctive movement gave it away, a sinister forward-and-back scuttle across the tiles of the pool patio. In my opinion, there wasn't a more evil-looking creature in existence than a scorpion. Usually the venom wouldn't kill you, but for the first couple of minutes after you'd been stung, you might wish it had.

The first rule for dealing with emergencies was: *Don't panic.* But as the scorpion skittered toward me with its grasping claws and upward-curved tail, I forgot all about rule number one and let out a shriek. Frantically I rummaged through my bag, a tote so heavy that whenever I set it on the passenger seat, the car would signal me to buckle it in. My hand fumbled past tissues, pens, bandages, Evian, hair products, deodorant, hand sanitizer, lotion, nail and makeup kits, tweezers, a sewing kit, glue, headphones, cough drops, a chocolate bar, over-the-counter medications, scissors, a file, a brush, earring backs, rubber bands, tampons, stain remover, a lint roller, bobby pins, a razor, double-sided tape, and cotton swabs.

The heaviest object I could find was a glue gun, which I threw at the scorpion. The glue gun bounced harmlessly on the tile, while the scorpion bristled to defend its territory. Pulling out a can of hair spray, I ventured forward with cautious determination.

"That's not going to work," I heard someone say in a low, amused voice. "Unless you're trying to give him more volume and shine."

Startled, I looked up as a stranger moved past me, a tall, black-haired man dressed in jeans, boots, and a T-shirt that had been washed to near annihilation. "I'll take care of it," he said.

I retreated a couple of steps, shoving the can back into my bag. "I . . . I thought hair spray might suffocate him."

"Nope. A scorpion can hold its breath for up to a week."

"Really?"

"Yes, ma'am." He crushed the scorpion beneath his boot, finishing with an extra grind of his heel. There was nothing a Texan killed more thoroughly than a scorpion or a lit cigarette. After kicking the exoskeleton into the mulch of a nearby flower bed, he turned to give me a long, considering glance. The purely male assessment jolted my heartbeat into a new frenzy. I found myself staring into eyes the color of blackstrap molasses. He was a striking man, his features bold, the nose strong, the jaw sturdy. The stubble on his face looked heavy enough to sand paint off a car. He was big-boned and lean, the muscles of his arms and chest as defined as cut stone beneath the worn layer of his T-shirt. A disreputable-looking man, maybe a little dangerous.

The kind of man who made you forget to breathe.

His boots and the raggedy hems of his jeans were skimmed with mud that was already drying to powder. He must have been walking near the creek that cut through the Stardust Ranch's four thousand acres. Dressed like that, he couldn't possibly have been one of the wedding guests, most of whom possessed unimaginable fortunes.

As his gaze swept over me, I knew exactly what he was seeing: a full-figured woman in her late twenties, with red hair and big-framed glasses. My clothes were comfortable, loose, and plain. "Forever 51," my younger sister Sofia had described my standard outfit of boxy tops and elastic-waist wide-legged pants. If the look was off-putting to men — and it usually was — so much the better. I had no interest in attracting anyone.

"Scorpions aren't supposed to come out in the daylight," I said unsteadily.

"We had an early thaw and a dry spring. They're looking for moisture. Swimmin' pool's going to draw 'em out." He had a lazy, easy way of talking, as if every word had been simmered for hours over a low flame.

Breaking our shared gaze, the stranger bent to retrieve the glue gun. As he handed it to me, our fingers touched briefly, and I felt a little jab of response beneath my lower ribs. I caught his scent, white soap and dust and sweet wild grass.

"You'd best change out of those," he advised, glancing at my open-toed flats. "You got boots? Running shoes?"

"I'm afraid not," I said. "I'll have to take my chances." I noticed the camera he had set on one of the patio tables, a Nikon with a pro-level lens, the metal barrel edged with red. "You're a professional photographer?" I asked.

"Yes, ma'am."

He had to be one of the second-shooters hired by George Gantz, the wedding photographer. I extended my hand. "I'm Avery Crosslin," I said in a friendly but businesslike tone. "The wedding co-ordinator."

He gripped my hand, the clasp warm and firm. I felt a little shock of pleasure at the contact.

"Joe Travis." His gaze continued to hold mine, and for some reason he prolonged the grip a couple of seconds longer than necessary. Unaccountable warmth swept over my face in a swift tide. I was relieved when he finally let go.

"Did George give you copies of the time-line and shot list?" I asked, trying to sound professional.

The question earned a blank look.

"Don't worry," I said, "we've got extra copies. Go to the main house and ask for my assistant, Steven. He's probably in the kitchen with the caterers." I fished in my bag for a business card. "If you have any problems, here's my cell number."

He took the card. "Thanks. But I'm not actually —"

11

"The guests will be seated at six thirty," I said briskly. "The ceremony will begin at seven and finish with the dove release at seven thirty. And we'll want some shots of the bride and groom before sunset, which happens at seven forty-one."

"Did you schedule that too?" Mocking amusement glinted in his eyes.

I shot him a warning glance. "You should probably spruce up before the guests are up and out this morning." I reached into my bag for a disposable razor. "Here, take this. Ask Steven where there's a place you can shave, and —"

"Slow down, honey. I have my own razor." He smiled slightly. "Do you always talk so fast?"

I frowned, tucking the razor back into my bag. "I have to get to work. I suggest you do the same."

"I don't work for George. I'm commercial and freelance. No weddings."

"Then what are you here for?" I asked.

"I'm a guest. Friend of the groom's."

Stunned, I stared at him with wide eyes. The creepy-crawly heat of embarrassment covered me from head to toe. "I'm sorry," I managed to say. "When I saw your camera, I assumed . . ."

"No harm done."

There was nothing I hated more than looking foolish, *nothing.* The appearance of competence was essential in building a client base . . . especially the upper-class clientele I was aiming for. But now on the day of the biggest, most expensive wedding my studio and I had ever orchestrated, this man was going to tell his wealthy friends about how I'd mistaken him for the hired help. There would be snickers behind my back. Snide jokes. Contempt.

Wanting to put as much distance as possible between us, I muttered, "If you'll excuse me . . ." I turned and walked away as fast as I could without breaking into a run.

"Hey," I heard Joe say, catching up to me in a few long strides. He had grabbed the camera and slung it on a strap over his shoulder. "Hold on. No need to be skittish."

"I'm not skittish," I said, hurrying toward a flagstone-floored pavilion with a wooden roof. "I'm busy."

He matched my pace easily. "Wait a minute. Let's start over."

"Mr. Travis —," I began, and stopped dead in my tracks as I realized exactly who he was. "God," I said sickly, closing my eyes for a moment. "You're one of those Travises, aren't you."

13

Joe came around to face me, his gaze quizzical. "Depends on what you mean by 'those.' "

"Oil money, private planes, yachts, mansions. *Those.*"

"I don't have a mansion. I have a fixer-upper in the Sixth Ward."

"You're still one of them," I insisted. "Your father is Churchill Travis, isn't he?"

A shadow crossed his expression. "Was."

Too late, I remembered that approximately six months earlier, the Travis family patriarch had passed away from sudden cardiac arrest. The media had covered his funeral extensively, describing his life and accomplishments in detail. Churchill had made his vast fortune with venture and growth capital investing, most of it related to energy. He'd been highly visible in the eighties and nineties, a frequent guest on TV business and financial shows. He — and his heirs — were the equivalent of Texas royalty.

"I'm . . . sorry for your loss," I said awkwardly.

"Thanks."

A wary silence ensued. I could feel his gaze moving over me, as tangible as the heat of sunlight.

"Look, Mr. Travis —"

"Joe."

"Joe," I repeated. "I'm more than a little preoccupied. This wedding is a complicated production. At the moment I'm managing the setup of the ceremony site, the decoration of an eight-thousand-square-foot reception tent, a formal dinner and dance with a live orchestra for four hundred guests, and a late night after-party. So I apologize for the misunderstanding, but —"

"No need to apologize," he said gently. "I should've spoken up sooner, but it's hard to get a word in edgewise with you." Amusement played at the corners of his mouth. "Which means either I'm going to have to speed up, or you're going to have to slow down."

Even as tense as I was, I was tempted to smile back.

"There's no need for the Travis name to make you feel uncomfortable," he continued. "Believe me, no one who knows my family is impressed by us in the least." He studied me for a moment. "Where are you headed to now?"

"The pavilion," I said, nodding to the covered wooden structure beyond the pool.

"Let me walk you there." At my hesitation, he added, "In case you run across another scorpion. Or some other varmint.

Tarantulas, lizards . . . I'll clear a path for you."

Wryly, I reflected that the man could probably charm the rattles off a snake. "It's not *that* bad out here," I said.

"You need me," he said with certainty.

Together we walked to the ceremony site, crossing beneath a motte of live oak on the way. The white silk reception tent in the distance was poised on a tract of emerald lawn like a massive cloud that had floated down to rest. There was no telling how much precious water had been used to maintain that brilliant grassy oasis, freshly rolled out and laid only a few days ago. And every tender green blade would have to be pulled up tomorrow.

Stardust was a four-thousand-acre working ranch with a main lodge, a compound of guesthouses and assorted buildings, a barn, and a riding arena. My event-planning studio had arranged to lease the private property while the owners were away on a two-week cruise. The couple had agreed on condition the property would be restored to exactly the way it had been before the wedding.

"How long you been at this?" Joe asked.

"Wedding planning? My sister Sofia and I started the business about three years ago.

Before that, I worked in bridal fashion design in New York."

"You must be good, if you were hired for Sloane Kendrick's wedding. Judy and Ray wouldn't settle for anyone but the best."

The Kendricks owned a chain of pawnshops from Lubbock to Galveston. Ray Kendrick, a former rodeo rider with a face like a pine knot, had laid out a cool million for his only daughter's wedding. If my event team pulled this off, there was no telling how many high-profile clients we might gain from it.

"Thanks," I said. "We've got a good team. My sister is very creative."

"What about you?"

"I take care of the business side of things. And I'm the head coordinator. It's up to me to make sure that every detail is perfect."

We reached the pavilion, where a trio of reps from the rental company were setting up white-painted chairs. Rummaging through my bag, I found a metal tape measure. With a few expert tugs, I extended it across the space between the cords that had been staked out to line up the chairs. "The aisle has to be six feet wide," I called out to the reps. "Move the cord, please."

"It is six feet," one of them called back.

"It's five feet and ten inches."

The rep gave me a long-suffering glance. "Isn't that close enough?"

"Six feet," I insisted, and snapped the measuring tape closed.

"What do you do when you're not working?" Joe asked from behind me.

I turned to face him. "I'm always working."

"Always?" he asked skeptically.

"I'm sure I'll slow down when the business is more established. But for now . . ." I shrugged. I could never seem to cram enough into one day. E-mails, phone calls, plans to be made, arrangements to nail down.

"Everyone needs some kind of hobby."

"What's yours?"

"Fishing, when I get the chance. Hunting, depending on the season. Every now and then I do some charity photography."

"What kind of charity?"

"A local animal shelter. A good photo on the website can help a dog get adopted sooner." Joe paused. "Maybe sometime you'd like to —"

"I'm sorry — excuse me." I had heard a ringtone from somewhere in the abyss of my bag, repeating the five notes of "Here Comes the Bride." As I retrieved the phone, I saw my sister's ID.

"I've been calling the dove handler, and he won't answer," Sofia said as soon as I answered. "He never confirmed which container we wanted for the release."

"Did you leave a message?" I asked.

"Five messages. What if something's wrong? What if he's sick?"

"He's not sick," I assured her.

"Maybe he got bird flu from his doves."

"His birds aren't doves. They're white pigeons, and pigeons are resistant to bird flu."

"Are you sure?"

"Try him again in a couple of hours," I said soothingly. "It's only seven. He may not even be awake yet."

"What if he's a no-show?"

"He'll be here," I said. "It's too early in the day to freak out, Sofia."

"When am I allowed to freak out?"

"You're not," I said. "I'm the only one who gets to do that. Let me know if you don't hear from him by ten."

"Okay."

I slipped the phone back into my bag and gave Joe an inquiring glance. "You were saying something about the animal shelter?"

He stared down at me. His thumbs were hooked in his pockets, most of his weight braced on one leg, in a stance that was both assertive and relaxed. I had never seen anything sexier in my life.

"I could take you along with me," he said, "next time I head over there. I wouldn't mind sharing my hobby until you get one of your own."

I was slow to respond. My thoughts had scattered like a flock of baby chicks at a petting zoo. I had the impression that he was asking me to go somewhere with him. Almost like . . . a date?

"Thanks," I said eventually, "but my schedule is full."

"Let me take you out sometime," he urged. "We could go out for drinks, or lunch."

I was rarely at a loss for words, but all I could do was stand there in baffled silence.

"Tell you what." His voice turned coaxing and soft. "I'll drive you to Fredericksburg one morning, while the day is still cool and we have the road to ourselves. We'll stop to buy some coffee and a bag of kolaches. I'll take you to a meadow so full of bluebonnets, you'll swear half the sky just fell over Texas. We'll find us a shade tree and watch the sunrise. How does that sound?"

It sounded like the kind of day meant for some other woman, someone who was accustomed to being charmed by handsome men. For a second I let myself imagine it, lounging with him on a quiet morning in a blue meadow. I was on the verge of agreeing to anything he asked. But I couldn't afford to take such a risk. Not now, not ever. A man like Joe Travis had undoubtedly broken so many hearts that mine would mean nothing to him.

"I'm not available," I blurted out.

"You're married?"

"No."

"Engaged?"

"No."

"Living with someone?"

I shook my head.

Joe was quiet for a few seconds, staring at me as if I were a puzzle he wanted to solve. "I'll see you later," he said eventually. "And in the meantime . . . I'm going to figure out how to get a 'yes' out of you."

TWO

Feeling somewhat dazed after the encounter with Joe Travis, I went to the main house and found my sister in the office. Sofia was beautiful and dark-haired, her eyes a rich hazel green. She had a curvy figure like me, but she dressed with flair, having no reservations about flaunting her hourglass shape.

"The dove handler just called back," Sofia said triumphantly. "The birds are confirmed." She gave me a concerned glance. "Your face is red. Are you dehydrated?" She handed me a bottle of water. "Here."

"I just met someone," I said after a few gulps.

"Who? What happened?"

Sofia and I were half-sisters who had been raised apart. She had lived with her mother in San Antonio, while I had lived with mine in Dallas. Although I had been aware of Sofia's existence, I hadn't met her until we were both grown. The Crosslin family tree had a few too many branches, thanks to our father Eli's five failed marriages and prolific affairs.

Eli, a handsome man with golden hair and a blinding smile, had pursued women compulsively. He had loved the emotional and sexual high of conquest. Once the excitement had faded, however, he'd never been able to settle into everyday life with one woman. For that matter, he'd never stayed with one job for more than a year or two.

There had been other children besides Sofia and me, half-siblings and innumerable stepsiblings. All of us had been abandoned by Eli, in turn. After the occasional call or visit, he would disappear for long periods, sometimes a couple of years. And then he would reappear briefly, magnetic and exciting, full of interesting stories and promises that I knew better than to believe.

The first time I met Sofia had been right after Eli had suffered a major stroke, an unexpected event for a man of his age and good physical condition. I had flown down from New York City to find an unfamiliar young woman waiting in his hospital room. Before she had even introduced herself, I had known she was one of Eli's daughters.

Although her coloring — black hair, glowing amber skin — had come from her Hispanic mother's side of the family, her fine, sculpted features had unmistakably been inherited from our father.

She had given me a cautious but friendly smile. "I'm Sofia."

"Avery." I had reached out for an awkward handshake, but she'd moved forward to hug me instead, and I'd found myself reciprocating and thinking, *My sister,* with a thrill of connection I wouldn't have expected. I had looked over her shoulder at Eli in the hospital bed, hooked up to machines, and I hadn't been able to make myself let go. That had been fine with Sofia, who was never the first to end a hug.

In the vast accumulation of Eli's offspring and exes, Sofia and I were the only ones who had shown up. I didn't blame any of the others for that: I hadn't even been sure why I was there. Eli had never read me a bedtime story, or bandaged a skinned knee, or done any of the things fathers were supposed to do. In his self-absorption, there had been no attention to spare for his children. Moreover, the pain and fury of the women he'd abandoned had made it difficult to contact their children, even if he'd wanted to. Eli's usual method of ending a relationship or a marriage was to have an exit affair, cheating until he was caught and kicked out. My mother had never forgiven him for that.

But Mom had repeated the same pattern, taking up with cheaters, liars, deadbeats, men who wore their red flags on their sleeves. Among the tumult of affairs, she had married and divorced two more times. Love had brought her so little happiness, it was a wonder that she kept searching for it.

In my mother's mind, the blame lay entirely with my father, the man who had started her on the self-defeating path. As I became older, however, I wondered if the reason Mom hated Eli so much was that they were so similar. I found no small irony in the fact that she was a temp secretary, going from office to office, boss to boss. When she had been offered a permanent position at one of the companies, she had refused. It would become too monotonous, she'd said, doing the same thing every day, always seeing the same people. I had been sixteen at the time, too mouthy to resist pointing out that with that attitude, she probably wouldn't have stayed married to Eli anyway. That had provoked an argument that had nearly resulted in me getting kicked out of the house. Mom had been so infuriated by my comment that I knew I was right.

From what I'd observed, the kind of love that flared brightest also burned out the fastest. It couldn't survive after the novelty and excitement had worn off and it was time to match socks from the dryer, or vacuum the dog hair off the sofa, or organize household debris. I wanted nothing to do with that kind of love: I couldn't see the benefit. Like the slam and fade of a destructive drug, the high never lasted long enough, and the low left you empty and craving more.

As for my father, every woman he'd supposedly loved, even the ones he'd married, had been nothing more than a stop along the way to someone else. He had been a single traveler on his life's journey, and that was how it had ended. The office manager of Eli's apartment complex had found him unconscious on the floor of his living room, after he'd failed to show up to renew his lease.

Eli had been rushed to the hospital in an ambulance, but he had never regained consciousness.

"My mother's not coming," I had told Sofia as we sat together in the hospital room.

"Mine either."

We had glanced at each other in mutual understanding. Neither of us had to ask why no one else had come to say good-bye. When a man abandoned his family, the hurt of it kept bringing out the worst in them long after he'd gone.

"Why are you here?" I dared to ask.

While Sofia considered her answer, the silence was punctured by the beeps from a monitor and the ventilator's constant rhythmic *whoosh.* "My family is Mexican," she finally said. "To them, everything is about togetherness and tradition. I always wanted to belong, but I knew I was different. My cousins all had fathers, while mine was a mystery. *Mamá* would never talk about him." Her gaze went to the bed where our father lay enmeshed inside a tangle of tubes and wires that hydrated, fed, breathed, regulated, and drained. "I only saw him once, when I was a little girl and he came to visit. *Mamá* wouldn't let him talk to me, but I ran after him when he walked out to his car. He was holding some balloons he'd brought for me." She smiled absently. "I thought he was the handsomest man in the world. He tied the ribbons around my wrist so the balloons wouldn't float away. After he drove off, I tried to bring the balloons into the house, but *Mamá* said I had to get rid of them. So I untied the ribbons and let them go, and I made a wish as I watched them float away."

"You wished that you would see him again someday," I said quietly.

Sofia nodded. "That's why I came. What about you?"

"Because I thought no one else would be here. And if someone had to take care of Eli, I didn't want it to be a total stranger."

Sofia's hand had covered mine, as naturally as if we'd known each other all our lives. "Now it's the two of us," she'd said simply.

Eli had passed away the next day. But in the process of losing him, Sofia and I had found each other.

At the time I had been working in bridal couture, but my career had been going nowhere. Sofia had been working as a nanny in San Antonio, planning children's parties on the side. We had talked about starting a wedding-planning studio together. Now, a little more than three years later, our Houston-based business was working out better than we had even dared to hope. Each small success had built on the next, allowing us to hire three employees and an intern. With the Kendrick wedding, we were on the verge of a breakthrough.

As long as we didn't screw up.

"Why didn't you say yes?" Sofia demanded after I told her about meeting Joe Travis.

"Because I don't believe for one minute that he was actually interested in me." I paused. "Oh, don't give me that look. You know that type of guy goes for trophy women."

I had been voluptuous since adolescence. I walked everywhere, took the stairs whenever possible, and went to a dance class twice a week. I ate healthy food and routinely consumed enough salad to choke a manatee. But no amount of exercise and or dieting would ever shrink me down to a single-digit dress size. Sofia often urged me to buy more body-conscious clothes, and I always told her I would do it later, when I was the right size.

"You're the right size now," Sofia would reply.

I knew that I shouldn't let a bathroom scale stand between me and happiness. Some days I won, but more often than not, the scale won.

"My grandmother always says, '*Sólo las ollas saben los hervores de su caldo.*' "

"Something about soup?" I guessed. Whenever Sofia related some of her grandmother's wisdom, it usually took the form of food analogies.

"Only pots know the boilings of their broths," Sofia said. "Maybe Joe Travis is the kind who loves a woman with a real figure. The men I knew in San Antonio always went for the women with big *pompis.*" She patted her rear end for emphasis and went to her laptop.

"What are you doing?" I asked.

"Googling him."

"Right now?"

"It will only take a minute."

"You don't have a minute — you're supposed to be working!"

Ignoring me, Sofia kept pecking at the keyboard, two-finger style.

"I don't care what you find out about him," I said. "Because I happen to be busy with this thing we've got scheduled . . . What was it? . . . Oh, yes, a wedding."

"He's hot," Sofia said, staring at her monitor. "And so is his brother."

She had clicked on a *Houston Chronicle* article headed with a photo of three men, all dressed in beautifully tailored suits. One of them was Joe, much younger and lankier than he'd been today. He must have packed on at least thirty pounds of muscle since the photo had been taken. A caption beneath the picture identified the other two as Joe's brother Jack and his father, Churchill. Both sons were a head taller than their sire, but they bore his stamp — the dark hair and intense eyes, the pronounced jaw-lines.

I frowned as I read the accompanying article.

HOUSTON, Texas (AP) In the aftermath of an explosion on their private boat, two sons of Houston businessman Churchill Travis tread water among fiery debris for approximately four hours as they waited for rescue. After a massive search effort by the Coast Guard, the brothers, Jack and Joseph, were located in Gulf waters off Galveston. Joseph Travis was airlifted directly to the level one trauma unit at Garner Hospital for immediate surgery. According to a hospital spokesman, his condition has been listed as critical but stable. Although details of the surgery have not been released, a source close to the family confirmed that Travis was suffering from internal bleeding as well as —

"Wait," I protested as Sofia clicked on another link. "I was still reading."

"I thought you weren't interested," she

said impishly. "Here, look at this." She found a Web page labeled "Houston's Top Ten Eligible Bachelors." The article featured a candid shot of Joe playing football on the beach with friends, his body sleek and hard-looking, muscular without being muscle-bound. The expanse of dark hair on his chest narrowed to a dark line that led to the waistband of his board shorts. It was a picture of unself-conscious masculinity, off-the-charts hot.

"Six foot one," Sofia said, reading his stats. "Twenty-nine years old. Graduate of UT. A Leo. Photographer."

"Cliché," I said dismissively.

"Being a photographer is a cliché?"

"Not for an ordinary guy. But for a trust fund baby, it's a total vanity job."

"Who cares? Let's see if he has a website."

"Sofia, it's time to stop fangirling over this guy and get some work done."

A new voice entered the conversation as my assistant, Steven Cavanaugh, walked into the office. He was a good-looking man in his mid-twenties, blue-eyed and blond and lean. "Fangirling over who?" he asked.

Sofia replied before I was able. "Joe Travis," she said. "One of *the* Travises. Avery just met him."

Steven glanced at me with acute interest.

"They did a story on him in CultureMap last year. He won a Key Art award for that movie poster."

"What movie poster?"

"The one for the documentary about soldiers and military dogs." Steven looked sardonic as he saw our mystified expressions. "I forgot the two of you only watch telenovelas. Joe Travis went to Afghanistan with the film crew as the stills photographer. They used one of his shots for the poster." He smiled at my expression. "You should read the paper more often, Avery. It comes in handy on occasion."

"That's what I have you for," I said.

Nothing escaped the intricate filing cabinet of Steven's mind. I envied his near total recall of details such as where someone's son had gone to college, or the name of their dog, or if they'd just had a birthday.

Among his many talents, Steven was an interior designer, a graphic design specialist, and a trained EMT. We had hired him immediately after starting Crosslin Event Design, and he had become so necessary to the business that I couldn't imagine doing without him.

"He asked Avery out," Sofia told Steven.

Giving me a dark glance, Steven asked,

"What did you say?" At my silence, he turned to Sofia. "Don't tell me she shut him down."

"She shut him down," Sofia said.

"Of course." Steven's tone was arid. "Avery would never waste her time with a rich, successful guy whose name would open any door in Houston."

"Drop it," I said curtly. "We've got work to do."

"First I want to talk to you." Steven glanced at Sofia. "Do me a favor and make sure they've started setting the reception tables."

"Don't order me around."

"I wasn't ordering, I was asking."

"It didn't sound like asking."

"Please," Steven said acidly. "Pretty please, Sofia, go to the reception tent and see if they've started setting the tables."

Sofia left the room with a scowl.

I shook my head in exasperation. Sofia and Steven were cantankerous with each other, quick to take offense, slow to forgive, in a way that neither of them was with anyone else.

It hadn't started off that way. When Steven had first been hired, he and Sofia had become fast friends. He was sophisticated and meticulously groomed and had such an acid wit that Sofia and I had automatically assumed he was gay. It had been three months before we had realized that he wasn't.

"No, I'm straight," he had said in a matter-of-fact tone.

"But . . . you went clothes shopping with me," Sofia had protested.

"Because you asked me to."

"I let you into the dressing room," Sofia had continued, increasingly irate. "I tried on a dress in front of you. And you never said a word!"

"I said thank you."

"You should have told me you weren't gay!"

"I'm not gay."

"It's too late now," Sofia had snapped.

Ever since then, my sunny-natured sister had found it difficult to muster anything more than the barest degree of politeness toward Steven. And he responded in kind, his barbed comments never failing to hit the target. Only my frequent interventions kept their conflict from escalating to an all-out war.

After Sofia left, Steven closed the office door for privacy. He leaned back against it and folded his arms as he contemplated me with an unreadable expression. "Really?" he eventually asked. "You're really that insecure?"

"I'm not allowed to say no when a man asks me out?"

"When was the last time you said yes? When have you gone out for coffee, or drinks, or even had a non-work-related conversation with a guy?"

"That's none of your business."

"As your employee . . . you're right, it isn't. But at the moment I'm talking to you as a friend. You're a healthy, attractive twenty-seven-year-old woman, and as far as I know, you haven't been with anyone for over three years. For your own sake, whether it's this guy or someone else, you need to get back in the game."

"He's not my type."

"He's rich, single, and a Travis," came Steven's sardonic reply. "He's everyone's type."

By the end of the day I felt as if I'd walked the equivalent of a thousand miles, vectoring between the reception tent, the ceremony pavilion, and the main lodge. Although it seemed that everything was coming together, I knew better than to succumb to a false sense of security. Last-minute problems never failed to plague even the most meticulously planned ceremonies.

The members of the event production team worked in concert to handle any issues that cropped up. Tank Mirecki, a burly handyman, was proficient with carpentry, electronics, and mechanical repair. Ree-Ann Davis, a sassy blond assistant with a background in hotel management, had been assigned as the bride and bridesmaid handler. A brunette intern, Val Yudina, who was taking a gap year before starting at Rice, was managing the groom's family.

I used a radio earpiece and clip-on mike to stay in constant communication with Sofia and Steven. At first Sofia and I had felt silly using standard voice procedures for the hands-free radios, but Steven had insisted, saying there was no way he could tolerate both my voice and Sofia's in his ears without some rules. We had soon realized he was right; otherwise we would have constantly talked over each other.

An hour before the guests were scheduled to be seated, I went to the reception tent. The interior had been floored with eight thousand feet of rare purpleheart hardwood. It looked like a fairy tale. A dozen twenty-foot-high maple trees, each weighing half a ton, had been brought inside the tent to create a lavish forest, with a scattering of LED fireflies winking among the leaves. Strands of unpolished rock crystal hung in loops from a row of bronze chandeliers. Luxuriant live moss crossed the long tables in organically shaped runners. Each place setting had been accented with a wedding favor of Scottish honey sealed in a tiny crystal jar.

Outside, a row of ten-ton Portapac units pumped nonstop, chilling the air inside to a blissful sixty-eight degrees. I breathed deeply, relishing the coolness as I looked at my final countdown list. "Sofia," I said into my mike, "has the bagpiper arrived? Over."

"Affirmative," my sister said. "I just took him to the main lodge. There's a crafts room between the kitchen and the housekeeper's room where he can tune up. Over."

"Roger. Steven, this is Avery. I need to change my clothes. Can you handle things while I take five? Over."

"Avery, that's a negative, we've got an issue with the dove release. Over."

I frowned. "Copy that, what's going on? Over."

"There's a hawk in the oak grove next to the wedding pavilion. The dove handler says he can't release his birds with a predator in the vicinity. Over."

"Tell him we'll pay extra if one of them

gets eaten. Over."

Sofia broke in. "Avery, we can't have a dove snatched from the sky and killed in front of the guests. Over."

"We're at a South Texas ranch," I said. "We'll be lucky if half the guests don't start shooting the doves. Over."

"It's against state and federal law to capture, harm, or kill a hawk," Steven said. "How do you propose we deal with it? Over."

"Is it illegal to scare the damn thing off? Over."

"I don't think so. Over."

"Then have Tank figure it out. Over."

"Avery, stand by," Sofia interrupted urgently. After a pause, she said, "I'm with Val. She says the groom has cold feet. Over."

"Is this a joke?" I asked, stunned. "Over." All through the engagement and wedding planning, the groom, Charlie Amspacher, had been rock-solid. A nice guy. In the past, some couples had given me cause to wonder if they'd make it to the altar, but Charlie and Sloane seemed to be genuinely in love.

"No joke," Sofia said. "Charlie just told Val he wants to call it off. Over."

THREE

Over. The word seemed to echo in my head.

A million dollars, wasted.

All of our careers were on the line.

And Sloane Kendrick would be devastated.

I was filled with what felt like the equivalent of a hundred shots of adrenaline. *"No one is calling this wedding off,"* I said in a murderous tone. "I will handle this. Tell Val not to let Charlie talk to anyone until I get there. *Quarantine* him, understand? Over."

"Copy. Over."

"Out."

I stalked across the grounds to the guesthouse where the groom's family was getting ready for the ceremony. I fought to keep from breaking into a run. As soon as I entered the house, I blotted my sweating face with a handful of tissues. The sounds of laughter, conversation, and clinking

40

glasses floated from the living room of the main floor.

Val was at my side instantly. She was dressed in a pale silver-gray skirt suit, her microbraids pulled back in a controlled low bun. High-pressure situations never seemed to fluster her; in fact, she usually became even calmer in the face of emergency. As I looked into her eyes, however, I saw the signs of panic. The ice in the drink she held was rattling slightly. Whatever was happening with the groom, it was serious.

"Avery," she whispered, "thank God you're here. Charlie's trying to call it off."

"Any idea why?"

"I'm sure the best man has something to do with it."

"Wyatt Vandale?"

"Uh-huh. He's been making comments all afternoon, like how marriage is nothing but a trap, and Sloane's going to turn into a fat baby machine, and how Charlie better make sure this isn't a mistake. I can't get him out of the upstairs parlor. He's stuck to Charlie like glue."

I cursed myself for not having anticipated something like this. Charlie's best friend, Wyatt, was a spoiled brat whose family's money had afforded him the luxury of delaying adulthood for as long as possible.

41

He was crude and obnoxious and never wasted an opportunity to demean women. Sloane despised Wyatt, but she had told me that because he had been friends with Charlie since first grade, he would have to be tolerated. Whenever she complained about Wyatt's vileness, Charlie told her that Wyatt was good at heart but tended to express himself badly. The problem was, Wyatt expressed himself perfectly.

Val handed me the glass filled with ice and amber liquid. "This is for Charlie. I know about the no-booze rule, but trust me, it's time to break it."

I took the drink from her. "All right. I'll take it to him. Charlie and I are about to have a come-to-fiery-Jesus moment. Don't let anyone interrupt."

"What about Wyatt?"

"I'll get rid of him." I gave her my headset. "Keep in touch with Sofia and Steven."

"Should I tell them we're going to start late?"

"We are going to start precisely on time," I said grimly. "If we don't, we lose the best light for the ceremony, and we also lose the dove release. Those birds have to fly back to Clear Lake, and they can't do it in the dark."

Val nodded and put on the headset, adjusting the microphone. I ascended the stairs, went to the parlor, and tapped at the partially open door. "Charlie," I asked in the calmest tone I could manage, "may I come in? It's Avery."

"Look who's here," Wyatt exclaimed as I entered the room. His expensive tux was disheveled and his black tie was missing. He was full of swagger, certain that he'd ruined Sloane Kendrick's big day. "What did I tell you, Charlie? Now she's gonna try and talk you out of it." He shot me a triumphant glance. "Too late. His mind's made up."

I glanced at the ashen-faced groom, who sat slumped on a love seat. He didn't look at all like himself.

"Wyatt," I said, "I need a moment alone with Charlie."

"He can stay," Charlie said in a subdued voice. "He's got my back."

Yes, I was tempted to say, *that knife he stuck in it sure makes a nice handle.* But instead I murmured, "Wyatt needs to get ready for the ceremony."

The best man smiled at me. "Didn't you hear? Wedding's been canceled."

"That's not your decision," I said.

"What do you care?" Wyatt asked. "You'll get paid anyway."

"I care about Charlie and Sloane. And I

43

care about the people who've worked hard to make this a special day for them."

"Well, I've known this guy here since first grade. And I'm not gonna let him be pushed around by you and your flunkies just because Sloane Kendrick decided it was time to put a noose around his neck."

I went to Charlie and handed him the drink. He took it gratefully.

I pulled out my cell phone. "Wyatt," I said in a matter-of-fact tone as I scrolled through my contacts list, "your opinions are not relevant. This wedding is not about you. I'd like you to leave, please."

Wyatt laughed. "Who's gonna make me?"

Having found Ray Kendrick's number on my contact list, I autodialed him. As a former rodeo rider, Sloane's father was a breed of man who, despite cracked ribs and bruised organs, willingly climbed atop an enraged two-thousand-pound animal for a ride that was the equivalent of being whacked repeatedly between the legs with a baseball bat.

Ray answered. "Kendrick."

"It's Avery," I said. "I'm next door with Charlie. We're having an issue with his friend Wyatt."

Ray, who had been visibly annoyed with Wyatt's behavior at the rehearsal dinner, asked, "That little sumbitch trying to stir up trouble?"

"He is," I said. "And I thought you'd be the one to explain to him how to behave on Sloane's big day."

"You got that right, honey," Ray said with untrammeled enthusiasm. As I had guessed, he was more than happy to have something to do rather than stand idly in his tuxedo and make small talk. "I'll be right over to give him a talkin'-to."

"Thank you, Ray."

As I ended the call and Charlie heard the name, his eyes bulged. "Shit. Did you just call Sloane's father?"

I turned a cool stare in Wyatt's direction. "I'd get lost, if I were you," I told him. "Or in a couple of minutes there won't be enough of you left to wad a shotgun."

"Bitch." Glaring at me, Wyatt stormed from the room.

I locked the door behind him and turned to Charlie, who had gulped down his drink.

He couldn't bring himself to look at me. "Wyatt's just trying to look out for me," he mumbled.

"By sabotaging your wedding?" I pulled up a nearby ottoman and sat to face Charlie, steeling myself not to look at my watch or think about how I needed to change my clothes. "Charlie, I've seen you with Sloane from the beginning of the engagement until right now. I believe you love her. But the fact is, nothing Wyatt said would have made a bit of difference unless something was going on. So tell me what the problem is."

Charlie's gaze met mine, and he gestured helplessly as he replied, "When you think about how many couples divorce, it's crazy that anyone wants to try it in the first place. A fifty-fifty chance. What guy in his right mind would go for those odds?"

"Those are the general odds," I said. "Those aren't your odds." Seeing his bewilderment, I said, "People get married for all kinds of wrong reasons: infatuation, fear of being alone, unplanned pregnancy. Does any of that apply to you or Sloane?"

"No."

"Then when you cut those people out of the equation, your statistics are a lot better than fifty-fifty."

Charlie rubbed his forehead with an unsteady hand. "I have to tell Sloane that I need more time to be sure about all of this."

"More time?" I echoed dazedly. "The wedding ceremony is going to start in forty-five minutes."

"I'm not canceling. I'm just postponing it."

I stared at him incredulously. "Postponement isn't an option, Charlie. Sloane has planned and dreamed about this wedding for months, and her family's spent a fortune. If you call it off at the last minute, you're not going to get another chance."

"We're talking about the rest of my life," he said in rising agitation. "I don't want to make a mistake."

"God help me," I burst out. "Do you think Sloane has no room for doubt? This wedding is an act of trust on her part too. It's a risk for her too! But she's willing to take a chance because she loves you. She's going to show up at that altar. And you're *seriously* telling me that you're going to humiliate her in front of everyone you both know and make her a laughingstock? Do you understand what that's going to do to her?"

"You don't know what this is like. You've never been married." As Charlie saw my face, he paused and said uncertainly, "Have you?"

My fury faded abruptly. In the process of planning and coordinating a wedding, especially one on this scale, it was easy to forget how terrifying the process was for the two people with the most at stake.

Taking off my glasses, I shook my head. "No, I've never been married," I said, cleaning the glasses with a tissue from my bag. "I was jilted on my wedding day. Which probably makes me the worst possible person to talk to you right now."

"Hell," I heard him mutter. "I'm sorry, Avery."

I replaced the glasses and balled the tissue in my fist.

Charlie was facing a life-altering decision, and he had the look of a five-month hog on butchering day. I had to make him aware of the consequences of what he was doing. For his sake, and especially for Sloane's.

I cast a longing glance at the empty glass in Charlie's hands, wishing I could have a drink, too. Hunkering down on the ottoman, I said, "Calling off this wedding isn't just canceling a social event, Charlie. It's going to change everything. And it's going to hurt Sloane in ways you haven't considered."

He stared at me alertly, his brow furrowed. "Sure, she'll be disappointed," he began. "But —"

"Disappointment is the least of what she's going to feel," I interrupted. "And even if she still loves you after this, she won't trust you. Why should she, when you've broken your promises?"

"I haven't made any promises yet," he said.

"You asked her to marry you," I said. "That means you promised to *be there* when she walks down the aisle."

As a heavy silence descended, I realized that I was going to have to tell Charlie Amspacher about the worst day of my life. The memory was a wound that had never fully healed, and I wasn't exactly eager to rip it open for the sake of a young man I didn't really know. However, I couldn't think of any other way to make the situation clear to him.

"My wedding was supposed to happen about three and a half years ago," I said. "I was living in New York at the time, working in bridal fashion. My fiancé, Brian, did equity research on Wall Street. We'd gone out for two years, and then we lived together for another two, and at some point we started talking about getting married. I planned a small, beautiful wedding. I even flew my deadbeat dad up to New York, so he could walk me down the aisle. Everything was going to be perfect. But on the morning of the wedding, Brian left the apartment before I woke up, and called to tell me that he couldn't go through with it. He'd made a mistake. He said he thought he'd loved me, but he didn't. He wasn't sure he ever had."

"Damn," Charlie said quietly.

"People are wrong when they say that time will mend a broken heart. It doesn't always. My heart stayed broken. I've had to learn to live with it that way. I'll never be able to trust anyone who says he loves me." I paused before forcing myself to say with stark honesty, "I'm so afraid of being dumped again that I'm always the first to leave. I've broken off potential relationships because I'd rather be lonely than hurt. I don't like it, but that's who I am now."

Charlie stared at me with concern and kindness. He looked like himself again, no longer spooked. "I'm surprised you stayed in the wedding business after being jilted."

"I thought about quitting," I admitted. "But somewhere inside, I still believe in the fairy tale. Not for myself, but for other people."

"For me and Sloane?" he asked, unsmiling.

"Yes. Why not?"

Charlie turned the empty glass around in his hands. "My parents divorced when I was eight," he said. "But they never stopped trying to use my brother and me against each other. Lying, backstabbing, arguing, ruining every birthday and holiday. That's why my mom and stepdad weren't on the guest list: I knew if they were here, they'd cause all kinds of problems. How am I supposed to have a good marriage when I've never seen it done right?" His gaze lifted to mine. "I'm not asking for a fairy tale. I just need to be sure that if I get married, it won't turn into a nightmare someday."

"I can't promise you'll never get divorced," I said. "Marriage doesn't come with guarantees. It's only going to work for as long as you and Sloane both want it to. For as long as you're both willing to keep your promises." I took a deep breath. "Let me see if I've got this straight, Charlie . . . You haven't gotten cold feet because you don't love Sloane . . . you have cold feet because you *do* love her. You want to call off the wedding because you don't want the marriage to fail. Is that right?"

Charlie's face changed. "Yeah," he said in a wondering tone. "That . . . kind of makes me sound like an idiot, doesn't it?"

"It makes you sound a little mixed up," I said gently. "Let me ask you something . . . has Sloane given you any reason to doubt her? Is there something about the relationship that's not working for you?"

"Hell, no. She's terrific. Sweet, smart . . .

I'm the luckiest guy on earth."

I was quiet, letting him work it out for himself.

"The luckiest guy on earth," he repeated slowly. "Holy shit — I'm about to screw up the best thing that ever happened to me. To hell with being scared. To hell with my parents' sorry-ass marriage. I'm going to do this."

"Then . . . the wedding's on?" I asked cautiously.

"It's on."

"You're sure?"

"I'm positive." Charlie met my gaze directly. "Thanks for telling me about what you went through. I know it wasn't easy for you to talk about."

"If it helped, I'm glad." As we both stood, I discovered that my legs were shaky.

Charlie looked down at me with a slight grimace. "We don't have to mention this to anyone . . . do we?"

"I'm like a lawyer or doctor," I assured him. "Our conversations are confidential."

He nodded and heaved a sigh of relief.

"I'm going to go now," I told him. "In the meantime, I think you should keep your distance from Wyatt and his nonsense. I know he's your friend, but frankly, he's the worst best man I've ever seen."

Charlie grinned crookedly. "I won't argue with that."

As he walked me to the door, I reflected that it took courage for him to make the commitment he was most afraid of. A kind of courage I would never have. No man would ever again have the power to let me down the way Brian had . . . the way Charlie had nearly let Sloane down just now. Feeling relieved and wrung-out, I picked up my bag.

"See you soon," Charlie called after me as I left the room and went downstairs.

I supposed it was somewhat hypocritical, having urged someone to take a chance on getting married when I had no intention of ever doing the same. But my instincts told me that Charlie and Sloane would be happy together, or at least they had as good a chance as anyone.

Val was waiting downstairs by the front door. "Well?" she asked anxiously.

"Full steam ahead," I said.

"Thank God." She handed me the radio headset. "I figured you had everything under control when I saw Wyatt trying to hightail it out of here. Ray Kendrick caught him at the front doorstep. Literally gripped him by the back of the neck like a dog with a rat."

"And?"

"Mr. Kendrick dragged him off somewhere, and no one's seen hide nor hair of either of them since."

"What's happening with the dove release?"

"Tank asked Steven to help him find some ABS pipe and a barbecue igniter, and he told me to rustle up a can of hair spray." She paused. "And he sent Ree-Ann to fetch some tennis balls."

"Tennis balls? What is he —"

I was interrupted by an earsplitting whistle followed by a violent blast. We both jumped and stared at each other with wide eyes. Another blast caused Val to cover her ears with her hands. *Boom . . . boom . . .* and in the distance I heard a masculine chorus of hoots and hollers.

"Steven," I said urgently into the headset, "what's happening? Over."

"Tank says the hawk's flown off. Over."

"What the hell was that noise? Over."

There was a distinct note of enjoyment in Steven's voice. "Tank rigged up a grenade launcher and made some exploding tennis balls. He emptied out some black powder from a handful of bullet cartridges, and . . . I'll tell you the rest later. We're about to start seating. Over."

"Seating?" I echoed, looking down at my

dusty, sweat-stained outfit. "Now?"

Val practically shoved me outside. "You've got to change. Go straight to the main house. Don't stop to talk to anyone!"

I raced to the lodge and entered through a kitchen filled with busy caterers. As I proceeded to the nearby crafts room, I heard a strange musical bellow, fading into something like a moan. I saw Sofia standing at a large wooden table beside an elderly man dressed in a kilt. Both of them were looking at a tartan-covered bag bristling with black pipes.

Sofia, wearing a pink fit-and-flare dress, gave me an appalled glance. "You haven't changed yet?"

"What's going on?" I asked.

"The bagpipes are broken," she said. "Don't worry. I can get a couple of musicians from the reception orchestra to play for the ceremony —"

"What do you mean they're broken?"

"Bag's leaking," came the bagpiper's glum reply. "I'll refund your deposit like we agreed in the contract."

I shook my head wildly. Sloane's mother, Judy, had set her heart on a bagpipe processional. She would be deeply disappointed with a substitution. "I don't want a refund, I want bagpipes. Where are your backups?"

"I don't have backups. Not at two thousand dollars a set."

I pointed an unsteady finger at the plaid heap on the table. "Then fix that."

"There's not enough time, and no supplies. The seam of the inner bag's come loose. It has to be sealed with heat-sensitive tape, and cured with infrared light to — *Lady, what are you doin'?*"

I had gone to the table, seized the bag, and pulled out the Gore-Tex lining with a determined tug. The pipes moaned like an eviscerated beast. Digging into my handbag, I found a role of silver duct tape, pulled it out, and tossed it to Sofia. She caught it in midair. "Patch it," I said tersely. Ignoring the bagpiper's howls of protest, I raced off to the housekeeper's supply room, where I had hung a black top and midcalf skirt on a closet door. The top had slipped from the hanger to the dirty floor. Picking up the garment, I saw to my horror that a couple of ugly grease splotches had soaked into the front.

Swearing, I searched through my bag for antibacterial wipes and a fabric-cleaning pen. I tried to remove the stains, but the more I worked on them, the worse the top looked.

"Do you need help?" I heard Sofia ask in

a couple of minutes.

"Come in," I said, my voice strung with frustration.

Sofia entered the supply room and took in the scene with a disbelieving gaze. "This is bad," she said.

"The skirt is fine," I said. "I'll wear it with the top I've got on now."

"You can't," Sofia said flatly. "You've been out in the heat for hours. That top is filthy, and there are sweat stains halfway down your sides."

"What do you suggest I do?" I snapped.

"Take the top I was wearing earlier. I've been in the air-conditioning for most of the day, and it still looks fine."

"That top won't fit me," I protested.

"Yes, it will. We're almost the same size, and it's a wrap top. *Hurry,* Avery."

Clumsy with haste, I took off my dusty pants and top and scoured myself with a handful of antibacterial towelettes. With Sofia's help, I changed into the black skirt and the borrowed top, a stretchy ivory blouse with three-quarter-length sleeves. Since my proportions were more generous than Sofia's, the V neckline that had been relatively modest on her was a definite plunge on me.

"I'm showing cleavage," I said indignantly,

tugging the sides of the top closer together.

"Yes. And you look twenty pounds thinner." Busily, she yanked the pins from my hair.

"Hey, stop that —"

"Your updo was a mess. There's no time for a new one. Just leave it loose."

"I look like an alpaca in a lightning storm." I tried to flatten the wild mass of curls with my hands. "And this top is too tight, I'm all bound up —"

"You're just not used to wearing something that fits. You look fine."

I gave her a tortured glance and picked up my headset. "Have you checked in with Steven?"

"Yes. Everything's under control. The ushers are seating the guests, and the dove handler is ready with the birds. And Sloane and the bridesmaids are all set. Go. I'll bring the bagpiper as soon as you give me the okay."

By some miracle, the ceremony started on time. And the wedding unfolded more perfectly than Sofia or I could have imagined. Lavish arrangements of thistle, roses, and field flowers had been wrapped around every column of the pavilion. The bagpipe processional established a solemn but electrifying tone for the bridal party's entrance.

As Sloane proceeded along the flower-strewn aisle runner, she looked like a princess in her white lace gown. Charlie looked entirely happy as he stared at his bride. No one could have doubted that he was a man in love.

I doubted anyone even noticed the sullen scowl on the best man's face.

After the vows were exchanged, a flock of white pigeons burst into flight and soared through the coral-glazed sky in a moment so picturesque that the entire congregation let out a collective breath.

"Hallelujah," I heard Sofia whisper in the earpiece, and I grinned.

Much later, while the guests danced to orchestra music in the reception tent, I stood in a quiet corner and spoke to Steven on the headset. "I see a potential carry-off," I said quietly. "Over." On occasion, we had to perform a discreet assisted removal for guests who'd had too much to drink. The best way to avoid problems was to catch them early.

"I see him," Steven replied. "I'll have Ree-Ann handle it. Over."

Aware of a woman approaching, I turned and smiled automatically. She was whippet-thin and elegant in a beaded panel-construction dress. Her blond bob was perfectly highlighted with a bar code of platinum streaks.

"Can I help you?" I asked with a smile.

"You're the one who planned this wedding?"

"Yes, along with my sister. I'm Avery Crosslin."

She sipped from a glass of champagne, her hand weighted with an emerald the size of an ashtray. Noticing that my gaze had flickered to the beveled square-cut gem, she said, "My husband gave it to me for my forty-fifth birthday. A carat for each year."

"It's remarkable."

"They say emeralds bestow the power to predict the future."

"Does yours?" I asked.

"Let's say the future generally happens the way I want it to." She took another dainty sip. "This turned out nice," she murmured, surveying the scene. "Fancy, but not too formal. Imaginative. Most weddings I've been to this year have all looked the same." She paused. "People are already saying this was the best wedding they've been to in years. But it's only the second best."

"What's the best wedding?" I asked.

"The one you're going to do for my daughter, Bethany. The wedding of the decade. The governor and an ex-president will be attending." Her lips curved in a slender, catlike smile. "I'm Hollis Warner. And your career's just been made."

FOUR

As Hollis Warner sauntered away, Steven's voice came through my earpiece.

"Her husband is David Warner. He inherited a restaurant business and parlayed it into casino resorts. Their fortune is obscene even by Houston standards. Over."

"Do they —"

"Later. You've got company. Over."

Blinking, I turned to see Joe Travis approaching. The sight of him kicked my heart into a drumfire rhythm. He was dazzling in a classic tux, wearing it with unself-conscious ease. The white edge of his collar formed a crisp contrast to an amber tan that seemed to go several layers deep, as if he'd been steeped in sun.

He smiled at me. "I like your hair down like that."

Self-consciously, I reached up to try to flatten it. "It's too curly."

"For God's sake," I heard Steven's acid

voice in the earpiece. "When a man gives you a compliment, don't argue with him. Over."

"Can you take a break for a few minutes?" Joe asked.

"I probably shouldn't —," I began, and I heard both Steven's and Sofia's voices at the same time.

"Yes, you should!"

"Tell him yes!"

I yanked off the earpiece and mike. "I don't usually take a break during the reception," I told Joe. "I need to keep an eye on things in case anyone has a problem."

"I have a problem," he said promptly. "I need a dance partner."

"There are a half-dozen bridesmaids here who would love to dance with you," I said. "Individually or collectively."

"None of them has red hair."

"Is that a requirement?"

"Let's call it a strong preference." Joe reached for my hand. "Come on. They can do without you for a few minutes."

I flushed and hesitated. "My bag . . ." I glanced at the bulk of it wedged beneath the chair. "I can't just —"

"I'll watch over it," came Sofia's cheerful voice. She had appeared out of nowhere. "Go have fun."

"Joe Travis," I said, "this is my sister Sofia. She's single. Maybe you should —"

"Take her away," Sofia told him, and they exchanged a grin.

Ignoring the dirty look I gave her, Sofia murmured something into her radio mike.

Joe kept possession of my hand, pulling me past tables and potted trees until we'd reached a semisecluded area at the other side of the reception tent. He signaled a waiter who was holding a tray of iced champagne.

"I'm supposed to be running things," I said. "I have to stay vigilant. Anything could happen. Someone could have a heart attack. The tent could catch on fire."

After taking two glasses of champagne from the waiter, Joe handed one to me and retained the other. "Even General Patton took a break sometimes," he said. "Relax, Avery."

"I'll try." I held the crystal flute by the stem, its contents shimmering with tiny bubbles.

"To your beautiful brown eyes," he said, lifting his glass

I flushed. "Thank you." We clinked glasses and drank. The champagne was dry and delicious, the chilled fizz like starlight on my tongue.

My view of the dance floor was obstructed by orchestra instruments, speakers, and ornamental trees. However, I thought I caught sight of Hollis Warner's distinctive white-blond bob in the milling crowd.

"Do you happen to know Hollis Warner?" I asked.

Joe nodded. "She's a friend of the family. And last year I took pictures of her house for a magazine feature. Why?"

"I just met her. She was interested in discussing ideas for her daughter's wedding."

He gave me an alert glance. "Who's Bethany engaged to?"

"I have no idea."

"Bethany's been going out with my cousin Ryan. But last time I saw him, he was planning to break up with her."

"Maybe his feelings went deeper than he thought."

"From what Ryan said, that doesn't seem likely."

"If I wanted to land Hollis as a client, what advice would you give me?"

"Wear garlic." He smiled at my expression. "But if you handle her right, she'd be a good client. What Hollis would spend on a wedding could probably buy Ecuador." He looked at my champagne glass. "Would you like another?"

"No, thanks."

He drained his own glass, took mine, and went to set them on a nearby busing tray.

"Why don't you do weddings?" I asked when he returned.

"It's the hardest job in photography, except for maybe working in a war zone." He smiled wryly. "When I was starting out, I managed to land a position as a staff photographer for a West Texas quarterly. *Modern Cattleman.* It's not easy trying to get an ornery bull to pose for a picture. But I'd still rather shoot livestock than weddings."

I laughed. "When did you first take up photography?"

"I was ten. My mom sneaked me off to a class every Saturday, and told my dad I was working out to get ready for Pop Warner football."

"He didn't approve of photography?"

Joe shook his head. "He had definite ideas about how his sons should spend their time. Football, 4-H, working outside, all that was fine. But art, music . . . that was taking it too far. And he thought of photography as a hobby, but nothing a man should try to make a career of."

"But you proved him wrong," I said.

His smile turned rueful. "It took a while. There were a couple of years we weren't exactly on speaking terms." He paused. "Later it worked out that I had to stay with Dad for a couple of months. That was when we finally made our peace with each other."

"When you stayed with him, was it . . ." I hesitated.

His head bent over mine. "Go on."

"Was it because of the boat accident?" Seeing his quizzical smile, I said uncomfortably, "My sister looked you up on the Internet."

"Yeah, it was after that. When I got out of the hospital, I had to stay with someone while I healed up. Dad was living by himself in River Oaks, so it made the most sense for me to go there."

"Is it hard for you to talk about the accident?"

"Not at all."

"Can I ask how it happened?"

"I was fishing with my brother Jack in the Gulf. We were heading back to the marina at Galveston, stopped near a seaweed mat, and managed to hook a dorado. While my brother was reeling it in, I started the engine so we could follow the fish. Next thing I knew, I was in the water and there was fire and debris everywhere."

"My God. What caused the explosion?"

"We're pretty sure the bilge blower malfunctioned, and fumes built up near the engine."

"That's awful," I said. "I'm so sorry."

"Yeah. That dorado was a five footer at least." He paused, his gaze flickering to my mouth as I smiled.

"What kind of injuries —" I broke off. "Never mind, it's not my business."

"Blast lung, it's called. When the shock waves from an explosion bruise the chest and lungs. For a while I couldn't work up enough air to fill a party balloon."

"You look pretty healthy now," I said.

"One hundred percent." A wicked glint entered his eyes as he observed my reaction. "Now that you're all sympathetic . . . come dance with me."

I shook my head. "I'm not *that* sympathetic." With an apologetic smile, I explained, "I never dance at an event I've planned. It's sort of like a waitress seating herself at a table she's supposed to be serving."

"I had two operations for internal bleeding while I was in the hospital," Joe informed me gravely. "For almost a week, I couldn't eat or talk because of the ventilator tube." He gave me a hopeful glance. "Now

68

do you feel sorry enough to dance with me?"

I shook my head again.

"Also," Joe said, "the accident happened on my birthday."

"It did not."

"It did."

I lifted my gaze heavenward. "That's so sad. That's . . ." I paused, fighting my better instincts. "Okay," I found myself saying. "One dance."

"I knew the birthday would do it," he said in satisfaction.

"A *quick* dance. In the corner, where as few people as possible can see."

Joe took my hand in a warm grip. He led me past sparkling groves of potted trees and palms, back to a shadowy corner behind the orchestra. A sly, jazzy version of "They Can't Take That Away from Me" floated through the air. The female singer's voice had an appealing rough-sweet edge, like broken candy.

Joe turned me to face him and took me in a practiced hold, one hand at my waist. So this would be a real dance, not a side-to-side sway. Tentatively, I placed my left hand on his shoulder. He pulled me into a smooth pattern, his movements so assured that there could be no doubt about who was leading. As he lifted my hand to guide me into a twirl, I followed so easily that we didn't miss a step. I heard his low laugh, a sound of pleasure at discovering a well-matched partner.

"What else are you good at?" he asked near my ear. "Besides dancing and wedding planning."

"That's about it." After a moment, I volunteered, "I can tie balloon animals. And I can whistle with my fingers."

I felt the shape of his smile against my ear.

My glasses had slipped down my nose, and I briefly broke our hold to push them back up to the bridge. I made a mental note to have the earpieces adjusted as soon as I got back to Houston. "What about you?" I asked. "Do you have any hidden talents?"

"I can scissor dribble a basketball. And I know the entire NATO phonetic alphabet."

"You mean like Alfa, Bravo, Charlie?"

"Exactly."

"How did you learn it?"

"Scouting badge."

"Spell my name," I commanded, testing him.

"Alfa-Victor-Echo-Romeo-Yankee." He twirled me again.

It seemed the air had turned into champagne, every breath filled with free-floating giddiness.

My glasses slipped again, and I began to adjust them. "Avery," he said gently, "let me hold those for you. I'll keep them in my pocket until we're done."

"I won't be able to see where we're going."

"But I will." Carefully he drew the glasses from my face, folded them, and slipped them into the breast pocket of his tux. The room turned into a blur of glitter and shadow. I didn't understand myself, why I had surrendered control to him so easily. I stood there blind and exposed, my heart beating like a hummingbird's wings.

Joe's arms went around me. He took me in the same hold as before, except now we were closer, our steps intimately constrained. This time he no longer followed the orchestra rhythm, only settled into a slow, relaxed pace.

As I breathed in the scent of him, burnished with sun and salt, I was confounded by the yearning to press my mouth against his neck, taste him.

"You're nearsighted," I heard him say on a questioning note.

I nodded. "You're the only thing I can see."

He looked down at me, our noses nearly

touching. "Good." The word was scratchy-soft, like a cat's tongue.

My breath caught. I turned my face away deliberately. I had to break the spell, or I was going to do something I would regret.

"Get ready," I heard him say. "I'm going to dip you."

I clutched at him. "Don't, you'll drop me."

"I'm not going to drop you." He sounded amused.

I stiffened as I felt his hand slide to the center of my back. "I'm serious. Joe —"

"Trust me."

"I don't think —"

"Here we go." He lowered me backward, supporting me securely. My head tipped back, my vision filled with the twinkling firefly lights entwined in the tree branches. I gasped as he pulled me upright with astonishing ease.

"Oh! You're strong."

"It has nothing to do with strength. It's knowing how to do it." Joe caught me against him, closer than before. Now we were matched front to front. The moment was charged with something I'd never felt before, a soft voltaic heat. I was quiet, unable to make a sound if my life had depended on it. I closed my eyes. My senses were busy gathering him in, the hard strength of his body, the caress of his breath against my ear.

All too soon, the song ended with a bittersweet flourish. Joe's arms tightened. "Not yet," he murmured. "One more."

"I shouldn't."

"Yes, you should." He kept me against him.

Another song started, the notes flaring softly. "What a Wonderful World" was a wedding staple. I'd heard it about a thousand times, interpreted every way imaginable. But every now and then an old song could pierce your heart as if you were hearing it for the first time.

As we danced, I tried to gather every passing second for safekeeping, like pennies in a Mason jar. But soon I lost track, and there was only the two of us, wrapped in music and dream-colored darkness. Joe's hand covered mine, and he pulled my arm around his neck. When I didn't resist, he reached for my other wrist and pulled that one up, too.

I had no idea what song played next. We stood locked in a subtle sway with my arms linked around his neck. I let my fingers drift over the nape of his neck, where the thick hair was tapered in close layers. A feeling of unreality swept over me, and my imagination kept veering in the wrong directions. . . . I wondered what he would be like in intimacy, the ways he might move and breathe and tremble.

His head lowered until his jaw grazed my cheek, the touch of shaven bristle delicious.

"I have to work," I managed to say. "What . . . what time is it?"

I felt him lift his arm behind me, but apparently it was too dark to read his watch. "Must be close to midnight," he said.

"I have to set up the after-party."

"Where?"

"The swimming pool patio."

"I'll go with you."

"No, you'll distract me." Realizing my arms were still linked around his neck, I began to pull free.

"Probably." Joe caught one of my wrists and turned his mouth to the inside of my wrist. A shock of sweetness went through me as I felt his lips touch the thin, tender skin, grazing the frantic thrum of a pulse. From inside his pocket, he withdrew my glasses and gave them back to me.

I couldn't stop staring at him. There was a crescent mark on the left side of his jaw, a thin white line amid the shadow of shaven bristle. And another mark near the outward corner of his left eye, a subtle parenthetical scar. Somehow the tiny imperfections made him even sexier.

I wanted to touch the marks with my fingertips. I wanted to kiss them. But the desire was hemmed by the instinctive knowledge that this wasn't a man I could ever be casual about. When you fell for a man like this, it would be an all-consuming bonfire. And afterward, your heart would resemble the contents of an ashtray.

"I'll meet you when you finish setting up," Joe told me.

"It may take a long time. I don't want you to wait."

"I've got all night." His voice was soft. "And you're how I want to spend it."

Desperately, I tried not to feel so flattered and overwhelmed. And I hurried away with the sense that I was running through a minefield.

FIVE

"Well?" Sofia asked, removing her radio mike as I reached her.

How could she look so relaxed? How could everything seem normal when it was the opposite of normal?

"We danced," I said distractedly. "Where's my bag? What time is it?"

"Eleven twenty-three. Your bag is right here. Steven and Val have already started the setup for the after-party. Tank helped the live band with all their speakers and power cords. Ree-Ann and the caterers are working on the pie buffet and the wine and coffee service. And the waitstaff is about to begin the reception cleanup."

"Everything's on schedule, then."

"You don't have to sound so surprised." Sofia smiled. "Where is Joe? Did you have a good time dancing?"

"Yes." I picked up my bag, which seemed to weigh a thousand pounds.

"Why do you look nervous?"

"He wants to meet me later."

"Tonight? That's wonderful." At my silence, Sofia asked, "Do you like him?"

"He's . . . well, he's . . ." I paused, floundering. "I can't figure out the angle."

"What angle?"

"Why he's pretending to be interested in me."

"Why do you think he's pretending?"

I scowled. "Come on, Sofia. Do I look like the kind of woman that a man like Joe Travis would go for? Does that even make sense?"

"Ay, chinga." Sofia did a face palm. "A big, sexy man wants to spend time with you. This is not a problem, Avery. Stop worrying."

"People do stupid things at weddings —" I began.

"Yes. Go be one of them."

"My God. You give the worst advice."

"Then don't ask me for it."

"I didn't!"

Sofia regarded me with fond concern. A sisterly gaze. "*Mija.* You know how people always say 'You'll find someone when you stop looking'?"

"Yes."

"I think you've gotten too good at not

looking. You've decided not to look even if the right man happens to be standing right in front of you." Taking my shoulders, she turned me around and gave me a little push. "Go on. Don't worry if it's a mistake. Most mistakes turn out okay."

"The *worst* advice," I repeated darkly, and left her.

I knew that Sofia was right: I had developed some bad habits since my catastrophic engagement. Solitude, avoidance, suspicion. But those coping mechanisms had warded off a hell of a lot of pain and damage. It wouldn't be easy to get rid of them, even if I wanted to.

By the time I reached the swimming pool patio, a couple of the bridesmaids had already changed into bikinis and were laughing and splashing in the pool. Noticing that no towels had been set out, I went to Val, who was arranging lounge furniture. "Towels?" I asked.

"Tank is assembling the towel stand."

"That should have been done earlier."

"I know. Sorry." Val made a little grimace. "He said he'll have it out here in ten minutes. We didn't expect anyone to be in the pool this early."

"It's fine. For now, go get a half-dozen

towels and set them out on the lounge chairs."

She nodded and began to leave.

"Val," I said.

Pausing, she gave me an inquiring glance.

"It looks great out here," I said. "Terrific job."

A smile lit her face, and she went in search of the towels.

I went to the long table where the pie-and-coffee buffet had been artfully arranged, with a trio of white-jacketed servers lined up behind it. Three-level French wire stands held gold-crusted pies of every flavor imaginable . . . caramel apple, glazed peach, dense slabs of buttermilk custard, strawberries mounded over lofty cushions of cream cheese.

Nearby, Steven separated stacks of chairs and arranged them around cloth-draped tables in the adjoining courtyard. I approached him, raising my voice to be heard over the band. "What can I do?"

"Nothing." Steven smiled. "All under control."

"Any sign of scorpions?"

He shook his head. "We saturated the perimeter of the patio and courtyard with citrus oil." He gave me an intent glance. "How's it going with you?"

"Fine. Why?"

"Glad to see you took my advice. About getting back in the game."

I frowned. "I'm not back in the game. I danced with someone, that's all."

"It's progress," he said laconically, and went for another stack of chairs.

When the setup was complete and guests were lining up at the pie buffet, I caught sight of a man sitting at one of the tables near the pool. It was Joe, relaxed and casual, the black tie hanging on either side of his neck. Giving me an expectant glance, he lifted a plate invitingly.

I went to him. "What flavor is that?" I asked, looking at the perfect wedge of pie, topped with a thick layer of meringue.

"Lemon icebox," he said. "I have two forks. Want to share?"

"I suppose as long as we sit way back in the courtyard, off to the side —"

"Where no one can see," Joe finished for me, a sparkle of amusement in his eyes. "Are you trying to hide me, Avery? Because I'm starting to feel cheap."

I couldn't help laughing. "Of all the adjectives I might use for you, 'cheap' is not one of them."

He followed me, plate in hand, as I went into the courtyard and headed to a far-off table. "What adjectives would you use?" he asked from behind me.

"Are you fishing for compliments?"

"A little encouragement never hurts." He set down the plate and pulled out a chair to seat me.

"Since I'm not available," I said, "I have no intention of encouraging you. Although if I did . . . I'd say you were charming."

He handed me a fork, and we both dug into the slice of pie. The first bite was so good, I closed my eyes to focus on it. A foamy mantle of meringue collapsed on my tongue, followed by a rich filling infused with saliva-spiking tartness. "This pie," I said, "tastes like one lemon fell in love with another lemon."

"Or three lemons had a ménage." Joe grinned at my mock-reproving glance. "Usually it's never sour enough for my taste," he said, "but this is about right."

When there was one bite of pie left, Joe picked up my fork and fed me the last morsel. To my astonishment, I opened my mouth and let him. The gesture was at once casual and oddly intimate. I chewed and swallowed with difficulty, my cheeks turning hot.

"I need something to drink," I said, and at that very moment someone approached our table.

It was Sofia, carrying two wineglasses and a bottle of chilled white Bordeaux. Setting them on the table, she said brightly, "Steven said to tell you we've got everything covered, so you can take off now."

I frowned. "I'm the one who decides if I can take off, not Steven."

"You've had less sleep than any of us —"

"I'm not tired."

"— and there's nothing left except to manage the cleanup crew. We can do that without you. Have a drink and enjoy yourself." Sofia left before I could reply.

I shook my head as I watched her go. "I'm not as irrelevant as they seem to think." Relaxing back in my chair, I said, "However . . . they did well today. And they probably can manage the cleanup without me." I stared up at the sky, where the mottled white band of the Milky Way glowed against the plenitude of stars. "Look at that," I said. "You can't see that from a city."

Gesturing with his glass, Joe said, "See the dark lane running along the center?"

I shook my head.

He moved his chair closer and pointed with his free hand. "There, where it looks like someone scribbled through it with a Sharpie."

Following the line of his arm, I saw the ragged stripe. "Yes. What is that?"

"It's the Great Rift, a big cloud of molecular dust . . . a place where new stars are forming."

I stared in wonder. "Why haven't I seen it before?"

"You have to be in the right place at the right time."

We glanced at each other with a shared smile. The wash of starlight had turned the little crescent scar on his jaw a faint silver. I wanted to trace it with my fingertip. I wanted to touch his face and stroke the hard contours of his features.

I picked up my wineglass. "I'm going to turn in after I finish this," I said, drinking deeply. "I'm beat."

"Are you staying at the ranch, or at one of the hotels in town?"

"Here. There's a little cabin along the drive to the back pasture. The trapper's cabin, they call it." I made a face. "There's a stuffed coon on the mantel. Hideous. I had to put a pillowcase over it."

He smiled. "I'll walk you over."

I hesitated. "Okay."

The conversation turned quiet, halting, as I drank the rest of my wine. It seemed as if some secondary, unspoken dialogue were filling up the space between the words.

Eventually, we stood and left the bottle and two empty glasses on the table.

As we walked on the side of the paved drive, Joe said, "I'd like to see you again, Avery."

"That's . . . well, I'm flattered. Thank you. But I can't."

"Why not?"

"I've enjoyed your company. Let's leave it at that."

Joe was silent the rest of the way to the cabin. Our pace was leisurely, but my thoughts raced, my brain cataloging a jumble of ideas about how to keep him at a distance.

We stopped at the front door. While I fumbled in my bag for the key, Joe spoke quietly. "Avery . . . I don't mean to presume. But I know what it feels like to want someone who doesn't want me back." A long pause. "And I don't think that's the case here."

Shaken, I managed to say, "I'm sorry for whatever I've said or done to give you that impression."

"Then I'm wrong?" he asked gently.

"It's . . . no . . . but it's a matter of timing."

Joe didn't react, didn't appear to believe

that, and Jesus, why should he? Why would anyone? He was like something from a dream as he stood there in a wash of moonlight, sexy in his rumpled tux, his eyes midnight dark.

"Can we talk about it for a minute?" he asked.

Reluctantly, I nodded and opened the door.

It was a one-room cabin, designery rustic with a handwoven rug and leather furniture and modern light fixtures that looked like crystal antlers. I flipped on a switch that illuminated a sconce in the corner and set down my bag. Turning to face Joe, I saw him standing with his shoulder braced against the doorjamb. His lips parted as if he were about to say something, but he appeared to think better of it.

"What?" I asked in a hushed voice.

"I know there are rules for this. I know I'm supposed to play it cool." A rueful smile touched his lips. "But to hell with it. The fact is, I liked you the first moment I saw you. You are a beautiful, interesting woman, and I want to see you again." His tone softened. "You can say yes to that, can't you?" Seeing my uncertainty, he murmured, "Pick the time and place. I promise you won't regret it."

Pushing away from the door, Joe approached me without haste. My heart began to work in sharp jolts, and I went hot and cold with nerves. It had been too long since I had been alone with a man in a bedroom.

Studying me intently, Joe touched the side of my face, his hand curving beneath my jaw. I knew he could feel the way I was trembling.

"Should I leave?" he asked, and began to draw back.

"No." Before I could stop myself, I caught his wrist. A few minutes earlier, I'd been calculating how to push him away, and now the only thing I could think about was how to make him stay. My fingers curved around the thickness of bone and sinew, the strong rhythm of his pulse.

I wanted him. Every part of me wanted him. We were alone, and the rest of the world was far away, and I knew somehow that if I slept with him, it would be extraordinary.

To a woman who'd lived twenty-seven years of ordinary, one night with a man like this didn't seem too much to ask.

I pulled his hand to my waist, and I stood on my toes, deliberately molding my body against his, and he was warm and sturdy, his arms anchoring me firmly. He began to kiss me slow and deep, as if the world were about to end, as if it were the last minute of the last hour of the last day. The things he did with his mouth, his tongue . . . it was like a conversation, like sex, the way he found what I wanted and gave it to me. There was more pleasure in that kiss than in any act of physical intimacy I had ever known.

After drawing his mouth away, Joe cupped my head to his shoulder. We stayed like that for a hard-breathing minute. I was dismantled, everything inside me thrown into chaos. All I knew was that I had to be close to him, I had to feel his skin. I grasped the lapels of his tux jacket, pushing them back. He stripped off the garment and dropped it to the floor. Without hesitation, he gripped my head back and his mouth found mine again, ardent and intent, as if he were feeding on something delicious. Somewhere in the midst of all those kisses, he reached down to my bottom, cinching me closer against a ridge of hard, impatient flesh. The need sharpened until it seemed I would die of not having him. Nothing had ever felt like this. Nothing ever would again.

You had to run with a feeling like that, all the way to sunrise.

"Take me to bed," I whispered.

I heard a quick, rough-sawn breath, and I sensed the conflict of desire and indecision.

"It's okay," I said anxiously. "I know what I'm doing, I want you to stay —"

"You don't have to —" he began.

"Yes. I have to." I kissed him again, excitement pulsing through me. "You have to," I whispered against his lips.

Joe responded voraciously, caught up in the heat just as I was, his hold on me changing as he sought to make the fit between us even closer, tighter. After a while he began to undress me, and himself, clothes littering the floor in a trail to the bed. The light was switched off, the darkness relieved only by the starlight sifting through the mesh of the window blinds.

I pulled back the covers and lay on the mattress, shaking from head to toe. He lowered over me, the feel of hair-roughened limbs stimulating my skin into excruciating sensitivity. I felt the hot whisk of his breath against my throat.

"Tell me if you want to stop," I heard him say hoarsely. "No matter what, I'll stop if you decide —"

"I know."

"I want you to understand —"

"I understand." I pulled him down to me. Nothing was real in that quiet room.

Things were being done to me, and by me, in an ecstasy of sexual greed that I knew I would be shamed by later. His mouth was at my breast, his tongue articulating delicate circles until the tip budded, and he began to lap and tug until the pleasure went singing to the quick of my body. I gripped his shoulders, the tough muscle of his back, massaging blindly.

Skilled and sure, his fingers teased along the insides of my thighs, coaxing them to part. The pad of his thumb brushed a place so tender that I cried out, my hips lifting. His finger slid inside me, caressing deep into a frantic wet pulse. My body tightened to hold the sensation, drawing the pleasure inward.

His weight slid over me, his legs spreading mine, and I gasped out a few words . . . we had no protection, we needed to use something . . . He reassured me with a hoarse murmur, reaching over to the bedside table for his wallet, which I hadn't even been aware of him setting there. I heard the rip of a plastic packet. Momentarily distracted, I wondered when that had happened, how he had managed —

My thoughts imploded as I felt the pressure of him working slowly, circling intimately. He entered me in a low, thick slide, sensation blooming within sensation, hot and sweet and maddening. A cry stirred in my throat.

Joe nuzzled at my ear. "Shhhh . . ." He slid an arm beneath my hips, pulling them high. Every thrust was a full-bodied caress, the hair on his chest teasing my breasts. I'd never felt so much at once, raw sensation eliding the spaces between every heartbeat and breath until I was blind and silent. The release wrung pleasure from every muscle, tightening until I shuddered in long, liquescent spasms. Joe held me tightly, breathing in rough gasps as he reached the pinnacle. He kissed my neck and shoulders, his hands moving over me gently. His fingers traversed my stomach, down between my legs to the verge of our joined flesh, and I felt him caressing intimately, teasing around the small centered ache. Moaning in astonishment, I sank into an erotic darkness where there was no thought, no past, no future, only pleasure that made me twist in helpless ecstasy.

I awakened alone in the morning, aware of the slight aches left by another body's intrusion into mine, the faint whisker burns on skin that had been kissed and kissed, the tender pull of inner thighs.

I wasn't sure what to think about what I'd done.

Joe had said little when he'd left, other than the obligatory, "I'll call you." A promise that no one ever kept.

I reminded myself that I had the right to sleep with someone if I wanted to, even a stranger. No judgments were necessary. No one had to feel bad.

Still . . . I felt as if something had been taken from me, and I didn't know what it was or how to regain it. I felt as if I would never be the same again.

Letting out a shuddering sigh, I used the bedsheet to blot my eyes as tears threatened to well up.

I pressed hard against my eyes. "You're okay," I whispered aloud. "Everything's okay."

As I huddled back into the damp pillow, I remembered how, when I was in grade school, we had studied butterflies for a science project. Samples of a butterfly's wing under a microscope had revealed that it was covered with tiny scales like feathers or roof shingles.

If you touched a butterfly's wing, the teacher had said, it would knock off some of the scales and they would never grow back. Some butterflies had clear patches on their wings where you could see right through the membrane. But even with some lost scales, a butterfly would still be able to fly after you let it go.

It would get along just fine.

Six

During the long drive home, Sofia and I talked about the wedding and rehashed every detail. I did my best to keep the mood light, forcing myself to laugh from time to time. When Sofia asked casually if anything had happened with Joe Travis, I replied, "No, but I gave him my number. He might call sometime." I could tell by her quick, speculative glance that she didn't entirely believe me.

After Sofia plugged her phone into the car audio and started a jaunty Tejano song, I let myself think about the previous night and tried to figure out why I felt so guilty and worried. Probably because having a one-night stand was so unlike me . . . except that since I'd done it, it *was* like me.

The new me.

Feeling a stirring of panic, I pushed it back down.

I thought back to when I'd first met Brian,

trying to remember how long I'd waited until sleeping with him. Two months, at least. I had been cautious about intimacy, having no desire to careen from one man to the next the way my mother had. Sex would be on my terms, within the margins that I established. Brian had been fine with that, patient, willing to wait until I was ready.

We had been introduced by mutual friends at a cocktail party held in the outdoor sculpture garden at the Met. We had been instantly comfortable with each other, so naturally in tune that our friends had laughingly accused us of already knowing each other. We'd both been twenty-one at the time, full of ambition and energy, both of us having just moved from other places, me from Dallas, Brian from Boston.

It had been the happiest time of my life, that first year in New York, a city that had infused me with the perpetual feeling that something great, or at least interesting, was just around the corner. Having been accustomed to the lazy, sunstruck pace of Texas, where the heat forced everyone to ration their energy, I had been galvanized by Manhattan's cool autumn vitality. *You belong here,* the city seemed to say, with the honking of canary-colored taxicabs and the screeching and grinding of construction equipment, the sounds of street musicians and bars and rattling subways . . . all of it meant that I was in a place where things were happening.

It had been easy to find friends, a group of women who filled their spare time with volunteer work, clubs, lessons in things like foreign languages, dancing, tennis. The Manhattanite's passion for self-improvement had been contagious — soon I'd found myself signing up for clubs and lessons, trying to make every minute of the day purposeful.

In retrospect, I had to wonder how much of my falling in love with New York had been the adjuvant to falling in love with Brian. Had I met Brian in another place, I wasn't certain that we would have lasted as long as we had. He had been a good lover, considerate in bed, but his Wall Street job had entailed sixteen-hour workdays and preoccupations with things such as the upcoming nonfarm payroll numbers or what was happening on Bloomberg at one A.M. It had made him perpetually tired and distracted. He had used alcohol to relieve the stress, and that hadn't exactly helped our love life. But even at the beginning of our relationship, I had never experienced anything with Brian that even remotely resembled what had happened last night.

I had been like an entirely different person with Joe. But I wasn't ready to be someone new — I'd grown too accustomed to being the woman Brian Palomer had jilted at the altar. If I let go of that identity, I wasn't sure what would happen. I was afraid to imagine the possibilities. All I knew was that no man would ever hurt me the way Brian had, and I was the only one who could protect myself from that.

Later that night, as I sat in bed reading, my cell phone rang and vibrated on the night-stand.

I stopped breathing as I saw Joe's caller ID.

My God. He'd meant it when he'd said he would call.

My heart throbbed against a painful tight-ness, as if it had been wrapped in a million rubber bands. Covering my ears with my hands, closing my eyes, I didn't respond to the insistent ringtone. I waited it out. I couldn't talk to him — I wouldn't know what in the hell to say. I knew him in the most intimate way possible, yet I didn't know him at all.

As wildly pleasurable as it had been to sleep with Joe, I didn't want it to happen again. I didn't have to have a reason, did I? No. I didn't owe him any explanations. I didn't even have to explain it to myself.

The phone went silent. The tiny screen flashed a message that a voice mail had been left.

Ignore it, I told myself. I picked up the book I'd been reading and focused blindly on a page. After a couple of minutes, I realized that I'd read the same page three times without comprehending a word.

Exasperated, I tossed the book aside and grabbed the phone.

My toes curled beneath the covers as I heard his message, that unhurried drawl seeming to sink inside me and dissolve like hot sugar. "Avery, it's Joe. I wanted to find out how your drive back to Houston was." A pause. "I thought about you all day. Give me a call when you feel like it. Or I'll try you again later." Another pause. "Talk to you soon."

Blood heat had turned my cheeks red and prickly. I set the phone back on the night-stand.

The adult thing, I reflected, would be to call him back, talk to him in a calm and reasonable manner, and tell him that I wasn't interested in seeing him again. *It's just not going to click for me,* I could say.

But I wasn't going to do that. I was going to ignore Joe until he went away, because the thought of talking to him made me break out in a nervous sweat.

The phone rang again, and I stared at it in disbelief. Was he calling *again*? This was going to get annoying, fast. As I looked at the caller ID, however, I saw that it was my best friend from New York, Jasmine, who was the fashion director of a major women's magazine. She was a friend and a mentor, a woman of forty who seemed to do everything well and was never afraid to be opinionated. And her opinions were usually right.

Style was religion to Jasmine. She had the rare gift of translating street trends, shopping blogs, Internet chatter, and cultural influence into a clear-eyed assessment of what was happening in fashion and what was coming around the corner. From her friends, Jasmine demanded and gave absolute loyalty, friendship being the only thing she valued nearly as much as style. She had tried to stop me from leaving New York, promising to use her connections to secure me a job as a special fashion correspondent for a local entertainment show or possibly doing a retail collaboration with some bridal designer who wanted to tap into a more affordable market.

I had appreciated Jasmine's efforts to help, but I had refused. I'd felt defeated and tired, and I'd needed a break from fashion. Most of all, I had wanted to live with my newfound sister and form a relationship with her. I had wanted to have someone in my life whom I was related to. And part of me had liked the way Sofia looked up to me — I'd needed that. Jasmine hadn't necessarily understood, but she had relented and backed off, after telling me that someday she would find a way to lure me back to New York.

"Jazz," I exclaimed, delighted. "How are you?"

"Sweetie. Do you have time to talk?"

"Yes, I —"

"Great. Listen, I'm about to run to a party, but I have some news that can't wait. Here's the thing: You know who Trevor Stearns is."

"Of course."

I had been in awe of Trevor Stearns since I'd been in design school. The legendary celebrity wedding planner was also a mega-successful bridal fashion designer, author, and host of a cable show titled *Rock the Wedding.* The show, based in L.A., was an effervescent mix of style, sentiment, and drama. Every episode featured Trevor and his team creating a dream wedding for a bride who didn't have the budget or the vision to do it on her own.

"Trevor and his producers," Jazz continued, "are planning to do a spin-off series based in Manhattan."

"Isn't that going to cause wedding show fatigue?" I asked. "I mean, how many people are willing to watch?"

"If there's a limit, they haven't found it yet. The cable channel is airing reruns of Trevor's show all the time, and the ratings are *huge.* So the thinking is, Trevor wants to mentor someone. Preferably a woman. He's going to create a star. Whoever he decides on will be the host of *Rock the Wedding: NYC,* and Trevor will make guest appearances on the show until it's established." Jazz paused. "Do you get where this is going, Avery?"

"You think *I* should give it a shot?" I asked in bewilderment.

"It's perfect for you. I still remember those interviews you did during Bridal Week — you looked amazing on camera, and you had so much personality —"

"Thanks, but Jazz . . . there's no way they would pick someone with so little experience. Besides —"

"You can't assume that. You don't know what they're looking for. They may not even know what they're looking for. I'm going to put together a video of various things you did on camera, and you're going to send me your résumé and a decent head shot, and I'll make sure Trevor Stearns's producers take a look at everything. If they're interested, they'll fly you up here to talk in person, so if nothing else, you'll get a free trip out of it and you can see me."

I smiled. "Okay. For that reason alone, I'll give it a try."

"Wonderful. Now, tell me quickly — everyone doing okay there? Your sister?"

"Yes, she's —"

"My ride's here. Let me call you later."

"Okay, Jazz. Take care of —"

The call ended. I looked down at my phone, still bemused by the rapid-fire conversation. "And Joe said *I* talked fast," I said aloud.

For the next week and a half, I received two more calls and several texts from Joe, the relaxed tone of his messages turning into perplexed impatience. Clearly he understood I was avoiding him, but he didn't give up. He even tried the event-planning studio's number and left a message that, although innocuous, provoked considerable interest from my employees. Sofia quieted them in a deliberately light, amused tone, telling them that whether or not I was going out with Joe Travis, it was no one's business but mine. After work, however, she cornered me in the kitchen and said, "You're not yourself, *mija*. You've been acting strange ever since the Kendrick wedding. Is everything okay?"

"Of course," I said quickly, "everything's fine."

"Then why have you been having an OCD meltdown?"

"I've been doing a little cleaning and reorganizing," I said defensively. "What's wrong with that?"

"You put all the takeout menus in color-coded folders, and stacked all the magazines in order of their dates. Even for you, that's too much."

"I just want everything to be under control." Uneasily, I opened a nearby drawer and began to rearrange the utensils. Sofia was silent, waiting patiently while I made certain that all the spatulas were in one compartment and slotted spoons were in another. "Actually," I said in a rush, fumbling with a set of measuring spoons, "I slept with Joe Travis the night of the wedding, and now he wants to go out with me, but I don't want to see him again and I can't make myself tell him, so I've been avoiding his calls and hoping he'll just go away."

"Why do you want him to go away?" she asked in concern. "Did you have a bad time with him?"

"No," I said, relieved at being able to talk about it. "Oh my God, it was so amazing that I think I lost brain cells, but I shouldn't have done it in the first place, and I *really* wish I hadn't, because now I feel weird, like I have emotional jet lag or something. I can't catch up to myself. And I'm embarrassed every time I think about how I jumped into bed with him like that."

"He's not embarrassed," Sofia pointed out. "Why should you be?"

I gave her a dark glance. "He's a man. Just because I don't agree with the double standard doesn't mean it's not there."

"In this situation," Sofia said gently, "I think the only person carrying around a double standard is you." Closing the utensil drawer, she turned me to face her. "Call him tonight," she said, "and tell him yes or no. Stop torturing yourself. And him."

I swallowed hard and nodded. "I'll text him."

"Talking is better."

"No, it has to be texting so there won't be any paraverbals."

"What are paraverbals?"

"All the things you communicate besides the words," I said. "Like the tone of your voice, or the pauses, or how fast or slow you talk."

"You mean the things that help to convey the truth."

"Exactly."

"You could just be honest with him," she suggested.

"I'd rather text."

Before I went to sleep, I opened the messages on my phone and forced myself to read Joe's most recent text.

Why aren't you answering?

Gripping the phone tightly, I told myself that I was being ridiculous. I had to deal with the situation.

I've been busy, I texted back.

His reply appeared with startling immediacy. *Let's talk.*

I'd rather not. After a long silence, in which he was no doubt trying to figure out how to reply, I added, *No possibility of this going anywhere.*

Why not?

It was perfect for one night. No regrets. But I'm not interested in anything more.

After a few minutes had passed, it was clear that there would be no answer.

I spent the rest of the night struggling to fall asleep, battling my own thoughts.

Pillow's too flat. Covers are too hot. Maybe I need some herb tea . . . a glass of wine . . . melatonin . . . more reading . . . I should try deep breathing . . . I need to find a nature-sounds app . . . a late-night show . . . no, stop thinking, stop. Is three o'clock too early to get up? . . . maybe I should wait till four . . .

I finally started to doze just as the alarm sounded. Groaning, I crawled out of bed. After a long shower, I pulled on some leggings and a roomy knit tunic and went down to the kitchen.

Sofia and I lived in a partially renovated building, a former cigar factory in Montrose. We both loved the eccentric neighborhood, which was filled with art galleries, upmarket boutiques, and quirky restaurants. I had bought the warehouse at a steal, owing to its ramshackle condition. So far we had converted the ground floor into a spacious studio with exposed brick walls and endless rows of multipaned factory windows. The main-floor plan included an open kitchen with granite countertops, a central seating area anchored by an electric-blue sectional sofa, and a design section with an idea wall and tables piled with books, swatches, trims, and samples. My bedroom was on the second floor, and Sofia's was on the third floor.

"Good morning," my sister said brightly. I flinched at her cheery tone.

"God. Please. Turn it down a notch."

"The light?" she asked, reaching for the dimmer.

"No, the perkiness."

Looking concerned, Sofia poured a cup of coffee and gave it to me. "You didn't sleep well?"

"No." I stirred sweetener and creamer into the coffee. "I finally texted Joe back last night."

"And?"

"I was blunt. I said I wasn't interested in seeing him again. He didn't reply." I shrugged and sighed. "I'm relieved. I should have done it a few days ago. Thank God I don't have to worry about it anymore."

"You're sure it was the right decision?"

"Without a doubt. Maybe I would have gotten another night of great sex, but I'm not interested in being some rich guy's cheap entertainment."

"Someday you'll run into him," Sofia said.

"Another wedding, or some other event —"

"Yes, but by then it won't matter. He'll have moved on. And we'll both behave like grown-ups."

"Your paraverbals seem worried," Sofia said. "What can I do, *mija*?"

I didn't know what would have become of my life without Sofia in it. Smiling, I leaned sideways so our heads touched briefly. "If I ever get arrested," I said, "you will be my one phone call. Bail me out — that's what you can do."

"If you ever get arrested," Sofia said, "I'll already be in jail as your accomplice."

That morning, Val came to the studio at her usual time of nine o'clock. It was a mark of her innate tact that although she obviously noticed my unkempt condition, she said nothing, only went to take care of e-mails and answering machine messages. However, Steven showed no such reticence when he walked in a few minutes later.

"What's the matter?" he asked, giving me an appalled glance as I sat with Sofia on the blue sectional.

"Nothing," I said curtly.

"Then why are you wearing a Boy Scout tent?"

Before I could reply, Sofia retorted, "Don't you dare criticize how Avery looks!"

Steven inquired acidly, "So you *like* what she's wearing?"

"Of course not," Sofia said. "But if I didn't say anything about it, you shouldn't either."

"Thanks, Sofia," I said dryly. I sent Steven a warning glance. "I had a rough night. Today is not a good day to push me."

"Avery," Val called urgently from her desk in the design area, "we've gotten an e-mail from Hollis Warner's social secretary. You've been invited to a private party at the Warner mansion on Saturday. A black tie fundraiser. It's their big annual contemporary art auction and dinner."

Sofia let out a little yelp of excitement.

The atmosphere in the studio seemed instantly diluted — my lungs had to work harder to obtain the necessary amount of oxygen. I strove to sound calm. "Did she mention a plus-one? Because I'd like for Sofia to come with me."

"There was no mention of that," Val said. "If you'd like me to call and ask —"

"No, don't," Sofia said instantly. "Let's not be pushy. Hollis may have a reason for inviting just you."

"She probably does," Steven said. "But that's irrelevant."

"Why?" Sofia, Val, and I all asked at the

same time.

"Because the Warners are out of our league. If the wedding is scaled bigger than Amspacher-Kendrick, which Hollis told you it would be, we haven't developed our vendors and suppliers list enough to handle it. The big event planners in Houston and Dallas have the best professionals and venues all sewn up with exclusive contracts. We're still relatively new on the scene."

"Working for Hollis would put us on the fast track," I pointed out.

"It's a bargain with the devil. She'll expect you to cut our percentage to the bone in return for the prestige of having her as a client. This won't help the business, Avery. It's more than we can handle right now. We need to keep growing by focusing on smaller projects."

"I'm not going to let anyone take advantage of us," I said. "But I'm definitely going to the party. No matter what happens, it's an opportunity to make some great contacts."

He looked sardonic. "What are you planning to wear to this black-tie event?"

"My formal gown, of course."

"The black one you wore to the hospital fund-raiser? The one with the big shoulder pouf? No, you're not going to the Warner mansion in that." Steven stood and began to hunt for his keys and wallet.

"What are you doing?" I asked.

"I'm taking you to Neiman's. We have to find something decent off-the-rack and get it altered by Friday."

"I'm not spending money on a new dress when I've already got a perfectly good one," I protested.

"Look, if you want to dress like a parade float on your own time, it's your business. But when you're networking and trying to land a high-profile client, it becomes my business. Your appearance reflects on the studio. And your personal taste is a tragic misuse of some fine genetic endowments."

I directed my outraged gaze from him to Sofia and Val, silently commanding them to back me up. To my disgust, Sofia had suddenly become preoccupied with checking her text messages, and Val was intently straightening the piles of magazines on the coffee table.

"Okay," I muttered, "I'll get a new dress."

"And a new hairstyle. Because that one does you no favors."

"I think he's right," Sofia ventured before I could reply. "You wear it in an updo all the time."

"Every time I get my hair cut, it ends up

looking like a Darth Vader helmet."

Ignoring my protests, Steven spoke to Sofia. "Call Salon One and ask them to squeeze in an appointment for Avery. If they give you any problems, remind them that they owe us a favor after we found a last-minute caterer for the owner's wedding. Also call Avery's optometrist for a contact lens fitting."

"No way," I said. "No contacts. I have a problem with touching my eyeballs."

"That's the least of your problems." Steven found his keys. "Come on."

"Wait," Sofia exclaimed, pulling something from a drawer. She hurried to hand it to Steven. "In case you need a backup," she said.

"Is that the studio credit card?" I asked indignantly. "That's only supposed to be used in case of emergency."

Steven gave me an assessing glance. "This qualifies."

As I picked up my bag and Steven ushered me to the front door, Sofia called out after us, "Don't let him in the dressing room, Avery. Remember, he's not gay."

I hated trying on clothes, hated it, *hated* it.

More than anything, I despised the department store dressing room. The three-way mirror that magnified every little indulgence and unwanted pound. The fluorescent lighting that gave me the complexion of a bridge troll. The way the salesgirl trilled, "How's everything working out for you?" right at the moment I was tangled up in a garment that had turned into a straitjacket.

When trying on clothes was unavoidable, a dressing room at Neiman Marcus ranked above all others. From my perspective, however, deciding on a favorite department store dressing room was about as appealing as choosing my favorite way to be executed.

The Neiman Marcus dressing room was spacious and beautifully decorated, with lit columns on either side of the full-length mirrors and dimmable ceiling lights.

"Stop," Steven said, carrying in a half-dozen gowns he had pulled from the racks as we walked through the premier designer apparel.

"Stop what?" I hung up the two black dresses I had picked out in defiance of Steven's objections.

"Stop looking like one of those caged puppies on the SPCA commercials."

"I can't help it. That mirror with the pedestal in front of it makes me feel threatened and depressed, and I haven't even tried anything on yet."

Steven took a few garments from a helpful saleswoman, closed the door, and hung them on the double wall rack. "The person in that mirror is not your adversary."

"No, at the moment that would be you."

Steven grinned. "Start trying on dresses." He took the dresses I had chosen and began to walk out.

"Why are you taking those away?"

"Because you're not wearing black to Hollis Warner's party."

"Black is slimming. It's a power color."

"In New York. In Houston, color is a power color." The door closed behind him.

The saleswoman brought a long-line bustier bra and a pair of high heels and left me in privacy. I undressed as far as possible from the three-way mirror, hooked the placket at the back of the bra, and twisted it around to my front. The bra, with its boning and angled seaming, hoisted my breasts to shameless prominence.

I took the first dress from the hanger. It was a canary-yellow sheath with a beaded bodice and a stretch satin skirt. "Yellow, Steven? Please."

"Any woman can wear yellow if it's the right shade for her coloring," he said from the other side of the door.

I struggled into the gown and reached

113

back to the zipper. It refused to budge. "Come in, I need help with the zipper."

Steven entered the room and gave me an assessing glance. "Not bad." Standing behind me, he closed the back of the dress with difficulty.

Tottering toward the mirror, I struggled to breathe. "Too tight." I was suffused with gloom as I saw the strained and distorted seams. "Could you get me the next size up?"

Steven lifted the tag dangling from one armhole and frowned as he read it. "This is the largest size it comes in."

"I'm leaving now," I informed him.

Steven unzipped me decisively. "We're not giving up."

"Yes, we are. I'm going to wear the dress I already have."

"It's gone."

"What do you mean, it's gone?"

"Right after we left, I texted Sofia and told her to get rid of it while you were out. You're at the point of no return."

I scowled. "I'm going to kill you with one of these stiletto heels. And I'm going to kill Sofia with the other one."

"Try another gown."

He left the dressing room while I fumed and reached for a floor-length aqua silk with an overlay of silver-beaded organza. The gown was sleeveless with a V neck. To my relief, it slid easily over my hips.

"I've always wanted to ask you this," I said. "Did Sofia really try on clothes in front of you?"

"Yes," Steven replied from the other side of the door. "But she wasn't naked, she was wearing underwear." After a pause, he added in a preoccupied tone, "A matched set. Black lace."

"Are you interested in her?" I asked, slipping my hands through the armholes and pulling up the rest of the dress. At his silence, I said, "Never mind, I know you are." I paused. "And it's not all one-sided."

His tone was decidedly less casual as he asked, "Is that opinion or confirmed fact?"

"Opinion."

"Even if I were interested in her, I never mix work with my personal life."

"But if you —"

"I'm not discussing Sofia with you. Are you almost done?"

"Yes, I think this one may actually fit." I wriggled to zip up the back. "You can come in."

Steven entered the dressing room and glanced over me approvingly. "This works."

The weight of the geometric-patterned beading made the gown pleasantly slinky. I had to admit that the modified Empire cut of the gown flattered my shape, the flared fullness of the skirt balancing my proportions.

"We'll have alterations cut it to knee-length," Steven said decisively. "Legs like yours should be flaunted."

"It's a nice dress," I admitted. "But the color is too bright. It competes with my hair."

"It's perfect with your hair."

"It's not me." I turned and gave him an apologetic glance. "I'm not comfortable in something that makes me look so . . ."

"Confident? Sexy? A dress that encourages people to look at you? Avery . . . nothing interesting ever happens to people who stay in their comfort zones all the time."

"Having gone outside my comfort zone in the past, I can say with authority that it's an overrated experience."

"All the same . . . you're never going to get what you want if you refuse to change. And we're not even talking big changes here. These are clothes, Avery. It's minor stuff."

"Then why are you making such a big deal out of it?"

"Because I'm tired of seeing you dressed like a Viking nanny. And so is everyone else.

You're the last person on the planet who should be hiding her figure. Let's buy you a nice dress, and maybe some designer jeans and a couple of tops. And a jacket. . . ."

In no time at all, Steven had enlisted the help of two saleswomen who proceeded to fill the dressing room racks with a rainbow of garments. The three of them informed me that I had been buying bigger sizes than I needed, in styles that were the opposite of what someone with my body shape should wear. By the time Steven and I left Neiman Marcus, I had bought the aqua dress, a print blouse, a couple of silk-blend tees, designer jeans and slim-fitting black pants, silk shorts, a plum-colored leather jacket, an open peach cardigan, an eggshell-white skirt suit, and four pairs of shoes. The outfits were sleek and simple, with waist-defining silhouettes.

Aside from making a hefty down payment on the warehouse in Montrose, I had never dropped so much money at one time in my life.

"Your new wardrobe is smoking hot," Steven informed me as we left the store with bags in each hand.

"So is my credit card."

He checked his messages. "We're going to the optometrist now. After that, the salon."

"Just out of curiosity, Steven . . . is there anything about my personal style that you *do* like?"

"Your eyebrows aren't bad. And you have nice teeth." As we drove away from the Galleria, Steven asked casually, "Are you ever going to tell me what happened with Joe Travis at the Kendrick wedding?"

"Nothing happened."

"If that were true, you would have told me right away. But you haven't said anything for a week and a half, which means something happened."

"Okay," I admitted. "You're right. But I don't want to talk about it."

"Fine by me." Steven found a soft-rock station on the radio and adjusted the volume.

After a couple of minutes, I burst out, "I slept with him."

"Did you use protection?"

"Yes."

"Did you enjoy it?"

After an uncomfortable hesitation, I admitted, "Yes."

Steven lifted one hand from the wheel to high-five me.

"Wow," I muttered, returning the high five. "No lectures about one-night stands?"

"Of course not. As long as you use a

condom, there's nothing wrong with commitment-free pleasure. That being said, I wouldn't advise using someone as a fuck-buddy. One of you always starts to have feelings. Expectations. Eventually someone gets hurt. So after the one-night stand, it's better to pull the plug right away."

"What if the other person asks to see you again?"

"I'm not a Magic Eight Ball."

"You're smart about these things," I insisted. "Tell me — is there any chance of a relationship after you've had a one-night stand?"

Steven gave me a wry sideways glance. "Most of the time, a one-night stand means you've both already decided it wasn't going to be serious in the first place."

It was nine o'clock before Steven finally brought me back home. The stylist at Salon One had worked diligently on my hair for three hours, subjecting it to a regimen of relaxing chemicals, creams, and serums, heating and drying in between each step. She had proceeded to cut off eight inches, leaving me with a lob that fell to my shoulders in loose, silky waves. The salon's cosmetician had done a mani-pedi in pale taupe, and while the polish was drying, she had shown me how to apply makeup. I had subsequently bought a small bag of cosmetics that had cost as much as my monthly car payment.

As it turned out, the salon visit was worth every penny. Steven, who had decided to have a rejuvenating facial during the last hour of my treatments, emerged just as my makeup was finished. His reaction was priceless. His jaw dropped, and he let out a disbelieving laugh.

"My God. Who the hell are you?"

I rolled my eyes and blushed, but Steven persisted, walking a full circle around me, finally pulling me into his arms for a rare embrace. "You're gorgeous," he murmured. "Now *own it.*"

Later, as we walked into the studio with a multitude of bags, Sofia came downstairs from her third-floor room. She was already dressed in pajamas and fuzzy slippers, her hair pulled up in a high ponytail. She gave me a questioning look and shook her head, as if she couldn't believe her eyes.

"We're bankrupt," I informed her with a grin. "I spent all our money on hair and clothes."

To my consternation, my sister's eyes welled up. Erupting into a stream of fluid Spanish, she embraced me so tightly that I could hardly breathe.

"Is it bad?" I asked.

She began to laugh through her tears. "No, no, you're so *beautiful,* Avery. . . ."

Somehow, in the confusion of hugging and rejoicing, Sofia ended up kissing Steven on the cheek.

He went still at the innocent gesture, looking down at her with an odd, flummoxed expression. It lasted only a second before his face went carefully blank. Sofia didn't seem to notice.

If I'd had any doubts about whether Steven felt something for my sister, I knew what a Magic 8 Ball would have said:

Signs point to yes.

SEVEN

The night of Hollis Warner's art auction was humid and hot, the air pungent with wax myrtle and lantana. I pulled up to a valet stand beside a parking area filled with luxury vehicles, and a uniformed attendant helped me from the car. I was wearing the aqua beaded dress, its shortened hem now swirling around my knees. Thanks to Sofia's help with my hair and makeup, I knew I had never looked better.

Live jazz drifted through the air like smoke as I walked into the Warner mansion, a southern colonial built on a two-acre lot in River Oaks. The home had been one of the original residences back when River Oaks had been established in the twenties. Hollis had nearly doubled the size of the historic building by adding a modern glass extension at the back, a showy but jarring combination. The outline of a huge white tent loomed behind the roof line.

A rush of chilled air surrounded me as I entered a spacious foyer with antique parquet floors. The mansion was already crowded, and the evening had just started. Assistant hostesses handed out catalogs of the artwork that would be up for auction later. "They'll hold the dinner and auction in the tent," one of the hostesses told me, "but right now the house is open for viewing the artwork. The catalog describes the auction items, and lists where they're located."

"Avery!" Hollis appeared in a pink chiffon dress with a slim-fitting silhouette, the skirt a swirl of pale pink ostrich feathers. Her husband, David, a lean, attractive man with salt-and-pepper hair, accompanied her. Pressing an air kiss near my cheek, Hollis enthused, "We're going to have such fun tonight! My, don't you look gorgeous!" Glancing up at her husband, she prompted, "Sugar, tell Avery what you just said when you saw her."

He obliged without hesitation. "I said, 'That redheaded gal in the blue dress is proof that God's a man.' "

I smiled. "Thank you for inviting me. What an incredible house this is."

"I'll show you the new addition," Hollis told me. "All glass and granite. It took forever to get it right, but David supported me every step of the way." She stroked her husband's arm and beamed at him.

"Hollis loves to entertain more than anyone you'll ever meet," David Warner said. "She raises money for all kinds of charities. A woman like this deserves any kind of house she wants."

"Sugar," Hollis murmured, "Avery's the one who did that wedding for Judy and Ray's daughter. I'm going to introduce her to Ryan tonight, so she can help push things along with him and Bethany."

David looked at me with new interest. "Glad to hear it. That was some shindig, the Kendrick wedding. Lotta fun. Wouldn't mind doing something like that for Bethany."

Wondering exactly what Hollis had meant by the phrase *push things along,* I asked, "Has there been an official proposal yet?"

"No, Ryan's trying to figure out a special way to pop the question. I told him you'd be here tonight to give him some ideas."

"Whatever I can do to help."

"We couldn't have asked for a nicer young man for Bethany," Hollis said. "Ryan's an architect. Smart as a whip. His family, the Chases, are close kin to the Travises. Ryan's mama died young — so unfortunate — but his uncle Churchill looked after the family and made sure the kids got educations. And when Churchill passed on, the Chases were included in his will." Hollis gave me a significant glance as she continued. "Ryan could live off the interest of his trust fund and never work a day in his life." She grasped my wrist with a clatter of multiple cocktail rings. "David, I'm going to tour Avery around the house. You can do without me for a few minutes, can't you?"

"I'll try," her husband said, and she winked at him before pulling me away.

Hollis chatted with the ease of an accomplished hostess as she guided me through the house toward the modern addition. She stopped to show me some of the auction paintings displayed throughout the house, each lot numbered and accompanied by information about the artist. Along the way, Hollis texted Ryan to meet us in what she called "the skyroom."

"He's going to slip away from Bethany for a few minutes," Hollis explained, "so he can talk to you without her. He wants the proposal to be a surprise, of course."

"If he'd rather come to our Montrose studio," I said, "we could discuss it there. That might be easier and more private —"

"No, it's better to take care of it tonight,"

125

Hollis said. "Otherwise Ryan will drag his feet. You know how men are."

I smiled noncommittally, hoping that Hollis wasn't trying to push Ryan into proposing. "Have he and Bethany been dating for a while?" I asked as we entered a small glass-sided elevator.

"Two or three months. When you meet the right one, you just know. David proposed to me just a couple of weeks after we met — and look at us now, twenty-five years later."

As the elevator ascended to the third floor, I had a perfect view of the tent in the back. It was connected to the house by a carpet runner of fresh flowers arranged in geometric swirls.

"Here's my skyroom," Hollis said with pride, showing me a spectacular gallery with steel-framed glass walls and a segmented glass ceiling. Sculptures perched on Lucite pedestals at various places in the room. The floor itself was made of clear glass with few visible supports. A tiled outdoor swimming pool glittered three stories directly below. "Isn't it fabulous? Come, I'll show you one of my favorite sculptures."

I hesitated, staring uneasily at the glass floor. Although I had never thought of myself as having a fear of heights, I didn't like the looks of it. The glass didn't look nearly substantial enough to support my weight.

"Oh, it's safe as could be," Hollis said as she saw my expression. "You get used to it right away." Her heels clinked like cocktail ice as she walked into the gallery. "This is the closest you'll ever get to walking on air."

Since I'd never had any desire to walk on air, that assurance wasn't exactly motivating. I reached the edge of the glass and my feet stopped, toes curling in my pumps. Every cell in my body warned that walking onto that expanse of clear glass would result in sudden and ignominious death.

Steeling myself not to glance at the sparkling swimming pool below, I ventured out onto the slick surface.

"What do you think?" I heard Hollis ask.

"Amazing," I managed to reply. I was tingling all over, not in a happy, excited way, but in an epic-freak-out way. Perspiration collected beneath my bra.

"This is one of my favorite pieces," Hollis said, guiding me to a sculpture on a pedestal. "It's only ten thousand. Such a bargain."

I found myself staring blankly at a cast polyurethane head that had been divided in half. A collection of found objects — things such as a broken dish, a plastic ball, a cell phone case — had been wedged between the two sides. "I'm not sure how to interpret postmodern sculpture," I admitted.

"This artist takes ordinary objects and changes their context —" Hollis was forced to pause as her phone vibrated. "Let me check this." Reading the message, she gave an exasperated sigh. "I can't slip away for ten minutes without someone needing me to do something. This is what I hired my secretary for. I swear, that girl is one twist short of a Slinky."

"If there's something you need to take care of, please go right ahead," I said, inwardly relieved at the prospect of being able to escape from the skyroom. "Don't worry about me."

Hollis patted my arm, her rings clattering like castanets. "I'll find someone for you to meet. I can't run off and leave you here alone."

"I'm fine, Hollis. Really —"

She pulled me even farther across the treacherous floor. We passed a trio of women chatting and laughing and an elderly couple examining a sculpture. Hollis tugged me toward a photographer who stood in the corner taking candid shots of the old couple. "Shutterbug," Hollis called out playfully, "look who I've got with me."

"Hollis," I protested faintly.

Before the man lowered his camera, I knew who he was. My whole body knew. I felt his presence instantly, even before I looked up into the eyes that had haunted me every night since we had met. Except that now they were as hard as onyx.

"Hi, Joe," I managed to whisper.

EIGHT

"Joe's doing us a favor by taking some pictures for the website," Hollis said.

He set his camera by the sculpture, his gaze pinning me like a butterfly to a spreading board. "Avery. Nice to see you again."

"Would you mind keeping company with Avery while she waits here for your cousin Ryan?" Hollis asked.

"My pleasure," Joe said.

"There's no need —" I began uncomfortably, but Hollis had already disappeared in a flurry of ostrich feathers.

Silence.

I hadn't expected it would be this difficult to face Joe. The memories of everything we had done surrounded us like scorch marks in the air. "I didn't know you'd be here," I managed to say. Taking a deep breath, I let it out slowly. "I haven't handled this well," I said.

His face was unreadable. "No, you

haven't."

"I'm sorry —" I stopped, having made the mistake of letting my gaze drop too far. A brief glimpse of the glass floor had given me a bizarre tilting sensation, as if the entire house had begun to rotate sideways.

"If you don't want to see me again," Joe said, "that's your decision. But I'd at least like to know —"

"Jesus." The room wouldn't stop moving. I wobbled and reached out to grasp the sleeve of Joe's jacket in a desperate bid for balance. My evening clutch dropped to the floor. I made the mistake of looking down at it and wobbled again.

Reflexively Joe reached out to steady me. "You okay?" I heard him ask.

"Yes. No." I gripped one of his wrists.

"Too much to drink?"

It was like standing on the deck of a ship in a rolling sea. "No, it's not that . . . the floor, it's giving me vertigo. Shit, *shit* —"

"Look at me." Joe gripped my wrist and reached for my other arm. I stared blindly at the dark blur of his face until my eyes refocused. The rocklike steadiness of his hold was the only thing that kept me from tipping over. "I've got you," he said.

A wave of nausea drained the color from my skin. Beads of cold sweat broke out on my forehead.

"The floor does this to at least half the people who try to walk on it," Joe continued. "The effect of the water below throws you off balance. Take a deep breath."

"I didn't want to walk out here," I said desperately. "I only did it because Hollis insisted, and I'm trying like hell to land her as a client." The sweat was going to ruin my makeup. I was going to dissolve like a chalk drawing in the rain.

"Would it help you to know that the floor is made out of layers of structural safety glass that's at least two inches thick?"

"No" came my woebegone reply.

The corner of his mouth twitched, and his expression softened. Carefully he released one of my arms and took my hand. "Close your eyes and let me lead you."

I gripped his hand and tried to follow as he moved us forward. After a couple of steps I stumbled, panic clamoring through my body. His arm locked around me immediately, hauling me against him, but the tumbling sensation persisted.

"Oh God," I said in dazed misery. "There's no way I'm getting off this stupid floor without falling."

"I'm not going to let you fall."

"I feel sick to my stomach —"

"Easy. Stay still and keep your eyes closed." Keeping his arm around me, Joe reached into his tux jacket and pulled out a handkerchief. I felt the soft folded cloth press gently against my forehead and cheeks, absorbing the film of sweat. "You just got yourself a little worked up, that's all," he murmured. "You'll feel better once your blood pressure goes down. Breathe." Pushing a lock of hair away from my face, he continued to hold me. "You're fine." His voice was quiet, soothing. "I won't let anything happen to you."

Feeling how solid he was, the strength of him all around me, I began to relax. One of my palms pressed against his chest, riding the steady rhythm of his breath.

"You look beautiful in that dress," Joe said quietly. His hand moved gently through the soft waves of my hair. "And I like this."

I kept my eyes closed, remembering the way he had gripped his hands in my hair that night, holding my head back while he'd kissed my throat —

I felt the movement of his arm as he gestured to someone.

"What are you doing?" I asked weakly.

"My brother Jack and his wife just got off the elevator."

"Don't call them over here," I begged.

"You'll get nothing but sympathy from Ella. She got stuck out on this floor when she was pregnant, and Jack ended up having to carry her off."

An affable voice entered the conversation. "Hey, bro. What's going on?"

"My friend has vertigo."

I opened my eyes cautiously. It was obvious that the striking man standing next to Joe was from the same supernally blessed Travis gene pool. Dark hair, alpha charisma, a raffish quality in his grin. "Jack Travis," he said. "Nice to meet you."

I began to turn to shake his hand, but Joe's arms tightened.

"No, keep still," he murmured. He told his brother, "She's trying to get her bearings."

"Fuckin' glass floor," Jack said ruefully. "I told Hollis to add a layer of smart glass, and then she could turn the whole thing opaque just by flipping a switch. People should listen to me."

"*I* listen to you," a woman said, approaching us with small, painstaking steps.

"Yeah," Jack replied, "but only so you can argue." He smiled down at her and slid an arm around her shoulders. She was slim and pretty, with chin-length blond hair, her eyes denim blue behind a delicate pair of cat's-eye glasses. "What are you doing, tiptoeing out here?" Jack asked her in a gently scolding tone. "You're going to get stuck again."

"I can handle it now that I'm not pregnant," she told him. "And I want to meet Joe's friend." She smiled at me. "I'm Ella Travis."

"This is Avery," Joe said. "Let's put off the rest of the introductions for now. The floor's making her dizzy."

Ella gave me a sympathetic look. "The same thing happened to me the first time I walked out on it. A see-through floor is such a ridiculous idea — do you realize that anyone in the swimming pool could look right up our skirts?"

I couldn't help glancing down in reflexive alarm, and the room lurched again.

"Whoa, there." Joe steadied me immediately. "Avery, *do not* look down. Ella —"

"Sorry, sorry, I'll shut up."

Laughter rustled through Jack's voice as he asked, "Anything I can do to help?"

"Yeah, see the rug they hung on that wall over there? Take it down, and we'll lay it across the floor like a bridge. That'll give Avery a fixed visual reference."

"Won't reach all the way," Jack pointed out.

"It'll be close enough."

I glanced at the rug on the distant wall. The artist had applied dozens of strips of colored duct tape to the surface of an antique Persian carpet and melted them onto the textile.

"You can't," I said. "That's an auction item."

"It's a rug," Joe replied. "It's supposed to go on the floor."

"It was a rug before. Now it's art."

"I was thinking about buying it," Ella volunteered. "The choice of materials represents a fusion of the past with the future."

Jack grinned at his wife. "Ella, you're the only one here who actually reads the catalog. You know I could duct-tape a rug and make it look just like that."

"Yes, but it wouldn't be worth a dime if you did it."

His eyes narrowed. "Why not?"

Ella's fingers walked playfully up the lapel of his tuxedo jacket. "Because, Jack Travis, you do not have the mind of an artist."

His face lowered until their noses nearly touched, and he said in a sexy purr, "Good thing you married me for my body."

Joe looked exasperated. "Cut it out, you two. Jack, go get the damn rug."

"Wait," I said desperately. "Let me try walking again. Please."

Joe didn't bother to hide his skepticism. "You think you can?"

I was feeling steadier now that my heart rate had returned to normal. "As long as I don't look down, I think I'll be okay."

Joe gave me an assessing glance, while his legs bracketed mine and his hands gripped my waist. "Take off your shoes."

I felt color flooding my face. Clinging to him, I slipped off my pumps.

"I'll get those," Jack said, retrieving the pumps and evening clutch.

"Close your eyes," Joe told me. After I complied, he slid an arm around my back. "Trust me," he murmured. "And keep breathing."

I obeyed the pressure of his hands and let him guide me.

"Why are you meeting with Ryan?" Joe asked as he steered me forward.

Grateful for the distraction, I said, "Hollis told me he needs help with ideas on how to propose to Bethany."

"Why would he need help with that? All he has to do is ask the question and give her a ring."

"Nowadays people make the proposal into an event." The soles of my feet were sweating. I hoped I wasn't leaving damp footprints on the glass. "You can take someone on a hot-air balloon ride and propose in midair, or go scuba diving and propose underwater, or even hire a flash mob to sing and dance."

"That's ridiculous," Joe said flatly.

"Being romantic is ridiculous?"

"No, turning a private moment into a Broadway musical is ridiculous." We stopped, and Joe turned me to face him. "You can open your eyes now."

"We're there?"

"We're there."

When I saw that we were safe on solid granite flooring, I let out a sigh of relief. Discovering that my fingers were still wrapped tightly around his wrist, I forced my grip to loosen. "Thank you," I whispered.

He leveled a steady gaze at me, and I writhed inwardly as I understood that before the evening was over, we were going to talk.

"I'll get my camera," he said, and went back to the skyroom.

"Here you go," Jack said, handing me the evening pumps and clutch bag.

"Thanks." I set the shoes on the floor and stepped into them. "I think that qualified as my first nervous breakdown," I said with chagrin.

"A little nervous breakdown never hurt anyone," Jack assured me. "I gave 'em to my mom all the time."

"You've given me one or two," Ella informed him.

"You knew what you were getting into, marrying a Travis."

"Yes, I knew." Ella smiled and reached over to adjust his tie. "After something this traumatic," she told me cheerfully, "you need to self-medicate. Let's go sit somewhere and have a drink."

"I would love to," I said, "but I can't. I have to wait here for Joe's cousin Ryan."

"Have you met him before?"

"No, and I have no idea what he looks like."

"I'll point him out to you," Ella said. "Although the family resemblance is unmistakable. Big, hairy, lots of attitude."

Jack bent to brush a casual kiss on her lips. "That's just how you like 'em," he said. "Want me to get you some champagne?"

"Yes, please."

Jack glanced at me. "Same for you, Avery?"

Although I would have loved some, I shook my head reluctantly. "Thank you, but

I'd better stay as clearheaded as possible."

As he left, Ella turned a friendly gaze to me. "How long have you and Joe known each other?"

"We don't," I said quickly. "I mean . . . we met several days ago at a wedding I'd planned, but we're not . . . you know . . ."

"He's interested," she told me. "I could tell from the way he was looking at you."

"I'm too busy to even think about going out with someone."

She gave me a patently sympathetic look. "Avery, I'm an advice columnist. I write about this stuff all the time. No one is ever too busy for a relationship. Katy Perry's busy, but she dates, right? A-Rod's busy, but he has a new girlfriend every month. So I'm guessing you were burned in your last relationship. You've lost faith in the entire male half of our species."

There was something so perky and engaging about her that I couldn't help smiling. "That about sums it up."

"Then you need to —" She broke off as Joe returned with his camera.

"Ryan's heading over here," he said. "I just saw him get off the elevator."

A tall, well-dressed man approached us. His thick hair had been clipped conservatively short, the locks the color of dark chocolate. With his high cheekbones and icehouse-blue eyes, he was remarkably handsome, more austere and polished than the Travis brothers. He possessed a self-contained quality, with no hint of the Travises' consummate charm or easy humor, but rather a sense that he was a man who would let his guard down only reluctantly, if at all.

"Hi, Ella," he said as he reached us, leaning down to kiss her cheek. "Joe."

"How's it going, Rye?" Joe asked as they shook hands.

"I've been better." Ryan turned to me, his expression masked with politeness. "You're the wedding planner?"

"Avery Crosslin."

His grip was firm but careful as we shook hands. "We'll have to make this quick," Ryan said. "I only have a few minutes before Bethany tracks me down."

"Of course. Would you like to talk in private? I'm not familiar with the house —"

"Not necessary," Ryan said. "Joe and Ella are family." His gaze was cool. "What has Hollis told you about my situation?"

I answered readily. "She said that you're going to propose to her daughter, Bethany, and you wanted to talk to me about ideas for the proposal."

141

"I don't need proposal ideas," Ryan said flatly. "Hollis only said that because she's afraid I won't go through with it. She and David are trying to hold my feet to the fire."

"Why's that?" Joe asked.

Ryan hesitated for a long moment. "Bethany's pregnant." The battened-down tension in his reply made it clear that the news had been neither expected nor welcome.

A sober silence descended.

"She said she wants to have the baby," Ryan continued. "I told her I'd stand by her, of course."

"Ryan," Ella ventured, "I know you're traditional about these things. But if that's the only reason you're proposing to Bethany, the marriage doesn't have a great chance of working out."

"We'll make it work."

"You can be part of your child's life without having to get married," I said quietly.

"I'm not here to discuss the pros and cons. The wedding is going to happen. All I want is a say in how it turns out."

"So you want to take an active part in the planning?" I asked.

"No, I just want to set some reasonable parameters and have them enforced. Otherwise, Hollis will have the entire wedding party riding on elephants dressed in gold chain mail, or worse."

I was troubled by the prospect of planning a wedding for a reluctant groom. It seemed doubtful that he and Bethany would make it to the altar, but even if they did, the process would likely be miserable for everyone involved. "Ryan," I said, "there are several very experienced and well-established event planners in Houston who could do a wonderful job —"

"They're all in the Warners' pocket. I've already made it clear to Hollis that I won't put up with any event planner who's worked for her in the past. I want someone she doesn't own. It doesn't matter to me about how good you are, or what kind of flowers you pick, or any of that. All I want to know is if you can stand up to Hollis when she tries to take over."

"Of course I can," I said. "I'm a pathological control freak. And I happen to be great at my job. But before we discuss this any further, why don't you come to my studio and —"

"You're hired," he said abruptly.

I responded with a startled laugh. "I'm sure you'll want to run it by Bethany first."

Ryan shook his head. "I'll stipulate that hiring you is a requirement for the engagement. She won't say a word about it."

"Usually the procedure for this starts with a studio visit. We look at a portfolio and discuss ideas and possibilities —"

"I don't want to drag this out any longer than necessary. I've already decided to give the job to you."

Before I could reply, Joe intervened with a flicker of amusement in his eyes. "Rye, I don't think the question is whether you want to hire Avery. I think she's trying to figure out if she wants to take you on."

"Why wouldn't she?" Ryan's perplexed gaze arrowed to mine.

While I was busy trying to come up with a diplomatic reply, we were interrupted by Jack's return. "Hey, Rye." He had arrived with Ella's champagne in time to overhear the last of the conversation. "What are you hiring Avery for?"

"Wedding planning," Ryan said. "Bethany's pregnant."

Jack stared at him blankly. "Damn, son," he said after a moment. "There are precautions for that."

Ryan's eyes narrowed. "No method's a hundred percent except abstinence. Explain that word to him, Ella — God knows he's never heard it before."

Jack grinned briefly. "She knows me well

enough not to bother."

Privately, I reflected that beneath Ryan's high-handed manner, he had to be feeling what any man would in this situation: anxiety, frustration, and a tremendous need to obtain control over *something*. "Ryan," I said gently, "I understand your desire to start making decisions right away, but this isn't the way to pick a wedding planner. If you're interested in hiring me, come to my studio at your earliest convenience and we'll talk." As I spoke, I fished a business card from my clutch and gave it to him.

Frowning, Ryan tucked the card into his pocket. "Monday morning?"

"That works fine for me."

"Avery," Ella said, "may I have a card too? I need your help."

Jack gave her a quizzical glance. "We're already married."

"Not for *that,* it's for Haven's baby shower." Ella took the card I gave her and gave me an imploring look. "How good are you at salvaging a disaster in the making? I had to arrange a baby shower for my sister-in-law Haven, because our other sister-in-law is swamped with a salon opening — she's starting her own business — and I'm a terrible procrastinator, so I put it off for way too long. And Haven just told me that she'd rather not have a traditional girly shower, she'd rather it be appropriate for families. The whole thing is only half-planned, and it's a mess."

"When is it?" I asked.

"Next weekend," Ella said sheepishly.

"I'll do the best I can. I can't promise miracles, but —"

"Thank you, what a relief! Anything you can do will be great. If you want to —"

"Wait a minute," Ryan interrupted. "Why does Ella get an instant 'yes' and I don't?"

"She needs the help more," Joe said, perfectly deadpan. "Have you been to one of Ella's parties?"

Ella gave him a warning glance, although her eyes sparkled with laughter. "Careful, you."

Joe grinned at her before turning his attention to Ryan. "Let's catch a game on Sunday," he said.

"Sounds good." Ryan paused before asking with a subtle smile, "Does Jack have to come along this time?"

"You'd better hope I do," Jack said. "I'm the only one who ever pays for the damn beer."

Joe took my elbow. "We'll see y'all in a bit," he said easily. "I want Avery's opinion on some paintings I might bid on."

Ella winked at me as Joe drew me away.

"Do you think your cousin is really going to go through with it?" I asked Joe in a low tone. "If he takes some time to think it through —"

"Rye won't change his mind," Joe said. "His dad died when he was ten. Trust me, he'd never let a kid of his grow up fatherless."

We stepped into the elevator. "But it doesn't sound as if he's considered all his options."

"There are no options. If I were in his place, I'd do the same thing."

"You'd propose to a woman you'd accidentally gotten pregnant, even if you didn't love her?"

"Of course I would. Why do you look surprised?"

"It's just . . . an old-fashioned notion, that's all."

"It's the right thing to do."

"I don't necessarily agree. The chances of divorce are very high when a marriage starts out that way."

"In my family, if you get a woman pregnant, you take responsibility."

"What about what Bethany wants?"

"She wants to marry a man with money. And she's not too particular about who it is, as long as he can afford her."

"You have no way of knowing that."

"Honey, everybody knows it." Joe cast a grim glance at the scenery on the other side of the elevator glass. "Ryan's spent most of his life with his nose to the grindstone, and then when he finally decides to take a break and have some fun, he hooks up with Bethany Warner. A party girl. A professional socialite. You don't get caught by a girl like that. I don't know what the hell he was thinking."

The doors opened, and we were on the main floor again. Joe took my free hand and began to tow me through the crowd.

"What are we doing?" I asked.

"I'm finding us a place to talk."

I blanched, knowing exactly what he wanted to discuss. "*Here? Now?* There's no privacy."

Joe sounded sardonic. "We could have had plenty of privacy, if you'd picked up your phone when I called."

We proceeded through one packed room after another, pausing occasionally for brief conversations. Even in this exalted gathering of insiders, it was clear that he was something special. The combination of his name, money, and looks was all a man needed to unlock the world. But he adroitly deflected people's eager interest, turning it around to focus on them as if they were infinitely more worthy of attention.

Eventually, we entered a room lined with dark paneled wood and bookshelves, the ceiling low and coffered, the floor covered with a thick Persian rug. Joe closed the door, muffling the sounds of conversation, laughter, and music. His polite social mask disappeared as he turned to face me. In the silence, my heartbeat gathered momentum, rolling into a hard repeated wallop.

"Why did you say there was no chance of this going anywhere?" he asked.

"Isn't it obvious?"

Joe gave me a caustic glance. "I'm a guy, Avery. Nothing about relationships is obvious to me."

No matter how I tried to explain, I knew I would end up sounding self-pitying or pathetic. *I don't want to end up being hurt the way you're going to hurt me. I know how these things work. You want sex and fun, and when it's over you'll move on, but I won't be able to, because you'll have broken what's left of my heart.*

"Joe . . . one night with you was all I expected, and it was wonderful. But I . . . I need something different." I paused, trying to think of how to explain.

His eyes widened, and he said my name on a quiet breath. Confused by the change in his demeanor, I backed up reflexively as he came to me. One of his arms slid around me, while his free hand lifted to cradle the side of my face. "Avery, sweetheart . . ." There was a slight rasp in his voice, something concerned . . . raw . . . sexual. "If I didn't give you what you needed . . . if I didn't satisfy you . . . all you had to do was tell me."

NINE

Realizing that Joe had misunderstood, I stammered, "No, that — that's not — I didn't mean —"

"I'll make it up to you." He caressed my cheek with his thumb, and his mouth grazed mine with an erotic gentleness that left me gasping. "Let me have another night with you. You can ask me for anything. Anything. I'll make it so good for you, honey . . . there are so many ways . . . All you have to do is come to bed with me, and I'll take care of you."

Dazed, I tried to explain that he'd gotten it all wrong, but as I opened my mouth, Joe kissed me again and again, murmuring promises about the pleasure he would give me, the things he would do for me. He was so remorseful, so determined . . . and to my shame, I found it sexy as hell to be caught in the grasp of a big, aroused male who wouldn't stop apologizing and kissing me.

Gradually, it seemed less important to break free. His mouth ravished mine, all silk and hunger, draining me of strength. The insane chemistry between us didn't just feel good, it felt necessary, as if I needed him to breathe, as though my body would stop functioning if I couldn't keep touching him.

He reached down to anchor my hips against his, aggressive hardness nudging into a lush, intimate ache. I quivered and began to breathe in long sighs. Remembering what it had been like — the way he had filled me — I was overcome with disorienting heat, and all I wanted to do was sink to the floor with him and have him take me right there. I welcomed the stroke of his tongue, opened for it, and a groan resonated in his throat. His hand slid to my breast.

Dimly realizing that the situation was about to blaze out of control, I struggled and pushed at him until his arms loosened. Panting, I wrenched free. Just as he reached for me again, I held up a staying hand, my fingers trembling.

"Wait . . . Wait . . ." I was breathing as if I'd sprinted a hundred yards. So was Joe. I made my way to a big upholstered chair and sat on the arm of it. My legs were weak. Every nerve shrilled in protest. "I don't think we can talk without a buffer zone.

Please, just . . . stay over there and let me say a couple of things, okay?"

Sliding his hands in his pockets, Joe gave me a nod of assent. He began to pace slowly.

"Just to be clear," I said, my face throbbing hotly, "I was more than satisfied that night. You're great in bed, as I'm sure a lot of women have told you. But I want an ordinary guy, someone I can be sure of, and you . . . you are not that guy."

The pacing stopped. Joe gave me a confounded glance.

I licked at my dry lips and tried to think over the clamor of my pulse. "You see, it's like . . . a long time ago, my mother wanted a Chanel bag for her birthday. She taped a magazine picture of it to the fridge and never stopped talking about it. My stepfather bought it for her. She kept it on the top shelf of her closet in the special protective cover it came with. But she never carried the bag. So a few years later I asked her why the Chanel bag had always stayed in the closet, and why she'd never taken it out. She said it was too nice for every day. Too fancy. She didn't want to worry about it getting damaged or lost, and besides that, it didn't go with any of her clothes. It didn't fit who she was." I paused. "Do you understand what I'm trying to say?"

Joe shook his head with baffled annoyance.

"You're the Chanel bag," I said.

His scowl deepened. "Let's drop the metaphors, Avery. Especially ones where I'm in a damn closet."

"Yes, but do you get what I —"

"I want a real reason for why you won't go out with me. Something I can understand. Like you don't like the way I smell, or you think I'm an asshole."

Looking down at the fabric of the chair, I traced the geometric pattern with the tip of my fingernail. "I love the way you smell," I said, "and you're not at all an asshole. But . . . you are a player."

An unaccountably long pause followed before I heard his bewildered reply.

"Me?"

I lifted my head. I hadn't expected him to look so stunned.

"Where did you get that idea?" he asked.

"I've *been* with you, Joe. I'm a personal witness to your hookup skills. The conversation, the dancing, the way you knew exactly how to play it so I'd feel comfortable with you. And when we were in bed, you had a condom conveniently ready, right there on the nightstand, so there was no pause in the action. Obviously you'd figured out every step beforehand."

He shot me an affronted glance, color heightening his tan to a shade of rosewood. "You're mad because I had a condom? You'd rather have done it without one?"

"No! It's just that the whole thing was so . . . so practiced. So smooth. A routine you've perfected."

His voice was quiet but biting. "There's a difference between having experience and being a player. I don't score women. I don't have a routine. And setting my wallet on the nightstand doesn't make me fuckin' Casanova."

"You've been with a lot of women," I insisted.

"How are you defining 'a lot'? Is there a number I'm not supposed to go over?"

Stung by the note of scorn, I asked, "Before last weekend, had you ever slept with a woman the first time you met her?"

"Once. In college. The rules were understood beforehand. Why does that matter?"

"I'm trying to make the point that sex doesn't mean the same thing to you that it does to me. This was the only one-night stand I've ever had, not to mention the first time I've slept with someone since Brian. You and I have never even been out on a date. Maybe you don't think of yourself as a player, but compared to —"

"Brian?" He looked at me alertly.

Regretting my slip of the tongue, I said curtly, "My fiancé. I was engaged, and we broke it off. That's not important. My point is —"

"When did that happen?"

"It doesn't matter." I stiffened as Joe began to approach me.

"When?" he insisted.

"A while ago." I stood from the chair and took a step back. "Joe, the buffer zone —"

"When was the last time you slept with him? With anyone?" He reached me, taking hold of my arms as I shrank back. I ended up against the bookshelves, crowded by his big frame.

"Let go," I said faintly. My gaze ricocheted as I tried to look anywhere but directly at him. "Please."

Joe was ruthless. "One year?" A pause. "Two?" As I kept silent, he stroked my upper arms, his warm hands bringing up gooseflesh. His voice turned gentle. "More than two years?"

I had never felt more vulnerable or mortified. Too much of my past had just been revealed, along with an avalanche of self-doubt and naïveté. As I wilted in the heat of exposure, it occurred to me that I may have judged him differently from how a more emotionally secure woman would have.

I threw a longing glance at the door, desperate to leave. "We have to get back to the party —"

Joe pulled me against him. I writhed in protest, but his arms tightened, restraining me easily. "I understand now," I heard him say after a moment. Although I wanted to ask what, exactly, he thought he understood, I could only stand there in a trance. A minute passed, and another. I began to say something, but he hushed me and kept holding me. Clasped securely against the rise and fall of his chest, steeped in his body heat, I felt myself relaxing.

I was filled with the bittersweet knowledge that this was the last time he would ever hold me. After this we would cut our losses. We would put the memory of that night behind us for good. But I was going to remember this embrace, because it was the best, safest, warmest feeling I'd ever had in my life.

"We slept together too soon," he said eventually. "My fault."

"No, it wasn't —"

"It was. I could tell you didn't have much experience, but you were willing, and . . .

hell, it felt too good to stop. I wasn't trying to play you. I'm —"

"Don't apologize for having sex with me!"

"Easy." Joe began to smooth my hair. "I'm not sorry that it happened. Only that it happened too soon for you to feel comfortable with it." He bent his head and kissed the soft skin around my ear, making me shiver. "It wasn't casual," he murmured. "Not for me. But I would never have let it go so far if I'd known it would scare you."

"It didn't scare me," I said, nettled by the implication that I was behaving like some terrified virgin.

"I think it did." His hand went to the back of my neck, kneading the small muscles gently, easing the ache into pleasure. It was all I could do not to arch and purr like a cat.

I tried to summon more indignation. "And what do you mean, you could tell I didn't have experience? Did I do something wrong? Was I a disappointment? Was I —"

"Yeah," Joe said, "it's a hell of a disappointment when I come so hard, I see stars. It was such a downer that I've been chasing after you ever since." He braced his hands on either side of me, gripping the edges of the bookshelf.

"It's over now," I managed to say. "I think

158

we should chalk it up to — to a spontaneous moment —" I broke off with an incoherent sound as he leaned forward to kiss my
neck.

"It can't be over when it never even
started," he said against my skin. "I'll tell
you what's going to happen, brown-eyed
girl: You're going to answer the phone when
I call. You're going to let me take you out,
and we're going to do some talking. There's
too much we don't know about each other."
He found a pulse, and his lips lingered on
the tiny, rampant rhythm. "So we're going
to take it slow. I'll get to know you. You'll
get to know me. And then it's up to you."

"It's too late," I managed to say in between
shivering breaths. "Sleeping together ruined
the getting-to-know-you part."

"It's not ruined. It's just a little more
complicated."

If I agreed to go out with him again, I was
asking for heartbreak. *Begging* for it. "Joe, I
don't think —"

"No decisions right now," he said, his
head lifting. "We'll talk later. For now . . ."
He retreated a step and held out his hand.
"Let's go back out there and have dinner. I
want a chance to prove that I can behave
around you." His hot gaze chased over me.
"But I swear, Avery Crosslin . . . you don't

make it easy."

Dinner was an elaborate six-course affair, with a piano-and-violin duet playing in the background. The tent had been decorated in black and white, with white phalaenopsis orchid centerpieces, all of it a perfect setting for the art auction. I sat with Joe at a table for ten, along with Jack, Ella, and a few assorted friends.

Joe was in a relaxed good mood, at times casually resting his arm at the back of my chair. The group was chatty and animated, making small talk with the ease of people who did it often, who knew exactly how to keep the conversation fluid. As the Travis brothers exchanged quips and good-natured jabs, it was obvious that they genuinely enjoyed each other's company.

Joe recounted a recent road trip he'd taken to do photos for a Texas magazine's "bucket list" issue, featuring activities and places that no Texan should miss during his life, among them to go two-stepping at Billy Bob's in Fort Worth, eat chicken-fried steak topped with white gravy at a particular diner in San Antonio, and visit Buddy Holly's grave in Lubbock. Ella volunteered that she didn't like white gravy on her chicken-fried steak, at which point Jack half covered his face. "She eats it dry," he confessed, as if it were blasphemy.

"It's not dry," Ella protested, "it's fried. And if you ask me, battering and deep-frying cube steak *and* drowning it in biscuit gravy is the worst —"

Gently, Jack laid his fingers over her mouth. "Not in public," he cautioned. As he felt the shape of her grin, he promptly removed his hand and kissed her.

"I've eaten chicken-fried steak for breakfast," Joe volunteered. "With two fried eggs on the side."

Jack gave him an approving glance. "That there's a real man," he told Ella.

"That there is a cardiovascular tragedy waiting to happen," she retorted, making her husband grin.

Later, as Ella and I walked to the restroom together, I remarked, "There is no shortage of testosterone at that table."

Ella smiled. "It's the way they were raised. The oldest brother, Gage, is just the same. But don't worry: Despite all the brawn and bluster, Travis men are pretty enlightened." With a rueful grin, she added, "By Texas standards."

"So Jack helps with things like household chores and changing the diapers?"

"Oh, absolutely. But there are certain

man-rules, like opening the door, or holding your chair, that are never going to change. And since Joe is obviously interested in you, I'll tell you right now, don't bother trying to split the check when he takes you out. He'd sooner commit hari-kari with a steak knife."

"I don't know if Joe and I will go out," I said cautiously. "It's probably better if we don't."

"I hope you do. He's a terrific guy."

We exited the tent and walked along the flowered pathway to the house. "Would you say he's a player?" I asked. "A heartbreaker?"

"I wouldn't put it that way." After a pause, Ella said frankly, "Women like Joe, and Joe likes women, so . . . yes, there have been one or two who wanted more of a commitment than he was willing to give. Let's face it, a lot of women would snap him up right away just because of the Travis name."

"I'm not one of them."

"I'm sure that's one of the reasons Joe likes you." We stopped beside an outdoor steel sculpture made of thick plates almost fifteen feet high, its edges curved and shaped in organic lines. Ella's voice lowered. "The Travises set quite a store by normalcy. They want to be part of the real world, experience it like everyone else, which is practically impossible at their level. Most of all they want to be treated like regular people."

"Ella . . . they're not regular people. I don't care how much chicken-fried steak they eat, they're just not. The money, the name, the looks . . . nothing about them is normal, no matter how they pretend otherwise."

"They're not pretending," Ella said thoughtfully, "it's more like . . . a value they want to live by. Trying to erase the distance between themselves and other people. They keep their egos in check, and they try to be honest with themselves." She shrugged and smiled. "I figure they deserve some credit for making the effort . . . don't you?"

TEN

At nine o'clock on Monday morning, Ryan Chase arrived at the Crosslin Event Design studio, determined to do or say whatever was necessary to "solve the problem" and move on. Except that a wedding wasn't supposed be a problem, it was supposed to be joyful. A union of two people who wanted to spend their lives together.

However, at this point in my career, I had learned that some weddings didn't match the fairy-tale template. So the goal in this case was to figure out what *was* possible. What might be appropriate for a bridegroom who viewed his wedding as an obligation.

I welcomed Ryan into the studio and introduced him to Sofia, who would be the only other person present at the meeting. I had told everyone else, including Steven, not to come in until noon. As we showed Ryan around, he seemed pleasantly surprised by the studio, looking closely at our renovations, the rows of factory windows left intact. "I like this place," he said. "I thought everything was going to be pink."

Sofia and I laughed.

"We have to live here," I said, "so it had to be comfortable and not too fussy. And on occasion, we do plan events other than weddings."

"It's nice that you kept some of the industrial elements." Ryan glanced up at a couple of exposed pipes overhead. "I do a lot of restoration projects. Old courthouses, theaters, and museums. I like buildings with character."

We sat on the blue sofa, while a video monitor played a photo stream from past weddings that the studio had planned and coordinated. "Ryan," I began carefully, "I've given a lot of thought to your circumstances. Every wedding comes with a certain amount of built-in stress. But when you add the stress of Bethany's pregnancy, and the drama Hollis brings to the table, it's going to be . . ."

"A nightmare?" he supplied.

"I was going to say 'challenging,' " I said wryly. "Have you considered talking Bethany into an elopement? Because we could arrange something simple and romantic, and I think it would be much easier on you."

Sofia shot me a startled glance. I knew she was wondering why I would risk the loss of a huge opportunity for our business. But I had to bring up the idea of eloping — I couldn't have lived with myself otherwise.

Ryan shook his head. "There's no way Bethany would ever go for that. She told me she's been dreaming her whole life about a big wedding." He relaxed a little, his blue eyes warming several degrees. "But it was nice of you to mention it. Thanks for taking my feelings into consideration." This was said without a trace of self-pity, only a matter-of-fact friendliness.

"Your feelings are important," I said. "And so are your opinions. I'm trying to get a sense of how much involvement you'll want in the wedding-planning process. Some men prefer to take part in every decision, whereas others —"

"Not me," he said flatly. "I'll leave all that to Bethany and Hollis. Not that I'd have a choice, anyway. But what I don't want is for the wedding to turn into something . . ." He paused, trying to think of the right word.

"*Una paletada hortera,*" Sofia supplied. At our questioning glances, she said, "There's not really a phrase for it in English . . . the best translation is 'a shovelful of tacky.' "

Ryan laughed, the flash of humor and warmth transforming his face. "That's exactly what I meant."

"All right, then," I said. "During the planning process, I'll give you updates as things are decided. If there's something you don't like, I'll shut it down. There may be a couple of things we'll have to compromise on, but overall, the wedding will be elegant. And it will not turn into *The Hollis Warner Show*."

"Thank you," Ryan said feelingly. He looked at his watch. "If that's it for now —"

"Wait, what about the proposal?" I asked.

A slight frown crossed his brow. "I'll probably propose to Bethany next weekend."

"Yes, but do you know how you're going to do it?"

"I'll get a ring and take her out to dinner." His frown deepened as he saw my expression. "What's wrong with that?"

"Nothing at all. But you could do it in a more imaginative way. We could come up with something cute and fairly easy."

"I'm not good at cute," Ryan said.

"Take her to Padre Island," Sofia suggested. "Stay at a beachside villa for a night. The next morning, the two of you could go for a walk on the beach . . ."

"And you'll pretend to find a message in

a bottle," I said, brainstorming.

"No, no," Sofia interrupted, "not a bottle . . . a sand castle. We'll hire some professional sand sculptors to do it —"

"Based off a sketch that Ryan's provided," I said. "He's an architect — he can design a special sand castle for Bethany."

"Perfect," Sofia exclaimed, and we high-fived each other.

Ryan had been glancing back and forth between us as if he were attending a tennis match.

"Then you'll get down on one knee and propose," I continued, "and —"

"Do I have to take a knee when I ask her?" Ryan asked.

"No, but it's traditional."

Ryan rubbed the lower half of his jaw, clearly not liking the idea.

"Men used to kneel when they were being knighted," Sofia pointed out.

"Or beheaded," Ryan said darkly.

"Kneeling will look nicer for the pictures," I said.

"Pictures?" Ryan's brows lifted. "You want me to propose to Bethany with camera guys there?"

"One photographer," I said hastily. "You'll hardly notice him. We'll camouflage him."

"We'll hide him in a sand dune," Sofia added.

Frowning, Ryan raked his hand through the close-cut layers of his brown hair, the light picking out glints of mahogany.

I looked at Sofia. "Never mind. A camera at the proposal sounds like a shovelful of tacky to me."

Ryan lowered his head, but not before I saw a reluctant smile emerge. "Damn it," I heard him mutter.

"What?"

"Suggesting you as the wedding planner is turning out to be the first nice thing Hollis has ever done for me. Which means I might have to thank her."

"You answered," Joe said later that night in a tone of mild surprise.

I smiled, leaning back against the pillows with my cell phone in hand. "You told me to."

"Where are you right now?"

"In bed."

"Should I call another time?"

"No, I'm not sleeping, I always sit in bed and do some reading at the end of the day."

"What do you like to read?"

I glanced at the pile of candy-colored novels on the nightstand and replied with self-conscious amusement, "Love stories. The kind with the happy endings."

"Do you ever get tired of knowing how the book's going to end?"

"No, that's the best part. Happily-ever-afters are hard to come by in real life, even in the wedding business. But at least I can count on one in a book."

"I've seen some great marriages in real life."

"They don't stay that way, though. Every marriage starts as a happy ending, and then it turns into a marriage."

"How did someone who doesn't believe in happily-ever-after end up as a wedding planner?"

I told him about my first job after graduating in fashion design, how I'd apprenticed under a New York designer for a bridal fashion label, managing the sample room, learning to analyze sales reports, developing relationships with buyers. I had worked on a few of my own designs and had even won a prize as an emerging designer. But when I'd tried to start my own label, it had never gotten off the ground. No one had shown any enthusiasm for backing me.

"I was honestly stunned," I told Joe. "The collection I'd designed was beautiful. I had a great reputation, and I'd built up all these amazing contacts. I couldn't figure out what was wrong. So I called Jasmine, and she said —"

"Who's Jasmine?"

"Oh, I forgot I hadn't told you about her. Jasmine's my best friend in New York. A mentor. She's the head fashion director at *Glimmer* magazine. She knows everything about style, and she can always tell which trends will be huge, and which ones will never get off the ground–" I paused. "Is this boring?"

"Not at all. Tell me what she said."

"Jasmine said there was nothing wrong with my collection. It was competently designed. Everything was in perfect taste."

"Then what was the problem?"

"That was the problem. I didn't take any risks. I didn't push my ideas enough. The extra *something*, that spark of originality . . . it wasn't there. But she said I was a fantastic businesswoman. I was good at networking and promoting; I got the business side of fashion like no one else she knew. I didn't like hearing any of this; I wanted to be a creative genius. But I had to admit that the business was what I'd really enjoyed, way more than the design work."

"Nothing wrong with that."

"I know that now. At the time, though, it

was hard to let go of something I'd worked so hard for. Not long after that, my father had a stroke. So I flew down to visit him in the hospital, and I met Sofia, and my whole life changed."

"And the broken engagement?" Joe surprised me by asking. "When did that happen?"

The question made me tense and uncomfortable. "I hate talking about that."

"We don't have to." The gentleness of his voice eased the tightness in my chest. I settled back deeper into the pillows. "Do you miss New York?" he asked.

"Sometimes." I paused and said ruefully, "A lot. But there are some days when I don't think about it as much as others."

"What do you miss most about it?"

"My friends most of all. And . . . it's hard to put it into words, but . . . New York is the only place where I could be the person I want to be. It speeds me up and makes me think bigger. God, what a city. I still dream about going back someday."

"Why did you leave in the first place?"

"I was sort of . . . not myself . . . after the broken engagement, and my father passing away. I needed a change. And I especially needed to be with Sofia. We had just found each other. It was the right decision to move down here. But someday, when Sofia is ready to take over, I'm going to go back to New York and give it another shot."

"I think you'll do fine wherever you live. In the meantime, you can go visit, can't you?"

"Yes, but I've been too busy the past three years. Soon, though. I want to see my friends in person. I want to go to a couple of plays, and some of my favorite restaurants, and find a street fair with five-dollar pashminas, and have a slice of really good pizza, and there's this rooftop bar on Fifth where you get the most perfect view of the Empire State Building . . ."

"I know that bar."

"You do?"

"Sure. The one with the garden."

"Yes! I can't believe you've been there."

Joe sounded amused. "I've been outside the state of Texas, despite appearances to the contrary."

He told me about a couple of his past trips to New York. We exchanged stories about places where we'd traveled, about ones we'd want to go back to and the ones we wouldn't. About the freedom of traveling alone, but also the loneliness.

When I realized how late it was, I couldn't believe the conversation had lasted for over two hours. We agreed it was time to call it a night. But I had no desire to stop. I could have gone on talking.

"This was fun," I said, feeling warm and even a little giddy. "I wish we could do it again." In the short silence that followed, I covered my eyes with my free hand, wishing I could take back the impulsive words.

There was a smile in Joe's voice. "I'll keep calling," he said, "if you'll keep answering."

ELEVEN

As it turned out, we talked every night for a week, including the night Joe was driving back late from a photo shoot in Brownwood. He'd done a session for a young congressman who'd just been elected to the U.S. House in a special runoff. The congressman had been a difficult subject, controlling and awkward, posing like a politician, roosterlike, despite Joe's efforts to catch him in a relaxed moment. And the guy was a braggart, a name-dropper, qualities that were nearly intolerable to a Travis.

While we talked during Joe's long drive to Houston, he told me about the photo shoot, and I filled him in on the planning for Haven's baby shower. It was going to be held at the Travis River Oaks mansion, which had gone unoccupied ever since Churchill's passing, mostly because no one knew what to do with it. None of the Travises particularly wanted to sell the place

— it was where they'd grown up — but neither did any of them want to live in it. Too big. Too reminiscent of their parents, who were both gone now. However, the pool and patio on the mansion's three-acre lot would provide the perfect setting for a party.

"I went to the River Oaks house today," I said. "Ella showed me around."

"What did you think?"

"Very impressive." The massive stone house had been designed to look like a château, surrounded by vast tracts of mowed green lawn, precisely trimmed hedges, and elaborate flower beds. After seeing walls sponged with a Tuscan faux finish and windows smothered with swag draperies, I had agreed with Ella's assessment that someone needed to "de-eighties" the place.

"Ella said that Jack had asked if she wanted to move there," I continued, "since they have two kids and the apartment's getting cramped."

"What did she say?"

"She told him the house is too big for a family of four. And Jack said they should move there anyway and just keep having children."

Joe laughed. "Good luck to him. I doubt he'll ever talk Ella into moving there, no matter how many kids they end up with.

It's not her kind of place. Or his, for that matter."

"What about Gage and Liberty?"

"They've built their own house in Tanglewood. And I don't think Haven and Hardy have any more interest in living in River Oaks than I do."

"Would your father have wanted one of you to keep it?"

"He didn't say anything specific." A pause. "But he was proud of that place. It was a measure of what he'd achieved."

Joe had previously told me about his father, a tough bantam of a man who'd come from nothing. The deprivation of Churchill's childhood had instilled a fierce drive to succeed, almost a rage, that had never fully left him. His first wife, Joanna, had died soon after giving birth to a son, Gage. A few years later, Churchill had married Ava Chase, a glamorous, cultured, supremely elegant woman whose ambition was equal to Churchill's, and that was saying something. She had smoothed some of his rough edges, taught him about subtlety and diplomacy. And she had given him two sons, Jack and Joe, and a petite dark-haired daughter, Haven.

Churchill had insisted on raising the boys with responsibility and a sense of obligation, to become the kind of men he approved of. To be like him. He had been a man of absolutes: A thing was either good or bad, right or wrong. Having seen how the children of some of his well-to-do peers had turned out — spoiled and soft — Churchill had been determined not to raise his offpring with a sense of entitlement. His boys had been required to excel in school, especially math, a subject that Gage had mastered and at which Jack had been proficient and Joe, on his best days, had never been more than adequate. Joe's talents had been in reading and writing, pursuits Churchill considered somewhat unmanly, especially because Ava had liked them.

His youngest son's lack of interest in Churchill's private equity investments and financial management consulting business had finally resulted in a huge blowup. When Joe turned eighteen, Churchill had wanted to put him on the board of his holding company, as he'd done with Gage and Jack. He'd always planned on having all three sons on the board. But Joe had flat-out refused. He hadn't even accepted a nominal position. The mushroom cloud had been visible for miles. Ava had passed away from cancer two years earlier, and there had been no one to mediate or intervene. Joe's relationship with his father had been ice cold for a couple of years after that and hadn't entirely recovered until Joe had stayed with him after the boat accident.

"I had to learn patience fast," Joe had told me. "My lungs were shot, and it was hard to argue with Dad when I was breathing like a Pekingese."

"How did you two manage to reconcile?"

"We went out to play golf. I hated golf. Old-man sport. But Dad insisted on dragging me to the driving range. He taught me how to swing a club. We played a couple of times after that." A grin emerged. "He was so old, and I was so busted up, neither of us could break one thirty on eighteen holes."

"But you had a good time?"

"We did. And after that, everything was fine."

"But . . . it couldn't have been. If you didn't talk about the issues . . ."

"That's one of the great things about being a guy: Sometimes we fix things by deciding it was bullshit and ignoring the hell out of it."

"That's not fixing," I had protested.

"Sure it is. Like Civil War medicine: Amputate and move on." Joe had paused. "Usually you can't do that with a woman."

"Not usually," I had agreed dryly. "We like

179

to solve problems by actually facing them and working out compromises."

"Golf's easier."

In less than a week, my team had put together a vintage-boardwalk-themed party for Haven Travis's baby shower. Tank had enlisted a local theater set crew to help him construct and paint a dessert station that resembled a boardwalk game arcade. Steven hired a landscaper to install a temporary mini golf course on the grounds of the Travis mansion. Together Sofia and I met with caterers and agreed on an outdoor party menu featuring gourmet burgers, grilled shrimp kebabs, and lobster rolls.

The forecast for the day of the party was ninety degrees and humid. The event team arrived at the Travis mansion at ten A.M. After helping the tent company reps to set up a row of open-sided cabana tents by the pool, Steven returned to the kitchen, where the rest of us were unboxing decorations.

"Tank," he said, "I need you and your guys to assemble the boardwalk arcade, and after that —" Steven broke off as he saw Sofia. His gaze traveled over the sleek length of her legs. "That's what you're wearing?" he asked, as if she were half-naked.

Sofia gave him a perplexed glance, a large

bleached starfish in her hand. "What do you mean?"

"Your outfit." Scowling, Steven turned his attention to me. "Are you actually going to let her wear that?"

I was dumbfounded. Sofia was dressed like a forties pinup girl in red-and-white polka-dotted shorts with a matching halter top. The outfit showed off her curvy figure, but there was nothing immodest about it. I couldn't fathom why Steven would object.

"What's wrong with it?" I asked.

"It's too short."

"It's ninety degrees outside," Sofia snapped at Steven, "and I'm going to be working all day. Do you expect me to wear an outfit like Avery's?"

I sent her an irritated glance.

Before getting dressed that morning, I had considered wearing some of my new clothes, most of which had hung in my closet untouched. However, old habits were hard to break. Rather than choose something silky and colorful, I had reverted to one of my old standbys: a relaxed-fit white cotton tunic. It was loose and sleeveless, worn over a pair of billowy gathered-hem pants that — despite their charming name of "poet pants" — were admittedly unflattering. But the outfit was comfortable, and I felt safe wearing it.

Steven gave Sofia a caustic glance. "Of course not. But it's still better than dressing like the featured performer at a strip club."

"Steven, that's enough," I said sharply.

"I'm going to fire you for sexual harassment," Sofia cried.

"You can't fire me," Steven informed her. "Only Avery can fire me."

"She won't have to if I kill you first!" She leapt toward him, holding the starfish like a weapon.

"Sofia," I yelped, grabbing her from behind. "Take it easy! Put that down. Jesus, have you both lost your minds?"

"Someone around here has," I heard Steven say. "Unless the plan is to flaunt Sofia as millionaire bait."

That did it. *No one* insulted my sister that way. "Tank," I said in a murderous tone, "get him out of here. Throw him into the pool to cool him off."

"Literally?" Tank asked.

"Yes, literally throw him into the pool."

"Not the pool" came Steven's muffled voice. Tank already had him in a headlock. "I'm wearing linen!"

One of the qualities I appreciated most about Tank was his unqualified allegiance to me. He hauled Steven out of the kitchen, lumbering like a small bear. No amount of struggling and swearing would dissuade him.

"If I let go of you," I said to Sofia, who was straining to break free, "promise not to follow them outside."

"I want to watch Tank throw him into the pool."

"I understand. So do I. But this is our *business,* Sofia. We have work to do. Don't let Steven's lapse of sanity interfere with it." When I felt her relax, I dropped my arms from around her.

My sister turned to face me, looking furious and crestfallen. "He hates me. I don't know why."

"He doesn't hate you," I said.

"But why —"

"Sofia," I said, "he's an asshole. We'll talk about it later. For now, let's get to work."

When I saw Steven two hours later, he was mostly dry. He worked on the finishing touches of the mini golf course, positioning an old-fashioned diver's helmet so a golf ball could roll up a ramp into the front porthole.

As I approached, he spoke tersely while adjusting the ramp. "Dolce and Gabbana shorts. Dry-clean only. You owe me three hundred bucks."

"You owe me an apology," I said. "This is the first time you've ever been less than professional during a job."

"I apologize."

"You owe an apology to Sofia."

Steven remained mutinously silent.

"Care to explain what's going on?" I asked.

"I've already explained. Her outfit is inappropriate."

"Because she looks cute and sexy? It's not a problem for anyone else. Why does it bother *you* so much?"

Another stony silence.

"The caterers are here," I finally said. "The band is arriving at eleven. Val and Sofia have almost finished decorating the indoor areas, and then I'll have them start on the patio tables."

"I need Ree-Ann to help with the cabanas."

"I'll send her out." I paused. "One more thing. From now on, I insist that you treat Sofia with respect. Even though I'm technically in charge of hiring and firing, Sofia and I are equal partners. And if she wants you gone, you're gone. Understood?"

"Understood," he muttered.

As I headed back to the house, I passed Tank, who was carrying two huge bunches of helium-filled balloons for the dessert arcade. "Thanks for helping me with Steven," I said.

"You mean tossing him into the pool? No problem. I'll throw him in again if you want."

"Thank you," I said with grim amusement, "but if he steps out of line again, I'll throw him in myself."

I returned to the kitchen, where Ree-Ann and the caterers were uncrating sets of plates and glassware for the indoor dining area.

"Where's Sofia?" I asked.

"She went to say hi to some of the Travises. They just arrived."

"When you're done with the plates, Steven needs you to help him with the cabanas."

"Sure thing."

I went to the main living room to find the group standing at the row of long windows with Sofia. They looked out at the pool and patio area, exclaiming and talking and laughing. A small dark-haired boy jumped up and down and tugged on the hem of Jack's shirt. "Daddy, take me outside! I wanna go see! Daddy! Daddy —"

"Hold your horses, son." Jack ruffled the boy's hair gently. "They're not ready for us yet."

"Avery," Ella exclaimed as she saw me, "what an amazing job you've done. I was just telling Sofia that it looks like Disneyland out there."

"I'm so glad you're happy with it."

"I'm never having a party without the two of you again. Can I keep you on retainer like lawyers?"

"Yes," Sofia said immediately.

Laughing, I turned my attention to the baby in Ella's arms. The infant was adorably chubby and pink-cheeked, with big blue eyes and curly blond hair pulled up in a topknot.

"Who is this?" I asked.

"That's my sister, Mia," the little boy answered before Ella could reply, "and I'm Luke, and I want to go to the party!"

"It'll be ready soon," I promised. "You can be the first one to go outside."

Deciding that it had fallen to him to make introductions, Luke pointed to the couple nearby. "That's my aunt Haven. She's got a big tummy. There's a baby in there."

"Luke —" Ella began, but he continued earnestly.

"She eats more than Uncle Hardy, and he could eat a whole *dinosaur.*"

Ella clapped a hand to her forehead. "Luke —"

"I did once," Hardy Cates said, lowering to his haunches. He was big and ruggedly built, a good-looking man with the bluest eyes I had ever seen. "Back when I was a boy camping in the Piney Woods. My friends and I were chasing armadillos across a dry river bottom, and we saw a big shape moving through the trees . . ."

The child listened, enraptured, as Hardy told him a tall tale about a dinosaur being pursued, lassoed, and eventually barbecued.

No doubt the prospect of marrying the only daughter in the Travis family would have deterred more than a few men. But Hardy Cates didn't seem like the type who was capable of being intimidated. He was a former roughneck who had started his own oil recovery company, going into spent fields to extract leftover reserves that bigger companies had left behind. Ella had described him as hardworking and wily, covering up his outsize ambition with plenty of laid-back charm. Hardy seemed so affable, Ella had said, that people were fooled into thinking they'd gotten to know him, even though they hadn't. But the Travises all agreed on one thing: Hardy loved Haven intensely, would have died for her. According to Ella, Jack had facetiously claimed he almost felt sorry for the guy, being wrapped around his little sister's finger like that.

I reached out to shake Haven's hand. She was delicately pretty, with dark winged brows. A Travis, unmistakably, although she was so much slighter and smaller than her towering brothers that she seemed to be a half-scale version. She was far along in her pregnancy, her ankles swollen and her stomach so heavy that it made me want to wince in sympathy.

"Avery," she said, "it's so nice to meet you. Thanks for doing this."

"We had a lot of fun," I said. "If there's anything we can do to make the party more enjoyable, just tell me. Can I get you some lemonade? Ice water?"

"No, I'm fine."

"She should be drinking something continuously," Hardy said, coming to his wife's side. "She's dehydrated and retaining water."

"At the same time?" I asked.

Haven smiled ruefully. "Apparently so. Who knew it was possible? We just came from my weekly checkup." She leaned against Hardy, and her smile widened. "We also found out that we're having a girl."

Luke received this announcement with a look of disgust. *"Awwww . . ."*

Amid the general congratulations, I heard

a familiar deep voice. "That's good news — we need more girls in the family." My heart kicked into a faster pace as Joe entered the room, lean and athletic in a pair of board shorts and a blue T-shirt.

He went straight to Haven, gathering her in a careful hug. Keeping her at his side, he reached out to shake Hardy's hand. "Let's just hope she has her mama's looks."

Hardy chuckled. "No one's hoping for that more than me." They prolonged the handshake for a couple of extra seconds, in the way of good friends.

Joe looked down at Haven affectionately. "How are you, sis?"

She looked up at him with chagrin. "When I'm not throwing up, I'm starving. I have aches and pains, mood swings and hair loss, and this past week I sent poor Hardy out for chicken nuggets at least a half-dozen times. Other than that, I'm great."

"I don't mind going out to get you the chicken nuggets," Hardy told her. "The hard part is watching you eat them with grape jelly."

Joe laughed and grimaced.

While Ella engaged the parents-to-be in a conversation about the doctor's visit, Joe came to me and bent to kiss my forehead. The touch of his mouth, the soft rush of his breath, sent a ripple of excitement down my spine. After the long talks we'd had, I should have felt comfortable with him. Instead I was nervous and oddly shy.

"You been busy today?" he asked.

I nodded. "Since six."

His fingers tangled gently with mine. "Can I help with something?"

Before I could reply, more of the family arrived. Gage, the oldest Travis sibling, was tall and athletic like his brothers, but his manner was quieter, composed, in comparison with their rough-and-tumble charm. His eyes were a striking pale gray, the light irises contained in darker rims.

Gage's wife, Liberty, was an attractive brunette with a warm, open smile. She introduced me to her son, Matthew, a boy of about five or six, and his big sister, Carrington, a pretty blond girl in her early teens. Everyone was laughing and talking at once, at least a half-dozen conversations happening simultaneously.

Even without prior knowledge of the Travises, I would have perceived instantly that they were a close-knit bunch. You could see and feel it in the way they interacted, with the familiarity of people who knew one another's schedules and habits. The genuine liking between them was unmistakable.

These were not relationships that would be set aside lightly or taken for granted. Having never been part of such a group, or anything remotely similar, I was fascinated but leery. I wondered how you could become part of a family like that and not be subsumed.

I stood on my toes to murmur near Joe's ear, "I have to carry some things out to the mini golf course."

"I'll come with you."

Although I began to tug my hand free, Joe's grip tightened. Amusement sparkled in his eyes as he murmured, "It's okay."

But I pulled away, reluctant to make any kind of demonstration in front of his family.

"Uncle Joe," I heard Luke ask, "is that your girlfriend?"

I turned crimson, while someone choked back a laugh.

"Not yet," Joe said easily, holding one of the French doors for me. "You have to work a little harder to get one of the good ones." He accompanied me out to the patio and reached down for a bag of miniature golf clubs and a bucket of balls. "I'll carry these," he said. "You lead the way."

As we walked across the patio and past the row of poolside cabanas, I debated inwardly about saying something to him, about giving his family the wrong impression. I didn't want them to think there was anything going on between us other than friendship. However, this didn't seem to be the right time or place to discuss it.

"Everything looks great," Joe said, taking in the arcade dessert buffet, the band setting up near the house.

"Considering how little time we had, it's not bad."

"Everyone appreciates the effort you put into it."

"I'm glad to help." I paused. "Your family seems really close. Even a bit clannish."

Joe considered that and shook his head. "I wouldn't say we're clannish. We all have outside friends and interests." As we walked over a section of mowed green lawn, he said, "I'll admit, we've seen a lot of each other since Dad died. We decided to start a charity foundation, with the four of us as the board of trustees. It's taken some time to get it up and running."

"When you were growing up," I asked, "did you have the usual fights and sibling rivalries?"

Joe's mouth twitched as if he were amused by a distant memory. "You could say that. Jack and I nearly killed each other a couple of times. But whenever we got too rough,

Gage would come and beat on us until we settled down. The way to earn a surefire killing was to do something mean to Haven — kidnap one of her dolls or scare her with a spider — Gage would come after us like the wrath of God."

"Where were your parents when all of that was happening?"

Joe shrugged. "We were left on our own a lot. Mom was always cochair of one charity or another, or busy with her friends. Dad was usually gone doing TV appearances or flying overseas."

"That must have been difficult."

"The problem wasn't Dad being gone. The problem was when he tried to make up for lost time. He was afraid we were being raised soft." Joe gestured with the bag of clubs. "See that retaining wall over there? One summer Dad had a truck unload three tons of stone in the backyard, and he told us to build a wall. He wanted us to learn the value of hard work."

I blinked at the sight of the dry-stacked wall, three feet high, extending approximately twenty feet before tapering to the ground. "*Just* the three of you?"

Joe nodded. "We cut rock with chisels and hand sledges, and stacked it, all in hundred-degree heat."

"How old were you?"

"Ten."

"I can't believe your mother allowed that."

"She wasn't happy about it. But once Dad put his foot down, there was no changing his mind. I think when he'd had a chance to think about it, he was sorry about having made the job that big. But he couldn't back down. To him, changing his mind was a weakness."

After setting down the clubs, Joe went to pour the golf balls into a painted wooden container. He glanced at the wall, squinting against the sun. "It took the three of us a month. But when we finished building the son of a bitch, we knew we could rely on each other. We'd made it through hell together. From then on we never raised a fist against each other again. No matter what. And we never took Dad's side against each other."

I reflected that while the family's wealth had conferred many advantages, none of the Travis offspring had escaped the pressures of expectation and obligation. No wonder they were close — who else would understand what their lives had been like?

Pensively, I wandered to the first hole of the mini golf course. The ramp on the diver's helmet didn't look quite straight, and I went to fiddle with it. I rolled a ball up the ramp and frowned as it bounced off the edge of the helmet's porthole. "I hope this is going to work."

Joe pulled a club from the bag, dropped a ball to the green, and putted. The ball rolled neatly across the green, up the ramp, and into the porthole. "Seems fine." He handed me the club. "You want to give it a try?"

Gamely, I placed a ball on the green and took a swing. The ball careened up the ramp, bounced off the helmet, and rolled back to me.

"You've never played golf before."

"How can you tell?" I asked dryly.

"Mostly because you're holding the club like a flyswatter."

"I hate sports," I confessed. "I always have. In school, I avoided gym class whenever possible. I faked sprains and stomachaches. On three different occasions, I told them my parakeet died."

His brows lifted. "That got you out of gym class?"

"The death of a parakeet is not an easy thing to get over, pal."

"Did you even have a parakeet?" he asked gravely.

"He was a metaphorical parakeet."

Laughter danced in his eyes. "Here, I'll

show you how to hold the club." He reached around me. "Wrap your fingers around the handle . . . No, left hand. Rest your thumb farther down the shaft . . . Perfect. Now take hold below with your right. Like this." He shaped my fingers around the grip. I took an extra breath to make up for the one that had stuck in my throat. I could feel the rise and fall of his chest, the solid, vital strength of him. His mouth was close to my ear. "Feet apart. Bend your knees a little and lean forward." Releasing me, he stood back and said, "Swing easy and follow through."

I swung, connected gently, and the ball rolled into the porthole with a satisfying *plunk.* "I did it!" I exclaimed, whirling to face him.

Joe smiled and caught me close, his hands at my waist. I looked up at him and time stopped, everything stopped. It seemed as if an electric current had locked up every muscle, and all I could do was wait help-lessly with the awareness of him flooding me.

His dark head lowered, and his mouth came to mine.

In the privacy of my imagination, I had relived his kisses, I had tasted them in my dreams. But nothing was close to the reality of him, the heat and soft, searching pressure, the intense sensuality of the way he brought up the desire slowly.

Gasping, I managed to pull back. "Joe, I . . . I'm not comfortable with this, especially in front of your family. And my employees. Someone might get the wrong impression."

"What impression would that be?"

"That there's something going on between us."

A series of expressions crossed his face: puzzlement, annoyance, mockery. "There's not?"

"No. We're friends. That's all it is for now, and that's all it's ever going to be, and . . . I have to work."

With that, I turned and strode toward the house in a subdued panic, feeling more relieved with every footstep I could put between us.

TWELVE

The band played jaunty surfer-pop as guests began to arrive. In no time at all, the house and patio were packed. People swarmed around the buffet and went out to the boardwalk arcade for dessert. A bartender served tropical drinks at a grass hut near the pool, while waitstaff walked around with trays of ice water and glasses of non-alcoholic punch.

"The mini golf course is a hit," Sofia said as we passed each other on the patio. "So is the dessert station. In fact, everything is a hit."

"Any problems with Steven?" I asked.

She shook her head. "Did you say anything to him?"

"I made it clear that anyone who disrespects you will be out on his ass."

"We couldn't afford to lose Steven."

"Out on his ass," I repeated firmly. "No one talks to you like that."

Sofia smiled at me. *"Te amo."*

For the rest of the afternoon, I stayed busy, taking care not to cross paths with Joe. A couple of times, when I passed by him, I could feel him trying to catch my gaze, but I ignored him, afraid that he would pull me into a conversation. Afraid that my face would reveal too much or that I would say something foolish.

Seeing Joe in person forced me to contend with him not as a friendly voice on the phone, but as a robust male who made no secret of the fact that he wanted me. Any notion I might have had of trying for a platonic friendship with Joe was gone. He wasn't going to settle for that. Neither would he let me slip away without a confrontation. My mind buzzed with ideas about how to handle him, what to say.

After lunch had been cleared and the caterers were washing dishes, I found Sofia and Ree-Ann standing just outside the kitchen door, drinking glasses of iced tea. They stared intently in the direction of the pool, neither of them sparing me a glance.

"What are you two looking at?" I asked.

Sofia made a shushing motion with her hand.

Following their gazes, I saw Joe emerging from the pool, shirtless and dripping. The sight of his athletic body, bronzed and taut, all those wet muscles gleaming in the sun, was spectacular. He shook his head like a dog, sending water drops flying.

"That is the hottest guy I've ever seen," Ree-Ann said reverently.

"A *papi chulo*," Sofia agreed.

Joe lowered to sit beside the pool as his nephew Luke came to him with an orange plastic water wing, the kind that slid over the upper arms. Joe pried open the valve on the plastic wing and blew air into it. I noticed a neat diagonal surgical scar on his side, parallel to his ribs, extending upward almost to his back. The line was nearly invisible, only a shade or two darker than the surrounding skin, but I could tell from the way the light hit it that the scar was slightly raised. After turning Luke around, Joe repeated the procedure on the other water wing.

"I wish he'd inflate my flotation devices," Ree-Ann said wistfully.

"Can't either of you find something productive to do?" I asked in annoyance.

"We're taking our ten-minute break," Sofia said.

Ree-Ann shook her head in admiration as Joe stood, his board shorts riding low on his hips. "Mmmn. Look at that rear view."

Scowling, I muttered, "It's not right to objectify men any more than it is for them to do it to us."

"I'm not objectifying him," Ree-Ann protested. "I'm just saying his ass is cute."

Before I could respond, Sofia said, "I think our break is over, Ree-Ann." She was struggling to hold back a laugh.

The three of us went to work in the kitchen with the catering staff as they boxed up untouched food to be taken to a women's shelter directly afterward. Glassware, dishes, and table accessories were washed and dried, table linens were put into laundry bags, the garbage was bagged, and the kitchen was scrubbed until it was spotless.

As the last of the party guests went inside to mingle with the family in the main room, Steven and Tank supervised the breakdown of the cabana tents and the dessert station, while the rest of the crew cleaned the pool and patio. After the caterers and cleanup staff had left, I walked around to make certain we had left everything exactly as we'd found it.

"Avery . . ." Sofia came out to the patio, looking satisfied but tired. "I just went through the house — it's perfect. The Travises are relaxing in the living room. Ree-Ann can drop me off at home, or I can stay here with you."

"Go with Ree-Ann. I'll ask Ella if there's anything else they'd like me to do."

"You sure?"

"Absolutely."

Sofia smiled. "I probably won't be home when you get back. I'm going to the gym."

"Tonight?" I asked incredulously.

"There's a new combo class with spinning and core training."

I gave her an arch glance. "What's his name?"

Sofia smiled sheepishly. "I don't know yet. He always takes bike twenty-two. Last spin class, he challenged me to a race."

"Who won?"

"He did. But only because I was distracted by his glutes."

I laughed. "Have a good workout."

After Sofia left, I continued to walk around the pool. Sunset wouldn't occur for another couple of hours, but the low-slung light was already braised with the last red fire of day. I was hot and sticky, and my feet were sore from walking back and forth across the patio. Sighing, I slipped off my sandals and flexed my toes and arches.

As I glanced into the water, I noticed a small, brightly colored object at the bottom of the pool. It looked like a child's toy. The cleanup crew had left by then; I was the only one outside. I walked to the shed where pool supplies were kept and found a long-handled net hung on a wall rack. It was the kind of net used for skimming debris. After fumbling to extend the telescoping handle to its fullest length, I crouched at the edge of the pool and sank the net as deep as I could. Unfortunately, it wasn't long enough.

One of the patio doors opened and closed. Somehow I knew it was Joe, even before I heard him ask casually, "Need a hand?"

I felt a thrill of worry, shrinking inwardly as I wondered if he would want to talk.

"I'm trying to get something out of the pool," I replied. "It looks like a kid's toy." Standing, I offered the pool net to Joe. "Do you want to give it a try?"

"That won't reach. It's about fourteen feet deep. We used to have a diving board at that end." Joe stripped off his shirt and dropped it to the sun-warmed tile.

"You don't have to —" I began, but he had already dived cleanly into the water, heading straight to the bottom with powerful, efficient strokes.

He emerged with a red-and-yellow toy car. "It's Luke's," he said, setting it on the side. "I'll take it in to him."

"Thank you."

Joe seemed in no hurry to get out of the pool. After pushing back his wet hair, he braced his folded arms on the tiled edge. Feeling that it would seem rude to just walk away, I lowered myself to sit on my heels, bringing our gazes closer to the same level.

"Did Haven enjoy the party?" I asked.

Joe nodded. "It was a good day for her. For all of us. The family doesn't want to clear out yet — they're talking about sending out for Chinese." A brief hesitation. "Why don't you stay and have dinner?"

"I should probably go home," I said. "I'm tired and sweaty. I wouldn't be good company."

"You don't need to be good company. That's the point of family: They have to tolerate you anyway."

I smiled. "It's your family, not mine. Technically they don't have to tolerate me."

"They will if I want them to."

Hearing a mockingbird's raggedy cry, I glanced at the distant tangle of trumpet vines and wax myrtle that bordered the bayou. Another mockingbird responded. Back and forth, one aggressive shriek after another.

"Are they fighting?" I asked.

"Could be a boundary dispute. But this time of year, there's still a chance they're courting."

"So it's a serenade?" The birds shrieked with all the musicality of torn sheet metal. "God, how romantic."

"It gets better when they reach the chorus."

I laughed and made the mistake of looking into his eyes. We were too close. I could smell his skin, sun and salt and chlorine. His hair was disheveled, and I wanted to smooth the wet locks, play with them.

"Hey," Joe said gently. "Why don't you come in here with me?"

The look in his eyes sent a rush of hot color over my face. "I don't have a swimsuit."

"Jump in with your clothes on. They'll dry out."

I shook my head with a flustered laugh. "I can't do that."

"Then take them off and swim in your underwear." His tone was practical, but I saw the mischief in his eyes.

"You," I informed him, "are out of your mind."

"Come on. It'll feel good."

"I'm not going to do something stupid with you just because it feels good." After a pause, I added with chagrin, "Again."

Joe laughed in that soft way he had, smoky

and deep in his throat. "Come in here." He caught my wrist lightly with one hand.

"There's no way I'm . . . *Hey.*" My eyes widened as I felt him exerting tension on my wrist. "Joe, I swear I'll kill you —"

One gentle tug was all it required to pull me off balance. I toppled forward with a little scream, into the water, readily enclosed in his waiting arms.

"Damn you!" I began to splash him furiously, flailing. "I can't believe you did that. . . . Stop laughing, you idiot! This is not funny!"

Snorting and chuckling, Joe grabbed me and pressed kisses wherever he could, on my head and neck and ear. I struggled indignantly, but his arms were too strong and his hands were everywhere. It was like wrestling an octopus.

"You are so damn cute," he gasped. "Like a little wet cat. Sweetheart, don't wear yourself out, you can't kick someone underwater."

As he played and I struggled, we slid to deeper water, and my feet left the bottom. Instinctively I clutched at him. "It's too deep."

"I've got you." Joe was still standing, one arm locking low on my hips. Some of his playfulness melted into concern. "Can you swim?"

"It would have been nice to ask before pulling me in," I said testily. "Yes, I can swim. But not well. And I don't like deep water."

"You're safe." He pulled me closer. "I'd never let anything happen to you. Now that you're in here, you might as well stay for a few minutes. Feels good, doesn't it?"

It did, although I wasn't about to give him the satisfaction of admitting it.

My clothes turned virtually transparent, the wet cotton billowing and undulating like the fins of exotic sea creatures. One of my hands encountered the diagonal scar at the side of Joe's chest. Hesitantly, I let my fingertips follow the slight ridge.

"This is from the boat accident?"

"Uh-huh. Surgery for a blood clot and a partially collapsed lung." One of his hands ventured beneath the drifting hem of my tunic to find the bare skin of my waist. "You know what that whole damn experience taught me?" he asked softly.

I shook my head, staring into his eyes, seeing reflected glimmers of sunset like tiny rushlights.

"Don't waste a minute of your life," he said. "Look for every reason you can to be happy. Don't hold back, thinking you'll have more time later . . . none of us can ever be sure about that."

"That's what makes life so scary," I said soberly.

Joe shook his head, smiling. "That's what makes it great." He lifted me higher, closer, and my hands crept around his neck.

Just before his lips met mine, a sound attracted his attention. He glanced over his shoulder as someone approached. "What do you want?" he asked irritably.

I started as I heard his brother Jack's laconic reply. "Heard someone holler."

Mortified to be caught in the pool with nowhere to hide, I shrank against Joe's chest.

"Did Avery fall in?" I heard Jack ask.

"No, I dunked her."

"Nice move" came the deadpan reply. "Want me to bring y'all a couple of towels?"

"Yeah, later. For now, I'd like some privacy."

"Sure thing."

After Jack left, I wriggled free from Joe and swam toward the shallow end. He kept pace with me, surging through the water with the ease of a dolphin. When I could stand with the water at chest level, I stopped and turned to face him with a scowl. "I don't like to be embarrassed. And I don't like to be pulled into swimming pools!"

"Sorry." He tried to look and sound contrite, with only limited success. "I wanted to get your attention."

"My *attention*?"

"Yeah." He moved around me slowly, his gaze holding mine. "You've been ignoring me all day."

"I was working."

"And ignoring me."

"All right," I admitted, "I was ignoring you. I don't know how we're supposed to behave in front of people. I'm not even sure what we're doing, and —" I broke off uneasily. "Joe, stop circling like that. I feel like I'm in the pool with a bull shark."

He reached for me, pulling me forward until I was lifted off my feet, the momentum floating me against him. Pressing a scorching kiss to my neck, he murmured, "I'd like to take a bite out of you."

As I tried to wriggle out of his arms, he gathered me up, deliberately keeping me off balance. "Come back here."

"What are you doing?"

"I want to talk to you." He took me to deeper water, where I was forced to cling to the hard slopes of his shoulders.

"About what?" I asked anxiously.

"About the problem we're having."

"Just because I don't want to have a relationship with you doesn't mean I have a problem."

"I agree. But if you wanted to have a relationship and you couldn't because you were afraid of something . . . then you would have a problem. And it'd be my problem, too."

The skin of my face tightened until I could feel my cheeks pulsing. "I want to get out of the pool."

"Let me say something — just give me a couple of minutes — and then I'll let you go. Deal?"

I responded with a quick nod.

There was something spare and focused in the way he spoke. "Everyone has secrets they don't want anyone to know. When you reckon all of it up . . . all those things we did or were done to us . . . all our sins and mistakes and guilty pleasures . . . those secrets are the sum of who we are. Sometimes you have to take a chance on letting someone in, because your gut tells you that person's worth it. But then all bets are off. You have to trust them, and hope they won't rip your heart out, and fuck it, sometimes you make the wrong call." He paused. "But you have to keep taking chances on the wrong people till you find the right one. You quit too damn early, Avery."

I felt suffocated and miserable. It didn't matter that he was right; I wasn't ready for this. For him. "I'd like to get out now." My voice came out thin and rickety.

Joe began to tow me to the shallow end. "Have you ever looked yourself up online, honey?"

Bewildered, I shook my head. "Steven handles most of the Internet stuff —"

"I don't mean your business. I mean your own name. The first results page is all related to your work: some blogs that mention you, a link to a Pinterest board, that kind of stuff. But on the second page, there's a link to an older article in a New York paper . . . about a bride who was jilted on her wedding day."

I felt myself turn bleach white.

Sometimes when I thought about that day, I could will myself into a state of detachment and view it as if it had happened to someone else. I tried to do that right now, but I couldn't manage to put any distance between me and that memory. I couldn't be detached about anything when Joe was holding me. And he was going to force me to explain how, on what should have been the happiest day of my life, I'd been rejected, abandoned, and humiliated in front of everyone whose opinion mattered to me. For a woman with normal self-esteem, that day would have been devastating. For a woman whose self-esteem hadn't been all that robust to begin with, it had been annihilating.

I closed my eyes as shame scalded every vein like poison. People who had experienced true shame didn't fear death the way regular people did . . . we knew that death would be a lot easier to tolerate. "I can't talk about it," I whispered.

Joe guided my wet head to his shoulder. "The groom called it off that morning," he continued evenly. "No one would have blamed the bride for falling apart. But instead she started making calls. She changed all the plans she'd made, so she could donate the wedding reception — which she'd paid for — to a local charity. And she spent the rest of the day with two hundred homeless people, treating them to a five-course dinner with live music. She was a fine, generous woman, and well rid of the asshole."

It was a long time before I could speak. Joe's fingers shaped to my skull and he kept his hand there, as if he were protecting me from something. I needed this more than I would have believed, latched so securely against him that his body formed the necessary margin, the boundary between me and the rest of the world.

It was more intimate than sex, to have someone hold the broken pieces of you together like that.

Gradually, I felt warmth coming back into my body, sensation returning until I was aware of his bare shoulder against my cheek, how hot and smooth the skin was. "I didn't want it in the paper," I said. "I asked the shelter not to say anything."

"It's hard to keep a gesture like that secret." Turning his mouth to my ear, he kissed it gently. "Can you tell me just a little, sweetheart? About what he said that morning?"

I swallowed hard. "Brian called and told me he wouldn't be at the ceremony. I thought he meant he was going to be late, so I asked if he was caught in traffic, and he said no, he wasn't coming at all. I was so shocked, I couldn't say anything. I couldn't even ask why. He said he was sorry, but he wasn't sure if he'd ever loved me . . . or maybe he'd loved me but it had just gone away."

"If it's real," Joe said quietly, "it doesn't

go away."

"How do you know?"

"Because that's what real is."

We moved slowly through the water, turning, floating in a lazy push and pull. I had no connection to anything except Joe, no contact with solid ground. He was in absolute control, leading me in a languid glide, and I was lulled by the peculiar sensuality of it.

"Brian didn't cheat on me, or anything like that," I found myself saying. "He had a terrible lifestyle — no one who works on Wall Street should even try to have a relationship until they're at least thirty. The schedule was insane. Eighty-hour workweeks, heavy drinking, no exercise, no spare time . . . Brian could never stop long enough to figure out what he really wanted."

As Joe turned in a slow circle, I found myself wrapping around him like a mermaid. "Sometimes you think you love someone," I said, "but it's really just that they've become a habit. At the last minute, Brian realized that was how he felt about me."

Joe pulled my arms around his neck, locking my fingers together at his nape. I brought myself to look into his eyes, lost in the dark, steady heat. Our progress around the pool resumed, and I held on to him, drifting easily. Whatever Joe's opinions were about Brian — and no doubt he had some strong ones — he kept to himself for now. He was quiet, waiting patiently for whatever I might want to tell him. Somehow that made it easier to confide the rest, the part that only Sofia knew.

"I went to my father after Brian called," I said. "I'd paid for him to fly up from Texas, so he could walk me down the aisle. My mother was livid when she found out. She and I were never all that close — I think we were both relieved when I left home to go to school. I love her, but I've always known that something wasn't right between us. She got married and divorced twice after Dad left us, but of all the men in her past, he was the one she hated the most. She always said that getting involved with him was the worst mistake she ever made. I don't think she can ever look at me without thinking of me as the daughter of the mistake."

We were in deep water now. I tightened my arms around Joe's neck.

"I've got you," he said, his tone reassuring. "Go on."

"My mother said she wouldn't come if Eli was there. She said I had to choose between them. And I chose him. That was pretty much the end of our relationship — she and I have hardly talked since then. I've invited her to come to Houston and meet Sofia, but she always refuses." I relaxed as Joe eased us to shallower water. "I don't know why I wanted Eli there so badly. He'd never done any of the things fathers were supposed to do. I guess I thought having him walk me down the aisle would make up for some of that. It felt like it would make everything right."

Joe's face was unreadable as he looked down at me. "What happened when you told him that Brian had called off the wedding?"

"He gave me a tissue, and hugged me, and I remember thinking, *This is my dad, and he's here for me, and I can lean on him when I'm in trouble, and it might even be worth losing Brian to find that out.* But then he said . . ."

"What?" Joe prompted when I fell silent.

"He said, 'Avery, it was never going to last anyway.' He told me that men weren't cut out for monogamy — you know, the biological thing — and he said most men ended up disappointed with their wives. He said he wished someone had told him a long time ago that no matter how much in love you were — no matter how convinced you

216

were that you'd found 'the one' — you would always find out when it was too late that you'd been lying to yourself." I smiled bleakly. "It was my father's way of being kind. He was trying to help me by telling me the truth."

"His truth. Not everyone else's."

"It's my truth too."

"The hell it is." Joe's voice had changed, no longer quite so patient. "You spend most of your time planning one wedding after another. You started a business doing that. Some part of you believes in it."

"I believe in marriage for some people."

"But not for yourself?" When it became clear that I wasn't going to reply, he said, " 'Course you don't. The two most important men in your life gave you a hell of a one-two punch, at a time when you couldn't protect yourself." Fervently he added, "I'd like to go back and kick both their asses."

"You can't. My father's gone, and Brian's not worth it."

"I still might kick his ass someday." Joe's hold on me altered, his hands becoming bolder, more intimate. The sky had turned blood orange, the hot evening air pungent with lantana. "When do you think you'll be ready to try another relationship?"

In the electric silence that followed, I didn't dare tell him what I really thought . . . that rehashing the sad, bitter memories had reminded me how much I wanted to avoid becoming involved with him. "When I find the right kind of man," I said eventually.

"What kind is that?"

I tensed as I felt his fingers sliding beneath the back placket of my bra. "Independent," I said. "Someone who agrees that we don't have to experience everything together. A guy who doesn't mind if we have separate interests and separate friends, and separate households. Because I like a lot of alone time —"

"What you just described isn't a relationship, Avery. It's friends with benefits."

"No, I wouldn't mind being part of a couple. I just don't want a relationship to take over everything."

We had stopped at the side of the pool, my back to the wall. My toes wouldn't quite touch the bottom, obliging me to cling to the hard slopes of his shoulders. I dropped my gaze and found myself staring at his chest, mesmerized by the way the water had darkened and flattened the coarse hair.

"That sounds like the same setup you had with Brian," I heard him say.

"Not exactly the same," I said defensively.

"But yes, something like that. I know what's right for me."

I felt a deft tug at the back of my bra, the heavy padded cups loosening. I gasped, my legs churning in a search for traction. His hands slid to my breasts, caressing me under the water, teasing the hardening tips. He pressed me back against the wall, his thigh intruding between mine. "Joe —" I protested.

"Now it's my turn to talk." The sound of his voice in my ear was pure sin. "I'm the guy who's right for you. I may not be what you're looking for, but I'm what you want. You've been alone long enough, honey. It's time for you to wake up with a man in your bed. Time for the kind of sex that lays you out, owns you, leaves you too shaky to pour your morning coffee." He pulled me more fully against his thigh, the intimate pressure making me weak with desire. "You're going to have it every night, any way you want it. I have the time for you, and I sure as hell have the energy. I'll make you forget every man you ever knew before me. The catch is, you have to trust me first. That's the hard part, isn't it? You can't let anyone get too close. Because someone who knows you like that, he could hurt you —"

"That's enough." I floundered and pushed

at him clumsily, dying to make him shut up.

His head lowered, and he kissed the side of my neck, using his tongue, making me squirm. In the middle of the twisting and splashing, he wedged both legs between mine and slid a hand over my bottom. I whimpered as he pulled me up against him, *there,* making me feel how big he was, how ready, and all my senses focused on that stiff, tantalizing pressure.

Gripping his hand in my hair, Joe brought my mouth to his and kissed me, deep and hungry. His other hand kept urging my hips closer, forcing me to ride him in an erotic protean rhythm, and I couldn't believe how damned shameless he was, and how good he felt, his body so hot and hard against mine. He was deliberate, doing exactly as he pleased, feeding every sensation with raw lust.

As the pleasure climbed, I couldn't stand it anymore, I had to wrap my legs around him, my nerves screaming, *yes, yes, now,* and nothing mattered except his hands and mouth and body, the way he was taking me over, bringing more and more pleasure to my dazzled senses. All I wanted was to kiss him and writhe against that relentless heat. I needed this so badly, the feeling that had begun to roll up to me with visceral force —

"Baby, no," Joe said hoarsely, pulling away with a shiver. "Not here. Wait. This isn't . . . no."

Clinging to the side of the pool, I stared at him with bewildered fury. I couldn't think straight. I was throbbing in every limb. My brain was slow to process that we weren't going to finish.

"You . . . you . . ."

"I know. I'm sorry. Hell." Breathing heavily, he turned away, the muscles of his back bunched and sharply delineated. "I didn't mean to take it that far."

I was temporarily incoherent with rage. Somehow this man had gotten me to confide in him until I was more vulnerable than I'd ever been with anyone, and then after driving me half-crazy with sexual frustration, he'd called a halt at the last minute. *Sadist.* I made my way toward the shallowest part of the pool and tried to fasten the back of my bra. But I was shaking and unsteady, and my wet shirt clung obstinately to my skin. I struggled with the sopping mess.

Joe came up behind me and rummaged beneath the back of my shirt. "I promised we'd take it slow," he muttered, hooking up my bra. "But I can't seem to keep my hands off you."

"You don't have to worry about that now," I said vehemently. "Because I wouldn't touch you with a ten-foot pole, unless you were dangling off the edge of a cliff, and then I would use that pole to *clobber* you."

"I'm sorry —" Joe began to put his arms around me from behind, but I shrugged him off and sloshed away in high dudgeon. He followed, continuing apologetically, "After our first time turning out like it did, I couldn't let the second time happen in a swimming pool."

"There's not going to be a second time." With effort, I hauled myself out of the pool. The wet clothes felt as heavy as chain mail. "I'm not going into the house like this. I need a towel. And my purse, which is on one of the kitchen counters." I sat on a lounge chair, trying to look as dignified as possible while water streamed off me.

"I'll get it." Joe paused. "About dinner . . ."

I gave him a withering glance.

"Forget dinner," he said hastily. "I'll be right back."

After he had brought the towels and I had dried off as much as possible, I walked to my car, with Joe at my heels. My hair was stringy and my clothes were clammy. The evening air was still warm, and I was overheated, almost steaming. As I sat in my car seat, I could feel the upholstery soaking up the water from my clothes. *If my car interior turns moldy,* I thought furiously, *I am going to make him pay to have the seats re-covered.*

"Wait." Joe held the edge of the car door before I could close it. To my outrage, he didn't look at all remorseful. "Are you going to answer when I call?" he asked.

"No."

That didn't seem to surprise him. "Then I'll show up at your place."

"Don't even think about it. I've had enough of your manhandling."

I could tell from the way he chewed on his lip that he was trying to hold back a smart-ass comment. Losing the battle, he said, "If I'd manhandled you just a little longer, honey, you'd be a hell of a lot happier right now."

I reached for the car door and slammed it shut. Extending my middle finger, I flipped him off through the window. As I started the car, Joe turned away . . . but not before I saw the flash of his grin.

THIRTEEN

Sunday night went by without a word from Joe. So did Monday night. I waited with growing impatience for him to call. I kept my cell phone with me at all times, pouncing on every call or text.

Nothing.

"I don't give a damn if you call or not," I muttered, glaring at the silent phone on its charger. "I couldn't be less interested, as a matter of fact."

Which was a lie, of course, but it felt good to say it.

The truth was, I couldn't stop reliving those weightless floating moments with Joe in the swimming pool, the memory cringe-inducing and haunting and wildly pleasurable. The way he had talked to me . . . unsparing, sexual . . . I'd felt his words sinking inside me, right through my skin. And the promises he'd made . . . was any of that even possible?

The idea of letting go, with him, was terrifying. Feeling that much. Flying that high. I didn't know what would happen afterward, what internal mechanisms might be shattered by the altitude, how much oxygen would be robbed from my blood. Or if a safe landing was even an option.

On Tuesday morning, I had to turn my full focus on Hollis Warner and her daughter, Bethany, who were visiting the studio for the first time. Ryan had proposed over the weekend, and from what Hollis had told me on the phone, Bethany had been delighted with the sand-castle proposal. The weekend had been romantic and relaxing, and the newly engaged couple had discussed possible wedding dates.

To my consternation — and Sofia's — the Warners wanted the ceremony to be held in four months.

"We're on a time limit," Bethany told me, her hand sliding to her flat stomach. "Four months is all we've got before I show too much for the kind of wedding dress I want."

"I understand," I said, keeping my expression impassive. I didn't dare look at Sofia, who was seated nearby with her sketch pad, but I knew she had to be thinking the same thing: No one could pull off a megawedding that fast. Every decent location would be booked up, and the same could be said for all the good vendors and musicians. "However," I continued, "a time frame that narrow is going to limit our options. Have you thought about having the baby first? That way —"

"No." Bethany gave me a chilling blue-eyed glare. In the next moment her face relaxed, and she smiled sweetly. "I'm an old-fashioned girl. To me, the wedding has to come before the baby. If that means the wedding has to be a little smaller, Ryan and I are fine with that."

"I'm not fine with a smaller wedding," Hollis said. "Anything less than four hundred guests is not possible. This occasion is going to show the old guard that we're a family to be reckoned with." She gave me a small smile that didn't quite coordinate with her fierce, fixed stare. "This is Bethany's wedding, but it's my show. I just want everyone to remember that."

This was not the first time I'd planned a wedding in which people had brought different agendas to the table. But it was the first time the mother of the bride had been so blunt about wanting the occasion to be her show.

It couldn't have been easy to grow up in the shadow of such a mother. Some children of dominating parents turned out to be timid and insecure, desperate not to attract attention. Bethany, however, seemed to be have been made in the same tough, diamond-hard mold. Although Bethany wanted a stylish wedding, it was clear that above all she desired expediency. I couldn't help wondering if she was worried about Ryan wriggling off the hook.

The pair sat side by side on the blue sectional, their legs crossed identically on the diagonal. Bethany was a gorgeous young woman, lean and lanky, her hair long, white blond, and stick straight. A large engagement solitaire glittered on her left hand as she draped her arm gracefully along the back of the sofa.

"Mother," she said to Hollis, "Ryan and I have already agreed that we're only going to invite guests that we have personal connections to."

"What about *my* personal connections? An ex-president and first lady —"

"We're not going to invite them."

Hollis stared at her daughter as if she had just spoken in tongues. "Of course we are."

"I've been to weddings with Secret Service, Mother. Bomb-sniffing dogs, the magnetometers, everything in lockdown for a five-mile radius . . . Ryan wouldn't stand for it. There's only so far I can push him."

"Why isn't anyone worried about pushing *me*?" Hollis asked, and laughed angrily. "Everyone knows the mother is in charge of the wedding. It's all going to reflect on *me*."

"That doesn't mean you can bully everyone into doing what you want."

"I'm the one being bullied. I'm the one everyone's trying to sideline!"

"Whose wedding is this?" Bethany asked. "You had your own. Do you have to take mine too?"

"Mine was *nothing* compared to this." Hollis shot me an incredulous glance as if to convey how impossible her daughter was. "Bethany, do you know how much you have in your life that I didn't get?"

"Of course I do. You never stop talking about it."

"No one is being sidelined," I interceded hastily. "We all have the same goal, for Bethany to have the wedding she deserves. Let's get the contractual obligations out of the way, and then we can start working on a master guest list. I'm sure we can find some ways to pare it down. We'll consult with Ryan, of course."

"Isn't it up to me to decide —" Hollis began.

"I'm positive we can have Bethany

featured as bride of the month in *Southern Weddings* and *Modern Bride,*" I interrupted, trying to distract her.

"And *Texas Bride,*" Sofia added.

"Not to mention some local media coverage leading up to the wedding," I continued. "First we'll come up with a compelling narrative —"

"I know all that," Hollis said irritably. "I've been interviewed dozens of times about my galas and fund-raisers."

"Mother knows everything," Bethany said in a saccharine tone.

"One of the most appealing angles to this story," I said, "is about a mother's and daughter's joy in planning a wedding together while the daughter is expecting her own child. That could be a great hook for —"

"We're not going to mention the pregnancy," Hollis said decisively.

"Why not?" Bethany asked.

"The old guard won't approve. It used to be that these situations were covered up and kept quiet, which is still the best way, if you ask me."

"I didn't ask you," Bethany retorted. "I haven't done anything to be ashamed of, and I'm not going into hiding. I'm marrying the father of my child. If the old bitches don't like it, they should try living in the twenty-first century. Besides, my bump is going to be obvious by the time the wedding takes place."

"You'll have to watch your weight, sweetheart. Eating for two is a myth. During my entire pregnancy, I only gained fifteen pounds. You're already looking puffy."

"Bethany," Sofia broke in with artificial cheer, "you and I need to arrange a time to brainstorm ideas and color palettes."

"I'll come too," Hollis said. "You'll want my ideas."

After the Warners had left the studio, Sofia and I collapsed on the sectional and groaned in unison.

"I feel like roadkill," I said.

"Are they going to act like this the whole time?"

"This is only the beginning." I stared up at the ceiling. "By the time we make it to the seating plan, blood will have been shed."

"Who is the old guard?" Sofia asked. "And why does Hollis keep talking about him?"

"It's not a him, it's a them. An older, established group that wants everything to stay the same. There can be an old guard in a society, in politics, a sports organization, pretty much any group you can come up with."

"Oh. I thought she meant someone in the army."

It was probably because of the contentious meeting we'd just been through, and the sudden release from tension, but Sofia's innocent remark struck me as irresistibly funny. I began to laugh.

A throw pillow came flying out of nowhere, hitting me in the face.

"What was that for?" I demanded.

"You're laughing at me."

"I'm not laughing at you, I'm laughing at what you said."

Another pillow struck me. I sat up and fired it back at her. Giggling wildly, Sofia leapt over the back of the sofa. I leaned over and whacked her with a pillow and ducked as she popped up to swat me again.

We were so busy that neither of us noticed the front door opening and closing.

"Uh . . . Avery?" came Val's voice. "I brought sandwiches for lunch, and —"

"Just set it on the counter," I called, leaning over the back of the sofa to wallop Sofia. "We're having an executive meeting." *Thwack.*

Sofia launched a counterattack, while I flung myself to the sofa cushions. *Thwack.*

Thwack.

"*Avery.*" A note in Val's voice caused my sister to stop. "We have a visitor."

I lifted my head and peeked over the sofa back. My eyes widened as I saw Joe Travis standing there.

Mortified, I dropped back out of sight. I lay back on the sofa, my heart thundering. He was here. He had shown up, as he'd said he would. I felt light-headed. Why hadn't he chosen a moment when I'd been composed and professional, instead of finding me in the middle of a pillow fight with my sister like a couple of twelve-year-olds?

"We were letting off steam," I heard Sofia say, still breathless.

"Can I watch?" Joe asked, making her laugh.

"I think we're done now."

Joe walked around the sectional and came to stand over me as I lay on my back. His gaze skimmed briefly over the length of my body. I was wearing another one of my shapeless but expensive dresses, black and sleeveless. Although the hem usually reached to midcalf, it had ridden above my knees when I'd flopped onto the sofa.

I couldn't look at him without remembering the last time we'd been together, the way I'd writhed and kissed him and told him everything. Mortified color blanketed me head to toe. What made it worse was that Joe smiled as if he understood exactly what was causing my distress.

"You have great legs," he said as he reached down for me, his fingers closing around mine. I was hauled to my feet with easy strength. "I told you I'd show up," he murmured.

"A little more advance notice would have been nice." Hastily I pulled my hand away from his and tugged my dress into place.

"And give you a chance to run?" He pushed back a wave of hair that had fallen over my eyes and tucked another behind my ear with unmistakable familiarity.

Conscious of Sofia's and Val's interested regard, I cleared my throat and said in a professional voice, "What can I help you with?"

"I came by to see if you wanted to go out to lunch. There's a Cajun diner downtown — it's not fancy, but the food is good."

"Thank you, but Val already brought sandwiches."

"I didn't bring anything for you, Avery," Val called from the kitchen. "Just for me and Sofia."

Like hell. I looked around Joe's shoulder, ready to call Val on it, but she ignored me, staying busy in the kitchen.

Sofia smiled at me, her eyes mischievous. "Go have lunch, *mi hermana.*" Deliberately she added, "Take as long as you want — your schedule is clear for the rest of the afternoon."

"I had plans," I said. "I was going to look over everyone's expense accounts."

Sofia gave Joe an imploring glance. "Keep her away as long as possible," she said, and he laughed.

"I'll do that."

The Cajun diner was lined with a counter and steel-framed stools on one side and a row of booths on the other. The atmosphere was agreeably boisterous, the air filled with brisk conversation, the scrape of flatware on melamine plates, and the rattling of ice cubes in tall glasses of sweet tea. Waitresses carried plates filled with steaming food . . . étouffée thick with plump crawfish tails, ladled over patties of grits fried in butter . . . po'boy rolls stuffed with lobster and shrimp.

To my relief, our conversation stayed in safe territory, with no mention of our last encounter. As I described the meeting with the Warners, Joe was amused and sympathetic.

The waitress brought out our order, two

plates of pompano that had been stuffed with shrimp and crabmeat and baked in foil pouches with a butter-and-wine velouté sauce. Every bite was creamy and tender, melting luxuriously on my tongue.

"I have an ulterior motive for asking you out today," Joe said as we ate. "I need to stop by an animal shelter and take some pictures of a couple of new dogs. Want to come and help?"

"I'll try . . . but I don't think I'm good with dogs."

"Are you afraid of them?"

"No, I've just never been around them."

"It'll be fine. I'll tell you what to do."

After lunch, we drove to the shelter, a small brick building with abundant windows and crisp white trim. A sign featuring cartoon cats and dogs read "Happy Tails Rescue Society." Joe pulled a camera bag and a duffel bag from the back of his Jeep, and we walked into the shelter. The lobby was bright and cheerful, featuring an interactive screen where visitors could browse through photos and descriptions of available animals.

An elderly man with a shock of white hair came from behind the counter to greet us, his blue eyes twinkling as he shook hands with Joe. "Millie called you about the latest group?"

"Yes, sir. She said four had been sent by a city shelter."

"Another one arrived this morning." The man's friendly gaze turned to me.

"Avery, this is Dan," Joe said. "He and his wife, Millie, built this place five years ago."

"How many dogs do you keep here?" I asked.

"We average about a hundred. We try to take the ones that other places have trouble adopting out."

"We'll go to the back and set up," Joe said. "Bring out the first one whenever you're ready, Dan."

"You bet."

Joe led me to an exercise area in the back of the building. The room was spacious, the rubber floor designed like a black-and-white checkerboard. One wall was lined with a low-slung red vinyl sofa. There was a basket of dog toys and a plastic children's playhouse with a ramp.

After taking a Nikon from a camera bag, Joe attached a lens and adjusted the exposure and scene modes. All of it was accomplished with the quickness and ease of someone who'd done it a million times before. "First I take a couple of minutes to get to know the dog a little," he said. "Some of them are nervous, especially if they've been neglected or abused. The important thing to remember is not to approach a dog directly and step into his space. He'll see that as a threat. You're the pack leader — the follower is supposed to come to you. No eye contact at first, just stay calm and ignore him until he gets used to you."

The door opened, and Dan led in a large black dog with raggedy ears. "This here's Ivy," he said. "A Lab-retriever mix. Blinded in one eye after she got caught into a bob-wire fence. No one can get a good picture because of the coloring."

"Solid black is tricky for lighting," Joe said. "Do you think she can handle it if I bounce a flash from the ceiling?"

"Sure, Ivy was a gun dog. A flash won't bother her a bit."

Setting aside the camera, Joe waited as Ivy came to sniff his hand. He petted her and scratched her neck. Her one good eye closed in ecstasy, and she panted happily. "Who's a good girl?" Joe asked, lowering to his haunches, rubbing her chest and neck.

Ivy padded over to the basket of toys, pulled out a stuffed gator, and brought it to Joe. He tossed the toy into the air, and Ivy caught it deftly. She brought the toy back, her tail wagging enthusiastically, and the process was repeated a few more times. Eventually Ivy dropped the toy and wandered toward me, sniffing curiously.

"She wants to meet you," Joe said.

"What should I do?"

"Stand still and let her smell your hand. Then you can rub under her chin."

Ivy sniffed a fold of my skirt, and then her cold nose touched against my hand. "Hello, Ivy," I murmured, stroking her beneath the chin and on her chest. The dog's jaw relaxed and she sat promptly, her tail thumping the floor. Her one good eye closed as I continued to pet her.

At Joe's direction, I held a reflector board while he took some shots of Ivy. She turned out to be a willing photography subject, lounging on the red sofa with a toy between her paws.

Three more dogs were brought out in turn, a beagle mix, a Yorkshire terrier, and a short-haired Chihuahua that Dan said would be the most difficult to adopt out. She was beige and white, with an adorable face with big, soft eyes, but she had two things going against her: She was ten years old, and toothless.

"Her owner had to go into assisted living," Dan explained, carrying the tiny creature into the room. "Dog's teeth went bad and every last one had to be pulled."

"Can she survive with no teeth?" I asked.

"As long as she gets soft food." Carefully, Dan set the Chihuahua on the floor. "Here you go, Coco."

The dog looked so fragile that I felt a pang of concern. "How long do they usually live?"

"This one might could last five years, maybe more. We've got a friend whose Chi lived to be eighteen."

Coco surveyed the three of us uncertainly. Her tail wagged once, twice, in a hopeful gesture that caused a sharp twinge in my heart. To my surprise, she came to me in a fit of bravery, miniature feet pattering on the floor. I leaned down to pick her up. She weighed nothing; it was like holding a bird. I could feel her heart beating against my fingers. As she strained to lick my chin, I could see hairline cracks at the tip of her tongue.

"Why is her tongue so dry?" I asked.

"She can't hold it in because of the missing teeth." Dan left the room, saying over his shoulder, "I'll let y'all get to work."

I carried the Chihuahua to the sofa and placed her on it carefully. Her ears drooped and her tail tucked between her legs. Staring up at me, she began to pant in distress.

"Everything's okay," I encouraged, backing away. "Stay still."

But Coco looked increasingly worried, creeping to the edge of the sofa as if preparing to jump and follow me. I returned and sat on the sofa. As I petted her, she crawled into my lap and tried to curl up. "What a love sponge," I said, laughing. "How do I make her sit by herself?"

"I have no idea," Joe said.

"I thought you knew how to handle dogs."

"Honey, there's no way I could convince her that a cold vinyl seat is better than your lap. If you'll keep holding her, I'll zoom the shots and make the depth of field as shallow as possible."

"So the background will be blurry?"

"Yes. See if you can get her to relax. With her ears flattened like that, she looks scared."

"What do you want her ears to do?"

"See if you can get them perked up and facing forward."

I held Coco in different poses, calling her a sweetheart, an angel, a sugar-pie, saying if she behaved, I would give her all the treats she wanted. "Are her ears perked up now?" I asked.

His mouth twitched. "Mine sure as hell are." Lowering to his haunches, he took multiple shots, the camera shutter clicking nonstop.

"Do you think someone will adopt her?"

"I hope so. It's not easy to get someone to take a senior dog. Not much time left, and health problems on the horizon."

Coco looked up at me with shining eyes and a gummy grin. I felt a sinking sensation as I thought of what would probably happen to this vulnerable, not-pretty creature.

"If life were simpler . . . ," I heard myself say, "if I were another kind of person . . . I'd take her home with me."

The shutter clicks stopped. "Do you want to?"

"It doesn't matter. I can't." I was surprised by the plangent sound of my own voice.

"That's okay."

"I have no experience with pets."

"I understand."

I held Coco up and looked at her. She regarded me earnestly with that little-old-lady face, paws dangling, tail wagging in midair. "You have too many problems," I told her.

Joe approached, looking amused. "You don't have to take her."

"I know. It's just . . ." I let out a tight, disbelieving laugh. "Somehow I can't stand the idea of walking away from her."

"Leave her here and think about it

overnight," Joe said. "You can always come back tomorrow."

"If I don't take her now, I won't come back." I held her in my lap, smoothing her fur, wondering what to do. She curled up into a little donut and closed her eyes.

Joe sat next to me, sliding an arm around my shoulders. He stayed silent, letting me think it through.

"Joe?" I asked after a couple of minutes.

"Mmm-hmm?"

"Can you give me a practical reason for taking this dog home with me? Anything at all? Because she's not big enough to protect me, and I don't need her as a service dog or to herd sheep. So give me a reason. Please."

"I'll give you three. One, a dog will give you unconditional love. Two, having a dog reduces stress. Three . . ." His arm slid away, and he turned my face toward his, his thumb stroking the edge of my jaw. He looked into my eyes and smiled. "Hell, do it because you want to," he said.

On the way back home, we stopped at a pet store for some basic supplies. Along with the basics, I bought a tote with mesh panels on the sides and a soft padded interior. As soon as I put Coco inside, she poked her head through an opening at the top and looked around. I was now a woman with a purse-dog, except that instead of a fluffy Pomeranian or a teacup poodle, mine was a toothless Chihuahua.

The studio was empty and silent when we arrived. Joe carried my purchases in from the car, including a pet crate and a case of premium canned dog food. I arranged a foam mat and a soft blanket in the crate. Coco crawled in eagerly.

"I'd like to give her a bath," I said, "but she's had enough excitement for now. I'll let her adjust to her new surroundings."

Joe set the dog food on the counter. "You sound like an expert already."

"Ha." I began to stack cans in the pantry. "Sofia's going to kill me. I should have asked her before doing this. Except that she would have said no, and I would have brought Coco home anyway."

"Tell her I pressured you."

"No, she knows I wouldn't do this unless it was something I really wanted. But thanks for offering to take the rap."

"Anytime." Joe paused. "I'll head out now."

I turned to face him, my nerves humming with anticipation as he approached. "Thanks for lunch," I said.

His warm gaze swept over me. "Thanks

243

for helping at the shelter." He reached around me, bringing me against a wealth of hard muscle. My hands crept up his back. The clean, earthy scent of him was becoming familiar, and it was a thousand times better than cologne. Finishing the hug, he let go.

"Bye, Avery," he said huskily.

I watched with wide eyes as he headed to the door. "Joe . . ."

He paused with his hand on the knob, glancing over his shoulder.

"Aren't you . . ." I blushed before continuing, "Aren't you going to kiss me?"

A slow grin crossed his face. "Nope." And he left, closing the door gently behind him.

While I stared at the door with astonished indignation, Coco ventured cautiously out of her crate.

"What is this?" I asked aloud, pacing in a tight circle. "He takes me out for lunch and brings me back with a secondhand Chihuahua, and on top of that, no kiss good-bye or any mention of when or if he's going to call. . . . What kind of game is he playing? Was this even a date?"

Coco watched me expectantly.

"Are you hungry? Thirsty?" I pointed to a corner of the kitchen. "Your bowls are over there."

She didn't move.

"Want to watch some TV?" I asked.

Her spindly tail wagged.

After scrolling through channels on the flat-screen TV, I found an episode of a telenovela that Sofia and I had been following. Despite the eye-rolling theatrics and the eighties-style hair and makeup, the story was as addictive as crack. I had to find out how it ended.

"Telenovelas teach important life lessons," Sofia had once told me. "For example, if you're in a love triangle with two handsome men who never wear shirts, remember that the one you reject will become a villain and plot to destroy you. And if you're beautiful but poor and mistreated, you were probably switched at birth with another baby who has taken your rightful place in a powerful family."

I entertained myself by reading the English subtitles to Coco, infusing high emotion in the dialogue: "I swear you will pay dearly for this outrage!" and "Now you must fight for your love!" While misting Coco's tongue with Evian spray during the commercial, I said, "Wait a minute, you don't need translation. You're a Chihuahua. You already speak Spanish."

Hearing the front door open and close, I

glanced over the back of the sofa. Sofia came in, looking demoralized.

"How's it going?" I asked.

"Remember the guy in spin class?"

"Bike twenty-two?"

"Uh-huh. We went out for drinks." She heaved a sigh. "It was *awful.* The conversation kept stalling. It was more boring than watching bananas ripen. All he does is exercise. He doesn't like to travel because it interferes with his workout schedule. He doesn't read books or keep up with the news. But the worst thing was that he kept looking at his phone for an entire hour. What kind of guy reads his phone and texts during a date? Finally I put a twenty-dollar bill on the table to pay for my share of the drinks, and said, 'I don't want to interfere with your phone time,' and I left."

"I'm so sorry."

"Now I can't even enjoy watching his glutes during spin class." Sofia plugged her phone into a charger on the counter. "How did your lunch go?"

"Great food."

"What about Joe? Did you have a good time? Was he charming?"

"It was fun," I said. "But I have something to confess."

She gave me an expectant glance. "Yes?"

"After lunch, we went shopping."

"For what?"

"A bed and a dog collar."

Her brows lifted. "That's a little kinky for a first date."

"The bed and dog collar are for an actual dog," I said.

Sofia's face went blank. "Whose?"

"Ours."

My sister walked around the sofa. Her incredulous gaze dropped to the Chihuahua in my lap. Coco shrank back against me, trembling.

"This is Coco," I said.

"Where's the dog? All I see is a mole rat with bulging eyes. And I can smell her from here."

"Don't listen to her," I told Coco. "You just need a better stylist."

"I asked you once if I could get a dog and you said it was a terrible idea!"

"I was right. It's a terrible idea if we're talking about a regular-sized dog. But this one is perfect."

"I *hate* Chihuahuas. Three of my aunts have them. They need special food and special collars and special stairs to get on the couch, and they pee five hundred times a day. If we get a dog, I want one that can go running with me."

"You don't run."

"Because I don't have a dog."

"Now we do."

"I can't run with a Chihuahua! She would drop dead after a half mile."

"So would you. I've seen you run."

Sofia looked infuriated. "I'm going to go out and buy a dog too. A *real* dog."

"Fine, go get one. Bring home a half dozen."

"Maybe I will." She scowled. "Why is her tongue hanging out like that?"

"She has no teeth."

Our gazes clashed in the charged silence.

"She can't keep her tongue in," I continued, "so it's chronically dry. But a lady at the pet store suggested massaging it with some organic coconut oil every night, and misting it with water throughout the day — Why is that funny?"

Sofia had started to choke with laughter. In fact, she could barely talk, she was snorting and wheezing so hard. "You have such high standards. You love beautiful, tasteful things. And this dog is so ugly and scraggly, and . . . *Dios mío,* she's a lemon." Sitting beside me, she reached out to let Coco smell her hand. Coco sniffed daintily and let Sofia pet her.

"She's not a lemon," I said, "she's *jolie laide.*"

"What does that mean?"

"It's a term for a woman who's not conventionally beautiful, but she's beautiful in a unique way. Like Cate Blanchett or Meryl Streep."

"Did Joe talk you into this? Are you doing it to make him think you're compassionate?"

I gave her a haughty glance. "You know that I've never wanted anyone to think of me as compassionate."

Sofia shook her head in resignation. "Come here, Meryl Streep," she said to Coco, trying to coax her out of my lap. *"Ven aquí, niña."*

Coco shrank back, panting anxiously.

"An asthmatic lemon," Sofia said, settling back in the corner of the couch with a sigh. "My mother's coming to visit tomorrow," she said after a moment.

"God, is it that time again?" I made a face. "Already?"

Every two or three months, Sofia's mother, Alameda, drove from San Antonio to visit for a night. These occasions always consisted of hours of relentless interrogation about Sofia's friends, her health, her work, and her sexual activities. Alameda had

249

never forgiven her daughter for moving so far away from the family and for ending a relationship with a young man named Luis Orizaga.

Sofia's entire family had tried to pressure her to marry Luis, whose parents were respectable and had money. According to Sofia, Luis had been overbearing and egotistical, and terrible in bed, besides. Alameda blamed me for helping Sofia to leave Luis and start a new life in Houston. As a result, Sofia's mother could barely bring herself to be civil in my presence.

For Sofia's sake, I tried to be nice to Alameda. On one level I felt sympathy for her, as I would for anyone whom my father had hurt. However, the way she treated Sofia was hard to tolerate. Since Alameda couldn't vent her anger on her ex-husband, she had made their daughter the scapegoat. I knew all too well how that felt. Sofia was always depressed for a day or two after her mother visited.

"Is she staying here?" I asked Sofia.

"No, she doesn't like sleeping on our pullout. It hurts her back. She's checking into the hotel tomorrow afternoon, and coming here for dinner at five."

"Why don't you take her out to eat?"

Sofia rested her head on the back of the

couch and rolled it in a slow negative shake. "She wants me to cook so she can tell me everything I'm doing wrong."

"Do you want me to leave while she's here?"

"It would be better if you stayed." With a half hearted smile, Sofia said, "You're good at deflecting some of the arrows."

"As many as I can," I said, feeling a rush of love for her. "Always, Sofia."

FOURTEEN

After brainstorming and mulling over ideas, Sofia had come up with two concepts for the Warner wedding. The first was a traditional formal wedding, perfectly feasible and impressive. Following a grand ceremony at Memorial Drive Methodist, a fleet of pearl-white limos would transport the guests to a crystal-and-roses ballroom reception at the River Oaks Country Club. It would be tasteful and elegant, the kind of affair that everyone would expect. But not the one we wanted the Warners to choose.

The second wedding plan was a knockout. The location was the Filter Building at White Rock Lake, near Dallas. The historic building was a spectacular lakefront industrial design, with corbeled brick and exposed iron trusses and big windows overlooking the lake. It was almost a guarantee that Ryan would love the location, which would appeal to his architectural taste.

Inspired by the Depression-era building, Sofia had conceived of a lavish Gatsbyesque wedding in creams, tans, and gold, with bridesmaids wearing drop-waist dresses and ropes of beads and the men in dinner suits. The tables would be covered in beaded fabric, and the flower arrangements would feature orchids and plumes. Guests would be transported from a hotel in Dallas to White Rock Lake in a succession of vintage Rolls-Royces and Pierce-Arrows.

"We'll make it fresh," Sofia said. "Fancy but modern. We want it to be inspired by the Jazz Age without making it too accurate, or it will look like a costume party." The team at the studio all loved the Gatsbyesque concept.

Everyone except Steven.

"You all know that Gatsby is a tragic story, right?" he asked. "Personally I wouldn't care for a wedding based on themes of power, greed, and betrayal."

"What a shame," Sofia said. "It would be so perfect for you."

Val interrupted before they could start bickering. "*The Great Gatsby* is one of those books that everyone's heard of but no one reads."

"I did," Steven said.

"Required high school reading?" Sofia asked disdainfully.

"No, for my own enjoyment. It's called literature. You should try it sometime, if you ever manage to tear yourself away from those Spanish soap operas."

Sofia's brows lowered. "You're a fine one to judge, with all the silly sports games you watch."

"That's enough, you two," I interceded, giving Steven a blistering glance.

He ignored me, picking up his phone. "I'm going to make a couple of calls. I'll be outside. I can't hear with all of you yammering."

"Go easy on him today," Tank suggested as soon as Steven wandered out of earshot. "He and his girlfriend broke up over the weekend."

Sofia's eyes widened. "He has a girlfriend?"

"They just started going out a couple of weeks ago. But on Sunday, they were watching football at his place, and all of a sudden she turned down the volume and told Steven she didn't think they should see each other again, because he was emotionally unavailable."

"What did he say?"

"He asked if they could wait to talk about it until half-time." At our looks of disgust, Tank said defensively, "We were playing the Cowboys."

The doorbell rang.

"It's *Mamá*," Sofia muttered.

"All hands to their battle stations," I said, only half kidding. Since everyone at the studio had encountered Alameda on previous occasions, they wasted no time in collecting their belongings quickly. No one had any desire to make small talk with a woman who was so utterly humorless. Every conversation with her was the same, a litany of complaints concealed within complaints, like a set of toxic Russian nesting dolls.

Sofia stood, tugged at the hem of her turquoise top, and went reluctantly to welcome her mother. She squared her shoulders before opening the door and saying brightly, "*Mamá!* How was the drive? How was —"

Breaking off abruptly, Sofia backed up as if confronted with a rearing cobra. Without thinking, I leapt from the sofa and went to her. My sister's face was leached of color except for bright pink streaks across the crest of each cheek, like signal flags sent up for a panic alert.

Alameda Cantera was at the threshold,

looking the same as always, her eyes stony and her mouth set with the bitterness of someone who had been defrauded by life. Alameda was an attractive woman, her figure small and trim in a suit jacket and hot-pink blouse and trouser jeans. The wealth of jet-black hair was pulled tightly back from her face and pinned into a controlled bun at her nape. It was an unfortunate style for someone whose hard features could have used some softening around the edges. But when Alameda had been young, before Eli had soured her, she must have been beautiful.

She had brought someone with her, a young man still in his twenties. He was black-haired, a bit heavyset, his short but muscular frame clad in pressed khakis and a crisp button-down shirt. Although he was handsome, his expression conveyed an impression of smug, sly machismo that I instinctively disliked.

"Avery," Sofia said, "this is Luis Orizaga."

Holy shit, I thought.

Even knowing Alameda, I couldn't believe she had brought her daughter's ex-boyfriend here, uninvited and *very* unwelcome. Although Luis had never been physically abusive, he had dominated Sofia in every other way, determined to extinguish every spark of independence.

Apparently, it had never occurred to Luis that Sofia might not have been happy in the relationship. It had been a shock to him when she had ended their engagement and moved to Houston to start a business with me. Luis had gone into a monthlong rage that had involved heavy drinking, multiple bar fights, and broken furniture. Less than a year later, he'd married a seventeen-year-old girl. They'd had a child, Alameda had informed Sofia peevishly, and had gone on to say that it should have been her grandchild, and Sofia should be having babies.

"Why are you here?" Sofia asked Luis. She sounded so young and vulnerable that I was tempted to push her behind me and snap at the pair in the doorway to leave her alone.

"I invited Luis to come with me," Alameda replied, aggressively cheerful, her eyes birdlike. "It's lonely to drive all that way by myself, which I have to do since *you* never come to visit *me,* Sofia. I told Luis that he never left your heart — that's why you've stayed single."

"But you're married," Sofia said, giving Luis a bewildered glance.

"We're divorced now," he said. "I gave my wife too much. I was too good to her. All that spoiling made her want to leave me."

"Of course it did," I couldn't resist saying acidly.

My comment was roundly ignored.

"I have a son named Bernardo —" Luis told Sofia.

"The most beautiful child," Alameda chimed in.

"He's almost two years old," Luis continued. "I have him every other weekend. I need help to raise him."

"You are the luckiest girl in the world, *mija*," Alameda said to Sofia. "Luis has decided to give you another chance."

I turned to Sofia. "You've hit the jackpot," I said dryly.

She was too shaken to smile. "You should have asked me first, Luis," she said. "I told you when I left Houston that I didn't want to see you again."

"Alameda explained everything," he replied. "Your sister talked you into moving away when you were grieving your father's death. You didn't know what you were doing."

I opened my mouth to protest, but Sofia made a shushing motion without even looking at me. "Luis," she said, "you know why I left. I'll never go back to you."

"Things are different. I've changed, Sofia. I know how to make you happy now."

"She's already happy," I burst out.

Alameda gave me a dismissive glance. "Avery, this does not concern you. It's a family matter."

"Don't be rude to Avery," Sofia said, flushing angrily. "She is my family."

A rapid volley of Spanish ensued, all three of them speaking at once. I couldn't follow more than a few words. In the background, Ree-Ann, Val, and Tank waited with their bags and laptops.

"Need help?" Tank asked meaningfully.

Grateful for his presence, I murmured, "Not sure yet."

Sofia looked increasingly distressed as she tried to defend herself. I inched closer, longing to intervene on her behalf. "Could we do this in English, please?" I asked crisply. No one appeared to have heard. "The fact is," I tried again, "Sofia has a great life here. A successful career. She's an independent woman." When none of that had any discernible effect, I added, "She has a new man."

To my satisfaction, an abrupt silence descended.

"That's right," Sofia said, seizing on the excuse. "I have a man, and we're engaged."

Alameda's eyes narrowed into spider-lashed slits. "You never said anything about him before. Who is he? What is his name?"

Sofia's lips parted. "He's —"

"Excuse me," Steven said, shouldering his way back into the studio through the half-open door. He paused with a quizzical frown, glancing at our blank faces in the fraught silence. "What's going on?"

"*Querido,*" Sofia exclaimed, and flung herself at him.

Before Steven could react, she wrapped her arms around his neck, tugged his head down, and pressed her mouth against his.

FIFTEEN

Taken by surprise, Steven froze as Sofia kissed him. I held my breath, silently willing him not to shove her away. His hands, suspended in the air as if by marionette strings, descended by slow degrees to her shoulders. *Take pity on her, Steven,* I thought desperately. *Just this once.*

But Steven's reaction had nothing to do with pity. His arms slid around her, and he began to kiss her as if he never wanted to stop. As if she were a dangerously addictive substance that had to be handled with care, rationed slowly, or he might die from a fatal overdose. The concentrated hunger of that blind, impassioned kiss seemed to radiate outward and heat up the entire room.

Somewhere behind me, I heard a thud on the floor. Tank had dropped his laptop. He and the two interns stared at the entwined couple with slack-jawed astonishment.

Bending to retrieve the laptop, Tank

reported, "It's okay. Fell on the carpet. Not even dinged."

"Nobody cares," Ree-Ann said, her dumbfounded gaze still locked on Steven and Sofia.

"You can all go now," I told them, pointing in the direction of the back door.

"I forgot to clean the coffeemaker," Val said.

"I'll help," Ree-Ann added.

"Out," I commanded.

Reluctantly, they all shuffled through the kitchen and out the back entrance, glancing repeatedly over their shoulders.

Abruptly, Steven broke the kiss and shook his head as if to clear it. His gaze went from Sofia's flushed face to the pair at the door. "What the —"

"*Mamá* is here to visit," Sofia told him hastily. "She brought my old boyfriend Luis."

My hands clenched as I waited for Steven's reaction. He knew enough about Sofia's past to understand how devastating the situation was. If he'd ever wished for an opportunity to humiliate Sofia . . . no, *decimate* her, it had just been handed to him.

"There's been a misunderstanding," Sofia continued, her desperate gaze locked on his.

"*Mamá* thought there was a chance that I would go back to Luis, so she talked him into coming here with her. But I was just starting to explain that it's not possible, because . . . because . . ."

"You and I are together," Steven said, the last word tipped with a faint questioning note.

Sofia nodded vigorously.

"I've seen him before," Alameda said to Sofia in an accusatory tone. "He works here. You don't even like him!"

I couldn't see Steven's face, but as he spoke, his voice was warm and wry. "It wasn't love at first sight," he conceded, keeping his arm around Sofia. "But the attraction was there from the beginning."

"For me too," Sofia said immediately.

"Sometimes when the feelings run deep," Steven said, "it's hard to know how to deal with them. And it's not like Sofia was the kind of woman I ever thought I would fall in love with."

Sofia looked up at him with a frown. "Why not?"

Staring into Sofia's eyes, Steven began to play with a lock of her hair. "Let me count the ways: You're an insufferable optimist, you start decorating for Christmas three months early, and you put glitter on anything that can't run away from you." His fingertips ran over the curve of her ear and caressed the side of her face. "When you get excited about a project, you start rubbing your hands together like a villain with an evil plan. You routinely eat peppers hot enough to make a normal person pass out. There are some words you never pronounce right. Salmon. Pajamas. Every time you hear a phone ring, you think it's yours, except when it actually is yours. The other day I watched you park in front of the studio, and I could tell that you were singing at the top of your lungs." He smiled slowly. "I've finally accepted that these are perfectly legitimate reasons to love someone."

My sister was speechless.

All of us were.

Steven tore his gaze from Sofia and reached out to shake Luis's hand. "I'm Steven Cavanaugh," he said. "I don't blame you for wanting Sofia back. But she's definitely taken."

Luis refused to reciprocate, only folded his arms and glared.

"You didn't ask for my permission," Alameda snapped at Steven. "And Sofia has no ring. There is no engagement without a ring."

Absorbing the information, Steven looked

down at Sophia. "You . . . told her about the engagement," he said slowly.

Sofia's head dipped in a nervous bob.

"Technically, they're engaged to be engaged," I broke in. "Steven was planning to discuss it with you tonight, Alameda. After dinner."

"He can't have dinner with us," Alameda said. "I invited Luis."

"I invited Steven first," Sofia said.

"Enough!" Luis growled. He grabbed for Sofia. "I want to talk to you outside. Alone."

Steven blocked the movement with a startling swiftness, knocking Luis's arm away. "Back the fuck off," he said in a tone that raised the hair on the back of my neck. This was not at all like Steven, who prided himself on never losing his cool.

"Steven," Sofia interrupted, trying to keep the situation from getting out of hand. *"Querido mío,* it's fine, I . . . I'll do what he wants. I can talk to him."

Steven stared at Luis, his gaze hard. "She's mine."

Antagonism thickened the air as the two men faced each other. I sorely regretted having sent Tank away. In the past he had done his share of breaking up fights, and this one promised to be a doozy.

"Luis," Alameda said uneasily, "maybe

265

you should go back to the hotel, and I'll handle my daughter."

"No one is going to handle me," Sofia burst out. "I'm not a puppet. *Mamá,* when are you going to accept that I can make decisions for myself?"

Alameda's mouth trembled and her eyes filled with tears. She fished in her handbag for tissues. "I've done everything for you. My whole life has been for you. I'm only trying to stop you from making so many mistakes."

"Mamá," Sofia said in exasperation, "Luis and I are wrong for each other." Alameda was sobbing too loudly to hear. Sofia turned to Luis. "I'm sorry. I wish all the best for you and your son —"

"Eres babosa," Luis exploded. From the way Sofia stiffened, I knew it an insult. He gestured toward Steven. "When he finds out how stupid and lazy you are, the way you lie in bed like a dead fish, he'll throw you out. He'll leave you fat and pregnant with his bastard, just like your father left Alameda."

"Luis," Alameda exclaimed, shocked out of her tears.

Luis continued bitterly, "Someday you'll come crawling to me, Sofia, and I'll tell you that it's what you deserved for being so —"

"And that is absolutely all we need to hear about your opinions," I said briskly. Seeing that Steven was about to lose it, I strode to the door and shoved it wide open. "If you need a taxi, I'd be happy to call one for you."

Luis stormed out without another word.

"How will he get back to the hotel?" Alameda asked in a watery voice. "We came in my car."

"He'll figure it out," I said.

Alameda blotted her eyes, which were surrounded with raccoon-like rings of mascara. "Sofia," she whined, "you made Luis so angry. He didn't know what he was saying."

Biting back a sarcastic reply, I put a hand on the older woman's shoulder and guided her toward the back of the studio. "Alameda, there's a powder room past the kitchen, down the hall to the left. You'll probably want to fix your makeup."

With a muffled exclamation, Alameda proceeded to the bathroom.

I turned to discover that Sofia was in Steven's arms. ". . . sorry to involve you," she was saying in a miserable voice. "It was all I could think of."

"Don't be sorry." Bending his head, Steven kissed her fully on the mouth, one hand at the back of her neck in a light cradling hold. I could hear her sharp intake of breath.

Flabbergasted, I walked by them to the kitchen as if nothing untoward were happening. Mechanically, I began to unload the clean dishes from the dishwasher. "I'll help with dinner," I heard Steven say eventually. "What are we having?"

Sofia sounded dazed. "I can't remember."

For the rest of the evening, Steven was the picture of the perfect boyfriend. I'd never seen him act like this before. Affectionate. Easygoing. I couldn't tell how much of it, if any, was real. He insisted on helping Sofia cook, and before long Alameda and I were sitting on bar stools at the counter, watching.

Steven and Sofia had spent countless hours working together, but they had never seemed comfortable in each other's company. Until now. They had just discovered a new kind of together. They were finding the right level, warming to each other.

Having worked in her family's restaurant, Sofia was an accomplished cook. Tonight she was making chicken mole, Alameda's favorite dish. For an appetizer, Sofia set out a bowl of home-fried tortilla chips, delicately thin and crisp, along with salsa pureed into a smoky liquid that made my tongue pulse with heat.

While Steven made margaritas, I went to find Coco, and I brought her out to meet Alameda. Although Sofia's mother and I had almost nothing in common, we had finally found something to bond over. Alameda and every one of Sofia's aunts adored Chihuahuas. She held Coco in her lap, cooed over her in Spanish, and admired her pink leather collar studded with rhinestones. Discovering that I was a willing audience on all Chihuahua-related matters, Alameda proceeded to dispense feeding and grooming advice.

Steven tossed a salad made with fresh-roasted corn, crumbled white cheese, chopped cilantro, and a tangy, creamy lime dressing. "How does this look?" he asked Sofia.

She smiled and replied in passing as she went to the refrigerator.

"What was that?" he asked.

Sofia took out a container of coffee-marinated chicken. "I said maybe add a little more dressing."

"I got that part. I was asking about the Spanish words. What did they mean?"

"Oh." Blushing, Sofia set a heavy iron skillet on the cooktop. "Nothing. Just an expression."

Steven put his hands on the counter, caging her from behind. Nuzzling her cheek, he murmured, "You can't call me names and not tell me what they mean."

Her color deepened. "It wasn't a name, it was . . . well, it makes no sense when I translate."

He wouldn't relent. "Tell me anyway."

"Media naranja."

"Which is?"

"Half of the orange," Alameda said. A frown pleated her forehead as she reached for her margarita glass. "We say it to mean 'better half.' Soul mate."

Steven's expression was difficult to interpret. But he lowered his head and kissed Sofia's cheek before moving away. Sofia began to stir the contents of a nearby pot without seeming to be entirely aware of what she was doing.

If Alameda had any doubts about whether or not the relationship was genuine, I was fairly certain they had just vanished. Steven and Sofia were damned convincing as a couple. Which worried me. With the Warner wedding still ahead of us, this was not the time for a tempestuous relationship and all the accompanying Sturm und Drang.

There was also a chance that Steven would revert to his regular self tomorrow morning. As well as I knew Steven, I couldn't tell what was going on in his mind. Would he totally compartmentalize this entire experience? No doubt Sofia was wondering about that, too.

The chicken turned out to be a masterpiece, bathed in a velvety dark sauce of unsweetened Oaxacan chocolate, spices, and the earthy heat of guajillo chiles. Steven exerted himself to be charming, readily answering Alameda's questions about his parents, who lived in Colorado. His mother was a florist and his father was a retired teacher, and they'd been married for thirty years. Under Alameda's probing, Steven admitted that he might not want to stay in event planning forever; he could see himself managing bigger, corporate-related projects or maybe going into public relations. For now, however, he had a lot more to learn at the studio.

"If only I wasn't so incredibly underpaid," he added in a deadpan tone, and both Sofia and I started laughing.

"After your last bonus?" I asked in mock indignation. "And your upgraded health plan?"

"I need more perks," Steven said. "What

about a company yoga class?" Comfortably, he slung an arm around the back of Sofia's chair.

Sofia held a folded tortilla up to his mouth to quiet him. Obligingly, he took a bite.

Alameda smiled thinly as she watched them. She would never like Steven, I thought. I felt certain he must have reminded her of my father. Even though Steven didn't technically look like Eli, he was tall and blond and possessed a similar WASPy handsomeness. I could have told Alameda that Steven was cut from an entirely different cloth, but it wouldn't have made a bit of difference. Alameda was determined not to approve of any man Sofia chose for herself.

We had flan for dessert and small, strong cups of cinnamon coffee. Eventually, Alameda announced that it was time to leave. The good-byes were awkward, interpolated with the awareness of what wasn't being said. Alameda wouldn't apologize for having brought Luis to Houston, and Sofia was still inwardly seething about having been ambushed. Alameda was only marginally civil to Steven, who, for his part, was scrupulously polite.

"May I walk you out to the car, Mrs. Cantera?" he asked.

"No, I want Avery to come with me."

"Absolutely," I said, thinking, *Anything. Anything to get you out of here.*

We walked outside to the parking spaces in front of the studio. I stood beside Alameda's car while she climbed into the driver's seat. She sighed heavily and sat with the door open.

"What kind of man is he?" she asked without looking at me.

I answered seriously. "A good man. Steven doesn't bail when things get tough. He's always calm in an emergency. He can drive anything on wheels, and he can do CPR and basic plumbing. He'll work an eighteen-hour day without a word of complaint, longer if necessary. I can promise you this, Alameda: He's not like my father."

A humorless smile flitted through the shadow patterns on her face. "They're all like your father, Avery."

"Then why were you trying to push Sofia and Luis together?" I asked, bewildered.

"Because at least he would bring her back to live close to her family," Alameda said. "Her *real* family."

Infuriated, I strove to keep my voice calm. "You know, Alameda, you have a nasty habit of taking shots at your own daughter, and I'm not sure what that's supposed to accomplish. If you expect it to provide incentive for Sofia to be near you, it doesn't seem to be working. You might want to try another tactic."

Glaring at me, Alameda slammed the car door shut and started the engine. After she drove away, I went back into the studio, where Sofia was closing the dishwasher and Steven was drying the blender pitcher. Both were quiet. I wondered what, if anything, had been said between them while I'd been outside.

I scooped up Coco and turned her to face me. "You behaved very well tonight," I told her. "You're such a good girl." She strained to lick me. "Not on the lips," I said. "I know where that mouth has been."

Steven picked up his keys from the counter. "Time to roll out," he said. "And after that meal, I mean it literally."

I smiled at him. "You saved the day," I said. "Thank you, Steven."

"Yes, thank you," Sofia said in a subdued voice. All the animation had drained from her expression.

Steven's tone was carefully neutral. "Don't mention it."

I pondered how to make a graceful exit. "Would you like me to —"

"No," Steven said quickly. "I'm going now.

I'll see you both tomorrow."

"Okay," Sofia and I both said in unison.

We both occupied ourselves with casual tasks while Steven let himself out. I picked up a paper towel and wiped the already clean counter. Sofia sprayed the interior of the sink, which had just been rinsed. As soon as the door closed, we burst into conversation.

"What did he say?" I demanded.

"Nothing special: He asked me if I wanted to save the rest of the salsa, and where did we keep the plastic bags." Sofia covered her face with her hands. "I *hate* him." I was startled to hear a sob escape.

"But," I said, bewildered, "he was really nice to you tonight. . . ."

"Exactly," Sofia said venomously. Another sob. "Like a Disney prince. And I let myself pretend it was real, and it was w-wonderful. But now it's over, and tomorrow he'll turn into a pu-pumpkin."

"The prince doesn't turn into a pumpkin."

"Then I turn into a pumpkin."

I reached for the paper towel stand and tugged one off the roll. "No, you don't turn into a pumpkin, either. The coach turns into a pumpkin. You end up walking home with one shoe and a bunch of traumatized rodents."

A laugh quivered out between Sofia's fingers. She took the paper towel. Wadding it against her wet eyes, she said, "He meant those things he said. He cares about me. I knew it was the truth."

"Everyone knew, Sofia. That's why Luis got pissed off and left so fast."

"But that doesn't mean Steven wants a relationship."

"Maybe you don't either," I said dryly. "Sometimes starting a relationship is the worst thing you can do to someone you love."

"Only one of Eli Crosslin's children would say that" came her voice from behind the paper towel.

"It's probably true, though."

Sofia glared at me over the sodden white pulp of the towel. "Avery," she said vehemently, "*nothing* our father ever said to you was true. Not one promise. Not one word of advice. He's the worst half of each of us. Why does his half always get to win?" Crying, she jumped up and went to her room.

Sixteen

To my satisfaction, not to mention Sofia's, Bethany Warner loved the concept of the Jazz Age wedding at the Filter Building. Hollis was slower to be convinced, worrying that the Art Deco elements might seem too cold. However, once Sofia showed her sketches and samples of lavish details, including fresh flower arrangements ornamented with strings of pearls and glittering crystal brooches, Hollis became more enthused.

"Still, I always imagined Bethany in a traditional wedding gown," Hollis fretted. "Not something trendy."

Bethany frowned. "It's not trendy if it's been around since 1920, Mother."

"I don't want you prancing around in something that looks like a costume," Hollis persisted.

I intervened quickly, grabbing a sketch pad from Sofia and sitting between the Warners. "I understand. We need something classic but not too theme-y. I wasn't thinking about drop-waist for you, Bethany. More something like this. . . ." I picked up a pencil and sketched a slim, high-waisted gown. On impulse, I added a split-front skirt draped in panels of sheer silk and tulle. "Most of the bodice would be done in linear beading and sequins." I filled it in with a light geometric pattern. "And instead of a veil, a double-strand headband of diamonds and pearls going across the forehead. Or if that's a little too dramatic —"

"That's it," Bethany said in excitement, jamming her finger directly on the design. "That's what I want. I love that."

"It's beautiful," Hollis admitted. She gave me a pleased look. "Did you just come up with this, Avery? You're very talented."

I smiled at her. "I'm sure we can have something similar to this made —"

"No, not similar," Bethany interrupted. "I want *this* one."

"Yes, you design it, Avery," Hollis said.

I shook my head, disconcerted. "I haven't designed for a few years. And my old contacts are in New York."

"Find someone to collaborate with," Hollis told me. "We'll take the plane up to

New York as often as we need for the fittings."

After the meeting was over and the Warners had left, Sofia exclaimed, "I can't believe they liked the Jazz Age wedding. I thought there was a fifty-fifty chance they'd choose the country club."

"I was pretty certain that Hollis would go for the more stylish option. She wants to be seen as forward-thinking and fashionable."

"But not if it offends the old guard," Sofia said.

I grinned as I went to get Coco from her crate. "I'll bet some of the old guard were there during the original Jazz Age."

"Why did you keep Coco in there while the Warners were here?"

"Some people don't like having a dog wandering around."

"I think you're embarrassed by her."

"Don't say things like that in front of the baby," I protested.

"That dog is not my baby," Sofia said with a reluctant smile.

"Come on, help me do her nails."

We sat side by side at the counter while I held Coco in my lap. "One of us should call Steven and tell him that the Warners liked the Gatsby wedding," I said. I uncapped a puppy-nail-polish pen, the same shade of pink as her rhinestone collar.

"You do it," Sofia said.

So far, Sofia and Steven had been at a stalemate. He had been unusually nice to her the past couple of days, but there had been no sign of the tenderness he had shown the night of Alameda's visit. When I had urged Sofia to say something to him, she had confessed that she was still trying to work up the nerve.

"Sofia, for heaven's sake, go talk to him. Be proactive."

She took one of Coco's delicate paws and held it steady. "Why don't you take your own advice?" she retorted. "You haven't talked to Joe since he took you out to lunch."

"My situation is different."

"How?"

Carefully I applied a coat of polish to Coco's nails. "For one thing, Joe has too much money. There's no way I can go after him without looking like a gold digger."

"Does Joe look at it that way?" Sofia asked dubiously.

"Doesn't matter. It's how everyone else does." The Chihuahua looked solemnly from one of us to the other as we talked. I capped the polish pen and blew gently on Coco's glossy pink nails.

"What if he's decided to outwait you? What if you're both too stubborn to make the next move?"

"Then at least I'll have my pride."

"Pride buys no meat in the market."

"You're hoping I'll ask you what that means, but I'm not going to."

"You might as well start sleeping with him," Sofia said, "since everyone already thinks you are."

My eyes widened. "Why would anyone assume that?"

"Because you bought a dog together."

"No, we didn't! *I* bought the dog. Joe just happened to be there."

"It's a sign of commitment. It shows that you're both thinking about a future together."

"Coco isn't a couples dog," I said heatedly, but as I glanced at her, I realized she was teasing. Rolling my eyes, I relaxed and set Coco carefully on the floor.

As I returned to my chair, Sofia gave me a pensive look. "Avery . . . I've been thinking about a lot of things since I saw Luis the other day. I've decided that bringing him here was one of the nicest things that *Mamá* has ever done for me."

"If so," I said, "trust me, it was purely accidental on her part."

Sofia smiled faintly. "I know. But it helped. Because facing Luis after all this time made me realize something: By not moving on, I've been giving Luis power over me. It's like he's been holding me hostage. He belongs in my past — I can't let him influence my future." Her hazel eyes took in my stricken expression as she continued. "You and I are too much alike, Avery. Thin-skinned people shouldn't feel things as deeply as we do — we bruise too easy."

We were both quiet for a moment.

"Whenever I think about moving on," I eventually said, "it's as terrifying as the idea of parachuting out of a plane. At night. Over a cactus field. I can't seem to make myself do it."

"What if the plane were on fire?" Sofia suggested. "Could you jump out of it then?"

An uneven grin spread across my face. "Well, that would definitely provide some motivation."

"Then the next time you're with Joe," Sofia said, "try telling yourself the plane's on fire. Then the only choice is to jump."

"Over the cactus field?"

"Anything's better than a burning plane," she said reasonably.

"Good point."

"Then you're going to call Joe?"

I hesitated, surprised by the flare of yearning I felt at the question. Two days, and I missed him badly. I didn't just want him, I *needed* him. *I'm doomed,* I thought, and sighed in resignation.

"No," I said, "I'm not going to call him. I'd rather figure out a way to make him come here without having to ask him."

She gave me a bemused glance. "Like fake your own kidnapping or something?"

I laughed. "I wouldn't go that far." After a few seconds of pondering, I said, "But that gives me an idea. . . ."

On Saturday afternoon I closed the studio and took a long, luxurious bath. Afterward I left my hair down in loose waves and misted my wrists and throat with a light cologne. I dressed in lavender silk lounge pants and a matching lace-trimmed top that showed more cleavage than I ever would have displayed in public.

"I'm leaving for a girls' night out" came Sofia's voice as I went downstairs.

"With who?"

"Val and some other friends." Sofia was busy rummaging through her handbag. "Dinner, a movie, and probably drinks afterward." She glanced at me and grinned. "I may crash at Val's place. You'll want the whole house to yourself once Joe sees you in that outfit."

"He may tell me off for the prank I pulled, and leave right afterward."

"I don't think so." Sofia blew me a kiss. "Remember the plane," she said, and left.

Wandering around the empty house, I turned down most of the lights, lit some candles in blown-glass votives, and poured a glass of wine. As I sat on the sofa in front of the TV, Coco climbed up a little set of steps to sit next to me.

We were about a third of the way into a movie when the doorbell rang.

Coco trotted down the sofa steps and hurried to the front door with an abbreviated yap. My nerves jangled wildly as I stood and followed, carrying my wineglass. After taking a deep breath, I cracked open the door to find Joe leaning against the door frame. He was heart-stoppingly handsome in a dark suit, dress shirt, and tie.

"Oh, hello," I said in a tone of mild surprise, opening the door a couple of inches wider. "What are you doing here?"

"I'm supposed to take pictures at a fund-raising event tonight. But just as I was leaving, I found out my camera bag was empty. Except for this." Joe held up a piece of paper covered with letters that had been cut from a magazine and arranged ransom-note style. It read:

Call me or the camera gets it.

"Happen to know anything about this?" he asked.

"I might." As I stared into his dark eyes, I saw to my relief that he wasn't angry. In fact, I got the impression that he was considerably entertained.

"This was an inside job," Joe said. "Jack has a key to my place, but he knows better. So it had to be Ella who helped you."

"I admit nothing." I opened the door fully. "Would you like to come in for a glass of wine?"

Joe was about to reply, but his gaze had flickered to the valley of my cleavage and my half-exposed breasts, and then he couldn't seem to look away.

"Wine?" I prompted.

Joe blinked and forced his gaze back up to my face. He had to clear his throat before replying. "Please."

Coco trotted back to the sofa as Joe and I went to the kitchen.

"You were expecting company?" Joe asked, seeing the extra wineglass waiting beside the open bottle.

"One never knows."

"One knows the chances are pretty high

when a three-thousand-dollar Nikon is missing."

"It's safe." I poured some chilled pinot grigio and gave it to him.

Joe took a swallow, the crystal stem of the wineglass glimmering in his strong fingers.

Being with him again, having him within arm's reach, filled me with an emotion bordering on exhilaration. For me, happiness was as elusive and fragile as one of those balloons Eli had once brought Sofia. At the moment, however, it seemed to have been woven all through me, stitched deep in my bones and muscles, enriching my blood.

"I hope I'm not making you late for your event," I said.

"It was canceled."

"When?"

A smile touched his lips. "About a minute and a half ago." He set aside his wine, then took off his jacket and draped it over the backrest of a bar stool. Next the shirt cuffs were unbuttoned and rolled up twice, revealing forearms dusted with dark hair. Excited flutters awakened in my stomach as he proceeded to remove his tie.

After unfastening his top shirt button, Joe picked up his wineglass and gave me a level glance. "I haven't called because I've been trying to give you space."

I tried to sound injured. "There's a difference between giving someone space and ignoring them."

"Honey, I'm not ignoring you, I'm trying not to act like a stalker."

"Why didn't you kiss me after we went out the other day?"

The creases at the outer corners of his eyes deepened. "Because I knew that if I started, I wouldn't be able to stop. You may have noticed that I have trouble putting on the brakes with you." He stood and took hold of the sides of my chair, effectively caging me. "Now that you've taken my camera hostage . . . what kind of ransom are we talking about?"

I had to work up my nerve before replying. "I think we should negotiate upstairs. In my bedroom."

Joe contemplated me for a long moment before shaking his head. "Avery . . . when it happens, I'm going to want things that are hard for you to give. It'll be different from the first time. And I can't take the chance that you're not ready."

I rested my hands on his forearms, taut with corded strength. "I've missed you," I said. "I missed talking to you at night and hearing about your day, and telling you about mine. I've even been dreaming about you. Since you're already occupying some of my head space, we might as well sleep together."

Joe was very still, his gaze locked on my reddening face. By now he knew how difficult it was for me to admit how I felt.

"I don't know if I'm ready for this," I continued, "but I know that I trust you. And I know that I want to wake up with a man in my bed tomorrow morning. Specifically you. So if you —"

Before I could finish, Joe leaned forward and kissed me. My fingers tightened on his arms in a bid for balance. I took an extra breath, another, my lungs striving amid a storm of heartbeats. The kiss turned stronger, more voracious, his mouth opening mine. Without breaking the kiss, he pulled me from the chair and pinned me against the counter, as if I needed to be held in place, restrained, and the hint of male aggression was wildly exciting.

"Joe," I panted when his mouth slid to my throat, "I . . . I have a big bed upstairs, covered with . . . Italian linens and a hand-quilted silk cover . . . and feather and down pillows . . ."

Joe drew his head back to look at me, a dance of laughter in his eyes. "You don't have to sell me on the bed, honey."

He paused at the sound of a phone emanating from his discarded jacket. "Sorry," he said, reaching for the garment. "I only get this ringtone when it's family." He began to hunt through the pockets.

"Of course."

He pulled out the phone and looked at his text messages. "Christ," he said, his expression changing.

Something bad had happened.

"Haven's in the hospital," he said. "I have to go."

"I'm coming too," I said instantly.

Joe shook his head. "You don't have to —"

"Wait two minutes," I said, already running to the stairs. "I'll put on a shirt and some jeans. Don't leave without me."

SEVENTEEN

It occurred to me on the way to the hospital that I might have been too pushy, insisting on accompanying Joe. Whatever was wrong with Haven, it was a family matter, and they might not appreciate having an outsider there. On the other hand, I wanted to help in any way possible. And more important, I wanted to be there for Joe. Having gained some understanding of how much the Travises meant to one another, I knew it would devastate him if anything happened to his sister.

"What does the text say about Haven's condition?" I asked.

Wordlessly Joe handed the phone to me.

"Preeclampsia," I said, reading the message from Ella.

"I've never heard of it before."

"I have, but I'm not sure exactly what it is." In a couple of minutes, I'd found a page on preeclampsia. "It's a hypertensive disease. High blood pressure, severe water retention, and toxic buildup in the kidneys and liver."

"How serious is it?"

I hesitated. "It can get really serious."

His hands clenched on the steering wheel. "Life-threatening?"

"Garner is a world-class hospital. I'm sure Haven will be fine." The phone rang, and I looked at the caller ID. "It's Ella. Do you want to —"

"Talk to her while I drive."

I answered the call. "Ella? Hi, it's Avery."

Ella's voice was quiet, but I could hear the stress threaded through her subdued tone. "We're in the waiting room at the neonatal ICU. Are you and Joe headed over?"

"Yes, we're almost there. What's happening?"

"This morning Haven woke up with a headache and nausea, but Jesus, that's routine for her. She couldn't keep anything down, and she went back to bed. When she woke up this afternoon, she was starting to have problems breathing. Hardy brought her to the hospital and they checked her vitals and did some tests. Her blood pressure is through the roof, and her protein levels are triple what they should be, and she's acting confused, which scared the shit out of Hardy. The good news is, the baby's heartbeat is normal."

"How many weeks before the baby is full term?"

"Four, I think. But she'll probably be fine, even being born this early."

"Wait. Are you saying Haven's in labor?"

"They're going to do a C-section. Okay, gotta go — Liberty and Gage are just walking in, and they'll want an update." The call ended.

"They're doing a C-section," I told Joe.

He swore softly.

I looked back at the Web page on the phone. "Preeclampsia is usually resolved within forty-eight hours after the baby's delivered," I said. "They'll give Haven medicine for the hypertension. The baby will be premature, but she's developed enough at this point that there probably won't be any long-term problems. So everything will be okay."

Joe nodded, looking far from reassured.

The waiting room of the NICU was furnished with clusters of blue upholstered chairs and small tables and a sofa. Harsh overhead lighting imparted a lunar whiteness to the atmosphere. The assembled members of the immediate Travis family were understandably tense and subdued as they welcomed Joe and me. Jack, however, summoned a hint of his usual humor. "Hi, Avery," he said, giving me a brief hug, adding in feigned surprise, "You're still hanging out with Joe?"

"I insisted on coming with him," I said. "I hope I'm not barging in, but I thought —"

"Not at all," Liberty interrupted, her green eyes warm.

"We're glad you're here," Gage added. His gaze traveled from my face to Joe's. "No news about Haven yet."

"How's Hardy doing?" Joe asked.

"He's been solid so far," Jack replied. "But if she goes downhill any further . . . he won't take it well."

"None of us will," Joe said, and the group fell silent.

We rearranged a few chairs and settled in the waiting room. Joe and I sat on the sofa. "You sure you want to stay?" Joe asked me sotto voce. "I can have you sent home in the hospital's private car. This won't be over any time soon."

"Do you want me to leave? Is it better for the family if there are no outsiders here? Just be blunt, because I —"

"You're not an outsider. But you don't

have to suffer in a hospital waiting room just because I'm here."

"I'm not suffering. And I want to stay, as long as it's okay with you." I curled my legs beneath me and leaned into his side.

"I want you here." He cuddled me closer.

"What did you mean, the hospital's private car?" I asked. "Is that a new service?"

"Not exactly. The hospital has what they call a VIP program for benefactors. The family made some donations in the past, and Dad left them a bequest in his will. So now if any of us comes to the hospital, we're supposed to wait in a VIP room, which is stuck in some distant wing of the hospital, with people hovering over you every minute. We've all agreed to avoid the VIP treatment whenever possible." He paused. "But I'd break the rules if you wanted a ride home in a town car."

"If you're not going to be a VIP," I told him, "don't try to turn me into one."

Joe smiled and pressed his lips to my temple. "Someday," he murmured, "I'm going to take you out for a nice, normal date. No drama. We'll go have dinner at a restaurant like civilized people."

After several long, quiet minutes, Jack said he was going to get some coffee and asked if anyone wanted some. The group shook their heads. He left and returned soon with a Styrofoam cup filled with steaming liquid.

Ella frowned in worry. "Jack, it's not good to drink hot liquid out of those kinds of cups — the chemicals leach into the coffee."

Jack looked sardonic. "I've drunk hot coffee out of Styrofoam for most of my life."

"That explains it," Joe said.

Although Jack sent him a warning glance, there was a betraying twitch at the corner of his mouth as he took his seat beside Ella. He offered her a pack of plastic-wrapped cookies.

"You got that from a vending machine, didn't you?" Ella asked suspiciously.

"I couldn't help myself," Jack said.

"What's wrong with vending machines?" I asked.

"The food is junk," Ella replied, "and the machines themselves are deadly. They kill more people per year than sharks."

"How could a vending machine kill someone?" Liberty asked.

"Fall over and crush them," Ella said earnestly. "It happens."

"There's no vending machine in existence that could take out a Travis," Jack informed her. "We're too hardheaded."

"I'll vouch for that," Ella said. Surreptitiously she took a cookie from the open packet and began to nibble on it.

I smiled and rested my head on Joe's shoulder. His hand began to sift through the loose locks of my hair.

Abruptly, the soothing motion of his hand stopped, a new tension entering his body. Lifting my head, I followed the direction of Joe's gaze.

Hardy had entered the waiting room, not seeming to recognize or notice anyone. His face was haggard and skull white, his eyes electric blue. He went blindly to the farthest corner and sat, his broad shoulders hunched as if he were trying to recover from a mule kick to the chest.

"Hardy —" someone said quietly.

He flinched and gave a little shake of his head.

A doctor had come to the doorway. Gage went to him, and they conferred for a couple of minutes.

Gage's expression was unreadable as he returned. The group leaned in to catch every word as he spoke quietly. "There's a complication with preeclampsia called HELLP syndrome. Basically the red blood cells are rupturing. Haven is heading toward liver failure and a possible stroke." He paused and swallowed hard, his gaze meeting Liberty's. "Delivering the baby is the first step," he continued in an even tone. "After that they'll give her steroids and plasma, and likely a blood transfusion. We'll probably get some news in about an hour. For now, we hunker down and wait."

"Shit," Joe said softly. He glanced at the far corner of the room, where Hardy leaned forward with his forearms braced on his thighs, his head down. "Someone should sit with him. Should I —"

"I will, if you don't mind," Gage murmured.

"Go right ahead."

Gage stood and went to the solitary figure in the corner.

I was surprised by Gage's desire to sit with Hardy, recalling some of what Joe had once told me, that there was no love lost between the two men. Joe had been somewhat vague about the details, but he'd indicated that Hardy had caused some kind of trouble for Gage and Liberty. It seemed there was history between Hardy and Liberty — they had known each other growing up and had even been childhood sweethearts for a time.

"How did Hardy end up marrying Haven?" I had asked.

"Not exactly sure how or when it started," Joe had said. "But once Hardy and Haven took up with each other, it was like trying to stop a runaway train. And eventually we all realized that Hardy loved her, which is all that matters. Still . . . Gage and Hardy generally keep their distance from each other, unless there's an occasion when the entire family gets together."

I stole a discreet glance at the corner of the room, where Gage sat beside Hardy and gave him a rough brotherly pat on the back. Hardy didn't even appear to notice. He was trapped in some private hell, where no one could reach him. In a couple of minutes, however, Hardy's shoulders lifted and fell in a sigh. Gage asked him something, and he shook his head in response.

For the next hour, Gage stayed beside Hardy, murmuring from time to time but mostly offering silent companionship. No one else approached, understanding that Hardy's emotions were too raw, that one person's proximity was all he could handle.

Why that person should be Gage, however, was difficult to understand.

I gave Joe a questioning glance. Leaning close, he murmured, "Haven's always been a favorite of Gage's. Hardy knows if anything happens, Gage would be nearly as torn up about it as he would. And besides . . . they're family."

A young nurse entered the waiting room. "Mr. Cates?" He rose to his feet, his face contorted with a raw anguish that I doubted she or anyone else would ever forget. She hurried over to him with her phone. "I have a picture of your daughter," she said. "I took it before they put her in the incubator. She's a perfect four pounds. Seventeen inches long."

The Travises all gathered around the phone with exclamations of excitement and relief.

Hardy took a glance at the image and said hoarsely, "My wife . . ."

"Mrs. Cates came through the surgery without any major issues. She's waking up in recovery — it'll take a little while. The doctor will be here in just a minute, and he'll let you know —"

"I want to see her," Hardy said brusquely.

Before the disconcerted nurse could reply, Gage intervened. "Hardy, I'll talk to the doctor while you're with Haven."

Hardy nodded and strode from the waiting area.

"He really shouldn't be doing that," the nurse fretted. "I'd better go follow him. If y'all want to take a peek at the baby, she's in the special care nursery."

I headed to the nursery with Joe, Ella, and

Jack, while Gage and Liberty stayed in the waiting room to talk to the doctor.

"Poor Hardy," Ella murmured as we walked along the hallway. "He's been worried sick."

"My sympathy's with Haven," Joe said. "I don't know the details of what she's been through, and I don't want to. But I do know she's gone through one hell of a battle."

We entered the special care nursery, where the newborn had been placed in an incubator. She had been hooked up to an oxygen tube and monitoring leads, and her midsection was wrapped in a glowing blue pad.

"What is that?" I asked in a hushed voice.

"A biliblanket," Ella replied. "Mia had one after she was born. It's phototherapy for jaundice."

The baby blinked and appeared to drift to sleep, her rosebud mouth opening and closing. Her head was covered with fine dark hair. "Hard to tell what she looks like," Jack commented.

"She'll be beautiful," Ella said. "How could she not be, with Haven and Hardy as parents?"

"Hardy's not what I'd call pretty," Jack said.

"If you did," Joe remarked, "he'd kick your ass."

Jack grinned and asked Ella, "Did Haven tell you what the baby's name was?"

"Not yet."

We returned to the waiting room, where Gage and Liberty had just finished talking with the doctor. "They're cautiously optimistic," Gage reported. "It's going to take three or four days before the HELLP issues are resolved. They've already given her a blood transfusion, and they'll probably do another to help with the platelet count. They're also going to put her on corticosteroid therapy and monitor her closely." He shook his head, looking troubled. "They're keeping her on the magnesium drip to ward off seizures. Apparently it's a son of a bitch."

Liberty rubbed her face and sighed. "Why don't they have a bar in a hospital? It's usually the place you most need a drink."

Gage wrapped his arms around his wife and snuggled her against his chest. "You need to go home and check on the kids. What if Jack and Ella drop you off while I stay here a little while longer? I'm going to stick around and talk to Hardy."

"That sounds good," Liberty said against his shoulder.

"You need me for anything?" Joe asked.

Gage shook his head and smiled. "I think

we're fine here. You and Avery go on and get some rest. You've earned it."

Eighteen

I woke up in the morning with the groggy awareness that I was not alone. Climbing through the blurred layers of consciousness, I recalled the events of the previous night . . . coming home from the hospital with Joe . . . inviting him upstairs to sleep with me. We had both been exhausted, sore from hours spent on uncomfortable waiting room furniture, emotionally drained. I had changed into a nightgown and climbed into bed with Joe. The feeling of being held against his big, warm body had been delicious, and in a matter of seconds I had passed out.

Joe was behind me, one arm tucked beneath my head, his legs drawn up under mine. I lay quietly and listened to the even cadence of his breathing. Wondering if he was awake, I let my toes delicately investigate the contours of his foot. Slowly his mouth came to my neck, finding a place so sensitive that I felt a shot of delight down to my stomach.

"There's a man in my bed," I remarked, groping back with my hand, feeling a hairy muscular thigh, the lean smoothness of a masculine hip. My wrist was gently captured, my hand guided downward until my fingers encountered hard, distended flesh and silky male skin. I took a quick breath, my eyes widening. "Joe . . . it's too early."

His hand traveled to my breast, caressing the shape through the thin knit fabric of my nightgown, softly pinching the nipple, enticing sensation from the stiffening points.

I tried again, sounding ambivalent even to my own ears. "I'm not a fan of morning sex."

But he continued to kiss my neck and pulled the hem of my nightgown up past my knees.

I let out a giggle of nerves and dismay, crawling toward the other side of the bed.

Joe pounced, pushing me back down. He covered me, thighs clamping on my hips, deliberately letting me feel some of his weight, his body charged with lust. The moment was playful, but there was intent in the way he handled me, an assertiveness that stole my breath away.

"At least let me take a shower first," I said plaintively.

"I want you like this."

I began to wriggle. "Later. Please."

Lowering his head, Joe murmured, "You're not in charge. I am."

I went still. For some reason, hearing those soft words while he was pinning me down like that sent a deep, deranged thrill through me. His voice curled hotly in my ear. "You belong to me, and I'm going to have you. Here and now."

I couldn't seem to get enough air. I had never been so intensely aroused.

His position altered, his hand sliding beneath the nightgown and between my thighs, searching intimately. I quivered as he massaged into the wetness, two fingers entering in a gentle glide. My hips began to rock back in a tight, unthinking rhythm, and he matched it exactly, pressing deep into the pulse, building sensation until I began to clench at each impetus.

Turning me to my back, he knelt between my thighs and propped them up so my knees were bent. He kissed my ankle, my calf, working his way upward. I bit my lips and writhed as the kisses crept closer to the juncture of my thigh and groin. "Don't —" I began to protest, right before I felt a hot glassy stroke across my twitching flesh. I couldn't escape the firm wet tug of his mouth. I began to sob, my defenses breaking down beneath the weight of pleasure.

He was unrelenting, concentrating on the shivery-hot place with his tongue, the caresses acquiring a rhythm that guided every impulse and sensation and heartbeat into a single focused current. My legs spread out and I was making sounds like I'd been hurt as the blinding release began. Too much to bear, too intense, my body seized with violent quivers.

Joe spent long minutes drawing out the afterglow even after I quieted, his mouth caressing me with diabolical gentleness. Eventually his head lifted and he kissed my stomach. I was so decimated that I barely registered when he rolled away for a moment and reached for something on the nightstand. He levered himself fully over my body, nudging my legs apart, and I reached up for him with weak arms. Entering me in a demanding drive, he pulled back just enough to thrust again, the deliberate measure of each lunge forcing me deliciously open, my hips lifted with each stroke.

Sometimes the rhythm was teasing and slow, sometimes fast and deep. He paid attention to every response, no matter how subtle, learning what excited me, what gave me pleasure. Joe was making love to me as no one ever had, and although the experience was unfamiliar, I could recognize it for what it was. Devastated, I closed my eyes as he ground into me with a steady circling. Whimpers broke from my throat. There was no holding anything back, no modesty, no control. More racking spasms, my pleasure feeding his. Joe growled in his chest and throat and began to shudder in my arms. I held him, kissing the side of his neck, loving the weight of him on me.

Eventually he turned and pulled me halfway over him, and we lay entangled for a long time afterward. I was in a stupor, random thoughts hovering just out of reach. The smells of sweat and sex mingled in an erotic fragrance, infusing every breath. Beneath my head, Joe's chest lifted and fell in a relaxed pattern. One of his hands wandered over me, stroking gently.

I kissed his shoulder. "I'm going to take a shower now," I said, my voice husky. "Don't try and stop me."

He smiled and turned to his side, watching me leave the bed.

I went into the bathroom on unsteady legs and started the shower. My throat was tight with the effort to hold back tears. It was difficult to feel so defenseless . . . unguarded . . . and yet at the same time, there was an unspeakable relief in it.

Before the water had heated sufficiently for me to step in, Joe entered the room. His acute gaze caught every nuance of my expression before I could manage to hide it. Reaching a hand into the shower spray, he tested the temperature. He went with me into the glass-fronted stall. Blindly I turned my face into the water.

Joe slicked his hands with soap and began to wash me, his touch tender rather than sexual. I leaned against him passively, making no protest even when his soapy fingers slid between my legs and parted the soft folds for the rinse of hot water. He turned me so the spray was at my back, and I was pressed all along the wet, muscled surface of his front.

"Too soon?" I heard him ask.

I shook my head, arms locked around his waist. "No . . . But it was different from the first time."

"I told you it would be."

"Yes, but I . . . I'm not sure why."

He murmured close to my ear, "Because it means something now."

I could respond only with a shaken nod.

■ ■ ■ ■

After a quick breakfast of coffee and toast, Joe had to leave. He would rush home to change his clothes before meeting with one of the directors of the Travis charitable giving foundation, to discuss the latest initiatives the family had agreed to focus on. "After everything that happened last night," Joe said, "I may be the only Travis who shows up." He stole a quick kiss. "Dinner tonight?" Another kiss before I could answer. "At seven?" One more kiss. "I'll take that as a yes."

I stood there with an idiotic grin on my face as he left.

A little while later, while I was drinking a second cup of coffee, Sofia came downstairs in a pink robe and matching bunny slippers. "Is Joe still here?" she asked in a whisper.

"No, he's gone."

"How was last night?"

I smiled wryly. "Eventful. We spent most of it in a waiting room at Garner Hospital." As we sat next to each other at the counter, I told Sofia all about Haven's pregnancy complications, and the baby's birth, and how the Travises had interacted.

"It was sort of eye-opening," I said. "I've seen families celebrating together, and families on the verge of brawling over incredibly stupid stuff. But I've never actually seen a family, up close, in a situation like that. The way they supported each other . . ." I paused, finding it difficult to put into words. "Well, it surprised me that Gage, who's had problems with Hardy in the past, would be the one to sit with him and comfort him, and Hardy let him, and it was because of the family bond, this . . . this weird connection that's so important to all of them."

"It's not weird," Sofia said. "That's what a family is."

"Yes, I know what a family is, but I've never seen what a family *does*. Not like that." I paused, frowning. "I've never been part of an extended family. I'm not sure I'd like it. They all seem to know each other so well. Too well. There wouldn't be enough privacy for me."

"There are obligations when you're part of a family," Sofia conceded. "And problems. But taking care of each other . . . the feeling of belonging somewhere . . . that part is wonderful."

"Do you miss not being close to your relatives?" I asked.

"Sometimes," Sofia admitted. "But when you're not accepted for who you are, it's not really a family." She shrugged and took a swallow of coffee. "Tell me the rest," she prompted. "When Joe brought you back."

A light blush covered my face. "He spent the night, obviously."

"And?"

"I'm not giving you details," I protested, and Sofia laughed gleefully as my color deepened.

"I can tell it was good just by looking at your face," she said.

I tried to divert her. "Let's figure out our plans for the day. Later this afternoon we need to review what's been done on the Warner wedding so far, and send a report to Ryan. I think he'll be fine with most of it, but I want to make sure —" I broke off as the doorbell rang. "That must be a delivery. Unless you're expecting someone?"

"No." Sofia went to the front entrance and peeked through one of the narrow side windows. She whirled around and plastered her back to the door like a knife thrower's assistant during warm-up practice. "It's Steven," she said, her eyes wide. "Why is he here?"

"I have no idea. Let's ask him."

She didn't move. "What do you think he wants?"

"He works here," I reminded her patiently. "Let him in."

My sister nodded tensely. She turned to unlock the door, then opened it with unnecessary force. "What do you want?" she asked without preamble.

Steven was dressed casually in jeans and a polo shirt. His expression was difficult to interpret as he looked down at her. "I left my phone case here yesterday," he said warily. "I came by to pick it up."

"Hi, Steven," I said. "Your phone case is on the coffee table."

"Thanks." He walked inside with an air of extreme caution, as if he suspected the studio had been booby-trapped.

Coco ascended the steps to the sofa and watched Steven retrieve his phone case. He paused to pet her tiny head and scratch the back of her neck. As soon as he stopped, Coco pawed at his hand and shoved her head beneath his palm, demanding that he continue.

"How's it going?" I asked.

"Fine," Steven replied.

"Would you like some coffee?"

It appeared to be a question with no easy answer. "I'm . . . not sure."

"Okay."

As Steven continued to pet Coco, he stole a glance at Sofia. "You're wearing bunny slippers," he said, as if it confirmed a suspicion he'd had for some time.

"And?" Sofia asked darkly, expecting a sarcastic comment.

"I like them."

Sofia gave him a confused glance.

They were both so focused on each other that neither of them noticed my discreet exit from the kitchen.

"I'm going to the farmer's market," Steven said. "There should be some good peaches. Would you like to come along?"

Sofia replied in a slightly higher-pitched voice than usual. "Okay, why not?"

"Good."

"I just have to change out of my pajamas into some regular clothes and . . ." Sofia paused. "Pajamas," she repeated. "That's how to say it. Right?"

Unable to resist, I stopped to glance at them from my vantage on the stairs. I had an unobstructed view of Steven's face. He was smiling down at Sofia, his eyes glowing. "The way you pronounce it," he said, "it always sounds like pa-yamas." He hesitated and lifted his hand to caress her cheek gently.

"Pajamas," Sofia repeated, sounding exactly like before.

Seeming to lose all restraint, Steven pulled her into his arms and murmured something low.

A long silence. A little sobbing breath. "So have I," I heard Sofia say.

He kissed her, and Sofia molded herself against him, her hands climbing into his hair. The two of them seemed overwhelmed with mutual tenderness, clumsy with it as they kissed each other's cheeks, chins, mouths.

Not long ago, I thought as I hurried up the stairs, the sight of Steven and Sofia passionately embracing would have been unthinkable.

Everything was changing so fast. The long, steady road I had plotted out for Sofia and me was turning out to have so many unexpected twists and detours that I found myself wondering if we were going to end up in entirely different places from those we'd originally planned.

I received frequent updates on Haven's condition from Ella and Liberty and, of course, Joe. Although Haven's health was improving rapidly, she wouldn't be well enough to receive visitors outside of immediate family until she was back home.

Her daughter, named Rosalie, was thriving and gaining weight and was frequently brought to Haven for what was called "kangaroo time," resting on her chest for skin-to-skin contact.

As I scrolled through photos that Joe had taken and loaded onto his tablet, I paused at a striking image of Hardy cradling Rosalie tenderly in his big hands, his smiling face lowered so that one of her miniature palms rested on his nose.

"Her eyes look blue," I said, zooming in on the picture.

"When Hardy's mom visited yesterday, she said his eyes were exactly that color when he was born."

"When will Haven and Rosalie be able to leave the hospital?"

"One more week, they think. Hardy will be over the moon, bringing his two girls home." Joe paused. "But I hope my sister's not going to want to have any more children. Hardy says he couldn't survive this again, even if Haven wants to take the chance."

"Is there a risk of preeclampsia if she gets pregnant again?"

Joe nodded.

"Haven may be fine with just having one child," I said. "Or Hardy may change his mind. You never can predict what people will do." Having reached the last picture, I handed the tablet back to Joe.

We were at his house in the Old Sixth Ward, a charming bungalow with a slightly smaller companion house in the back. Joe had painted the interiors of both buildings a soft, creamy white and stained the trim a rich walnut. The decor was spare and masculine, with a few pieces of beautifully restored furniture. Joe had spent more time showing me the smaller house, where he worked and kept his photography equipment. To my surprise, there was even a darkroom, which he admitted he seldom used, but would never get rid of.

"Every now and then, I'll shoot a roll of film because there's still something magical about developing a print in the darkroom."

"Magical?" I repeated with a quizzical smile.

"I'll show you sometime. There's nothing like seeing an image appear in the developer tray. And it's all about craft: You can't tell if the exposure is too light or dark, you can't see the details of burning and dodging, so you have to go with what feels right, what past experience has taught you."

"So you prefer that to Photoshop?"

"No, Photoshop has too many advantages.

But I still like the idea of having to wait to see a picture in the darkroom. Taking time, and seeing the image with a fresh perspective . . . it's not as practical as digital, but it's more romantic."

I loved his passion for his work. I loved it that he thought of a tiny windowless room filled with trays of caustic chemicals as romantic.

Scrolling through files of photos on a computer monitor, I found a series of shots he'd taken in Afghanistan . . . beautiful, stark, riveting. Some of the landscapes were otherworldly. A pair of old men sitting in front of a turquoise wall . . . a soldier's silhouette against a red sky as he stood on a mountain path . . . a dog, seen from an eye-level perspective with a soldier's booted feet in the foreground.

"How long were you there?" I asked.

"Only a month."

"How did you end up going?"

"A friend from college was filming a documentary. He and his camera crew were embedded with troops at a firebase in Kandahar. But the stills photographer had to leave early. So they asked if I would step in and finish. I was sent to the same two-day training session the rest of the crew had gone through, basically how not to screw things up in a combat environment. The dogs at the front lines were incredible. Not one of them flinched at the sound of a gunshot. One day on patrol, I watched a Lab sniff out an IED that the metal detectors didn't catch."

"That was incredibly dangerous."

"Yes. But she was a smart dog. She knew what she was doing."

"I meant dangerous for you."

"Oh." His lips quirked. "I'm pretty good at staying out of trouble."

I tried to return the smile, but there was a stabbing sensation in my chest as I thought of him taking that kind of risk. "Would you do something like that again?" I couldn't resist asking. "Take a job where you could be hurt or . . . or worse?"

"Any of us could be hurt, no matter where we are," he said. "When your number's up, it's up." His gaze held mine as he added, "But I wouldn't go into a situation like that if you didn't want me to."

The implication that my feelings might sway such a decision was a little unnerving. But part of me responded to it, craved that kind of influence over him. That worried me even more.

"Come on," Joe murmured, leading me

out of the small building. "Let's go into the house."

Exploring, I went into the small bedroom. The queen-size bed was covered with simple white sheets and a white quilt. I admired the headboard, a panel made of wooden vertical slats. "Where did you get this?"

"Haven gave it to me. It was the door of an old freight elevator in her apartment building."

Inspecting the piece more closely, I saw a long-faded word stenciled in red letters on the side — DANGER — and I smiled. I ran my hand across the smooth surface of a turned-over sheet. "These are nice. Looks like a high thread count."

"I don't know the thread count."

I kicked off my shoes and crawled onto the queen-size bed. Reclining on my side, I shot him a provocative glance. "Apparently you don't share my appreciation for luxury linens."

Joe lowered himself next to me. "Believe me, you're the most luxurious thing that's ever been on this bed." Slowly his hand followed the curve of my waist and hip. "Avery . . . I want to take your picture."

My brows lifted. "When?"

"Now."

I looked down at my sleeveless top and

jeans. "In this outfit?"

Idly, he traced a pattern on my thigh. "Actually . . . I was thinking you could take it off."

My eyes turned huge. "Oh, my God. Are you seriously asking me to pose for naked pictures?"

"You can cover yourself with a sheet."

"No."

From the way Joe looked at me, I could tell he was calculating how to get what he wanted.

"What is the point?" I asked anxiously.

"My two favorite things in the world are you, and photography. I want to enjoy both at the same time."

"And then what will happen to these pictures?"

"They're just for me. I won't show them to anyone. Later I'll delete every single one if that's what you want."

"Have you done this before?" I asked, suspicious. "Is it some ritual you have with your girlfriends?"

Joe shook his head. "You're the first." He paused. "No, you're the second. Once I was hired to shoot a car ad with a model wearing only silver paint. I went out with her a couple of times after that. She was never actually a girlfriend."

"Why did you break up?"

"After the silver paint came off, she wasn't all that interesting."

I couldn't hold back a reluctant laugh.

"Let me take your picture," Joe coaxed. "Trust me."

I gave him a furiously pleading glance. "Why am I even considering this?"

His eyes flashed with satisfaction. "That means yes." He left the bed.

"It means I'm going to kill you if you betray me," I called after him. Hearing myself, I rolled my eyes. "I'm talking like a telenovela character." I undressed quickly and climbed into bed, shivering at the coolness of the sheets.

In a minute, Joe returned to the room with his Nikon and a small stand-alone flash. He opened the shades, leaving the windows covered with sheers that softened the brilliant afternoon light. As he pulled away the top cover on the bed, I jerked the sheet up high under my chin.

Joe looked at me in a different way from ever before, assessing highlights, shadows, visual geometry.

"I'm not comfortable being naked," I told him.

"The problem is that you're not naked often enough. You need to go without clothes about ninety-five percent of the time, and then you'll get used to it."

"You'd like that," I muttered.

Joe grinned and leaned over to kiss the exposed skin of my shoulder. "You're so pretty without your clothes," he murmured, working his way toward my neck. "Every time I see you in one of those big loose shirts, I think about all those sexy curves underneath, and it makes me as hot as hell."

I slid him a perturbed glance. "You don't like the way I dress?"

He paused in his kissing just long enough to say, "You're beautiful no matter what you wear."

The puzzling thing was, I knew he actually meant it. I could tell it was the truth, had been the truth for him since the beginning. My figure flaws weren't flaws to Joe — he had always regarded my body with a mixture of appreciation and lust that was pretty damned flattering.

I thought it was possible that I'd been testing him without being aware of it, trying to find out if the sack dresses and big tops and baggy pants would make any difference to him. Clearly they hadn't. Joe thought I was beautiful. Why should I think less of myself than he did? What point was there in letting those beautiful clothes hang in my closet unworn?

"I have some really stylish new outfits that Steven helped me pick out," I said. "I just haven't found the right time to start wearing them."

"You don't have to change anything for me."

Perversely, that made me wish I'd worn something new and pretty today, something that measured up to the way he saw me.

At Joe's direction, I lay on my side, awkwardly propping my head on my hand.

Lowering to his haunches, Joe positioned the camera. The shutter clicked and the nightstand unit flashed, covering me with fill light to balance the brilliance from the window behind me. "You've got no reason to be shy," he said. "Every inch of you is luscious." He paused to adjust the stand-alone flash, tested it again, and focused on me. His voice was soft and encouraging. "Can you show me your leg?"

I hesitated.

"One leg," he coaxed.

Cautiously, I slid out my top leg and hooked it over the top of the sheet.

Joe's gaze traveled along my exposed limb, and he shook his head as if presented with more temptation than a man could stand.

Setting aside the camera, he bent to kiss my knee.

I reached out to stroke his dark hair. "You're about to drop your camera."

"I don't care."

"You will if it smashes on the floor."

His hand began to insinuate itself beneath the sheet. "Maybe before I start taking pictures, we should —"

"No," I said. "Stay on task."

He withdrew his hand. "After?" he asked hopefully.

I couldn't restrain a grin. "We'll see."

My smile was captured with an immediate click of the shutter. Joe proceeded to shoot pictures from different angles, adjusting the focus ring with expert precision.

"Why do you have it on manual?" I asked, tucking the sheet more securely beneath my arms.

"In this lighting, I can find the right focusing point faster than auto mode can."

It was sexy, watching his hands on the camera, the skillful way he held and manipulated it. There was a particular pleasure in watching a man do something he was that good at. His expression was absorbed and intent as he took a series of shots with me lying on my stomach, my hips covered with the sheet, the length of my back exposed. I rested my head in the crook of my folded arms and gave him a sideways glance. The shutter clicked several times.

"Damn, you're photogenic," he murmured, approaching the bed. "Your skin catches the light like a pearl." As he continued to take shots from various angles, praising and flirting, fondling whenever he got the chance, I found myself beginning to have a good time.

"I'm beginning to think you're just using this as an excuse to feel me up," I commented.

"Side benefit," he said, climbing onto the bed with me. Still holding his camera, he straddled my hips in an easy movement, his denim-clad thighs on either side of me.

"Hey," I protested, tugging the sheet higher over my breasts.

Rising on his knees, Joe angled the camera directly above me and took a few shots. As close as we were, it was impossible not to notice that the button-fly crotch of his jeans was straining. Playfully, I walked my fingers up to his crotch and wiggled them into the spaces between the metal buttons.

Joe fumbled to adjust the focus ring. "Avery, don't distract me."

"I'm trying to help you." I unfastened the top button.

"That's not helping. In fact" — he let out an unsteady breath as I began on the second button — "that's the opposite of helping." He pried my hand from the placket. "Be a good girl and let me take a few more shots. I like this pose." After pressing a kiss into my palm, he positioned my arm up around my head in an abandoned posture. His fingers adjusted my elbow, softening the angle. With every alteration of his weight, I felt the enticing pressure of him against my groin.

Picking up his camera, Joe rose to his knees again. I looked into the lens while he looked at me, and I thought of the last time we'd had sex, how he'd stood at the side of the bed and pulled my legs up to his shoulders, how he'd teased and entered me slowly.

As I lay there, warmed by the erotic memory, I felt a deep, unfamiliar sense of ease, of languorous openness. My inhibitions had dissolved, and for once I wasn't trying to hide anything. It was so completely the opposite of what I'd expected that my lips parted with a faint, wondering smile.

The shutter clicked a few more times. "That's it," Joe said softly, the camera lowering.

"What do you mean?"

"I got the shot I wanted."

I blinked. "How can you tell?"

"Sometimes I can feel it even before I see it. Everything lines up. The second I push the shutter, I know I've found the sweet spot."

As he stretched to set the camera on the nightstand, I went for the buttons of his fly again, and I heard his quiet laugh. He stripped off his T-shirt and tossed it aside. Intent on my task, I worked at the fastenings, my hair pooling and sliding over his bare stomach. I licked at the line of crinkled hair leading into his jeans, my tongue sliding over roughness and silk. He made a fervent sound, his hands coming to my head, a slight tremor in his fingers. Another button, another, and then I pulled at the waist of his boxers.

Joe moved to help me. Before he could shove his jeans all the way off, I was on him, grasping the thick shaft with both hands. It was scorching hot, the thin skin moving easily over hard flesh. I put my mouth on him, and he went still, his jeans bunched around his knees, his lungs working in powerful bursts. I painted him with my tongue, taking in the salt and satin and a rampaging pulse, his pleasure so intense that I could feel its echoes in my own body. When I heard his muffled pleading groan, I lifted my head inch by inch, sucking wetly all the way. His entire body was rigid, his face flushed.

I crawled over him and he tangled one of his hands in my hair, forcing my head down to his. As he kicked off his jeans, I straddled him and reached down to guide him in place. With a hoarse murmur, he moved to help me, his hand closing over mine.

I began to ride fast and hard, pumping in reckless abandon. Wanting to make it last, Joe reached for my hips, forcing me to ease the pace. His hands played over me gently, caressing, coaxing me to lean forward. Lifting his head, he caught my nipple and pulled it deep. I writhed with the heat of him inside me, my body filled and brimming with sensation. He pulled me down farther, and we tried to find ways to pull each other even closer, using arms, legs, hands, mouths, breathing the same air, matching kisses and caresses and heartbeats.

Much later, Joe showed me the photo after he'd loaded it onto his laptop. A bright wash of light had imparted a pearly glow to my skin and turned my hair ember red. The eyes were heavy-lidded, the lips full and slightly parted. The woman in the photo was seductive, inviting, radiant.

Me.

As I stared at the image in wonder, Joe wrapped his arms around me from behind and whispered in my ear, "Every time I look at you . . . this is what I see."

NINETEEN

"Everyone be quiet," Sofia said, adjusting the TV volume. "I don't want to miss a word."

"You're recording it, right?" Steven asked.

"I think so, but sometimes I don't get the settings right."

"Let me check," he said, and she handed him the remote.

Everyone in the studio had gathered to watch the broadcast of a local television-magazine show. The producers had sent a camera crew and reporter to the Harlingen wedding we had done recently. The hour-long wedding special featured the latest tips, fashions, and trends, as well as profiling Texas-based businesses. The last segment of the show focused on practical advice for wedding planning. A Houston planner named Judith Lord had been asked to discuss choosing venues and vendors. I had been invited to follow up with advice about day-of preparation and logistics.

The Judith Lord segment was elegant and dignified, exactly what I hoped mine would be like. Judith, a long-established grande dame of the business, possessed a fondant-over-steel composure that I admired immensely. The reporter asked her a few easy questions, the interview cut to a shot of Judith and a client browsing through a row of wedding dresses and another showing them enjoying wedding cake samples, with Mozart playing in the background.

All semblance of dignity vanished, however, as soon as *my* segment started. The music changed to a manic comic-opera piece. "Why are they playing that?" I asked in surprised distaste.

At the same time, Tank exclaimed, "Hey, I like that song. It's the one from the Bugs Bunny cartoon with the barber chairs."

"Otherwise known as Rossini's overture to *The Barber of Seville*," Steven said dryly.

The reporter's voice-over started. *"In the elite world of Texas society weddings, Avery Crosslin has been aggressively building a client list with her take-no-prisoners style —"*

"Aggressive?" I protested.

"That's not a bad word," Steven said.

"Not for a man. But it's bad when they say it about a woman."

"Come here, Avery," Joe murmured. He was half sitting on an arm of the sofa, while Sofia and the rest of the studio team clustered in front of the television.

I went to him, and he slid an arm around my hip. "Am I aggressive?" I asked with a frown.

" 'Course not," he replied soothingly, at the same time that everyone else in the room said in unison, *"Yes."*

In the month since Joe and I had started sleeping together, we had grown closer at a rate that would have alarmed me if I'd allowed myself enough time to really think about it. Instead I stayed busy planning two small weddings as well as the Warner extravaganza. Every day was filled with work. My nights, however, belonged to Joe. Time moved at a different pace when I was with him, the hours blazing by at light speed. I always dreaded the shock of the alarm clock in the morning, when we had to go our separate ways.

Joe was a physical man, demanding in bed, endlessly patient and creative. I was never quite certain what to expect from him. Sometimes he was playful and spontaneous, ravishing me against the kitchen counter or on the stairs, doing exactly as he pleased despite my outraged modesty. Other times he would make me lie completely still while he caressed and teased endlessly, his hands so skilled and gentle that it drove me wild. Afterwards we had long, lazy conversations in the darkness, in which I confided things that I would probably regret later. But I couldn't seem to hold anything back with Joe. His attention was like some damned addictive drug that was impossible to kick.

Understanding me far too well, Joe gave my hip a comforting pat as I frowned at the TV. There I was on camera, stressing the importance of maintaining a strict timeline for the wedding day events.

Sofia turned briefly from the television and grinned at me over her shoulder. "You look great on TV," she said.

"Your personality is larger than life," Ree-Ann added.

"So is my ass," I muttered as the television-me walked away and the camera focused on my backside.

Joe, who would tolerate no criticism of my posterior, discreetly pinched my rear. "Hush," he whispered.

For the next four minutes, I watched with growing dismay as my professional image was demolished by quick-cut editing and whimsical music. I looked like a screwball comedy actress as I repositioned microphones, adjusted flower arrangements, and went out to the street to direct traffic so the photographer could get a shot of the wedding party outside the church.

The camera showed me talking to a groomsman who had insisted on wearing a cowboy hat with his tux. He was clutching his hat as if fearing I might rip it from him. As I argued and gestured, Coco stared up at the obstinate groomsman with a grumpy expression, her front paws flopping up and down in perfect timing to the opera music.

Everyone in the room chuckled. "They weren't supposed to film me with Coco," I said with a scowl. "I made that clear. I only brought her because the pet hotel didn't have room that day."

They cut back to the interview. *"You've said that part of your job is to prepare for the unexpected,"* the reporter said. *"How exactly do you do that?"*

"I try to think in terms of worst-case scenarios," I replied. *"Unexpected weather, vendor mistakes, technical difficulties . . ."*

"Technical difficulties such as . . ."

"Oh, it could be anything. Issues with the dance floor, problems with zippers or buttons . . . even an off-center ornament on the wedding cake."

I was shown walking into the reception site kitchen, which had been declared off-limits to the camera crew. But someone had followed me with a head-cam.

"I didn't say anyone could film me with a head-cam," I protested. "They didn't do that to Judith Lord!"

Everyone shushed me again.

On the TV screen, I approached two de-liverymen who were settling a four-tiered wedding cake on the counter. I told them they had brought it inside too soon — the cake was supposed to stay in the refriger-ated truck or the buttercream would melt.

"No one told us," one of them replied.

"I'm telling you. Take it back to the truck and —" My eyes widened as the heavy wedding cake topper began to slide and tilt. I reached up and leaned forward to catch it before it could damage all four tiers on the way down.

Someone in editing had bleeped out my swearing.

Noticing the way the deliverymen were staring at me, I followed their avid gazes, discovering I had leaned so close to the cake that my breasts were covered with white buttercream swirls.

By this point, everyone in the room was cracking up. Even Joe was trying manfully

335

to choke back his amusement.

On the TV screen, the reporter asked me a question about the challenges of my job. I paraphrased General Patton, saying you had to accept the challenges so you could experience the exhilaration of victory.

"But what about the romance of the wedding day?" the reporter asked. *"Doesn't that get lost when you treat it like a military campaign?"*

"The bride and groom supply the romance," I replied confidently. *"I worry about every detail, so they don't have to. A wedding is a celebration of love, and that's what they should be free to focus on."*

"And while everyone else is celebrating," the reporter said in a voice-over, *"Avery Crosslin is taking care of business."*

I was shown making a beeline to the back of the church, where the chain-smoking father of the bride was lurking with a lit cigarette in his mouth. Without a word, I took the can of Evian from my bag and extinguished the cigarette while he stood there blinking. Next I was kneeling on the floor, duct-taping the torn hem of one of the bridesmaid's dresses. Finally the camera panned to the groomsman's cowboy hat shoved under a chair, where I'd secretly stashed it.

Someone had turned the hat upside down, and Coco was sitting in it. She stared directly into the camera, her eyes bright, her tongue hanging out, while the piece concluded with a grand orchestral finale.

I picked up the remote controller and turned off the TV. "Who put Coco in that hat?" I demanded. "She couldn't have gotten in there by herself. Sofia, did you do it?"

She shook her head, snickering.

"Then who?"

No one would admit to it. I looked around the room at the entire lot of them. I had never seen them so collectively entertained. "I'm glad you all find this so amusing, since we'll probably be out of business in a matter of days."

"Are you kidding?" Steven asked. "We're going to get more business from this than we can handle."

"They made me look incompetent."

"No, they didn't."

"What about the frosting?" I demanded.

"You saved the cake," Steven pointed out. "While at the same time boosting the testosterone level of every guy in the audience."

"It was a wedding show," I said. "You, Tank, and Joe are the only three straight men in Houston who watched it."

"Give me the remote," Ree-Ann said. "I want to see it again."

I shook my head emphatically. "I'm going to delete it."

"Doesn't matter," Tank told Ree-Ann. "The station will put it on their website."

Joe closed his hand over the remote and removed it carefully from my grip. His gaze was lit with amused sympathy.

"I want to be elegant like Judith Lord," I told him plaintively.

"Avery, there are a million Judith Lords out there, and only one you. You were beautiful and funny on that program, and you gave off the energy of someone who was having a hell of a good time. You accomplished everything Judith Lord did, except that you were a lot more entertaining." Joe handed the remote to Steven and took my hand. "Come on, I'm taking you out for dinner."

By the time he and I had reached the front door, they had rewound the interview and were watching it again.

Returning to the studio a couple of hours later, Joe and I encountered Sofia and Steven, who were on their way out to eat.

Sofia was happy and animated, almost illuminated from within. That undoubtedly had something to do with the fact that she and Steven had recently started sleeping together. Sofia had divulged to me that, unlike Luis, Steven knew about foreplay. I could tell from seeing them together that everything was going very, very well. In fact, Sofia and Steven treated each other with a kindness that I wouldn't have expected, given their past animosity. They had once looked for thousands of small ways to hurt each other, searching for each other's weaknesses. Now they seemed to share an uncomplicated joy in being unguarded with each other.

"Do you feel better?" Sofia asked, hugging me as I walked in.

"Actually, yes," I said. "I've decided to put that stupid television show behind me and pretend it never happened."

"I'm afraid you can't do that," Sofia said, delight glimmering in her hazel eyes. "The producer called this morning and said you're all over their Twitter feed, and everyone loves you. And a half-dozen people have asked about adopting Coco."

I picked up the Chihuahua protectively. Her dry little tongue swiped at my chin.

"I told them we'd think about it," Sofia continued, her gaze teasing.

Within a week, the segment had been picked up by the station's national affiliate. The schedule at the studio was crammed with appointments, and both Steven and Sofia were insisting that we needed to hire more people.

On Friday afternoon, I received a text from my friend Jasmine, a command to call her instantly.

Although I always loved talking with Jasmine and hearing about her life in Manhattan, I was reluctant to dial her. If she'd seen the interview, I was certain she disapproved. Jazz had always said it was imperative that a woman maintain a professional façade no matter what. No crying, no displays of anger, no loss of composure. A television appearance in which I had cursed, carried around a Chihuahua, and ended up with buttercream on my boobs was not what Jazz would consider an appropriate work persona.

"Did you see it?" I asked as soon as Jasmine said hello.

"Yes, you hot shit. I saw it."

That surprised a laugh out of me. "You didn't hate it?"

"It was fabulous. Like a perfectly timed sitcom. You *owned* the screen. You and that little dog — what's her name?"

"Coco."

"I never knew you were a dog person."

"I didn't either."

"The part with the cake — did you plan that?"

"Good Lord, no. I'll never live it down."

"You don't want to live it down. You want to do more of that."

I frowned, puzzled. "What?"

"Remember that opportunity I told you about a while back, the one for *Rock the Wedding*?"

"The Trevor Stearns show."

"Yes. I sent them your résumé and portfolio, and the video, and never heard back from them. They've interviewed dozens of candidates, and as far as I know, they've auditioned three. But they're not one hundred percent happy with any of them, and Trevor is going to freak out if they don't find someone soon. The host not only has to be capable of the job, she also has to have the *thing*. That quality that makes it impossible to take your eyes off her. So a couple days ago, one of the producers, Lois, saw the YouTube video, with you and — sorry, what's the dog's name again?"

"Coco," I said breathlessly.

"Right. Lois saw that and sent the link to Trevor and the others, and they *died*. They took another look at your résumé, and now they think you're *exactly* what they've been looking for. They want to meet you. They're going to bring you up here for an interview." Jasmine paused. "You're quiet," she said impatiently. "What are you thinking?"

"I can't believe it," I managed to say. My heart was pounding.

"Believe it!" Jasmine cried triumphantly. "Now that I've told you, I'll give your contact info to Lois, and she'll arrange a flight. Trevor's in L.A., but the *Rock the Wedding* producers are in Manhattan, and they're the ones you'll talk to initially. We'll have to get you an agent — we won't be able to find anyone in time for the first meeting, but that's okay at this stage. Don't make any commitments or promises. Just let them get to know you, and listen to what they have to say."

"They don't need to fly me to New York, if they can wait a few days," I said. "I'm coming up next Wednesday for a dress fitting with one of my brides."

"You were coming here and you didn't mention it?"

"I've been busy," I protested.

"I'm sure you have. How are things with Joe Travis, by the way?"

I had told her recently about my relationship with Joe, but I hadn't explained how I really felt about him . . . the deep tenderness and happiness and fear, and the painful ambivalence I felt about becoming ever more dependent on him. Jasmine wouldn't have understood. When it came to her own love life, she chose relationships that were convenient and ultimately disposable. Falling in love was something she didn't allow herself. "Love doesn't care if you get your work done," she had once told me.

In response to her question, I said, "He's divine in bed."

I heard her familiar husky laugh. "Enjoy that hot Texas stud while you can. You'll be moving back to New York soon."

"I wouldn't count on that just yet," I said. "Trevor and his people will probably end up deciding not to cast me. Also . . . there's a lot for me to think about."

"Avery, if this works out, you'll be a celebrity. Everyone will know you. You can get the best table at any restaurant, the best tickets, a penthouse apartment . . . what is there to think about?"

"My sister is here."

"She can move up here too. They'll find something for her to do."

"I don't know if that's what she would want. Sofia and I have worked hard to build this business. It wouldn't be easy for either of us to abandon it."

"All right. Do your thinking. In the meantime, I'm giving Lois your info. And I'll see you next week."

"I can't wait," I said. "Jazz . . . I don't know how to thank you for this."

"Don't be afraid of this chance. It's the right thing for you. New York is where you belong, and you know it. Things are happening up here. Bye, sweetie." She ended the call.

Sighing, I plugged my phone back into its charger. "Things are happening here too," I said.

TWENTY

"I've always known you were meant for something like this," Sofia said after I'd told her about Jazz's call. Her reaction to the news had been similar to mine: She seemed a little shaken but excited. She understood the potential of such an opportunity, what it could mean. Shaking her head slowly, she looked at me with wide eyes. "You're going to be working with Trevor Stearns."

"It's just a possibility."

"It will happen. I can feel it."

"I would have to move back to New York," I said.

Her smile dimmed a little. "If you do, we'll make it work."

"Would you want to come with me?"

"You mean . . . move to New York with you?"

"I don't think I could ever be happy living away from you," I said.

Sofia reached out and took my hand.

"We're sisters," she said simply. "We're together even when we're not, do you understand, *mi corazón*? But New York is not the place for me."

"I'm not going to leave you by yourself here."

"I won't be alone. I have the business, and our friends, and . . ." She paused and colored.

"Steven," I said.

Sofia nodded, her eyes sparkling.

"What is it?" I demanded. "What?"

"He loves me. He told me."

"And you said it back?"

"I did."

"Did you say it back because you didn't want to hurt his feelings or because he's the first man you've ever experienced foreplay with, or because you really love him?"

Sofia smiled. "I said it back because I love him for his heart, his soul, and his interesting, complicated brain." She paused. "The foreplay doesn't hurt."

I gave a wondering laugh. "When was the moment you realized you loved him?"

"There wasn't a moment. It was like uncovering something that was there all along."

"It's serious, then? Living-together serious?"

"Talking-about-marriage serious." Sofia hesitated. "Do we have your approval?"

"Of course you do. No one's good enough for you, but Steven's as close as you're going to get." I braced my elbows on the table and pressed my fingertips against my temples. "The two of you could handle the business," I mused aloud. "Steven can do what I do. You're the only truly indispensable person around here — you're the creative engine. All you need are people to make your ideas happen."

"What would it be like for you," Sofia asked, "hosting a show like *Rock the Wedding*? Would you have to come up with ideas?"

I shook my head. "I imagine most of it will be preplanned and staged. My role will be to flail around like Lucy Ricardo and then pull everything together at the end. There'll be pratfalls and manufactured crises, and countless views of my cleavage and my weird dog."

"It's going to be such a big hit," Sofia said in awe.

"I know," I said, and we both squealed.

Sobering after a minute, she asked, "What about Joe?"

The question made my stomach hurt. "I don't know."

"Lots of people do long-distance," Sofia said. "If two people want to make it work, they can."

"That's true," I said. "Joe's got enough money to travel as much as he wants."

"It could make the relationship even better," Sofia volunteered. "You would never get sick of each other."

"Quality time instead of quantity."

Sofia nodded vigorously. "Everything will be fine."

Deep down I knew all of that was bullshit, but it sounded so good that I wanted to believe it. "I don't think there's any need to mention this to Joe until after I go to New York, do you?" I asked. "I don't want to worry him unnecessarily."

"I wouldn't say anything until you know for sure."

I lasted for most of the weekend without saying a word to Joe, but it nagged at me. I wanted to be up front with him, even though I was afraid of what he might say. I had problems sleeping, waking up repeatedly throughout the night and going through the next day exhausted. This cycle was repeated for two more days, until finally Joe turned on the light at midnight. "I feel like I've got a sack of puppies in bed," he said, a note of exasperation in his voice, but his eyes were warm. "What's going on, honey? Why can't you sleep?"

I looked at him in the lamplight, at his concerned face and disheveled hair and that broad chest. I was suffused with a terrible feeling of longing, as if no matter how closely he held me, it would never be close enough. I huddled against him, and he murmured quietly, tucking the covers around us both. "Tell me. Whatever it is, it's okay."

I told him everything, talking so fast that it was a wonder he could follow. I told him everything Jasmine had said about Trevor Stearns and *Rock the Wedding*, and how this was a chance that wouldn't come my way again, and how it was everything I'd ever dreamed of.

Joe listened carefully, interrupting only to ask a question now and then. When I finally paused to take a breath, he eased my face away from his chest and looked down at me. His expression was unreadable. "Of course you have to talk to the producers," he said. "You need to find out what the options are."

"You're not mad? Upset?"

"Hell, no, I'm proud of you. If this is what you want, I'll support you all the way."

I nearly gasped with relief. "Oh, God. I'm

so glad to hear you say that. I was so worried. When you think about it, a long-distance relationship doesn't have to be bad at all. As long as the two of us —"

"Avery," he said gently, "I haven't agreed to a long-distance relationship."

Bewildered, I sat up to face him, pulling the silk straps of my nightgown back to my shoulders. "But you just said you'd support me."

"I will. I want you to have whatever makes you happy."

"I'd be happy if I could get this show and move to New York, and also keep my relationship with you." Realizing how selfish that sounded, I added sheepishly, "So basically I want to have my cake, and also have my cake travel back and forth to visit me."

I saw his quick grin, although there wasn't much real amusement in it. "Cake doesn't generally travel well."

"Would you at least be willing to give it a try?" I asked. "With a long-distance relationship, you could have the benefits of being single, but you'd also have the security of —"

"I tried that a long time ago," Joe interrupted quietly. "Never again. There's no benefit, honey. You get tired of being lonely. Tired of all the miles between you. Every time you're together, you're giving a dying relationship CPR. If it's a short-term separation, that's different. But what you're talking about . . . an open-ended arrangement with no stopping point . . . it's a nonstarter."

"You could move. You would have incredible opportunities in New York. Better than here."

"Not better," he countered calmly. "Just different."

"Better," I insisted. "When you consider —"

"Hold on." Joe held up a hand in a staying gesture, a wry smile touching his lips. "First you're going to go talk to those people and find out if you're right for the job, and if the job's right for you. For now, let's get some sleep."

"I can't sleep," I grumbled, dropping to my back, huffing in frustration. "I couldn't sleep last night, either."

"I know," he said. "I was with you."

The light was extinguished, the room so dark that it was shadowless.

"Why didn't this happen three years ago?" I asked aloud. "*That* was when I needed it. Why did it have to be now?"

"Because life has shitty timing. Hush."

My nerves had knotted in agitation. "I refuse to believe you would dump me just because I didn't happen to be conveniently located in Texas."

"Avery, quit working yourself up."

"Sorry." I tried to relax and regulate my breathing. "Let me ask just one thing: Your family has a private plane, right?"

"A Gulfstream. For business."

"Yes, but if you wanted to use it for personal reasons, would your brothers and sister object?"

"*I* would object. It's five thousand bucks per flight hour."

"Is it a light jet, or a midsize, or —"

"It's a Gulfstream large-cabin super-midsize jet."

"How long in advance do you have to call before they can have it ready?"

"For a trip like that, two or three hours." The covers were drawn back from my legs.

"What are you doing?" I couldn't see him, could only feel him moving in the darkness.

"Since you're so interested in my plane, I'm going to tell you all about it."

"Joe —"

"Quiet." The hem of my nightgown inched upward, and I felt a soft, hot kiss on the side of my knee. "The Gulfstream has Internet, TV, a Global Satcom phone system, and the worst coffeemaker in existence." A kiss descended to my other knee, followed by the long ticklish streak of his tongue trailing upward along my thigh. "The two upgraded Rolls-Royce engines," he continued, "provide about fourteen thousand pounds of thrust each." I drew in a sharp breath as I felt the slither of his tongue high on the inside of my leg.

His breath stirred private curls until each hair stood on end, individuate with sensation. "The plane takes about forty-four hundred gallons of fuel."

A single, idle lick. I whimpered, all my focus zinging to that soft place. He nuzzled deeper into the tenderness.

"Fully fueled, it flies nonstop for forty-three hundred nautical miles." His fingertips nudged me open while his lips descended, forming a hot, wet seal. I was dazed and silent, my hips catching a tight upward arch. Just as the pleasure approached an unimaginable spike, his mouth lifted.

"It's been updated with thrust reversers that shorten the landing," he murmured, "and an enhanced vision system with an infrared camera mounted on the front." A long finger slid inside me. "Is there anything else you'd like to know?"

I shook my head, beyond speech. Although he couldn't have seen the movement, he must have felt it, because I heard his quiet sound of amusement. "Avery, honey," he whispered, "you're gonna sleep so good tonight. . . ."

I felt his mouth and tongue again as he worked me with delicately ruthless precision, and I was lost in a tumble of heat. Pleasure gathered, lifted, refracted. When it became too much to bear, I tried to twist away, but Joe wouldn't let me, persisting until my groans had broken into long sighs.

After he was finished with me, I didn't fall asleep so much as I fell unconscious. I slept so long and hard that I barely registered Joe kissing me good-bye the next morning. He leaned over the bed, showered and fully dressed, murmuring that he had to leave.

By the time I was fully awake, Joe was gone.

Two days later, I boarded a private Citation Ultra with Hollis Warner. A flight attendant served us Dr Pepper on ice while we waited for Bethany, who was running late. Fashionably dressed and heavily made up, Hollis relaxed in the cream leather seat next to mine. She explained that her husband, David, offered compensation plans to some of the top executives in his restaurant and casino businesses to have the jet for a specified number of personal-use hours, with the company picking up the tab. Hollis and her friends often used the Citation for shopping trips and vacations.

"I'm so glad we're staying two nights instead of just one," Hollis said. "I'm having dinner with some girlfriends tomorrow night. You're welcome to join us, Avery."

"Thank you so much, but I'm having dinner with friends I haven't seen in much too long. And there's a meeting I have to attend tomorrow afternoon." I told her about the meeting with the producers of *Rock the Wedding* and being interviewed as a potential host of a spin-off. Hollis seemed delighted by the news and said that when I became a celebrity, she was going to take credit for helping to launch me. "After all, if I hadn't picked you as Bethany's wedding planner, you wouldn't have gotten on that show."

"I'll tell everyone it was you," I assured her, and we clinked glasses.

After taking a sip, Hollis tucked a lock of smooth blond hair behind her ear and asked in an off hand tone, "Are you still going out with Joe?"

"Yes."

"What does he say about this opportunity?"

"Oh, he's being very supportive. He's

happy for my sake."

I knew without being told that should the television opportunity come through, Joe was determined not to influence my decision. He would not ask me to stay or give up anything. Most of all, he would make no promises. There were no guarantees about what our relationship might become or how long it would last. Whereas there *would* be guarantees, contractual ones, if I was hired by Trevor Stearns's production company. Even in case of failure, I would have some incredible takeaways. Money, connections, a heavily bolstered résumé.

I was spared the necessity of replying when Bethany boarded the plane. She was dressed in a vibrant Tory Burch tunic and capris, her hair gilded with fresh highlights. "Hi, y'all!" she exclaimed. "Isn't this *fun*?"

"Look at how pretty she is," Hollis said with a mixture of pride and rue. "The prettiest girl in Texas, her daddy always says." Hollis's expression went blank as she saw another passenger board after Bethany. "I see you've brought Kolby."

"You said I could bring a friend."

"I sure did, sugar." Hollis flipped open a magazine and began to page through it methodically, her mouth tight. It didn't appear that Kolby, a muscular young man in his twenties, was the kind of friend Hollis had had in mind.

Bethany's companion was dressed in board shorts, a Billabong button-down shirt, and a sports cap from which a shock of sun-bleached hair protruded in the back. He was tanned a deep shade of walnut, his eyes light blue, the teeth toilet-bowl white. From an objective viewpoint, he was handsome in the bland, deeply boring way that only someone with perfectly symmetrical features could be.

"Bethany, you look fabulous, as usual," I said as she leaned down to hug me. "How are you feeling? Are you up to this flight?"

"I sure am!" she exclaimed. "Feeling awesome. My OB-GYN says I'm his star patient. The baby's kicking hard now — sometimes you can see my stomach move."

"Wonderful," I said, smiling. "Was Ryan excited to feel the baby kicking?"

She made a face. "Ryan's so serious about everything. I won't let him come to my checkups, because he brings my mood down."

Hollis spoke while continuing to leaf through the magazine. "Maybe you could work on getting him to smile more often, Bethany."

The young woman laughed. "No, I'll let

him fiddle with his drawings and computer designs . . . I've got someone right here who knows how to have a good time." She squeezed the man's arm and smiled at me. "Avery, you don't mind me bringing Kolby on our girls' trip, do you? He won't bother anyone."

The man looked at her with a sly grin. "I'm gonna bother you plenty," he said.

Erupting in a fit of giggles, Bethany dragged him to the bar, where they rummaged through canned beverages. Looking perturbed, the flight attendant tried to persuade them to have a seat and allow her to bring the drinks.

"Who is Kolby?" I dared to ask Hollis.

"No one," she murmured. "A waterskiing instructor Bethany met last summer. They're just friends." She shrugged. "Bethany likes to keep fun people around her. As much as I adore Ryan, he can be a stick-in-the-mud."

I let the comments pass, although I was tempted to point out that it wasn't fair to judge Ryan for not being fun when he was preparing to marry a woman he didn't love and be a father to a baby he didn't want.

"Nothing needs to be mentioned about this," Hollis said after a moment. "Particularly to Joe. He might say something to Ryan and stir up trouble for no reason."

"Hollis, if there's anyone in the world who wants this wedding to go off without a hitch even more than you do, it's me. Trust me, I'm not going to say anything about Kolby to anyone. It's not my place."

Satisfied, Hollis shot me a glance of genuine warmth. "I'm glad we understand each other," she said.

Another disconcerting moment occurred at the hotel reservations desk, where I was checking in. As the desk clerk ran my credit card and we waited for the charge to go through, I glanced at the other clerk at the desk, who had just checked Bethany and Kolby into a single room. I supposed some part of me had hoped that Bethany and Kolby really were just friends. They had behaved like teenagers during the flight from Houston, whispering and giggling, watching a movie together, but there had been nothing overtly sexual in their interactions.

This arrangement, however, left no room for doubt.

I dragged my gaze back to the clerk in front of me. He returned my credit card and gave me a form to initial and sign. I had meant what I'd said to Hollis — I wasn't going to mention anything about this to anyone. But it made me feel guilty and sordid to be part of this secret.

"See y'all later," Bethany said. "Don't expect Kolby and me for lunch — we're ordering room service."

"Let's meet at the concierge desk in two hours," I said. "The fitting appointment is at two o'clock."

"Two o'clock," Bethany repeated, walking to the bank of elevators with Kolby in tow. They paused to look at a display window filled with glittering jewelry.

Hollis came to stand beside me, tucking her phone back into her bag. "You try to raise a daughter someday," she said, sounding tired and a little defensive, "and tell me how easy it is. You'll teach her right from wrong, how to behave, what to believe. You'll do your best. But someday your smart girl will do something stupid. And you'll do anything you can to help her." Hollis sighed and shrugged. "Bethany can do whatever she wants until she's a married woman. She hasn't said any vows yet. When she does, I'll expect her to keep them. Until then, Ryan has the same freedom."

I kept my mouth shut and nodded.

At two o'clock on the dot, we were

welcomed into Finola Strong's studio and bridal salon on the Upper East Side. The salon was decorated in understated smoky colors, the furniture in the private seating areas upholstered in velvet. Jasmine had referred me to Finola, who had agreed to turn my rough sketches into an appropriate design. Known for her love of clean lines and opulent detail, Finola was well suited to pull off the period beading and intricate paneled construction of the high-waisted skirt. Her team was second to none at creating couture gowns that started at thirty thousand dollars.

Two months earlier, an assistant from the studio had flown to the Warner home in Houston to render the drafted pattern into a muslin mock-up, pinning it meticulously to fit Bethany's body. Since Finola had been told about the pregnancy, she had designed the gown to be easily adjusted to Bethany's changing shape.

This fitting was the first for the actual gown, with much of the beading and trim already added. Today the garment would be adjusted so the fabric would drape and fall perfectly. One of Finola's assistants would fly down with the finished gown a few days before the wedding, for one last fitting. At that time, additional alterations would be made if necessary.

As we lounged in a dressing room with a giant three-way mirror and a private seating area, an assistant brought champagne for Hollis and me and a flute of club soda and juice for Bethany. Soon Finola appeared. She was a slender, fair-haired woman in her thirties, with an easy smile and a lively, discerning gaze. I had met her three or four times during the years I had been in design, but each encounter had lasted for mere seconds during Fashion Week or at some crowded society function.

"Avery Crosslin," Finola exclaimed. "Congratulations on the new gig."

I laughed. "Thank you, but I'm not nearly as convinced as Jazz that I'm going to get it."

"You're no good at modesty," she informed me. "You look positively smug. When do you meet with the producers?"

I grinned at her. "Tomorrow."

After I introduced Finola to the Warners, she pronounced that Bethany would be one of the most beautiful brides she had ever dressed. "I can't wait to see you in this gown," she told Bethany. "It's a global creation: silk from Japan, lining from Korea, beaded embroidery from India, an underlay from Italy, and antique lace from France.

We'll leave for a few minutes while you try it on. My assistant Chloe will help you."

After a tour of Finola's salon, we returned to the dressing room. Bethany stood before the mirror, her figure slim and glittering.

The gown was a work of art, the bodice made of antique lace that had been hand-embroidered in a geometric pattern and encrusted with crystal beading as fine as fairy dust. It was held up with thin crystal straps that glittered against Bethany's golden shoulders. The skirt, adorned with scattered beads that caught the light like mist, flowed gently from the high-cut bodice. It was impossible to imagine any bride more beautiful.

Hollis smiled and put her fingers to her mouth. "How magnificent," she gasped.

Bethany smiled and swished her skirts.

However, there was a problem with the dress, and Finola and I both saw it. The drape of the front panels wasn't right. They split much wider over her stomach than I had sketched them. Approaching Bethany, I said with a smile, "You're gorgeous. But we'll have to make a few alterations."

"Where?" Bethany asked, perplexed. "It's already perfect."

"It's the way it drapes," Finola explained. "In the month between now and the wedding, you'll grow enough that the overskirts will fall on either side like theater curtains, which, adorable as your tummy is, will not be flattering."

"I don't know why I've gotten big so fast," Bethany fretted.

"Everyone's pregnancy is different," Hollis told her.

"You're not big at all," Finola soothed. "You're slender everywhere except your stomach, which is just as it should be. Our job is to make this dress fit like a dream, which we will certainly do." She went to Bethany, grasping folds of the paneling, repositioning fabric and viewing the drape with an assessing gaze.

Suddenly Bethany jumped a little and put her hand to the front of her stomach. "Oh!" She laughed. "That was a strong kick."

"It was," Finola said. "I could see it. Do you need to sit down, Bethany?"

"No, I'm fine."

"Good. I'm just figuring out this paneling situation. I'll be done in a second." Finola's gaze was filled with warm interest as she looked at Bethany. "I'm trying to figure out how much your bump will grow in the next month. . . . Are you by chance expecting twins?"

Bethany shook her head.

"Thank goodness. One of my sisters had twins, and that was an unholy challenge. And the due date . . . has that been revised?"

"No," Hollis answered for her.

Finola glanced at her assistant. "Chloe, please help Bethany out of the dress while I talk with Avery about the alterations. Bethany, may we leave your mother here with you?"

"Sure."

Finola went to Hollis and picked up the empty champagne glass on the little table beside her. "More champagne?" she asked. "Coffee?"

"Coffee, please."

"I'll tell one of my assistants. We'll be back soon. Come, Avery."

Obediently, I followed Finola out of the dressing room. She gave the empty flute to a passing assistant and directed her to brew some fresh coffee for Mrs. Warner. We proceeded along a quiet hallway to a corner office lined with windows.

I sat in the chair that Finola indicated. "How tough is the paneling to fix?" I asked in concern. "You won't have to take the whole skirt apart, will you?"

"I'll have my pattern maker and draper take a look at it. For what they're paying, we'll remake the entire fucking dress if necessary." She stretched her shoulders and rubbed the back of her neck. "You know what the problem with the paneling is, don't you?"

I shook my head. "I'd have to take a closer look."

"Here's the cardinal rule of designing for a knocked-up bride: Never trust the due date."

"You think she's off by a little?"

"I think she's off by at least two months."

I gave her a blank stare.

"I see it all the time," Finola said. "Maternity is the fastest-growing department in bridal ready-to-wear. Approximately one in five of my brides are pregnant. And many of them fudge the dates. Even in this day and age, some women worry about their parents' disapproval. And there are other reasons. . . ." She shrugged. "It's not for us to judge or comment. If I'm right about the timing, then Bethany's belly will be considerably larger than we expected when she walks down the aisle."

"Then we should forget the paneling and replace the entire overlay," I said distractedly. "Although there's probably not enough time to get new beadwork done."

"We'll have some hideously expensive local person do it. How long will Bethany be in town? Can we schedule an additional fitting for her tomorrow?"

"Absolutely. In the morning?"

"No, we'll need more time than that. How about in the afternoon after your meeting?"

"I'm not sure how long it will last."

"If you can't make it, just have Bethany come here by four. I'll take pictures and send jpegs so you can see exactly what we've done."

"Finola . . . are you absolutely sure about the due date?"

"I'm not a doctor. But I guarantee that girl is more than four months pregnant. Her belly button's popped out, which usually doesn't happen until the end of the second trimester. And the way that baby's kicking? Impressive for a fetus that's only supposed to be about five inches long. Even though Bethany's kept her weight down, the bump doesn't lie."

I went out to dinner that night with Jasmine and an assortment of old friends from the fashion industry. We sat at a table for twelve in an Italian restaurant, with at least three or four conversations going on at any given moment. As always, they had the best gossip in the world, exchanging tidbits about designers, celebrities, and society icons. I had forgotten how exciting it was to be in the middle of everything new and fresh, to know things before the rest of the world did.

Plates of beef carpaccio were brought out, the raw meat sliced into translucent sheets even thinner than the scattered flakes of shaved Parmesan on top. Although the waiter tried to bring baskets of bread along with the salad course, everyone at the table shook their heads in unison. I stared forlornly at the retreating bread, which left wafts of sweetly fragrant steam in its wake.

"We could each have just one piece," I said.

"No one eats carbs," replied Siobhan, the beauty director at Jasmine's magazine.

"Still?" I asked. "I was hoping they'd come back by now."

"Carbs will never come back," Jasmine said.

"God, don't say that."

"It's been scientifically proven that eating white bread is so bad for you, you're better off emptying packets of granulated sugar into your mouth."

"Send Avery a copy of the KPD plan," Siobhan said to Jazz. She gave me a significant glance. "I lost twelve pounds in a week."

"From where?" I asked, looking at her rail-thin frame.

"You'll love KPD," Jasmine assured me. "Everyone's doing it. It's a modified ketogenic-Paleo-detox plan, starting with an intervention phase similar to Protein Power. The weight comes off so fast, it's almost as good as having a tapeworm."

When the entrées were brought out, I realized I was the only one in the group who had ordered pasta.

Jett, an accessories designer for a major fashion label, glanced at my penne and said with a sigh, "I haven't eaten pasta since Bush was in office."

"First or second?" Jasmine asked.

"First." Jett looked nostalgic. "I remember that last meal. Carbonara, extra bacon."

Becoming aware of their intent gazes, I paused with my loaded fork halfway up to my mouth. "Sorry," I said sheepishly. "Should I eat this at another table?"

"Since you're technically an out-of-town guest," Jasmine said, "you can keep your penne. When you move back here, however, you'll have to say good-bye to refined carbohydrates."

"If I move back here," I said, "I'll have to say good-bye to a lot of things."

At one o'clock the next afternoon, I took a

cab to midtown and walked into the Stearns production offices. After five minutes of waiting, a young woman with a messy bob and a skinny black pantsuit came to escort me to an elevator. We rode a few floors up and entered a reception area with a spectacular ceiling paved in a lavender-and-silver mosaic tile design and furniture upholstered in a deep shade of eggplant.

Three people were there to greet me with such lavish enthusiasm that I relaxed immediately. They were all young and beautifully dressed, smiling widely as they introduced themselves. The woman introduced herself as Lois Ammons, a producer and executive assistant to Trevor Stearns; after that came Tim Watson, a casting producer, and Rudy Winters, a producer and assistant director.

"You didn't bring your sweet little dog?" Lois asked with a laugh as we went into a spacious office with a dazzling view of the Chrysler Building.

"I'm afraid Coco is a little too old and high-maintenance to do much traveling," I said.

"Poor thing. I'm sure she misses you."

"She's in good hands. My sister Sofia is taking care of her."

"You work with your sister, right? Why

don't you tell us how that started. Wait, would you mind if we record our chat?"

"Not at all."

The next three hours went so fast that they seemed like three minutes. We started by discussing my past experience in the fashion business and then what it had been like to start the studio with Sofia. As I recounted some of the quirkier weddings we had designed and coordinated, I had to pause while the trio burst out laughing.

"Avery," Lois said, "Jasmine told me that you're still in the process of getting an agent."

"Yes, although I wasn't certain it would even be necessary, so I haven't —"

"It's necessary," Tim said, smiling at me. "If this all works out, Avery, we'll be negotiating issues such as public appearances, licensing and merchandising rights, product endorsements, publishing, residuals . . . So you need to find an agent right away."

"Got it," I said, pulling a tablet from my bag and making a note. "Does this mean we'll be meeting again?"

"Avery," Rudy said, "as far as I'm concerned, you're our girl. We'll have to do some more testing, perhaps send a camera crew to the Warner wedding."

"I'll have to clear it with them," I said breathlessly, "but I don't think they'd object."

"You and this show would be a perfect match," Tim said. "I think you could take Trevor's concept and make it your own. You'll bring great energy. We love the sexy redhead image, love how comfortable you are with the camera. You'll be on a fast learning track, but you can handle it."

"We need to get her together with Trevor and see how they click," Lois said. She smiled at me. "He already loves you. Once you get an agent, we can start talking about tailoring the show to your personality, and working on the pilot treatment. In the first episode we'd like to push the idea that Trevor is mentoring you . . . set up some dilemmas and have you call him for advice, which you don't necessarily have to follow. Ideally the dynamic would have hints of tension . . . Trevor and his sassy protégée, with a lot of snappy dialogue . . . how does that sound?"

"Sounds fun," I said automatically, although I was unnerved by the feeling that a persona was being created for me.

"And there'll have to be a dog," Tim said. "Everyone at the L.A. offices loved seeing you carry that dog around. But a cuter one.

What are those fluffy white ones, Lois?"

"Pomeranian?"

Tim shook his head. "No, I don't think that's what I mean. . . ."

"Coton de Tulear?"

"Maybe. . . ."

"I'll pull up a list of breeds for you to look at," Lois said, making notes.

"You're getting me another dog?" I asked.

"Just for the show," Lois said. "But you wouldn't have to take it home with you." She laughed lightly. "I'm sure Coco would have something to say about that."

"So," I asked, "the dog would be a prop?"

"A cast member," Tim replied.

While the two men talked, Lois reached out and gripped my nerveless hand, beaming at me.

"Let's make this happen," she said.

Sitting in the hotel room that night, staring down at my cell phone, I practiced what to say to Joe. I tried a few lines out loud and wrote a few words on a nearby notepad.

When I realized what I was doing . . . *rehearsing* for a conversation with him . . . I pushed away the notepad and made myself dial.

Joe picked up right away. The sound of his voice, that familiar, comforting drawl, made me feel good all over and at the same time filled me with wrenching longing. "Avery, honey. How are you doing?"

"I'm fine. Missing you."

"I miss you too."

"Do you have a few minutes to talk?"

"I've got all night. Tell me what you've been up to."

I sat back farther on the bed and crossed my legs. "Well . . . I had the big meeting today."

"How did it go?"

I described it in detail, everything that had been said, everything I'd thought and felt. While I did most of the talking, Joe was deliberately reserved, refusing to express an opinion one way or the other.

"Did you talk numbers?" he asked eventually.

"No, but I'm pretty sure the money will be big. Maybe life-changing."

He sounded sardonic. "Whether or not the money's life-changing, the job sure as hell will be."

"Joe . . . this is the kind of opportunity I've always dreamed of. It looks like it really could happen. They made it pretty clear that they want to make it work out. If so . . . I don't know how I can turn it down."

"I told you before, I won't stand in your way."

"Yes, I know that," I said with a touch of annoyance. "I'm not worried that you'll try to stand in the way. I'm worried that you won't try to stay in my life."

Joe answered with the weary impatience of someone whose thoughts had been chasing in circles, just like mine. "If your life moves fifteen hundred miles away, Avery, it's not going to be all that easy for me to stay in it."

"What about moving there with me? We could share an apartment. There's nothing tying you to Texas. You could pack everything up and —"

"Nothing except my family, friends, home, business, the foundation I agreed to help manage —"

"People move, Joe. They find ways to stay in touch. They make new beginnings. It's because I'm the woman, isn't it? Most women move when their boyfriends or husbands have a job opportunity, but if the situation's reversed —"

"Avery, don't give me that shit. It has nothing to do with sexism."

"You could be happy anywhere if you make up your mind to be —"

"It's not about that, either. Baby . . ." I

heard a short, tense sigh. "You're not just choosing a job, you're choosing a life. A career on rocket fuel. You won't have one damn minute of spare time. I'm not moving to New York so I can see you for half of one day on the weekend, and twenty minutes every night between the time you get home and the time you go to bed. I can't see any room in that life for me, or for kids."

My heart plummeted. "Kids," I echoed numbly.

"Yes. I want kids someday. I want to sit on the front porch and watch them run through the sprinkler. I want to spend time with them, teach them how to play catch. I'm talking about having a family."

It was a long time before I could say anything. "I don't know if I would be a good parent."

"No one does."

"No, I *really* don't. I never had any kind of family. I lived with parts of broken families. One time I came home from school and there was a new man and new kids in the house, and I found out my mother had gotten married again without even telling me. And then one day they all disappeared without warning. Like some magician's trick."

Joe's voice turned gentle. "Avery, listen —"

"If I tried to be a parent and failed, I'd never forgive myself. It's too much of a risk. And it's too soon to be talking about this. For God's sake, we've never even said —" I broke off as my throat closed.

"I know. But I sure as hell can't say it right now, Avery. Because at the moment it would seem like nothing more than a pressure tactic."

I had to end the call. I had to retreat.

"At the very least," I said, "we can make the most of the time we have left. I have a month until Bethany's wedding, and after that —"

"A month of what? Trying not to care about you any more than I already do? Trying to back away from how I feel?" There was something wrong with his breathing, something broken. His voice was no less intense for its quietness. "A month of checking off the days until the final countdown . . . Damn you, Avery, I can't do that."

Tears brimmed and slid down my cheeks in burning paths.

"What should I say?"

"Tell me how to stop wanting you," he said. "Tell me how to stop —" He broke off and swore. "I'd rather put an end to this right now than drag it out."

The phone was trembling in my grip. I was scared. I was as scared as I'd ever been about anything. "Let's not talk any more tonight," I said breathlessly. "Nothing's changed. Nothing's been decided, okay?"

More silence.

"Joe?"

"I'll talk to you when you get back," he said gruffly. "But I want you to think about something, Avery. When you told me the story about your mom's Chanel bag, you got the metaphor dead wrong. You need to figure out what it really stands for."

TWENTY-ONE

Ravaged and exhausted from a sleepless night, I applied a heavier layer of makeup than usual the next morning. If the hollow-eyed look was in, I thought bleakly, I was definitely on-trend. I packed my bag and went downstairs a few minutes before I was supposed to meet Hollis, Bethany, and Kolby in the lobby. From there we would travel by limo to Teterboro Airport, about twelve miles away. The small airport, located in the New Jersey Meadowlands, was popular for private aircraft.

Heading to a lounge off the lobby, I saw Bethany sitting alone at a small table by a window. "Good morning," I said with a smile. "You're up early too?"

She smiled back at me, looking tired. "Can't sleep too good with all the city noise at night. Kolby's taking a shower. Want to sit with me?"

"Yes, I'll get some coffee."

In a minute, I returned to the table with my coffee and sat opposite Bethany. "I looked at the jpegs Finola sent last night," I said. "What did you think about the skirt redesign?"

"It was pretty. Finola said they would put beading on it."

"So you're happy with it?"

Bethany shrugged. "I liked the panels better. But there's no choice with my bump getting so big."

"It will be a gorgeous dress," I said. "And you'll look like a queen. I'm sorry I wasn't there yesterday."

"You didn't need to be. Finola was real nice to me and Mother." She paused. "She didn't say anything . . . but she knows. I could tell."

"About what?" I asked without expression.

"The due date." Bethany swirled a spoon aimlessly in her coffee cup. "I'm just about to start the last trimester. I may not even fit into that dress by the wedding."

"That's what the last fitting is for," I said automatically. "It'll be fine, Bethany." I drank some coffee and fastened my gaze on the scene outside the window, watching the pedestrians with their necks swathed in stylish scarves . . . a chic woman on a bicycle . . . a pair of elderly men, both in fedoras. "Does your mother know?" I asked.

She nodded. "I tell her everything. I always swear I'm going to keep some things private, and then I end up telling her, and I'm always sorry. But I do it anyway. I guess I always will."

"You may not," I said. "Believe me, I don't do a lot of the things I thought I'd always be doing."

Bethany left the spoon in the mug and pushed it aside. "Mother says you'll keep quiet about Kolby," she said. "Thank you."

"Please don't thank me. It's not my place to say anything."

"You're right. It's not. But I know you like Ryan, and you probably feel sorry for him. You shouldn't, though. He'll be fine."

"Is the baby his?" I asked softly.

Bethany flicked a derisive glance at me. "What do you think?"

"I think it's Kolby's."

Her slight smile faded. She didn't answer. She didn't have to.

We were both quiet for a minute.

"I love Kolby," Bethany said eventually. "It doesn't make a difference, but I do."

"Have you talked to him about it?"

"Of course."

"What does he say?"

"Stupid stuff. He said he wanted to get married and live in a beach house in Santa Cruz. Like I'd be sending our kid to public school." She let out a little huff of laughter. "Can you imagine me marrying a waterskiing instructor? Kolby has no money. No one would invite me anywhere. I wouldn't be anyone."

"You'd be with the person you love. The father of your child. You'd have to work, but you've got a college degree and connections —"

"Avery, no one makes money from working. Not real money. Even if you get that TV show job, you'll never earn anything close to what a Travis or a Chase or a Warner has. I wasn't raised to live in the top one percent, I was raised to live in the top tenth of the top one percent. That's who I am. You can't go down from that. No one would give up the kind of life I have just because they love someone."

I didn't reply.

"You think I'm a bitch," Bethany said.

"No."

"Well, I am."

"Bethany," I asked, "what are you going to tell Ryan when the baby is born two months early and it's obviously not a preemie?"

"It won't matter then. We'll be legally married. Even if Ryan decides to deny paternity and divorce me, he'll have to pay through the nose. I'll threaten to fight the prenup in court. Mother says Ryan will pay rather than go through a big public embarrassment."

I worked to keep all expression from my face. "Are you sure Kolby won't say anything? He won't cause trouble?"

"No, I told him all he has to do is wait. Once the divorce has gone through and I've got money, Kolby can live with me and the baby."

I couldn't speak for a moment. "What a perfect plan," I finally said.

I was quiet for most of the flight back, my thoughts seething. Plugging in a pair of earbuds, I started a movie on my laptop and stared blindly at the screen.

Any trace of compassion or pity I might have felt for Bethany had been obliterated when she had revealed that the wedding was nothing but a means to extort money from Ryan Chase. Bethany and her parents already knew that the marriage wouldn't last. They knew that he wasn't the father of the baby. They were taking advantage of Ryan's innate decency, and he would end up screwed to the wall while Bethany and Kolby lived off his money.

I was pretty sure I couldn't live with that.

In the periphery of my vision, I saw Bethany gesture to Hollis, who joined her on the long sofa at the back of the plane. They whispered together for at least twenty minutes, the discussion becoming increasingly animated, as if the subject were urgent. My guess was that Bethany regretted having told me so much earlier, and she was confessing to her mother. At one point, Hollis looked up and met my gaze directly.

Yes. I had been identified as a potential problem that would have to be addressed.

I returned my gaze to the laptop screen.

Thanks to the time zone change, we arrived at Houston's Hobby Airport at eleven A.M. "How nice," I said with a tacked-on smile, sliding my laptop into my carry-on. "Most of the day is still ahead of us."

Hollis smiled thinly. Bethany didn't respond.

I thanked the pilot and flight attendant while Bethany and Kolby left the plane. Turning toward the exit, I saw that Hollis was waiting for me.

"Avery," she said pleasantly, "before we get off the plane, I want to have a little chat."

"Certainly," I said, equally pleasant.

"I need to explain something because I'm not sure you fully understand our kind of people. The rules are different at our level. If you have any illusions about Ryan Chase, let me tell you something: He's no better than any other man. Don't you realize Ryan's going to keep some sweet young thing on the side? A man with his looks and money, he'll go through three or four wives at least. What do you care if Bethany's one of them?" Her eyes narrowed. "You're not being paid to make judgments or interfere with your clients' personal lives. Your job is to make this wedding happen. And if anything goes wrong . . . I'll make sure no one touches your business. I'll do whatever's necessary to ruin your chances of being on that TV show. David and I have friends who own media empires. Don't even think about crossing me."

My cordial expression didn't falter for one second of her speech.

"As you said at the beginning of the trip, Hollis, we understand each other."

After holding my gaze for a moment, she seemed to relax. "I told Bethany you wouldn't be a problem. A woman in your situation can't afford to act against your own interests."

"My situation?" I echoed, puzzled.

385

"Working."

Only Hollis Warner could have made that sound like a dirty word.

I deliberately took a roundabout route on the way home from Hobby, so I would have the time I needed. I always did my best thinking in the car, especially on longer drives. Somehow the tortured maze of thoughts at forty thousand feet became miraculously untangled as soon as I set foot on the ground.

There was no denying the importance — the necessity — of having a fulfilling career. But a job was never the most important thing. People were.

The fact was, I already had a career I loved. I had built it from scratch with my sister, and it was all ours, and I was in control of it, and we were damned success-ful. We could create our own opportunities.

Talking with Trevor Stearns's producers had given me a fleeting taste of what it would be like to be managed and supervised and have everything laid out for me. A fluffy white Pomeranian? . . . No thanks. I was just fine with my toothless Chihuahua, who, although not pretty, was at least not a stage prop.

I realized I had been so swept away by the

idea of getting the big break I had always dreamed of, and returning to New York in triumph, that I hadn't paused to consider whether that was still what I wanted.

Sometimes dreams changed when you weren't looking.

The things I'd accomplished and learned, and even lost, had all helped me to look at the world in a different way. But most of all, I had changed because of the people I had chosen to care about. It was as if my heart had been unwrapped and could feel everything more deeply. As if . . .

"My God," I said aloud, swallowing hard as I realized what the Chanel bag metaphor was.

My heart was the carefully protected object on the shelf. I had tried to keep it safe from damage, tried to use it only when necessary.

But some things became more beautiful with frequent use. The nicks and scuffs and cracks, the places that had been worn smooth, the areas that had been broken and repaired . . . all of that meant that an object had served its purpose. What good was a heart that had been grudgingly used? What value did it have if you'd never risked it on anyone? Trying not to feel had never been the right answer to my problems, it *was* the problem.

Happiness and fear were pressed together inside me, a double-sided coin that kept spinning. I wanted to go to Joe right then and make sure I hadn't lost him. I wanted things it was probably better not to think about at the moment.

That life he'd described . . . God help me, I wanted it. All of it, including children. Until this moment, I'd always been too scared to admit that, even to myself. I'd been too encumbered by the fear of turning out like my father.

Except that I wouldn't.

Unlike Eli, I was good at loving people. It was the first time I'd ever realized that.

I had to take off my sunglasses as the bottom rims became slick with tears.

Right now, I had to take care of a couple of urgent matters. Later I would go to Joe when I could find enough time and privacy. His feelings, and mine, were too important to fit in between errands.

I pulled into the drive-through at a Whataburger. Waiting in line to order a Diet Dr Pepper, I fished my phone out of my purse and dialed a number.

"Hello?" came a brusque voice.

"Ryan?" I asked, wiping my wet cheeks. "It's Avery."

His tone warmed. "Back from the big city?"

"I am."

"How was the trip?"

"Even more interesting than I expected," I said. "Ryan, I need to talk to you privately. Is there any way you could take a break and meet me somewhere? Preferably a place with a bar? I wouldn't ask unless it was important."

"Sure, I'll buy you lunch. Where are you?"

I told him, and he gave me directions to a bar and grill not far from Montrose.

I bought a Diet Dr Pepper, bolstered myself with a cold, crackling swallow, and made one more call before leaving the parking lot.

"Lois? Hi, it's Avery Crosslin." I tried to sound regretful. "I'm afraid I've had to make a tough decision about *Rock the Wedding.* . . ."

For the maximum amount of privacy at a bar and grill, the place had to be either completely packed or mostly empty. The restaurant where I met Ryan was so crowded that we were obliged to occupy two seats at the end of the bar and order our lunch from there. I always liked eating at a bar where the full menu was served, and for this particular conversation, it would be ideal. We could sit close without having to maintain eye contact, which was the perfect way to discuss something this difficult.

"Before I start," I said to Ryan, "I should tell you that it's bad news. Or maybe it's good news disguised as bad news. Either way, it's going to sound bad when I tell you. If you'd rather not know, I apologize for wasting your time, and lunch is on me, but you're going to know eventually, so —"

"Avery," Ryan interrupted, "slow down, honey. You've been turbocharged."

I smiled crookedly. "New York," I offered by way of explanation. I was surprised but pleased by the endearment, which he'd said in a brotherly way, as if I were part of the family.

The bartender brought a glass of wine for me and a beer for Ryan, and we gave him our orders.

"As far as bad news goes," Ryan told me, "I prefer to have it right away. I don't like it sugarcoated. And don't tell me the bright side. If it's not obvious, it's not a bright side."

"Good point." I considered various ways to break the news, wondering if I should start with Kolby's appearance on the plane or Bethany's fallacious due date. "I'm trying to think of how to explain all of this."

"Try five words or less," Ryan suggested.

"The baby's not yours."

Ryan stared at me blankly.

I repeated it more slowly. "The baby's not yours." I wondered if it was bad that it felt so good to tell him.

With extreme care, Ryan closed his hand around his beer glass and drank the contents without stopping. He signaled the bartender for another. "Go on," he murmured, bracing his forearms on the edge of the bar, looking straight ahead.

For twenty minutes, Ryan listened while I talked. I couldn't read him at all — he was incredibly good at concealing his emotions. But gradually I sensed that he was relaxing, in the deep and elemental way of someone who had carried a heavy burden for months and was finally being allowed to let it go.

Eventually Ryan said, "What Hollis said about hurting your business . . . don't you worry about that. I'll handle the Warners, so you —"

"Jesus, Ryan, your first concern doesn't have to be for me. Let's talk about you. Are you okay? I was afraid maybe you had feelings for Bethany, and —"

"No, I tried. The best I could do was be kind to her. But I never wanted her." Reaching out, Ryan hugged me while we remained sitting on the bar stools. The embrace was fervent and strong. "Thank you," he murmured in my hair. "God, thank you."

I wasn't certain if he was saying it to me or actually praying.

Drawing back, Ryan looked at me with impossibly blue eyes. "You didn't have to tell me. You could have gone ahead with the wedding and collected your percentage."

"And then stand back and watch the Warners take you to the cleaners? I don't think so." I gave him a concerned glance. "What are you going to do now?"

"I'm going to talk to Bethany as soon as possible. I'll do what I should have done in the first place: tell her we'll wait until after the baby's born, and do a DNA test. In the meantime, I'll demand to meet her doctor and find out the accurate due date."

"So the wedding is off," I said.

"Pull the plug" came his decisive reply. "I'll compensate Hollis for the costs that you can't recoup. And I want to pay you and your people for the hours you've put in."

"That's not necessary."

"Yes, it is."

We talked for a while longer, while the lunch crowd gradually cleared out and the waitstaff was busy running back and forth with credit card folders, cash, and receipts. Ryan paid the check for our lunch and gave the bartender a mammoth tip.

As we left the restaurant, Ryan held the door open for me. "You didn't mention how your meeting with the TV producers went."

"It went well," I said in an off hand tone. "I got the impression they were working up to a nice offer. But I turned them down. They couldn't make me a deal that would top what I've already got here."

"Glad you're going to stay. By the way . . . are you going to see Joe anytime soon?"

"I expect so."

"He's been as ornery as a two-headed bull while you were gone. Jack says the next time you go anywhere, you have to take Joe with you. None of the rest of us can stand him like this."

I laughed, while nerves fluttered in my stomach. "I'm not sure how things are between Joe and me right now," I confessed. "Our last call didn't end too well."

"I wouldn't worry." Ryan smiled. "But don't put off talking to him. For all our sakes."

I nodded. "I'll get my team started on un-planning the wedding, and then I'll call him." We parted company and headed to our separate cars. "Ryan," I said. He stopped to look back at me. "Someday you're going to hire me to plan another wedding. And the next time, it'll be for the right reasons."

"Avery," he replied sincerely, "I'm going to hire someone to shoot me if I ever get engaged again."

TWENTY-TWO

As soon as I came through the front door, I heard Coco begin to yip frantically. She hurried to me from the main seating area, almost beside herself with excitement. "Coco!" I exclaimed, dropping my bag and scooping her up.

She licked me and tried to cuddle closer while yapping as if to nag me for having been away so long.

I heard a chorus of welcomes from various places around the studio.

It was good to be home.

"Dogs have no sense of time," Sofia said, reaching me in a few strides. "She thinks you were gone for two weeks instead of two days."

"It felt like two weeks," I said.

She kissed me on both cheeks, while Coco wriggled excitedly between us. "Oh, it's good to have you back! I got some of your texts, but you were so quiet yesterday, and nothing at all last night."

"The events of the past two days would surpass even the most overwrought tele-novela," I said. "Prepare to be shocked."

Steven laughed and came to me for a hug. After enfolding me in a hearty embrace, he drew back and looked down at me with twinkling blue eyes. "I'm shockproof now," he said. "I've watched enough of those idiotic shows that I can see every plot twist from a mile away."

"Trust me, I'm about to put you to the test." I frowned as Coco kissed my cheek and I felt how raspy her tongue was. "Didn't anyone put coconut oil on her tongue while I was gone?" I demanded. "It's like an emery board."

"She won't let anyone touch it," Sofia protested. "I tried. Tell her, Steven."

"She tried," he acknowledged. "I watched."

"He laughed until he fell off the sofa," Sofia said.

I shook my head and looked into Coco's soulful eyes. "I don't want to think about what you've endured."

"It wasn't that terrible —" Sofia began.

"Sweetheart," Steven interrupted, "I think she's talking to the Chihuahua."

After taking care of Coco's tongue, I asked

everyone to stop what they were doing and sit at the long table. "For the rest of the day," I said, "we're all going to be busy with a special project."

"Sounds fun," Val said lightly.

"It's not going to be fun in the least." I looked at Ree-Ann. "Have the Warner wedding invitations gone out yet?" I asked, thinking, *Please say no, please say no . . .*

"Yesterday," she said proudly.

I uttered a word that made her eyes widen.

"You told me to," she protested. "I was only doing what you —"

"I know. It's fine. Unfortunately it means extra work, but we can handle it. I need you to print out the master list, Ree-Ann. We're going to have to contact everyone on it and obtain verbal confirmation of the cancellation."

"What? Why? What are you talking about?"

"We have to unplan the Warner-Chase wedding."

"How much of it?" Steven asked.

"All of it."

Tank looked bewildered. "It's postponed?"

"It's off," I said. "Permanently off."

Everyone looked at me and asked in unison, *"Why?"*

"It doesn't go beyond this room. We do not gossip about clients. Ever."

"Yes, we all know," Steven said. "*Explain,* Avery."

Two hours later, my team still appeared to be dazed by the turn of events. I had assured them that we would all be compensated for the time we'd spent. There would be other weddings, other chances to make our mark. Still, that was small consolation when they had been tasked with unraveling a wedding that was only a month away. Steven had already succeeded in canceling the fleet of Rolls-Royces and one of the wedding favor orders. Sophia had contacted the caterers and the chair and table rental company and was waiting for callbacks. Val and Ree-Ann had both been assigned to call every name on the guest list and inform them of the cancellation, while claiming ignorance as to the reason why.

"How long do we have to do this?" Ree-Ann moaned. "It's five o'clock. I want to go home."

"I'd like you to work until six, if possible," I said. "Depending on how the unplanning goes, we'll all have to put in some overtime this week, so you may want to —" I stopped as I heard a key turn in the front door.

The only people with keys were Sofia, me, Steven . . . and Joe.

He let himself in. His searing gaze found me at once.

A potent silence infused the room.

Joe looked the worse for wear, sleep-deprived, with no reserve of patience left. He was big and brooding and surly . . . and he was all mine.

The sound of my heartbeat filled my head with ragged music.

"Ryan called me." Joe's voice was like gravel in a blender.

The studio was quiet. Everyone listened avidly, making not even the slightest pretense at minding their own business. Even Coco had climbed to the top of the sofa back to watch us with prurient interest.

"Did he tell you —" I began.

"Yes." It was clear that Joe didn't give a damn about who was there or what they saw. His focus was riveted exclusively on me. His color had heightened, and his jaw was hard, and despite his obvious effort at control, I could tell he was on a hair trigger.

I had to get everyone out of the studio. Fast.

"Let me clear a couple of things out of the way," I said distractedly, "and then we can talk."

"I don't want to talk." Joe moved toward me and paused as I stepped back instinctively. "In thirty seconds," he warned, "you're mine. You'll want to be upstairs when it happens." He glanced at his watch.

"Joe . . ." I shook my head with an agitated laugh. "Come on, you can't just —"

"Twenty-five."

Shit. He wasn't kidding.

I cast a wild glance at Ree-Ann and Val, who were having the time of their lives. "You can go home now," I told them curtly. "Good work, everyone. Be back bright and early tomorrow morning."

"I'm going to stay and keep working until six," Ree-Ann said virtuously.

"I'll help," Val chimed in.

Tank shook his head and sent me one of his rare grins. "I'll kick 'em out, Avery."

Steven picked up his keys. "Let's go to dinner," he suggested to Sofia in a casual tone, as if nothing untoward were happening. As if I weren't just about to be ravished in the living room.

"Eighteen seconds," Joe said.

Outraged and giddy, I rushed to the stairs in a panic. "Joe, this is ridiculous —"

"Fifteen." He began to follow me at a measured pace. Feeling like a hunted creature, I scrambled up the steps, which seemed to have turned into an escalator.

By the time I reached my room, Joe had

caught up to me. I ran inside and turned to face him as he closed the door. He tensed in readiness to catch me, no matter which direction I bolted. But then I saw the shadows beneath his eyes, and the flush beneath his tan, and my heart ached. I headed straight for him.

His hard arms closed around me. His mouth took mine, and he growled softly in what could have been pleasure or agony. For a few minutes there was nothing but darkness and sensation, those deep kisses demolishing every thought. I was never quite certain how we ended up on the bed. We rolled across the mattress fully clothed, grappling and kissing in a fury, breaking apart only when the need for oxygen was imperative. Joe kissed my neck and tugged at my shirt, more aggressive than he'd ever been before, until I heard threads snapping and felt a button pop off.

With a shaky laugh, I put my hands on either side of his face. "Joe. Take it easy. Hey —"

He kissed me again, shivering with the effort of holding back. I felt the hot, ready pressure of him against me, and I wanted him so badly that a moan rose in my throat. But there were things that needed to be said.

"I'm choosing the life I want," I managed

to tell him. "There's no obligation for you. I'm staying because this is my home and I can make my own dreams come true right here, with my sister and my friends and employees and my dog, and all the things I —"

"What about me? Was I a part of your decision?"

"Well . . ."

He frowned, his gaze raking over me as I hesitated.

"Joe, what I'm trying to say is . . . I don't expect a commitment from you because of this. I don't want you to feel pressured in any way. It may be years before we figure out how we feel about each other, so —"

He smothered my words with his mouth, kissing me until I was drunk on the taste and feel of him. After a long time, his head lifted. "You know right now," he whispered, staring at me with those midnight eyes. Tender amusement lurked in the corners of his mouth. This was the Joe I was accustomed to, the one who loved to tease me without mercy. "And you're going to tell me."

My heart began to thump, not in a good way. I wasn't sure I could do what he wanted. "Later."

"Now." He rested more of his weight on

me, as if he were settling in for a prolonged siege.

I abandoned all pride. "Joe, please, please don't make me —"

"Say it," he murmured. "Or in about ten minutes you'll be screaming it with me inside you."

"Jesus." I squirmed and fidgeted. "You are the most —"

"Tell me," he insisted.

"Why do I have to be the first?"

Joe held me with his relentless gaze. "Because I want you to."

Realizing there would be no compromise, I began to wheeze as if I'd just run a marathon. Somehow I got out the words in one fraught breath.

To my outrage, Joe began to laugh softly. "Honey . . . you say it like you're confessing to a crime."

I scowled and wriggled beneath him. "If you're going to make fun of me —"

"No," he said tenderly, keeping me pinned in place. He took my head in his hands. A last chuckle escaped, and then he stared into my eyes, seeing everything, hiding nothing. "I love you," he said. His mouth caressed mine, soft as velvet. "Now try it again." Another gentle, smoldering stroke of his lips. "You don't have to be scared."

"I love you," I managed to say, my heart still thundering.

Joe rewarded me by covering my mouth with his, searching deeply. After a kiss that dismantled my brain entirely, he finished with a soft nuzzle. "I can't kiss you enough," he told me. "I'm going to kiss you a million times in our life, and it will never be enough."

Our life.

I had never known a happiness like this, reaching all the way down to the place in my heart where sorrow usually started, siphoning up tears. Joe wiped at the wetness with his fingers and pressed his lips to my cheeks, absorbing the salty taste of joy.

"Let's practice some more," he whispered.

And before long, I discovered that with the right person, saying those three words wasn't difficult at all.

It was the easiest thing in the world.

EPILOGUE

The Happy Tails Rescue Society has been decorated for Christmas, with lights strung high near the ceiling and a tree in the lobby covered in bone-shaped doggie treats. Although Millie and Dan have enforced a no-adoption policy during the weeks before and after Christmas, to prohibit impulse buying that might lead to later regrets, the shelter and its website have still been busy. People are allowed to visit the dogs and ask for one to be kept on hold until January 1, when adoptions start up again.

Joe sets up his camera in the dogs' exercise room, while I pick out a few toys from the box. We're here for our monthly visit to take pictures of the shelter's newest arrivals. Later in the day, we're going to the Galleria to shop for Christmas presents, which Joe hates nearly as much as I enjoy it. "Shopping is a competitive sport," I'd told him. "Stick with me, pal — I'll show you how it's done."

"Shopping's not a sport."

"It is the way I do it," I had assured him, and he had allowed it was probably worth going just to see me in action.

Even before Dan opens the door to bring in the first dog, I can hear a tumult of high-pitched barking. I make a comical face. "What's going on out there?"

Joe shrugs innocently.

The door opens, and a pack of golden retriever puppies rushes in. I laugh in delight at the roly-poly creatures swarming around us, all bright eyes and wagging tails. Five of them. "All at once?" I ask. "I don't think there's any way I can get them to . . ." My voice fades as I notice that each puppy has a sign tied around its neck. Name tags? Perplexed, I pick up a puppy and read the word printed on its sign while it struggles to lick me. "You," I read aloud. I pick up another. "Me." I glance quickly at Joe, who nudges another puppy in my direction. I look at the sign. "Will."

And then I understand.

I blink against a sudden blur. "Where's the other one?" I ask, sniffling as the rambunctious little bodies scamper around me.

"Guys," Joe says to the yapping, unruly

bunch, "let's do it the way we rehearsed." He reaches for the puppies and tries to set them in a line, except the order isn't right.

Will. Me. Marry. You.

The fifth puppy, wearing a ?, has wandered off to investigate the toy box, while the others race around in circles.

"You're proposing with puppies?" I ask, my lips stretched in a crooked smile.

Joe pulls a ring from his pocket. "Bad idea?" he asks.

I love this man beyond reason.

I use my sleeve to blot my eyes. "No, it's wonderful . . . maybe a little ungrammatical, but you can't help it if you lack puppy-herding skills." I move some of the puppies out of the way so I can straddle his lap. My arms link around his neck. "How do I say yes? Do you have any more signs?"

"There was a sixth puppy who was supposed to wear a reversible 'yes' or 'no,' but she was adopted last week."

I kiss him passionately. "The 'no' option wouldn't have been necessary."

"Then . . ."

"*Yes,* of course it's yes!"

Joe slides the diamond ring on my finger, and I admire the flash of cool, brilliant fire. "I love you," he says, and I say it back with a tremor of emotion. Leaning hard on him,

I try to push him to the floor.

Joe eases down obligingly and wraps his arms around me as I lower my mouth to his. After a minute, he rolls me to my back and makes the kiss deeper, more intimate. Our soulful embrace is interrupted as puppies begin to clamber over us, and we discover that it's nearly impossible to kiss when you're laughing.

But we try anyway.

ABOUT THE AUTHOR

Lisa Kleypas is the RITA Award-winning author of many contemporary and historical romance novels, including *A Wallflower Christmas, Christmas Eve at Friday Harbor,* and *Love in the Afternoon.* Her books are published in fourteen languages and are bestsellers all over the world. Kleypas graduated from Wellesley College and published her first novel at the age of 21. In 1985, she was named Miss Massachusetts in the Miss America competition. She lives in Washington with her husband and two children.

The employees of Thorndike Press hope you have enjoyed this Large Print book. All our Thorndike, Wheeler, and Kennebec Large Print titles are designed for easy reading, and all our books are made to last. Other Thorndike Press Large Print books are available at your library, through selected bookstores, or directly from us.

For information about titles, please call:
(800) 223-1244

or visit our Web site at:
http://gale.cengage.com/thorndike

To share your comments, please write:
Publisher
Thorndike Press
10 Water St., Suite 310
Waterville, ME 04901